DESTINATION PEACE

DESTINATION PEACE

Three Decades of Israeli Foreign Policy

A Personal Memoir

GIDEON RAFAEL

STEIN AND DAY/ *Publishers* / New York

To Nurit and our children
with love.

First published in the United States of America in 1981
Copyright © 1981 by Gideon Rafael
All rights reserved
Printed in the United States of America
Stein and Day/*Publishers*/Scarborough House
Briarcliff Manor, New York 10510

Rafael, Gideon.
    Destination peace.

    Includes index.
    1. Israel -Foreign relations. 2. Rafael, Gideon.
3. Diplomats - Israel - Biography. I. Title.
DS119.6.R33   1981   327.5694   80-9060
ISBN 0-8128-2812-7   AACR2

Contents

Illustrations   vii

Preface   ix

Part One: CONFRONTATION
  1 Opening Night at the Foreign Ministry   3
  2 The Year of Decision   11
  3 The First Steps in World Affairs   21
  4 Belligerence in Action   30
  5 Towards the Brink   40
  6 Ben Gurion Prepares the Nation   53

Part Two: CONSOLIDATION
  7 The Aftermath of the Sinai-Suez Campaign   71
  8 Leap Over the Arab Wall   78
  9 Israel in Asia   86
 10 The China Disconnection   91
 11 Relations with Western Europe   100
 12 Eastern Europe   113
 13 A Decade of Growth and Consolidation   123

Part Three: CONFLAGRATION
 14 Moscow Prelude   129
 15 The Ides of May   136
 16 The East Side Story   143
 17 Six Days and Seven Nights   153
 18 Consultations in Jerusalem   167
 19 Emergency Session   173
 20 Resolution 242   186

Part Four: CONCILIATION

21 The Jarring Mission   193
22 War of Attrition   201
23 The Rogers Plan – First Steps   207
24 Suspension of Arms Deliveries to Israel   214
25 Cease-Fire and Diplomatic Deadlock   221
26 US-USSR: Common Denominators and Conflicting
    Objectives   233
27 Upheaval in Jordan   238
28 The Ascension of Sadat and the Decline of Jarring   250
29 Suez Approaches   258
30 The Great Surprise   273
31 The Watershed   289
32 Airlift, Cease-Fire and Oil   304
33 Disengagement   315
34 London – The Last Post   330
35 Inside the Foreign Ministry   376
36 Peace   388

Index   395

Illustrations

The first Israeli delegation to the United Nations, May 1948 (*Leo Rosenthal*).

Golda Meir and Gideon Rafael *en route* to New York, 18 May 1948.

Trygve Lie and Warren Austin, 1949 (*Photo Krongold, London*).

With Abba Eban, Jacob Malik and Seamyon Tsarapkin, 1950.

With Charles Malik, Foreign Minister of the Lebanon, 1953 (*Leo Rosenthal*).

Ben Gurion and Moshe Sharett with British Foreign Secretary Selwyn Lloyd, March 1956 (*David Rubinger*).

Ben Gurion visits the United Nations Headquarters, 1955.

Digging for victory, 1956 (*P. Goldman*).

With Queen Elisabeth of Belgium and Isaac Stern, 16 May 1959 (*Belga*).

With UN Secretary-General Dag Hammarskjöld (*Leo Rosenthal*).

With Pandit Nehru, 1961.

The author presents his credentials to UN Secretary-General U Thant, May 1967.

At a meeting with UN Undersecretary-General Ralph Bunche, 15 May 1967 (*Max Machol*).

In conversation with Nikolai Fedorenko, 24 May 1967 (*United Nations*).

Ambassador Gunnar Jarring in conversation with the author and President Shazar in Jerusalem, 1967 (*Israel Press and Photo Agency*).

At a reception with UN Secretary-General and Mrs Kurt Waldheim, 1967.

With Romanian Deputy Foreign Minister George Macovescu, 1971 (*News Phot*).

'Number one on the Palestinian terrorists' hit list' – arriving under heavy guard at Heathrow airport, January 1971 (*Press Association*).

En route to Buckingham Palace, February 1971 (*Keystone*).

With Prime Minister Harold Wilson, 1976 (*Sidney Harris Ltd*).

'In that day shall Israel be the third with Egypt and Assyria, a blessing in the midst of the earth, and the Lord shall bless them: Blessed be Egypt my people, and Assyria the work of my hands and Israel mine inheritance.'

Isaiah XIX, 24–25

Preface

'Parlez-vous français?' asked Eliyahu Golomb, the formidable commander of the Haganah. 'Oui, monsieur,' I answered deferentially. This was apparently all he needed to know about my linguistic proficiency. My affirmative reply to his next and final question – whether our kibbutz could provide me with a presentable suit – concluded my entrance exam into Israel's public service.

Dismissing me with a warm handshake and a reassuring look, Eliyahu summed up my travel orders in one sentence: 'You will proceed to Paris where you will report for duty to our man in charge.'

The year was 1939. The intensity of Nazi Germany's war preparations was matched by the ferocity of its anti-Jewish persecutions. We were engaged in a desperate race between ruin and rescue. The British administration had blocked the safe haven of the Jewish homeland to the escapees from Hitler's hell. The struggle for Jewish survival centred on our capacity to force open the locked gates.

Our armada was a motley collection of ramshackle boats; our captains were farmers turned sailors and our cargo ragged refugees. The odyssey of the Jewish 'boat people' of the 1930s was the warning signal of the approaching fire-storm. When it had burned out five years later, Europe's soil was hallowed by countless graves of the victims of Nazi barbarity and covered with the cinders of millions of martyred Jews.

The rescue of the survivors of the Holocaust and their fight to settle in the only land anxious to offer them refuge and rehabilitation formed a decisive stage in the struggle for the restoration of Jewish independence. Participation in it was not only a rugged experience, but also a solid preparation for future service.

Vision was the moving force of Israel's renaissance. Intuition rather than experience guided its founding fathers; ingenuity rather than premeditation determined the actions of its pioneers. The fabric of Israel's society was not woven by master craftsmen but by apprentices. Most of the first generation of the state's public servants, whether civil or military, had graduated not from staff colleges but from field service. The fledgling foreign service, much like other branches of government, had to make up with enthusiasm and originality what it lacked in worldly wisdom.

The style of Israeli diplomacy was largely shaped by the ability of its practitioners and the oddity of the challenges they had to cope with. The pattern of Israeli foreign policy emerged from its spiritual distinctiveness, its traumatic Jewish experience, its sense of international responsibility and its defence requirements in an inimical environment.

Initially Israel tried to steer an independent course, charted by its own concepts and scale of values, away from the turbulence of the big power contest. But the ill winds of hostility forced it to change direction. Its land borders sealed by siege, it had to seek its friends beyond the sea. While the supreme goal of its policy was peace, war became its inescapable challenge. Confronted constantly with unforeseen situations, Israeli foreign policy perfected the art of improvisation rather than of planning.

In dealing with the evolution of Israeli foreign policy during the first three decades of the state's existence, I propose to present its underlying concepts and main features, to elucidate the motivations of its decision-makers, to dispel some of the myths that did not shape the course of events and to display some of the hazards that did. I have tried to evaluate the developments against their regional and global backgrounds and examine the transformation of a state of obdurate confrontation into a process of cautious conciliation.

This book is not intended to be an all-inclusive compilation of Israeli diplomacy, nor is it meant to be an autobiographical account of one of its practitioners. Its touchstone is documentary evidence, which is referred to in the text within the limits of official regulations. Memory and personal experience are invoked to illustrate the record and complete it where it is wanting.

In the history of nations thirty years are a fleeting moment; in the life of a man they equal the span of a generation. The first thirty years of the State of Israel were a momentous epoch. The state was forged on the anvil of adversity into a hardy nation, and was driven by a compelling urge of creativity to fulfil the prophetic vision of Amos: 'My people Israel shall rebuild deserted cities and live in them, they shall plant vineyards and drink their wine, make gardens and eat their fruit. Once more I shall plant them on their own soil and they shall never again be uprooted from it.' Its first generation was harrowed by the memory of the Holocaust, elated by the emergence of the state and agonized by the ravages of four wars. It was a generation that yearned for peace, which eluded it for three decades. The closer we came to it, the higher towered the obstacles. When we set out on the tortuous road towards destination peace on the very day Israel proclaimed its independence, we used to exclaim in wonder at every step: 'This is the first time in 2000 years.' Thirty years later, when we had reached the first station of peace, our historical count had changed to 'The first time after thirty years.'

It was the first time that the vast stretch of territory from the headwaters of the Jordan to the sources of the Nile had become an area of peace; that the only land link between Africa and Asia – the Sinai desert, so long a barrier – had been transformed into a bridge; that Cairo became the nearest capital accessible to Jerusalem. It was the first time that Israel had breached the wall of regional segregation and attained Arab recognition of its sovereign legitimacy; and the first time that the cry of battle had given way to the vow of 'no more war'.

This solemn pledge, pronounced in Jerusalem by the President of Egypt and the Prime Minister of Israel, became the foundation stone of the first edifice of Arab-Israeli peace. It is now a commitment by the people of Egypt and Israel from which they cannot retreat, because the road of return would lead them into the abyss. It is some recompense for the irredeemable debt we owe to all who gave their lives to frustrate the futile attempt to eradicate Israel.

In retracing the road to peace I wish not only to offer my contribution to the understanding of Israel's foreign policy, but to pay my tribute to the generation which paved the way: to the fighting men and women who did not return from the field of battle and their anguished families on the home front; to the people toiling in towns, villages and kibbutzim; to the fellahin tilling their land in the sweat of their brow; to the visionaries dreaming of a peaceful and bountiful world; and to the statesmen and my colleagues, the diplomats, grappling with its adverse realities. They all joined forces to accomplish the first stage of the unfinished journey. They will complete it if they continue to advance together.

Jerusalem

Part One

CONFRONTATION

1

Opening Night at the Foreign Ministry

Moshe Sharett, Israel's first Foreign Minister after 2,000 years as he whimsically liked to introduce himself, was a man of many talents and endearing qualities. His intellectual discipline was proverbial and his flair for precision and detail unmatched. It provoked the admiration of the uninvolved spectator and the exasperation of his close associates.

He was a tireless traveller in the cause of Jewish national redemption. He prepared his journeys with clockwork precision, but impish spirits always upset his meticulous planning. Arriving at his destination, he would discover that his luggage had travelled in a completely different direction. The efforts to achieve a tolerable measure of synchronization between the man and his belongings and their eventual reunion were sometimes no less exciting and tiring than the endless exertions needed to goad the divergent branches of government into co-ordinated action. The last baggage crisis, immediately preceding the proclamation of Israel's independence, occurred in Athens. It preceded one of the first diplomatic achievements of the new-born state. But we shall not pre-empt events; history must follow its orderly course.

The termination of the British Mandate was set for midnight, 14 May 1948. Sharett was flying from New York to Tel Aviv to participate in the final deliberations before the proclamation of the Jewish state and the preparation of its declaration of independence. Shortly before his departure, Secretary of State General George Marshall had urged him to come to Washington. Sharett was afraid that Marshall might use the full weight of his high office and forceful personality to press the Jewish representatives to postpone the proclamation of independence. He wished to avoid the meeting, claiming that his presence at home was indispensable. We felt the summons to Washington was inescapable and argued that if the United States government was determined to communicate a policy decision, it would reach its addressee wherever he may be. A man to man talk on the other hand might help clarify and alter American views.

Sharett went to Washington. He did not regret it. He sent me ahead to wait for him in Geneva and to meet Shaul Avigur, one of the founding fathers of the Jewish self-defence organization and at the time, chief of the Haganah's arms-purchasing mission in Europe. The prospect of arms acquisition and their arrival in the country were vital factors for the Jewish authorities in determining their next move. Ben Gurion expected an all-out Arab military assault against the fledgling Jewish state. He had no doubt about the tenacity and valour of the people in a fight against overwhelming odds, but he knew that without a sufficient quantity of arms Israel would not emerge victorious from the ordeal. The political circumstances under which Israel would encounter the Arab onslaught, and in particular America's fidelity to the United Nations partition decision of 29 November 1947, would play a vital role in the outcome of the struggle.

Sharett's plane arrived in Geneva late at night. It was bound for Cairo, and we were supposed to change in Athens for Tel Aviv. Before we reached Rome, Sharett gave me a detailed report of his conversation with General Marshall. He had been neither encouraging nor discouraging. He had stressed the military risks to which Israel would be exposed without an organized and well-equipped military force in a war fought against it by seven regular Arab armies. He had persuasively stated the facts, but refrained from offering an effective remedy. It was up to the Jews either to defend themselves, or to defer the establishment of their state to a more propitious time. Whatever they decided the United States wished them well and hoped that the Lord would bless His people. Silently we pondered the words of the Secretary of State. Sharett asked my opinion. I thought that there was no indication of active American opposition; General Marshall, in assessing the military equation, had sounded a warning. It was more a counsel of caution than an act of censure. Sharett did not argue; he simply said that this was his own conclusion. There was now no way of turning back or stopping in the middle of the road. It was not the inescapable decision which was fateful, but its consequences. Then he made a philosophical observation on missed opportunities in history which never recur, and dozed off until our landing in Athens was announced.

Sharett became fidgety. All airlines had ceased flying to Tel Aviv. Our authorities had promised that our one and only passenger plane, a DC 3 of Second World War vintage, would pick us up in Athens Sharett's faith in the eternity of Israel was unshakable, but his trust in the reliability of this one-man-one-plane air service was less steadfast. 'Now we'll be stuck here in Athens,' he lamented, 'and I haven't even got a Greek visa.' When it came to conjuring up difficulties, he had no peer. At this critical stage the TWA ground hostess announced that a Mr Shertok (later known as Sharett) was requested to identify himself. After a short dramatic pause she added with marked respect, 'Your plane for Tel Aviv, sir, is ready for take-off.' We followed her over the tarmac with an air of forced nonchalance. But as usual, one of Moshe Sharett's suitcases was missing.

There was another surprise on board. A charming girl supplemented the one-man crew. She served as air hostess and assistant navigator, and presided over two cartons of sandwiches and beverages and a large map – a worthy beginning for a national airline. At dusk the plane landed on the Tel Aviv landing-strip, illuminated by kerosene torches. Reuben Shiloah, a close confidant of Ben Gurion and trusted adviser of Sharett, met us. A young man in the uniform of the British supernumerary police introduced himself as being in charge of the airfield. The British administration had already evacuated the Tel Aviv area, a few days in advance of its withdrawal from the rest of the country, and *de facto* governmental jurisdiction had been transferred to the Jewish authorities. In this capacity the one-man manager of the airfield, customs, police and immigration services decided that Sharett's arrival was a suitable occasion to manifest the powers of his multiple functions. He lined up his six policemen as a guard of honour, personally stamped our passports, and announced that he exempted us from customs inspection because he had decided to grant us diplomatic immunity. Sharett was too busy talking to Shiloah to register the full impact of this act of Jewish sovereignty performed in our ancestral land for the first time after 2,000 years. He rushed off to a meeting with Ben Gurion.

Credentials but no credit

Three days after our diplomatic recognition by the Tel Aviv authorities, the new State of Israel requested recognition from the governments of the world. This was the first major assignment of the newly formed Ministry of Foreign Affairs. When we left the brief, sober and solemn ceremony of the Proclamation of Independence, Sharett curtly instructed me to present myself at eight p.m. sharp at the 'Foreign Ministry'. The new General Services Administration – or whatever the preparatory committee charged with planning the government services of Israel had called itself – had allocated two rooms to our Ministry in an old building by the seashore. It was known as the 'red house', not for its ideological interior but for the pinkish paint of its exterior. The fact that it housed a branch of the Haganah's High Command was not a matter of common knowledge.

Sharett went to work without preliminaries. His staff consisted of two assistants: an elderly lady and a young man. Eiga Shapira was a highly educated person, as gracious in her manners as she was perfect in her style of typing. Her output in terms of quantity and quality was superb. Myself, the other assistant, was entrusted with a dazzling variety of assignments. One of them was to answer the telephone with the inevitable '*Shalom*' and the less credible '*Misrad ha Chuz*' – 'the Foreign Ministry'. The invariable reply was, 'We don't want to speak to what's-your-name, please hurry and transfer us to Moshe Sharett.' People felt they had to make up for a lot of time lost during the last two millennia. A more erudite occupation to which I was assigned was to make up a list of the capitals to be officially informed of the establishment of the State of Israel. My reference library consisted of a respectable atlas and an old edition of the *Statesman's Year Book*. Sharett, sitting in his corner, was completely immersed in composing the telegrams. The only interruption which he allowed himself was to down, at fixed intervals, cups of piping hot tea, an immutable rite to this day for the transaction of any sort of governmental business in Israel.

In those days the ascent of colonial populations to sovereign statehood was not an event of universal interest. But the restoration of Israel's independence evoked deep emotions which went far beyond the Jewish world and the Arab environment. Peoples living far apart from one another – Icelanders and New Zealanders, Guatemalans and Czechs – distant from the scene of the event, were gripped by the drama of the rebirth of Israel. They were linked to it by the teachings and the images of the ancient Scriptures and the recent guilt-laden memories of the Holocaust. The concurrence of the United States and the Soviet Union, justifying and supporting the establishment of the Jewish state, consecrated its act of birth.

Nonetheless Israel, from the very hour of its creation, had to fend for its place among the nations. It emerged in awe but in solitude. There was no other people who had contributed so much and for so long to enlighten so many on the spiritual and moral imperatives which govern the ways of mankind. It seemed that Sharett was absorbed in these thoughts as he laboured on his drafts. He tried to condense in his message to the nations of the world the history of the Jewish people from Abraham the patriarch to Herzl the visionary; he referred to the salient points of the epoch-making United Nations decision; he quoted the central parts of Israel's declaration of independence and highlighted the social and political aspirations of the new state to live in peace with all states near and far. He produced a beautifully written but rather lengthy manifesto. When we transcribed it, we pointed out somewhat irreverently that the number of words in the telegram equalled the length of the Jewish exile from the promised land. Meanwhile we had prepared our list of recipients. It comprised all the member states of the United Nations and those countries of Western and Eastern Europe which at the time were still outside the world organization. It excluded the Arab states, more for technical than for ideological reasons. We felt no harm could be done by advising them officially of the establishment of Israel and the peaceful intentions of its government, but all the Arab capitals had severed their lines of communication with the new state.

At two o'clock in the morning we had completed our work, but we were soon jolted out of our complacency. We sent our driver with the sizeable bundle of telegrams to the Tel Aviv Central Post Office. He returned them – undispatched. Had it closed its night service with the advent of the State of Israel? Far from it. The telegraph service was operating perfectly. There was only one snag. The postal clerk refused to accept the cables without cash payment. The thought of such petty mercantilism at Israel's finest hour had never occurred to us. And even if it had, we were not in a position to do anything about it. The Foreign Ministry simply had no funds at its disposal. We did not even possess our own stationery. Our only equipment was the typewriter and a tea kettle.

I telephoned the man who was holding up the happy news of Israel's birth, and tried to impress on him that destiny had chosen him to play a historic role. My wooing was of no avail. He worked to rule, and the rule-book was still that of the British administration. Of course, he knew that the State of Israel had been proclaimed, but he was less certain about the existence of an institution which called itself the Foreign Ministry.

I asked him to suggest a way out of the impasse. He pondered while the time ticked away. Then, suddenly, he saw the light. He had read in the papers that there was a man by the name of Seev Sharef who had been entrusted with the establishment of the new governmental administration. If I could provide him with an authorization from this man, he would send the telegrams and charge us later. 'For heaven's sake, where can I find Sharef at three o'clock in the morning?' I asked him, exasperated. 'That's your problem,' he replied. Sharett, who had listened intently to this first diplomatic exchange, knew where the all-powerful dispenser of authorizations could be found in Tel Aviv, and we went there, woke him up and explained our predicament. He wrote the redeeming note, hardly concealing his pride in the nocturnal recognition of his authority. In no time at all the wires were humming with the proclamation of Israel's birth.

Recognition

At dawn, Israel received its first signal of foreign recognition. The Egyptian airforce bombed Tel Aviv's airfield and power station. The smoke rose in a cloud which for decades to come was to darken the skies of the Middle East. But at the same hour an exhilarating message arrived from Washington. As expected by the initiated few, but surprising in his swiftness, President Truman announced the *de facto* recognition of the State of Israel and its government. The presidential announcement lifted our spirits and cemented the friendship between the two peoples, which has remained the corner-stone of Israel's foreign relations. American recognition had placed the new state firmly on the political map of the world. The Soviet Union followed suit. Dispensing with juridical subtleties, it granted full *de jure* recognition to Israel. A spate of similar messages arrived from capitals all over the world. Among the important countries only British recognition remained conspicuously absent. London had not yet decided to close the Palestine file and to open a new chapter. The pundits of Whitehall were more reserved than the master of the White House. For them, Israel's attainment of independence was still an unfinished journey. Yet a few months later, under the impact of events, HMG was forced to recognize the fact that we had arrived.

The crop which the Foreign Ministry had harvested during the first forty-eight hours of its operation was more bountiful than we had expected. After the first rush was over, we had to get organized for the tasks ahead. Policy, personnel and premises became the preoccupations of the new minister. Of course, Sharett consulted Ben Gurion on the main problems and key appointments, but the Prime Minister's time and mind were absorbed by the immense task of organizing the defence of the country against the invading Arab armies. In a fit of old world courtesy the Secretary-General of the Arab League had deemed it opportune officially to inform the Secretary-General of the United Nations on 15 May 1948 that the Arab states had decided to take up arms against the State of Israel. This was a declaration of war which went against a decision of the United Nations, whose members had pledged themselves 'to refrain in their international relations from the threat or use of force against the territorial integrity and political independence of any state and to settle their international disputes by peaceful means'.

The United Nations took notice of the violation of its Charter, but no action in its defence. The burden fell on Israel's shoulders alone. It was the first occasion in which the world organization failed in the fulfilment of its principal task as guardian of international peace and security. Its failure had fateful consequences not only for peace in the Middle East, but for the United Nations itself.

Since 1947 the United Nations had become the centre of Israel's political efforts. The concerted Arab military response to the proclamation of its independence made the United Nations one of the most active diplomatic front-lines of the new state and one of the most favoured political battlegrounds for its adversaries.

This situation prompted Foreign Minister Sharett to take a quick decision about the organization of Israel's representation at the United Nations. Abba Eban, a young member of the Jewish Agency team, had distinguished himself in his diplomatic work for Israel's right to statehood and in the ensuing international struggle in the United Nations. He had excelled in preparing the briefs of the delegation and in drafting some of the most remarkable speeches of its members. His first personal appearance as speaker in the United Nations debates in April 1948 aroused wide public acclaim and Sharett's admiration. Eban became his natural choice as Israel's representative and spokesman in the assembly of the nations. Sharett also thought that, in the light of my own experience at the United Nations and my familiarity with the situation in Israel and perception of the realities in its neighbouring countries, I would make a useful contribution to the work of our new delegation. In his view, the critical military and political developments required my urgent departure for New York to assist Eban and help to inform American public opinion about Israel's perils and prospects.

It was easier to decide than to leave. All airlines had ceased their flights to and from Israel. It had become an air- and land-locked country under siege. I had two companions while waiting for means of transportation: Golda Meir and Teddy Kollek had also been asked to go to the United States on urgent missions. Golda was to mobilize desperately-needed funds, and Teddy to enlist volunteer manpower and vital supplies. He was not only a good organizer, he was also endowed with a sharp ear for unusual news. He had learnt that a private Beachcraft plane, piloted by two Frenchmen, had landed in Haifa with a group of war correspondents. Teddy asked the military authorities to make the plane available to us. Within twenty-four hours we were on our way.

I spent my last day in Tel Aviv in a series of meetings. The Chief of Military Operations, General Yigael Yadin, gave me a situation report. The Arab armies were closing in from the south, east and north. The situation of besieged Jerusalem, pounded by Jordanian artillery, was grave. The outlying villages of the Kfar Etzion region near Hebron had been captured by the Arab Legion. The army stores were at their lowest, but the fighting spirit was incredibly high. Yadin concluded that if military supplies arrived in time and in sufficient quantities, the defence forces could repel the combined Arab attack. Colonel Mickey Marcus, an American Jewish volunteer with wide combat and staff experience, added to General Yadin's assessment. He believed that the Arab war-machine would soon run out of steam. The more the Egyptians advanced, the longer and more vulnerable their lines of supply and communication would become. The convergence of the Arab armies in Palestine was militarily unco-ordinated and would lead to in-fighting. Mickey Marcus sent me off in good spirit: 'If you fellows will pass on the ammunition and hold the front line in New York, we shall win,' were the last words which I heard from this soldier with a great heart and a keen mind. A few weeks later at the height of the fighting he was killed, accidentally, by one of our own guard posts.

The first envoys sent abroad by the new state did not only encounter a problem of transportation, but also of accreditation. Israel had not yet issued its own national passports; more urgent matters preoccupied its government. Sharett decided that the three of us would have to travel on our defunct Palestinian passports, but he felt that international protocol required that the envoy proceeding on a mission on behalf of the Foreign Ministry should be duly accredited. He composed the text of the letter and eventually typed it himself, after having detected some misspellings in the one produced by one of the volunteer helpers. He wrote it on a blank page:

STATE OF ISRAEL   FOREIGN OFFICE
Provisional Government   Tel Aviv, May 17, 1948

TO WHOM IT MAY CONCERN

This is to certify that Mr Gideon Ruffer [later Rafael] is a senior member of the staff of
the Foreign Office of the State of Israel, who is proceeding on duty to the United States.
Any assistance which will be rendered to him in the course of his travels and in the
discharge of his functions will be appreciated.

signed M. Shertok [later Sharett]
Foreign Secretary
Provisional Government of Israel

Equipped with this momentous document and his last-minute instructions
to recover his suitcase in Athens, I took off the following morning from Haifa
airport in the company of Golda and Teddy. The plane had just enough fuel to
reach Cyprus. We boarded the aircraft unescorted and silently, each of us deep
in his own thoughts on the future, but bound together by a feeling of joint
responsibility for the accomplishment of our tasks.

Landing in Athens I went about my first diplomatic assignment. The arrival
of a plane with three envoys from the embattled Holy Land aroused
understandable excitement. We were received like messengers from another
planet – with circumspection, curiosity and courtesy. I asked to see the man in
charge of the airport. He directed me to the lost property department, and
there it was – the object of my search. The official was most forthcoming, but
how could I prove that I was entitled to receive the suitcase? I produced my
credentials. Was it not clearly stated by the owner of the valise himself,
the Foreign Secretary, that assistance should be rendered to me in the
discharge of my functions? The customs officer found the logic irresistible and
the credentials impeccable. He made me sign a receipt, explaining that he
needed the signature not so much for his files but rather for his son's collection
of autographs.

I sent a jubilant telegram to Sharett: 'Mission accomplished. Suitcase
salvaged. Gideon.' Cryptographers all along the line must have racked their
brains to crack Israel's new code.

2

The Year of Decision

The restoration of Jewish independence in the land where the Hebrews had established their national and spiritual identity had been a compelling force in the life of the Jewish people since its dispersion. It was a principal article of its faith and an inexhaustible well from which it drew the strength to survive its trials and tribulations. From the end of the nineteenth century the urge to regain its statehood had become its central political goal. The horrors of the Nazi Holocaust welded the religious longings and the political aspirations into an irresistible force. The United Nations recognized its moral validity and political legitimacy; it was not the progenitor of the Jewish state but it issued its birth certificate. The State of Israel, conceived in the hearts and minds of generations of Jews and born into a ravaged world, grew up in an environment of hostility.

From the first day of its regained independence Israel had to struggle alone for its existence. The United Nations did not assume the role of its protector; it contented itself with exhorting the parties to cease fighting and invited them to settle their differences by peaceful means. It lacked the will and the means to enforce its decisions. The absence of international action shaped the pattern of the armed conflict which continued over a period of thirty years, marked more by its recurrent eruptions than its temporary interruptions. It was a cycle of war revolving with planetary regularity around the axis of belligerency, touching off in its path fiery flare-ups, passing through cooling-off zones of cease-fires, heating-up periods of increasing hostile activity and leading back, full circle, to renewed all-out war.

War-armistice-war became the pattern of the Middle Eastern scene for three decades, and it dominated the conduct of the foreign affairs of Israel and the Arab states. The War of Independence was Israel's first and most severe test. It demanded the mobilization of all its resources in its fight for survival, and they were wanting in every respect. Men and material became a matter of highest priority; the gathering of political support to secure their unimpeded flow was a vital necessity. Procurement of military supplies, availability of financial support, the movement of immigrants and the enlistment of international goodwill became the four pillars of Israel's external endeavours. Not all of them were the direct responsibility of the Foreign Ministry, but the issues were interrelated, and all of them required extensive activity in foreign countries. The new state had still to gain experience in inter-departmental co-operation and work out a system of co-ordination. What the government lacked in method it tried to make up by ingenious improvisation. The swiftly-changing and unforeseen situations confronting Israel transformed improvisation from a necessary evil to a cherished national cult. It added a dynamism, but also a wastefulness, to the life-style of the nation.

The beginnings of the Foreign Service

The conduct of a coherent foreign policy required some method and manner and not merely mental agility. In the months between the United Nations decision of November 1947 and the proclamation of the state in May 1948 some work had been done to prepare a chart of the future organization of the Foreign Ministry. Israel was the forerunner of the wave of independence which swept the globe after the Second World War. Its beginnings were dramatic and modest at the same time. Its territory was smaller than Wales, its population hardly exceeded the half-million mark, and the country was surrounded by fifty million implacable foes. The task to achieve even survival was monumental and the tools at hand minimal. This was the root of the Israeli dilemma and has ever since formed a mighty stimulant to gather strength, self-reliance and national cohesion.

Unlike other ex-colonial people who enjoyed international acclaim and support from their former rulers in their quest for independence, Israel had to struggle for every inch of its national territory and every ounce of international succour.

At the time that Israel proclaimed its independence, it did not possess a professionally-trained foreign service, although some of its first senior members had acquired useful political experience in the course of the struggle and while representing the Zionist organization abroad. These people became the first envoys of the new State: Eliyahu Eilat in Washington, Abba Eban at the United Nations, Maurice Fischer in Paris. Golda Meir reluctantly accepted her appointment to Moscow, and only after some powerful prime ministerial persuasion. She really wanted to stay at home where the action was. Who didn't?

Foreign Minister Moshe Sharett decided that Israel's foreign represent-ation should be limited in scope, unpretentious in style, high in quality, and low in cost. Arriving in New York I drove from the airport straight to Lake Success, where the Security Council was in session in its provisional quarters. The press, which received its reports mainly from correspondents stationed in Cairo and Beirut, featured the advance of the Arab armies on Tel Aviv and Israel's untenable military situation. I met a group of United Nations correspondents and explained the war situation with the help of a detailed map and the briefing received before my departure, reassuring the people from the press that Israel would repel the invaders provided it received in time some urgently needed supplies.

The first truce

The Security Council debated a draft resolution calling for an immediate cease-fire with considerable anxiety. The United States and the Soviet Union concurred; France was in favour, but hesitant to state her position; Britain preferred to remain on the sidelines; and the Arab states strongly rejected any move intended to bring the fighting to an end. The Soviet representative, Andrei Gromyko, rebuked them firmly: 'This is not the first time that the Arab states which organized the invasion of Palestine have ignored the decisions of the United Nations. It is not in the interest of the United Nations to tolerate a situation where decisions of the Security Council designed to put an end to warfare in Palestine have been flouted by the Arab governments primarily responsible for the present situation.'

Senator Warren Austin, the United States representative, an elderly gentleman of great forbearance and courtesy from Vermont, tried to separate the adversaries by appeals to their good sense and tenets of human morality. But when the war continued and the violence of the debate did not abate, he tried his ultimate argument. In exasperation he exclaimed: 'Why can't you Jews and Moslems settle this conflict in the true Christian spirit?' This was certainly a novel but unfortunately not very promising prescription.

The Security Council eventually compromised on a thirty-day truce and ordered the United Nations mediator to take the necessary steps for its implementation in the field. Communications between Israel and New York at the time were rudimentary and cumbersome. The Foreign Minister in Tel Aviv had interpreted the day of the adoption of the resolution as coinciding with the date for the cessation of all fighting. Accordingly, orders had been issued to the Israeli forces to discontinue all military activity from that date. The Arab armies, however, did not lay down their arms. The Foreign Ministry managed to establish a radio-telephone link with our delegation through a roundabout circuit of RCA relayed via Tangiers. It was a poor connection more likely to cause misunderstandings than elucidation. We heard Sharett hollering that we were to submit an urgent complaint about the violation of the cease-fire. He, on his side, had difficulty in understanding our explanation that the resolution would become effective only after the UN mediator had made technical agreements with both parties. Sharett incredulously repeated: 'But we have already stopped fighting and interrupted our promising advance in a certain sector.' All that I could get over to him was, 'Keep on fighting and advance as long as the going is good. The hour for the cease-fire to become operative will be arranged by Count Bernadotte.' We heard Sharett's voice fading away, saying something like 'I accept this on your responsibility.' Our answer that this was the correct meaning of the Security Council decision never reached him. The circuit had broken down under the over-load of scores of unauthorized, but understandably curious, listeners-in. This was the first time in the state's young history that the thrust of the fighting was directed by overseas telephone. With the improvement of telecommunications and the intensification of the conflict over the years, the telephone was to become an indispensable instrument in critical situations.

1948 was as turbulent a year as it was a critical one. While the United States and the Soviet Union co-operated in the Middle East conflict, though for different ends, they clashed in Europe. Moscow hoisted the storm signal of the Berlin blockade and Washington decided to ride the storm.

The United Nations reflected like a global mirror the converging and divergent currents of the policies of the two great World War allies. Wherever they confronted each other directly or by proxy, the world organization was excluded from playing a meaningful role in the settlement of the conflict.

The unique international constellation of 1948 came when the United States and the Soviet Union concurred in their opposition to the armed Arab attack, and this had a salutary effect on Israel's military situation and its international standing. When the first cease-fire came into effect, at the beginning of June, the outcome of the war was far from being decided. The situation in Jerusalem was precarious after the Jordanian army had occupied the Old City and its Jewish Quarter. The Jewish defence forces were still in the first and accelerated state of their transformation into a regular army. The fighting men and women, grossly outnumbered by the enemy and pitifully under-equipped, were in desperate need of rest, regrouping and training. Survivors of the Nazi camps, refugees detained in Cyprus by the British government and scores of Jews from oriental countries escaping the Arab fury, streamed through the open gates of the reborn Jewish state.

Their arrival was the ultimate vindication of Israel's fight for freedom. It achieved the central objective of its struggle to hold the keys of the gates to the land in its own hands. But the tens of thousands of newcomers had to be housed, fed and gainfully employed. It was a staggering task under normal circumstances, but a crushing charge in time of war. Yet the seemingly unbearable burden was accepted by the people as a blessing.

Renewal of fighting

The rest of 1948 passed in a fast-moving sequence of broken truces, renewed fighting and feverish political action, leading by the end of the year to an agreement to negotiate armistice agreements between the combatant Arab states and Israel. The Arabs had paid a high price for their rejection of the Security Council injunction to extend the first cease-fire. When they renewed hostilities in July, the Israeli forces, retrained and better-equipped, succeeded in rolling back the Arab armies from sizeable stretches of territory that they had occupied in the first round of the fighting. However, they still maintained important positions in the northern Negev and the Gaza area, perilously close to Israel's urban centres. In its precipitate advance towards Tel Aviv and Jerusalem, the Egyptian army had left at their rear Israeli villages which they had failed to capture. They were now cut off from the rest of the country. Their fate depended solely on the capacity of the Israeli army to break through the Egyptian forward lines.

At the beginning of August, I received instructions to go for a short visit to Israel for consultations of an unspecified nature. Upon arrival I was told to present myself at the house of Prime Minister Ben Gurion the next day. It was a humid and hot Tel Aviv Sabbath morning when I rang the bell. It was the first time that I had been privileged to meet him privately since he had assumed the premiership. Although we had always been informal, I decided that the occasion required a modicum of decorum and donned a sports jacket. The Prime Minister answered the door himself. He was dressed in a pair of pyjama trousers, and nothing else. He eyed me for a moment with incredulity and asked with a straight face: 'Gideon, is it cold outside?'

Not given to small talk he immediately plunged into his subject. We had settled down in his book- and manuscript-crowded studio, and he shot his question at me without preliminaries: 'How long does it take from the beginning of fighting until a cease-fire ordered by the Security Council becomes operative?' Collecting my wits I replied that our experience in this field was still rather limited. Much depended on the field reports of the United Nations observers and even more on the wishes of the great powers. It might take five days, plus another twenty-four hours perhaps for additional clarifications, but after that the situation would become sticky for anyone defying the Security Council. Ben Gurion pondered silently and then growled: 'That's not enough. I need at least seven fighting days.' I would not change my estimate, but replied jokingly: 'If it depended on me, I would be glad to oblige you with a whole month.' He snapped: 'I don't need a month, I want a week.' He explained the military plan and its requirements and I explained the workings of the Security Council. He sent me to General Yadin for further discussion, with the request that I enlighten him about the way the United Nations operated.

A few months later Yadin went to see Sharett in Paris, where he was attending the United Nations annual assembly. Ben Gurion had sent Yadin to consult with the Foreign Minister on the political aspects and the timing of the planned operation. Sharett recognized that any further delay in lifting the Egyptian siege of the Negev villages would spell their doom. He considered the political repercussions to be far-reaching, but the military concerns were overriding. At the end of October a special task force relieved the embattled villages and in intermittent fighting which lasted for a few weeks the Egyptian army was driven out from Beersheba and most of the Negev. Part of the forces were surrounded in a tight pocket at Faluja, where a young major, Gamal

Abdul Nasser, negotiated their fate with the Israeli commander. And another part retreated into the Gaza Strip, where they were saved by the unavoidable cease-fire resolution which, as anticipated, became mandatory and fully operative five days after the Security Council had been convened to deal with the renewal of the hostilities. Upon the insistence of the British representative, Harold Beeley – an influential adviser of Foreign Secretary Ernest Bevin – the resolution called on the fighting sides not only to observe the cease-fire, but also to withdraw their forces to the truce lines which had been established prior to the flare-up. In practice, this would mean the restoration of the Egyptian siege and the return of their forces to the positions they had occupied in the wake of their invasion of Israel. Lester Pearson, the Canadian Foreign Minister, valiantly led the opposition to this absurd proposition, possible only in the world of surrealistic policies which in the course of time the United Nations became increasingly inclined to foster. But his efforts were cut short by Beeley's fast and indefatigable footwork. He virtually circled the Council table like a sheepdog gathering his straying flock. The Russians and Americans made some braying noises of disaffection, but were not inclined to frustrate the exercise by casting their veto. Apparently they did not feel that this was an opportune moment to annoy the United Nations.

Armistice

The position in which the Council had put itself was completely untenable. It was obvious that Israel would not withdraw to allow Egypt to advance anew. But it is not the practice of the United Nations to change its resolutions because they are impractical – unwarranted or outdated though they may be. Its way is to erect its new structures on the ruins of the dilapidated ones, without first removing the accumulated debris. To avoid unnecessary conflict with the Security Council and strain our international position even more, the Israeli delegation initiated the introduction of a new resolution. Its aim was to consolidate the volatile situation and stop the pendulum-swing between temporary truces and renewed fighting.

The General Assembly was held that year in Paris and the Security Council had transferred its activities there. I felt it would be useful to consult a good friend who worked in the political department of the United Nations secretariat on how to go about the new venture. It occurred to me that one could not withdraw to old truce lines if they were superseded by some other form of demarcation. 'What about armistice lines instead?' I probed. Drawing on his solid international experience, my friend gave a logical reply. Armistice lines, he thought, was as useful a term as it was a good idea, provided there was an armistice agreement. He shared my view that the time was ripe for the Security Council to decide on three steps: a permanent cessation of the armed conflict; the conclusion of an armistice agreement to be negotiated between the parties, fixing the demarcation of the lines separating the opposing forces;

and an injunction that the new agreement should serve as a first step towards the establishment of permanent peace without delay. It was a tall order, but we believed it was possible. We drafted an outline of the new resolution on the back of a menu card and rushed over to the hotel where Sharett and Eban were staying. In our excitement we showed him the savoury side of the menu card. The Foreign Minister looked at it, bemused, assuming it was a practical but ill-timed joke. 'And what else brings you here at this unusual hour of midnight?' he inquired. We swiftly discovered the error and turned the card over. Eban accepted the idea and immediately asked who would sponsor such a resolution.

Lester Pearson, Canada's Foreign Minister, agreed to take the lead. He assured himself of the support of Philip Jessup, an eminent jurist and deputy United States representative. Circumventing the opposition of the British Middle East professionals and disregarding strident Arab objections, they pushed the armistice resolution through the Security Council. The decision adopted on 16 November opened a new chapter. Although the Syrian and Egyptian representatives had proclaimed that their countries would under no circumstances participate in any negotiations, only a few weeks passed before the government of Egypt announced its acceptance of the invitation of Dr Ralph Bunche, the acting United Nations mediator, to send representatives to the island of Rhodes for armistice negotiations with Israel. At the end of February 1949 the agreement was signed, sealed and celebrated. In the course of the next six months Jordan, Lebanon and lastly, obdurate Syria followed suit.

The Bernadotte plan

Concurrent with the action of the Security Council, the political committee of the General Assembly discussed the non-military aspects of the conflict. It rejected a plan based on the recommendations of the late Count Bernadotte which clearly revealed the fingerprints of the British Foreign Office, proposing in essence the severance of the Negev from Israel and the annexation of all of Jerusalem by Jordan. Though the new plan had been designed to take into account the demands of the Arab states, they rejected it out of hand because it envisaged the establishment of peace with a sovereign Jewish state. Israel's delegation, resisting as it did the truncation of its parsimoniously small territory and the imposition of Arab control over all of Jerusalem, worked under a severe handicap. Not yet admitted as a member of the United Nations, its representatives participated in the debates merely as observers. But much graver than this inferior status was the dark cloud which was hovering over the young state.

Shortly before the opening of the Assembly at the Palais de Chaillot in September, the United Nations mediator Count Folke Bernadotte had been assassinated in Jerusalem by two Jewish assailants. It was a dastardly act committed by self-styled avengers. The government expressed its abhorrence but, despite efforts not always vigorously pursued, it failed to apprehend the murderers. The primary preoccupation of the provisional government at the time was to impose national discipline on the dissident militant underground organizations, and integrate them into the newly-formed Israel Defence Army, based principally on the formations of the pre-state defence organization, the Haganah. Its overriding consideration was to rally all available and desperately needed forces for the joint war effort. In later years the government felt that a determined prosecution of the investigation might open old wounds and weaken national unity in the face of unrelenting external hostility. Both motivations, to say the least, are questionable. National discipline and unity must be founded on fundamental values in a free society and particularly in a Jewish state which derives its strength for survival from its spiritual inheritance. Assassins must be brought to justice, regardless of the motives which perverted their minds. And political differences must be settled in open debate and not papered over with shallow notions of national consensus.

Twenty-three years later, on the occasion of an official visit to Sweden, Countess Bernadotte received my wife and myself at her home in Stockholm. By that time terrorism was burgeoning like poisonous weeds in the political wasteland of many countries. Our hostess received us like friends. She tactfully avoided mentioning the tragedy which had brought us to pay our respects and regrets to her. Terrorism was a plague, whatever its reason and origin, and was an unpardonable crime. It threatened free society. It was the duty of its elected organs to combat it wherever and under whatever ideological guise it appeared. When we took our leave the Countess promised to visit Jerusalem.

The virulent life of international organizations, however, is more animated by the fervour of animosity than the spirit of generosity. The Bernadotte tragedy cast a long and sombre shadow over the work and standing of the Israeli delegation, the first to represent the new state at the assembly of the nations of the world.

Admission to the United Nations

Although the rejection of the Bernadotte plan had created an impasse in the political debate, the principal powers did not relent in their search for new approaches to the peaceful settlement of the conflict. After lengthy negotiations they agreed on a composite resolution and secured its adoption, despite Arab opposition. It served for many years as one of the basic documents of United Nations policy on the outstanding issues of the Arab-Israeli dispute. It set forth as its principal aim the termination of the conflict by a peaceful settlement, negotiated by the parties directly or with the assistance of a specially appointed Conciliation Commission. Moreover, the resolution recommended an alternative solution for the refugees who had left the country in the course of the fighting. Those who were willing to live in peace in Israel should be permitted to return. Others, who preferred to stay abroad, should receive compensation.

The Paris Assembly had determined for a long period to come the direction of Arab-Israeli affairs. It had initiated the armistice agreements; called for a peaceful settlement of the conflict; prescribed guidelines for the solution of the refugee question and accepted the territorial consequences of the unsuccessful Arab military attempt to eliminate the State of Israel.

The crowning event of the dramatic year 1948 for the Jewish people was the establishment of the State of Israel and its victorious defence against overwhelming odds. We felt that it was befitting to apply for United Nations membership before the year came to an end. Eban agreed that 29 November, the first anniversary of the adoption of the resolution endorsing the establishment of the Jewish state, was an auspicious date for the submission of Israel's application to the Secretary-General. Trygve Lie received us, as always, with warmth and good humour. He assured us that if the decision had depended on him, Israel would have been admitted at the hour of the proclamation of its independence; but we needed seven votes from the Security Council and he doubted whether they would be forthcoming. Nonetheless, he thought it was worth trying. He put the application on the agenda of the Council and it failed, as he had correctly anticipated. It was passed a few months later, after the conclusion of the armistice agreement between Israel and Egypt.

On 11 May 1949 the United Nations voted Israel's admission to membership. With visible emotion and accompanied by warm applause Moshe Sharett led the first delegation of the Jewish state to their seats in the General Assembly hall.

Sharett went up to the rostrum to make the acceptance speech. He recalled the tribulations of the Jewish people, so tragically ravaged in the Second World War, when three out of every four Jews had been put to death. The United Nations represented an anti-Nazi coalition born of a common war against the darkest forces of evil. The triumph of the allied nations over the scourge of humanity would have remained incomplete if the Jewish people had still remained without a country of their own. At the historic juncture of its admission, Israel's first thoughts were for the Jews of all countries, and it expressed fervent wishes for the security, dignified existence and equality of rights of Jews everywhere. The Foreign Minister referred to the historical coincidence of Israel's admission on the day the agreement between the United States and the Soviet Union on the lifting of the Berlin blockade entered into force, and hoped that both events would lead to a reduction of tension between the great powers. Both the United States and the Soviet Union had supported Israel's struggle for statehood and welcomed its admission to the United Nations.

Addressing himself to the Arab people he declared that Israel was deeply aware of the common destiny uniting it with them forever. Israel had no higher ambition or more urgent task than to attain a relationship of good neighbourliness and friendly collaboration with the peoples of that vital area. He concluded his address with the pledge that Israel would strive to live up to the noble record of Jewish tradition. It was the prophets of Israel who had bequeathed to the world the vision that 'nation shall not lift up sword against nation, neither shall they learn war any more'.

The next day Israel's flag was hoisted in front of the United Nations building. It joined the emblems of the other member states. It signified the legitimacy of Israel's place in the world community of sovereign nations, and was an elating and unforgettable moment for all of us present.

3

The First Steps in World Affairs

Until its admission to the UN, Israel's foreign policy had as its overriding aim the establishment of formal relations with the greatest possible number of states, the repulsion of the political onslaught accompanying the Arab military assault and the mobilization of political, moral and material support.

But now, as a member of the world organization with equal sovereign rights and obligations, Israel had to assume new responsibilities in world affairs far beyond the horizon of the Arab-Israeli conflict. Inexperienced and uninvolved in the intricacies of foreign relations, its representatives would have to express Israel's views and cast its vote on issues ranging from the Kashmir dispute to South African apartheid, from diplomatic sanctions against Franco Spain to the determination of the future of the former Italian colony Libya.

The Libyan vote

The day after the Israeli delegation had taken its seat in the Assembly hall, it had to cast its first vote. Ernest Bevin and Count Sforza, the Foreign Ministers of Britain and Italy, had submitted to the United Nations a joint proposal on the future of Libya, still occupied by Commonwealth forces. The Arab states and the Soviet bloc strongly opposed the draft resolution placing the ex-Italian colony under a trusteeship regime for the duration of ten years. The Soviet Union's claim to participate in the trusteeship administration had been dismissed by its Western allies.

The trusteeship resolution required a two-thirds majority for its adoption, which was not assured. Every vote counted. Both camps engaged in fierce lobbying, with the undecided countries their prey. The Israeli delegation wavered. It had neither a voting record nor a thought-out policy. Having gained our independence from British rule, we sympathized with the anti-colonial aspirations of other peoples. On the other hand the combined strength of Arab hostility unleashed against Israel naturally dampened our enthusiasm for the addition of another sovereign member to the Arab war coalition. While our delegation was still swaying between its ideological temptation and its pragmatical consideration, a member of the Iraqi delegation, the head of the political department of Baghdad's Foreign Ministry, approached one of our Arabic-speaking representatives with a startling appeal. The Arab delegations, he said, were asking themselves: Whither Israel? Did it want to become an integral part of the area or serve as a bridgehead for foreign interests? The Libyan question was a test. Israel's vote might be decisive.

The very fact that an Arab official had approached an Israeli representative was in itself exciting news. His message was heady wine: it tasted well but dulled the senses. Foreign Minister Sharett, with the full support of his delegation, decided to meet the challenge half way. Israel would not support the resolution, but abstain. The resolution failed to obtain the required two-thirds majority by one vote. Admitted to the United Nations, Libya joined the anti-Israel chorus to become, under Colonel Qaddafi's direction, one of its most frenetic vocalists. When Israel's abstention helped frustrate the trusteeship plan, it did not expect to gain Libya's friendship but neither did it anticipate its rabid hostility.

Atoms for peace

The great number of international disputes which mushroomed in the aftermath of the war, and the growing tensions between the former allies, impelled Israel to formulate a more coherent foreign policy. It needed a 'guide for the perplexed' to navigate the stormy seas. The developments in its immediate surroundings continued, of course, to constitute Israel's principal concern. But they were affected by the happenings in the wider world. Four principal themes occupied the minds of the policy planners: the quest for peace, the retention of American support and Soviet sympathy, the fostering of the fraternal relationship with the Jewish diaspora, and the making of a meaningful contribution to the solution of international problems. The reborn nation believed that the teachings of its prophets were meant to be more than a source for its spiritual pride; they ought also to be a code of its worldly conduct. It was not an easy task to translate the four guiding principles into a workable foreign policy in a world moved by fierce contests of power rather than by the lofty principles of the United Nations Charter. Israel thought, however, that it would be able to reconcile its aspirations with the existing realities and assert its own identity by a policy which it liked to call 'non-identification'. In substance this meant: to keep out of the big power struggle, to avoid involvement in controversies, to support international conciliation and to urge the peaceful settlement of disputes.

But this policy did not mean mere abstention from political action. Israel's policy-makers gave much thought at the time to how to make positive contributions to the solution of global problems concerning humanity as a whole or affecting the underprivileged part of it. The use of the atom bomb had had a devastating effect – not only on its immediate targets in Japan. The nuclear threat hovering over the planet gripped humanity everywhere with a frightful anguish.

At the end of 1949, I made the acquaintance in New York of a man who had played an important part in advising President Roosevelt to embark on the 'Manhattan project'. Alexander Sachs was a genius; a mathematician by inclination, an economist by acquired experience and a financier by profession. His erudition was wide and profound. His personality radiated originality of thought and power of persuasion. At the end of the 1930s he had received information from some physicists who had escaped Nazi Europe that German nuclear research was advancing towards the application of atomic energy to military purposes. Sachs discussed the frightening news with Professor Albert Einstein. The great scientist recognized the fearful implications of a German nuclear monopoly with Hitler's finger on the trigger, and at Sachs's prompting wrote to President Roosevelt. His letter of warning, presented by Sachs, played an important role in convincing the President that the survival of the United States and its allies required an American scientific, technological and financial mobilization of hitherto unknown scope and priority. The combined forces of European scientific genius and American technological ingenuity succeeded in producing the atom bomb before it became available to Nazi Germany.

After the first nuclear device had become operative, Sachs and a number of his physicist friends, who had worked on its development, objected to the use of the terrible weapon without forewarning. They suggested that its devastating power should be demonstrated to foes, friends and neutrals alike in a test drop on an uninhabited island in the Pacific Ocean. The trial should be accompanied by an ultimatum to Japan to surrender, if it wanted to be spared from nuclear disaster. Roosevelt died before he could deal with the proposal. According to Alexander Sachs it was never brought to the attention of his successor, President Harry Truman. After the bomb had been dropped on Japanese towns, Alex Sachs and his friends felt pangs of conscience for their participation, in one form or another, in the creation of forces which, if uncontrolled, would threaten the existence of mankind.

Since then, Sachs had given much thought to a system of international nuclear control, disarmament and the use of atomic power for peaceful purposes. He felt that Israel should become the standard-bearer of the protection of humanity from the nuclear menace. As the result of our talks, we drew up the outlines of a plan which we called 'Atoms for Peace'. We decided to seek the advice of Dr Weizmann, the President of the State and its fore-most scientist, and, with his blessing, the government's consent to submit the proposal at the forthcoming session of the United Nations.

President Weizmann received me at his residence in Rehovoth at the beginning of April 1950. He was ailing, although regally poised in his straight-backed armchair. He felt much attracted by the 'Atoms for Peace' idea and in particular that Israel should take a leading part in promoting it. He had always felt that Israel's vocation was to reach out into the world, and that the genius of the Jewish people should apply itself not solely to matters of Israel's immediate concern, but also to the solution of problems of universal significance. He asked Professor Ernst Bergmann to study the details of our project and lend his assistance in its implementation.

Then the venerable old man asked me what my impression of life in Israel was after a year's absence from the country. I said it seemed somehow unreal. At the United Nations, Israel's adversaries subjected the country to constant assault and battery, its legitimacy was questioned and its very existence threatened; and yet here at home, on this glorious spring day, the people went about their work, seemingly unperturbed by these ill winds and unaware of the perils beyond the borders. President Weizmann's tired face lit up with a smile of satisfaction. 'The secret of our fortitude', he said, 'is this pluckiness of our people. If they busied themselves in figuring out every day what could happen to us, they would become broken reeds in no time. They are not unconscious at all of the perils, but they have confidence in our future here. It will be a sad day for Israel, if we lose our sense of self-reliance.'

Heartened by the President's equanimity and his support of our 'Atoms for Peace' plan, we elaborated it in New York in more precise terms during further consultations with Alexander Sachs. Abba Eban intended to present our proposal to the meeting of the General Assembly in September 1950. But on 25 June North Korea invaded the south. The Korean War changed all the international priorities; for the next three years it became the central concern of the United Nations. The confrontation between the United States and the Soviet Union created by the war did not come at the most opportune time for the promotion of an innovative project, based on international co-operation and especially on that of the two rival superpowers. 'Atoms for Peace' was shelved. It reappeared in another version as an American plan personally presented by President Eisenhower to the United Nations in December 1953.

Abba Eban, the head of our delegation, welcomed the American initiative: 'Out of successful co-operation on the peaceful use of atomic energy there may well emerge processes of supranational thought and action which may assist the evolution of the United Nations towards a broader universalism in other questions, including the problem of atomic weapons.' He then spoke of Dr Weizmann's concern, both as scientist and as architect of the nation, 'with the problem of compensating for natural deficiencies by the results of advanced scientific research'. New materials and new power appealed to Dr Weizmann's scientific imagination, as well as to his vision of a broader welfare for Israel and other small countries than their existing conventional resources seemed to promise. Thus, from the concluding days of the Second World War he was in contact with leading figures in the world of nuclear physics.

Referring to the practical aspects of peaceful use of atomic power, Eban said: 'Countries afflicted with deserts and plagued by centuries of erosion are deeply interested in processes for adapting sea-water to irrigation purposes.

This may well be one of the first practical problems which the international atomic energy organization could try to solve, with incalculable benefits to countries in the Middle East and elsewhere in which the shortage of water for irrigation prevents the attainment of self-sufficiency in food production.'

'For good or ill,' Eban concluded, 'atomic science has set us on the crossroads from which two paths branch forth – the one leading to immeasurable abundance, the other towards disaster beyond comprehension by heart and mind. May our deliberations be guided with wisdom and humanity, as we stand within the shadow of this fateful choice.'

Korean mediation

The Korean War was the first major post-war conflagration and became not only a tremendous test for the United States policy of the inviolability of boundaries and lines of demarcation agreed upon by the Western Allies and the Soviet Union, but compelled the member states of the United Nations to take a stand. It was the first major trial for Israel's policy of non-identification. The gravity of the conflict and its far-reaching international implications made political escapism a hopeless undertaking for a country like Israel which was so closely tied in friendship, concept and national need to the United States. Cautiously Israel moved away from its earlier policy. It did not commit itself outright to one side. Trying instead to avoid a frontal clash with the other, it attempted to steer a middle course. Resistance to aggression had been the compelling motivation of Israel's foreign policy from its inception. The peaceful settlement of conflicts was its other corner-stone. These two principles guided its course like directional beams. Thus, Israel aligned itself in the Korean conflict with the anti-aggression coalition and supported the efforts of the non-aligned countries to bring the war to an end by peaceful means.

In the United Nations debate and in the behind-the-scenes diplomatic activities, Israel's representatives soon became actively involved. We helped formulate a number of guidelines acceptable to both sides as a basis for negotiations. The heads of the delegations of India (Sir Benegal Rau), of Mexico (Padilla Nervo) and the Foreign Minister of Canada (Lester Pearson), all maintained an intensive exchange of ideas with our delegation. Likewise, Israel backed the American plan of 'Uniting for Peace', presented by Secretary of State Foster Dulles. It was designed to empower the General Assembly to take action against breaches of international peace, a prerogative which had hitherto belonged exclusively to the Security Council. The functioning of this principal United Nations organ in matters of international peace and security had been paralysed by the veto cast by the Soviet Union with regularity against any resolution which did not suit its policy.

Before the hostilities in Korea broke out, the Soviet Union had decided not to participate in the work of the Security Council as a protest against the continued representation of China by the Government of Taiwan. The Russian absence enabled the Council to take fateful decisions, endorsing United States military action in Korea under the auspices of the United Nations. During the first month of the war neither the Soviet voice nor its veto frustrated the work of the Security Council. Ambassador Jacob Malik, the permanent representative of the Soviet Union, was scheduled to preside over the Council in August. The diplomatic and journalistic guessing-game reached its peak in the final days of July. Reporters buttonholed ambassadors and vice versa – will he or won't he come back?

A few days before the decisive date, Tom Hamilton, the chief of the *New York Times* UN bureau, approached me in the delegates' lounge with the ominous question. I answered without hesitation that we had good reason to believe that Malik would take up his presidency on the first of August. The experienced journalist dismissed my guesswork. He did not know, nor did I reveal, that the source of my information was unimpeachable. It came from the mouth of a Soviet official, the United Nations Undersecretary in charge of Security Council affairs. He gave the secret away inadvertently. Eban and I had discussed with him, sometime in July, a matter related to the Arab-Israeli conflict which we thought might come up before the Security Council. The Undersecretary advised us to defer the issue until August when his countryman Ambassador Jacob Malik would be in the chair. From previous experience we knew of the close contact that existed between Soviet officials of the United Nations Secretariat and the Soviet mission and had, therefore, no doubt about the authenticity of the Undersecretary's fortuitous revelation. Two or three days after my chance meeting with Tom Hamilton, Jacob Malik announced officially that he would assume his presidential duties. Hamilton called me in a mood of self-flagellation – however could he have slipped the scoop? He had failed to grasp that 'I have good reason to believe' is the diplomatic equivalent for 'I know'.

The reasons for the absence of the Soviet Union from the Security Council in the decisive days of the outbreak of the war have intrigued diplomats and historians ever since. The Kremlin's archives are locked up and the Soviet press is leak-proof. Speculations range widely from diplomatic miscalculation to well-planned political strategy. In the light of later Soviet performance it appears that it was a combination of both. The Soviet government must have been well aware of the planned attack on South Korea when it decided to boycott the Council. It apparently assumed that the forces of the North would overrun the Republic of Korea in a short campaign, and that the United States would confine its reaction to angry protests and diplomatic activity which the Soviet Union would tackle after South Korea had been conquered. Seemingly, it had not anticipated American military intervention, sanctioned by the United Nations and carried out under its flag. A Soviet veto would probably not have deterred the United States from rushing to the rescue of its ally, but would have denied it the legitimacy of United Nations endorsement, a politically valuable asset under the circumstances. In any case, in the course of the war the Soviet Union had ample opportunity to use its veto.

In the debates on the 'Uniting for Peace' resolution, Abba Eban took a prominent part. By his interventions he helped strengthen the legal and political structure of the plan as well as its conceptual foundations. None of us suspected then that six years later the United States, together with the Soviet Union, would use the 'Uniting for Peace' resolution in the wake of the Suez campaign as a powerful lever against Israel, Britain and France. Yet the objective of the United States initiative in 1950 was to muster worldwide support against unprovoked aggression. Israel, itself still a recent victim of aggression by seven Arab states, had good reason to strengthen the capacity of the United Nations, and its most powerful member, the United States, to resist it. The 'Uniting for Peace' plan stipulated the establishment of a body which it euphemistically called the 'Peace Observation Committee'. In view of Israel's manifest support of the resolution and believing that peace observation was a useful means of crisis management, it accepted its nomination to the committee. For years I served as its rapporteur. It was my most leisurely assignment; the Committee did not observe any peace and I had nothing to report.

In our Korean mediation efforts, however, we were somewhat more successful. At the end of December 1950, after the People's Republic of China had intervened massively in the Korean War, a delegation of the Peking government was invited to state its case before the United Nations. The large measure of curiosity the newcomers aroused was matched by the extreme secrecy with which they shrouded their views about the terms of an eventual settlement of the conflict. In the hope of warming up the strangers and drawing them out, Trygve Lie, the UN Secretary-General, arranged a dinner at his home in their honour. He invited the heads of the delegations of the states which had recognized the People's Republic. There were nine, Israel among them – represented by its Foreign Minister.

Moshe Sharett had not followed closely the developments of the Korean conflict in the United Nations. He knew, of course, of our consultations with a group of delegations engaged in a mediation effort. On the day of the dinner-party he asked me to brief him and furnish him with some ideas which he would try out on the Chinese emissaries. I put down on a piece of paper points which appeared to offer to my mind the best chance for a consensus. The following morning Trygve Lie's secretary called me with a curt request to find Sharett and to come with him immediately to see the Secretary-General in his office.

Sharett was puzzled, but obliged. He inquired whether anything disturbing had occurred overnight in Israel. Nothing of the kind; all was quiet on the Eastern front. On our way to the United Nations building he described in great detail the happenings at Trygve Lie's party. He enumerated the various courses of the menu and commented on their culinary quality. He gave a picturesque account of the Chinese envoys, their height and weight, their bearing and their Mao dress. I interrupted him impatiently: 'Did you speak to them?' 'Of course,' Sharett replied, 'there was one who spoke Russian. I recited to him like a good student your seven-point plan.' 'What was his reaction?' I asked, hoping against hope that he had revealed an indication of Peking's thinking. 'Reaction,' pondered Sharett. 'None whatsoever, only a broad friendly grin. As a matter of fact I began to doubt later whether he understood Russian at all. But at table I distinctly heard him speak Russian. You never know with these people,' he concluded with a sigh of resignation.

Trygve Lie received us in high spirits. 'Tell me, Moshe,' he came straight to the point, 'what did you discuss yesterday at the dinner with my Chinese guests?' Sharett answered warily: 'We spoke about Korea. Why do you ask?' Trygve Lie beamed. That morning the Chinese delegation had visited him and, unlike previous conversations where they had refused to give the slightest indication of their ideas on a negotiated compromise, their leader had made a cryptic remark. He said: 'Yesterday night at dinner-party I spoke with little man with small moustache. He talked Russian and it made sense.' The Secretary-General told us that he had immediately consulted his guest list and the only one who corresponded to the colourful description was the Foreign Minister of Israel. 'Now, come on Moshe, tell me everything. This may be the key to the solution.' Sharett reiterated our seven-point plan and asked me to elaborate on it. Trygve Lie said it made sense to him, too. He urged us to discuss it with Lester Pearson and a number of other like-minded delegates and then circulate it in form of a draft resolution. We left the office of the Secretary-General more reassured than when we had entered.

Sharett reported with visible satisfaction to Eban and directed him to initiate the necessary steps. We consulted with a number of delegations who accepted our proposal with a few amendments. Sir Benegal Rau and Padilla Nervo urged us to submit it in the form of a draft resolution to the Political Committee. Foster Dulles was more reserved; he found that some of its provisions were too far removed from the American position. Nonetheless he did not try to dissuade us from going ahead. It appeared that he wished to protect the United States' bargaining stance, anticipating that the other side might insist on major changes in the text.

When Eban announced his intention to introduce the draft resolution, various Arab delegations protested against Israel's insolence in defying the rules of the Arab diplomatic boycott, which barred Israel from sponsoring resolutions and election to office in international organizations. They threatened to thwart the consensus if it were to be achieved as a result of the Israeli proposal. Their determination to manifest their hostility against Israel on all fronts had precedence over all other considerations, including the restoration of international peace. We decided to yield our sponsorship to Norway, who presented the resolution with due credit to its authors. It was adopted and became the diplomatic basis for the Korean armistice negotiations. In his memoirs, Trygve Lie commented on Israel's role in the peaceful settlement of the Korean War: 'At this dinner Mr Sharett broached the principles of the cease-fire resolution which the General Assembly later adopted.'

Twenty years later on the occasion of a visit to the Republic of Korea, the United Nations Command invited me to tour the Armistice Zone at Panmunjom. The compound where the Armistice Commission was meeting was an eerie place. The demarcation line between North and South Korea crossed the conference table. It was marked by a wire connecting the microphones. Two doors led into the hall where the meetings took place; one door for the North Koreans and the other for the United Nations representatives. Under normal circumstances they met once a month. Their sessions followed a rigid rite: without greetings or preliminaries, the head of the North Korean delegation would read a strident indictment against the United States, listing the crimes of imperialism in general and alleged armistice violations in particular. His American opposite number would listen stoically, and then either briefly refute the irrelevancies, present a number of United Nations claims or ignore the other side altogether.

Thinking of the working of the Israeli-Arab Armistice Commissions, I asked the American general how they reached decisions. He gave me an astonished look, wondering at such fathomless innocence, and snapped: 'Decision? But we have never taken any formal decisions since the signing of the armistice agreement. All that is happening here is an interminable North Korean exercise of harassment and a test of United States stamina.' I pondered whether Israel was more fortunate in its armistice relations with its neighbours. Outwardly perhaps there was less hectoring and more handshaking, but in substance the observance of the agreements was in constant jeopardy, because the Arab signatories used them as a sanctuary from which to launch their sorties against Israel. In the surrealistic setting of Panmunjom they relentlessly played out a weird game of propaganda offensive and political attrition, but were careful not to step on the tripwire which could detonate a new explosion. The chessmen on their board were the peoples from north and south of the great Korean divide whose peace and safety depended on the accuracy of the calculations of their leaders and allies and the boldness of their moves. For more than a quarter of a century the Korean armistice has weathered the fierce storms which have swept South East Asia. The early practitioners of Israel's foreign policy can look back with the satisfaction of having supplied a few bricks to the foundations of the structure.

4

Belligerence in Action

The armistice agreements concluded between Israel and its Arab neighbours in 1949 envisaged a swift passage from war to peace. They stipulated the unconditional end of all belligerent acts and all crossing of the lines for hostile purposes, and the lifting of the ban on Israeli shipping through the Suez Canal and in the Gulf of Aqaba. But Israel's neighbours chose to practise belligerence under the protective cloak of the armistice agreements. They regarded them as a recuperative interval in an unfinished war and not as a stepping-stone to peace. The more the Arab states recovered their political and military strength, the less they were inclined to accept the existence of Israel. Instead of negotiating a final peace settlement with Israel, they stepped up hostile activities, maintaining the maritime blockade, reinforcing the economic boycott, promoting the political and propaganda warfare and supporting ruthless incursions into Israel. Against this background the advent of Gamal Abdul Nasser in Egypt and the tragic death of King Abdullah of Jordan, who had secretly been engaged in peace negotiations with Israel, sharpened the tensions and accelerated the military preparations on both sides.

In response to deadly raids carried out with growing frequency and severity against the civilian population by Arab marauders operating from sanctuaries across the borders, Israel's defence forces adopted a doctrine and stern practice of forceful counteraction against selected targets on the other side of the line. The concept was endorsed by Ben Gurion, Premier and Defence Minister at the time. But the application of overdoses of the prescribed remedy, instead of curing the malady, caused in quite a number of cases severe affliction to the dispenser. It usually produced harmful international repercussions, strengthening the Arab position and encouraging them to pursue their hostile campaigns against Israel with greater virulence.

Most of the difficulties arose from ill-timed and ill-conceived actions. Sometimes their scope exceeded the planned proportions and in other cases their timing completely ignored the effect on wider political and regional developments of foremost significance to Israel and its friends. What became known as the policy of retaliation was essentially a sort of tribal action of raids and counter-raids. Their limited and local nature excluded the possibility of quelling hostile Arab activities altogether by a decisive use of Israel's military superiority. The application of periodic shocks, on the other hand, increased the Arab political potential.

The proponents of the policy of retaliation advanced two reasons for its support. Its deterrent effect would curb the scope and intensity of the terrorist attacks and would constrain the Arab governments to take effective measures against the perpetrators of such acts denying them the use of their territory. Furthermore it was a necessary outlet for the wrath of the harassed people. This may have been true in cases of signal viciousness, but it provided only temporary relief gained sometimes at an unduly high cost in Israeli lives. The counteractions failed to restrain the Arab governments from aiding and abetting terrorism, because the United Nations granted them immunity from international censure, let alone from the adoption of suppressive measures. Nor did retaliation deter the attackers for long; they invariably returned to their invidious *métier* of maim and murder.

Over the years, the frequency of strike and the vehemence of counterstrike escalated and assumed at various times the dimensions of small-scale war operations. Their inability to check Arab violence became obvious to the civilian and military branch of government alike. But General Moshe Dayan, the then Chief of Staff, strongly insisted on the continuation and intensification of retaliatory operations, although he also realized that they did not serve their purpose. His intention, which he later expounded, was to create a situation of such gravity that it would force the Arab states to take up open battle with Israel. He held the view – shared by Ben Gurion – that time worked in favour of the accumulation of Arab strength. The Arab states would employ it against Israel without hesitation when they felt assured of their military preponderance. They therefore had to be kept off-balance and their anticipated attack pre-empted. In the opinion of Dayan and his associates of the defence establishment, any effective action, open or covert, likely to retard the progress of Arab reinforcement was an unavoidable necessity which would ensure Israel's territorial integrity and political independence.

The assessment of the General Staff prevailed in the councils of government not only in military matters – the field of their competence and responsibility – but also in the domain of foreign relations. The military roughly divided the world into five compartments: the belligerent Arab states which could be persuaded only by military means to change their ways; friendly countries from which armaments and material support could be obtained; the Soviet bloc which was in league with the enemy and a constant source of danger; the vast group of secondary powers and uninvolved countries which were considered useless from the military point of view; and Israel, which had ceaselessly to assert its strong military posture regardless of international considerations, gather strength from whatever source it could, and, in the final analysis, simply rely on its own resources.

Foreign Minister Sharett's view of the utility of the policy advocated and practised by the Chief of Staff was rather different. He did not dismiss out of hand the necessity of an occasional show of strength, but in many cases he objected to its dimension and timing. In others he felt that as a practical politician he had to compromise. The pressures exerted were powerful; their advocates were strong-minded; their answers to vexing problems were clear-cut and instantaneous; their argument was supported by Ben Gurion. Military reaction was more impressive and plausible to the general public than refined political reasoning. It took Sharett a while to recognize that the growing thrust and volume of the counteraction was not merely accidental, resulting from local tactical considerations, but an integral part of the plan to break the backbone of Arab belligerence and end the unfinished war by decisive military action when international circumstances were propitious. When he realized that this was the basic aim of Dayan's policy, his opposition to particular actions hardened. To Ben Gurion's dismay he succeeded on several occasions in swinging the cabinet to his side and out-voting the Prime Minister. No head of government anywhere would relish such a state of affairs; Ben Gurion was no exception. Slowly the storm was gathering which would eventually sweep Sharett from his post.

My first professional involvement in the policy of retaliation occurred shortly after my return to Jerusalem in autumn 1953 after a prolonged tour of duty in New York as a member of our permanent mission to the United Nations. The Foreign Minister had appointed me Counsellor in charge of Middle East and United Nations affairs. On my desk I found a file stamped 'urgent and secret'. It dealt with one of Israel's most imaginative and constructive ventures – the conduit of water from the Jordan river in the north of the country to the parched lands of the Negev desert. The project encountered virulent Syrian objection, not because it would infringe on the water rights of a small number of riparian farmers, but because it was designed to make a major contribution to the development of the State of Israel. The United Nations officials in the area, in charge of the supervision of the armistice agreements, tended to yield to Syrian pressures and insist on the temporary interruption of the work.

Sharett was deputizing for Ben Gurion who had gone on an extended vacation devoted to rest and contemplation. Pinchas Lavon replaced Sharett as acting Minister of Defence. On 12 October Sharett convened him and a group of advisers for a consultation on the Jordan project. The Chief of Staff, General Dayan, had tried to force the issue by giving orders that a diversionary channel be dug. The chief representative of the United Nations considered the action a challenge to his authority and demanded the cessation of the work. While we were discussing the matter with Lavon, I was called to the telephone. One of my colleagues informed me that news had reached him of an impending major retaliatory action planned for the same night against an Arab village located on the Jordanian side of the border. I handed Sharett a short note asking him whether he had approved the action. Instead of replying he interrupted the meeting and asked Lavon to step outside with him. After a short while the two men returned. Lavon's mien was nonchalant; Sharett's face was ashen. He quickly wound up the discussion and asked me to stay behind.

'Your information was correct,' snapped Sharett. His voice was trembling, his features drawn. Lavon had confirmed the planned operation. Sharett asked him how he could ever have arrogated to himself the authority to decide on a matter of such heavy responsibility without first asking the acting Prime Minister. Lavon replied without hesitation that he had consulted Ben Gurion, the vacationing Prime Minister. Sharett urged his colleague to countermand the orders. He refused, invoking Ben Gurion's alleged authorization. He pointed out that since 1950 Israel had suffered 421 casualties from raids launched from terrorist bases in Jordan. The latest outrage of the murder of a mother and her children in a village near the border could not pass unpunished. Sharett was in a state of high excitement, not only because his authority had been challenged so coarsely, but because he foresaw that the action might cause grievous harm to the country. I suggested he should verify with Ben Gurion the contentions of the acting Defence Minister, and if necessary argue it out with him. In the course of the evening he tried repeatedly to reach Ben Gurion by phone, but he was unavailable. Nobody knew how and where to locate him.

The following morning it was my painful task to inform Sharett of the result of the strike against the village of Kybia. More than sixty civilians, most of them women and children, had met their death under the ruins of the dynamited houses. Ariel Sharon had commanded the operation. Moshe Dayan claimed that for unforeseen reasons it had exceeded its planned scope and anticipated number of casualties. Ben Gurion stated that he had never given his consent. The seed was laid for the notorious Lavon affair. It mushroomed into one of Israel's gravest internal crises.

The same morning I sent a short memorandum to the Foreign Minister summarizing the events preceding the action, and drawing attention to the expected international repercussions, to the failings of intergovernmental co-ordination and the erosion of moral standards. Under these conditions I felt unable to fulfil my assigned duties as the Foreign Minister himself had defined them and asked to be relieved of my functions. Sharett's reaction was fast and firm. He returned my submission with every paragraph marked 'correct' with the exception of the last one which he annotated, 'nonsensical conclusion, proposition rejected'.

A few days later he sent a short note to me from the cabinet room: 'Prepare for travel tonight, wait for me in the office.' The government had decided to dispatch Dayan and myself to New York immediately, to assist Abba Eban in defending Israel's case before the Security Council. During our long flight I failed to elicit from Dayan an explanation of why things had gone wrong at Kybia. At our first meeting with Eban and the senior members of our UN mission, Dayan analysed the background of the operation, stated that continued fedayeen raids made the escalation of our counteraction unavoidable, and predicted that the cycle of violence would eventually spark off full-scale war. In his view the terrorist incursions sponsored by the Arab governments were an intermittent stage of, and not a substitute for, total war which they were prepared to renew at the time of their choice. I contented myself with repeating what I had suggested to Sharett before our departure: we should base the presentation of our case on the state of belligerence sustained by the Arab governments and its application by hostile activities of their choice. Warfare was a two-way street in which neither side could unilaterally impose its own rules on the other. This was the cause for the recurrent incidents. Israel sincerely regretted the loss of life. The strict observance of all the provisions of the armistice agreements and in particular the termination of the state of war and its transformation into permanent peace would break the tragic chain of grievous incidents.

With masterful oratory, incisive logic and persuasive argument Eban defended the justification of Israel's military policy, although he personally was far from being convinced of the political and moral soundness of excessive acts of reprisal. The perspectives so bluntly depicted by Dayan increased his doubts and anxieties. The Security Council was no different from the other organs of the United Nations. The mightiest flow of rhetoric, though evoking admiration, was incapable of diverting the set direction of the international current. The lengthy debate concluded with the condemnation of Israel's action, qualified by the censure of Jordan for its violations of the armistice agreement. The adoption of the resolution did not come as a surprise except for the abstention by the Soviet Union, the only member of the Council which had refrained from voting for it. We were pleasantly puzzled by this show of Soviet sympathy. We attributed it to the fact that, only a few weeks before, the Soviet Union had renewed its diplomatic relations with Israel. It had severed them in retaliation for Israel's strong reaction to the libellous anti-Jewish allegations of the so-called 'doctors' plot' concocted in Moscow in the final stage of Stalin's physical and mental decline. Besides, the Soviet government had not much love lost then for the Kingdom of Jordan, closely associated as it was with Britain.

The sharpness of the United Nations response to Israel's action at Kybia spurred the terrorist organizations and their political supporters to accelerate their operations and extend the scope of their violence. Nor did the resolution deter Israel from its policy of forceful counteraction. The more the United

States curried Arab favour, the more Israel felt itself isolated, and the prospects of a peaceful settlement receded while the risks of renewed war grew. The icy gusts of the Cold War did not spare the Middle East. It was an area too close to Europe and too vital to strategic interests to be bypassed. The chill did not cool tempers in the area; on the contrary it inflamed them even more.

Britain withdraws from Egypt

The United States made a major attempt to draw the new Nasser regime in Egypt onto its side. It planned to make it the linch-pin of a regional defence system tied to NATO. When this failed they concluded the Baghdad pact, setting up the celebrated but short-lived northern tier designed to bolster the defences in the rear of Turkey and Iran and to bar the front to Soviet penetration of the Middle East. But Nasser had a different order of priorities. His first aim was the termination of British military presence on Egyptian soil. Foster Dulles, in his eagerness to gain Nasser's favour, added American leverage to the pressure exerted by the new Egyptian regime. The Secretary of State fully supported the demand that the British should hand over to Egypt all their military installations which were mainly located in the Suez area. To smooth the path of rapprochement the State Department generously suggested throwing a part of Israeli territory into the bargain. Nasser coveted the southern Negev; he desired to establish a land connection between Egypt and Jordan, to advance his pan-Arab ambitions in the Asian part of the Arab domain. As could easily be foreseen, the scheme aroused Israel's resolute resistance and nourished its suspicions of future developments after the British military evacuation of Egypt.

Two schools of thought emerged in Israel. The military planners saw unmitigated disaster in the agreement and recommended that it be frustrated by diplomatic intervention or otherwise. The latter term was a code word in the military and intelligence lexicon for rather undefined non-conventional operations. They believed that existence of a foreign barrier separating Egypt from direct physical contact with Israel was advantageous to its security. Thus they preferred the continued military presence of Britain in the Suez area. Later, after the Sinai campaign in 1956, the United Nations Emergency Force assumed that role and after the Yom Kippur War they resumed it as part of the separation of forces agreements.

The Foreign Ministry's experts on Arab affairs considered that once Nasser had achieved the central objective of all Egyptian governments since the beginning of the century – the removal of the British – he would adopt an 'Egypt first' policy and become more amenable to a settlement with Israel. Any objection by Israel to the treaty, a futile exercise in any case, could only foil the slender chances of a future accommodation with Egypt. When the debate between these two concepts reached its climax, Ben Gurion's opinion was not clear. He lived at Kibbutz Sde Boker in retirement but not as a recluse.

His friends in the party and the defence establishment continued to keep him briefed and consulted him on all important concerns. Yet there is no record of whether he sided with any of the options discussed during the first months of 1954.

By then it had already become the practice of Israel's foreign policy-makers to find ways of accommodating the views held by the military. The more strongly the defence people insisted on their position and plan of action, the more the compromise was tilted in their direction. But in quite a few cases its implementation was not co-ordinated between the two branches of government, nor was the knowledge of their course of action reciprocal. While our ambassadors in London and Washington expressed their concern at the possible harmful effects of the British evacuation on the security of Israel, other representatives established contact with envoys of Nasser in order to reassure him of Israel's understanding of his aspirations and its keen interest in negotiating a peaceful settlement with him. The contrast was not prompted by Machiavellian duplicity, but rather by the inherent contradiction of the compromise between two incompatible views. We were trying to ride two horses simultaneously, one named contact, and the other contest – we fell between the two.

The Cairo trial

However, there was another participant in the race, concealed from our eyes: a stalking horse called 'otherwise'. It was groomed in an inaccessible stable of the military intelligence branch. The defence people did not have much patience with the slow diplomatic process. They considered it more as a prelude to forcible action. They were no different in their approach from their comrades-in-arms in other countries, and they preferred to see tangible results.

The trouble begins when they step beyond the bounds of their military competence and civilian control, and attempt to apply militant short cuts to international complexities. In this case the prevailing opinion of the defence establishment, represented by the director of military intelligence, Colonel Benjamin Gibli, was that the British-Egyptian negotiations must not succeed. We had lively arguments with him when he unhesitatingly revealed his ideological cunning, but carefully concealed his operational planning. His minister, Pinchas Lavon, who had assumed the defence portfolio in Sharett's newly-formed cabinet, startled his colleagues by his swift transmutation from moderate labour leader to militant activist. Without any thorough exploration of the situation, he discerned in any internal Arab upheaval – be it the replacement of General Naguib by Colonel Nasser or the overthrow of Adib Shishakli in Syria – an auspicious occasion for Israeli military intervention. He created the impression of being engaged in a desperate race of activism with the Chief of Staff and his aides. It was an uneven competition. Dayan would either overtake him or abandon him.

But in mid-summer a sudden rumble from Cairo halted this contest. The warning signal was audible only to the initiated; it foreshadowed disaster and they ran for cover. A series of mysterious explosions had occurred in a number of buildings housing British or American institutions in Cairo. One young man was caught running from a crowded cinema with an incendiary device burning in his pocket. The police quickly arrested a group of local young Jewish men and women, and accused them of belonging to a sabotage ring operated by Israeli military intelligence. Colonel Gibli had prepared them to commit, at a given moment, acts of sabotage which he thought would blast the negotiations to smithereens. This, of course, was unmitigated folly.

Yet the explosions in Egypt touched off a chain reaction of shattering effect in Israel. At first its tremors remained underground, strictly confined to the defence hierarchy. The Minister of Defence, the Chief of Staff and last but by no means least, the Head of Intelligence, chose to conceal their knowledge of the affair from Prime Minister Sharett. But Lavon and Gibli went to work immediately to prevent repercussions and obscure any record of responsibility. For more than two months they and the Chief of Staff managed to withhold information on the Cairo calamity from their own Prime Minister.

As I was in charge of Middle Eastern affairs, I used to receive every morning a summary of Arab broadcasting from our monitoring service. On 5 October, I found a startling bulletin from Radio Cairo on my desk. It told about the arrest of members of an Israeli sabotage network. The story was detailed; it announced that the arrested persons would shortly be put on trial and it smacked of authenticity rather than of propaganda. I asked the opinion of my associates. They consulted the original Arab text and confirmed my initial impression. I took the bulletin to Sharett and gave him our assessment, asking him point-blank whether he had any information on the matter. He denied all knowledge without the slightest hesitation. Then he pondered for a moment and said firmly that the story could not be true, such operations just could not be ordered without the knowledge of the Prime Minister and, if a mishap had occurred, he would have been informed immediately. Since I knew no more than what the broadcast said, I felt there was no point in arguing with him and simply suggested that he had better check the story with the Minister of Defence. He did and was flabbergasted.

It was a weird tale of political delusion, moral infirmity, governmental lassitude and professional deficiency. Sharett ruled that the saving of the lives of the young captives in Cairo, misguided by their superiors, must take priority over all other considerations. Investigations into those responsible for the action had to take second place. Any unguarded remark, any irresponsible press leak could seal the fate of the accused. Any hope for rescue depended on the closest co-operation between the few of us in the Foreign Ministry who knew the secret, and the people dealing with the affair in the Ministry of

Defence. The Prime Minister entrusted me with the co-ordination of the efforts. We decided to activate all available personal connections and public bodies who might influence Nasser. Members of parliament, representatives of the Church, human rights organizations and friendly governments intervened in Cairo. Through our direct contacts we tried to impress on the President of Egypt Israel's friendly intentions towards his desire to free his country from foreign interference.

The frequent exchanges widened the secret channel of communications between the two governments. They centred on two themes: the nature of their future relations and the immediate fate of the unfortunate captives. Nasser consistently avoided linking the two subjects. On the first he professed to favour a process of peaceful evolution, on the second he gave repeated but, in the final analysis, noncommittal assurances of leniency. The exchanges culminated at the end of December 1954 in a message from Sharett and a response from Nasser, both informal, typed on blank paper, accompanied by oral explanations and transmitted through Nasser's personal representative in Paris. On 21 December Sharett wrote:

I have noted with deep satisfaction that it is your desire to bring about a peaceful solution of the problems outstanding between Egypt and Israel. I welcome particularly your readiness to consider measures for improving the present situation and reducing the prevailing tensions. We for our part are eager to co-operate in efforts directed towards this end.

Many of us admire your brave idealism and tenacity of purpose and wish you the fullest success in attaining the emancipation of the Land of the Nile from the last vestiges of foreign domination and the initiation for the masses of the people of an era of social regeneration and economic welfare.

We feel sure that your aims are peace and progress and that you fully realize the interdependence of the two.

It is for this reason that we are keenly looking forward to more tangible evidence that you and your friends are preparing the ground for an eventual settlement with Israel by educating your public opinion to appreciate the vital importance of peace within the Middle East.

There are two matters in particular the handling of which may well have a decisive effect on the development of relations between our countries.

In the first place, freedom for all shipping to and from Israel to pass through the Suez Canal would be in keeping with Egypt's international obligations and would be widely acclaimed by the international community.

Secondly, there is the urgent question of the trial now proceeding in Cairo. I cannot emphasize too strongly the gravity of the issue which is there in balance. I fervently hope that no death sentences will be passed, as demanded by the prosecution. They would inevitably produce a violent crisis, kindle afresh the flames of bitterness and strife and defeat our efforts to curb passion and to lead our people into the ways of peace.

We look forward to counsels of far-sighted statesmanship prevailing over considerations of the moment, for the sake of the goal which I assume we pursue in common – a settlement between Egypt and Israel and a state of peace and contentment inside the region as a whole.

This message which I am addressing to you above the din of daily conflict in a spirit of sincere quest for peace and friendship will, I hope, evoke a corresponding response.

Nasser replied ten days later with an unsigned message dated 31 December 1954:

I have received your letter of 21 December. I have instructed my special emissary to transmit a verbal answer to the questions you have mentioned in your letters. I am glad that you realize the efforts spent from our side to bring our relations to a peaceful solution. I hope that they will be met by similar efforts from your side thus permitting us to achieve the results we are seeking for the benefit of both countries.

After having handed over the sphinx-like message, Nasser's envoy read us the specific answers. Egypt was interested, so the statement went, in a quiet border and was taking measures to ensure this. Reciprocal steps were expected from Israel. The present state of relations between the two countries did not allow the raising of the level of the existing contacts. The time was not appropriate for talks between high-ranking representatives. The present envoy was authorized to remain in touch with representatives of Israel. Israel's activities against the signature of the Anglo-Egyptian treaty and in particular the revelations of the Cairo trial had deeply disturbed the atmosphere between the two states. Before any practical arrangement for Israel's shipping through the Suez Canal could be discussed, the present tensions must be reduced. The Egyptian government could not intervene in the proceedings of the Cairo trial which was being conducted with strict observance of fair procedure. The defendants were receiving all the legal aid they had requested. In the personal view of the envoy there would be no execution of death sentences.

The reply was typical of Nasser's delaying tactics which he perfected over the years into an art. He would proceed towards his predetermined objective by a number of lanes not necessarily running in the same direction. He would adjust the presentation of his views to the sensitivities of the ear of his interlocutor. Where necessary he would stress his willingness – real or feigned is a matter of historical judgement – to establish peaceful relations with Israel, but would avoid any act of commitment. Pretexts of inappropriate timing and expectations of unilateral gestures were the mainstays of his elusiveness. At the same time he would take practical steps to advance his true objective – the establishment under his leadership of Egypt's hegemony in the Arab and the Third World. While secretly professing peaceful intentions towards Israel, he openly supported the intensification of fedayeen raids against it. While covertly discussing the relaxation of the maritime blockade, he tightened it in the Suez Canal and extended it to the Gulf of Aqaba. While soliciting American support in his negotiations with Britain, he surreptitiously approached the Soviet Union to obtain military assistance.

5

Towards the Brink

Tragically, Nasser had betrayed the expectations of the many influential people who believed that they had elicited from him a promise to spare the lives of the defendants of the Cairo trial. Two of the men were condemned to death and the others received harsh prison sentences. The executions shocked the intermediaries, dismayed public opinion, struck the Israeli government like a whiplash and fanned the passions of the people, who were ignorant of the sombre background of the tragedy. Questioners who asked Nasser for an explanation remained unconvinced by his replies. He claimed that unforeseen circumstances had forced his hand and the execution of seven members of the Moslem Brotherhood tried for conspiracy made it impossible for him to commute the death sentences on the two Jews.

The aftermath of the Cairo calamity determined the fate of Sharett's premiership, now in its second and last year. It also exerted a significant influence on the future direction of Israeli-Egyptian relations. The disastrous intelligence operation, aggravated by relentless hostile Egyptian activities, widened the gap of mutual distrust and sharpened the sensitivities of both sides. When, in February 1955, fedayeen gangs from the Gaza Strip penetrated deep into the country, General Dayan asked for authorization for reciprocal action against strongholds in the Gaza area. Knowing that the military were in a bad mood after what had happened in Cairo, the Prime Minister directed the Chief of Staff to exercise restraint and keep the number of Arab casualties to a minimum. The action took place on 28 February. The Egyptian forces suffered eighty-five casualties, among them forty soldiers killed.

The raid took place only a few days after Nasser had proclaimed his resolute resistance to the newly concluded Baghdad pact. After the first shock the Egyptian leader accused Israel of having acted as a tool of Western imperialism. Nothing was further from the truth. Nobody in authority in Israel had given the slightest thought to the wider aspects of the operation. It was not the first or last time that decisions on armed action were taken oblivious to their effect on international developments concerning Israel.

Normally it takes some forty-eight hours for the gravity of world reaction to begin to dawn upon the leaders of Israel and to disturb its public opinion.

Because of our unsettled situation we instinctively choose to surround ourselves with a protective psychological wall. But once breached, the floods of strident argument begin to inundate the political countryside. Lavon's position had become untenable. He had not only kept the knowledge of the affair from his Prime Minister, but had also become involved in a cycle of vicious recrimination with the director of military intelligence about the responsibility for the original order launching the Cairo operation. Lavon denied authorizing Colonel Gibli to transmit the command signal. The findings of a commission of inquiry, chaired by the President of the Supreme Court, were inconclusive. The Chief of Staff, Moshe Dayan, and the Director-General of the Ministry of Defence, Shimon Peres, pressed hard for Lavon's resignation. Leading members of the ruling Labour Party impressed on Sharett that the dissension in the defence establishment was undermining the morale of the army and was jeopardizing the party's prospects at the forthcoming elections. Golda Meir and her colleagues strongly advocated the recall of Ben Gurion as the only possible candidate for the post of Minister of Defence. They implored him to come out from his retirement at Sde Boker and serve under Prime Minister Sharett. Recognizing the terrible dilemma facing the government, the party and the army, both men agreed.

The day before Ben Gurion's consent was made public, Sharett briefed Walter Eytan, then Director-General of the Foreign Ministry, and myself on the latest developments of the cabal and the imminent return of Ben Gurion. He quietly but tensely explained that this was the only way out of the Lavon crisis and then added calmly: 'You understand, my friends, that this is the end of my political career.' We tried in vain to dissuade him from his sombre thoughts. But events proved that his insight was greater than our wishful thinking. In November that year Sharett would hand the premiership back to Ben Gurion.

But Lavon's dismissal – and, later, Sharett's resignation – did not exorcise the ghost of the Cairo affair. For years to come it continued to bedevil Israel's political life. It damaged its moral fabric, envenomed relations between the political leaders, broke up the unity of the Labour Party, cast a heavy shadow over the ways of governance, drove Ben Gurion to entrench himself in grim opposition, and contributed to the eventual downfall of the Labour Party which had become a house divided against itself. Its international ramifications were no less dismal and enduring. As Sharett had warned in his message to Nasser, 'the death sentences would kindle afresh the flames of strife'. After the executions the situation deteriorated steadily. In the preceding year direct contacts between Israel and Egypt had been developed. Although, despite their intimacy and intensity, they did not yield significant political results, still they were an important link for the exchange of views between the two hostile countries. Now, after the Gaza reprisal, Cairo stopped these contacts altogether. We tried to establish alternative lines of communication through third parties. Washington conveyed Israel's proposals to Cairo for talks on joint measures for the reduction of border tension, but Egypt preferred the continuation of incursions into Israel to the holding of meetings with its representatives. Since early 1954 the United States government had tried to arrange such talks, and preparations had been made for them to open in April. But because of border incidents culminating in the heavy shelling of Gaza shortly before the agreed date of the meeting, Egypt cancelled its participation.

Border clashes, which reached new heights in frequency and vehemence in the summer of 1955, coincided with a fresh attempt to establish direct communication between Nasser and Sharett. This time the Egyptian government had initiated the move. In July, the Egyptian Ambassador in Washington, Ahmed Hussein, and his Foreign Minister, Mahmud Fawzy, approached a prominent person in the American Friends organization, commonly known as the Quakers. They suggested that Elmore Jackson should help establish contacts between the governments of Egypt and Israel and visit the two countries for that purpose. They stressed that the time for a settlement with Israel was propitious and the prospects promising. Unhesitatingly, Sharett and Ben Gurion gave their consent to the mission. He arrived in Jerusalem in the middle of August and met Sharett and Ben Gurion. They emphasized Israel's interest in the establishment of contacts as a necessary prelude for the negotiation of a peaceful settlement. Ben Gurion glowingly depicted his vision of a Middle East restored to its ancient glories by a new peaceful encounter between the Jewish and Egyptian people, and dramatically declared that if the leaders of the two countries were to meet face to face they could settle all outstanding issues in less than a day.

Endowed with Israel's blessings and assurances of its keen desire to reach a peaceful agreement with Egypt, Elmore Jackson left for Cairo. A few hours after his departure we learnt that a retaliatory raid in the Gaza Strip was planned for the same night. Sharett phoned Jacob Herzog, a close adviser, and myself to come immediately to his residence. He was pacing up and down, fuming and growling like a caged tiger. From time to time he snapped: 'This is impossible, it would be deceit, it must be stopped.' We suggested that he call his Minister of Defence, who might not be aware of the unfortunate coincidence. Sharett declined. He could not talk to Ben Gurion, he would turn him down. He asked us to go and see the old man and, reluctantly, we accepted the delicate mission. Still there was hope. Herzog had the ear and confidence of Ben Gurion and I trusted his sense of fairness and political wisdom. He lived at the time in a hotel not far from the Foreign Minister's residence. We found him alone in his little room, stretched out on the bed suffering from a bout of lumbago. He immediately grasped what was at stake, picked up the telephone and instructed Colonel Nehemia Argov, his military aide, to ask General Dayan to cancel the operation. After a short while Nehemia called back from Tel Aviv to report that the Chief of Staff had left his home for the forward command post from which the commandos were to set out on their mission. Ben Gurion suggested that Nehemia should send a signal through military or police channels to stop Dayan *en route* and request him to get in touch with him. Colonel Argov argued against this procedure. It would stir up unnecessary commotion and unwarranted speculation, and probably arouse Dayan's anger. Ben Gurion listened patiently to his trusted aide and then said slowly and calmly: 'Nehemia, I would like you to do me a favour. If you are not too tired please drive down yourself to the jump-off point near the Gaza Strip and tell Dayan in my name to rescind the orders and the reasons for my decision. If the troops have already crossed the lines and started action he should do nothing which would endanger their safety.'

Nehemia loyally fulfilled his unusual mission. Dayan cancelled the operation and the next day submitted his resignation to Ben Gurion after he had learnt of Sharett's intervention. The Prime Minister, faced with the unexpected crisis, convened Ben Gurion, the Chief of Staff and a few senior cabinet colleagues for an emergency meeting. He asked Herzog and myself to attend. Sharett had hoped that Ben Gurion would begin the unpleasant conversation by explaining to Dayan that his move had been completely unwarranted, that he had shared the Prime Minister's opinion of the necessity for calling off the action and took full responsibility for countermanding the orders. But Ben Gurion kept silent and let Sharett bear the burden of argument alone. Dayan made a strong case for the policy of retaliation as the only effective means with which to stem the tide of Arab aggression. He claimed that the repeal of the orders harmed the morale of the forces. Sharett tried to soothe him, explaining again the special conditions that had prompted him to intervene and assuring him of his readiness to authorize actions if circumstances warranted them. Dayan insisted that Nasser must be taught lessons which he as a military man would understand. Diplomatic goodwill messages intended to improve him were useless.

To wind up the futile argument Ben Gurion asked Dayan to acquaint the gathering with his plans for an operation against Khan Yunis, an Egyptian military stronghold in the Gaza Strip. Dayan, visibly ruffled, tried to side-step the request. He claimed it was premature to give details. The forces which had been concentrated the other night had returned to their bases after the operation was called off. Why should the Foreign Ministry suddenly be so eager to see action? He would not jeopardize the lives of his men just to overcome an unpleasant situation. The participants of the meeting stepped up their prodding and appeals. A few days later a reconciled General Dayan gave the order to launch a massive retaliatory attack on a strongly fortified position at Khan Yunis.

Elmore Jackson had returned from his talks with Nasser and was about to go back to Cairo. He was supposed to carry a message which Sharett had drafted. But after the Khan Yunis operation, which had caused a considerable number of Egyptian casualties, Sharett felt that blood and ink would not mix well. Instead of sending a letter, we briefed Jackson in detail for his second meeting with Nasser and Foreign Minister Mahmud Fawzy. Our principal proposal was to arrange forthwith a high-level meeting between representatives of the two sides to discuss measures for the enforcement of a complete and lasting cease-fire. Furthermore we suggested that an exchange of prisoners, including those condemned at the Cairo trial, would help calm the highly inflamed situation. Reiterating Israel's continued readiness to explore the possibilities of an overall or a partial settlement with Egypt, we renewed the proposal, previously discussed with Egypt, to terminate as a first step the state of belligerence as decreed already by the Security Council in 1951. In this connection we suggested practical arrangements for the free passage of Israeli shipping through the Suez Canal, which would neither affect Egypt's prestige nor infringe on Israel's inherent rights. Any interference with Israeli shipping to and from Eilat through the Straits of Tiran should end. In addition, both sides, in preparation for the normalization of relations, should cease all hostile propaganda.

In his talks with the American envoy, Nasser maintained that Israel's February operation against his forces in Gaza constituted a turning-point. Until that date he had believed that the interests and aspirations of the two countries were reconcilable, provided that Israel made the necessary concessions. But the Gaza shock had been an eye-opener for him; Egypt had to reckon with a formidable adversary and the army command urged the build-up of the country's military strength. Nasser informed Elmore Jackson that the proposal he had brought had been discussed previously between an Israeli team led by myself and his special envoy. The Gaza incident had brought the talks to a bitter end. He was agreeable to the restoration of quiet along the armistice line, but could not consent to a high-level meeting. As a matter of fact he issued orders then temporarily suspending attacks across the Gaza line. But at the same time his *chef de cabinet* – and right-hand man, as we learned from unimpeachable sources – instructed the Egyptian liaison officer with the fedayeen gangs in Jordan to intensify their raids across Israel's eastern border. He agreed in principle to an exchange of prisoners-of-war and other detainees, but in fact they were only released two years later after the Sinai campaign. The prisoners of the Cairo trial had to wait another twelve years for their freedom, until after the Six Day War. Although nothing of substance had come out of Elmore Jackson's three visits to Jerusalem and Cairo, he felt that they had helped prevent the situation from getting out of control. Back in Washington he recommended to the State Department that President Eisenhower himself should initiate a mediation process by inviting the two heads of government, one after the other, to see him at the White House, a proposal which the President took up in a modified form when, a few months later, he dispatched Robert Anderson as his personal envoy on a top secret mission to Egypt and Israel.

The Czech arms deal

Shortly after Jackson's return to the United States, Nasser startled the world with the announcement of his massive arms deal with Czechoslovakia. Czechoslovakia acted as stand-in for the Soviet Union, which at that time conducted not only its wars but also its arms transactions by proxy. The unexpected development raised anxieties in Israel, and also prompted political and strategic reassessments in the major capitals. Elmore Jackson himself had second thoughts about the motivations of the Egyptian Foreign Minister and his Ambassador in Washington who had invited him earlier that summer to undertake his mission of mediation. He concluded that both men had been eager to dissuade Nasser from entering into the portentous deal with the Soviets. There was only one way in their view to prevent it, the supply of American arms to Egypt. But they also assumed that without a basic change in Egypt's relations with Israel, Washington would not oblige.

The arms deal was Nasser's first major surprise move. Over the years he developed his technique, adding experience to boldness. In 1956 he nationalized the Suez Canal without prior warning. In 1967 he expelled the United Nations forces from Sinai as a prelude to massing his troops on Israel's southern border. Two years later he started the war of attrition along the Suez line and then, in 1970, suddenly died. His successor, President Anwar Sadat, refined the art of surprise and stratagem when in 1972 he expelled without forewarning the corps of Russian military advisers. A year later he attacked Israel with deadly suddenness and stunned the world with his astonishing visit to Jerusalem five years later.

But even the best guarded secret requires time to prepare. If there ever was a discernible turning-point in the fortunes of the Middle East, it was not the Gaza action of February, but the Bandung conference in April 1955. This was the first world gathering of countries meeting under the banner of non-alignment, and it was Nasser's *première* on the international stage. Arab opposition had foiled Israel's strenuous efforts to be invited to the conference. At Bandung, Nasser met Chinese Premier Chou En-lai, who offered him his assistance in obtaining arms from the Soviet Union – a bizarre proposition considered in terms of contemporary Chinese-Russian relations but far from being impractical at the time. Upon Nasser's return to Cairo the Soviet Ambassador presented himself and launched the negotiations which were consummated a few months later in the Czech arms deal.

The sudden mass injection of advanced Soviet armaments into Egypt jolted Israel like an electric shock. Its security margin had always been precarious, its manpower outmatched at a rate of twenty-five to one and its sources of arms supplies as limited as its resources. Even under the best of conditions the quantity of its military equipment never exceeded the three to one ratio in favour of its hostile neighbours. Now the fresh flow of arms into Egypt added a new dimension to the perilous imbalance.

In October 1957 a Harvard professor, noted for his original writings on modern strategy and diplomacy, analysed the causes which had sparked off the Suez crisis and Sinai campaign one year earlier. In an unpublished lecture to a prestigious research institute in New York, Dr Henry Kissinger told his audience: 'When the Soviet arms deal was announced I happened to be in Washington. My recommendation at the time was that it had to be stopped by all means – even by the use of force. It seemed quite clear that the entry of Soviet arms into Egypt would, if nothing else, force Israel to take some steps because a state like Israel, which cannot afford to lose a single battle, whose territory can be cut in half by one defeat, will not permit a threat to become unambiguous. A state whose margin of survival is narrow will seek to anticipate armed attack.'

Such considerations, however, were alien to a United States surrounded by immense oceans, firmly implanted in one of the most fertile and productive continents of the world, and secured by overwhelming material and military strength. Irrespective of the threat created by the injection of Soviet arms into such a highly explosive area, the United States government continued to abide by its policy of abstention from arms supplies to the contending parties in the Middle East.

Now, more than ever, Israel had to redouble its efforts. A few weeks after the announcement of the Soviet-Egyptian arms deal a conference of the Foreign Ministers of the Big Four was scheduled to take place in Geneva. I thought it could offer a suitable opportunity to express our concern and suggested that Premier and Foreign Minister Sharett should individually meet the four participants. Of course, we did not expect to obtain commitments on the spot from the three Western Foreign Ministers nor to persuade Mr Molotov to mend the ways of Soviet policy. But we believed that the Prime Minister's tour of the Geneva conference would draw world attention to Israel's predicament and possibly evoke new and, hopefully, sympathetic thinking in at least the three Western capitals, and perhaps cause some measure of restraint in Moscow. Sharett acquitted himself of his mission with his customary aplomb. *En route* to Geneva he met in Paris with Prime Minister Edgar Faure, who pledged to sell Israel a squadron of Mystère jet-fighters. Encouraged by this breakthrough we continued to the Geneva conference; Sharett heading a formidable array of Israeli ambassadors to the four capitals, an assortment of advisers and a selection of experts. Whether our diplomatic invasion impressed the assembled Foreign Ministers was hard to say, but undoubtedly it stirred the curiosity of the sizeable corps of media representatives. The wide and friendly coverage our delegation received was not exactly matched by its political conquests.

Pinay would only confine himself to generalities since the central issue of arms to Israel had been taken care of in Sharett's talk with his Prime Minister, Edgar Faure.

Macmillan was attentive and evasive. He was reluctant to let new Middle East anxieties intrude on the conference which had been called to deal with European controversies.

Molotov simply denied that the delivery of arms to a hostile neighbour was a matter of Israel's concern. All that the Soviet Union wanted was to assist Egypt in protecting itself against the designs of the imperialist powers. Israel was safe and had no reason to worry. It was as simple as that.

Foster Dulles was alert to the implications of a massive flow of Soviet arms into a belligerent Arab country, but he declined to take the matter up with his Soviet colleague. That would in his view constitute an American legitimization of Soviet aspirations in the Middle East which the United States refused to recognize. His legal doctrine was questionable to say the least, but the political wisdom of his position was calamitous. The events occurring less than a year later proved this. The Soviet Union, not encountering any serious American resistance to its attempt to penetrate the Middle East, accelerated the pace and enlarged the scope of its involvement to a point where the red warning-light not only alerted Israel but also alarmed the United States and its allies. One thing Dulles did realize in Geneva was that Israel's concern and claims were justified. He understood that sending Sharett away empty-handed would probably encourage Soviet-Arab daring and make Israel despair. He therefore invited Sharett to visit Washington the following December to discuss in detail Israel's requirements; in the meantime the State Department would reassess the situation. The Geneva visit was Sharett's last mission in his capacity as Prime Minister. During his absence Ben Gurion, who had led the labour list in the recent elections, had returned to the premiership. He reappointed Sharett as Foreign Minister.

The Ben Gurion-Sharett rift

In the intervening months border tensions had shifted from the Gaza Strip to the Syrian-Israeli boundary. Syria decided that it was its turn to activate its forces and, entrenching them in positions on the Golan Heights, dominating the Huleh valley and the Lake of Tiberias, began sporadically to shell Israeli villages and interfere forcibly with fishing in the lake. Moreover they persuaded Syrian villagers to cross the border and start unauthorized fishing in violation of the armistice agreement. After a series of warnings had gone unheeded, Prime Minister Ben Gurion authorized a deterrent raid against Syrian positions located in the vicinity of the lake. The timing and the dimension of the operation were devastating. More than seventy Syrians were killed. Israel suffered six fatal casualties and many more wounded and missing. The severity of the action aroused indignation in world public opinion. Washington deferred *sine die* its reply to Israel's arms request which Sharett had been discussing with the administration at that time, and Sharett returned to Jerusalem frustrated and despondent. Eban defended Israel's case before a furious Security Council, golden-tongued as ever, but heavy-hearted as never before. Even his most sparkling performance could not avert a stern and unbalanced condemnation of the untimely and disproportionate operation.

Sharett reported on his mission to Geneva and Washington to a meeting in Jerusalem of the political committee of the Labour Party. The atmosphere was leaden. He plunged into a minutely detailed account of each and every one of his activities and then reached his climax – the ruinous effect of the Kinnereth action. 'Satan could not have chosen a worst timing,' he exclaimed, his voice high pitched in anger. Ben Gurion had taken a seat between Yitzhak Navon, his political secretary, and myself at the side of the room; he had declined the invitation of the chairman to sit at the head of the table. When he heard the word Satan, the same in English as in Hebrew and more sinister in its meaning than the more colloquial 'devil', he jerked as if he had been hit by a bullet, then leaned back without uttering a sound. I could physically feel how the word had hurt him. The audience gasped, as if witnessing a tightrope walker losing his balance. Sharett continued his report, apparently oblivious of anything untoward. After he had finished, the chairman invited Ben Gurion to take the floor. He declined curtly. The members of the political committee dispersed in a mood of gloom and I went home with the nagging thought that the brittle Ben Gurion-Sharett relationship had reached breaking-point.

The Anderson mission

A few days later, on 2 January 1956, Ben Gurion reviewed the security situation in a speech in the Knesset:

It is my duty to inform the Knesset of the deadly purpose involved in the flow of Soviet arms to Egypt. I have not the slightest interest in the motives of the arms suppliers. All that concerns me is the unmistakable aim of the recipients.

On 16 October 1955, Nasser himself told the editor of the *New York Post* that he was not fighting Israel alone, but also international Jewry and Jewish capital.

The flow of Soviet and British arms gives these threats immediate and dangerous significance, and we shall imperil our existence if we ignore them. But we shall be able to hold our ground if we prepare for whatever is in store and muster all our strength to forestall the blow.

The warning was clear. The growing danger of a heavily armed Egypt would compel Israel to take pre-emptive action. In January President Eisenhower endorsed the proposal of his Secretary of State to tackle the brewing crisis between Egypt and Israel at the highest level and in the most direct manner. He appointed Robert Anderson, an influential Texan, a former Secretary of the Navy and later Secretary of the Treasury, as his personal emissary. He recommended him to the Prime Ministers of Egypt and Israel and entrusted him with the task of preparing the ground for negotiations on a peace settlement.

Extreme secrecy was imperative for the success of the mission. Only a handful of us in the Prime Minister's office and the Foreign Ministry knew about it. Ben Gurion and Sharett conducted the talks. I was assigned to prepare the background and position papers. The 'Nasser file', a small volume, contained concise reports on contacts and negotiations with Egypt from 1949 onward; summaries of talks with Egyptian leaders; the sad history of our attempt to forestall the death sentences at the Cairo trial; recommendations on the conduct and content of the current negotiations; copies of messages exchanged between the Prime Ministers of Israel and Egypt and a profile of Gamal Abdul Nasser – the man, his aims and tactics. The summary of this portrait was:

Nasser's character is marked by a strong conspiratorial streak, formed over the long period of his political underground activity. His political stature grew considerably after his first appearance on the international stage at the Bandung conference, where he acquired foreign experience and personal esteem. His success reached a high mark with the Czech arms deal, which raised his prestige in the Arab countries and established him as an international figure to be reckoned with.

Nasser's political tactics are intricate and flexible. He switches from moderation to extremism by cool, unemotional calculation. In his struggle with Britain and his fight against Israel, he uses alternately moderation and extremism, violence and appeasement in accordance with the tactical needs of the hour. The amount of force he is ready to use is adjusted to his immediate objective. He tries to avoid tests of strength for which he is not yet prepared.

His method is to demand an advance for any action he is asked to undertake, carefully avoiding to commit himself explicitly to defray the payment. He generally formulates his assurances in a noncommittal way: 'if you will cease to do so and so and if you grant me this and that, I will be in a better position to do what you expect from me'. He displays an astonishing talent for inventing pretexts when asked to fulfil his undertakings. His system of dodging obligations is remarkably cunning. The right way to deal with Nasser is to put his promises, big or small, to the test of performance.

Robert Anderson arrived from Cairo on 23 January 1956 and reported on his meetings with Nasser, all held at night and in utmost secrecy. The Egyptian leader gave him his version of the events which had led to the present tensions and compelled him to seek aid from the Soviet Union. He reiterated his claim that the action of 28 February had triggered off the chain reaction. He was not hostile to the United States, but he was inimical to the Baghdad pact designed by the British to undermine Arab independence. He was basically not opposed to a settlement with Israel, but it would require in the first instance the restoration of calm along the borders between Israel and all its Arab neighbours. He was prepared to co-operate in such an attempt, but Egypt was responsible not only for the fate of its own country, it was also committed to the struggle and the security of all its Arab brethren. A satisfactory solution must be found for the Palestinian refugees, not necessarily by massive repatriation, but by giving them the opportunity of free choice. Jerusalem was not Nasser's major concern. In his view it was mainly a question between Jordan and Israel, and the present territorial division was preferable to the internationalization of the town. But it was vital for Egypt to have territorial contiguity with Jordan, now severed by Israel's possession of the Negev. Without the establishment of a territorial link under Arab, i.e. Egyptian sovereignty, connecting Africa and Asia, no settlement with Israel could be envisaged. It had to yield the Negev or at least a substantial part of it. All other outstanding problems were secondary. In summing up, Nasser asked Anderson to assure Ben Gurion that he did not want any further acts of hostility. He would consider punishing people responsible for such acts and even publish a statement on this subject.

Past experiences had taught Israel's leaders not to take general assurances from Nasser for granted. Throughout the talks Ben Gurion and Sharett tried to probe into the specifics. First of all, said Ben Gurion, there was the important question of whether Nasser wanted to align with the Soviet bloc. Egypt could be the key to the Soviet conquest of Africa, and the Russians had always wanted to penetrate Africa. Now they were in Egypt. Whether Nasser liked it or not, he would facilitate their penetration of Sudan and of Syria. He thought he was using the Soviet Union for his own aims, but in reality he was only serving theirs.

Israel, of course, was ready to conclude a peace with Egypt and, if Ben Gurion were to meet Nasser, he would make the settlement attractive. But a minimal basis of confidence had to be established. Direct contacts between the two sides were an indispensable prerequisite, if not yet by the two heads of government, then at least by other authorized representatives. The first step must be to stop all shooting along the cease-fire lines.

When Anderson at his third visit to Cairo finally pressed for a definite reply on a meeting between Egyptian and Israeli representatives, Nasser suggested that the exchanges should be channelled exclusively through the United States. Direct meetings were impossible. During the two months of his travails and travels between Cairo and Jerusalem the special envoy was unable to obtain from Nasser a formal, written undertaking to restore the cease-fire and to abide by all the provisions of the armistice agreement.

Repeatedly in their conversations with Anderson, Ben Gurion and Sharett stressed that, while Nasser had failed to provide tangible proof of his peaceful intentions, he had not concealed his military preparations. He was piling up powerful Soviet weapons to attack Israel at a date of his choice. Nasser had explained to the presidential envoy that internal and external pressures prevented him from entering into peace negotiations, but the same forces could propel him, even against his better judgement, into war with Israel. It would be irresponsible for Israel's leaders to ignore the possibility that Nasser was playing for time. He feigned interest in peace as long as he was not ready for war. The continued American denial of arms to Israel worsened the situation immensely, and brought the day nearer when Egypt, taking advantage of the imbalance, would turn its newly acquired arms against Israel in a strike which might cripple it, if not jeopardize its whole existence. In the stillness of his nightly talks with the emissary Nasser protested his desire for peace, but all day long his organs of propaganda trumpeted Israel's doom.

On 14 February, while the Anderson mission was still under way but had failed to show any visible signs of progress, Ben Gurion gave vent to Israel's anxieties in a letter to President Eisenhower:

No government responsible for the fate and survival of its people can watch with equanimity an enormous accumulation of arms of a neighbouring power, which vigorously insists on war, without making every effort to acquire arms, if not in the same quantity, at least of the same quality. . . .

An Israel capable of defending itself – an Israel which cannot be destroyed can bring peace nearer. . . .

I therefore appeal to you, Mr President, not to leave Israel without adequate capacity for self-defence, which only arms from a great power can provide, and to issue instructions that the United States supply Israel with arms we must have to prevent or repel an attack.

The ominous wording 'prevent an attack' was before long to reveal its operational meaning. The President replied on 27 February, all goodwill in general and irritating evasiveness on the specific issue:

I have taken sympathetic note of your statement of Israel's need for arms. Your request is being given the most careful consideration in light of need both to ensure Israel's security and to create a situation which will be most conducive to peace in the area.

The reply was as disappointing as were Nasser's elusive tactics in the trilateral talks conducted by Anderson. The final meeting between President Eisenhower's emissary and Ben Gurion took place on 9 March. Despite consistent American prodding, Nasser had turned down all the practical proposals for an amelioration of the perilous relationship; no direct contacts in any shape or form, no new commitment to abide by the obligations of the armistice agreement, no agreed measures to halt the daily border incidents – only general and non-binding promises and professions of good intention, closely concealed from his own people. This was the yield of a mission in which the United States had invested presidential prestige, Robert Anderson his remarkable talents and Israel's leaders much thought, considerable hope and willingness to compromise. Instead of bringing the

parties to the conflict together it widened the gulf between them.
In taking leave of the peace envoy Ben Gurion sounded a note of alarm:

If we should get a negative answer from the President on our request for arms, or none
at all after you have submitted your report to him, then we will have only one task: to
look to our security. Nothing else will interest us. We shall strengthen our morale,
fortify our settlements, build shelters in the cities and see what we can do. If we
get help – good. But we must be prepared to defend ourselves without help from the
outside . . . .

Nasser will feel free to do whatever he likes. He will have every reason to make war.
If we have to fight, we shall fight desperately. We will have to devote the last drop of our
energy to preparing our people to meet Nasser and all his Migs.

Thus ended in gloom and foreboding a peace mission conceived in the
noblest of spirit, conducted with the greatest of tact, the deepest of discretion
and the utmost of perseverance.

6

Ben Gurion Prepares the Nation

The failure of the Anderson mission removed the last barrier before the brink of war. Ben Gurion meant what he said and did what he had threatened to do: he prepared the nation for the approaching ordeal. He instructed the procurement people of the Defence Ministry to look high and low for new sources of arms. France was an obvious target. It possessed a first-class military industry, pursued ambitious trade policies, faced strong Arab antagonism because of its Algerian struggle and harboured considerable popular sympathy for Israel. Its agreement to sell Israel twelve latest-model jet fighters was a promising opening for a continuing supply relationship. In the months to come it began to deliver weapons systems and technology urgently needed by Israel to catch up with Egypt. Every step taken by Nasser against Western interests and every setback France suffered in North Africa fostered the intimacy of Franco-Israeli political understanding and military co-operation. The United States, still reluctant to become a major arms supplier to the strife-torn region, encouraged France to proceed, and consented to the release by Canada of a number of American-made fighter planes which in the end Israel could dispense with because of other acquisitions.

Ben Gurion called upon the people to rally round its government and strengthen its home defences. He launched a movement of volunteers who went to border villages to build fortifications. The newspapers showed him stringing barbed-wire, and the Chief of Staff digging trenches. A group of us went to a kibbutz near the Jordanian line and, although some of us had in our younger years done manual work, we found that moving rocks was somewhat more arduous than pushing pens.

The defence forces perfected their call-up system and intensified their training programme. They absorbed with alacrity and skill the new weapons which were mostly of French origin – ranging from Mystère jets to Ouragan fighter bombers, from anti-tank rockets to heavy artillery. But mounting numbers of Soviet tanks, Mig fighters and artillery of all sizes continued to arrive in Egypt, outnumbering by far the shipments reaching Israel. The more Nasser felt assured of Egypt's growing military strength, the more he flexed his oratorical and political muscle. In June, after the last British forces had evacuated the Suez Canal zone, he proclaimed: 'The Egyptian army has enough strength to wipe Israel off the map of the earth.'

Meanwhile, Nasser was applying his persuasive powers to Washington in order to obtain financial and technical aid for his favourite project: the construction of the monumental Aswan dam. The logic of his policy of equilibrium was simple. The Soviet Union would grant him the necessary military aid and the United States the required economic support. And the more the one was forthcoming, the more the other side would feel constrained to do its part. But the mechanics of foreign power-relations cannot be manipulated as simply as Nasser tried to do it; obviously the donor also expects from the recipient some measure of consideration. By midsummer 1956 the United States government concluded that Nasser had failed its cautious expectations. He had frustrated the success of the Anderson mission, tightened Egypt's links with the Soviet Union, mounted a fierce campaign against the Baghdad pact and ignored the appeals for restraint in the sensitive Egyptian-Israeli border area. Consequently Secretary Foster Dulles informed Ambassador Ahmed Hussein, without any preliminaries and with marked bluntness, that the United States felt unable under the prevailing circumstances to lend its support to the Aswan project. Nasser's reaction was swift and vehement. On 26 July he abrogated the international status of the Suez Canal and proclaimed its nationalization. In an impassioned speech to the excited masses he recommended to the United States 'to jump in the lake' if it did not like his policy. In one stroke he had achieved the realization of Egypt's national aspirations and an international crisis of the first order.

The Suez crisis accentuated the looming danger and accelerated the convergence of French, British and Israeli interests. The two Western powers considered Egypt's unilateral control over the canal as a threat to their far-flung maritime and economic interests east of Suez. They also thought that any accretion of international status could only spur Nasser on to pursue his designs in Africa with greater vigour.

Israel was convinced that Nasser would provoke a confrontation with it after he had weathered the Suez storm. Its margin of security was too narrow to absorb the shock of surprise. It felt that in its solitude and exposure, it had to seize the unique opportunity offered by France to obtain access to much needed armaments and to develop a political and military working relationship, even if temporary in nature and based on limited common interests. France became the connecting link for British participation in the anti-Nasser coalition. Both countries, supported by their European and Commonwealth allies, tried in the first instance to meet Nasser's challenge by determined and united diplomatic resistance. But their efforts to establish an impressive common front were frustrated by the prevarications of Foster Dulles. He had decided at an early stage of the crisis to yield to what he believed the inevitable, and to concentrate his considerable talents of tactical elasticity on preventing Britain and France from attaining by forcible intervention what the maritime community was incapable of achieving by diplomatic means. His method was to drag the issue from conference to conference and to whittle it down with every new meeting. His only allowance to the mounting frustration of his allies was to join in high-sounding but low-powered declarations against Nasser's action.

These tactics neither appeased Britain and France nor gained Egyptian goodwill. They strengthened the determination of the leaders of the two countries to go it alone and proceed surreptitiously in their own way.

Sharett resigns, Golda Meir takes over

Together with the mounting international tension, the situation on Israel's borders deteriorated markedly. The defence forces toughened and their counteractions became more widespread. The number of casualties on both sides increased alarmingly. The threat of a re-armed Egypt, defying with impunity a disunited Western world and drawing its military strength and political audacity from the Soviet Union, assumed fearful proportions in the eyes of Israel. At the beginning of 1956, Ben Gurion had formed the opinion that the active involvement of the Soviet Union in the Arab-Israeli conflict on the side of Egypt would lead to another round of war. He became convinced that in the course of the year the government would be faced with fateful decisions requiring, as he saw it, a united cabinet under his unchallenged leadership. Moshe Sharett, because of his moral integrity, power of rational argument and precision of thought, held in the government a position of influence second only to Ben Gurion. He was highly respected in his party and enjoyed vast popularity among the people. His personal effervescence was moderated by his political rationality and sense of fairness. As a man of deep-seated peaceable sentiments the pursuit of peace was second nature to him. Of course, he recognized the realities of a situation in which Israel had to fight for its existence and devote maximum effort to strengthening its defence capacity. But he also believed that the possession of arms in itself and the show of military muscle, indispensable as they may be, were not sufficient to ensure Israel's security. He tended to judge proposals for military action by a balanced blend of these criteria. These qualities made him not only a highly esteemed member of the cabinet but also an opponent to be reckoned with.

Since Ben Gurion's return to the premiership Sharett had succeeded on a number of occasions in thwarting the adoption of proposals for military action recommended by the Chief of Staff and presented by Ben Gurion. The fact that he was able occasionally to muster a cabinet majority against the Prime Minister caused Ben Gurion considerable concern and personal pain. When his plans for preventive action against Egypt matured in June he convinced himself that Sharett might eventually frustrate them. Without any substantive discussion or an explanation of his true reasons he asked for Sharett's resignation from the post of Foreign Minister. Sharett, who had often contemplated handing in his resignation, was flabbergasted by the suddenness of the Prime Minister's blow. His relationship with him over the previous few years was far from harmonious, but Sharett had never suspected that Ben Gurion would terminate their close association of nearly twenty-five years with such painful abruptness. Although Sharett had confided in us, when Ben Gurion returned from Sde Boker to join his government, that he believed his days were numbered, he did not imagine that they would end without his own consent and mutual understanding with Ben Gurion.

At the height of the Lavon crisis of confidence, after the Cairo trial, he had wrestled with himself about how he should tell his Minister of Defence that his time was up. John Strachey, a former cabinet minister and prominent member of the British Labour Party, was visiting Israel at the time. Sharett invited him for lunch and asked me to attend. The first course passed with general talk, but when the entrée was served Sharett came to the point. 'Tell me, John,' he inquired, 'how does the British Prime Minister proceed when he feels it necessary to relieve a cabinet member of his duties?' 'That's very simple,' replied Strachey. 'I can speak from experience. One fine morning, Attlee called me in to Number Ten and said: "John, I want your resignation." I did not have the slightest forewarning and asked: "Why?" Attlee answered dryly, "Because you are not up to standard."' 'What did you say to him?' asked Sharett, amazed. 'Very simply, "Yes, Mr Prime Minister",' answered Strachey. 'And then?' probed Sharett. 'And then, nothing. That was it,' replied the ex-minister. Sharett found this procedure incredible, but being a perfect host he would not subject his guest to further cross-examination. Later, however, he felt impelled to return to the subject: 'Tell me, John, when Attlee dismissed you, you said "yes, Prime Minister". Why so formal – after all party friends are customarily on first-name terms?' With mild astonishment Strachey answered: 'But he did not dismiss me in his capacity as leader of the party. It was the Prime Minister of Britain who had asked for my resignation.'

This was certainly not the Israeli way of doing things. Good form required that the candidate for resignation had to abide by a rigid ritual. It normally began with a press story predicting his imminent political demise. This was promptly denied by the 'competent authorities'. After a short while, not always a decent interval, the rumours blossomed into facts. The heat was on and together with it the public debate. At that point the candidate usually indicated, preferably through third parties, his intention to resign, provided he had in his view sufficient party backing to pull him back from the brink. Then began the processions of delegations to his office or home. The number of participants and repeat performances was strictly regulated by the standing and popularity of the candidate. The lack of supplications was the humiliation an Israeli politician dreaded the most. It was his doom.

I once asked Golda Meir, after she had resigned from the premiership, how she had wielded the abdication threat. She had used it repeatedly in her illustrious public career, either in protest against vexing departmental interference or as a means to achieve her ends. Golda pondered a minute and said: 'It is a dangerous tool. One must use it with utmost care, never too often and always ready to take the risk. This is the only way to make the threat credible and effective.'

When Ben Gurion struck his blow, Sharett lulled himself in the belief that his party and cabinet colleagues would rally around him and resist Ben Gurion's peremptory decision. It was not his attachment to his ministerial office which prompted him to refuse to vacate it voluntarily. He felt that good government as practised in Israel was at stake, that the Prime Minister was arrogating to himself powers which neither the Knesset nor his party had conferred upon him. He was concerned that without his moderating and balancing influence, Ben Gurion could lead the government into ventures fraught with inestimable danger to the state. He had reason to believe that his view was shared by a number of cabinet ministers and a large segment of his party's leadership.

A few of us, his trusted aides, followed the unfolding drama blow by blow. Sharett kept away from the public, but remained close to his personal friends. He shared with them his hurt feelings and sense of outrage, but never asked us to intercede on his behalf. But he counted on his political friends. Indeed they came to see him not in processions but one by one, to express discreetly their sympathies and indignation, but not to pledge solidarity. The party counsels had tried to avert the rift, but they were powerless to heal it. Ben Gurion refused, even in his most intimate circle, to reveal his reasoning for his resolute insistence on Sharett's removal.

But what distressed Sharett more than anything else was what he called the spinelessness of his closest party colleagues in the last stages of his losing battle. They came to plead with him to remove himself voluntarily from the scene. Pinchas Sapir, a top wheel in the party machine and a staunch supporter of Sharett's policies, administered the final blow. As Sharett told us at the time, he arrived at his home, accompanied by a few friends, and bluntly told him that any further resistance to Ben Gurion's will was not only useless, but worse, it was harmful. 'I bowed my head to the Lord High Executioner,' as Sharett put it when telling us of his painful final hours.

But what embittered him most, beyond reconciliation until his dying day, was Golda Meir's consent to succeed him. Shortly after she had taken over the Ministry she invited me for a private talk. She knew that Arthur Lourie, Jacob Herzog and myself had offered to resign in protest and solidarity with our offended minister. But Sharett had rebuked us sternly, saying that such an act would add our injustice to his injury. Golda maintained that although she could understand our feelings, she could not dispense with our co-operation.

When Ben Gurion called her into his office to offer her Sharett's position, she was resolute in her decision to reject it. But when the Old Man pleaded with her on grounds of national emergency, her resistance broke down. 'If he had ordered me to jump out of the window', a figure of speech which Golda used to highlight dramatic events, 'I would have done it for him.' I was somewhat baffled by this revelation of blind devotion and muttered to myself, but apparently distinctly enough for Golda's ears, that I would never accept a proposition against my better judgement and contrary to my basic beliefs. This remark hit a sensitive spot. She recorded it as an irredeemable irreverence.

War in Sinai and Suez

After the removal of the Sharett obstacle, Ben Gurion proceeded singlemindedly on his course. Confident in Golda's dutiful compliance, he gave free rein to Shimon Peres, Director-General of the Ministry of Defence and one of his closest collaborators, to tighten the French connection. He reported directly to the Prime Minister and followed his own diplomatic style, not always to the pleasure of the new Foreign Minister. But the arrival of arms in steadily increasing quantities compensated for the ill-feelings. Hand in hand with the flow of supplies the planning of military and political co-operation with France progressed. It culminated in the then very secret and now highly publicized meeting at Sèvres, a place better known for the manufacture of exquisite china. The story of the meeting between Ben Gurion, Christian Pineau and Selwyn Lloyd and their suites of aides has been told by insiders and outsiders in a dazzling variety of colourful versions, ranging from suspense stories to factual, but still undocumented, narrations adorned with the predilections of their authors. There is no need to retell it here. Suffice it to say that at the Sèvres meeting Ben Gurion hesitated until the last moment to participate in the joint venture. He feared that at the decisive hour Britain and France would not fulfil their commitments to provide Israel with the indispensable protective air umbrella and necessary international support. He finally yielded to the strong urgings of Dayan and Peres. When the operation was launched on 29 October, it surprised not only Egypt, but also the United States, the closest ally of Britain and France and the most important of Israel's friends.

Yet, perhaps more amazing was the rapidity of the advance of the Israeli forces, the fast and thorough collapse of the Egyptian army, and the way the Franco-British expeditionary corps moved so slowly and indecisively. The most stunning surprise came from Washington. The reaction of the Eisenhower administration was irate and utterly uncompromising. It insisted on an immediate halt of the operation and took instant steps to enforce its decision. The planners in Israel had given some general thought to the international implications, but had sought very little expert advice on how the events on the battlefield would reflect in the political arena. They completely miscalculated the American response, reckoning that in the last week before the presidential election the American government would be too hamstrung to take any meaningful action. They were correct in their assumption that the Security Council would be convened, but erred in their conclusion that the promised Franco-British veto would terminate all further United Nations intervention. The American President hit hard, regardless of, or probably because of, his election campaign. The most powerful man in the world was offended by the unilateral action of his friends and allies and decided to assert his authority. He was particularly incensed by what he thought to be an act of British infidelity.

When I served in the mid-seventies as Ambassador to the Court of St James's my wife and I struck up a warm friendship with Lord and Lady Avon, the former Anthony Eden, who was Prime Minister at the time of the Suez affair. He used to invite us to his unostentatious manor, appointed with exquisite taste, nestling in the serene rolling hills of Wiltshire. His striking good looks were well preserved despite his delicate state of health and the disappointments he had suffered. He was still smarting at the deviousness of Foster Dulles. On the first day of the British Suez intervention, Foster Dulles had conveyed to HMG, in outspokenly sharp terms, the President's indignation. Eden telephoned Eisenhower and suggested that he leave the same night for Washington to explain what had prompted him to join battle against Nasser. Eisenhower welcomed his initiative without the slightest hesitation. Content with the prospect of regaining the confidence of the United States, Eden set out for the House of Commons to cool the boiling tempers with the announcement of his imminent consultation with the President. But as he entered his car, his private secretary rushed out to summon him back to the transatlantic telephone. President Eisenhower was on the line. He had just consulted his diary, meaning his Secretary of State, and found to his regret that every date was booked for at least a week. He suggested that Eden should contact him again after the end of the operations which he firmly hoped would be suspended without further delay. To quote Lord Avon, he was 'slamming the door in the face of the British Prime Minister *à la* Foster Dulles'. In his view presidential pique and state department myopia had jointly defeated a unique chance to turn the fortunes of the Middle East and those of the Western world. These were the thoughts of Anthony Eden, the founding father of the Arab League in 1945, who had come full circle thirty years later to regret that he had sired a miscreation.

Ben Gurion had his own version of Lord Avon's metamorphosis. He once told me that Eden had been much obliged to him for his discretion on the British participation in the Sèvres agreement. In a statement made in the House of Commons, Eden had strongly denied the existence of any agreement of collusion with Israel prior to the Suez campaign. Ben Gurion, although in possession of a copy of the accord, had never contradicted Eden's denial even with the slightest hint. And Eden had never forgotten this act of good faith of his former Israeli colleague. As a matter of fact, years after the event Eden met Ben Gurion in Paris for the sole purpose of expressing his gratitude to his loyal comrade in arms and conspiracy.

The Security Council, paralysed by the British and French veto, did not lose an hour in invoking the 'Uniting for Peace' resolution of Korean War fame and convened the General Assembly in a special session. I arrived in New York on 6 November, the day the Israeli forces had attained all their targets and had stopped their advance along a line twelve miles east of the Suez Canal. Abba Eban had just communicated to Dag Hammarskjöld, the UN Secretary-General, Israel's acceptance of the cease-fire resolution and the issuing of the relevant orders to its forces. Dag Hammarskjöld demanded a similar statement from the British Ambassador. Sir Pierson Dixon was taken aback to learn of Israel's unilateral step. Upon instructions from London he urged Eban to withdraw his communication. Actually there was no diplomatic co-ordination between the delegations of Israel, Britain and France in New York. Insofar as it existed, it was handled in the capitals of the three confederates. As the latest addition to his tired forces, Eban commissioned me to untangle the mess.

The Franco-British forces had got stuck on the way to their targets. According to the official version they were supposed to inject themselves between the two fighting sides and form a buffer zone on both sides of the canal. But where there was no fighting, there was no need for a buffer. I went up to the Secretary-General's lofty tower office and acquitted myself with considerable embarrassment of my mission, explaining that an error of transmission had occurred, thus invalidating Eban's earlier message. Hammarskjöld fumed and threatened to expose the whole plot, as he preferred to call the Suez campaign. He calmed down when I suggested a not exactly heroic, but under the circumstances practical, compromise. We would check our 'transmissions' and he would withhold his communication. This little interlude provided the two allies with some more marching-time, but they advanced in slow motion. The mounting pressure from Washington and Moscow, amplified by a frenetic United Nations chorus, made them stop in their tracks, far from their original objectives.

Soviet threats

Meanwhile Moscow was threatening London and Paris with missiles which it did not possess at the time and Washington was manifesting its aloof indifference to the fate of its threatened allies. At one of our pleasant Wiltshire luncheons, Anthony Eden told me the story of the great Khrushchev missile revelation. Some time in 1955, allied intelligence had obtained disquieting information of Soviet missile development, but lacked details of their range and effectiveness. British intelligence had been hard at work, so far unsuccessfully, to get information on the specifics. In the spring of 1956, Khrushchev steamed into Plymouth on a battle-cruiser at the head of an impressive delegation. It was his first official visit to Britain. The talks with the temperamental Chairman were lively. At one point Prime Minister Eden stressed the vital necessity 'for Britain to ensure the undisturbed flow of Middle East oil to its shores. We would have to go to war if this lifeline were cut,' he said calmly but resolutely. Khrushchev heaved in his seat, banged his fist on the table and shouted: 'Don't threaten me. We have missiles with a range of 150 kilometres. You had better think twice before you talk to me about war.' What British intelligence had failed to discover, the irascible Chairman had volunteered to reveal. Eden still chuckled at the recollection of the scene.

In the autumn crisis of 1956, however, the Khrushchev-Bulganin duo did not content itself with missile threats, it accompanied them with raging missives to Israel's Prime Minister, predicting the doom of the Jewish state unless it instantly ceased all military action. The Soviet threats, which stunned Jerusalem, London and Paris, were aimed at two objectives: to save the Nasser regime from succumbing to the tripartite operation, and to divert world attention from the Soviet military suppression of the Hungarian uprising. Both eruptions, completely different in nature and motivation, coincided to the detriment of the insurrectionists of Budapest and the interventionists at Suez. The former Yugoslav Ambassador to the Soviet Union, Veljko Micunovic, recounts in his memoirs, *Moscow Years 1956–8*, that in a secret meeting between Khrushchev and Tito on the island of Brioni, the Chairman told the Marshal that the Russians were able to intervene in Hungary only because of the simultaneous action of Britain, France and Israel against Egypt. He did not fear any serious Western reaction: 'They were as deeply bogged down in the mud of Egypt as we were in that of Hungary.'

But there was one fundamental difference. In its intervention in Hungary the Soviet Union did not get stuck in the United Nations quagmire. It simply ignored the pile of ineffectual resolutions deploring, appealing to and pleading with it; and, with Tito's consent, squashed without quavering the first people's rebellion in a Soviet-controlled People's Republic. The United Nations buried in its archives its mound of Hungarian resolutions, never again to see the light of day. But how different was the reaction of the world organization to Israel's attempt to break the siege, blockade and impending threat to its very existence emanating from a belligerent neighbour, and to the Franco-British undertaking to restore international legality where Nasser had taken the law into his own hands. The United States and the Soviet Union – at loggerheads over Hungary, the rebellious Soviet satellite – became brothers-in-arms against the United States' friends and allies acting against Egypt, the Soviet client-state. It was a strange mix-up of positions. It unbalanced the established

East-West equilibrium and upset the traditional Middle Eastern constellation of power for years to come.

US pressure

United States pressures, supplemented by Soviet threats, rose to irreversible levels. The General Assembly decided on the immediate withdrawal of the occupying forces and adopted a Canadian proposal to replace them with a special United Nations Emergency Force. Ben Gurion, carried away by the resounding military success and his elation at the nation's deliverance, proclaimed from the rostrum of the Knesset the restoration of King Solomon's patrimony stretching from the island of Jotphata in the south to the foothills of the Lebanon in the north. It was a short-lived daydream. The morning after, a nerve-racking presidential message jolted the jubilant Prime Minister back to reality. Eisenhower demanded Israel's compliance with the United Nations resolution. Simultaneously the American media reported that units of the Atlantic fleet had put to sea from the Norfolk naval base. Whether this move was meant to deter the Soviet Union or to impress Britain, France and Israel, has never been disclosed. But one thing was clear: it highlighted the gravity of the crisis and scared America's friends more than its foes.

Ben Gurion was endowed with the unique gift of being able to switch instantaneously from high flights of fancy to earthy realism without any intermediary stages. He immediately recognized that the United States resolution to put an end to the Sinai-Suez venture and undo its territorial consequences was unshakable. He instructed Eban to inform the White House immediately of Israel's unconditional acceptance of the withdrawal order. We in New York were linked to Jerusalem and Washington by a conference telephone hook-up. Eban consulted us while Ben Gurion was on the line, and we came to the conclusion that neither the Eisenhower message nor the United Nations situation warranted a post-haste evacuation. We recommended confining the government's announcement to its decision to withdraw Israeli forces in accordance with arrangements to be made with the United Nations. Ben Gurion feared that such delaying tactics would be furiously rejected and merely aggravate the crisis. He consulted his colleagues who were assembled in the cabinet room and asked Eban whether he could take personal responsibility that Washington would content itself with such an answer. We nodded in unison and Eban firmly assured Ben Gurion that nothing more than the proposed statement was required for the moment. Eban contacted Washington. His communication was welcomed by the White House with audible relief.

Our qualified reply blunted the edge of the political sword hanging over Israel and bought it time to gain at least some of its most important objectives. But time as such is a nondescript and valueless commodity in human terms without a purpose and an awareness in the users of its limited availability. The government had instructed us to focus on two main issues: a binding undertaking on the complete cessation of all hostile activities and the guaranteed freedom of navigation through the international waterways of the region, in particular the unhampered access to Eilat, Israel's only port on the Red Sea. Of course the conclusion of final peace remained the principal goal but it was out of reach as long as the great powers pursued opposing policies and the United Nations treated basic ills with nothing but streams of paper.

Abba Eban and a small team of associates conducted the negotiations with the Secretary-General, assisted by an array of his deputies and experts. It was an unequal contest. Hammarskjöld, relying on his massive support from the General Assembly and on Soviet-American backing, was dead against any concessions to Israel. Israel was entirely alone. Its French and British partners had abandoned the field, folding up like a travelling circus which had pitched its tents on forbidden ground. With tenacity, tiring and exasperating the Secretary-General, we tried to defend every inch of our position against the United Nations bulldozer. Eban, the lonely swordsman, wielded his rapier with admirable skill, while Hammarskjöld at the head of his phalanx brandished the United Nations club. Whenever he felt in need of aid to break an impasse, he would activate the General Assembly, which dutifully supplied him with more ammunition. The longer the negotiations lasted, the fiercer the resolutions became. The little support which Israel had enjoyed at the beginning now dwindled away completely. Henri Spaak, Belgium's outstanding statesman and a powerful orator, was one of the last of the just. Answering the representative of Iraq who had denounced the Western powers as abominable offenders of human rights, Spaak, with a fervour worthy of Emile Zola, pointed his accusing finger at the Arab delegations from the rostrum of the huge Assembly hall, and asked in his ringing voice: 'Who are you to teach La France human rights and Britain justice? What are your credentials, the rolling heads and the cut-off hands in the market-places of Saudi Arabia?' He was given enthusiastic applause, mainly from the public gallery. His courageous appearance raised the spirits of the desolate delegates.

While the talks on the thirty-eighth floor were dragging on inconclusively, Golda Meir followed them with growing anxiety from her hotel suite at the Savoy Plaza. It was her first attendance of the General Assembly in her capacity as Foreign Minister. At a particularly difficult point in the negotiations she decided to join us. It was one of those late-night sessions necessitated by the full daytime schedule of the participants. Golda had decided to take the Secretary-General to task for his callous disregard of Israel's dilemma. She did not mince her words, nor spare Hammarskjöld personal reproach. He was normally a patient, but tense listener. Yet with every new cadence of Golda's indictment, he became more and more fidgety until he lost his self-control. His face flushing red, he interrupted her icily: 'Why are you so bitter, madam?' His words hit Golda like a stone. For a moment she was stunned, but rallied quickly. 'Because I am anguished by the thought of the bitter fate awaiting our people, if we are deprived of our capacity to defend ourselves,' answered Golda with a heavy heart but a much softer voice.

The exchange did not alter anything of substance, except that from now on Golda accorded Hammarskjöld a prominent and lasting place on her list of *personae non gratae*. The deadlock in New York stirred Foster Dulles to renewed activity. The talks were transferred to Washington and conducted personally by the Secretary of State and Ambassador Eban. One working-paper after another was discarded after laborious consultations between Washington and Jerusalem. Ben Gurion insisted on the non-return of the Egyptians to Gaza and the retention of Sharm el-Sheikh by Israel. In February 1957 Foster Dulles presented his final proposal. His *aide-mémoire* stipulated United Nations responsibility for border security in the Gaza Strip and along the international boundary between Egypt and Israel. It offered international guarantees for the non-interference with Israeli shipping in the Straits of Tiran and the Gulf of Aqaba.

Golda opposed the withdrawal from Gaza. She did not trust the United Nations' ability to secure the observance of the cease-fire and prevent the return of the Egyptians. Ben Gurion did not share the concern of his Foreign Minister; he recognized that his options were extremely limited. The choice before him was either to secure Israel's position on the Red Sea, or to remain in occupation of a strip of land which was densely populated by more than 300,000 Arabs. He told Eban that he regarded Israel's rule over this compact mass of irreconciled people as being as dangerous as dynamite placed at the foundations of the state. His previous insistence on the Gaza issue, which Golda had taken at face value, was meant to improve Israel's negotiating position on Eilat, its gateway to Africa and Asia and terminal of the then vital supply-line of Iranian oil. Golda resigned herself reluctantly to the inevitable and Eban concluded the agreement with Foster Dulles, but not before we had gone through a gruelling final session with the Secretary of State and his host of assistants. He had prepared the text of a statement which Golda was to deliver at the General Assembly, Hammarskjöld to concur with and Cabot Lodge, the United States representative, to endorse in his reply. Foster Dulles accepted a number of Eban's amendments and entered them into the text, but he was somewhat elusive when we asked to see the wording of the American reply. He enumerated its main topics, but claimed that for lack of time he had been unable to draft the full text which would, he solemnly promised, conform to exactly the points he had mentioned.

On 1 March 1957 Golda made the statement in the General Assembly on the withdrawal of all Israeli forces from Sinai and Gaza under the terms agreed in Washington. Israel's commitments were expressed in precise language, but the obligations of the international community were couched in less specific formulations. Israel was entitled to expect and hope that the United Nations would assume direct responsibility for the civil and military administration of the Gaza Strip, that the shattered armistice agreement would eventually be replaced by a peace settlement, that tranquillity would reign along the borders and that freedom of navigation in the Gulf of Aqaba would be guaranteed. On this last point the Foreign Minister stated Israel's position, as endorsed by the United States, in unmistakably clear terms: 'Interference, by armed force, with ships of Israeli flag exercising free and innocent passage in the Gulf of Aqaba and through the Straits of Tiran will be regarded by Israel as an attack entitling it to exercise its inherent right of self-defence under Article 51 of the Charter and to take all measures as are necessary to ensure the free and innocent passage of its ships in the Gulf and in the Straits.' As events were to prove ten years later when Egypt reimposed its maritime blockade, this clause became the central pillar of Israel's case.

What distressed Golda above all was the speech of Ambassador Cabot Lodge. Foster Dulles had assured Eban that the United States response would fit Israel's outstretched hand like a glove, but soon we were to discover to our consternation that the glove had gaping holes. The United States representative deviated more implicitly than explicitly from a number of essential points which the Secretary of State had undertaken to include. Golda, justifiably, was up in arms. Eban's remonstrations with Foster Dulles elicited lame excuses and ardent professions of good faith, but no official correction. General Eisenhower dispatched a letter urgently to Ben Gurion expressing 'his deep gratification at the decision of your government to withdraw promptly and fully behind the armistice lines'. The President's hope was 'that the carrying-out of these withdrawals will go forward with the utmost speed. I know that this decision was not an easy one. I believe, however, that Israel will have no cause to regret having conformed to the strong sentiment of the world community.' It was a textbook letter of noncommital diplomatic correspondence, adding anger to Israel's other anxieties.

Golda, still smouldering from what she called the Dulles dupery, reached boiling-point when she was informed that the United Nations Secretariat was discussing arrangements with Cairo for the Egyptian return to Gaza. It was late in the evening when she called Eban and myself to see her in her suite on the twenty-seventh floor of the Savoy Plaza Hotel. She presented us with the confidential report and her decision to ask Ben Gurion to cancel the orders for the evacuation of the Gaza Strip which was scheduled for 7 March. Eban explained that we were beyond the point of no return. Israel could not go back on its solemn pledge without causing itself irreparable harm. Its relations with the United States would not endure the strain and its position in the world would be demolished. He suggested that Golda herself should warn Foster Dulles of the incalculable consequences of a breach of the agreement. That was the last straw for the Foreign Minister. 'Now you want me to repair the mess', she fumed, 'after you have confronted me with a *fait accompli.*' Her pent-up frustrations erupted like a geyser. Her ambassador, she claimed, had not deigned to report to her personally on all stages of his negotiations with Dulles and Hammarskjöld, let alone consult her. Of course, he was covered by the instructions of the Prime Minister, but after all she *was* the Foreign Minister.

Eban was stupefied and speechless, a condition as abnormal for him as my attendance at a ministerial dressing-down of an ambassador. Then, without any further comment, Golda demanded that Eban cable the Prime Minister right then and there to postpone the withdrawal. Eban simply refused and, visibly shaken, suggested that if she felt so strongly on the matter, she should send the telegram in her own name. Now it was Golda's turn to be stupefied. It was apparently the first time that she had encountered Eban in a rebellious mood. She was beside herself and cried that she would jump out of the window. In her state of mind, I feared it was not just a figure of speech. I tried to calm her down, but to no avail. She raised her voice from demand to command level. Without saying a word Eban got up, marched out and shut the door behind him with audible emphasis.

Golda slumped down in an armchair and held her head between her hands. After a short while she asked me quietly to take down the text of her message to Ben Gurion. I felt it was useless to argue with her in her condition. She first had to get it out of her system. She dictated the gist of what she wanted to say and left the drafting to me. After I had read the finished product to her, I said pensively: 'Golda, on second thoughts, do you really believe it necessary to send the cable? The information is not new to Ben Gurion. He certainly received it through his own channels. If he thinks that it is so weighty as to make a momentous change in the government's decision, he'll do it without prodding. But if he concludes that it is not warranted, you are going to make things even more difficult for him than they already are. If he has to turn your advice down, it will be embarrassing for both of you.' She pondered a moment, sighed deeply and without any further comment said: 'OK, forget it.' She offered me a cup of coffee, her equivalent of a peace pipe, and then we chatted leisurely about the occurrences of the day.

Forgetting was not one of Golda's distinctive qualities. The clash with Eban continued to hover over their relations like a dark cloud, never to dissipate. But of more far-reaching consequence was her disappointing experience of the political aftermath of the Sinai campaign. Rationally, she realized that Israel had exhausted all its political potential and obtained the maximum it could expect from the drawn-out negotiations, but emotionally she felt we had surrendered. We should never have withdrawn from Sinai and Gaza without a peace treaty with Egypt. Perhaps her expectations had been too high when she counted on the steadfastness of the British and French partners and the benevolence of the United States. Probably, also, her assessment of the combined political strength of Israel's adversaries had been faulty. Be that as it may, her appearance on the rostrum of the United Nations on 1 March to announce the final withdrawal, had become for her a traumatic experience. Over the years she hardened her resolve that it should never happen again. The trauma of 1957 was probably the key to an understanding of her unyielding position as Prime Minister. Her instincts had not betrayed her. The Egyptians returned to Gaza and ten years later, when Nasser was ready for a confrontation with Israel, the United Nations forces melted away like butter in the desert sun.

Part Two

CONSOLIDATION

7

The Aftermath of the Sinai-Suez Campaign

The Sinai campaign and the Suez intervention did not produce permanent territorial changes. Still, their military and political repercussions were far-reaching. They altered the balance of power between Israel and the Arab states, reduced the confidence and cohesion of the Western alliance and accelerated the process of North African de-colonization and Arab radicalization. In the wake of the short but fierce war of 1956, the Soviet Union strengthened its position in the Middle East, overtaking the United States in the race to make friends and gain influence in which both countries had jointly engaged against America's friends. Nasser, saved by the skin of his teeth by the Soviet-American rescue mission, lustily returned to his subversion against those Arab states which tried to resist his coercion, but showed appreciable – if only temporary – restraint towards Israel. Egypt's attempts to dominate the Arab countries, the relentless Soviet drive and the endemic internal weaknesses and external rivalries of the growing number of independent Arab states, turned the Middle East into one of the most unstable regions of the world.

Upheaval in Baghdad
The pro-Western regime in Iraq of King Feisal and Premier Nuri Said was overthrown by a military coup fifteen months after the last Israeli forces had left Sinai. The King and his family were shot and the bodies of the Prime Minister and his entourage dragged through the streets of Baghdad. The President of the Lebanon, Camille Chamoun, called for United States troops to save the independence of his country from a Nasserist take-over attempt. And young King Hussein of Jordan, tossed by the ill winds, appealed to Britain to help him hold onto his shaky throne. I was serving at the time as Ambassador to Belgium. Contrary to widespread popular belief, an ambassador's lot is not an easy one. He normally divides his time between standing up in defence of his country's interests or standing around, the obligatory cocktail glass in his hand. Steady legs are no less a prerequisite of his craft than a sound head. The sinister news from Baghdad reached us in the early afternoon of 14 July. Shortly afterwards Abba Eban called from London. He was on his way from his ambassadorial post in Washington for

routine consultations in Jerusalem. He suggested that we meet in London right away to discuss the crisis. I agreed to go there later in the evening , since that afternoon I had to attend the traditional Quatorze Juillet reception at the French embassy. The usual exercise at such parties is to pump the hand of the host, say a few polite words of congratulation, flatter the hostess, march around in a wide circle straining your neck muscles with friendly nods, watch out not to bump into an Arab colleague, avoid a harmless bore, balance your glass, make your way to the laden buffet besieged by multitudes of starving humanity, avoid being crushed in the assault and eventually withdraw unharmed – if possible unobserved – through a side exit.

However, the routine changes when there is a happening. And the sensational news from Baghdad, on this festive summer day in 1958, was indeed a happening. Groups of ambassadors huddled on the lawn like teams in the game of American football, their heads bent, listening attentively to the coach. Arriving on the scene, my British colleague resolutely drew me into the nearest huddle. He carried the respectable name of Labouchère. This had once caused a slight misunderstanding with Foreign Minister Henri Spaak. He had phoned the British Ambassador, who answered the call simply: 'Labouchère.' Whereupon the Foreign Minister, with undisguised irritation, shouted: 'I don't want the butcher, I asked for the British Ambassador.'

In these familiar surroundings, however, Her Majesty's plenipotentiary had no problem of recognition. 'Here is our Israeli colleague, let's hear what he thinks is going to happen,' he suggested. I politely declined the honour of diplomatic soothsayer, commenting that I had the greatest respect for the prophets of Israel but that I had none of their gifts. But my assembled colleagues would not let me go. I had to catch my plane to London so, trying to extricate myself and admittedly caught in a moment of inconsistency, said off-handedly: 'Well, if you insist on knowing, I believe the Americans will land marines on the shores of Tripoli in Lebanon.' This bold pronouncement based on no knowledge of American intentions whatsoever, but rather on intuition, aroused general hilarity and was proclaimed as the joke of the day. Yet it facilitated my planned early escape from the party and got me to the airport on time. After my return the following day from London I received a number of how-did-you-know calls. My firm protestations of innocence were either accepted with suppressed doubt or earned me professional credit.

Eban was waiting for me at Grosvenor House. He thought we would be less disturbed at his parents' nearby flat, where he believed we could speak more freely to Washington and Jerusalem. We hailed a taxi and settled down for a short ride, but we got so involved in our conversation – of course conducted in Hebrew – that we became oblivious to time and surroundings. After about thirty minutes Eban glanced out of the window and noticed the familiar sight of Grosvenor House. This startled even him, as he was not always fully aware of his environment when deeply immersed in thought and conversation. With appropriate caution and humility, advisable when questioning the sense of direction of a taxi driver anywhere in the world, he inquired whether we were not slightly off target and somewhat behind schedule. The driver, turning around with a big grin and with an authentic East End accent, explained: 'Ambassador Eban, it is such a thrill having you in my cab and listening to your voice . . .. I wanted to stretch the pleasure and drove back and forth, listening to your talk. I didn't understand a bit of it, but I enjoyed every word. Don't worry about the meter, you are my guest.' In no time he dropped us at our destination, but his curiosity was not yet satisfied. He wanted to know the other passenger's station in life. Eban duly introduced me. 'By God,' he said, 'what a day! Two Israeli ambassadors on one fare.'

It was after midnight when we reached Jacob Herzog, Eban's deputy in Washington, by telephone. The line was clear, but his language oblique. Herzog had always been inclined to circumspection, but now his transatlantic lingo was so conspiratorial that only with a lot of guessing could we make out what he was trying to convey. The Americans were considering some kind of move, but before committing themselves to action they needed more information. Herzog assured us 'that there would be action before the sun rose', but Eban should not change his travel plans.

Eban proceeded to Jerusalem the next morning and then returned to Washington with up-to-date instructions. The Americans had decided to land the marines on the beaches of Beirut and the British were airlifting troops to Jordan, flying straight over Israel, asking for clearance only while the mission was already under way. The combined operation preserved the independence of the Lebanon and secured the survival of the Hashemite dynasty. Khrushchev blustered and calmed down. Hammarskjöld convened an Emergency Session of the United Nations which adjourned after a flood of words and not a drop of action. John Foster Dulles realized in his dying days that his diplomacy of joining hands with the Soviets against America's allies in 1956, had been an ill-fated miscalculation. But the Middle Eastern cauldron continued to sizzle. In Syria one military dictator ousted another in regular sequence. In Iraq the savage regime of Colonel Kassem succumbed to the bloody *putsch* of a rival military faction. In Jordan, King Hussein had his hands full trying to keep a riotous West Bank population under control. In Sudan, the southern African tribes rose against their Arab rulers. Egypt, its expansion towards the north barred by Israel, turned east against Yemen, trying to gain a foothold in the Arabian peninsula which floated on a sea of oil. New inter-Arab alliances mushroomed and disappeared, but the national rivalries and sectional feuds endured.

Arab-Israeli contacts
Yet the Arab world, however divided against itself, remained united in its enmity against Israel. The Arab League served as its rallying-point. It was the

repository of joint bellicose declarations, but rarely a vehicle of united action. It instigated more than it perpetrated. It kept the stone wall of hostility around Israel intact and watched jealously that none of its members should breach it. Nevertheless, before and after independence, and undeterred by rebuff and hostility, Israeli envoys continuously cultivated contacts with leading Arab personalities.

As early as 1950, representatives of Israel conducted lengthy negotiations with King Abdullah of Jordan and reached agreement with him on a draft peace treaty. But under the powerful influence of his British advisers, the king backed out at the decisive moment. The Foreign Office considered that the advantages emanating from the normalization of relations between the two successor states of the former mandatory territory of Palestine were not commensurate with the risks involved for the Hashemite dynasty and continued British predominance in Jordan.

None of the Arab countries was excluded from Israel's exertions to establish peaceful and good neighbourly relations. Discussions took place with Colonel Husmi Zaim, the head of the Syrian military regime. After his overthrow they were resumed with one of his successors, Colonel Adib Shishakli, but the talks were abortive. The turnover of Syrian governments was too fast for the exchanges to mature to a conclusive stage, nor was the political climate in Syria conducive to peace.

The dialogue between Israel and Lebanon had begun long before the attainment of their independence. It continued almost without interruption from the beginning of 1949, when Israel agreed to withdraw its forces from southern Lebanon, until the present day, when a large part of the country is occupied by the Syrian army and its future is threatened by internecine war. These contacts comprised Christian as well as Moslem leaders, and there were times when Lebanese officials could be seen in public places absorbed in conversation with Israeli representatives.

For years my right-hand neighbour in the United Nations political committee was Charles Malik, the distinguished representative of the Lebanon. Unabashedly he would shake hands with me when he took his seat and start his lively banter on the committee's proceedings and the events of the day. The watchful observers were amused, but not my left-hand neighbour, the representative of Iraq. He ignored me completely, but did not hide his scorn at Charles Malik's frivolities. When compelled to identify me in the course of his harangues, he would refer to me as 'Mr Gideon' and not, as customary, 'the representative of Israel'. It must have been an unbearable torment to him to style us correctly. The admission of Ireland to the United Nations finally relieved him of his anguish and provided us with a companionship on our left as sociable as that on our right.

The only other Arab mission which maintained contacts with us was the delegation of the Hashemite Kingdom of Jordan. During the UN debates on the status of Jerusalem in 1950 and 1951 we had kept in close touch with the Jordanian chief representatives, Fawzi Mulki and Ahmed Toukan. The interests of our two countries converged: both governments opposed the internationalization of Jerusalem and co-ordinated their policies to induce the majority of the United Nations to accept the *status quo* as established by the 1949 armistice.

Israel's main peace efforts had always focused on Egypt, its most powerful and least emotionally-involved neighbour. There was not one government in Egypt which was not in touch with the leaders of Israel over the whole period of the three decades of belligerency. The contacts ranged from meetings in New York with the Egyptian Secretary-General of the Arab League to clandestine rendezvous between the heads of the two countries' delegations to the peace talks in Lausanne, which opened in 1949 under the auspices of the Palestine Conciliation Commission. This was a body set up by the United Nations to assist the conflicting parties in the conduct of peace negotiations. Although it has been defunct now for nearly twenty-five years, it still appears as an existing institution in the statute books of the United Nations. This peace commission scored a record of futility which is unsurpassed even in the annals of the United Nations. It failed to convene the delegations to the conference around the same table, and succeeded in uniting the Arab countries on a common denominator of extremism imposed by their most radical participants. For its diplomatic standstill the Commission made up with lively gastronomic activity. It organized a ceaseless round of dinner parties in honour of the various delegations, either individually or collectively. The guests would assiduously return the hospitality. After a short while the scoreboard looked like the tabulation of an international soccer competition: the United States entertaining Jordan; Syria dining France; all three Commissioners hosting Israel – in short it was a culinary merry-go-round. After three months of wining and dining around the Lake of Geneva, without a single meal being taken together by the Arab and Israeli delegates, I felt the time had come to call a halt to this festival which was so high in calories but so low in yields. I invited the members of the Conciliation Commission for a farewell dinner. My toast was short and factual: 'Never have so few consumed so much and done so little.'

The outward sterility of their public clashes on the international stage did not deter Egyptian and Israeli representatives from meeting behind the scenes. As I have already said, the exchanges were also handled in a number of instances by intermediaries. Most of the initiatives came from Israel or third parties. Their frequency varied according to circumstances. In times of increased tension on the borders, the clandestine channels of communication hummed with traffic. The messages were mainly intended to avoid the extension of hostilities due to misinterpretation of certain actions or military moves.

The suspension of the work of the Israeli-Egyptian armistice commission after the fighting in 1956 made crisis management more difficult. The formal meetings of the commission, held under the chairmanship of a United Nations representative, had served more as a ledger of incidents than as an instrument for their prevention. They provided sufficient opportunities for the heads of the delegations to discuss the situation privately and to convey messages from one government to the other. Fortunately, in the wake of the Sinai campaign the situation along the Israeli-Egyptian border improved markedly, due to the deployment of the United Nations Emergency Force along the lines, the non-interference with Israeli shipping in the Gulf of Aqaba and greater restraint exercised by Egypt – an understandable precaution after its experience in the Sinai campaign and Gaza. However, its *débâcle* on the battlefield did not produce a strong enough stimulus for Egypt to seek a settlement of the conflict at the negotiating table. Enjoying the political support of the two superpowers and a stepped-up supply of Soviet arms, Nasser preferred the long-range military preparation for a new and more successful round with Israel to the short-cut of a peaceful settlement. Since he knew that Egypt needed several years and a good amount of foreign support to recover its strength, he lowered his militant profile when facing the West, while raising the level of his involvement with the East.

During the period between the wars of 1956 and 1967 the contacts between Egypt and Israel were at an ebb. Sometimes Nasser would assure a prominent Western interlocutor of his ultimate peaceful intentions towards Israel, but meticulously refrain from taking any step to advance the realization of this goal. Early in 1963, one of the visitors to Cairo, Sir Denis Hamilton of the London *Times*, gained the impression from his talks with Nasser that he had changed his position on Israel. He believed he had discovered a willingness on Nasser's part to meet secretly with Ben Gurion. Sir Denis went to Jerusalem and received the Prime Minister's enthusiastic response: he was ready to meet Nasser at any time, in any place, including Cairo. Ben Gurion waited anxiously for the answer. Before Hamilton's surprise visit the Prime Minister had made up his mind to retire to his kibbutz, Sde Boker, but the hopeful news prompted him to postpone his decision. He thought if there was even the slightest chance of bringing about a change in the destinies of Israel and Egypt, he felt it had overriding precedence over any other consideration. He waited impatiently for Nasser's reply. It did not come. And on 16 June 1963 the Prime Minister stunned his uninitiated cabinet with the announcement of his irrevocable resignation, instead, as he would have preferred, with the startling news of his impending visit to Cairo.

The gulf of distrust between the two countries widened, while the area of their contacts notably contracted. Just when means of communications were needed more than at any other time, at the outbreak of the crisis in May 1967, they had virtually faded away. In their absence the government instructed me, then serving as permanent representative to the UN, to convey by way of the Secretary-General a message to Egypt assuring it of Israel's peaceful intentions. We shall come back to this later. But until the eruption in June 1967, relations with Egypt had been rather uneventful: relative quiet had reigned along the borders since the end of the Sinai campaign.

8

Leap Over the Arab Wall

When Israel's policy-makers realized that their attempts at breaching the wall of Arab hostility were doomed to failure, they turned their sights elsewhere. Beyond the wall there were important countries in the Middle East and Africa which were accessible to Israel. The two most important of them, Iran and Turkey, though predominantly Moslem were guided in the conduct of their foreign policy by political rather than religious considerations. Turkey, although it had voted in 1947 against the establishment of the Jewish state, recognized the importance of Israel in the affairs of the Middle East after its victorious emergence from the War of Independence. It became the first Moslem country to establish diplomatic relations with Israel and, despite strains and stresses caused by outside pressures, maintained them without interruption.

The relations with Iran developed more slowly and cautiously. Although they were never formalized by an exchange of ambassadors, the amplitude of their substance outweighed the deficiency of their form. Nevertheless, both countries established governmental missions which enjoyed diplomatic privileges. Shaded from the limelight of publicity the intimacy between the two governments and the intensity of their economic and political exchanges prospered. Iran remained one of Israel's main suppliers of oil even in the turbulent post-Yom Kippur War period, until the Khomeini regime terminated the flow and the relations altogether. Turkey and Iran had been designated by the Western defence planners as front-line barriers against Soviet domination of the Middle East. The effectiveness and speed with which the Israel Defence Army acquitted itself in its first test of modern warfare in 1956, established Israel as a central military force of recognized competence.

Christian Ethiopia, feeling itself menaced by Arab expansionist designs, also valued a strong and self-reliant Israel and established diplomatic relations with it. From a modest beginning the co-operation between the two countries branched out into numerous fields. Agricultural experts directed rural expansion schemes, teaching Ethiopian farmers modern farming techniques; industrialists introduced new manufactures; geologists discovered natural resources and a military mission helped modernize the Ethiopian army.

The wars of 1967 and 1973 did not substantially affect Israel's relations with Ethiopia and Iran. They succumbed to the revolutionary upheavals which swept the two countries in 1978. The establishment of Soviet predominance in Ethiopia eliminated the last vestiges of Israeli-Ethiopian co-operation. In the wake of the Islamic upheaval, Iran joined the anti-Israel camp of Arab extremism. But history has its ironic twists. While in Teheran the PLO took over the building of the Israeli mission, in Cairo the flag of Israel was raised to greet Prime Minister Begin on his arrival in the Egyptian capital to celebrate the conclusion of the peace treaty between the Jewish state and the most important Arab country.

In its attempt to reach out beyond its hostile environment, Israel also made considerable but less co-ordinated efforts to establish ties with North African countries. Algiers was the pivot of the struggle for independence in which the three North African French dependencies had been actively engaged since the early 1950s. France desperately fought the fierce Algerian uprising, trying to prevent the secession of the territory. Israel's policy-makers were torn between their sympathy for the aspirations of the Algerians and their obligations of friendship with France. To limit Arab interventionist capacity, French policy-makers concluded that the strengthening of Israel, threatened by the same adversary, would best serve their objective. This policy corresponded with Israel's urgent needs, accentuated by the Soviet arms shipments to Egypt.

When the fighting in Algeria was approaching its climax, the co-operation between France and Israel had reached its peak. French armaments, especially of the latest type of aircraft, replenished its arsenals. Transferred technology helped modernize Israel's arms industry. All these were tangible things, strengthening the country's defence capabilities.

The cultivation of relations with France's adversaries at a decisive phase of their struggle was not only an uncertain investment in the future, but also a risk for the prosperity of Franco-Israeli co-operation. Israel tried to meet the dilemma with an ambivalent policy, which Dr Weizmann used to call 'warm frost'. Some cautious overtures to Algerian politicians, erroneously believed by Israeli experts to be the coming leadership, as well as full public support for the political and military policies of France, were self-cancelling efforts. They completely lost their meaning when, in 1962, De Gaulle reached a settlement with the FLN and it turned out that the new rulers of independent Algeria were the field commanders of the rebellion and not the Paris-based politicians. Immediately after its accession to power, Algeria joined the Arab League and became one of its most outspoken anti-Israeli members. Algeria, in step with the radicalization of its foreign policy in the wake of its growing co-operation with the Soviet Union, shifted from restrained antagonism to open enmity. It helped align the so-called non-aligned countries against Israel; it supplied fighting men and war material to the Arab states; it acted as a logistic and ideological support centre for terrorist organizations of all sorts and interceded with Moscow to bail Egypt and Syria out of their self-inflicted military *débâcles*.

The termination of the Algerian conflict not only relieved France of an unbearable burden, it also removed the main stumbling-block to the recovery of its position in the Arab world. To begin with Paris proceeded cautiously, step by step, with measured poise. De Gaulle continued to assure the Prime Ministers of Israel, first Ben Gurion and later Eshkol, of the unwavering fidelity of France to Israel, its 'friend and ally'. But the more Franco-Arab relations flourished the faster Franco-Israeli friendship wilted. Israel's policy-makers were not prepared for the steady decline. They refused to recognize the process of erosion, set in motion by the readjustment of French policy.

In our assessments at the Foreign Ministry we had from time to time pointed with moderate emphasis to disquieting symptoms of deterioration. The speeches and votes of French delegates at the United Nations became increasingly reserved towards Israel and steadily moved in the direction of the Arabs. The French position in the Security Council debate, initiated by Israel in the autumn of 1966 against Syria's support of aggressive incursions, appeared to our delegation to be particularly alarming. In a report to Foreign Minister Eban, I summed up our concern that the position of France, as it came to light in the Security Council, reflected its *rapprochement* with the Soviet Union, its estrangement from its Western allies and its desire to co-operate closely with the non-aligned and, in particular, the Arab countries. This alone was sufficient ground for Israel to be concerned, but in addition I felt it advisable to reassess our working assumption that the Soviet Union, though fanning the tension, was not interested in a military confrontation between Syria and Israel. I expressed the belief that Moscow might not be averse to a short and violent clash – short enough to avoid the intervention of the Western powers, and violent enough to compel Syria to ask for urgent Soviet support. In the ensuing Security Council deliberations the Soviet Union would lead the anti-Israel onslaught, rescue Syria from massive defeat and try to reap maximum Arab gains. In anticipation of such an eventuality Soviet propaganda exerted itself to decry alleged aggressive designs hedged by Israel on behalf of the imperialist powers. 'Were the Soviet Union genuinely concerned at the results of an Israeli military strike,' I added, 'it would have shown greater restraint and less hostility in the just concluded Security Council debate.'

The test of this prognosis was not to be long in coming. The events unfolding in May 1967 confirmed our premonitions. France imposed an arms embargo on Israel and the Soviet Union encouraged Syria and Egypt into war.

The efforts of Israel to win friends in North Africa included Tunisia and Morocco. Both states had attained their independence not so much by violent struggle but rather as a result of political attrition. The renaissance of Israel had deeply stirred the large and ancient Jewish communities in Tunisia and Morocco. Disturbed by manifestations of hostility, driven by their age-old yearnings and elated at the opportunity of finding a safe haven in Israel, they joined the stream of returning exiles. The Sinai campaign added impetus to their desire to leave. Nearly 300,000 Jews from North Africa – the majority from Morocco – reached Israel in the first twenty years of its independence. The organizational requirements of this mass movement created a framework of contacts between the authorities of the three countries, outgrowing in the course of the years the mere technical aspects of the migration movement.

This created a climate of trust conducive to co-operation in other fields of central importance to Morocco. Yet in public appearances Morocco's spokesmen did not fall behind their most radical Arab colleagues, nor did Morocco always confine itself to lip-service to the Arab cause. In the Yom Kippur War it dispatched to the Syrian front commando units which gained the dubious distinction of waging the most ruthless sort of fighting. Four years later King Hassan assisted in the establishment of the contacts between the representatives of Egypt and Israel which initiated the peace negotiations. In short, the policy of Morocco towards Israel was more a function of its conflicts and conciliations with its immediate North African neighbours than an ideological disposition. It was a mixed bag of discreet assistance and public hostility, of open participation in the war against Israel and undercover support of its peace efforts.

Co-operation with developing countries

The third area of no man's land on Israel's political map was the vast sub-Saharan territories of Africa. In the decade following the Sinai campaign, they gained their independence in a chain reaction of decolonization. The emerging states soon realized that, after having cast off their old shackles, they needed new supports. Wary of new economic and political dependence, they searched for helpmates, technologically advanced, development conscious, unattached to power blocs and belonging to the community of newly independent states.

Israel ideally fitted these conditions. From its early beginnings it felt ideologically committed to international co-operation and development aid. Its economic resources were poor, but the resourcefulness which it had displayed in the swift organization of its state had created a wealth of experience. Israel's innovative spirit and idealistic impulses prompted it to seek outlets for its pent-up energies. It was a sense of modern pioneering, an urge for solidarity with the underprivileged and a desire to share the fruits of experience, which inspired Israel to go out into unknown lands.

Israel tried to exemplify that small states can be linked by bonds of international solidarity and fruitful partnership on the grounds of functional affinity and not merely of geographical vicinity. Under the spirited leadership of Foreign Minister Golda Meir, Israel established relations of development co-operation with more than sixty countries in Africa, Asia and Latin America. Not all were newcomers to the community of independent states, but each of them was plagued by similar tribulations of want, neglect, disease and squalor. Projects ranged from rural rehabilitation programmes to integrated irrigation schemes, from the establishment of community centres to the training of medical personnel in field courses and at Israeli universities.

A special division of the Foreign Ministry administered these far-flung activities. It organized training programmes in Israel and abroad and dispatched several thousand Israeli experts for field work in three continents. They became known as the ambassadors in overalls, driving tractors and digging irrigation trenches, planting new strains of high-yield crops and setting up modern diary farming. They not only helped master the wilderness, but also conquered the hearts of the people with whom they worked. The Israeli instructors fired the imagination and gained the goodwill of the local people because they were the first foreigners who had come not to give orders but to set a personal example.

The work of development co-operation, bolstered by high-level diplomatic efforts, also yielded encouraging political results. At the peak of its achievement before the outbreak of the Six Day War, Israel maintained diplomatic relations with twenty-seven African states. While bilateral understanding between Israel and its friends in the developing countries was growing and its views supported by most of them in the intimacy of private conversations, in the international arena, however, its new friends swayed and bent under constant Soviet-Arab battering. Only a relatively small group of new faithfuls stood up at the United Nations in open defence of Israel. They joined European and Latin American initiatives calling upon the Arab states to enter into direct negotiations with Israel. But the majority of these new countries remained either neutral or supported the Arab side because of considerations of regional solidarity or identification with Third World interests. Yet their representatives would rarely pass up an opportunity to assure their Israeli colleagues in private of their enduring fidelity. Non-alignment, as originally conceived, aimed at sheltering the underdeveloped world from the conflicts of the superpowers. It was a well-intentioned but impractical proposition. As it worked out, non-alignment leant increasingly towards the more assertive Soviet side, if only because Soviet displeasure was more menacing than Western promises were enticing.

An African interlude

I had acquired only a rather sparse personal experience of African affairs, never having served in any of the developing countries, although I had gained some impressions on occasional official visits to Asia, Latin America and

Africa. In 1959, when I served as ambassador in Brussels, one of them brought me to the then Belgian Congo. It was my first contact with Africa. Its impact was as perplexing as it was illuminating, and I toured the country far and wide. It was full of contrast. The University of Leopoldville sported a nuclear research reactor, while the country did not have a single physician of Congolese origin. Although the call for independence sounded throughout the land, nobody seriously anticipated that its coming was only one year away. The story of modern Israel was surprisingly well known, but its association with the saga of the Jewish people was rather nebulous. One day we stopped in a little town in a remote part of the country, far off the beaten track. I went into the post office to mail some post cards. The African clerk accepted them with a friendly smile. He looked at them, obviously enjoying the picturesque landscapes, but when he examined their destination his face froze. 'Monsieur, you mean to send these cards to Jerusalem?' he questioned with a grimace of awe and disbelief. 'What's wrong with that?' I asked. 'But mon cher monsieur, Jerusalem is in heaven,' he said. Stunned by this startling revelation I hesitated a moment. Should I reply that we had a hot line to heaven? I preferred to tell him the simple truth that Jerusalem was the capital of the State of Israel. 'Oh, Israel,' he cried, enchanted. 'I have heard so many good things about this country.' Then he affixed the stamps, stood up, stretched out his hand and declared solemnly: 'May I offer you the stamps as a modest token of my deep admiration for Israel.' I was touched and promised to write to him from Jerusalem on earth.

Upon my return to Brussels Prime Minister Gaston Eyskens asked me to give him my impressions of the situation in the Congo which had been causing considerable headaches to his government. I told him that this immense land appeared to me to be like a slumbering giant resting on a bed of copper, cobalt and uranium studded with diamonds – unaware of its wealth and stirring before its sudden awakening. The Prime Minister asked for my suggestions. I summed them up in three points: firstly, Africanize the administration – there was not a single high official in the government of the colony; secondly, Europeanize the problem – Belgium should share its responsibilities and burdens with its fellow members of the European Community; thirdly, it should commit itself to a timetable for the granting of independence.

Circumstances constrained the Belgian government to implement the last recommendation within a year, but that was before it had been able to make any progress on the other two. The result was a total collapse of the administration and, following its withdrawal, an outbreak of chaotic violence which tore the new state asunder.

A few weeks before the proclamation of independence in the Congo, later to be known as Zaire, I paid a farewell visit to King Baudouin at the termination of my tour of duty in Brussels. The escorting protocol people withdrew at a move of the royal hand and the King settled down with me to what he called a man-to-man talk. After some courtesies he came straight to the point. He was deeply worried, he said, about what was going to happen in the Congo after the Belgian evacuation. It was a nightmare for him to think of the bloodshed that would erupt among the Africans after the Belgian withdrawal. But his country was no more capable of conducting a colonial war than France, already engaged in difficulties in Algeria. Furthermore, Belgium's resources were smaller than those of its neighbour, the public constraints greater and the Congo's distance of 6,000 miles constituted a formidable logistic burden, surpassing Belgium's military and economic capabilities.

The King, who knew that I had met a number of Congolese leaders in Brussels, inquired what I thought of them and of their intentions. I told him of a meeting with Patrice Lumumba. He had visited me at the embassy, as quite a few of his colleagues participating in the round table conference on the future of the Congo had done before. Unlike the others he came alone to offer his political assistance to Israel. He proposed to inform its competent authorities about the activities of its adversaries in Africa and to advise on appropriate action against them. His services deserved, as he put it, adequate remuneration. I explained to him politely and patiently that what we meant when we offered technical assistance was something quite different and spoke in reassuring terms of rural planning and urban housing. Lumumba dismissed all this as irrelevant and repeated his offer in greater detail and, in case I had missed the value of the bargain, he reminded me that I had the honour of speaking to the future Prime Minister of the Congo. I made it clear that I was duly impressed by his new station in life, but not with his present proposition, whereupon he terminated the visit, but not before asking me to provide him with transport to his next appointment. My driver returned after a short while with a mien of offended innocence. 'You know, sir, where he asked me to take him?' he said. 'To the Egyptian Embassy.' There he apparently reiterated his proposal, this time however in favour of the opposition.

The King laughed heartily, but he did not realize that three months later Prime Minister Lumumba would take advantage of the King's presence at the ceremony of the proclamation of independence in Leopoldville to insult him and his country. Nor did Lumumba suspect that he was a doomed man. He was swept away by the flood of violence unleashed by his own scheming. The man who had tried so valiantly but in vain to stem the tide, UN Secretary-General Dag Hammarskjöld, became its other victim.

In the period between the two wars of 1956 and 1967, Israel's efforts in the developing world produced fruitful results in the sphere of human progress, which was their principal purpose. They also contributed significantly to the strengthening of Israel's international standing. The impressive victory in 1956 gained it, if not admiration everywhere, all-round respect. Probably the fact that Israel had relinquished its occupation of Egyptian territory by 1957 facilitated the forging of its links with the newly emerging states. They were attracted by the effectiveness and prowess of a small fellow-member of the community of new states and the readiness of its people to extend a helping hand to others.

If Israel's investment in goodwill and physical exertion in the developing countries were to be measured merely in terms of political returns, the balance would be rather disappointing. The house of diplomatic relations which Israel had built, mainly in Africa, began to crack in the aftermath of the Six Day War. It crumbled under the blows of the political and propaganda tornado unleashed jointly by the Arab states and the Soviet Union after the Yom Kippur War. But until then the bare walls of the structure at least had not collapsed. Israel's diplomatic presence in Africa, though restricted in scope, remained intact until October 1973. It provided the basis for high-level contacts, enabling its representatives to present Israel's views and interpretation of the situation, and it served as a channel for the heads of state to convey their recommendations to Jerusalem.

9

Israel in Asia

Unlike the evolution of Israel's relations with the new African states, which proceeded on a more or less uniform pattern, its links with Asia developed not in one upsurge but gradually. Situated on the western extremity of the continent, Israel was remote to the people of East Asia. They were not linked to it by historical or spiritual encounter. The Bible telling the story of the Jewish people and defining its religious identity had no more meaning to them than other books relating the legends and philosophy of ancient civilizations. The contemporary revival of the Jewish people out of the ashes of the Nazi Holocaust evoked only faint echoes in distant Asia. These countries were emerging from the trauma of their own recent experience: the recovery from Japanese subjugation, the convulsions of the Chinese civil war, the rebuilding of the ruins of defeat and the nuclear holocaust of Hiroshima and Nagasaki. Their attention focused on the wars of liberation in Indonesia and Vietnam and not on the struggle in the Middle East.

The first Asian country to establish diplomatic ties with Israel was Japan. After its defeat it had ceased to play a role in world affairs. It was eager to dispel its reputation as an ally of Hitler and the enemy of the powers which had defended human civilization against him. To gain the friendship of the Jewish people, the principal target of Nazi savagery, must have appeared an attractive proposition to Japan, likely to further its moral rehabilitation. However, the historic and psychological distance separating Israel and Japan and the paucity of their trade and cultural relations impeded the growth of a close relationship between them. Nonetheless, increasing curiosity about their different backgrounds and lifestyles stimulated contacts. After Japan had joined the United Nations it adopted an attitude of benevolent neutrality towards Israel on Arab-Israeli issues. It tended to adjust its cautious policy to that of the United States and its European partners, but generally lagged a step or two behind them. For Israel it was an important diplomatic vantage-point, providing it with a foothold in a country destined to regain a leading position in Asia and in world economic affairs.

The establishment of relations with Thailand, Burma, South Korea, the Philippines, Laos and Cambodia followed in the ensuing years. The links, particularly those with Burma, were forged essentially by technical assistance programmes with numerous Israeli experts working on rural development and irrigation projects and many students from these countries acquiring knowledge and training in Israel.

However, the principal and most elusive objective of Israel's diplomatic efforts in Asia was India. It remained equally aloof under Mahatma Gandhi, Pandit Nehru and Indira Gandhi. Though India had recognized the State of Israel in 1950, it was slow to establish diplomatic relations. Its promises were as frequent as its evasions. The opening of the Sinai campaign surprised ex-Foreign Minister Moshe Sharett on the eve of a scheduled meeting with Pandit Nehru in Delhi. Sharett acquitted himself gallantly of the task of defending an action to which he was totally opposed. In the circumstances Nehru felt free to give vent to his criticism of Israel's policy in general and the military action in particular. Ignoring the fact that India had taken up arms when it felt its interests endangered in Kashmir, had defied United Nations resolutions on the peaceful settlement of the issue and had been actively involved in the forcible movement of millions of refugees to and from Pakistan, Nehru held forth on Israel's alleged aggressiveness and imperviousness to the fate of the Arab refugees. Sharett gave him chapter and verse, but it did not change Nehru's decision that India should remain aloof from Israel.

In 1961, our government sent me to the annual conference of the World Health Organization, assembled in Delhi. Although Israel's medical achievements and high professional standards were universally recognized and even admitted by the Soviet Minister of Health in his address to the conference, we had been barred from taking our rightful place in the executive body of the organization. The Foreign Ministry believed that the Delhi meeting offered an opportunity to overcome the Arab-sponsored ostracism. It likewise thought that my visit was an appropriate time to renew political contacts with the Indian government. Besides regular meetings with leading representatives of India at the United Nations, sporadic friendly talks with Mrs Pandit, Nehru's sister, and agitated and exasperating meetings with Krishna Menon, the Prime Minister's confidant, no official dialogue of consequence between the two countries had taken place in the intervening years. The small Israeli consulate, relegated to Bombay and to affairs of migration, trade and some closely restricted information work, was by the very nature of its location and the definition of its functions denied access to decisive levels of government in Delhi.

Mrs Lakshmi Menon, the Deputy Foreign Minister, responded quickly to our request for a meeting. She was well disposed towards Israel, admitted the justice of some of our grievances and the usefulness of our suggestions on how to advance the relations from their state of stagnation. But she also pointed out that only Pandit Nehru himself could do anything positive about it. We left it at that and agreed to meet again later in the week. A day or two later

Nehru's private secretary unexpectedly invited me to meet the Prime Minister or, as he asked with exemplary Indian courtesy laced with a dash of British Foreign Office style, 'whether his Excellency would be free to see the Prime Minister?' What a question! The answer was evident and the appointment was duly fixed.

The meeting took place the day Pandit Nehru had revealed to parliament the incursion of Chinese forces into Indian territory in the Himalayan region. The Prime Minister opened our conversation after the customary exchange of courtesies by referring to my talk with Mrs Lakshmi Menon. She had reported to him and he wished to be personally apprised of our views on the international situation. He leaned back in his chair behind a huge U-shaped desk decorated by a slender vase cradling a solitary red rose. Closing his eyes, as if absorbed in meditation, but keeping a narrow slit open for observation, Pandit Nehru gestured me to begin. I began my survey of the international scene. There were two epicentres at the moment: one was located in Central Africa where the upheaval in the former Belgian Congo had attracted foreign involvement including that of the Soviet bloc; the other centre lay in Indo-China and was extending to the border area between India and China. The Middle East, the link between Africa and Asia, was in itself a region of high volatility and inherent tension; any new explosion there could exacerbate the situation in the two affected areas. Increased antagonism of the two super-powers in the Middle East could ignite a conflagration which would extend beyond the confines of the region. The two focal points in Africa and Asia could be controlled as long as they remained isolated one from the other; but if open trouble erupted simultaneously in the Middle East, Africa and Asia the brushfires might link up and engulf vast continental expanses where Soviet ambitions challenged the vital interests of the Western world. The victims of such a clash, whatever its outcome, would be the masses of indigenous people. It was therefore, I continued, a primary task of statesmanship to assist in the pacification of Western Asia, the geographical term which the Indians preferred in referring to the Middle East.

Nehru answered after a short pause for reflection. He knew it was an enormous problem, far from any settlement. He had probed again and again, in his talks with Arab leaders and especially with Nasser, into whether there was an opening for reconciliation with Israel, but he had always come up against a wall of steel. The Arabs had repeatedly said to him that the time was not yet ripe for a settlement. They claimed that any Arab leader willing to seek peace with Israel would be assassinated. Nehru said this with a faint ironic smile, as if to express his disbelief or his contempt for the contrived argument.

The real reason for the reluctance of the Arabs to accept the existing reality of Israel, I went on, was the unqualified Soviet support granted to them. It made them believe that Moscow would provide them with sufficient military and political strength to eliminate Israel. It was a miscalculation, and a dangerous one, containing the seeds of more wars and Arab defeats. The present world situation and the endemic perils in the Middle East made it imperative for all peace-loving countries to make their contribution to the reduction of tensions in the area by encouraging the Arab states to adopt policies of peaceful accommodation. Of course, the parties to the conflict had to carry the main burden, but the sooner states closely linked with the Arab world equalized their relations with Israel, the easier it would become for the Arab governments to follow suit.

The unmistakable allusion drew Nehru's attention. He straightened up in his chair and said almost in a tone of command: 'Will you repeat this, please.' Dutifully I did, whereupon he reverted to his somnolent posture. After a short while he broke the silence: 'You mean to say that India should establish diplomatic relations with Israel?' I assured him that this item was not on my agenda, because all that Israel could say in the matter had been said, and all that India had to do it knew by heart. All our arguments were known to him and all his reasons for delaying the overdue decision were registered with us. But the great man thought differently: 'I hope you will permit me to speak about the problem,' he retorted pointedly. 'Who am I to give permission to the Prime Minister of India to speak his mind?' I rejoined. After this minuet of preliminaries Nehru took over. India had recognized Israel in 1950, he said, and indeed should have at that time established diplomatic relations. The sentiments in India towards Israel were good. Many people were keenly interested in its achievements. Of course, India had historic ties with the Arabs and in recent years they had become closer. The trouble was that there was a strong Arab reaction to the establishment of diplomatic relations between our two countries. In short it was the old Indian song of frustrated love.

I did not expect to change the Prime Minister's mind, but I felt that his routine rhyme should not be left unanswered. As much as Israel would appreciate normal relations with India, I said, it was faring not too badly in their absence. We were maintaining diplomatic relations with seventy countries on all five continents. Israel's diplomatic map stretched from Ghana to Madagascar, from Mali to Cyprus. Nehru commented that he had noticed our remarkable success with the new countries, but he admitted that he had not been fully aware how widespread the network of our relations was and was somewhat astonished that it included Cyprus. I told him how the little island, Israel's geographically closest friendly neighbour, had stood up to the threat of Arab diplomatic boycott of the 'either or' sort, with the result that Cyprus could pride itself in offering hospitality to the embassies of all states of the Middle East – Arab and Israeli alike.

At this point Nehru exclaimed with undisguised indignation: 'What right have the Arabs to threaten an independent country with diplomatic boycott?' I was startled by this manifestation of righteous anger and commented in an aside: 'Indeed what right do they have to threaten any state?' Nehru's remark was certainly amazing to anyone used to thinking in terms of logical sequence. Here I encountered for the first time that kind of stark ambivalence which, according to knowledgeable people, was the key to the understanding of Nehru's mind and policies. It seemed to be a kind of two-tier structure with no connecting staircase. When it came to far-distant Cyprus, a mini state with a population of 450,000, Nehru was a fearless admirer of its courage and a defender of international fortitude. But where India was concerned, a subcontinent with a population more than a hundred times as large, Nehru preferred evasion to valour and expediency to principle.

While I was still musing about this disturbing contrast, the Prime Minister paid a few friendly compliments to Israel's technological and scientific progress and its impressive work of technical assistance. He agreed that India and Israel should intensify their co-operation in these fields, commending the successes of Israel's experts in the development of water resources in the Rahjistan desert. He added that it was not only the multiplicity of India's problems which tormented him, but the multitude of the people afflicted. Any remedy we want to apply, we have to dispense in half a billion doses, he said. While Nehru's sigh about the plight of his people was moving and sounded sincere, his compliments about Israel proved to be no more than courtesies and his consent to co-operate with it remained an uncovered cheque which bounced on presentation.

At least we did not return empty-handed from the World Health conference – Israel was elected to its Executive Council. However, its representative came home with pneumonia. The doctors, treating it as a sturdy strain of Indian virus, were more proficient than the diplomats. They restored my health in a few weeks, yet our relations with India continue to ail to this day.

10

The China Disconnection

China is as distant from Israel in history and culture as it is in geography. The contacts between the Chinese and Jewish peoples had been sparse and sporadic. Although the ancient silk route traversed Palestine and Jewish traders travelled it, it never became a connecting link of significance between the two civilizations. Small Jewish communities dating back to antiquity, scattered through the huge empire, were submerged completely in their surroundings, in the course of time. A new influx of Jews took place in this century. In the 1920s, after the Bolshevik Revolution, about 15,000 Russian Jews settled in Harbin and other Chinese towns. And in the 1930s Shanghai became a safe haven for many thousands of German Jews fleeing Nazi persecution.

Nonetheless the Kuomintang government of China abstained from supporting the UN decision on the establishment of a Jewish state in 1947. China was then fighting the last and decisive battles of its civil war. Although the national government had lost the mainland, it retained its seat in the United Nations and its decisive vote in the Security Council as one of its five permanent members. Reconstituted in Taiwan, the Chiang Kai-shek government continued its attitude of aloofness towards Israel.

Israel, in its attempt to strike a better balance between its far-flung relations with the Occident and its slender ties with Asia, thought that the revolutionary changes in China offered an opportunity for progress. Early in 1950 it recognized the government of the People's Republic of China. But before Israel could consummate this step by establishing diplomatic relations with Peking, the Korean War broke out. It froze Israel's China policy for several years. Apart from the short encounter between Moshe Sharett and the representatives of the People's Republic attending the Korean debate at the United Nations, Israel refrained from developing its link with Peking. The Foreign Minister planned, however, to normalize relations after the termination of the fighting in Korea.

Our ambassador in Burma, David Hacohen, a veteran labour leader and a man of refreshing originality of mind and expression, had been urging the government for some time to expedite the establishment of diplomatic relations. He had met Chou En-lai in Rangoon and felt assured that China's response to an Israeli initiative would be positive. On the other hand Reuben Shiloah, the minister in Israel's embassy in Washington, counselled caution. The wounds of the Korean War were too fresh and painful and American public opinion would take a dim view of Israel establishing relations with a country which had been branded by the United Nations as an aggressor.

When the ninth session of the UN General Assembly discussed the perennial item of China's representation, the Israeli delegation for the first time cast a negative vote on a motion supporting the government of the People's Republic. Because of strong American lobbying, Eban had interpreted his directives from Jerusalem rather flexibly. The spokesman of the Foreign Ministry, trying to limit possible harm in Peking, stated that 'the delegation had not voted in accordance with the principal intention as originally laid down'.

Apparently the vote did not make a special mark in Peking. On 23 September 1954, two days after the UN vote, Foreign Minister Chou En-lai informed the National People's Congress that: 'Contacts are being made for establishing normal relations with Afghanistan as well as between China and Israel.' The professionals at the Foreign Ministry in Jerusalem favoured the move. The cabinet was divided. It did not deal with the issue in plenary session but instead contented itself with accepting the opinion of its ministerial committee for foreign affairs. Sharett presented the committee with the arguments of our embassies in Burma and Washington. He shared David Hacohen's view and firmly recommended the establishment of diplomatic ties. But he met with opposition mainly from Minister of Education Zalman Aranne, who was afraid of antagonizing the United States, and Minister of Defence Pinhas Lavon, who was eager to irritate Sharett. The majority of the committee voted against the motion of the Foreign Minister but authorized him to resume contacts with Peking.

Sharett directed David Hacohen to explore, with his Chinese colleague, the possibilities of his government receiving an Israeli trade delegation. Peking's affirmative reply arrived three months later and David Hacohen was appointed to lead the mission. Two weeks before it left Eban cabled from Washington that in his view: 'Relations with China would strengthen Israel's international position and should not be postponed. The US government would reconcile itself to the act. They too were seeking a path to relations with Peking. I tend to regret that we approached along the line of commercial and not diplomatic relations.' The mission arrived in Peking in February 1955 with explicit instructions not to propose diplomatic relations and to give a noncommittal reply if the Chinese took the initiative. The delegation held trade talks of a general nature, visited a number of cities, enjoyed the traditional Chinese hospitality, exchanged declarations of goodwill and returned greatly impressed but without any tangible agreements.

Upon their return David Hacohen, supported by Daniel Lewin, the head of the Ministry's Asian division, pressed hard for an immediate initiative to establish diplomatic relations. But the Foreign Minister only authorized Lewin to remind his opposite number that Israel would be glad to welcome the return visit of a Chinese trade delegation. Only after the conclusion of the Bandung conference in April 1955, with the prominent participation of Peking and the painful exclusion of Israel, did Sharett decide to propose the establishment of diplomatic relations at the earliest convenient moment. On 29 April 1955, Lewin conveyed the proposal in an official letter to the Foreign Ministry in Peking. A month later he received a noncommittal reply. It was the end of a short but friendly beginning, and the opening of a long period of inimical Chinese policy towards Israel.

The changing world situation was the principal reason for Peking's growing and lasting antagonism. 1955 was the year of the Bandung conference, the birth-place of what later came to be known as the Third World. Chou En-lai attended the gathering; so did Gamal Abdul Nasser and other Arab leaders. There, the People's Republic of China discovered the potential of the Arab world as an agent of fermentation, and supported the pro-Arab resolution adopted by the conference. From that time on China embarked on a steady anti-Israel course of ever-increasing harshness. Nine years after Bandung, on the occasion of a visit to Cairo in December 1964 Chou En-lai declared: 'We are ready to help the Arab nations to regain Palestine. We are willing to give you anything and everything: arms and volunteers.'

Ever since the visit of the trade delegation Israeli politicians, Foreign Ministry officials and Sinologists have been engaged in a lively controversy on the reasons for the disappointing evolution of Israel's relations with China. Most of them tend to place the responsibility on the government for hesitating to adopt an unambiguous policy, for having missed the opportunity of establishing diplomatic relations in 1950 when it recognized the People's Republic, and for failing to take a new initiative in 1954. The argument that Israel proceeded too cautiously can hardly be dismissed. It took half measures for which it paid the full price without achieving any real gain. But in the light of international developments, it seems highly doubtful that 1955 was a propitious year for strengthening Israel's ties with the People's Republic of China. Even if Israel had taken a bolder step, it would have come too late.

Israel, occupied with more immediate problems and rejected by China, relegated its Chinese policy to a state of low priority. As long as the Peking government was barred from representing China at the United Nations, there existed no direct point of contact or friction between the two countries. Still, twice in 1963 and 1965, Prime Minister Eshkol addressed himself to the government of the People's Republic to reconsider its negative policy towards Israel, but his appeals fell on deaf ears. Once a year the recurring question of China's representation at the UN briefly engaged the attention of Jerusalem, when the Foreign Ministry had to instruct its UN delegation on how to vote at the autumn rites. It normally abstained but, on rare occasions, voted in favour of Peking. The decision was mostly a compromise between conflicting expediencies: not to challenge Peking too much, nor to offend Washington excessively; to remain cognizant of Taiwan's vote in matters vitally affecting Israel and to protest against mainland China's support of Arab terrorist organizations; and, on the other hand, not to move too far away from its friends in the non-aligned camp and the West European wing which supported the People's Republic.

Moreover, how could Israel vote for the expulsion of a member state while its adversaries were plotting its own exclusion? But, again, how could it ignore the existing realities? The obvious compromise was dual representation of Taiwan and Peking at the United Nations, but the idea had a salient flaw: it was unacceptable to both sides and incompatible with the Charter.

The issue reached its climax at the September session of the General Assembly in 1971. After Dr Kissinger had visited Peking earlier in the year, the replacement of Taiwan at the UN by the People's Republic had become a foregone conclusion. The United States was fighting a rearguard action to cover its retreat and asked its friends for sympathetic understanding and, wherever possible, support. Foreign Minister Eban strongly advocated that Israel should cast an affirmative vote for Peking. The cabinet supported him with the exception of Prime Minister Golda Meir and Defence Minister Dayan. It was one of the rare occasions where the cabinet voted not in conformity with the views and wishes of Golda and Dayan, but in favour of Eban's recommendations.

A few days before the matter came up for the vote in New York, Dayan asked the cabinet to reconsider its decision. It was an unusual move. After all, the issue was not of primary importance. Knowledgeable ministers explained that Dayan felt a bad precedent had been established when the cabinet outvoted himself and the Prime Minister. The cabinet dismissed the appeal and reaffirmed its previous decision. When the representatives of the People's Republic took their seats at the United Nations, Eban sent a telegram of congratulations to his opposite number in Peking. It was returned with a note: 'Undelivered because of non-existing relations.' As it happened, Egypt established postal communications with Israel before China resumed theirs.

At the United Nations the new Chinese team kept on the sidelines of the Arab-Israeli conflict. It neither participated actively in diplomatic initiatives, nor did it prevent them by casting its veto. To outdo Soviet rhetoric and to please the Arab gallery, it confined itself to a routine of tirades against Israel whenever a suitable opportunity presented itself. Its permanent representative, courteous in his personal contact with his Israeli colleague, was interested to be informed about Israel and its policy, but was impervious to any suggestions about improving relations. Israel was too far away from China, not only in distance but also in dimension: it was too small a speck on the map to have any significance. On the other hand, the Arab world was wide and had a vast hinterland in Africa. It was there that China sought to counteract established and expanding Soviet influence.

On the occasion of a mission to a number of newly independent West African states in 1960, I came across some curious features of the budding Sino-Russian popularity contest. Guinea, a country better known for its rich bauxite deposits than its contribution to the welfare of humanity, was ruled then as today by a tough-fisted dictator. President Seku Toure, lacking the means to provide bread for his destitute people, compensated them with well-staged circuses. He treated the diplomatic corps as part of his exotic menagerie. At official ceremonies he liked to parade them in the streets of his capital, Conakry, following on foot the triumphant President riding in his car. The procession usually started at twelve noon with the hapless ambassadors dressed in full regalia from top hat to patent-leather shoes.

Shortly before I visited Conakry, the President of Liberia had been received with lavish honours, including the walking escort of the diplomatic corps. The American Ambassador, who told me the story, was a man of ardent devotion to his task. He would not shy away from any tribulations to humour the government of Guinea to make it accept generous American development aid, but the Liberian procession was more than even this humble servant was prepared to suffer. Sweltering in the midday sun after trotting for more than an hour behind the presidential car, he turned to his Soviet colleague and bravely proposed that they call it a day and go home. Ambassador Solod, who had won his spurs in Beirut and Cairo where in the 1950s he had laid the groundwork for Arab-Russian *rapprochement*, eagerly agreed with his American colleague. 'Truly, this is an abuse of our diplomatic dignity,' he snorted. 'We really should quit. There should be some solidarity among us. We diplomats should form an international trade union to protect our professional and human rights,' he exclaimed. Then lowering his voice to a conspiratorial whisper he pointed to the straggling ambassador of the People's Republic of China: 'But the Chinaman will never join us. He'll keep walking. He will not abandon the procession even if they have to carry him on a stretcher. Moscow would never forgive me leaving the field to him.' The three wilted Ambassadors continued their long march not towards liberation but exhaustion.

In Africa China kept walking, but in the Middle East it lacked the material means and the practical experience to compete with the Soviet Union and the Western powers to exert a notable influence on the course of events.

Israel renewed its active interest in a dialogue with the government of the People's Republic when at the end of its period of internal turmoil in the 1960s, it came out of its shell and pulled in its horns. The Foreign Ministry asked a number of influential visitors to China and friends of Israel to acquaint the leadership in Peking with Israel's aspirations, its position in the

Middle East and the vast reservoir of friendship it enjoyed in the United States and in the countries of the West. In the best of cases the Chinese interlocutors listened, noted and refrained from commenting. In the periodic meetings which I used to hold as Director-General of the Foreign Ministry with Deputy Foreign Minister Macovescu, he told me that Romania had succeeded in establishing close links of friendship with Peking while straining but not jeopardizing its relations with Moscow. On the occasion of President Ceausescu's visit to Peking in 1971, the Romanian delegation had gained the impression that the Chinese showed a certain interest in Romania's reasons for maintaining relations with Israel. Macovescu believed that this was the beginning of a lengthy process of adjustment of Chinese foreign policy which could last several years. In these talks they had given the first indication that they had taken notice of Israel as a factor in the Middle East. He counselled Israel not to precipitate matters – Romania would continue to monitor the development.

At that time nothing was known of the secret contacts between Washington and Peking in preparation for Dr Kissinger's surprise visit to mainland China. It appears that Romania had played the role of intermediary as it previously had done in Vietnam, when Macovescu and other Romanian officials had visited Hanoi and Washington at the height of the war to help establish contacts between the two sides. Shortly after Ceausescu's visit to Peking, Macovescu came to Jerusalem for one of our periodic consultations. At the end of our meeting, he suggested we have a private talk. I invited him to our home and we talked for two hours, unhampered by protocol and minutes. The conversation ranged over a wide range of topics, from the contacts which Romania was trying to establish between Cairo and Jerusalem to the vicissitudes of Soviet-Romanian relations; from Romania's efforts to strengthen its ties with the United States to Israel's claims for increased emigration of Romanian Jews. This was a subject which topped our list of concerns. Romania, on the other hand, was principally interested in enlisting Israel's influence in the United States for the improvement of its political and commercial relations with the leader of the Western world.

Shortly after the Soviet invasion of Czechoslovakia in August 1968, the Romanian Foreign Ministry invited me to pay an official visit to Bucharest to discuss the tense situation in Europe and the Middle East. In our talks, which took place in December, the Romanian government urged us to solicit goodwill for it in the United States. It recognized that the alleviation of its restrictions on Jewish emigration and the improvement of its relations with Israel would facilitate the attainment of its main objective. Romania agreed to liberalize its emigration policy, a process which still required lengthy negotiations, until it produced relatively satisfactory results. It also assented to expand its trade with Israel and promised to raise the level of diplomatic representation between both countries from the status of legation to embassy.

In June 1969 I visited Washington for discussions with the new administration on the state of affairs in the Middle East. In our talks with Dr Kissinger and Undersecretary of State Elliot Richardson I raised the Romanian issue and explained Israel's interest in the strengthening of its relations with the only member state of the Warsaw pact to have retained its ties with us. I recommended a favourable American response to Romania's solicitations for the improvement of its relations with the United States.

After my return to Jerusalem the Romanian Ambassador brought me a cordial message of thanks from George Macovescu, the Deputy Foreign Minister. The United States government had informed the Romanian government of President Nixon's desire to pay an official visit to Bucharest in August. Although this idea had not figured in our talks in Washington, Macovescu apparently assumed that our intercession had been instrumental in bringing it about. A few days after the completion of Nixon's visit, Romania announced the elevation of our missions to the status of embassies. More important, the trickle of Jews previously permitted to leave the country for Israel turned into a steady flow.

At the end of our private talk in the summer of 1971 Macovescu related his impressions of his recent visit to China. In counselling patience to Israel and commenting on possible changes in the relations between China and the United States, he made a somewhat cryptic remark that startling happenings might occur soon which would initiate new departures. He did not mention any specifics and did not make the slightest allusion to Dr Kissinger's planned visit. Neither had our embassy in Washington any inkling of his plans.

Israel and Romania, each in its own way, have continued their attempts at breaking the Chinese ice. The huge block has not melted yet, although some China-watchers believe they have seen some signs of a thaw. The Chinese government displayed a benevolent interest in President Sadat's visit to Jerusalem in November 1977 and refrained from critical comments on the signature of the peace treaty between Egypt and Israel. High officials in Peking are reported to have shown increased interest in Israel's views, objectives and capacities. In the configuration of China's concerns, Israel may actually constitute a more positive element than before, but in terms of their political quantum theory it is apparently still a negligible factor. The conclusion of peace between Egypt and Israel with its resulting new alignment in the Middle East may accelerate the process of adjustment of China's foreign policy.

Be that as it may, Ben Gurion, in his later years, was a firm believer in the powerful influence which China in the foreseeable future would exert on world affairs. In discussions with leading statesmen he frequently and ardently dwelt on the subject. 1971 was a year of good political vintage for Israel. Foreign Ministers from quite a few countries, among them the Federal Republic of Germany, paid official visits so that they could acquaint themselves with the thinking of Israel's leaders. Scheel's visit was the first of a German Foreign Minister to Israel. It was a precarious venture which required considerable tact and restraint. Scheel had expressed the wish to pay his respects to Ben Gurion who lived in retirement in the Negev. On the last day of his visit we flew down by helicopter to Sde Boker, the kibbutz where the old man worked, studied and wrote.

Scheel became somewhat discomforted when we approached Ben Gurion's wooden bungalow. He asked with unconcealed bewilderment whether this was indeed the place where the great man lived. He greeted Ben Gurion with pronounced and respectful formality, but the old man put him instantly at ease with his robust charm. He selected a peach the size of a large apple and urged the Foreign Minister to taste it. Mr Scheel obviously had other ideas than partaking of the fruits of the kibbutz. He intended to address Ben Gurion. But who could resist him, particularly when he told his guest the history of the juicy peach. 'Out of the desert it has blossomed,' he exclaimed. 'Water had to be carried here from far away. There was not a single tree here when our boys came to this place in the wilderness some twenty years ago.' Then he glanced at the peach with the pride of a father looking at his handsome and well brought-up child.

At this point Scheel thought that his turn had finally come. He positioned himself and began his speech. He had come to express the gratitude of the German people to the former Prime Minister who had led the way to recon-ciliation between the two peoples. His courage and foresight had been epoch-making and, when he had grasped the outstretched hand of Kanzler Adenauer, he had opened a new and promising chapter after the unspeakable horrors of the Nazi period. Ben Gurion raised his hands as if to say 'no more speeches' and without any transition began to speak about the subject which evidently preoccupied his mind.

America and China, he started abruptly, must come to terms. This was the only way to safeguard the peace of the world and to preserve it from Russian domination. The sooner the countries of Western Europe recognized this the better, because their own freedom was at stake. America should no longer hesitate to engage in the normalization of its relations with the People's Republic of China: 'I assure you, it is a matter of months and not of years.' Scheel tried mildly and politely to bring the visionary back to the realities of international life as he saw them. He argued that the time for such a bold move was not ripe, nor was the United States prepared to abandon its Taiwan ally. Ben Gurion dismissed the arguments of the realistic Foreign Minister in a friendly way and reiterated his conviction.

Scheel had to leave. His plane was waiting to take him back to Bonn. A few days later the news of Dr Kissinger's visit to China stunned the world. Ben Gurion had not been in possession of any advance information. It was his knowledge of the world and his legendary intuition which led him to the right conclusion. Just as his vision of the future of American-Chinese relations became reality at the beginning of the 1970s, so did his views on the inevitability of Arab-Israeli peace come true at the end of the decade.

11

Relations with Western Europe

In 1957 I was appointed Ambassador to Belgium and Luxembourg. Before taking up my new assignment I paid a customary farewell visit to the Prime Minister. I supposed that Belgium was of no significant interest to Ben Gurion and prepared myself to listen to one of his usually fascinating monologues on a theme which was preoccupying him at the moment, totally unrelated to my mission. I was in for a surprise. The Prime Minister used the occasion to brief me on his European views and their operational implications for my new tasks.

After the United States had assisted in the reconstruction of Western Europe with such striking success, Ben Gurion explained, the European countries – allies and former enemies alike – had embarked on their own road, leading through economic co-operation to political unity. This was the lesson the Europeans had learnt from the internecine wars which had ruined and torn them apart in the past. Their future economic well-being and social progress required the establishment of a closely-knit community which would become a central force in world affairs. Brussels was the centre of the community. Israel must forge close links with it. The task of the ambassador was to promote them. So much for the multilateral aspect of the assignment. But the bilateral one, continued Ben Gurion, also required our full attention. Belgium was a highly developed industrial country. Israel needed modern machinery and technology to build its own industry rapidly. Only a firm industrial infrastructure could ensure its defence, enable it to accommodate hundreds of thousands of newcomers and provide the people with a decent standard of living. Moreover we should not rely exclusively on France. Its solitary friendship with Israel should be shored up by its European partners. Belgium, closely linked to its neighbour, could help enlarge the area of support for Israel. After all, envisaged the Prime Minister, the war in Algeria would one day come to an end and the more friends Israel could count on in Europe, the safer its relations with France would be in the future. He concluded on an inspirational note: 'Tell the Europeans that they have inherited their spiritual values from that little but enduring people which you are going to represent among them. We have not only horrible memories of the recent past in common, but also a bright future ahead of us.' As usual with

Ben Gurion his vision was not removed from reality. His briefing was a practical programme for ambassadorial action.

The opportunity to present the Prime Minister with a tangible token of Belgian friendship arrived a year or so later. The Queen Mother, Elisabeth, grandmother of the reigning king, Baudouin, had been a lifelong friend of the Jews, an admirer of Dr Weizmann and a supporter of Israel. When my wife and I arrived in Brussels she graciously bestowed her friendship on us personally. She would invite us to her palace for intimate luncheons and the outspoken talk for which she was famous, and to concerts of which she was the celebrated royal patron. In the mid-1930s she had visited what was then Palestine with her late husband, King Albert. She was intrigued by the idea of revisiting the country, a suggestion which my wife intimated to her with that directness and naturalness which always added so much strength to the persuasiveness of her advice and gained Israel many friends wherever we served. But there were two difficulties: the Queen's advanced age and the reluctance of the Belgian Foreign Ministry to consent to an act of friendship which might evoke the displeasure of the Arab governments. The Queen suggested that we divide the task of removing the obstacles. She would convince the doubters of her ability to travel and I would have to persuade the government to let her go. We both acquitted ourselves successfully of our undertakings. On the eve of the royal departure, Foreign Minister Pierre Wigny phoned me with undisguised anxiety to elicit from me a solemn pledge that everything would remain quiet in the area during the Queen Mother's visit. I assured him of Israel's absolute pacific intentions and of our knowledge of no Arab plans likely to disturb the existing tranquillity.

Little did I know that only a few days later we would be in the middle of a completely unforeseen and self-inflicted crisis. The directors of operations and of military intelligence of the Israel Defence Force had the droll idea of testing the call-up system without any forewarning. Neither the Minister of Defence, who happened to be Prime Minister Ben Gurion, nor the Chief of Staff had any advance notice of the exercise carried out on 1 April 1959, making it a memorable April fools' day. On that morning there were as many red faces in the elevated echelons of the top brass as there were red roses in the Queen Mother's apartment. And all the generals, culpable or innocent, insisted on presenting their apologies personally to Her Majesty. After the initial agitation and sustained embarrassment, Ben Gurion re-established order among his worrying warriors and sent the Chief of Staff to present the apologies on behalf of the army. Unlike Queen Victoria, the Queen Mother was truly amused. She cheered up General Laskow, saying that in Israel's situation the army must be in a state of constant alert and inquiring whether the call-up exercise had been smooth and effective. She thanked the Chief of Staff for having added such a fascinating feature to her interesting programme. It gave her a special taste of the Israeli reality which she had come to experience. Now it was the turn of the Belgian Ambassador to be red-faced. In the first rush of his excitement he had insisted that Her Majesty interrupt her visit and return to Brussels.

Queen Elisabeth was a remarkable woman. She was the daughter of a Bavarian nobleman and ophthalmologist and before the First World War had married King Albert of Belgium. When the German armies invaded her new country in 1914, the Queen made the memorable declaration: 'An iron curtain has come down between me and Germany' – a figure of speech which Churchill inscribed indelibly in the political lexicon of the post-Second World War epoch. The Queen Mother's visit to an informal Israel was far from being a pomp and circumstance affair. It was more like a happening, full of human touches and good humour kindled by her quick wit and engaging naturalness. For the people of Israel, steeped in historic memory, it was a thrilling event, the first royal visit to the reborn state since the Queen of Sheba had paid her respects to King Solomon – Cleopatra's alleged attempt to inveigle King Herod into a dangerous liaison being discounted by the chroniclers.

In any case the visit of the Queen Mother was a *première* in modern Israel, an occasion arousing not only spontaneous enthusiasm but also calling for an appropriate measure of protocol hospitality. President Ben-Zvi, a man of proverbial modesty, presided over the state dinner. He insisted on holding it in the crammed dining-room which adjoined his offices and was located in a large wooden hut, symbolizing the simplicity of the early pioneer days. Our chief of protocol insisted that champagne was an indispensable requisite of a royal banquet. This was too much even for the mild-mannered President. Reinforced by his gallant wife he rebelled. Never had such a beverage of debauchery defaced his table. We were rapidly approaching a constitutional crisis. Where did the presidential prerogative end and the government's word begin? An ingenious last-minute compromise prevented the looming confrontation. The contending parties settled on a sparkling wine made in Israel and euphemistically called champagne.

The President's staff had unwittingly prepared for some unscheduled entertainment during the meal. A man entered from the kitchen, positioned himself in a corner of the dining-room clutching a bottle of Israeli champagne, and aimed it with visible concentration at the ceiling immediately above the table. The cork escaped with a booming sound and the contents showered the guests. The little that had remained in the bottle he poured gingerly into two glasses. His performance evoked some subdued but respectful giggling, the members of the royal party wondering whether this was an ancient Israeli ceremony to salute visiting royalty. But the presidential champagne-gunner was undeterred. He produced a second bottle and launched it with even greater aplomb and accuracy. Down flowed the sparkling liquid straight onto the crowned head. The Queen Mother broke into hilarious laughter and relieved everyone of painful embarrassment. It needed considerable persuasion to make the intrepid champagne-launcher retreat to the kitchen from where the muffled sounds of his fireworks continued to amuse the guests.

Before leaving, Ben Gurion took me aside. He beamed with enjoyment. The Queen had enchanted him. 'What a gracious lady,' he mused, 'what a keen intellect,' and with a twinkle in his eye, 'what a beautiful woman.' Then, the old warrior, feeling that he had perhaps revealed too much sentimentality, snapped curtly: 'But the best of the evening, I tell you Gideon, was the champagne salute. What targeting, what shooting.' Ben Gurion had already moved away and so did not hear my recommendation that he decorate the gunner with a military champagne ribbon.

The implementation of the first part of the Prime Minister's directives which he had given me on the eve of my departure for Brussels proceeded satisfactorily. Trade between Belgium and Israel expanded, credit facilities became available, an economic mission of leading Belgian industrialists and bankers visited Israel and the arms industries of the two countries developed mutually beneficial connections. In the United Nations, Belgium generally adhered to positions which were not harmful to Israel, closer in line with the attitude of friendly and understanding Netherlands than with that of the other somewhat more reserved Western European countries. The two countries raised the status of their diplomatic missions from legations to embassies.

Israel's first participation in the World Fair, held in Brussels in 1958, presented to millions of visitors the little known face of its new civilization, rebuilt in its ancient homeland, ravaged by centuries of neglect and set against the background of its tragedies and triumphs of the past. The original of the Isaiah Scroll, one of the Dead Sea Scrolls, exhibited at the entrance of the Israeli pavilion, aroused reverential admiration. In a dimly-lit passageway leading to an exhibit of present-day life in Israel, ghastly scenes of the Nazi Holocaust evoked abhorrence and tearful compassion. Looking at the gruesome pictures, Queen Juliana of the Netherlands broke out into sobs and muttered: 'It is so important that you show this. All people must see this lest they forget the horrors inflicted on the Jews.'

The Common Market

In the second sphere of my ambassadorial duties, the development of relations with the European Economic Community, progress was incomparably slower. To manifest the importance Israel attributed to its ties with the fledgling organization, the government decided to appoint me as representative to the Community, a status officially defined for non-member countries as that of a 'permanent observer'. The nomenclature of international organizations was still relatively new, and their diplomatic protocol in its swaddling-clothes. Why permanent? Why observer? Who was observing whom? When I later served as 'Permanent Representative' to the United Nations and was recalled to Jerusalem after eleven months to head the foreign service my permanency fell rather short of perpetuity. Anyway my accreditation to the Community, better known as the Common Market, created problems. Not, however, as one might expect, from the Arab states; at that time they were indifferent to the new and untested organization. The difficulty arose from an internal conflict of authority. The three observers who had been accredited before had presented their credentials to the President of the European Commission, the management of the community. Now the President of the Council of Ministers, the principal political organ of the Common Market, insisted on the presentation of the letter of accreditation to him in order to assert the preferential status of the Council. The intramural wrangling lasted several weeks while we were kept in the dark on the reasons for the delay of the ceremony. It was the perfect occasion for any diplomat to give free rein to his analytic or speculative talents. The prevailing theory was that the delay was due to opposition to Israel's application. It was a typical diplomatic figment of the imagination with not a grain of fact to substantiate the assumption. The internal community dispute was finally settled by Solomonic wisdom. The two presidents agreed to receive two identical letters appropriately addressed. And this is now hallowed community protocol.

The follow-up was meant to be more purposeful. The six original members of the European Economic Community constituted Israel's principal foreign trade partners. Jaffa oranges and grapefruit had become a European staple, later to be supplemented by sizeable shipments of out-of-season fruit. vegetables and flowers. The new tariffs envisaged by the Common Market were likely to seriously harm Israel's exports. Only a special agreement could facilitate them. The opinions among the economic experts and political people in Israel, on what kind of agreement was desirable and attainable, were divided. The representatives of trade interests favoured a preferential tariff accord as a first step. The more visionary political minds aspired to the status of associate membership, so as to set off the disadvantages deriving from Israel's regional isolation. The outcome of the discussion was a hybrid memorandum focusing on neither one issue nor the other. I submitted it in October 1958 to Professor Walter Hallstein, the incumbent German President of the European Commission. The Common Market was then still in its initial stages of organization and was defining its internal and external economic policy. It was anxious to avoid far-reaching commitments extending to non-member states. Hallstein and his associates recognized that Israel had a valid case. It was a valuable trading-partner of the six, not only because of its exports, but also because of the steadily increasing volume of its imports, which favoured Common Market countries. But realizing these inequities was still a far cry from trying to remedy them by the sweeping act of admitting Israel as an associate member. To alleviate some of the immediate hardships the Commission proposed an agreement on tariff reductions for Israel's citrus exports and negotiations on commercial credits to facilitate its European imports. Jerusalem was disappointed by the parsimony of the offer. It was aiming higher. My colleagues and I in Brussels were of the opinion that Jerusalem's target was beyond the reach of our political capabilities and far beyond the horizon of the new community.

The ensuing stalemate lasted several years. We intensified our high-level contacts in Brussels. Israel's then Minister of Commerce, Pinhas Sapir, and later Finance Minister Levi Eshkol held extensive talks with the commissioners and ministers of the European Community. But they failed to overcome the reluctance of their counterparts to enter into a comprehensive agreement. Nonetheless, Levi Eshkol left his mark in Brussels in a field in which at home he was not considered to be a practitioner of excellence. Public speaking had never been his strong point. The Minister of Finance had agreed to address a festive mass meeting celebrating the tenth anniversary of Israel's independence. He surprised us by insisting on delivering his speech in French, a language which we had the impression he was no more familiar with than the audience would be with Hebrew. To be a Minister of Finance anywhere one has to be a stubborn man, and in Israel even more so. A French text was prepared and our best French-speaking secretary coached him in phonetics like a latterday Professor Higgins.

Mr Eshkol addressed the packed hall with typical Israeli self-confidence. Whilst he was wrestling with his text, the crowd became increasingly restless. The applause greeting the Minister's performance was more a manifestation of their unshakeable solidarity with Israel than an enthusiastic acclaim of an oratorical treat. The next morning the press featured the event with headlines: 'Belgium can learn a lesson from Israel. French-speaking audience admires Israel minister's perfect Flemish pronunciation. Israeli solution of our language problem: Speak French and make it sound Flemish.' Eshkol, famous for his sound sense of humour, quipped: 'I didn't succeed in lowering the European tariffs, but at least I helped raise Israel's popularity.'

This had been my second bout with the intricacies of the linguistic problem. Belgian protocol postulates that a newly accredited ambassador pays his first visit to the President of the Parliament. When we arrived in Brussels, Camille Huysmans was Mr Speaker. He was a man in his middle eighties, endowed with a sharp wit and an enviable vitality. He had just married a lady fifty years his junior; when he received me, he was still in blissful honeymoon spirit. Although a born Walloon, he had been all his life a fierce fighter for Flemish rights. I thought he would appreciate it if I were to make my opening remarks in Flemish. I asked our embassy driver, a solid Flammand, to tutor me.

The great moment arrived. I was shown into the presence of the grand old man and delivered my speech. Huysmans listened attentively, but with a look of incredulity in his eyes. When he thought that I had finished, he planted himself straight in front of me and said slowly in French: 'Jeune homme' – this was the way he addressed anyone below the age of seventy – 'Young man, I have been a lifelong supporter of Zionism. I met your President Ben-Zvi at the

Congress of the Socialist International in Stuttgart in 1907. I have been a close friend of the Jewish community in Antwerp, since the time I was Mayor of the town. I have been a champion of Israel's rights and have visited the land six times. But I regret to say, I have never managed to learn Yiddish.' Then he toasted the success of my mission with a glass of champagne and a paternal pat on the shoulder.

In due course I was to find out after all that it was easier to master some Flemish than to find a common language with the Common Market. Although our mutual trade increased threefold in the intervening years and Israeli exports encountered sharp competition, it was only in 1964 that Israel succeeded in concluding its first trade agreement of rather limited scope with the European Economic Community. It took another decade before the organization, by then enlarged to nine members and Israel's mutual trade with them exceeding two billion dollars annually, signed a new comprehensive agreement with Israel. It envisaged the gradual reduction of tariffs over a lengthy period of time and their eventual abolition as part of an overall agreement with all the Mediterranean countries. Twenty years after its first application for association with the European Community, Israel, though by now closely connected with it, was still far from its original objective. The development of its relations with the Common Market was an object lesson on how to adjust far-flung aims to given opportunities commensurate with Israel's political limitations and corresponding to existing international realities.

Rapprochement with Germany

Three major trends marked the evolution of the bilateral relationships between Israel and Europe during the post-Sinai war decade, 1957–67. Firstly, the French connection, still going strong up till the early 1960s, steadily declined from then on at the same rate as France and Algeria became reconciled. Secondly, the relations with the Soviet Union and its Eastern European allies, under heavy strain since their arms deal with Egypt in 1955, deteriorated constantly until they reached breaking-point at the height of the fighting in 1967. Thirdly, the German-Israeli complexity, burdened by the indelible memory of the Nazi abominations and haunted by the ghastly shadows of its countless victims, began to undergo a slow and initially imperceptible change.

Germany's mounting importance in the affairs of Europe, its accumulation of economic power and its major contribution to the defence of the Western alliance, steadily raised its political influence in world affairs. This created a new reality which even the most powerful states could not afford to disregard, let alone a besieged and embattled Israel subjected to incessant Arab efforts to encumber its ties with friendly countries.

The beginning of a relationship of sorts between Israel and the new Germany went back to 1952 when the two countries signed in Luxembourg an important agreement on individual restitution to Nazi victims and a lump payment of indemnity to the State of Israel. The material side of this agreement was of incontestable value to the economic development of Israel and its ability to carry the enormous financial burdens imposed on it by its defence needs and the costs of settlement of hundreds of thousands of destitute newcomers. Yet the moral and political justification of the agreement was fiercely attacked by the parties of the radical left and the extreme right in Israel. The Herut Party, led by Mr Begin, carried the fight into the streets and for the first, and happily the last, time in the young history of the state, police had to use armed force to overcome a violent crowd of Herut demonstrators threatening to storm the Knesset.

Although the benefits deriving from the restitution payments became in the course of the years more and more evident, they removed neither the fabric of scars nor the mount of memories left behind by the Nazi Holocaust. Mammon cannot recompense the wilful destruction of millions of human beings. Yet the implementation of the agreement necessitated the development of contacts between individuals and the authorities of the two countries to an increasing degree. They initiated a slow process of outward normalization in the sphere of practical affairs.

In the absence of diplomatic relations between the two countries – unthinkable for Israel at that time – the Foreign Ministry had little, if any, say in German-Israeli affairs. Our large economic mission in Cologne lodged two lonely foreign service officers: a consul mainly dealing with the certification of documents and a counsellor whose political advice was rarely solicited. It appeared that both defence establishments in Tel Aviv and Bonn felt less encumbered in their dealings without the more rigid framework of diplomatic relations. And despite the fact that the policy-makers in our Ministry of Defence pressed constantly for the reduction of the restrictions regulating Israel's policy towards Germany, they were reluctant to support their diplomatic normalization. Connoisseurs of the military mind attributed this seeming contradiction more to a desire to preserve their primacy, unimpaired by ambassadorial scrutiny, than to ideological or emotive reasons.

Yet the growing status of Germany in the world and its unfailing observance of its undertakings towards Israel above and beyond its contractual obligations induced the government of Israel to take an important step towards Germany. It was principally Ben Gurion's initiative and he encountered serious grumblings from his left-wing cabinet colleagues, who later left the government upon the revelation of some of the transactions between the defence establishments of the two countries and, in particular, the secret visit of the then Chief of Staff, Moshe Dayan.

But Ben Gurion was convinced that for the good of Israel, it had to come to terms with the new reality. On the occasion of a visit to the United States in March 1960, where he had a satisfactory talk with President Kennedy on Israel's defence needs, a meeting was arranged between him and Kanzler Adenauer who happened to be in New York. The two leaders, old but still very much in command, secluded themselves without ceremony in the Waldorf Astoria Hotel. Adenauer was convinced that the test for the new Germany was its ability to establish a relationship of trust with Israel and the Jews in the world. It had to show the awareness of its responsibility for the past by its unwavering and manifest commitment to Israel's future.

Prominent Germans who had known the Kanzler intimately and had not been uncritical of his pragmatic flexibility, have confirmed that three basic beliefs formed his moral and political foundations: his religious faith, his trust in the inescapable necessity of European unity and his conviction that, without reconciliation with the Jewish people, Germany would not be accepted as a trusted and respected member of the international community.

Axel Springer, the prominent German publisher and outstanding friend of Israel, once related a conversation he had had with Konrad Adenauer in the last month of his long life. The Kanzler urged him to abide by two maxims: always to remain watchful in regard to the unbalanced German people, and always to stand loyally by the Jews and Israel.

Ben Gurion emerged from his meeting with the Kanzler reassured in his faith that a new Germany had arisen – a Germany determined to abide by its moral obligations towards Israel and pledged to alleviate its burdens by continued material aid. In the remaining three years of his premiership Ben Gurion pursued a steady course of *rapprochement* with Germany. Near the end of his tenure – or perhaps it was even one of the reasons which brought it to an end – the highly sensitive Israeli-German relations becar e strained by a sudden crisis. At the beginning of 1963 the head of the Mossad, Israel's Central Intelligence Agency, believed that he had discovered evidence of the involvement of German scientists in nuclear missile development in Egypt. There was no doubt that Egypt had embarked on a missile programme and established connections with German firms and individuals active in the related fields of science and technology, but there was no substantive evidence available that they were engaged in the development of nuclear weapons, nor that Egypt had made any serious progress in the field of ballistic missiles.

However, Isser Harel, the undaunted head of the Mossad, was not a man to suffer doubters. He was convinced that the rumours were facts and his conviction was contagious. He overwhelmed the otherwise rather sceptical Golda Meir, then Foreign Minister, not so much by the soundness of his evidence but by the power of his anti-German persuasion, shared to no small degree by Golda herself. 'Tiny Isser', as the formidable intelligence chief was called throughout the land, not for the smallness of his ambitions but for the diminutiveness of his stature, insisted that the great German danger should be smashed by a worldwide press campaign castigating its conspiracy with Egypt. Not relying on the governmental information services, he activated his own people. Golda herself made a tough statement in the Knesset, detailing the allegations which Isser had supplied and casting grave doubts on the moral and political integrity of the 'new Germany'. The consternation of the government in Bonn was no less than that of Ben Gurion vacationing in Tiberias. The vociferous press campaign and the statement of his Foreign Minister came to him as a complete surprise. He had been neither consulted on it beforehand, nor asked to give his approval. Shimon Peres, his number two in the Ministry of Defence, took Isser Harel to task for his unconsidered action based on speculative reports. Ben Gurion fumed about Golda's independent and unco-ordinated sally against Germany.

Before long, the smouldering tension caused by the incident broke out in a private talk between the two. Preceding the weekly Sunday cabinet meeting, the Prime Minister held his usual Saturday night consultation with the Foreign Minister. Ben Gurion, criticizing the handling of the German scientist affair, suggested steps to repair the damage caused to Israeli-German relations which would be likely to affect a number of vital defence matters under discussion with Bonn. Golda stoutly defended her way of dealing with the situation, which she continued to consider as a grave threat to Israel's security. She opposed the idea of calling off the campaign and discussing the issue directly and discreetly with Bonn. Recognizing that in such sensitive matters the opinion of the Prime Minister, who was also in charge of defence, was overriding, she suggested that she yield not her opinion but her office. Ben Gurion curtly rejected her offer and left it at that, but only for a few hours. The next morning he announced to the stupefied cabinet his irrevocable decision to resign. He did not elaborate on his reasons besides those contained in his public statement, neither did he point to any particular incident. He contented himself with stressing that his resignation was the result of thorough reflection and of his long-standing desire to shed the burdens of public office.

Friends close to Ben Gurion confirmed that his resignation was not a sudden act, but the culmination of a process of wear and tear in which the handling of the Lavon affair and the German scientist campaign had played an important role. But the Prime Minister's intimates would not dismiss at all the possibility that his tense meeting with his Foreign Minister might have been the crucial impulse for the timing of his decision. Golda's and Ben Gurion's ways parted now for ten years of bitter antagonism. Only when advanced age had mellowed them, and both were thinking about the last chapter of their lives, did they meet for reconciliation. Ben Gurion took the initiative, not because he merely wanted to be chivalrous to a lady, but because with all his foibles he was a great man to the end.

In April 1964, Bonn actively assisted Israel in signing its first trade agreement with the European Economic Community. It opposed moves, sponsored mainly by France, to tilt the balanced position of the Community on the Arab-Israeli conflict in favour of the Arab side. In the course of time, Germany became Israel's second best export market and overall trading partner. The influx of substantial quantities of German equipment into Israel's economy helped not only to expand and modernize its industry and agriculture, but also created a constantly widening network of connections between Israeli and German citizens. It was more a process of familiarization than a trend to fraternization – a sheer impossibility for any Israeli of this generation, still conscious of the Nazi outrage.

Yet both Germany and Israel realized that, despite these emotive barriers, the multiplicity and diversity of their already existing ties necessitated their integration into a permanent framework of formal diplomatic relations. In March 1965, Bonn sent a special envoy, Dr Kurt Birnbach, to Jerusalem to initiate the talks on the normalization. In August of the same year, Israel and Germany exchanged ambassadors. The arrival of a German ambassador in Israel caused considerable agitation. Survivors of concentration camps demonstrated, expressing their understandable wrath; but other participants in the protests, mostly youths sent into the streets by the right-wing opposition parties, were in their personal experience rather remote from the hideous Nazi period. Their leaders used them more to stir up trouble against their own government than to remind present-day Germany of its Nazi past.

The reaction of the Arab governments to the formalization of German-Israeli relations was virulent. Most of them severed their diplomatic relations with the Federal Republic, only to regret the political and economic harm they had inflicted upon themselves. Slowly, in a process lasting a few years, the Arab states accommodated themselves to the realities of German-Israeli relations and restored their own one by one with the Federal Republic.

The first German ambassador, Rolf Pauls, was a man endowed with patience, tact and understanding. Unostentatiously he created confidence in the sincerity of his personal goodwill and the integrity of his government's intentions. When he relinquished his post a few years later to become Ambassador to Washington, he left behind an astonishing residue of personal friendships. He had successfully negotiated quite a few rapids in the swirling stream of Israeli-German relations.

Some twelve years later the erstwhile leader of the anti-reconciliationists, Menachem Begin, by then Prime Minister, extended his hand to welcome Klaus Schuetz, the former Lord Mayor of Berlin and new ambassador. The process of diplomatic normalization proceeded on its customary course. Abba Eban was the first Israeli Foreign Minister to pay an official visit to Germany in 1970. Walter Scheel reciprocated a year later. Eban's visit began at Dachau and Scheel's at the shrine of the martyrs of the Holocaust in Jerusalem. And both ended with the pledge to nurture the new growth of understanding but also with the avowal that it could never erase the memory of the scorched earth underneath.

The new plague

Now, a new evil was spreading. International terrorism was striking at society in worldwide manifestations of savagery. Equipped with Soviet arms and Maoist ideological confusion, trained in Arab camps and financed by oil potentates, the motley crowd of killers committed their crimes on land, sea and air, wherever their peculiar minds believed bloodshed and publicity would further their nihilistic causes and satisfy their murderous compulsions. In autumn 1972, Arab terrorists descended on the Olympics held in Germany for the first time since they had been staged in Berlin under Hitler's auspices, thirty-six years before. In plain view of a stupefied world audience, the self-styled liberators captured and killed eleven members of the Israeli team. Shock swept the civilized world and many Germans bowed their head in shame that their land had again become the scene of a horrible crime committed against Jews.

In an article which I wrote for the *New York Times* in the aftermath of the events, I tried to express our feelings of abhorrence and voice a warning:

The Arab terrorists moved on to Munich to continue their deadly game. When they go into action, they do not attack armed forces. They assault defenceless civilians. They do not fight on the battlefield, they butcher in the bedroom. For these killers the ideal of the Olympic peace has no significance because they loathe the very idea of peace. For them sanctity does not exist, because they live beyond the pale of human values.

They do not come to the Olympics to compete in manly contest. Their sport is manhunt and mass murder. They triumphed in seizing eleven Israeli sportsmen in their sleep – and after twenty-four hours of captivity mowed their shackled prisoners down with Soviet Khalatchikov guns.

Moved by the ferocity of the outrage and the memories it evoked, the German government decided on stern measures to combat terrorism on its own soil. Realizing that the spreading of the plague could only be halted by joint European measures it initiated their adoption by the members of the Common Market. But when Arab terrorists hijacked a Lufthansa plane a year later, demanding the release of the Olympic murderers, Bonn yielded and dispatched them to Libya. It was a step back into the wilderness of anarchy and caused considerable dismay in Israel. Six years of trial and error passed until Germany, having been subjected to the most revolting outrages of kidnapping and murder with its own citizens as victims, was able and willing to strike a successful blow against a mixed gang of Arab and German terrorists. Encouraged by Israel's rescue mission at Entebbe, a specially trained German anti-terrorist force freed a plane-load of hijacked passengers in a swift operation at Mogadishu.

In 1973, a few months before the Yom Kippur War, the then German Kanzler, Willy Brandt, made a personal contribution to the strengthening of the developing relations. His official visit to Israel was more in the nature of a pilgrimage of atonement than a ceremonious affair of state. Government and public extended to him a friendly welcome, respecting his unblemished anti-Nazi record and appreciating his stand against the detractors of Israel in the international arena. Brandt, one of the main proponents of Germany's Ostpolitik which eased its relations with the Soviet Union and legitimized the Soviet post-war expansion in Europe, had firmly resisted Soviet attempts to persuade Germany to reduce its commitment to Israel. In the European Community, the government of Willy Brandt favoured Israel's requests, and in its political councils it distanced itself from French attempts to commit the Common Market to a joint policy of one-sided support of Arab policies. On the other hand, the restoration of diplomatic relations between Germany and the Arab countries and its membership in the United Nations exposed Bonn to mounting pressures. It induced it to follow a more cautious course towards Israel, a process which the oil squeeze exerted in the wake of the Yom Kippur War accelerated and exacerbated. Yet, by and large, Germany remained cognizant of its obligations towards Israel in a European environment which was more inclined to submit to Arab demands.

12

Eastern Europe

Until 10 June 1967, the Soviet Union and all its partners in the Warsaw pact had diplomatic relations with Israel. On the last day of the Six Day War, Moscow and its East European allies, regrettably joined by Yugoslavia, severed them. Only Romania refused to make common cause and remained a solitary oasis in the new diplomatic desert stretching from the Chinese border to the Berlin wall.

It was not the first time that the Soviet Union had used diplomatic sanctions against Israel, but the decision taken in 1967 inaugurated a period of aridity of record length. In 1953 Moscow broke its relations in retaliation for the strong reaction which the libellous anti-Jewish allegations of the doctors' plot had caused in Israel. It was one of the last acts of the Stalin era. A few months after the dictator's demise, Prime Minister Molotov initiated the resumption of relations.

The next demonstration of Soviet diplomatic ire occurred in 1956. At the outset of the Sinai campaign Moscow recalled its ambassador and suspended the relations, although not severing them. It is notable that it did not take the same steps against Israel's French and British partners. The Russian military suppression of the Hungarian uprising, coinciding with the flare-up in the Middle East, had apparently had a restraining influence on the decision-makers in the Kremlin. They were not too keen to use a diplomatic stick which furious Western public opinion could demand to be wielded against the Soviet Union. In any case, after a few weeks of sporadic and inconsequential debate, the United Nations with its selective register of moral outrage laid the Soviet intervention in Hungary to eternal rest in the vaults of its archives.

Soon after it had demonstrated its displeasure with Israel's participation in the Sinai-Suez venture, the Soviet Union sent its ambassador back to Israel. The relations, however, have never warmed up again since the beginning of the chill in the early 1950s. This turned into permafrost in the later 1960s. The intervening decade of diplomatic normality was on the whole a barren period, and the Soviet Union refused to resume its trade relations which it had suspended in 1956. Until then mostly barter agreements had regulated the exchange of goods – mainly citrus fruit against oil.

Yom Kippur in Odessa
Despite expectations of liberalization evoked by the successors of Stalin, the

Soviet government continued to suppress the rising protests of Soviet Jews against the denial of religious and cultural freedom and their claim of the right to leave for Israel. During one short private visit to Odessa, I had the opportunity to witness personally the full impact of these repressed aspirations. On the day of Yom Kippur 1956, accompanied by my fifteen-year-old son, I attended the service in the only remaining synagogue of the town. It was located far from the centre in a derelict neighbourhood and the building was too small to hold the mass of 3,000 worshippers. Spilling over into the densely packed courtyard and street, they formed a sea of humanity swaying in devotion. After we had been recognized as visitors from Jerusalem a hush embraced the community. Suddenly we were lifted up and carried bodily over the heads of the assembled into the centre of the synagogue where the elders of the community were praying on a raised platform. From all sides people crowded in on us, to whisper in our ears a word of anxiety or just to touch the 'messengers from Jerusalem' as they called us. When we reached the concluding prayer, 'Next year in rebuilt Jerusalem', the congregation emitted an outcry of such fervour, anguish and hope as if to make the walls crumble and raise the roof, and let their plaint and prayer be heard all over heaven and earth.

Four days later, we left for home on the last Israeli oil-tanker to sail from a Soviet port, the howl of anguish resounding in our hearts. It was an irrepressible protest, because it merged a never-forgotten yearning for the return to the land of Israel with the urge to escape the actual distress. It erupted collectively in this unforgettable Yom Kippur prayer, but we also encountered it when our Intourist guide and KGB chaperone, a young lady, burst into tears when she took leave of us. During the four days she had accompanied us in our wanderings through Odessa she had not revealed her Jewish origin. At the gates of the port she suddenly said: 'How much I envy you going home where we all belong.' We were perplexed, but still somehow on our guard; yet, before we could say anything, she continued: 'My father fought at the front and my mother managed to escape with us children to Tashkent before the Nazis occupied Odessa. We all survived and at the end of the war met here again in our home town. When we wanted to return to our miserable flat, it was occupied by strangers. We asked them for the belongings we had left behind, but they turned us away.' Our guide could no longer control her emotions and choking with sobs she said: 'You in Israel will never have to go through this. When you work, you work for your country; when you fight, you fight for your people. We all are so proud of you.' We passed through the gates of the port, open to us and locked to her.

As later evidence revealed, the existence of the Jews in the Soviet Union was at stake during the terminal stage of Stalin's rule. He had planned to deport the Jews to uninhabitable parts of the country where they would succumb to the rigours of climate, neglect and forced labour. The tremors preceding the approaching catastrophe had their shattering effect on the Jewish community, all of them witnesses of the Nazi Holocaust and most of them remnants of families wiped out by it. Premonition honed by age-old experience and the more recent memory of the Czarist pogroms sharpened their perception of imminent danger. Denied any chance to escape or resist the onslaught when it came, and cut off from the outside world, the Jews in the Soviet Union became conscious of their Jewish heritage from which the communist society had tried to alienate them without offering them unqualified acceptance. Even when Stalin's maniacal designs were buried with him, neither the anxieties nor the stirrings of the Russian Jews were laid to rest. The more the Soviet government stepped up its anti-Israel campaign, the more vitriolic its vilification of Zionism – meaning Judaism – became, the stronger grew the sense of vigilance of the Soviet Jews, their self-assertion and identification with Israel.

Hopes that Khrushchev's policy of de-Stalinization would also moderate the anti-Jewish attitudes of the Soviet government failed to materialize. Nor did it alter its anti-Israeli stance. The bias against Jews and Israel was not necessarily an organic part of Soviet ideology, but rather a function of its pro-Arab partiality. The Soviet Union increasingly attuned its position to the volume of Arab hostility against Israel, amplifying it through its worldwide propaganda machine. The sharper its attacks against Israel became, the more the Soviet Jews identified themselves with the Jewish state. The Soviet assault against Israel abroad and the repression of Jewish rights at home produced a movement of protest throughout the Jewish communities, constantly growing in vigour and participation. Many non-Jews, aroused by the reappearance of racial and religious discrimination so soon after the defeat of Hitler and apprehensive of the fate of the Jews in Russia, joined in the struggle for their defence. Prominent gentile politicians from opposite camps joined hands, and outstanding artists, scientists and members of the free professions rallied together with ordinary conscientious citizens to support the cause of Soviet Jewry.

The swelling volume of protest caused obvious embarrassment to the Kremlin. Yet for years their leadership continued to hold the view that any yielding to the claims of the Russian Jews and their foreign supporters would encourage other nationalities, larger in size and more important to the stability of the Soviet regime, to demand the recognition of their own rights, guaranteed by the constitution of the Soviet Union but ignored by its government. Moreover any relaxation of the ban on Jewish emigration would arouse Arab resentment. Whenever representatives of Israel raised the issue discreetly with the Soviet government they were rebuffed. It was an internal issue, they were told; no foreign interference would be tolerated.

The situation of the Russian Jews has remained one of the most important and contentious items on the agenda of Soviet-Israeli relations to this day. When Israel showed too strong a concern for the fate of Russian Jews, the Soviet authorities, in most cases, would react sternly. They expelled members of the Israeli embassy in Moscow and kept the mission under strict surveillance, actually installing a listening post in a specially dug tunnel which caused the KGB considerable embarrassment when it collapsed on the heads of their monitors. They arrested Jews trying to contact the embassy; their officials boycotted official Israeli receptions, and their press attacked the ambassador personally. But when the plight of Soviet Jewry began to arouse worldwide compassion and protests calling for sanctions against the Soviet Union, Moscow did not hesitate to let the Israeli government know that this agitation was the main obstacle to the improvement of relations. Whenever the Israeli Premier or Foreign Minister, in their indefatigable zeal to bring about a change, asked Soviet officials what Israel on its part could do, they would receive either the laconic answer that they should know without being told, or more outspoken ambassadors would say that Israel should cease its activities on behalf of Soviet Jewry.

The Soviet government has tried to meet the growing pressures of world concern with measures alternating between stepped-up repression and temporary relaxation, with diplomatic sanctions against Israel and unsubstantiated promises to improve mutual relations. It has flexed and constricted its muscles like someone trying to free himself from fetters, oblivious to the fact that it has chained itself by its own anti-Jewish policy. While internally the Soviet government has become increasingly permissive of anti-Jewish defamation which, of course, could only be disseminated with the consent or at least the tacit agreement of government and party, externally it has sought to mollify the aroused passions by slowly yielding on the emigration issue. Before its rupture of relations with Israel in 1967, an annual trickle of a maximum of 2,000 Jews, mostly from the newly acquired territories, were permitted to leave for Israel. But in 1973, at the height of Soviet hostility against Israel, more than 30,000 received their exit permits. This was not the result of a fundamental change of policy but rather the consequence of restrictive measures which the United States Senate had imposed on Soviet-American trade relations. Moscow considered these constraints as more harmful to its immediate interests than the gains of Arab sympathy deriving from the ban on Jewish emigration.

Moscow-Jerusalem ups and downs

When the Soviet Union emerged from the Second World War, bleeding from millions of wounds and with its Jewish population decimated and dispersed, its government realized that the Jewish question, far from having disappeared, had become even more acute and painful. Political expediency and the impact of the disaster which had befallen European Jewry made the Soviet leadership amenable to the idea of Jewish statehood. Andrei Gromyko, then the Permanent Representative of the Soviet Union to the United Nations, expressed the new policy in one of his speeches in the great debate which culminated in the United Nations decision in November 1947 endorsing the establishment of an independent Jewish state. These were his words:

The Jewish people have been closely linked with Palestine for a considerable period in history. As a result of the war the Jews as a people have suffered more than any other people. The total number of the Jewish population who perished at the hands of the Nazi executioners is estimated at approximately six million. The Jewish people are therefore striving to create a state of their own and it would be unjust to deny them that right.

But the warm and rather unusual spell of Soviet compassion and support of Jewish national aspirations did not last long. The interaction of a variety of factors effected the change. The Soviet government had not expected the exhilarating impact of the new Jewish state on Soviet Jewry. The appearance of the first Israeli ambassador in their midst at the High Holy Days' services in 1948, when thousands of worshippers streamed out into the streets to hail Golda Meir as the embodiment of the rebirth of Zion, was not only a unique event for the Jewish community but also a manifestation of independent spontaneity unheard of and intolerable to a regime which normally only allowed mass demonstrations of popular enthusiasm or rage by government or party fiat. The Golda tremor, which shook the Russian Jews after thirty years of solitary confinement, in a way blurred the judgement of the new Israeli embassy on the limits of its freedom of action and the tolerance of the Soviet government. It took swift and ruthless measures to put the Jews back into the place it had assigned to them. It separated them from the embassy and warned the Israeli envoys against any further trespassing. To leave no doubt in the minds of the Israeli diplomatic newcomers, and of the stirring community, the Soviet authorities reverted to harsh measures of repression against Jewish cultural and religious institutions, and did not shy away from the elimination of a number of the most prominent Jewish writers and artists.

On the other hand they continued to pursue their pro-Israeli foreign policy as if it was business as usual. Golda did not stay long enough in Moscow to fully recognize the perilous developments and to try to influence them. After a year of service as ambassador she preferred to join the newly formed Israeli government as Minister of Labour. It is arguable whether her continuation at her post in Moscow could have averted the worst to come for the Jews and Israel in the ensuing years, but it is not unthinkable that her powerful personality might well have mitigated the process.

Soviet policy towards Israel soon began to change. The heated reaction in Israel to the repression of Soviet Jewry was only a secondary factor. What counted foremost for the policy-makers in the Kremlin was that Israel had disappointed their hopes to serve as a wrecking tool of the Western position in the Middle East. Although the Israeli government had initially tried to steer a neutral course in the East-West conflict and the Korean War, its natural ideological and political inclination towards the Western world and its economic, human and security requirements impelled it to drift away from non-alignment. But, more important, with Nasser's advent to power, the Soviet Union concluded that Egypt, the leading Arab country, would serve as a far more effective and amenable instrument for its designs than Israel could ever be. It provided Soviet entry into the Arab world and into the burgeoning association of non-aligned states, and facilitated Soviet designs to keep the Arab-Israeli conflict simmering on a remote-controlled burner. The Soviet Union, anxious to cover up the post-war expansion of its own domain and to gain a foothold in the dismantled parts of the crumbling Western empires, presented itself as the champion of decolonization and wars of liberation. The Soviet discovery of the potential turbulence in the Arab world was certainly one of the predominant reasons for the reorientation of its policy towards Israel.

In the mid-1950s a small group of us in the Foreign Ministry prepared a memorandum on the new Soviet policy in the Middle East. The summary of our assessment was that:

- a. The anti-Israeli policy adopted by the Soviet Union was a matter of long-term policy;
- b. it was an integral part of the Soviet effort to forestall an American takeover of the positions which Britain and France would abandon in the Middle East in due time;
- c. in the competition to fill the vacuum created by the diminution of British and French influence in the area, the Soviet Union saw itself handicapped by the enormous economic potential of the United States. Therefore, while also giving the Arab states some economic assistance, it would concentrate mainly on political and military aid. This was a sphere in which Washington was unable to outdo Moscow, because American public opinion would not allow its government to take steps endangering Israel's security.

The bleak prospects for any *rapprochement* between the Soviet Union and Israel and the sharpening contest between the two superpowers in the Middle East envisaged by our Foreign Ministry were borne out by the evolution of the situation in the area. Nevertheless Israel did not abandon its attempts to bring about an improvement of its relations with the Soviet Union. The Soviet government, however, showed no inclination to reciprocate. While in Jerusalem Soviet ambassadors had free access to all the incumbent Prime Ministers, no Israeli ambassador in Moscow was ever received by the head of the government or party. The highest level an Israeli ambassador could reach to discuss the state of affairs was an occasional meeting with the Foreign Minister, and the most representative exchange of views between the two countries used to take place when their two Foreign Ministers met at the annual Assembly of the United Nations. Never did a Soviet Foreign Minister visit Israel despite innumerable invitations, nor was his Israeli counterpart allowed to set foot on Soviet soil.

The climate of Soviet-Israeli relations has remained shivery ever since the beginning of the great chill in the early 1950s. Admittedly there were brighter spots in the normally overcast sky, but they did not herald a general change in the dreary pattern. As far as it is possible to identify the reasons for any temporary moderation in Soviet attitudes towards Israel, a few motivations are discernible. When inner Arab conflicts burst into the open, the Soviet Union reduced its manifestations of enmity towards Israel in an effort to keep it on the sidelines, fearing that additional friction could induce Israel to take advantage of the situation. Moscow, embarrassed by the difficult choices in a dispute between two Arab countries, tried to limit the area of the conflict and avoid as much as possible any outside involvement likely to exacerbate its dilemma.

The Lebanese crisis of 1958, where the government embattled by Nasserist subversion called for United States military intervention, was one of the first instances of such a choice for the Soviet Union. It faced American unilateral action in an area which Moscow claimed to belong to its strategic hinterland situated 'in the proximity of its southern borders', a household word of Soviet diplomacy ever since; it had to restrain an impetuous Nasser, a recent Soviet acquisition, whom it had bailed out from military disaster only two years earlier with the friendly but short-lived co-operation of the United States; and it had to weigh its interests in Lebanon, where it was trying to promote Soviet influence. This set-up in itself was complicated enough for Soviet diplomacy and made it tread carefully to avoid involving additional countries, especially Israel. Moscow knew that in such circumstances bullying would not be effective; soothing talk would be more persuasive. It faced the same predicament when, in 1961, Iraq challenged the sovereign legitimacy of Kuwait; when later Damascus broke with Cairo; and during Egypt's war in Yemen. Occasionally when Moscow felt it lacked sufficient leverage to separate the quarrelling Arab states, it would make an ostentatious gesture towards Israel to scare the disputants with the prospect of an imminent Soviet-Israeli *rapprochement*. This normally brought the unruly Arab states back into the Soviet fold. After they had been safely trapped, Moscow would once again lower the temperature of its relations with Israel.

Israel, the Russian bogeyman

Another prop employed by the Soviet Union to control the volatile tempers of its Arab friends and manipulate tensions to its advantage was the evocation of the perennial Israeli war-scare. As long as Moscow felt certain that the bogey contrived by its own propaganda was harmless, it attacked it with undiminished fury. But when it began to realize that a situation was indeed serious, because Israel might strike a major blow in response to continued Arab provocation, its crisis management alternated between dire threats and tempting lure. Its menaces were couched in incisive terms, its promises offered in vague and convoluted language. None of them carried the strength of credibility, though no responsible government could afford *a priori* to disregard the threats. Marshal Bulganin, then chairman of the Council of Ministers, wrote a note to Prime Minister Ben Gurion on 5 November 1956: 'The government of Israel is playing with the fate of its own people. Its actions are putting a question mark on the very existence of Israel as a state.'

Yet ten years later, when relations between the new pro-Soviet regime in Syria and the Western powers had come under heavy strain because it had suspended the transit of TAP line oil and stimulated the intensification of terrorist raids from its territory against Israel, the Soviet Foreign Ministry sent a different sounding *aide-mémoire* to Jerusalem on 9 November 1966. It contended that external imperialist forces were plotting to overthrow the new Syrian regime because it was liable to jeopardize the interests of the oil companies. For this purpose, they were fanning existing tensions between Syria and Israel, or as the note said in its subtle way: 'It is impossible not to be disturbed by the fact that the rising tension on the Israeli-Syrian border manifests itself just when the great Western powers openly admit that they are not content with the progress of the discussions that are being held between the oil companies and the Syrian government about payments for the pipe line across Syrian territory.' The exposé continued by telling the apparently naive government of Israel that history offered abundant examples of provocation staged by imperialist masterminds against governments who were unwilling to submit to their dictates.

When an interest of the Soviet Union was at stake, it knew how to dangle the carrot and hide the stick with remarkable dexterity. Since the days of the British administration of Palestine the Soviet government had pressed in vain for the transfer of the sizeable property held by the White Russian Church in Jerusalem to Soviet ownership. Its negotiations with the government of Israel reached a decisive stage in 1964, which became the most restful year in Soviet-Israeli relations. There were no Soviet vetoes in the Security Council, anti-Israeli propaganda was reduced to a respectable minimum so as not to arouse Arab suspicions of unfaithfulness, promises of resumption of trade relations and cultural exchanges were the order of the day. It was not exactly a honeymoon but it was a pleasant vacation. After the church property deal was concluded the relations returned to 'normal'. Israel, the old imperialist stooge, threatened the innocent Arabs, the Soviet knight in shining armour came to their rescue, casting a veto here and raising a mailed fist there. The lure of Israeli oranges was forgotten and the undertaking to renew the supply of Soviet oil effaced from memory.

The issue of the fate of the Russian Jews and Soviet partiality in all matters pertaining to the Arab-Israeli conflict ruled out any chance of a basic improvement in Israeli-Soviet relations. In a conversation we had with Gromyko at the end of September 1966, Eban summed up the main differences between Moscow and Jerusalem:

1. The Soviet Union's incorrect contention that Israel was acting against Syria as an instrument of foreign forces with a view to bringing about a change of government in Damascus. All that Israel was interested in was that Syria should strictly adhere to its obligations under the Armistice Agreement;
2. The non-existence of trade and the highly limited cultural exchange, which emptied diplomatic relations between the two countries of all practical content;
3. The unbalanced attitude of the Soviet Union in the Arab-Israeli conflict was aggravating instead of pacifying it;
4. The erroneous idea in Moscow that there was no suitable atmosphere in Israel for closer relations with the Soviet Union;
5. The complicated problem of Soviet Jews, which the Soviet Union did not really try to understand.

Although it was a classic diplomatic understatement, it reflected the state of affairs in general terms. The next meeting between the two Foreign Ministers took place at the opening of the peace conference in Geneva, two wars and seven years later.

War scares, conjured up by the Soviet Union, had been a standard weapon in its arsenal of anti-Israeli propaganda for a long time. In 1957, a few months after the completion of the Israeli withdrawal from Sinai, long-standing tensions between Turkey and Syria reached a crisis point over the dispute between them about the Alexandretta district, annexed by Turkey. It had nothing whatsoever to do with Israel. Nonetheless, the Soviet press poured out accusations at the height of the crisis that 'Israel was preparing an aggression against Syria with the help of the United States', and warned 'the Israeli ruling circles not to forget that there are powers capable of making them abandon the policy of intimidation'. The tension subsided when the United States firmly advised Moscow to 'abandon its policy of intimidation' against Turkey or anyone else. In his speech of 22 October 1957 before the UN General Assembly, Gromyko grudgingly tried to cover the Soviet retreat by firing a last salvo at Israel: 'It was anticipated, when the US-Turkish plan of attack upon Syria was discussed, that Israel, too, would participate in certain stages of these operations. Experience has shown that Israel gives little heed to its very existence as a state. It seems to be hacking away at the branch on which it is sitting.' If this meant that Israel was perched on a Russian branch, then indeed there remained little to chop away.

Over the years Moscow turned its Israeli war-scare tap on and off at its convenience. Unfounded as the rumours were, they were sufficient to incite the Arab states to increase their dependence on Soviet protection and provided suitable pretexts for the expansion of Russian influence in the region. The exercise was simple, crude and effective. After a show of Soviet muscle-flexing, the Israeli scarecrow would disappear like a *fata morgana* and the Arabs would, hopefully, be ever grateful to the Soviet Union for having saved them from a non-existent threat.

But the Russian game was not fail-safe in an area which had its subsoil soaked with petroleum and its surface covered with inflammable cinders. The explosion of 1967 was not a sudden eruption, but was triggered off by a long fuse. From the moment the new Baath regime in Damascus revealed its pro-Soviet inclinations and the British government its intention to abandon its positions east of Suez, the Soviet Union stepped up its activities in the Middle East. It feared for its tender plant in Damascus and was tempted by the prospective power vacuum in the Persian Gulf. It resurrected the Israeli bogeyman as a convenient conveyance for its aspirations. As early as May 1966, Deputy Foreign Minister Semyonov summoned the Israeli ambassador in Moscow to warn him against alleged Israeli 'troop concentrations on the Syrian border', adding the ritual threat that 'the government of Israel will realistically recognize the dangerous consequences of its dangerous plans and not permit outside forces to play with the fate of the nation and the state'. The rules of the game stipulated, of course, widest diffusion and amplification of the warning.

The next blast came at the end of July from Nicolai Fedorenko, the Soviet Ambassador to the United Nations. He told an incredulous Security Council that Israel was preparing an army of a quarter of a million men for combat and, while it was concentrating its forces on the Syrian frontier, 'an imposing squadron of the American Sixth Fleet had appeared at Beirut and a British squadron had dropped anchor in Haifa'. And so the campaign went on until it reached its diplomatic climax on 26 April 1967, when the by-then-well-practised Semyonov handed to the by-now-well-experienced Israeli ambassador a note informing him 'that the Soviet government was in possession of information about Israeli troop concentrations on the borders', etc., and concluding with the friendly advice, normally used by the godfather of the *cosa nostra* before the execution of a contract, 'not to play with the fate of the State of Israel and its people'. This demonstrated a strange split in the Soviet political conscience. It was extremely alert to alleged Israeli suicidal tendencies and completely indifferent to the avowed genocidal intentions of Israel's neighbours. I was in Moscow at the time on an official mission to explain to the Soviet government the facts and true intentions of the government of Israel and its people. I made the point that the Soviet policy of incitement was fraught with grave dangers and that they were 'playing with the fate of peace in the Middle East'.

13

A Decade of Growth and Consolidation

In the decade between the two wars of 1956 and 1967 Israel grew from adolescence to manhood. It was a period of progress and consolidation. The swift victory of 1956, although disappointing in its political outcome, had imbued it with a sense of greater security and pride in its military prowess. It had put its army on the strategic map of the Middle East as a fighting force to be reckoned with. Its borders remained relatively quiet and its population generally safe from murderous marauding.

The harsh charge of military collusion with Britain and France, which had been ringing through the halls of the United Nations, lost its reverberation in the outside world soon after the territorial *status quo ante* had been restored in Sinai and the Suez Canal re-opened to shipping. Israel's relations with the non-aligned countries of Africa and Asia had recovered not only remarkably fast from the initial shock of the war but branched out into new areas of co-operation. The new states felt more secure in dealing with a small country which possessed valuable experience in tackling civilian tasks and military challenges and had no perilous political ambitions. The fact that Israel had so swiftly and effectively overcome the Arab menace earned it wide respect among the new nations. Denunciations of imperialism and militancy were a fashionable style for UN speeches and an inevitable requisite to gain favour with the communist bloc, but by no means did they express the true nature of the prospering relations between most of the participants in the verbal exercise and its object – Israel.

Israel's ties with most of the countries of Western Europe became firmer and gained in substance. While its relations with France, at their peak at the beginning of the decade, reached their nadir at its end under De Gaulle, its links with Britain under Harold Wilson improved satisfactorily in the second half of the 1960s. While the countries of the Iberian peninsula remained reserved towards Israel, its relationship with the Scandinavian states became considerably closer. In the same period Israel signed its first trade agreement with the European Economic Community, a stepping-stone to future extended co-operation.

In South America Israel established a number of new embassies and some of the Latin countries opened missions in Jerusalem. In the Middle East co-operation between Iran and Israel developed quickly and steadily. The Lion of Judah, Ethiopia's Emperor, exchanged ambassadors with the government in Jerusalem, where he had found refuge during the Italian occupation of his country. Turkey, the first Moslem country to have established diplomatic relations with the Jewish state, intensified its co-operation after an unpublicized meeting between the Prime Ministers of the two countries.

Relations with the Soviet Union remained dour and tense, and links with the communist countries of Eastern Europe reflected in substance, but not always in form, the attitude of the Soviet Union. Some of the states of Eastern Europe, however, followed a more liberal policy on matters of Jewish emigration to Israel, being conscious that their countries had been the main theatre of the Nazi horrors. They also maintained, in contrast to the Soviet Union, some limited trade with Israel. The ground was sufficiently firm to permit the first visit of an Israeli Foreign Minister to a communist state. In May 1966, Abba Eban convened all Israeli ambassadors serving in Eastern Europe in the capital of Poland. It was a curious conference where it was not only our diplomats who listened to the debates. Rumour has it that a technical hitch deprived the attentive Polish authorities of some of our wisdoms and induced them to ask for a repeat performance.

At the United Nations, Israel's position declined in direct proportion to the increase of the organization's membership and the change of its political composition. The Soviet bloc added numerical and political strength. The ex-colonial countries formed coalitions less for reasons of ideological affinity than for the purpose of asserting their combined parliamentary power in the new struggle between the poor and affluent countries. Invariably supported by the Soviet bloc, the alliance of the non-aligned became the principal broker, if not of power then of votes in the United Nations, and normally their bloc vote had little to do with the merits of the case at issue.

The central pillar of Israel's foreign relations was its bonds with the United States. We have dealt with them cursorily in the context of the Sinai-Suez crisis in 1956–7 and will come back to them later. The tripartite action against Egypt in 1956 had evoked an unexpectedly strong rejection from the Eisenhower administration. American-French relations have never been the same again, and the special relationship between the United States and Britain suffered a long time from the sudden strain. Yet the injuries caused in Washington and Jerusalem by the events of 1956 had healed by the time President Eisenhower left office. Under his successors, John Kennedy and Lyndon Johnson, a new dimension extended and strengthened the ties between the United States and Israel. The continued turbulence in the Arab part of the Middle East enhanced Israel's standing as a reliable factor of regional stability. In the surging sea of inter-Arab turmoil, Israel stood out like a lighthouse on a firm rock, saving quite a few Arab governments from running aground.

John Kennedy was the first President to recognize that Israel needed more than a friendly pat on the back for the safeguarding of its security. He responded favourably to Ben Gurion's call for the supply of sophisticated American weapons systems. On 12 May 1963, a month before his resignation, the old leader addressed a passionate letter to the young President. Ben Gurion was deeply worried about Nasser's intentions. 'I have thought it my duty to convey to you, Mr President, in all candour, what I think about the present situation in the Middle East and the dangers in store for my people.'

When we worked with Ben Gurion on the letter we did not realize that he meant it to be a kind of political testament and an appeal to Israel's most powerful friend to stand by it in the perils it might have to face in the years to come. Ben Gurion, who had always totally identified himself with the destiny of the state, was in a gloomy mood in the last months of his premiership. It was reflected in the Hebrew draft from which I had to prepare the English version of his letter. After he had dealt extensively with Nasser and his evil designs, Ben Gurion wrote that, after what had happened to the Jews during the Second World War, he could not dismiss the possibility that this might occur again if the Arabs continued to pursue their policy of belligerency against Israel. Then came a sentence which shocked Golda and the few of us who were working on the draft. 'It may not happen today or tomorrow, but I am not sure whether the state will continue to exist after my life has come to an end.' Golda asked me to do all I could to persuade Ben Gurion to delete this prophecy of doom, but he was adamant, as he always used to be on matters of great importance to him. He finally accepted my slightly modified phrasing, eliminating his dire reflection on the survival of Israel.

The text which was dispatched to President Kennedy read:

For many years the civilized world did not take seriously Hitler's statement that one of his aims was the worldwide extermination of the Jewish people. I have no doubt that a similar thing might happen to Jews in Israel if Nasser succeeded in defeating our army. . . .

It does not matter whether it will or will not happen during my lifetime. As a Jew I know the history of my people, and carry with me the memories of all it has endured over a period of 3,000 years and the effort it has cost to accomplish what has been achieved in this country in recent generations. I am confident that such a calamity, which might befall the remnant of Israel in its own land, can be prevented.

And then he made a startling proposal: the United States and the Soviet Union should issue a joint declaration that 'any country in the Middle East that refuses to recognize the territorial integrity and to live in peace with any other country in the area would receive no financial, political or military aid from the two powers'. The Prime Minister then summarized the measures he thought to be most conducive to ensuring peace and security in the Middle East: the complete demilitarization of the area of the West Bank under suitable international supervision in order to avert the danger to Israel emanating from any change in the regime in Jordan, and the conclusion of a Bilateral Security Agreement between the United States of America and Israel, with which allies of the United States be invited to associate themselves.

In conclusion, Ben Gurion wrote: 'I should not like you to think that I do not deeply appreciate the supply of the Hawk missiles.' The delivery of anti-aircraft Hawk missiles by the administration of President Kennedy was the beginning of a continuing arms supply relationship. It was deepened and strengthened by President Lyndon Johnson's authorization to sell Phantom jet fighters to Israel and culminated in Nixon's airlift of emergency shipments at the height of the Yom Kippur War. When it came to the crunch in 1967 the United States, unlike ten years earlier, was firmly on Israel's side, logistically and politically.

But what counted more than any outside help, when Israel had to face a new military confrontation, was the internal strength it had gained during its second decade of relative detente. In the first ten years of its independence, it had integrated into the life of the nation nearly one million newcomers. Clusters of new villages enlivened the land and farming reached heights of technical perfection and bountiful crops. New towns provided housing and modern industries gainful employment. Commerce flourished, and air and maritime communications connected the country with all parts of the world. The Arab population multiplied faster and its standard of living rose considerably above that in any of the neighbouring countries. Education strengthened the cohesion of the nation and literacy brought knowledge to masses of deprived immigrants from backward countries. Tourism prospered and thousands of trainees from developing countries availed themselves of rewarding opportunities to study in Israel. Its international relations were solid and extensive, linking Israel with nearly all the countries of the world outside the Arab domain. Public opinion, mostly in the Western and Third World, showed understanding and sympathy for Israel.

Although the harsh days of pioneering were over for most of the people and living conditions had eased, there were still pockets of hardship and much struggle ahead, to unite and solidify the nation to meet its peaceful tasks and military challenges. When, in the spring of 1967, the call came with brutal suddenness, Israel's army was well prepared, its equipment of high quality, its troops thoroughly trained and its mood reflecting the spirit of a nation determined to fight for its existence.

Part Three

CONFLAGRATION

14

Moscow Prelude

I arrived in New York on 2 May 1967 to take up my new post, having flown in directly from Moscow. Foreign Minister Abba Eban thought it might be useful for Israel's new ambassador to the United Nations, who was familiar with the American scene, to get acquainted with Soviet thinking and to expound to leading Soviet officials Israel's views on the worsening situation in the Middle East. Our ambassador in Moscow made the arrangements for the talks to be held in the second half of April.

Since Khrushchev's astonishing act in 1955 of vaulting over the northern tier of the Baghdad pact straight into the Land of the Nile, carrying with him a sizeable parcel of Soviet arms presented in Czechoslovakian gift wrapping, Soviet involvement in the affairs and destinies of the Middle East had become deeper and more threatening.

Changes in Syria

A new governmental upheaval which had occurred in Syria at the beginning of 1966 was seized on by the Soviet government as an opportunity to establish firm and influential ties with the new leftist Baath government. The Soviet Union now felt able to balance its position in the Middle East more evenly on two points of gravity: Cairo and Damascus. Yet Moscow was not certain whether the newly gained ground in Syria was solid enough to carry the full weight of Soviet 'assistance'. To strengthen its hold, it stirred up, by open and covert means, the anti-Israeli fervour of the new Syrian government.

In the early summer of 1966 we had reached the conclusion at the Foreign Ministry that the Soviet Union would in the course of the coming months considerably increase its activity in the area. It would try to push southwards from its newly established foothold in Syria. The British policy, announced at that time, of relinquishing its positions and responsibilities east of Suez, created a power vacuum in a coveted and turbulent area of strategic and economic global importance. The Soviet Union, barred from reaching the Persian Gulf by NATO-supported Turkey and Iran, would in our view try to develop an alternative route via Iraq and Syria in order to extend its influence in the direction of the Arabian peninsula and the adjacent gulf.

Israel formed a formidable obstacle on this road of penetration. Unless an alternative power filled the vacuum created by the British evacuation, we expected the Soviet push southwards to gather dangerous momentum. If undeterred by a credible manifestation of alternative Western strength, the Soviet Union would within a year provoke armed conflict between Israel and its Arab neighbours to remove the Israeli roadblock.

Since I had been the main proponent of this much discussed and gloomy prognosis, the Foreign Minister entrusted me with a special mission to Washington and London. By and large the British officials shared our analysis and concern. They suggested that we exert our influence on the United States to take over the strategic responsibilities abandoned by Britain.

In an exhaustive review of the Middle East situation with the top officials of the State Department we concurred on the inherent dangers of Soviet ambitions in the area, but differed on the means of countering them. In a final session, Secretary of State Dean Rusk bluntly summed up the American position. Israel and Britain should not cherish any illusion that the United States would take over any new commitments east of Suez. Its involvement in Vietnam was engaging all its strength and national attention. The war in the Far East was causing enormous internal strains and external stresses. Congress and the American people would strongly resist any new foreign defence obligations. The United States government was not oblivious of the concerns of its friends in the Middle East. It was prepared to help build up on a bilateral basis the defensive strength of Israel, Jordan and Iran. He did not mention Saudi Arabia, perhaps in deference to an understandable Israeli sensitivity after its king had proclaimed his intention to wipe out Israel even at the cost of ten million Arab lives.

A few months later, when Soviet stirrings in Syria became more blatant, Dean Rusk admitted in a talk with Abba Eban that the matters we had discussed in the summer merited further consideration. But the more the burdens in the Far East weighed on the United States, the easier it became for the Soviet Union to pursue its designs in the Middle East. Arab terrorist organizations intensified their deep incursions into Israel from their operational bases in Syria. The situation became critical in October 1966. The Israeli government was subjected to strong pressures to take military counteraction; but the opinion which advocated diplomatic measures prevailed in the cabinet. It decided to ask for an urgent meeting of the Security Council. In the light of its disappointing record over the decades of ignoring Israel's complaints against continuous active Arab hostility, hopes of finding redress were not excessive. Nonetheless we expected that a forceful stand by the United States, which had strongly advised us to try the remedy of the Security Council, would produce some moderating results.

Weeks were wasted in the wrangle of how to word a resolution which would enjoy immunity from Soviet veto. The text which finally emerged made an oblique reference to the 'Fatah organization' and contained a polite invitation to the government of Syria to stop using its territory for attacks against Israel. Syria was in no mood to respond to the appeal and the Soviet Union was only too eager to prove its unstinting support to its recently acquired friends. The hand of the Soviet representative was raised in veto, but not before he had given a stern warning against Israel's alleged sinister plans to mass forces on the Syrian border. In the months which followed, this piece of Soviet misinformation became a basis of their incendiary propaganda, until it lit the flames of war. The Soviet veto cast in November barred the United Nations from playing a significant role in averting the gathering storm. It gave free rein to the operations of 'Fatah' which reached their peak in April 1967 with widespread, murderous attacks against Israeli civilians, which compelled the Israel Defence Forces to take stern counteraction.

Travels in Russia

It was against this background that I arrived in Moscow in the middle of April 1967, a few days after our air force had brought down six Syrian Migs, which had been covering artillery fire from the Golan Heights on Israeli villages in the valley. In the Austrian airliner which we had boarded in Vienna I discovered a familiar fellow traveller. The man seated on my left at the United Nations for many years was on board. Adnan Pachachi, the Foreign Minister of Iraq, was also Moscow-bound; apart from the destination we had nothing in common. He had never exchanged a word or a greeting with me. Although he glanced from time to time in my direction, he displayed remarkable self-control in suppressing his obvious curiosity about the reasons for our joint flight and separate missions to Moscow.

Gromyko was waiting at the steps of the plane to greet his colleague. Pouring rain and the apprehension that I might descend into the midst of the reception festivities shortened the proceedings to a brief handshake and deprived Pachachi of his well-deserved bear-hug. He was swiftly whisked away. To be on the safe side, Soviet protocol allowed a decent interval to elapse before I was invited to disembark.

The stern masters of Soviet protocol found that Moscow was too small a place to welcome under its hospitable roof two representatives from opposing camps. They suggested to our ambassador that his special envoy might prefer to tour the country and celebrate Pessach with the Jewish community before embarking on his political talks; an acquaintance with the Soviet land and people might enhance their success. Ambassador Katz, realizing how keen the officials were to shunt us off into the provinces, asked for permission to visit Armenia, the forbidden land for foreign diplomats. Protocol countered by recommending visits to Leningrad and a *kolkhoz* which would be more suitable for our cultural curiosity. We accepted the suggestion as a welcome addition to our Armenian project. Time was pressing, the situation embarrassing, and permission was granted.

Our arrival in Erevan in the late evening after a three-hour flight was most impressive. Along the main streets rolled a long military column rehearsing for the First of May parade. Our escorts drove our car with admirable agility on the pavements, cutting through the thin crowd of spectators with authoritative blasts of their siren.

Our Armenian hosts were outgoing, relaxed and good-humoured people. Their programme included the traditional tourist sights, with a visit to the National Museum of ancient manuscripts scheduled as the crowning event. It was a rewarding and somehow moving visit. The curator, a lady who spoke fluent English, guided us through the magnificent collection. Many of the ancient books originated from the Holy Land, and relations with the Armenian community in Jerusalem were particularly close. With understandable pride the curator extolled the secret of the preservation of the manuscripts, some of them dating back to the fifth century AD. In times of persecution and dispersion, she explained, the people had carried the books with them as marks of their national identity and religious faith. Suddenly she paused and with a broad smile she turned to us: 'Who am I to explain all this to the representatives of the people of the Book, which has inspired so many other peoples with its attachment to its land and heritage?' We felt warmly that the bonds of spirit and tragic experience were stronger links than the political demarcation lines separating us.

We attended the Pessach service at the central synagogue of Moscow, seated in a special enclosure reserved exclusively for the embassy staff. The separation, which the elders presented to us as a mark of distinction, was instituted by the authorities as a means of quarantine to prevent any contact between the worshipping representatives of Israel and the members of the congregation praying for the peace of the Jewish state. The eyes focused on us expressed more than words could say.

We celebrated the traditional second Seder as guests of the Chief Rabbi Lewin at his modest flat. The permission granted to him by the authorities to invite us was seen by the experts on governmental good- or ill-will as a favourable omen. More sceptical members of our embassy staff, however, thought we also owed this special dispensation to the ill-timed presence of the Iraqi Foreign Minister in Moscow. Be that as it may, we read the Haggadah story of the exodus from Egypt in the straitened circumstances of a rabbinical home in Moscow.

The room was too small to hold the long table which extended into the corridor. The mood was festive but subdued. The venerable Rabbi, our host and reader, whispered into my ear a running commentary in Hebrew on the sombre realities of Jewish life in the Soviet Union and gave a warning about certain of our co-celebrants who had been entrusted not with the supervision of the Kashruth of the proceedings, but rather with the observance of the authorities' holy writ.

The Rabbi had warned me that the offering of the toast would be the critical moment of the evening. He had cautioned the president of the community that he would leave the table if he were to utter even a single sentence giving offence to Israel and its representatives. The bulky president got up, swaying between his official directives and the rabbinical admonition. The air was thick with foreboding and the room hushed in tense silence. The speaker dwelt with considerable feeling on the miserable conditions under which Russian Jews had lived under the Czarist regime. He extolled the virtues of the Bolshevik Revolution which had abolished all discrimination and restored freedom and dignity to the Jewish masses. He depicted the horrors of a new war. Here we all nodded in perfect unison and with unfailing conviction. He implored Israel to pursue peace and avoid any further bloodshed. The Rabbi became fidgety; the orator was approaching the trip-wire. A quick-minded guest came to his rescue. He offered the toast to peace and the good health of the honoured guests. We all drank with relish and relief.

With Pessach and Pachachi out of the way all was clear for the opening of our talks at the Foreign Ministry. Deputy Foreign Minister Vladimir Semyonov represented the Soviet side. He was then in overall charge of Near Eastern affairs. (Later he led the Soviet delegation in the SALT negotiations.) I tried to convince him that the one-sided Soviet policy of all-out support for Arab revanchism was fraught with danger. I argued that the reduction of tension in the Middle East required 'a more equal distribution of Soviet friendship' among all the states in the region. Alas, our arguments and facts fell on minds attuned only to the stereotype version of Soviet propaganda, preconceived ideas and premeditated actions. Semyonov and his colleagues claimed that Israel's policy was directed by the American oil companies whose aim it was to topple the new Syrian government. In a show of magnanimity, he conceded that Israel might perhaps have got itself enmeshed and was being used as an unwilling tool in this power plot.

I thought that I had at least made one point to my Soviet interlocutors when I explained to them that the boiling-point in the Middle East was much lower and the degree of excitement much higher than Moscow's remote-control thermostat experts could imagine. But we were soon to realize that, instead of reducing the heat, the Soviet government would continue to fan the flames. In one of my later exchanges with Soviet Ambassador Fedorenko at the Security Council, I referred to my visit to Moscow:

President Nasser himself revealed in his speech of 9 June, in which he gave the first hint to his people of the military disaster that had befallen his army, that responsible Soviet leaders had at the end of April informed a visiting Egyptian parliamentary delegation (headed by Anwar Sadat – now President of Egypt) that Israel had concentrated large forces on its northern borders and was about to attack Syria. As Nasser explained the course of events, this warning compelled him to dispatch massive forces to Israel's southern borders.

I was in Moscow at that time, and I encountered that Egyptian delegation on Red Square at the First of May celebrations. I wish I had had the opportunity to talk to them. I would have extended to them the same invitation to verify the facts that my government had extended to the Soviet ambassador in Israel. But they were exposed to Soviet admonitions and advice, the sole purpose of which was to advance Soviet political and strategic ambitions in the Middle East, which apparently have not changed since the day of the Ribbentrop-Molotov agreement, by which the Soviet government obtained Nazi recognition of its expansionist designs extending as far as to the Persian Gulf.

In further talks conducted with Ambassador Shchiborin, the head of the Foreign Ministry's Middle East division, we discussed the situation and aspirations of Soviet Jews. I had personally witnessed the burning attachment to Israel exhibited by many of them wherever I had the opportunity of meeting them – in the street, in front of the synagogue or individually by chance. They pleaded with us to help them reach Israel. When it had become known through broadcasts from Jerusalem that the new Israeli ambassador to the United Nations was holding talks with the Soviet government, people arrived at our embassy from places as far away as Alma Ata to ask for my intercession with the authorities to obtain exit visas.

The Soviet officials, after reiterating their standard story of the rescue of European Jewry from total annihilation by the victorious Red Army and the general state of happiness in which the Jews lived in the Soviet Union, were ready to discuss the question of reunion of families, a codeword for the urge of scores of Russian Jews to go to Israel. They pointed out that the number of exit visas granted in the last twelve months had increased to 2,000. A further and more substantial extension was not excluded, provided the Israeli government adopted a more restrained policy. What was the sense, they asked with a mien of contrived concern, in exposing good Soviet citizens to the perils of war in the Middle East? In our reply we vouchsafed their safety, reaffirmed Israel's peaceful intentions, but admitted that we did not feel reassured about Soviet moves which were likely to intensify the existing tensions in the area.

Upon my arrival in New York I presented my letters of accreditation to the Secretary-General and stated to the press that:

... under the Charter, Israel has its responsibilities towards the United Nations, as the United Nations has its responsibilities in regard to Israel. We favour the intensification of co-operation between all nations, to improve the lot of multitudes of people in large parts of the world, to eliminate all forms of human discrimination and intolerance and to safeguard the independence of all states and the inviolability of their frontiers. Israel will support all positive forces which strive to narrow the gap between United Nations principles and international practices.

Referring to my just completed visit to the Soviet Union I said: 'The impressions which I have gathered and the conversations which I have had, have enlarged my knowledge and I hope will serve the cause of mutual understanding.' A typical case of diplomatic wishful-thinking.

I started my routine rounds of visits to my new colleagues and prepared for the celebration of the nineteenth anniversary of Israel's independence. Ambassador Fedorenko received me on 9 May. It was the very day that Nazi Germany, twenty-two years previously, had signed the document of its surrender in Berlin. Fedorenko was in an expansive mood. He proposed a vodka toast 'to celebrate the victory over the common foe'. At this time, Israel and the Soviet Union were still, according to Ambassador Fedorenko, partners of the great allied coalition which had brought about the downfall of the Third Reich. My new Soviet colleague eagerly inquired about my impressions of recent talks and travels in his country and was particularly anxious to obtain confirmation that mazzot had been available in abundance to Jews celebrating Pessach. I told him of the ardour of prayer I had witnessed at the great synagogue in Moscow, the outcry '*L'shana haba'ah b'yerushalayim*' ('next year in Jerusalem') and the joyful outpouring of dancing Jewish youth in front of the synagogue. There was no indication that Mr Fedorenko would soon undergo a transformation from an amiable host into a formidable foe. Two weeks later, in the meetings of the Security Council, he defamed his former anti-Nazi ally as a representative of a Hitlerite government!

15

The Ides of May

Daily reports of terrorist attacks of ever increasing frequency and vehemence in the north of Israel came over our telex-line from Jerusalem. On 10 May 1967 I went to see Dr Ralph Bunche, the United Nations Undersecretary, in his office on the thirty-eighth floor of the UN glass house. I asked him to acquaint Secretary-General U Thant with the facts of the rapidly deteriorating situation and request him to express publicly his concern about the continuation of these attacks and warn the Arab states of their responsibility in supporting hostile activity against a member state of the United Nations. I also suggested that the Secretary-General should send a personal message asking the Syrian leaders to put an end to these actions launched from their territory.

Bunche believed that a personal message would not be effective with the Syrian leadership in their prevailing state of mind. However, he suggested the publication of a statement. A day or two later U Thant expressed in a firm statement his deep concern at the Fatah raids and placed the responsibility squarely on those governments which aided and abetted them.

All was set for our Independence Day Reception on 15 May. Early in the afternoon Mr Fedorenko's secretary called our delegation to convey the personal apologies of her ambassador but a cold kept him from attending our reception – a cold that started the diplomatic chill.

Reports and instructions which had reached us from Jerusalem that morning clouded our festive mood. The Syrian government had made claims of alleged Israeli troop concentrations along the northern borders. At the same time large Egyptian forces and heavy armour had passed through Cairo in an easterly direction, cheered by frantic mobs clamouring for war against Israel. Foreign Minister Eban cabled 'most immediately' that press agencies reported large Egyptian troop movements in response to alleged concentrations of Israeli forces on the Syrian border. He instructed me to inform Ralph Bunche that: a) no Israeli forces were concentrated along the Syrian border; b) as long as the Syrian side kept the border area quiet there was no cause for concern; c) it appeared that Syria intended to drag Egypt into confrontation with Israel. Bunche was free to communicate the three points to the Egyptian representative. The telegram concluded with the barbed remark that the only concentrations which could actually be found in Israel were the masses of tourists who had arrived in the country to attend the Independence Day celebrations.

Bunche confirmed that the reports of the United Nations observers on the spot agreed that no Israeli forces were concentrated on the Syrian border. A few hours later at our reception, Ralph Bunche informed me that the Secretary-General had already received confirmation from the Egyptian and Syrian representatives that the message had been duly transmitted to Cairo and to Damascus.

Eban's next telegram on the following day was more specific on the massive movement of Egyptian armour and the forward deployment of its air force in Sinai. The sardonic ring of his first communication was gone. He stressed the gravity of the tension created by these moves which were accompanied by vicious war propaganda spread by the Egyptian and Syrian media. He instructed the Israeli ambassadors to Washington, Paris and the United Nations to make representations that steps should be taken to control the mounting crisis.

From now on we were in daily, and sometimes in hourly, contact with the Secretary-General or with Ralph Bunche. The reel of events unrolled with break-neck speed. Completely disregarding the information which the United Nations had conveyed to the Egyptian government, the Egyptian liaison officer with the United Nations Emergency Force (UNEF) repeated, on 16 May, the allegation of Israel's troop concentrations on the northern border. Again the United Nations dismissed these reports as false. A few hours later, during the night, the Egyptian Commander in Sinai made his dramatic and fateful move. He asked General Rikhye, the Commander of the UNEF, to evacuate his troops along the Egyptian-Israeli border, to avoid any interference with the advancing Egyptian army. At midday, 17 May, I received a report that the United Nations spokesman in New York had issued a statement that should Egypt insist on its demand the Secretary-General had no alternative but to withdraw all the United Nations forces from all their positions along the border and to evacuate them completely from Egyptian territory.

I felt that this reaction was likely to precipitate events and rushed up to Ralph Bunche's office to express our apprehensions. He told me that General Rikhye had refused to accept the Egyptian eviction order, saying that he received his instructions from the United Nations Secretary-General and not from an Egyptian major-general – an answer worthy of the American reply 'nuts' to Marshal von Rundstedt's call for the surrender of the allied forces fighting the Battle of the Bulge.

U Thant had immediately requested an explanation from the Egyptian government, cautioning Cairo that any attempt to interfere with the freedom of movement of the UNEF would be regarded as an abrogation of Egypt's agreement to the stationing of United Nations forces and would, accordingly, compel the Secretary-General to evacuate all of them. I asked Ralph Bunche what had happened to the pledge given in 1957 by Secretary-General Hammarskjöld not to make any changes in the disposition of the United Nations forces without the prior consent of the United Nations General Assembly. Bunche replied with some visible embarrassment that the Secretary-General had recently been advised by his legal counsellor that the presence of United Nations forces depended solely upon the consent of the host government.

I reminded Dr Bunche that the agreements of 1957 constituted international guarantees given to Israel prior to the withdrawal of its forces. He himself had actively participated in the lengthy negotiations and had proved his drafting skill when we finalized the texts. It was clear from them that no unilateral action by Egypt could change the deployment of UN forces. Moreover, I warned him that the UN statement on the complete withdrawal of all UN forces in the case of interference with their freedom of movement was likely to force Nasser's hand and create a head-on collision between Israel and Egypt. Bunche did not share our opinion. He explained that in making that statement the Secretary-General intended to call Nasser's bluff. He was convinced that, confronted with the exigency of the withdrawal of the United Nations forces, Nasser would reconsider his action. I expressed my strong doubts at such an optimistic view of Nasser's reaction to weakness and confusion.

One day, when the relevant documents of the archives in Moscow and Cairo are made available to the public, it will be possible to ascertain the interrelation between events, causes and effects. Nasser claimed in an interview with a French journalist, Eric Rouleau, published in the London *Times* of 19 February 1970: 'I had not asked U Thant to withdraw United Nations troops from Gaza and Sharm el-Sheikh, commanding the entrance to the gulf, but only from a part of the frontier from Rafah to Eilat.' In the light of Nasser's permissive relationship to facts and truth and his unequalled facility to shift with abandon from fact to fiction there is sufficient reason to doubt the accuracy of this statement. Moreover, in that same interview Nasser claimed: 'It was not my intention to close the Gulf of Aqaba to Israeli ships.' That contention has been bluntly refuted by U Thant himself in his report to the General Assembly of 26 June 1967, where he describes his unsuccessful emergency mission to Cairo: 'It is also pertinent to note that in response to a query from the Secretary-General as to why the United Arab Republic had announced its reinstitution of the blockade in the Straits of Tiran, while the Secretary-General was actually *en route* to Cairo on 22 May, President Nasser explained that his government's decision to resume the blockade had been taken some time before U Thant's departure and it was considered preferable to make the announcement before rather than after the Secretary-General's visit to Cairo.' The known facts lend more credibility to Nasser's statement to the Secretary-General in 1967 than to his remarks to Eric Rouleau in 1970.

In a conversation with Abba Eban and myself some time later, U Thant gave us a colourful version of his talk with Nasser on this subject. Nasser told him that he and his colleagues had some heart-searching deliberations on the timing of the blockade proclamation. Were they to announce the measure before the departure of the Secretary-General for Cairo, it would be interpreted as a move to torpedo his mission. Were they to announce it after his departure, it would be regarded as a failure of U Thant's mission – and this would be an unpardonable lack of Arab civility and hospitality. Therefore Nasser decided to proclaim the blockade while U Thant was in mid-air *en route* to Cairo.

Shout before shooting

On 18 May, the day Nasser issued his evacuation order to the United Nations forces, I had a long and lively discussion with U Thant. I stressed again the dangers inherent in yielding to Egypt's demands, and read to him an excerpt from a United Nations document:

Despite almost a decade of relative quiet along the line on which the UNEF is deployed, relations between the peoples on the opposite sides of the line are such that if the United Nations buffer should be removed, serious fighting would, quite likely, soon be resumed.

U Thant, somewhat bewildered, asked me who wrote that report. I answered: 'It was submitted by yourself, Mr Secretary-General, on 7 September 1966 to the General Assembly.' U Thant glanced at Ralph Bunche forlornly. I pointed out that the Egyptian demand for withdrawal of the United Nations forces was a clear indication of their aggressive designs against Israel. The Egyptian government wanted to remove the United Nations buffer forces so that its army could directly and without hindrance come to grips with Israel. The withdrawal of the United Nations forces from Sharm el-Sheikh would reinstate Egyptian forces at the control of one of Israel's lifelines. Bunche agreed that the decisive question was whether Egypt would re-occupy Sharm el-Sheikh. He doubted it in view of its involvement in Yemen, where its forces were bogged down. I explained to the Secretary-General that in accordance with the 1957 agreement, the UNEF could not be withdrawn unilaterally, but I soon gathered from U Thant's perplexed expression that he was only remotely acquainted with these accords. He had not fully grasped that they were meant to serve as safeguards, exactly for such a contingency, and prevent an agitated situation from getting out of control.

I suggested to U Thant that he advise Nasser in a personal message to desist from his reckless venture and, instead of demanding the withdrawal of the UNEF, pull back from the brink of the precipice. U Thant accepted the idea and promised to summon the representative of Egypt. I hurried the end of our talk so as not to delay the arrival of my Egyptian colleague. He did indeed arrive quickly, but the message was not given. The Secretary-General himself revealed what happened a few weeks later in his report of 26 June to the General Assembly:

The Secretary-General expressed deep misgivings to the Permanent Representative of the United Arab Republic about the likely disastrous consequence of the withdrawal of the UNEF and indicated his intention to appeal urgently to President Nasser to reconsider the decision. Later in the day, the representative of the United Arab Republic informed the Secretary-General that the Foreign Minister (Mahmoud Riad) had asked the Permanent Representative by telephone from Cairo to convey to the Secretary-General his urgent advice that the Secretary-General should not make an appeal to President Nasser to reconsider the request for withdrawal of the UNEF and that, if he did so, such a request would be sternly rebuffed.

The next day I called again on the Secretary-General, this time with a pressing message from Foreign Minister Eban urging the Secretary-General not to allow the complete folding-up of the UNEF and again emphasizing that its withdrawal cleared the road for the advance of the Egyptian army. The message ended with an appeal to the Secretary-General 'to avoid condoning any change in the *status quo* pending fullest and broadest international consultation'.

U Thant again argued that he could not oppose the decision of a sovereign member-state and therefore had to bow to Egypt's demand. Dr Bunche added that if the Secretary-General were to insist on the UNEF staying put, it would be compelled to open fire against the Egyptian army. I repeatedly tried to impress on U Thant that a determined stand on his part would generate second thoughts on the other side. When all my representations were to no avail, I snapped: 'Before shooting at them at least you could have shouted at them.' By now it was clear that the Secretary-General had given up any resistance to the Egyptian decision to deploy its forces along Israel's southern border.

That day I discussed with Ambassador Arthur Goldberg, the United States representative, an idea which Jerusalem had authorized me to explore with him. We thought that the emergency warranted a supreme effort by the Secretary-General to deal personally with the crisis. We suggested that he should take off for Cairo, Jerusalem and Damascus on a 'prevent-the-war' mission. We thought that it would be more effective if this proposal was presented to U Thant by a party who was not directly involved. If the idea was acceptable to the United States, it seemed to us preferable that Ambassador Goldberg should present it as an American initiative. He reacted positively, and with the consent of the State Department he submitted the idea to the Secretary-General. U Thant's first reaction was cautious and hesitant. He contacted the Egyptian representative and asked him to inquire of his government whether the visit to Cairo would be welcomed. He ignored the suggestion of visiting Jerusalem and Damascus.

On 22 May, the day U Thant set out on his voyage to Cairo, I ascended once again to the thirty-eighth floor to present him with a message from Foreign Minister Eban. It stressed particularly the gravity of the situation caused by the concentration of Egyptian forces on Israel's southern borders and the potential threat to Israel's maritime freedom and to international shipping if Egypt reinstituted the blockade in the Straits of Tiran. The message did not leave any doubt that, should this occur, Israel would have no alternative but to act in self-defence of its maritime rights and territorial security:

The freedom of passage for Israeli-bound ships in the Straits of Tiran is a supreme national interest and right which it will assert and defend whatever the sacrifice. Israel's refusal to return to a position of blockade is firm and unconditional. We urgently request you to consider methods of ensuring the retention of a suitable United Nations presence at Sharm el-Sheikh.

U Thant replied that he was fully aware of the gravity of the situation and particularly of the dangers inherent in the renewal of the maritime blockade. He assured us that he would warn Nasser not to put the torch to the inflammable situation.

Later in the day I consulted with Ambassador Goldberg about the steps which the United States government could take to drive home to the governments of Egypt and the Soviet Union that the implementation of Nasser's threats to close the Straits of Tiran would detonate the powder-keg which he had rolled into Sinai. Goldberg promised to immediately get in touch with the President and hinted at certain initiatives which were under preparation. In his book *The Vantage Point*, President Lyndon Johnson reveals that on that day he sent a message to Soviet Chairman Kosygin suggesting a joint effort to calm the situation. In the same spirit Arthur Goldberg also made representations to U Thant a few hours before he left for Cairo. Other governments likewise asked the Secretary-General to apprise the Egyptian government of their view that the course it had embarked upon might lead to a head-on collision.

The next I heard about U Thant's mission was a telephone call late that night from the United States Delegation. U Thant had been stunned to hear at his stop-over in Paris that Nasser had proclaimed a blockade. He had consulted by phone with his colleagues at the United Nations Secretariat about whether he should proceed to Cairo. He also requested them to solicit the opinion of the American government. The United States Mission wanted to ascertain our views, too. I replied that although it seemed that the die was cast, one should not abandon an honourable effort to save the peace and that U Thant should forcefully press Nasser to revoke his decision. He should squarely place the responsibility for the consequences of his action on his shoulders. The United States Delegation concurred.

U Thant proceeded to Cairo. He held long talks with Nasser. The Egyptian leader did not yield an inch – his course was set. After two days U Thant left empty-handed and down-hearted for New York and submitted a negative report to the Security Council. Another diplomatic emergency move had failed to dam the torrent of overflowing emotions released by a reckless dictator. It ended up like so many of its precursors – in the waste-paper basket of history, marked 'too little and too late'.

16

The East Side Story

While U Thant was still in Cairo, the representatives of Canada and Denmark asked for an urgent meeting of the Security Council. It was by now obvious that the Egyptian step to decree the blockade on the eve of U Thant's arrival in Cairo had raised the temperature of the crisis. When the Council convened on 24 May, I made a short statement reiterating the salient points of Prime Minister Eshkol's declaration in the Knesset the previous night. It conveyed in terse terms the sense of gravity and urgency in a situation which the Secretary-General himself, in his report of 19 May to the Security Council, had described as 'extremely menacing'.

Although the facts were known, the Security Council, in the austere language of its minutes, adjourned 'without taking action'. The Soviet representative, Nicolai Fedorenko, supported by a well-disciplined and highly vocal chorus of Arab and Soviet bloc representatives, opened with his theme song of this new 'East Side Story': 'Why rush and be excited? Never will the Arabs be indicted.' For days and nights on end the drama, played out on the world stage of the Security Council, frightened, frustrated and thrilled tens of millions of people around the world. Fedorenko expressed his fierce indignation at the audacious initiative taken by Canada and Denmark. It was obvious that the Soviet and Arab representatives were not eager for the Security Council to dilute their plot while it was thickening.

On 25 May, Eban arrived in New York on his way to Washington to acquaint President Johnson with Israel's anxieties and consult with him on measures to cope with the menace. He asked me to join him. In a *tour de force* the previous day he had managed to meet General de Gaulle in Paris and Prime Minister Harold Wilson in London. Ambassador Harman met us at the airport. He carried in his briefcase a stunning surprise for Eban, a personal top secret telegram from the Prime Minister. It was short and Eban devoured it in one glance on the drive to his hotel. He did not utter a word, but his excitement was visible. When we reached his suite he paced up and down. He read the cable again, flung it on a table, as he used to do with papers which utterly displeased him, and in a tone of command completely unnatural for him he snapped: 'Read it.'

It contained the startling information from impeccable sources that the Egyptian armies in Sinai would launch their offensive within the next twenty-four hours. Eban was directed to meet the President immediately and, without consulting Jerusalem on any point, ask him to declare that any attack on Israel would be considered an attack on the United States.

This was such a sudden turn of events and abrupt change of direction that after some reflection I felt bound to express some cautious doubts about the authenticity of the information and the wisdom of the political prescription. Both ran against everything we had known before our arrival in Washington and also against what Eban had been asked by the government to accomplish on his mission. I counselled Eban to check with Eshkol regardless of the injunction, before embarking on a course which might jeopardize Israel's credibility and raise doubts about the soundness of its government's political judgement. However, Eban felt the responsibility was so immense and the described emergency so grave that any delay could cause irreparable harm.

The President was expected back in Washington from a visit to Canada only late that night. Eban asked to advance his scheduled meeting with the Secretary of State. He went straight to the point. He read the text of the telegram verbatim. Dean Rusk gasped. He asked Eban to repeat it at dictation speed and took it down word by word. So did his assembled aides. Without saying a word, he got up, opened a drinks cabinet and poured two glasses, one for himself and one for his distinguished visitor. Rusk gulped his drink silently. Then he wrote something on a piece of paper and gave it to Eugene Rostow to deliver. He returned after a few minutes and withdrew with the Secretary into a distant corner of his office, where he spoke to him with apparent emphasis.

When Dean Rusk rejoined us he said slowly and pointedly that none of the United States services were in possession of any intelligence which could confirm any aspect of the information from Jerusalem. Then he stared straight into Eban's eyes and said: 'Of course, I do not wish to assume that your information is meant to give us advance notice of a planned Israeli pre-emptive strike. This would be a horrendous error.' Eban assured him that the telegram meant what it said. At this point the meeting was adjourned, with Rusk's promise to seek further clarification, until the time we were to reconvene for a working dinner.

No further information was forthcoming from Jerusalem. The attack did not materialize on the anticipated date. We were puzzled and considerably disturbed by the whole affair. In the ensuing turmoil of the war and its aftermath these events remained shrouded in mystery. Only a few years later, when a spate of self-revelations inundated the Israeli press, did the story of the strange telegram come to light. General Rabin, who had been indisposed for a day or two at the height of the crisis and had been prevented from attending an important meeting of the General Staff, had come to Jerusalem to discuss with the Prime Minister his evaluation of the situation. Before entering his office, he stopped at the desk of Jacob Herzog, the Director-General and gifted political adviser of the Prime Minister. He showed him the text of a telegram which he had drafted for Eshkol to impress on Eban the urgency of the situation. Rabin felt that the text was not strong enough. In his opinion it was time to test the American position. A clear case had to be presented in order to obtain a clear commitment. Herzog had his doubts, but Rabin was firm. They re-drafted the cable and obtained Eshkol's consent.

The following afternoon I went back to New York to meet U Thant who had returned from Cairo that same day. He informed me of his talks in Egypt and pondered his next step. I suggested that he submit to the Security Council a factual report on his mission and let the Council face the realities of the situation, reminding him that Israel would under no circumstances acquiesce in the Egyptian blockade, which by all international norms was a flagrant act of aggression.

Eban returned to Israel after his meeting with the President. He stopped off in New York for two hours to consult with Ambassador Goldberg, who had already received a brief report from the White House. After he had explained the situation in the Security Council, where the United States was bound to seek the necessary votes for a resolution reaffirming the freedom of maritime passage as prelude for any further action, Arthur Goldberg came to his principal concern. He felt that he should draw the attention of the Foreign Minister to a subtle but decisive fact which had emerged in his talk with the President. L.B.J. had stressed that, before he could take any action which he certainly contemplated, he had to assure himself of Congressional support. Goldberg advised Eban to consider the presidential commitment as conditional. Dean Rusk and he himself were fully aware that the United States would refrain from any action in the field until it had been made absolutely clear to them that the President had committed himself. It would be a fateful error to rely on the opinion of the two Rostow brothers; their advice to the President was sometimes rather impetuous. Only after the President had made up his mind, could the Secretary of State loyally and effectively translate his decision into action. Goldberg advised Eban that whenever Israel felt bound to act on its own, it should not proceed without the prior knowledge of, and consultation with, the United States government. America had worldwide obligations and could not accept surprises.

We rushed from the Waldorf Towers to Kennedy airport. Eban's mind was already in the cabinet room, where his colleagues were anxiously awaiting his report. I tried to underline what we had just heard from Arthur Goldberg. His advice was in my opinion offered not only as an expression of his personal concern, but also upon the request of the administration, which was eager to avoid any misunderstanding of the President's position. Ambassador Goldberg later confirmed the accuracy of this assumption.

To ease the tense moments before take-off, Eban asked me about the prospects of the Security Council debate which, of course, compared to his

Washington meetings, was a secondary and rather hopeless affair. I told him about Fedorenko's contemptible attacks on Israel and the honour of the Jewish people. A columnist had written in the *New York Times* that his comparison of Israel to the Nazis was calculated to 'enrage the Israelis and comfort the Arabs without committing a single Soviet tank or Mig'. I assured the Foreign Minister that I would not let Fedorenko get away with it. He would hear some stinging reminders of the annexation of the Baltic republics and the Soviet invasion of Finland, seasoned with the Molotov-Ribbentrop pact and topped with the Moscow 'doctors' plot'. I trusted that this would be a sufficiently potent brew to have a tranquillizing effect on him.

Eban was absorbed in his own thoughts. He murmured something to the effect that it would be all right, but that I should speak only in terms of general principles and not elaborate too much. What precisely he meant remained obscure, because the departure of his plane ended our conversation. What I had in mind was clear to me and, after I had articulated it in a number of responses to Fedorenko's outbursts, Eban sent me an encouraging congratulatory telegram on my intrepid stand against the 'waves of vicious assault'. The Israeli public welcomed the incisiveness of the new look of Israel's diplomacy.

A few days after our first exchange of fireworks Ambassador Fedorenko approached me in the Security Council lounge, saying that we had exchanged enough views in the debate and perhaps a private talk might be preferable. I intimated that one did not exclude the other. What he called his views were nothing but sinister insinuations to which I had replied with facts. They might not always be pleasant for him to listen to, but nonetheless their accuracy was incontrovertible. 'Who is interested in facts in the United Nations?', Fedorenko persisted. 'What counts are the views of the governments and the votes of the delegates.' I reminded him that he had started the defamation campaign which he euphemistically called 'an exchange of views'. If he had now decided to call it off, it was all right with me. But if he were to continue, I promised him more facts annoying to him, but revealing to the audience. He did not desist from further vilification, either carried away by his own temper or carrying out the instructions of his superiors in Moscow. In any case, our 'exchange of views' continued with undiminished vigour.

The Security Council, stunned by Nasser's audacity, paralysed by Soviet procrastination and intimidated by Arab verbal vehemence, lingered in a state of lethargy. The meetings of 29 and 30 May passed in a sterile game of oratorical strikes and counter-strikes. Ambassador Goldberg denounced the illegality of the reimposed blockade, describing the crisis as 'more menacing than at any time since 1956'. He urged the Council to endorse the Secretary-General's appeal to all parties concerned 'to exercise special restraints, to forego belligerence and to avoid all other actions which could increase them'. Solemnly he warned the international community: 'What we do here today and in the days to come will affect not only the peace of the Near East but the good name and standing of this great organization.'

In our statements we focused on dispelling the fiction and revealing the facts. I said:

On Saturday, 13 May, the streets of Cairo reverberated with the sound of tanks and the cries of agitated crowds whipped up by the cheer-leaders chanting: 'We want war with Israel.'

We in Israel looked on this spectacle with detachment, thinking that this was just one more outburst of chauvinistic frenzy which is such a common feature of military dictatorships.

But the Egyptian military machine moved forward with ever-increasing momentum, while its propaganda poured out a torrent of threats against Israel and charges that it had massed large forces on its northern border in preparation for an attack on Syria.

By the alchemy of a process of constant repetition, the Egyptian propaganda machine tries to transmute the big lie into golden truth. This technique has been tried before, and not so long ago, with initial success and final disaster for its practitioners.

U Thant's last-minute appeal

It was on a Saturday morning, 28 May, that U Thant made up his mind about his next move. Ralph Bunche called me at home. He had a most urgent message from the Secretary-General for Prime Minister Eshkol. Until its text reached us in a short while, Bunche requested us to keep our lines of communication with Jerusalem clear so that the message could get through instantly.

We cleared the lines. The text arrived. It was a strong plea to:

H.E. Mr Levi Eshkol, Prime Minister of Israel

Excellency,

It is only because of my deep concern – a concern which I know you fully share – that the Near East should not again be plunged into the catastrophe of war that I take the liberty of addressing to you this strong and urgent personal appeal. As you know, intensive efforts are being made here and in other places to find means of averting that war. The imperative need is for time in which these efforts can have a reasonable chance to achieve constructive results. I am fully aware of your government's firm position with regard to freedom of innocent passage through the Straits of Tiran. However, I do wish to call especially to your attention what I said in paragraph 14 of my report to the Security Council dated 26 May 1967.

I now appeal to you, as I am appealing to President Nasser and to all concerned, to exercise the utmost restraint at this critical juncture. In particular, may I express the hope that information which has come to me that no ship flying the flag of Israel is likely to seek passage through the Straits of Tiran in the coming two weeks, will prove to be correct.

I can assure you, Excellency, that I personally and the international community generally, will greatly appreciate all possible helpfulness. My sole interest is to gain even a short period of time in which every effort may be exerted here and elsewhere to find a way to stave off a war in the Near East which, as I have said to the Security Council, I greatly fear could ensue from a clash over the Straits of Tiran.

Accept, Excellency, the assurances of my highest consideration.

U Thant

The Secretary-General made a similar appeal to President Nasser.

Shortly after I had received the text, I got another call from Dr Bunche, anxiously inquiring whether it had already been transmitted. 'They are working on it right now,' I replied eagerly. 'Please hold it', pleaded Bunche, 'until I have been in touch again with U Thant.' After an hour or so, Bunche called again. His voice was hesitant: 'Look, Gideon, about this message to Prime Minister Eshkol, forget about it. Don't send it. Please return it to me on Monday.'

'What happened?' I asked, not hiding my bewilderment. 'Did Nasser lift the blockade?'

'Unfortunately, it is not that,' answered Bunche in an embarrassed tone. 'I can't tell you the reasons right now.'

My guess was that Nasser had rejected the appeal. I checked with Arthur Goldberg. He confirmed my assumption.

This was the third time that the Secretary-General had abandoned his efforts in the face of Egypt's objection. He dispensed with his urgent representation to Nasser to reconsider his demand for the withdrawal of the UNEF when he was advised by Foreign Minister Riad 'that such a request would be sternly rebuffed'. He set out for Cairo to persuade Nasser not to reinstate the naval blockade but, while he was *en route*, Nasser took the fateful step. And now, on 27 May, Nasser refused to receive a last-minute appeal from the Secretary-General to withdraw from the brink. The Secretary-General yielded again and recalled his missive with the same alacrity as he had withdrawn the UN forces.

Le premier coup

Ambassador Goldberg made valiant and unrelenting efforts to whip the Security Council into action. He prodded, he pleaded, he proposed, but all his efforts bounced back from the stone wall of the Council's lethargy, trepidation and animosity. As a matter of fact, the United States draft resolution which he introduced at the meeting of the Security Council on 31 May was never put to the vote. It was fiercely attacked by the Arab and Soviet delegates and their camp followers.

In his memoirs, President Johnson summed up that stage of the proceedings:

With the deadline nearing, we asked the United Nations Security Council to endorse the appeal U Thant had made, after his return from Cairo, calling on all countries involved to avoid violence and provide time for further diplomatic and United Nations efforts. Because France abstained, we were unable to get nine votes in the Security Council to force the issue – a dismal comment on the effectiveness of that body.

The French delegate, Ambassador Roger Seydoux, hedged. He needed more time for 'careful study' – a United Nations synonym for 'do nothing'. He suggested the adjournment of the debate for a few days – another United Nations device for evading action and responsibility. As a matter of fact Ambassador Goldberg had sounded warnings over the previous year that we should be prepared for a painful change in France's policy of friendship towards Israel. In his contacts with French officials he had noted distressing signs of the coming estrangement, but he had also noticed that Israel's diplomatic antennae had not been adjusted to the disturbing atmospherics. The arms embargo imposed at the beginning of June was a sudden blow to the unsuspecting, and a logical but distasteful consequence to the initiated.

While time was running out in the Middle East, it was a surplus commodity at the United Nations. When the Council finally reconvened on 3 June to continue the consideration of the United States draft resolution, the French delegate declared that it would be 'useless and even dangerous' to vote on draft resolutions. He appealed instead for a breathing-spell, while military encirclement and maritime blockade were strangling Israel. He proposed '*le concert des quatre grandes puissances*' to deal with the situation. But at that time, the Soviet government was not inclined to attend such a '*concert*'. They rejected General de Gaulle's proposal for four-power consultations.

Ambassador Seydoux remonstrated on the responsibility of the party 'which would decide to take the initiative of military action' – completely oblivious of the fact that the Tiran blockade constituted aggressive action and that massive concentrations of Egyptian forces were poised at a distance of fifty miles from Tel Aviv, ready to invade Israel.

The day before Ambassador Seydoux made his statement, I had a rather animated conversation with him when he gave an advance warning that at the next meeting of the Council he would expound the French doctrine of the responsibility of '*qui tire le premier coup*'. What a strange and antiquated concept, I said. It fitted perhaps the period of the Battle of Fontenoy: '*Messieurs les Anglais, tirez, vous les premiers.*' For twenty years now Israel had been subjected to a state of belligerency and active hostility. Since the first day of its independence, it had been besieged, blockaded and embattled. The first shot was fired on 15 May 1948, when six Arab armies invaded Israel, and since then their firing had never ceased. Did it befit the honour and '*la gloire de la France*', I asked, to abandon a faithful friend in the hour of his mortal danger? Seydoux promised to report our conversation immediately to Couve de Murville, his Foreign Minister, and to ask for a softening of his instructions. The next morning, just before the opening of the Council's meeting, he came up to me and told me that Couve de Murville had been

impressed by our argument. He had redrafted the instruction to soften the
wording but did not change the substance of the French position.

Appeal to reason

The third of June was a Saturday. It was my turn to be the opening speaker at
the Council's meeting. I had had to put off the preparation of my speech until
after midnight the night before, since late that evening I had driven out to
Kennedy airport to meet our ambassador in Washington who was passing
through on his way for urgent consultations in Jerusalem. We exchanged
information on the latest developments and assessed the situation from our
respective vantage points in the capitals of the United States and the United
Nations, as we had done in close contact and co-operation during these fateful
weeks. I asked my colleague to tell our Foreign Minister that, in my view, all
political and diplomatic means to redress the situation had been exhausted.
The Security Council would not take any action of consequence. The United
States plan, code-named 'Regatta', to force the blockade by a multi-national
naval force, would never leave the safe haven of governmental chancelleries.
Nasser would neither lift the blockade nor withdraw his massed forces by
diplomatic persuasion. Israel stood alone. If it did not counter in time the acts of
war which Egypt had taken, it might succumb. If it yielded to Nasser's challenge,
it would totally compromise its political and security position. It would lose the
deterrent respect of its enemies and the countenance of its friends. Article 51 of
the United Nations Charter granted us the right of self-defence. The explicit
recognition in 1957 by the United States and other powers of Israel's right to take
action in case Egypt should renew the blockade in the Straits of Tiran was the
primary condition for our consent to withdraw our forces from Sinai.

From the airport I went back to our offices and began to work on the
speech, together with my good and learned friend, Ambassador Shabtai
Rosenne, the Deputy Chief of our mission. I was intrigued to read two years
later a well-argued dissertation, which maintained in minute analysis the
thesis that my statement of 3 June proved that by that date the government of
Israel had decided on its course of action and had instructed its UN representative accordingly on the contents of his statement. Far from it. I had not received
any specific directions from Jerusalem, apart from a general line for the
presentation of Israel's case at the outset of the Security Council's discussion
on 24 May. I was not informed about 'a decision of the government' which
had been taken. We had reached the conclusion on our own that the gravity of
the crisis and the immediacy of the threat to Israel warranted the kind of
statement I had prepared.

When the Security Council convened on the morning of 3 June, I addressed
it with 'A Last Call to Reason'.

The Arab governments have launched a campaign of unrestrained political warfare
here in the Security Council in preparation for the total war which they openly

proclaim to be their ultimate objective. As the Foreign Minister of Iraq himself said, 'the conflict will be total and uncompromising . . . there will be no retreat'. I say to him, you need not retreat if you do not advance.

Two heavily armed armies are facing each other, one poised to invade and destroy Israel, the other to defend it.

The war of 1948 was terminated by the conclusion of armistice agreements. I would remind the Arab representatives that the only valid basis for the Egyptian presence in the Gaza area and for the Jordanian presence on the West Bank is the armistice regime. They should therefore be more prudent before they disregard the significance and sanctity of the armistice demarcation lines.

Eilat, a thriving port and industrial centre, is Israel's outlet to the Red Sea. It links our country with Africa and Asia. Considerable trade passes through this essential maritime route.

Severing this maritime artery is an act as grave as an attempt to truncate part of our territory. It is a curious thing that those who are responsible for proclaiming the blockade come here and belittle the significance of their action for Israel. But if that were so, why do they go to such lengths and create a crisis fraught with such dangers?

They are following the same line as the Nazis did in 1939 when they took over Danzig. They launched the slogan – Why fight for Danzig? – and that is what we have heard here! Why fight for Eilat? Mr Shukairy has given us the answer in his broadcast: 'First the Gulf of Aqaba and then the Bay of Acre.' Israel is determined to make its stand on the Gulf of Aqaba. Nothing less than complete non-interference with free and innocent passage through the Gulf is acceptable to the government of Israel.

The situation with which the Council is confronted today has deteriorated since the Council first met on this question. The Arab governments have intensified their war preparations. It is not a breathing-spell which will avert the present danger. What is required is action, concrete steps to forego all acts of belligerence and to withdraw the armies back to their previous positions.

The call went unheeded. Egypt intensified its blockade measures and deployed its forces in Sinai in jump-off positions.

The Security Council decided not to vote on any resolutions and to adjourn over the weekend until Monday afternoon, 5 June. It neither prepared for the worst nor hoped for the best. All that could be said in the meetings of the Council had been said and all that should have been done, remained undone. In Macbeth's words: 'a tale of sound and fury signifying nothing' had come to its unhappy end.

The story of May is not only a record of the failure of the international community to defuse an explosive situation, but it also presents striking evidence that Israel did not leave a stone unturned to prevent the war. It appealed to the Secretary-General of the United Nations not to withdraw the United Nations Emergency Force. It asked him, while the evacuation was in progress, to maintain at least the United Nations units at Sharm el-Sheikh. U Thant admitted later in his report of 26 June that 'the direct confrontation between Israel and the United Arab Republic was revived after a decade by the decision of the United Arab Republic to move its forces up to the line'.

Israel suggested the mission of the Secretary-General to the three capitals in the Near East: Cairo, Jerusalem and Damascus. We were in the process of transmitting his last-minute appeal to the Prime Minister of Israel when he cancelled it.

Israel expounded its case in the capitals of the world and before the Security Council and gained the understanding of world opinion. It contacted the Soviet government as early as mid-April, to caution it against the dangers of fanning the flames of Arab ardour. However, the sympathy universally manifested for Israel's plight was frustrated by the apathy of the United Nations.

Israel appealed to the leaders of the three principal powers – France, Great Britain and the United States – to join in effective action to save the peace. It kept its mind cool and showed singular forbearance. But when nobody else ventured to remove the stranglehold, Israel itself had to cut the noose.

17

Six Days and Seven Nights

On Sunday, all the bustling diplomatic activity of the week had come to a halt. Even the unending telegram traffic with Jerusalem had petered out. The sudden silence of the teleprinters was more telling than their routine outpouring of messages, chasing one another with dazzling speed. All political means seemed exhausted. Israel was brooding over the fateful decision of when to break the stranglehold. In a last review of the situation the cabinet had concluded that no power in the world was willing or capable of making Nasser retract.

It was a placid, good-humoured and well-tempered Sunday in New York. But beneath the tranquil surface there was an air of tension. Washington was aware that the next twenty-four hours would be decisive. The plan to set up a joint task force, composed of the principal maritime powers committed to the freedom of passage through the Straits of Tiran, did not even reach the launching-stage. 'Regatta' never got off the ground. 'It was an amateur show that has collapsed,' said Justice Arthur Goldberg, when I went to see him that Sunday morning.

In a grim mood we reviewed the latest developments. Only four governments had indicated their readiness to participate in the naval demonstration in the Gulf of Aqaba. The Canadian Prime Minister, Lester Pearson, who had initially favoured the idea, had had second thoughts. He believed that worldwide political pressures and the enormous economic difficulties confronting Nasser would compel him to call off his adventure. We did not share this optimistic outlook. The crisis was too far advanced. Ambassador Goldberg recognized that Israel's survival as an independent nation, capable of defending itself, was at stake. Its future position among the nations depended on how it would face the challenge: lying down or standing up. If Israel recoiled, a strong alliance of Arab states would attack it at the time of their choice. But if Israel acted in self-defence it would not remain without support, continued Arthur Goldberg.

In Goldberg's opinion, the statement made the previous day by the Minister of Defence, Moshe Dayan, that Israel did not want any American soldiers fighting for it, was most timely and useful. As long as world opinion remained convinced that Israel had been provoked into fighting for its survival, Israel would be assured of American political and economic support. The Soviet Union was not too keen on the outbreak of full-scale war. It wanted Nasser to win a political victory. But events had overtaken the policy-planners in Moscow. Goldberg felt that an Egyptian attack on a vessel trying to pass the Straits of Tiran would be a manifest act of war. He commended my statement of the previous day that 'Israel is determined to make its stand on the Gulf of Aqaba'. Fifty million people in the United States alone were watching the televised Security Council debates. They were thrilled by our struggle. This was the principal arena in the contest for public support where, in Ambassador Goldberg's view, we had gained the upper hand. When we parted we were certain that zero hour was near.

The call from Jerusalem came before dawn. Joseph Tekoah, who was in charge of United Nations affairs at the Foreign Ministry, was on the line. Without ado he said: 'Please take paper and pencil and write down: Inform immediately the President of the Security Council that Israel is now engaged in repelling Egyptian land and air forces. Tell him that you wish to make an urgent statement on the situation before the Security Council.' This was my battle order. It was the shortest communication with the longest consequences.

'Tell him' was easy to say when it was nine o'clock in Jerusalem, but it was only three a.m. in New York. The Ambassador of Denmark, Hans Tabor, was the President of the Security Council for the month of June. He lived somewhere out in Long Island. His wife answered my call. She was somewhat bewildered about my nocturnal urgency; cautiously she inquired whether, after all, the matter could not wait until a little bit later in the day. 'No, unfortunately, I must speak to the ambassador right now,' I insisted. Reluctantly Mrs Tabor revealed that her husband might possibly be found in their town flat. My apologies were short and coupled with a promise that the morning sun would shed light on the mystery of my emergency call. Hans Tabor was fully alert when I reached him. After a moment of stunned silence he said: 'You mean to say that the war has started. Will you please repeat your message slowly.' He promised to do the necessary. My call to him was followed soon after by that of my Egyptian colleague. It was the beginning of many disturbed nights, and not only for the President of the Security Council.

Next on my list was my driver, a hardy Kurd born in Jerusalem, always reliable and good company. 'Harness your horses, Shmuel,' I said. 'The war is on.' In no time at all he was there and rushed me to our offices. The members of the staff alerted by the duty officer arrived one by one. Ambassador Goldberg called. His anxiety was noticeable. He wanted to know details of the fighting and the line I intended to follow at the meeting of the Security Council. I briefed him on the latter point, while on the first I was unable to satisfy him. We had in the meantime received strictest instructions to refrain from volunteering any military information.

At around 6.30 in the morning the chief cipher officer brought down a telegram in a sealed envelope marked: 'For the Ambassador, Personal – For Your Eyes Only.' It contained the stimulating news that by noon Israeli time the Israeli air force had destroyed more than 250 Egyptian planes. This exhilarating report was accompanied by a strict warning not to communicate it to any living soul. It was apparently meant as a booster shot for the head of the mission to get him in good trim for the forthcoming fierce UN debates. And indeed it did.

A few weeks later Ambassador Tabor asked me to enlighten him on a matter which had puzzled him ever since the morning of the fateful fifth of June. When we met in the Security Council chamber shortly before the opening of the meeting, he had told me how perturbed he was about the news broadcast by Radio Cairo that Egyptian forces were advancing on Tel Aviv, Jordanian shelling had caused severe damage to West Jerusalem and Syrian air-raids were incinerating Haifa. He had expressed his deep sorrow at Israel's distress.

'Yes,' I confirmed. 'I remember how I was touched by your concern.' 'But', continued Tabor, 'it perplexed me that apparently you were not sharing it. When I asked you to take your seat at the Security Council table, your face did not betray a trace of worry. I wondered how could a man be so detached in such a desperate situation.'

I thought that by that time it would do no harm to reveal to him the secret of the 'Eyes only' telegram. After all, I admitted, with 250 enemy planes in the bag, one sits more confidently at the Security Council table.

However, the meeting was far from comfortable. Having initiated the debate I was inscribed as the first speaker. The representative of India objected; he wanted to deprive Israel of the first move. I strongly opposed this unwarranted interference and informed the President of the Council that if I were denied the right to address it, I would withdraw and make my statement to the press and television reporters massed in strength in the lobby. He realized the absurdity of the situation and ruled accordingly.

My statement was brief and conformed with the text cabled to me by the Foreign Ministry in the early hours of the morning. I felt, however, that the scope and meaning of my announcement would be enhanced by appending to it the text of the order of the day issued by the Minister of Defence. It contained a passage of particular significance: 'We have no aim of conquest. Our sole objectives are to put an end to the Arab attempt to conquer our land and to lift the blockade and to terminate the state of belligerence enacted against us. We are a small but brave people. We want peace, but we are ready to fight for our land and our lives.'

For good measure I quoted also from General Murtaghi, the Egyptian field commander's order of 3 June: 'Reconquer the stolen land with God's help and the power of justice and with the strength of your arms and your united faith.' I concluded my statement: 'The Egyptian forces met with the response of the Israel Defence Forces, acting in self-defence in accordance with Article 51 of the Charter.'

This was the diplomatic opening shot in the first round of a long and tough battle of wits which culminated in November with the adoption of Security Council Resolution 242. That morning of 5 June the Security Council, after having heard the first sparse news of the fighting, preferred to await the unfolding of events before deciding on its course of action. It suspended its session. It was undeniably a rather animated state of suspension. The scene of activity shifted from the Council chamber to the delegates' lounge, where reporters competed with diplomats in the gathering of news. But more important was the intense diplomatic footwork. This was a crisis of the first order. It was a situation which required urgent contact between the delegations of the United States and the Soviet Republic, and their constant communication with the representatives of the countries at war. Unlike other cases of conflict discussed in the United Nations, there existed no contact whatever between the ambassadors of the Arab states and Israel. The Arab delegates religiously observed the ban on communications decreed by their governments when Israel attained its independence. They ignored us, because in their book Israel was not supposed to exist.

More ominous than this was the lack of contact between the Soviet and American delegations during the first critical hours after the outbreak of hostilities. Ambassador Fedorenko was unavailable for the greater part of the day. Ambassador Goldberg's repeated attempts to contact him were to no avail; the Soviet Ambassador was cooped up in his impenetrable embassy. He could not make a move without instructions from Moscow and apparently these were not forthcoming. The diplomatic steps taken in the Security Council were related to the movements on the battlefield. At five in the afternoon Ambassador Fedorenko emerged from his hide-out full of pent-up energy.

It was by then eleven at night in the zone of the hostilities. Although Israel was still withholding official news on the progress of the fighting, the Soviet government had realized that the advance of the forces was going in the opposite direction to that proclaimed by the Egyptian media. The armies of Egypt were not approaching the gates of Tel Aviv; instead the forces of Israel were heading towards the Suez Canal. Haifa was not burning; instead numerous military airfields in Egypt had been destroyed. As long as Moscow was uncertain of the direction of the fighting and the fortunes of war, it had been holding up its decision on how to proceed at the United Nations. It had no intention of hindering the proclaimed progress of its Arab allies by the adoption of a cease-fire resolution linked to a call for the withdrawal of forces. As soon as the true battle situation became clear, revealing that the Egyptian forces were in retreat, the Soviet Union started its political and propaganda machine to rescue them by high-speed UN action. Prime Minister Kosygin, using the hot line, asked President Johnson to take joint action against the

'Israeli aggressors', a term from which they and their Arab associates never deviated from that time on. The President replied that the Security Council was supposed to deal with the situation and New York was the appropriate place for discussions between the representatives of the two countries. After this tense exchange Mr Fedorenko immediately began consultations with Justice Goldberg. These lasted the better part of the night and the whole of the next day.

From the crisp instructions which I received from home, I understood that they expected me to carry out a diplomatic holding-action. The strategic outcome of the fighting was a race between time and space. Our armoured divisions would cover the space as fast as they could and our diplomatic corps was to provide the time for them to reach their objectives. When Arthur Goldberg asked me at the critical early stage what our most pressing requirement at the Security Council was, I answered: 'Time.' 'If Fedorenko continues to avoid me,' he replied wryly, 'you'll have plenty of it.' During the suspension of the session in New York, which lasted for nearly thirty-six hours, an entirely new situation was created in the Middle East. Jordan, which had disregarded a last-minute Israeli appeal to stay out of the fighting, occupied and ransacked the United Nations headquarters on the Hill of Evil Counsel which dominates part of Jerusalem. Israeli forces retook the Mount and shortly afterwards freed the erstwhile campus of the Hebrew University on Mount Scopus and the Hadassah Hospital, held under siege by Jordanian forces for nearly two decades. The first news of Israel's astounding victories in Sinai began to trickle through, but remained unconfirmed by the stony silence of our delegation. Rumours carried Syrian troops to the outskirts of Safed and news reports returned them to their original positions on the Golan Heights from which they had never departed.

By now cognizant of the real situation, the Soviet representative pressed hard for the adoption of a resolution ordering an immediate cease-fire and the withdrawal of forces. This was the standard drill of Soviet diplomacy when bailing out countries which had initiated armed action with the encouragement of the Soviet Union and had encountered unexpected set-backs. However, when the going was good and Soviet objectives were in reach they rejected with indignation all calls for a cease-fire. The United States was not inclined to support the kind of first aid that Ambassador Fedorenko had in mind. It rejected the Soviet draft resolution which insisted on the restoration of the situation that had prevailed on the eve of the outbreak of the fighting and placed the responsibility for the hostilities on Israel. The Soviet Union wanted to reinstate the broken armistice lines, retain the state of belligerence, continue blockades and boycotts – in short, preserve the conditions of war in a state of incubation until renewed Arab military preparations had fully matured.

Washington, for its part, was ready to agree to an immediate cease-fire linked to some steps for the restoration of an armistice regime, which would ensure the inviolability of the lines and serve as a basis for the eventual establishment of peace. We firmly rejected any reference to the defunct armistice agreements – they had already succumbed to incessant Arab assault and battering. The end of the hostilities must lead to a new Arab-Israeli relationship. The cease-fire resolution should, in our view, initiate a process of peace and not perpetuate a state of war. We intervened vigorously in New York and in Washington against any dubious compromise. We urged Ambassador Goldberg, a skilled and tenacious negotiator, to hold out. The anticipated progress in the field would not fail to soften the Soviet stand.

The talks dragged on. The other delegates became impatient, and they urged the resumption of the meeting. On the morning of 6 June, Jerusalem informed us that our Foreign Minister was on his way to New York. Our telephone communications with Israel were frequent and mostly clear, but on one occasion when the head of the Director-General's office called from Jerusalem there was a distinct disturbance on the line. When I asked him to speak up, he answered quietly: 'Sir, we have some disturbance here. The Jordanians are shelling us. This is the interference which causes the background noise.' I was deeply impressed with both his courtesy and his *sang-froid* under fire. The formal address of 'Sir' is most unusual in the foreign service. Its use by Shimon Amir could only be explained by the solemnity of the extraordinary circumstances.

Eban to the fore

While Abba Eban was crossing the Atlantic the pressure for the adoption of a resolution increased from hour to hour. I cabled him in-flight that he should be prepared to go directly from the airport to the Security Council, preferably with the text of his speech ready. His arrival was expected in the afternoon and provided me with an additional argument to stave off the resumption of the session until the early hours of the evening. The ambassadors of the United States and the Soviet Union were still engaged in their wrangle over the wording of a compromise draft. The stumbling-block remained the reference to the armistice system. While they were still closeted in negotiations I sent Arthur Goldberg a brief note: 'I appeal to you not to agree to any withdrawal clause which would establish an Egyptian claim for Israeli withdrawal before belligerence including Tiran blockade is terminated. Nasser should never again reap a political victory from a military defeat. This is vital not only for Israel but also for the Western position in the Middle East.'

Eban arrived in time and his primary concern was the text of the draft resolution. The armistice regime was not to be mentioned under any circumstances. Before settling down, he called Ambassador Goldberg. Without any preliminaries he gave him an intense lecture about the irreparable damage the reaffirmation of the armistice regime would inflict on post-war efforts to establish a durable peace. The much-tried Justice listened with inexhaustible patience and unmatched courtesy, until he finally got a word in: 'Abba, you don't have to rush over to see me. It's all finished, draft resolution and everything. You don't have to worry. You'd better get your speech ready. The Council is going to meet in an hour or so. Meanwhile, send Gideon over; I'll give him the draft. He deserves it. He has been on my back for the last thirty-six hours. He surely didn't break it, but if anyone broke, it was Fedorenko. He has yielded all along the line. And now back to work.'

This seemed to be comforting but still imprecise news. I rushed over to the United States Mission. The final draft carefully avoided any reference to withdrawal or the defunct armistice agreements. It called on the governments concerned 'as a first step to take forthwith all measures for an immediate cease-fire and for a cessation of all military activities in the area'. I congratulated Ambassador Goldberg on his negotiating skill, of which we were to see many more examples in the months to come. The United States draft resolution passed without objections. The Soviet representative abstained after his own draft had failed to obtain the necessary number of votes; he realized that a Soviet veto would stop the Council from taking any action likely to alleviate the growing plight of the Arab armies.

Eban's address was sombre and his poise reflected the singular burden of responsibility he carried for the successful outcome of Israel's struggle on the diplomatic front. He desisted from using rhetorical fireworks while the young of both sides were writhing in bloody battle. He depicted the background of blunder and bluster which had transformed a manageable political situation into an uncontrollable military confrontation. With a wide sweep he drew the lessons for the ancient peoples of the Middle East of getting inveigled in the power games of foreign countries, newcomers to the area. His vista of new horizons for the people of the Middle East, after the dust of battle had settled, was well received.

I was glad that Eban was back at the helm in New York. This was the time when the resonance of his voice was needed more than ever. His judgement of the political consequences of the war, seen from the American and United Nations vantage points, ought to carry a special weight in the decisions of the government in Jerusalem. Our long association dating back to the days before independence, our tests in many a diplomatic action and United Nations debate, had forged between us strong links of intellectual and personal affinity. But Eban was torn between his preoccupations in Jerusalem and the opportunities of New York. When the crisis became more poignant in the days preceding the outbreak of the hostilities, I had repeatedly urged Eban to come to New York. My colleagues at the Foreign Ministry expected him to heed the call and directed me accordingly to refrain from any major intervention in the debate of the Security Council. The Foreign Minister would deliver the principal address. People wondered about the reasons for my reticence, broken only occasionally to refute a particularly vicious Arab or Soviet verbal assault.

Eban was tempted to join the fight in New York, but he hinted in his phone calls to me that some internal difficulties delayed his departure. When he finally arrived on the second day of the war, he revealed the nature of 'the difficulties'. In the political turmoil which had seized the government and the Knesset in the days of the heightening military tension, some of the leading politicians were scheming to oust him from his post of Foreign Minister. A whispering campaign was launched, murmuring that he had failed to present a precise picture of President Johnson's position to the cabinet and that he had counselled patience while holding out promises for American action which, in the view of Eban's detractors, the administration in Washington never intended to take. Two senior officials of his Foreign Ministry helped fan the smouldering flames. They dropped a 'knowledgeable' remark here and there about their Minister's inaccurate reporting. Eban was deeply hurt and disappointed by the disloyalty of some of his party colleagues and members of his own staff. In cabinet deliberations he had sided with those who had accepted President Johnson's urging a delay of military action until the prospects of international intervention had been fully explored. At the beginning of June, when it became evident that Israel would have to face the peril alone, Eban resolutely supported Prime Minister Eshkol once he had come to the conclusion that there was no choice but self-defence.

It was a decisive week for the State of Israel and for Eban's own political fortunes. Both these concerns prompted him to remain in Jerusalem, knowing that 'les absents ont toujours tort'. When he arrived in New York his face was marked by the strains of the last turbulent days. With greater distance between him and the scene of events he tried to explain to himself and to his friends the background of what he called 'the cabal' to which he had nearly fallen victim. In the helter-skelter of transforming the cabinet on the eve of the war into a Government of National Unity, important influences in the leading Labour Party rooted for the transfer of Yigal Allon from the Ministry of Labour to Defence, a post held by the Prime Minister and aspired to by Moshe Dayan. To ensure Dayan's participation in the new coalition the idea was mooted of offering him Eban's portfolio, the Ministry of Foreign Affairs. Dayan's friends intimated that the conduct of foreign affairs was no less attractive to him than matters of defence, a supposition which proved correct ten years later. In the view of the cabinet-makers it was to be a simple operation: exit Eban, enter Dayan and transfer Allon to the post of his aspirations. But the plan encountered two hitches: Eban refused to jump overboard and Dayan insisted on the appointment of Minister of Defence. Under the pressure of the emergency Eshkol yielded. It was a fateful decision as the tragic events of Yom Kippur, six years later, were to show. Eshkol was then no longer among the living to witness the sad vindication of his resistance to the decision which had been forced upon him.

Verbal violence and cease-fire

After two days in New York Eban returned home. He felt that his presence in Jerusalem was more important than his stay at the United Nations. The events of the last days had completely transformed the situation. The Old City of Jerusalem, for nineteen years under Jordanian occupation, had surrendered to the Israel Defence Forces. The reunion of the Jewish people with the Western Wall of its ancient Temple was an occurrence which stirred every Jew in the deepest recesses of his soul. Israel's control of the other holy places, venerated by hundreds of millions of people all over the world, aroused initial consternation and uneasy expectation. It had never happened before in the long and eventful history of Jerusalem. It could not have happened before. When Rome ended Jewish independence, there was only one central holy shrine in the city: the Second Temple. It went up in flames followed by the destruction of Judea.

The West Bank occupied by Jordan fell shortly after. Syrian artillery, from its positions on the Golan Heights, continued its shelling of villages in Galilee – a situation which became more intolerable with every day. The Israeli forces in Sinai had overcome most of the Egyptian resistance and were approaching the Suez Canal. Israel had declared its acceptance of the cease-fire resolution with the normal proviso of reciprocity. Egypt was still stalling; Nasser appeared to be incapable of realizing the immensity of the military disaster which he had brought upon Egypt. The Soviet Union, by now fully aware of Egypt's desperate situation, pressed hard for its acceptance of the cease-fire. When Cairo finally made its decision, it appeared that the Soviet ambassador was informed of it earlier than his Egyptian colleague. Ambassador Fedorenko had requested the President of the Security Council to reconvene the meeting, but when the delegates took their seats, Ambassador El-Khuni refused to join them. He did not budge from his seat on the side-lines reserved for non-members of the Council. Fedorenko went over to him. His persuasion, though not audible, was clearly visible from his ample gesticulation. He showed him a paper; El-Khuni glanced at it with an incredulous look, but did not move from his place.

The President called the meeting to order and invited the representatives of Egypt and Israel to take their seats at the table. He gave the floor to Ambassador El-Khuni. Still hesitating, the ambassador made his way to the table and with tears in his eyes read his statement. It sounded more like a forced confession than a governmental declaration. He announced that Egypt accepted the cease-fire.

While the fighting on the Sinai front was nearing its end, the Arab and Soviet representatives continued their attack in the Security Council. Fedorenko led the forces of fury. Their blasts of fiery oratory did not spare the

American and British representatives either when they tried to brave the storm. When Fedorenko compared Israel to Nazi Germany and predicted its doom, I replied:

The representative of the Soviet Union has deemed it fit, in the course of the last few days, to hurl with ever-increasing vehemence insult after insult at my government and its representatives. Ambassador Fedorenko reached the heights of his crescendo today when he compared Israel's fight for its existence to Hitler's aggression. This is unheard of. He seems to believe that, representing a powerful country, he has the right to trample on the honour of a small state and a people which suffered more from Hitlerite aggression than any other people, one-third of which was exterminated by Hitler.

Neither Israel nor the Jewish people concluded a pact with Hitler's Germany, a pact which unleashed Nazi Germany's aggression against the world. The people of Israel volunteered from the first minute of that war to take up arms against the enemy of mankind, while the Soviet Union stood by, watching the developments.

Skilled in the craft of psychological warfare the Soviet delegates, supported by their Bulgarian helpmates and spurred by the clamour of their Arab associates, dragged the sessions out late into the night. Their tactic, well tested on home ground, was to unnerve and wear out their opponents by constant verbal battering and provocation. When one of their prosecutors was tired his substitute took over. They tried to transform the Council Chamber into a Russian courtroom.

The Syrian government delayed its acceptance of the cease-fire resolution somewhat longer than its Egyptian allies. Meanwhile, the Syrian army continued the shelling of Israeli villages in Upper Galilee. On the fifth day of the fighting the Director-General of our Ministry, in an early morning call from Tel Aviv, directed me to inform the President of the Security Council immediately that in response to the continued Syrian artillery attacks Israeli forces were now engaged in serious fighting to dislodge the Syrian forces from their positions on the Golan Heights. While I was still pondering whether it was an inescapable necessity to disturb again the sleep of the hardworking Ambassador Tabor, the secretary of the Security Council informed me that in view of the intense fighting on the Syrian front the Council would meet at nine o'clock. General Rabin, then Chief of Staff, later revealed that the decision to launch a full-scale attack against the Syrian positions was taken late at night by Defence Minister Moshe Dayan after a brief consultation with Prime Minister Eshkol. Only a day earlier, Dayan had opposed the plans of the General Staff to take decisive action on the Syrian front; he feared that it would create serious international complications. Rabin, tired and disappointed, had left his headquarters to snatch a few hours of undisturbed sleep at home. The commander of the northern front, General Elazar, had done likewise, resigned to the assumption that for him and his troops the war was over. Dayan alerted him that night to start operations in the early hours of the morning. General Rabin learned of the orders only when he was on his way back to his headquarters after a good night's sleep. Despite the short time for preparation the forces acquitted themselves of their task with admirable efficiency and outstanding courage.

While the heavy fighting proceeded with military precision, the debate in the Security Council got completely out of control. The Soviet delegation launched a verbal barrage unsurpassed in vehemence by anything heard before. The Council decided to renew its call for an immediate cease-fire and demanded that the two governments of Israel and Syria notify it instantaneously of their compliance. After the session had adjourned in considerable commotion the UN Undersecretary-General Aleksei Nesterenko, a Soviet appointee, asked myself and my Syrian colleague to follow him into an adjacent room. Though the seating order practised by the Council placed the representatives of Syria and Israel side by side, we had never met face to face privately. Realizing the oddity of the situation, the Undersecretary motioned us into two opposite corners like prize-fighters, and positioned himself like the referee in the middle of the ring. In his hands he held two copies of the resolution, one for each of us. He waved them at us with the distinct expectation that we would approach him together, so he could hand them to us simultaneously. I advanced. Mr Tome, the Syrian ambassador, stood as if petrified in his corner. 'I want an immediate reply,' commanded the hardy Russian. 'After I have received it from Jerusalem, I'll hand it to the President of the Council,' I retorted. 'So far it has been the practice that governments instruct their ambassadors and not the Secretariat of the United Nations, and we had better continue to abide by this principle.' Then I withdrew with a polite nod in the direction of my Syrian colleague.

The Council had decided to remain in session, waiting for the replies and even more impatiently for the definite cessation of hostilities. The Egyptian front was quiet by this time and the Jordanian army had evacuated the whole of the West Bank and retreated to the east of the Jordan river. The routed Egyptian forces, which had managed to extricate themselves from encirclement, streamed back home over the Suez Canal. But on the Syrian front fighting continued unabated. The difficult terrain and heavy Syrian resistance from strongly fortified positions slowed down the Israeli forces storming the Golan escarpment. In the late evening of Friday, 9 June, I notified the President of the Security Council that Israel was ready to cease operations provided that General Bull, the Chief of Staff of the UN observer corps, would discuss with the two combatant sides the necessary arrangements for the strict and mutual observance of the cease-fire. The Security Council was not satisfied and vented its disappointment in another stormy debate lasting into the small hours of the morning. The exhausted representatives – who had come to realize that man does not live by word alone, 'despite the fact that sometimes he has to eat his own', as Adlai

Stevenson once said in exasperation – decided to adjourn for a few hours to restore their depleted energies.

When the Council reconvened on the morning of 10 June, the fighting was still in full swing and Israeli forces were advancing eastwards over the flat Syrian plateau, stretching out to Damascus without any significant physical obstacles on the way. My Syrian neighbours at the Council table became increasingly edgy. While Mr Tome, the chief representative, let off his ire and frustration in a series of hard-hitting interventions, his aides seated behind him rushed in and out gathering the facts about the military situation. They had to rely on the news agencies, because their government had neither the time nor the inclination to furnish them with authentic information. At one stage, when the verbal clashes had reached heights of intensity over the question of whether the Israeli forces had taken the key town of Kuneitra, a member of the Syrian delegation tried unsuccessfully to pinpoint the location on a map. Ignorant not only of the geography of his country but apparently also oblivious of the seating arrangements of the United Nations, he turned to his neighbour on the right and asked him in Arabic: 'Where is that god-forsaken place, Kuneitra?' Politely, my colleague pointed it out on the map. His act of technical assistance was welcomed with an absent-minded 'Thank you very much' and a later side-glance of utter stupefaction. With more reports coming in on the advance of our forces, the Syrian, Soviet and Bulgarian representatives increased their pressure on me to give them a detailed report on their actual positions. I reiterated that I was under no obligation to provide the Council with military information. Fedorenko asked the President to rule that the Israeli representative must respond. Ambassador Tabor refused. There was no provision in the rules of procedure empowering the President of the Council to compel the representative of a sovereign state to make a statement.

As the session progressed and there was still no confirmation of the cessation of the fighting, Ambassador Goldberg asked me to join him in the delegates' lounge. Without any preliminaries he said: 'The situation has reached a point where you must immediately make a statement that Israel has ceased all military operations on the Syrian front. Fedorenko, any minute now, is going to make a statement in the form of an ultimatum. He will declare that "the Soviet government is prepared to use every available means to make Israel respect the cease-fire resolution".' This was grave news, but I had to tell Ambassador Goldberg that I could not make such a statement without the explicit authorization of my government. Goldberg was clearly dismayed. 'I speak to you on specific and urgent instructions from the President of the United States. We do not know whether and how the Soviets will materialize their threat. But what we do know is that the United States government does not want the war to end as the result of a Soviet ultimatum. This would be disastrous for the future not only of Israel, but of us all. It is your responsibility to act now.' The impact of his words was powerful. I pondered for a moment and replied: 'A statement made by an ambassador committing his government is valid only when it is covered by its authorization. I suppose your colleague in Israel has conveyed the President's message to our government.'

Just when we were on the point of ending our tense, but as always friendly exchange, I was called to the phone. Moshe Sasson, the director of military liaison in the Foreign Ministry in Jerusalem, was on the line. 'Please write down the following statement which you are asked to make immediately.' While I prepared myself for the ordeal, I thought to myself: here we go again, another of these circumlocutions, the diffusive product of draftsmanship by committee. But Sasson's first sentence was reassuring. General Dayan and General Bull had agreed on the modalities and time of the cease-fire. It would enter into force at 2 p.m. Greenwich Mean Time. I rushed back to Justice Goldberg with the good news. He went to the President of the Council and asked him to interrupt the debate to permit me to make the long-awaited statement. I slowly read it out, explaining that I was translating it from a Hebrew text which had just been transmitted to me:

General Dayan and General Bull have just concluded their meeting. Israel has accepted the proposals made by the UN representative for the implementation of the cease-fire resolution and the arrangements for the supervision of the cease-fire. General Dayan stated that on his part the cease-fire could enter into force at any hour. General Bull replied that this will take some time, because he has to contact Damascus. He also requested from Israel certain assistance in transport and equipment which General Dayan promised to make available to him. It was agreed that General Bull will fix the hour for the cease-fire entering into force and the technical arrangements for its supervision.

Fedorenko did not let it go at that. He was visibly frustrated that his diplomatic timebomb had been defused. As a parting-shot to our heated exchanges I remarked casually: 'I have hesitantly come to the conclusion that the representative of the Soviet Union does not seem to be too happy that the fighting has now finally come to an end.'

The Security Council adjourned with a deep sense of relief and in a state of complete exhaustion. In the area of battle the forces were deploying along the lines accepted by the high commands of Syria and Israel through General Bull's energetic intervention. In New York the diplomats went to bed for their first night of well-deserved, undisturbed sleep after six days of uninterrupted turbulence. We had good reason to look forward to a serene Sunday. But the Syrian ambassador felt differently. In the early hours of the day of rest he alerted the President of the Council with the news of alleged Israeli troop movements. Ambassador Tabor, audibly annoyed with this unexpected alarm, called me for verification. I assured him that we had not the slightest indication of the authenticity of the Syrian report, but I would, of course, check immediately with Jerusalem. A short while later I reported back that there were no forward movements in the field. The Israeli forces, under the surveillance of United Nations observers, had taken up their positions on the cease-fire line in conformity with the agreed map. In the light of the events of the last few days the Syrian jitters were understandable. Tabor said that he had consulted some of the permanent members of the Council as well as the Secretary-General, and they all shared his opinion that the situation did not warrant a new meeting.

In the course of the day, however, the Secretary-General received from his own sources in the area reports that an Israeli task force was moving beyond the cease-fire line in the direction of the little Syrian town, Sheikh Meskin. When my specific inquiry elicited only a vague reply from Jerusalem, I sent a strongly worded telegram to the Foreign Minister. I warned him of the grave international consequences of any infringement of the cease-fire agreement. Eban's reply was not long in coming. Firm orders had been issued to desist from any further military movements. The reports the Secretary-General had referred to stemmed from an attempt by some forward units to improve their positions.

The Syrian representative, obviously under pressure from Damascus, insisted on his request for a meeting of the Council. The President, after having held out for a few hours, yielded reluctantly and convened the Council for late Sunday evening. Although, by the time the meeting opened, there was no longer any reason for special agitation, and although the delegates were listless, the debate was nevertheless lively. Ambassador Fedorenko's absence was interpreted as a show of disapproval of Syria's unco-ordinated initiative. The seventh night of the Six Day War faded out in inconclusive debate. The military facts accomplished in the field remained unchanged for years to come.

When we returned late that night to the offices of our mission to report home about the abortive session, I found a telegram from Eban on my desk. He conveyed the government's deep appreciation to the head and members of our delegation on the steadfast course we had pursued in the political struggle. Our achievement in the international arena befitted the valour and victory of our fighting men in the field. Our resolute stand against the detractors of Israel had been warmly acclaimed at home. The cable ended with an invitation for a brief visit to Jerusalem to participate in consultations: 'We are on the point', wrote Eban, 'of taking fateful decisions affecting the future of the Middle East. Your presence here is vital to me and the Ministry.'

18

Consultations in Jerusalem

I arrived in Jerusalem late and tired on 13 June. Although I was expected to report to the Prime Minister and the Foreign Minister upon arrival, I felt an irresistible urge to visit the Old City first. We drove through the dismantled checkpoint at the Mandelbaum gate which had gained international fame as the only crossing-point between the two parts of the city, divided since 1948 when the Jordanian forces had captured eastern Jerusalem. The familiar guards and road-blocks had been removed as if by a magic wand. The driver continued through a maze of pitch-dark streets with complete self-assurance. 'You seem to know your way around here,' I said, impressed by his boldness. 'When did you drive here last?' I inquired cautiously. 'Twenty years ago,' he answered, driving on as if it had been yesterday. In a way I was glad he did not give the proverbial answer, 'Two thousand years ago.' After all the traffic regulations might have changed since. Indeed they had changed a few days before. The Israeli forces in command of east Jerusalem had imposed a strict ban on civilian driving and a complete night curfew. We soon encountered the raised hand of the new law. A sergeant stopped us, making his point nonchalantly but convincingly with his Uzi gun. 'Identity and authorization,' was his order. On the first we could oblige, but on the latter we were on rather weak ground. After he had examined my papers, he said benevolently: 'Ah, aren't you the guy who shook up that nasty Russian over there in New York. What's his name?' I misunderstood and replied obligingly: 'Gideon Rafael.' 'No,' he said, somewhat impatient with my lack of attention, 'I mean the other one.' 'Fedorenko' became the password. He waved us through, but warned us that we might run into trouble.

He was, of course, right. While my entire attention was absorbed by the unique experience of driving through old Jerusalem, so tangible now and so far removed from the table in the Council Chamber in New York, a flashlight suddenly signalled us to stop. A group of young officers and soldiers surrounded us. Introductions and explanations were to no avail. There was still sniping going on from time to time, the officer said. No unauthorized persons were allowed. Strict orders. Good-naturedly, the officer in charge enumerated his options. 'Under the curfew orders we could have shot you, but this could have caused a lot of uncontrolled shooting. And we want to keep it quiet here. So I must arrest you.' He scratched his head, contemplating the complexities of the situation and pronounced his judgement: 'Arresting is a hell of a lot of paperwork and a waste of time. So you'd better get out of here before I change my mind.' He escorted us to the checkpoint, where the sergeant greeted us with a broad grin and an 'I told you so'.

Abba Eban was full of understanding for the irresistible call of the Old City. Without losing any more time he plunged straight into the affairs of state. We first surveyed the course and outcome of our action in the United Nations since the eruption of the crisis in mid-May. We had fought the first two rounds of a political fight which none of us anticipated would continue for so many years. The first round had come to an abrupt end with the outbreak of the fighting on 5 June. We had failed to persuade the Secretary-General of the UN to reject Nasser's demand for the withdrawal of the United Nations Emergency Force from Sinai and Gaza. He had failed in his endeavours, supported by the United States and Britain, to impress upon Nasser the dangers involved in reinstating the maritime blockade at Sharm el-Sheikh. While it became evident that the war was inevitable, the Security Council dallied in debate and evaded action. But by exposing the Egyptian aggressive design and military preparations and biding our time, Israel had gained widespread public support and understanding in Washington.

The UN second round ended with the implementation of the cease-fire on all fronts on 10 June. The basic instruction which I had received at the beginning of this debate was to prevent, if possible until the arrival of the Foreign Minister, the adoption of a resolution by the Council. The government assumed that any resolution would automatically include a provision on the withdrawal of forces. Mindful of the disappointments of our struggle at the United Nations in the wake of the Sinai campaign in 1956, I outlined at the beginning of the fighting in 1967 the main objectives which should guide our delegation's work:

a. To provide Israel's army, Zahal, with sufficient time for a decisive elimination of the Egyptian military threat;

b. to prevent the adoption of any resolution calling for the withdrawal of forces prior to the establishment of peace;

c. to oppose any reconstruction of the collapsed armistice regime and urge its replacement by a lasting peace;

d. to co-operate closely with the United States, to avoid the re-activation of that fatal American-Russian vice which had cracked the position of America's friends and allies and enabled its foes to recuperate their strength.

The Arab states, on the other hand, staunchly supported by their Soviet allies, pursued three objectives, diametrically opposed to ours. After they had realized that the fortunes of war had turned against them they demanded:

a.   The immediate, unconditional and total withdrawal of Israel's forces from all the territories evacuated by the retreating Arab armies;
b.   the condemnation of Israel as aggressor;
c.   full compensation of the Arab states for all war damages.

It was a tall order. But in the light of their political success in 1956–7, they believed that joint American-Soviet action would again extricate them from the political and territorial consequences of their military defeat. Yet the United States had also drawn its own conclusions from previous experience. It had recognized that its policy in 1956 had advanced the Soviet aims of deepening its penetration of the Mediterranean area and the consolidation of its position in the Middle East. It had humiliated and estranged America's allies and resurrected Nasser, the implacable adversary of the West. Yet in 1967, after some brief wavering, the United States opposed the restoration of the dilapidated armistice regime and came out with growing determination for the complete termination of the state of war and the establishment of a just and lasting peace.

Eban concurred with this assessment and expressed his satisfaction at the close contacts we had maintained with the United States mission. This co-operation had strengthened substantially Israel's capacity to protect its diplomatic front-line. The Foreign Minster commented that the relationship of mutual trust and intimate consultation with the United States was the indispensable prerequisite for the attainment of Israel's central goal: the transformation of the Arab-Israeli confrontation into a state of good-neigh-bourly peaceful co-operation. He felt we had scored well in the second round. While the Arab states had failed to achieve any of their objectives, Israel had strengthened its positions. Yet a long uphill struggle was still ahead of us.

Prime Minister Levi Eshkol was alone in his office. Abba Eban and I reported to him on the state of affairs at the United Nations and listed a number of issues which, in our view, required the urgent attention of the government. Eshkol gave the impression that he was ready to grapple with the post-war problems in a practical and pragmatic way. To prepare the ground for a more formal cabinet discussion in the evening, he invited a select group of ministers to a meeting in the afternoon.

This meeting was held at the Prime Minister's residence and attended by Eban; Yigal Allon, then Deputy Prime Minister and Minister of Education; Moshe Dayan, Minister of Defence; Israel Galili, Minister Without Portfolio but not without influence of a singular but indefinable nature on all Prime Ministers under whom he served after Ben Gurion. Galili reached the peak of his clout during the premiership of Golda Meir. She regarded him as a fountain-head of statecraft and a master draftsman of ambivalent political statements. Among the small group of participants was also Professor Yigael Yadin, archaeologist and former Chief of Staff. Since the beginning of the crisis he had served as the Prime Minister's special adviser. It appeared that his functions were not limited to military matters, the field where he was thought to exert a moderating influence, but extended to all matters of state in which his experience was rather limited.

The deliberations centred basically on three questions. What immediate steps were to be taken to return the country to peace-time activity and to carry out the new reponsibilities in the Arab territories now under Israeli military administration? What were the prospects for Israeli peace initiatives? And how should we prepare for the political debate, expected to be renewed with full fury at the forthcoming Special United Nations General Assembly?

The discussion, true to Israel's political style, was rather freewheeling. Opinions were normally expressed with eruptive brevity or in the form of rambling dissertations. Dayan felt that the time was not yet ripe for peace moves. He thought that the Arabs were in a state of 'shell-shock', incapable of relating to the new realities. Eban strongly advocated an active peace policy. He claimed that if Israel were to miss the present opportunities, others would seize them with harmful consequences. Although we had succeeded in avoiding the adoption of a resolution calling for the withdrawal of forces, this issue still appeared at the top of the international agenda. Israel had to present peace proposals in order to influence the direction of future political decisions. Eshkol cautiously sided with Eban without committing himself at this stage to any definite programme of action. The general trend of the debate continued in the ensuing session of the cabinet security committee. The committee favoured the elaboration of peace aims and their early presentation. The prevailing opinion tended to accept the view that the attainment of peace warranted the return, with certain modifications, to the international boundaries between Israel, Egypt and Syria respectively. Opinions on the future territorial dispositions on the West Bank were less definite. Still, most of the participants favoured the restoration of the densely Arab-populated parts to Jordan. Minister Menachem Begin by and large did not differ from his colleagues on the territorial settlement with Egypt and Syria, although concerning the West Bank he opposed the adoption of any definite position at this time.

Summing up my report to the meeting I outlined three areas of particular international sensitivity, where the policies pursued by Israel could determine the measure of support we would be able to muster in the international arena. We were dealing with human, ideological and territorial problems. Firstly, the world, and especially our friends, would not tolerate the creation of a new Palestine refugee problem. Any action which could be interpreted as the encouragement of a second exodus would arouse strong anti-Israeli feeling.

Secondly, the question of Jerusalem was not only a matter of central significance for the Jewish people, but it was also apt to stir up deep-seated emotions in the Christian and Moslem world. It was of primary importance that the government proclaimed without delay its commitment to the safeguarding of freedom of worship and access to the holy places to all believers; its recognition of the existing rights of all the communities; the preservation of the religious *status quo* and the physical protection of the holy places. The situation in, and the fate of, Jerusalem commanded worldwide interest, not only motivated by the purity of religious sentiments, but also by the prejudice of feelings. In any peace negotiation Jerusalem might constitute the central problem, because it transcended the confines of the Arab-Israeli conflict. I advised the government to act in Jerusalem with circumspection and magnanimity, if it wished to obtain international acquiescence and the ultimate recognition of the old-new reality of Jewish sovereignty over the united city.

And thirdly, the territorial issue. I felt it did not become my station to give unsolicited advice to the government on the eventual configuration of Israel's map. I only pointed out that at this stage the international insistence on the evacuation of the 'territories occupied in the recent fighting' was stronger by far than the urge to transform the twenty-year-old state of war into permanent peace. The forces of restoration outnumbered the supporters of new beginnings in the United Nations by nearly two to one. But both sides were united in their objection to the endorsement of the newly created territorial situation. In these circumstances, I concluded, the only promising policy would be flexibility on withdrawal and firmness on peace.

The discussion, which had ranged over a wide field, touched at this early stage on the guarantees of free passage through the Suez Canal and the Straits of Tiran; the establishment of demilitarized zones as part of the final territorial settlement, and safeguards of access to the head waters of the Jordan on the Syrian border. Less than a week later, on 19 June, the government consolidated most of these ideas in a comprehensive plan which Foreign Minister Eban was authorized to submit as a first step to Secretary of State Dean Rusk.

Before my return to New York we discussed the composition of our delegation to the Special Assembly, due to open on 19 June. The Soviet Union, which had initiated its convocation, was reported to be considering the appointment of Prime Minister Kosygin as leader of its delegation. As a matter of fact they did send their strongest national team to the Assembly headed by Kosygin, who was flanked by Gromyko and an impressive selection of diplomatic stalwarts. They were supported by formidable delegations from the other Soviet bloc countries, mostly headed by their Prime Ministers.

Prime Minister Eshkol did not want to compete with them; he relied on his Foreign Minister. But others inside and outside the government discussed the idea that Eban should be accompanied by a group of ministers, led by Begin. It was sardonically referred to as a watchdog committee. Eban rebelled. He did not require a ministerial watch, nor was it clear to him who was meant to be the dog. He was already labelled as a dove and felt that too much zoology would not embellish Israel's image in the international arena. His firm refusal prevailed and the delegation was composed as usual of the permanent representative and a contingent of professional foreign service officers, assisted by a parliamentary advisory group.

19

Emergency Session

The United Nations Special Assembly opened in an air of tension and excitement which resembled the World Cup Final. Prime Minister Kosygin was honoured with the kick-off. He delivered his address, though full of political pep, with the monotonous voice of a town crier. It was as colourless as his general appearance. I had last seen him six weeks before, saluting the huge May Day parade from the top of the Lenin Mausoleum. He had stood there, motionless and ashen-faced. Only the next day did it become known that, the night before, his wife and life-long companion had succumbed to a long and incurable disease. The Soviet order of things made it impossible for him to absent himself from the festivities. The true reason would not be believed, but speculation that his non-appearance meant political disappearance would find widespread credence. For the preservation of his public life he had to forgo the privacy of mourning his wife's death.

Kosygin began his speech with a virulent condemnation of American intervention in the Congo, Cuba and Vietnam, climaxing in its collusion with Israel against the Arab states. Then he turned full blast against Israel, listing the whole register of Israel's sins according to the Soviet gospel. The famous ruling circles of Tel Aviv marched at the head of a long column, closely followed by sinister CIA battalions, pulling the wires of the misguided Israeli government. He did not deny Israel's right of existence, provided it followed the Soviet book of rules. It had to atone, until 'the consequences of its aggression were liquidated'. Liquidation is an ominous word in the Soviet vocabulary: whole ethnic minorities, millions of 'enemies of the state', returning prisoners of war, dissident intellectuals and unco-operative peasants have experienced its sinister meaning with their lives.

Concluding his address the Soviet Prime Minister asked the UN Assembly to return a verdict of guilty against Israel and to sentence it to unconditional and immediate withdrawal, condemnation as the aggressor and payment of reparations. The special UN session, although heavily stacked against Israel, deliberated for nearly two months, dismissing each and every one of the charges of the joint Soviet-Arab prosecution team.

The Russian propaganda planners had good reason to believe that the speech of the Prime Minister of the Soviet Union which had initiated the convocation of the Special Assembly would carry the day, at least on the front pages of the media. But they had neither accounted for the political agility of President Lyndon Johnson, nor the oratorical prowess of Foreign Minister Abba Eban. On the morning before the UN Assembly opened, Johnson made a surprise move. Without advance notice – politicians know how to keep secrets when it serves their purpose – the White House released the text of a speech President Johnson had made at a closed session of the National Foreign Policy Conference for Educators: 'During the past weekend at Camp David,' he opened his remarks, 'I thought of the General Assembly debate on the Middle East that opens now in New York.' Then he enunciated the five principles of American policy in the Middle East: the first and greatest principle was that every nation in the Middle East had a fundamental right to live in peace and be respected by its neighbours; secondly, a basic requirement for a settlement was justice for the refugees; thirdly, maritime rights of free passage through international waterways must be respected. 'If a single act of folly', said the President, 'was more responsible for this explosion than any other, it was the arbitary and dangerous decision announcing that the Straits of Tiran would be closed.'

The fourth principle President Johnson stated was that 'the responsibility for the arms race of the last twelve years rests not only on those in the area, but upon the larger states outside the area. Limits must be set on the wasteful and destructive arms race. The United States, for its part, will use every counsel of reason and prudence to find a better course.' Fifthly, the respect for the political independence and territorial integrity of all the states in the area could only become effective on the basis of peace between the parties. The nations of the region had had only fragile and violated truce lines for twenty years. What they now needed were recognized boundaries and other arrangements which would give them security against terror, destruction and war. 'Further,' he added, 'there must be adequate recognition of the special interest of the three great religions in the holy places of Jerusalem.'

The President concluded: 'These five principles, taken together, point the way from uncertain armistice to durable peace.' The well-timed presidential statement was widely acclaimed in the United States and sparked off a resounding echo throughout the world. The five principles have remained the fundamental tenets of American policy from L.B.J.'s reflective weekend at Camp David in 1967 to Jimmy Carter's lively summit meeting at the same presidential mountain retreat in 1978.

On stage
Abba Eban followed Kosygin on the rostrum with a powerful speech. We had expected the Foreign Minister to arrive from Jerusalem with a prepared text, but this was not his way of operating. Normally he would postpone his speech-writing to the very last minute. To deliver a great speech he apparently needed a sleepless night. Sitting in his hotel suite he filled page after page of yellow

legal pads with his neat handwriting, structuring his text with the precision of a master builder. His secretary passed the pages, one by one, to two typists located in an adjacent room. He competed with them in speed writing. Once part of the first draft was typed, it was passed on to me and one or two other friends for comment. Eban generally accepted changes and corrections easily, and would rarely argue or ponder, since time pressed. He would enter in his own hand the comments he agreed to, and those he rejected he would politely acknowledge and ignore. Since he always wrote abundantly, he did not mind suggestions to eliminate whole pages. With a generous gesture he would cross them out or tear them up, no author's pride hurt.

Exhausted from his travels and travails, Eban decided at dawn to catch some sleep and to complete the draft in time for the opening session of the Assembly. The hours advanced, but we could not get through to him. He was either sleeping or writing in absolute seclusion. 'He is capable of doing both at the same time,' wryly observed our press officer, who was in agony because media coverage required the advance distribution of the text and the demand for Eban's speech was naturally high. Shortly after 10 a.m. he emerged, scrubbed, shaved and composed, with a sizeable stack of sheaves in his hand. He seemed to be unaware that during the last few hours there had been an interruption in his production line, because he asked for our comments on parts of the text we had never seen. 'So you'll hear it,' he said laconically.

And indeed we heard it, and so did a rapt audience of delegates in the crowded Assembly hall. Kosygin, wired to his translation set, followed attentively. Unlike his predecessor, Khrushchev, he kept his shoes on and his temper controlled even when Eban accused the Soviet government of complicity with Arab aggression. At about 1 p.m. Kosygin left the hall while Eban was still speaking. The heads of the delegates turned to watch the prime ministerial procession. Rumour mills started to grind with high speed: Soviet Prime Minister left in protest; Russian attitude will harden. How much more it could harden was left to unsubstantiated speculation. The Soviet delegation soon informed inquiring reporters that Mr Kosygin had to leave to be in time for a luncheon engagement. We accepted this version with considerable relief. It was inconceivable to us that any civilized person would voluntarily detach himself from the spell of Eban's eloquence.

In the General Assembly, the Arab-Soviet coalition vigorously pursued their offensive which had been halted in the Security Council. They were determined to attain their three objectives: condemnation, compensation and evacuation. When they failed to mobilize the necessary votes for their extremist proposals, they sent their strategic reserves into the field. Yugoslavia, together with a number of delegations traditionally aligned with the Arab states, introduced a new draft resolution which, though more moderate in form and wording, aimed at the same central objective: unconditional Israeli withdrawal without an equivalent Arab advance towards peace. A group of Latin American countries adopted an intermediary position. They advocated that the termination of the state of war must precede the withdrawal of forces.

At the United Nations the Soviet government, ardent antagonist of religion in its own realm, joined the most fervent defenders of the faith in propagating religious rights in Jerusalem. News of legislation planned by the Knesset to extend Israel's jurisdiction over east Jerusalem made the temperature of the Assembly debate soar. Eban advised the government to proceed with prudence and refrain from any ostentatious action. He was supported in his strongly-worded plea by all the members of the Knesset advisory group, including the late Ben-Elieser, one of the most prominent leaders of the Herut Party. But the mood in Jerusalem was now or never, and the Knesset adopted the law at the end of June. It was not the first or the last time in Israel's young history that the government at home disregarded the opinion of its Foreign Minister conveyed from an important vantage-point abroad.

The plight of refugees moving eastward over the Jordan river understandably evoked feelings of compassion. In an era where television can carry human suffering right into the homes and hearts of every citizen, neither private persons nor public bodies can escape its impact. But the United Nations distinguished itself more by the selectivity of its compassion than by the universality of its humanity. It could leap into feverish activity to castigate abuses when the object of its just scorn was politically isolated, and then ignore unspeakable outrages when the perpetrators belonged to a powerful bloc of member states.

The plight of Arab refugees was one of the issues of manifest United Nations ambivalence. Wars and upheavals, wherever they occurred, have caused the tragic displacement of multitudes of people and have sometimes uprooted entire populations. Refugees are the tragic consequence of the inhumanity of war or of violent revolutionary change. They are the straggling witnesses of disaster inflicted by men upon men. The United Nations served as a potent catalyst in the transformation of the Arab refugee problem from a humanitarian issue of no wider scope than most of the post-war migrations, into an intractable political problem. Inexhaustible debates and repetitive resolutions dehumanized an essentially humanitarian and manageable problem and turned it into a weapon of war. Refugee camps maintained by United Nations relief organizations became military installations; storehouses were used as arms depots and United Nations-supported schools as drill grounds for military and doctrinal instruction, to hate and fight Jews. Arab governments which had considered the refugees a convenient tool in their struggle against Israel, became the first victims of their militarization. Throughout the 1970s Jordan and Lebanon carried the main brunt of the terrible in-fighting.

However, the principal sufferers remained the immovable mass of the Palestinian refugees themselves. Abused by their leaders, deprived of human dignity, depressed by hopelessness and tossed back and forth between the fighting fronts, they became a heavy political liability to some of the Arab governments and a weighty moral obligation for the humanitarian-minded part of the world community. Pictures appearing day after day on the front pages of the press and on television screens of refugees leaving their homes in the wake of the fighting on the West Bank, heightened the vehemence of the Assembly debate. Mounting international resentment began to cast a shadow over the sympathy Israel had enjoyed in the hour of its triumph. Constant American reminders, presented with growing impatience, had a restraining effect on the more activist organs of the military administration.

Behind the scenes

On stage the debate in the General Assembly tottered between recrimination and rebuttal, rarely sobered by a sprinkle of constructive thought. But the real action took place behind the scenes. Two days after the opening of the Special General Assembly Abba Eban was received by Dean Rusk at his suite in the Waldorf Towers. Ambassador Goldberg was assisting the Secretary of State; the Foreign Minister was accompanied by Abe Harman, the Israeli ambassador in Washington, and myself, permanent representative to the United Nations. Eban had been directed by the government to discuss the practical proposals for a peace settlement, which the cabinet had formulated a day after his departure for New York. When he received the telegram conveying the detailed summary, Eban was pleasantly surprised at its moderation. The proposals followed the lines of the cabinet discussion which I had attended a few days earlier in Jerusalem. But in their written rendition they impressed us not only by their decisiveness, but also by their soberness. The government had clearly subordinated territorial claims to the postulates of peace. The plan was based on the original international boundaries which had existed between British-administered Palestine and Egypt and Syria respectively. In the context of a peace treaty, Israel envisaged only such changes which security considerations in the south and the unimpaired free flow of the Jordan headwaters in the north necessitated. It contained provisions for the demilitarization of the evacuated areas and confirmed the government's readiness to consider a special status for the protection of, and free access to, the holy places in Jerusalem. On the future dispositions in the West Bank the cabinet had decided to make a pronouncement at a later stage, as the coalition partners had been unable to reach a consent. There were two conceptions on this: the first based on the assumption that there would be the possibility of an agreed settlement with King Hussein; and the second that there should be an association between the West Bank and Israel, involving autonomy for the West Bank and economic union. In this case the West Bank would be separated from Transjordan, and the government was looking into the constitutional precedents of such a solution. Rusk's response was brief and to the point: 'There is a constitutional precedent for letting people themselves decide.' This issue has remained ever since a bone of contention in Israel's internal and external policy.

The Secretary of State was visibly impressed by the realism and moderation of the proposals. His comments centred on two points: not 'to sell King Hussein short' and the question of Jerusalem. In his view Hussein had much more staying power than many of his foes or friends would concede. Though he had committed a great error in disregarding Israel's plea to stay out of the war, he might in due course prove his mettle as a man of peace. But Jerusalem, warned Rusk, was the most sensitive of all outstanding issues, which could potentially arouse strong anti-semitism. This remark grated on our ears, more so as the Secretary of State did not deem it necessary to dissociate himself personally from the spectre he evoked. He referred to deep-seated Christian sentiments which Jewish rule might antagonize. Eban reminded him curtly that during nineteen years of Jordanian Moslem rule over Jerusalem, which was internationally illegal and locally arbitrary, the Church had shown remarkable restraint in its sentiments.

The second part of the conversation dealt with strategy and tactics in the General Assembly. We counselled that the main objective should not be the adoption of a compromise resolution, because there was no common denominator between those who wanted to perpetuate a state of war and those who sought to establish a lasting peace. The inconclusive termination of the Special Assembly, convened by Soviet initiative, would serve as an object lesson to all those states which relied on Soviet political muscle to bail them out from self-inflicted *débâcles*. The United States delegation was not convinced that the Assembly would disperse without adopting a resolution. It aimed at the appointment of a UN special representative lending his good offices to the parties.

A futile compromise

By mid-July the debates of the Emergency Assembly and the behind-the-scenes diplomatic wrangling had reached a deadlock. Two opposing concepts were in conflict with no compromise in sight; neither side could muster the required voting majority. The Arab-Soviet bloc insisted on the restoration of the pre-June situation. On the other side a powerful group of delegations, led by the United States and composed mainly of pro-Western states and a number of developing countries, supported initiatives meant to bring the Arab-Israeli conflict to an ultimately peaceful conclusion. When the Soviet delegation realized that its diplomatic and propaganda offensive was doomed to failure, the Soviet ambassador in Washington, Anatoly Dobrynin, a crafty diplomat and old United Nations hand, contacted the Secretary of State in an effort to break the deadlock. He suggested a new formula, waiving demands for the condemnation of Israel and reparations for the Arab states. His proposal focused on the principal Arab-Soviet objective: the immediate withdrawal of all Israeli forces from all the territories in return for a vague and noncommittal undertaking by the Arab states to relinquish their active hostility.

Dean Rusk, well versed in Soviet negotiating practices, is said to have replied: 'What you are suggesting, Mr Ambassador, is to trade a horse for a rabbit.' Dobrynin asked for clarification. After all, when diplomacy deals in zoological terms – an innovation entered into the political vocabulary during the Cuban crisis – some scientific precision is not out of place. The Secretary of State explained that the horse was the Israeli withdrawal and the rabbit was the trifle the Soviet government was offering in exchange. But American diplomacy also abided by another rule which is always good politics: never dismiss a probing exercise until you know exactly what the other side is ultimately aiming at. Dean Rusk, therefore, suggested that Ambassador Goldberg should be available for further contacts with Soviet representatives in New York.

Dobrynin and Goldberg met on 18 July. They tried to work out a mutually acceptable draft. But their main difference centred around the 'horse-rabbit' equation. In conformity with President Johnson's five points the American representative insisted that withdrawal must be subject to a definite termination of the state of war. His Soviet negotiating partner, however, argued that though the USSR favoured this objective, its Arab friends, unfortunately, refused to accept a draft which explicitly stipulated the cessation of belligerence.

Our delegation viewed a gradual erosion of the American position with growing concern. We intervened strongly in New York and Washington to arrest the dangerous drift. The American desire, however, to reach a parliamentary understanding with the Soviet Union in the United Nations was, as matters stood, a more attractive proposition for the State Department than the adherence to a firm position favouring the promotion of lasting peace between Israel and the Arab states. It appeared that the professionals had little faith in its prospects.

To bolster its negotiating strength, the Soviet government circulated information repeatedly through 'reliable channels' that it would not remain indifferent to the continued occupation of Arab territories and would take appropriate steps in case the political efforts failed. The United States, deeply and painfully involved in Vietnam and torn at home by the war, felt that it should proceed with great caution in other international crises. It preferred a dubious diplomatic compromise to additional foreign complications. Moreover, there were American policy experts who believed that an accommodation with the Soviet Union would curb its expansionist ambitions in the Mediterranean area.

We had reason to conclude that these considerations had guided the State Department in directing Ambassador Goldberg to seek an American-Soviet compromise formula. When the talks with Ambassador Dobrynin failed to produce the desired result, Foreign Minister Gromyko took over personally. Eventually both sides agreed on a draft which was much closer to the Soviet position than to the policy enunciated by President Johnson. Both parties to the bargain were aware that their real differences had simply been papered over. As we learned later, at the end of the talks Gromyko suggested to Goldberg that they should agree on the wording and differ on its interpretation.

Our delegation heard officially of the American change of direction only on the morning after the transaction, when it was presented with the text of the agreed draft resolution. We were stunned by its wording:

The General Assembly:
1. Declares that peace and final solutions of this problem can be achieved within the framework of the Charter of the UN.
2. Affirms the principles under the Charter of:
   A. Withdrawal without delay by the parties to the conflict from territories occupied by them, in keeping with the inadmissibility of conquest of territory by war.
   B. Acknowledgement without delay by all member-states of the United Nations in the area: that each enjoys the right to maintain an independent national state of its own and to live in peace and security; and renunciation of all claims and acts inconsistent therewith.
3. Requests the Security Council to continue examining the situation in the Middle East with a sense of urgency, working directly with the parties and utilizing the United Nations presence to achieve an appropriate and just solution of all aspects of the problem, in particular bringing to an end the long-deferred problem of the refugees and guaranteeing freedom of transit through international waterways.

The reversal of the American position was the most hazardous of the many fluctuations of our political fortunes that we had encountered since the outbreak of the war. The United States, in its attempt to close the gap between its own and the opposing Soviet position, had departed from its proclaimed policy. This was a move we considered as dangerous to Israel's future as it was detrimental to the prospects of peace in the Middle East. The joint draft dispensed not only with the call for a lasting peace, but even with the demand for the termination of the state of war. It placed all its emphasis on a precipitate withdrawal of Israel's forces. The United States after all had come dangerously close to buying Dobrynin's rabbit.

A heated argument

We felt we had to meet the emergency head-on. Eban asked for an urgent meeting with Arthur Goldberg. He received us in his office, flanked by Joe Sisco, the Assistant Secretary of State in charge of International Organizations, and Dick Pedersen, a member of the US mission. Eban was not in the mood for preliminaries. He started from the end. The American-Soviet accord flouted the understanding which had existed between us. It made the five points of the President unrecognizable. While we had been told time and again that Israel should not evacuate a single inch of the occupied territories as long as the Arab states refused to conclude peace, the United States was now negotiating nebulous formulations which on the one hand stressed Israeli withdrawal and on the other did not commit the Arab side to take any positive practical action. The Soviet-American exchanges were likely to undermine our joint parliamentary position in the United Nations. The Soviet objectives were obvious. They meant unconditional withdrawal presented on a paper plate inscribed with a few meaningless slogans. To sum up, Eban flatly declared, nobody should be misled into believing that Israel would withdraw its forces on the basis of the draft which Ambassador Goldberg had worked out with the Soviet representatives.

Arthur Goldberg did not hide his dismay at the fury of Eban's charge, but replied with restraint. He explained how Washington assessed the situation, and how he interpreted the wording of the draft resolution. It was not the parliamentary constellation at the Special Session alone, but fundamental American interest in the peace and security of the Middle East which compelled the United States to explore any Soviet initiative likely to promote these aims. The draft did not change the policy proclaimed by the President. America aimed to encourage the more moderate and reasonable Arab governments to proceed on their own on the road to reconciliation with Israel. The resolution would require the Arab states to make public statements recognizing Israel's right to independent statehood. They would have to renounce all claims and actions incompatible with such recognition. The resolution would not harm Israel, but rather split the moderates from the extremists in the Arab world.

Ambassador Goldberg had tried his diplomatic and forensic best to soften the blow, but Eban went back to the charge. It was not an unlikely rift in the Arab camp at the expense of vital Israeli needs which interested us, but the true purpose of the Soviet exercise which was to drive a wedge between the United States and Israel.

Goldberg preferred to terminate the conversation on a more hopeful note. He would exert his influence to wind up the Special Assembly until the end of the week. In seeing us out, and apparently in a last effort to relieve our anger, he predicted that nothing would come of Soviet-American negotiations. His guess proved true, not so much from American reluctance to make concessions, but rather from Arab refusal to accept compromises.

Goldberg must have felt a bit piqued by the forcefulness of Eban's intervention, but he kept his feelings to himself. Only after the General Assembly had dispersed did he casually bring the matter up. 'Do you people really believe that I do not know how to negotiate? All my adult life I have been a negotiator of labour disputes', he turned to me. 'You both rather over-reacted at the time.' I thought I had to find a good-humoured way to close the lingering discord. 'Arthur,' I said, 'you are nationally and internationally famous as one of the best labour negotiators, and we admire you. But, I believe there is a slight difference between negotiating with General Motors and dealing with the Soviet Union. In industry the employers may differ with labour on wages and terms, but both pursue a common interest – to manufacture goods. The people in Detroit want to build cars which are steady on the road, but the designers of Moscow try to construct conveyances which produce road accidents.' Ambassador Goldberg took it in good spirit: 'Don't worry, over the years I have learnt to drive Soviet cars.'

The stage was set for a grand finale of the Emergency Session. The Soviet delegation undertook to secure Arab assent to the terms of the joint draft resolution, but Gromyko was in for a surprise. The Arab delegations rejected the proposal. The Algerian and Syrian delegations led the opposition and Egypt felt bound to follow suit. Their negative stand spelt the doom of the Soviet-American compromise and relieved Israel from a perilous diplomatic dilemma. When this last effort had failed the Special Assembly decided to wind up its session without further ado. At the end of two months of parliamentary tug-of-war, the balance-sheet showed a substantial deficit for Israel's adversaries.

Consultations with Washington

The danger of disagreements, highlighted by the Soviet-American negotiations, prompted the Foreign Minister to direct the Israeli represen-tatives in Washington and New York to request the State Department to enter into substantive talks with us on the co-ordination of future policies at the United Nations and in the capitals. The meetings took place in Washington and New York in the second half of August. They were chaired by Ambassador Goldberg, who was assisted by the Deputy Undersecretary of State, Eugene Rostow, and the Assistant Secretary for Middle East Affairs, Lucius Battle.

Despite the failure of previous American-Soviet negotiation attempts, Washington was not averse to renewing its contacts with the Soviet delegation. For such a second try the State Department had prepared a revised draft. It decided to consult Israel first, to avoid another round of misunderstandings, before circulating the new proposal. With the exception of London, so the officials in Washington assured us, no other government had seen the draft.

Israel's reaction to the new draft was pointedly negative. A senior official of the Foreign Ministry in Jerusalem had warned the American ambassador – easy-going, good-natured and sharp-minded Walworth Barbour – that with such a proposal the United States would embark on a collision course with Israel. The Secretary of State personally felt offended by such language and even the President later referred to it in anger in a meeting with Abba Eban. In our talks with Ambassador Goldberg and his colleagues we preferred to present Israel's reservations in a style more befitting the close friendly relationship between the two countries.

Our objections focused on three points. The draft referred to the withdrawal of forces in a way which lent itself to being interpreted to mean withdrawal to the defunct armistice lines. It did not ask the parties to negotiate a settlement. It defined a United Nations presence in terms which were likely to make it again a surrogate for a permanent peace, or a cover for continued belligerence. Moreover the new American draft contained the ominous formula of 'the inadmissibility of conquest of territory by war'. We again went over the arguments to make our case against the inadmissibility of this doubtful principle in relation to the Six Day War. Israel had fought in defence of its sovereignty and protection of its security. We recalled that the West Bank and the Gaza Strip had come under Jordanian and Egyptian rule as the result of their military intervention in 1948 against the fledgling State of Israel. If there were any justification for the application of that doctrine, it should be applied to these territories. Rostow admitted the cogency of our argument and pointed out that the United States had never recognized Jordan's frontiers on the West Bank as its final boundaries. Furthermore President Johnson, in turning down a recent one-sided peace proposal conveyed to him by Tito, had stated 'that withdrawal of Israeli forces to agreed and secured national boundaries' should be effected only as part of an overall Arab-Israeli settlement.

We argued against the advisability of the United States soliciting the co-operation of the Soviet Union at the United Nations. Their aims in the Middle East were widely divergent. Signs of Arab distrust and Soviet disillusionment marred Arab-Soviet harmony. Future developments in Soviet-Arab relations would be influenced by three factors: lack of capacity to dislodge the Israeli forces by military means; a fading belief in the possibility of achieving this through United Nations action; and a firm public posture by the United States stressing the continued validity of President Johnson's five principles. An American-Soviet compromise resolution would only revive Soviet and Arab illusions that Israel could be forced to withdraw without a negotiated settlement. It was inconceivable, we argued, that the transition to a new politico-juridical relationship and to a new map of recognized and permanent boundaries could be made without a process of negotiation between Israel and the Arab states.

In these talks Ambassador Goldberg and his colleagues conveyed to us the American assessment of the international implications of the situation. They involved global strategic United States requirements, bilateral relations with the Soviet Union, sizeable interest in the Arab East and tactical considerations at the United Nations. In substance, we were assured, the United States subscribed to Israel's ultimate aspiration to replace the fragile armistice structure with an edifice of permanent peace. But the vicissitudes encountered at the United Nations required tactical and semantic compromises which did not alter America's will to pursue its basic policy. The importance of American interests in the Middle East made it necessary not to alienate moderate Arab governments while securing Israel's basic security and national well-being. The perils and prospects inherent in the relations between the United States and the Soviet Union made it imperative to maintain a dialogue between the two governments on matters of world concern. Even if joint action was doubtful, separate miscalculation was dangerous. The United States was extremely reluctant to see the Soviets create in the Middle East a new 'Cuban crisis' as the result of lack of contact with them on one of the central issues of the area.

In surveying the current Middle East situation, Eugene Rostow and Luke Battle stressed that King Hussein had regained strength and was credited with considerable staying-power. He was interested in peace talks with Israel. Egypt's economic situation was assessed as 'nearly desperate'. Both estimates proved correct: King Hussein retained his rule and Egypt's economic situation remained calamitous. Our American interlocutors also explained that the British government was pressing hard for an arrangement to enable the reopening of the Suez Canal. We could confirm this from our personal experience. In lively talks between our Foreign Minister and the British Foreign Secretary, George Brown as usual did not mince his words when recounting the losses the closure of the canal was causing his country. Once, in the heat of the argument, I felt it opportune to dampen his ardour. Apologizing for my ignorance, I asked why Britain did not follow the example of other shipbuilding nations, such as Japan and the Scandinavian countries, and build supertankers in its under-employed shipyards. George Brown's reddish complexion turned purple. I was ready for one of his famous high-decibel outbursts. Pointing his finger at his Foreign Office entourage he shouted: 'Listen to that. It makes sense, what the ambassador says. This is what I told you chaps in London when you came pestering me with your bloody canal. But you turned me down. I won't have any more of that.'

At the conclusion of our talks Ambassador Goldberg assured us that, while Washington was not committing itself to abandoning its initiative, it would not proceed without further consultation with Israel. When the regular session of the General Assembly convened in September, the United States had shelved its plan. The Soviet reaction had been frosty, the Arab rejection icy and the Israeli opposition heated.

The great Soviet summer offensive had ended like Haydn's famous symphony, where one player after the other, after having finished his part, extinguishes the flickering candle and withdraws. Mr Kosygin had returned to Moscow shortly after he had realized that the American President was not inclined to sacrifice either Israel or his Middle East peace policy for the sake of a Soviet-American deal. Mr Gromyko was the last to go home, after all his moves had been checkmated.

Behind the scenes, however, diplomatic activity continued. Lord Caradon, Britain's permanent representative, led the group of activists. Early in October, he presented a draft resolution to the Israeli delegation. It was a kind of jigsaw puzzle which he had pieced together from bits of the defunct Gromyko-Goldberg formula, seasoned with ingredients of a forgotten Latin-American draft and topped with the idea of appointing a special United Nations representative to act as mediator. Yet Lord Caradon's new model was a non-starter. It did not commend itself either to Israel or to other delegations.

The diplomatic probings proceeded in a leisurely atmosphere, until the calm was suddenly broken on 21 October by the dramatic news that the Israeli destroyer *Eilat* had been sunk by a Soviet-made and Egyptian-launched missile. When Israel responded by shelling the refineries at Port Suez on 24 October, the Security Council was called into urgent session.

That same day President Lyndon Johnson vented his views in a freewheeling conversation with Abba Eban. He claimed that the further we got away from the territorial situation which had prevailed on 5 June, the further we moved away from peace. He was not happy that Israel had disregarded his advice before 5 June and had taken up arms, but he admitted that the provocation had been very great. Now the Soviets were trying to get a grip on all of the Middle East. They had suffered a humiliation in June 1967 and might try to recoup their positions. In the days following the outbreak of the war he had had to make some awesome decisions. The Israelis believed that the United States had influence on the Soviets and the Arabs believed that it had great clout with Israel. Both were wrong.

Eban reminded the President that the United States had proved its influence with the Russians when it got them to keep their hands off the area during the war. L.B.J. admitted that moving the US fleet 300 miles eastward 'had not harmed the situation', but he stressed that the mood of the United States was to withdraw from foreign commitments.

The two incidents – the sinking of the destroyer and the shelling of the refineries – raised the Middle East temperature to a degree which the Big Powers considered perilously inflammable. The international community was seized with anxiety that the cease-fire was about to collapse. The denial of access to water resources and the interference with free passage through waterways on the one hand, and the threat to the free flow of oil on the other, have been in recent decades the principal causes of military conflagrations in the area.

20
Resolution 242

The military incidents in Egypt stimulated the slow-moving diplomatic activity. The Soviet Union dispatched to New York its First Deputy Foreign Minister – Vasili Kuznetsov, a skilful and respected negotiator. He took over from Fedorenko who had allegedly been blamed by his government for the fiasco of the Soviet initiative. A day after the Special Assembly had fizzled out, Fedorenko ran into me in the delegates' lounge. He stopped and stretched out his hand. 'After all', he said, 'we are all human beings. In the Security Council we act in accordance with the instructions we receive from our governments. Let's shake hands.' I looked at him with some surprise and replied: 'I have no difficulty in returning your greeting. I am the same human being in the lobby as I am in the Council chamber.' With a sour smile he gripped my hand. A few months later Fedorenko was replaced as permanent representative and vanished into the oblivion of the vast Soviet Union.

Kuznetsov began his special assignment in Washington by informing the Secretary of State that the Arab governments were now prepared to accept the Gromyko-Goldberg formula and for good measure added his warning that the Middle East was nearing a new blow-up, a situation in which the Soviet Union could not remain indifferent. The United States, undeterred by the failure of the other members of the Security Council to agree on a joint course of action, pursued its independent efforts to enlist support for a resolution of its own drafting. On 7 November, when the American diplomatic activity was in full swing, the Egyptian delegation made a surprise move. It called for an urgent meeting of the Security Council. The United States delegation was deeply disappointed by Egypt's unexpected action, because Ambassador Goldberg had been engaged in secret and searching talks with the Egyptian Foreign Minister Mahmoud Riad, and with King Hussein who was in New York at the time. Goldberg had obtained the consent of the King to the principles and formulations of the American draft, after he had assured himself in advance that his point of view was shared by Nasser with whom he had co-ordinated his moves at a meeting in Cairo on 17 September. In their conversations with the Egyptian Foreign Minister, the American representatives were led to believe that he was anxious to come to an agreement with them on an acceptable draft resolution. The United States delegates realized later that, while they were holding their talks with Riad, he was at the same time urging the Indian delegation to proceed with the preparation of their own pro-Arab draft and to introduce it without any prior notice.

The morning Ambassador Goldberg learnt that the Egyptian delegation intended to spring its surprise, he tried to forestall them by tabling the United States draft resolution so as to ensure its priority of voting. To be fair he contacted me before going ahead. I asked him to hold off for an hour or so until I had clearance from Jerusalem, because my government had previously expressed serious reservations about the American text. In the light of the new parliamentary situation created by the Egyptian move, I urged the government to forgo its objections; but the Prime Minister, or whoever advised him, was not impressed by the urgency of the situation. I informed Goldberg of the negative reply. He did not conceal his anger: during the two hours we had been stalling, India had introduced its draft resolution and gained priority for it. A situation had been created which was to cause us and our friends many unnecessary difficulties. Golda Meir, who was in New York on a fund-raising mission, was present when I spoke with Goldberg. She was not then a member of the government and was puzzled by the government's lack of understanding, commenting that Jerusalem should have relied on Arthur Goldberg's judgement and my advice. She wondered whether it had been at all necessary for me to consult Jerusalem. I wondered how she would have reacted when she was Foreign Minister if her ambassador had acted on his own initiative in a similar situation. I knew the answer without asking.

When the Council met on 9 November it had before it the two rival draft resolutions, from America and India. The Indian draft appeared to have better prospects than the American. At that time the United States still refrained from using the ultimate United Nations weapon, the veto, to block unacceptable draft resolutions; it relied instead on its power of persuasion. It was obvious to most of the delegations that under the circumstances any resolution opposed by the United States and rejected by Israel would carry no real political weight and exert little influence on the situation in the Middle East.

In the face of this dilemma, Lord Caradon decided that the time was ripe to manifest his diplomatic skill and zeal, and try to bridge the gap between the two opposing draft resolutions. He now came forward with a proposal based in its essentials on the American draft, adding wording from former texts and some variations on the Indian resolution. Intrinsically, the new British design was not much different from the American model. It contained, however, two important modifications: a provision on 'the inadmissibility of the acquisition of territory by war' and the principle of agreement and acceptability by the parties which the United Nations Special Representative was instructed to promote. Lord Caradon incorporated the 'inadmissibility' clause, to forestall a separate Argentinian-Brazilian initiative which was likely to jeopardize his endeavours to secure a unanimously acceptable compromise. If the idea of the inadmissibility of the acquisition of territory by war was to have any meaning, it could relate only to territorial conquests resulting from wars of aggression. Caradon's clause, included only for the sake of parliamentary convenience, became in later years one of the main bones of contention in the interpretation and implementation of the resolution. The Soviet Union, which had acquired more territory by war than any other nation in recent history, posed at the United Nations as one of the most zealous champions of the principle of the unalterability of frontiers. Admittedly, it had been the victim of Nazi aggression and derived from it the justification of its territorial acquisitions. But so had Israel been subjected to unrelenting Arab warfare from the first day of its regained independence. But under the rules of Soviet dialectics, what was allowed to Russia in Eastern Europe was forbidden to Israel in the Middle East. To comply with the minimal demands of political logic, Soviet propaganda applied its long practised process of dialectic alchemy. It transmuted the victim of aggression into the aggressor.

After arduous and sometimes tense discussions between Lord Caradon and the representatives of Israel and the United States respectively, it was agreed that the resolution ought to reflect five guiding principles:

1. The establishment of a just and lasting peace between Israel and the Arab states was to constitute the central objective of the resolution;
2. withdrawal of Israeli forces to secure and recognized boundaries should take place when agreed upon within the terms of a freely negotiated peace treaty;
3. unrestricted freedom of navigation through all international waterways in the area must be ensured;
4. a just solution of the refugee problem should be found;
5. a United Nations Special Representative would be authorized to render his good offices to the parties, but not to act independently as mediator or arbitrator.

One difference between the American and British draft was the curious omission in the British text of the American provision 'to limit the wasteful and destructive arms race in the area'. The reason for the elimination has never been made clear. The suggestion that it was excluded in deference to Soviet intentions, to replenish the depleted Arab arsenals, ran against the fact that a Soviet draft resolution presented at the final stage of the debate included an almost identical provision to halt the arms race.

Before the British draft resolution reached the voting stage, the Arab delegations, strongly supported by the Soviet Union, made an all-out effort to alter the withdrawal paragraph. They demanded that the resolution should explicitly call upon Israel to withdraw *all its* forces *from all the* occupied territories. Lord Caradon tried to work out a compromise which would have altered the whole thrust of the resolution by the insertion of a single three-letter word, the definite article 'the', so that the text would read: 'withdrawal of Israeli forces from *the territories*'. He appeared disappointed when he encountered a resolute rejection from Israel and the United States of any alterations of the text.

When the Security Council reconvened on 17 November, the Soviet Deputy Foreign Minister made a brief and carefully worded statement which took everybody by surprise. He stressed that the Soviet Union supported the inalienable right of every state in the Middle East, including Israel, to national and independent existence. This was meant to be the prelude to his adamant demand that Israel must withdraw its forces from all the occupied territories. It was a well-tested practice of Soviet negotiators to wear out their opponents by prolonging the negotiating process until every political, tactical, psychological and propaganda ploy had been brought into full play. Only after they had reached the firm conclusion that the position of the other side was unalterable, would they yield, either step by step, or in a swift and final turnabout. The Soviet delegation continued its parliamentary war of attrition, even after it had become evident that Egypt and Jordan were prepared to accept the British draft without any changes. The Foreign Minister of Romania, who served as President of the General Assembly and was an expert in Soviet diplomatic tactics, assured us that, in the final analysis, the Soviet Union would vote in favour of the British draft resolution as it stood.

During a two days' interlude in the Council's debates, requested by the Soviet government, Moscow made a concerted effort to persuade Washington to accept the wording: 'withdrawal *from all the* occupied territories'. It carried its fight for the definite article to the highest level in Washington. When President Johnson politely but firmly declined, Chairman Kosygin proposed as a last resort to let the word 'all' fall by the wayside and agree to the wording: 'withdrawal from *the* occupied territories'. In his message of 21 November to President Johnson, Chairman Kosygin outlined the conditions under which the Soviet Union would vote together with the United States for the British draft resolution. Israel 'as the aggressor would have to withdraw its forces to the pre-war lines of June the fourth'; this would be the first necessary step to attain peace in the Middle East. 'If the President were sincere in what he was saying, he would agree to the Chairman's proposal', the message concluded. Kosygin's doubt in his sincerity aroused L.B.J.'s indignation. He shot back that what he meant he had said with clarity in his statement on 19 June and in the various pronouncements made by Ambassador Goldberg. This was the time to begin the peace effort and high time for the Soviet government to help promote a lasting peace in the Middle East. The President felt that the continuation of these messages would not serve any useful purpose. And as a parting shot he added: 'Peace will not be made in the corridors of the United Nations. It will be made if the parties reason together.'

When the Security Council reconvened on 22 November to take the vote, the Soviet representative raised his hand with his American colleague and all the other delegates in favour of the unamended British draft which entered into the annals of international diplomacy as 'Security Council Resolution 242'. The most conspicuous omission in Resolution 242 was any reference to the Palestinian people. The exclusion was deliberate. As a matter of fact, the term 'Palestine' appeared nowhere in the resolution. The sponsors of Resolution 242 were fully aware of the Arab design to forge the refugee problem into a formidable political weapon. They declined to support this pernicious intention, even if presented in ostensibly innocent wording. The resolution was meant to be a set of guide-lines for the establishment of a just and lasting peace between the Arab states and Israel, and to be the master key which would unlock a conflict which had endured for twenty years. It has shown an unexpected resistance to wear and tear in a swiftly changing world situation, enduring even the shock of the Yom Kippur War.

Ever since its adoption, Resolution 242 has dominated the diplomatic scene in the Middle East as the only accepted, though differently interpreted, common denominator. After the Yom Kippur War a companion piece was introduced in the form of Resolution 338, which prescribed the immediate opening of direct negotiations. Thirty years of hostility had to pass, four wars be fought and tens of thousands of dead be mourned, before Egypt and Israel moved from the battlefield to the negotiating table.

Part Four

CONCILIATION

21

The Jarring Mission

Resolution 242, although elaborate in its guide-lines, was austere in its operative instructions. It contained a single paragraph calling for the appointment of a United Nations Special Representative and defining his terms of reference. Secretary-General U Thant gave much thought to the choice of a suitable candidate. In consultations with us he mused about the widely supported nomination of the Finnish permanent representative, Per Jacobson, but found him unsuitable. He explained with disarming but disturbing candour that he was unacceptable to the Arabs because of his Jewish origin. Ralph Bunche, the highest-ranking black UN official, a Nobel prize-winner and fearless fighter against racial discrimination, tried to avoid embarrassment by pointing out that some of the Secretary-General's best friends were Jews. Unfortunately, however, the Arabs were unduly discriminating. Since we had not initiated the candidature of Ambassador Jacobson, we left it at that.

The choice fell on Gunnar Jarring, a veteran ambassador from Sweden who had served with distinction in Washington and was at the time representing his country in Moscow. His appointment conformed with the UN rules of equilibrium. The nominee was well-known and esteemed in Washington and in close touch with the authorities in Moscow. His political background was impeccable – traditional Swedish neutrality. Gunnar Jarring was a quiet man, more of a scholar than a dashing diplomat. Turkomanish languages were the field of his academic achievements. It was far easier for him to understand the fine nuances of Turkomanish dialects than the subtleties of oriental politics. He understood what the contenders said but not always what they meant. He was a cautious man, launching his rare initiatives only with the prior consent of the parties. Undeniably he was studious and conscientious in his efforts to help clarify the controversial issues, but he lacked the boldness needed to summon Israel and the Arab states to a peace conference. It eluded him, probably because of his inclination to disentangle painstakingly every thread of the Gordian knot, instead of cutting it with one well-aimed stroke.

Ambassador Jarring set out on his mission early in 1968. He returned from his first tour of the five capitals – Cairo, Amman, Damascas, Beirut and

Jerusalem – with a sharpened awareness of the contrasting concepts and objectives of the contending parties. Conscious of the fact that it was neither within his competence nor his capacity to propose solutions to the basic controversial issues, he tried to build procedural bridges and to remove some irritants which seemed likely to bar progress. The five young Jews condemned in the Cairo trial in 1955 were still languishing in prison. All our efforts to exchange them for detainees of interest to Egypt had failed. We approached Dr Jarring, and asked him to convey to the Egyptian government a proposal to include our five people in the general exchange of prisoners from the 1967 war. Israel was holding about 5,000 Egyptian POWs against 19 Israeli military personnel held by Egypt. Jarring agreed to support the proposition. After a few weeks of negotiations conducted in Cairo and Jerusalem in great secrecy, he brought us the good news of Egypt's agreement. It stipulated that all publicity must be avoided on the release of our security detainees to spare Egypt unnecessary embarrassment. They were to be freed after the return of the bulk of Egyptian POWs. There was no signed agreement; we had to rely on the word given by Foreign Minister Mahmoud Riad to Ambassador Jarring and on his assurance that Egypt would carry out its undertaking in good faith. It did, and we regarded this as a good omen for the future.

Another matter, although a side issue, had caused considerable diplomatic commotion. It did not concern the destiny of people, but the destination of ships. At the outbreak of the Six Day War, Nasser had ordered the blocking of the Suez Canal. As a result a number of foreign vessels were moored in the Bitter Lake. Naturally, their governments had become increasingly impatient with the prolonged detention which was causing losses to the owners and hardship to the crews. As long as Israeli and Egyptian forces were deployed along the banks of the canal, its re-opening was out of the question. After protracted negotiations, conducted by Ambassador Jarring, the idea took shape to clear only one end of the canal through which the ships could sail to liberty. Egypt insisted on clearing the northern exit at Port Said. Israel would agree to let the ships leave only through the southern passage at Port Suez. In short it was a typical diplomatic impasse with each side sitting tight on its geographical predilection.

It was obvious that neither Israel nor Egypt were really interested in solving the problem. The more both governments reiterated their willingness to oblige, the more they piled up arguments, contrived or real, to thwart a *dénouement* of the situation. It was not even a battle of wits; it was an exercise in mulish stubbornness. At one point, having apparently exhausted all other arguments, our defence people claimed that the opening of the northern end would induce the Soviet navy to steam into the canal and position itself in front of our lines. When we unimaginative diplomats meekly inquired what it was to do there and hinted at the possibility that, in case of trouble, the venturous gun-boats were nothing but sitting ducks, their exit from the canal less assured than their entry, the strategists just looked at us with that certain mixture of contempt for the ignorant and pity for the innocent.

After Dr Jarring had scooped up all the quicksand arguments like a canal-dredger without one of the moored ships moving a single inch, the Egyptians made an attempt to force the issue. One fine morning they sent a small boat up from Ismailia to survey the northern passage. Our military were not in the mood to acquiesce in that sort of thing. A few shots over the bow ended the sortie and scuttled Ambassador Jarring's maritime diplomacy. It was another eight years before the stranded ships could leave their moorings after the Yom Kippur War, and sail through the re-opened canal north or south at their own choice.

The elusive peace conference

Since the Arab perception of Resolution 242 had deviated essentially from its letter and spirit as interpreted by its sponsors, the government of National Unity in Israel, itself disunited in its attitude towards the resolution, adopted a posture of cautious probing in regard to the Jarring mission. Foreign Minister Eban, conducting the talks with Dr Jarring, was directed by the cabinet not to commit himself to any position before the government had had the opportunity to ascertain the true intentions of the Arab states on the central theme of the resolution: the establishment of a just and lasting peace. Accordingly, we asked Dr Jarring to obtain official clarification from the Arab governments of their position on the main issues. In the exercise of this function the UN Special Representative innovated a method of mobility, later to be labelled 'shuttle diplomacy'. His progress through the lands of Araby and Israel was somewhat less royal and spectacular than that of Henry Kissinger a few years later. His special plane was a modest ten-seater, and his security protection consisted of a lonely bodyguard. Not being a star performer, he was not followed by a comet's-tail of reporters. His back-up was the multi-faceted conglomeration of the United Nations, not the single-minded power of the United States. His style was Nordic – slow and deliberate – a far cry from that of the American go-getter. Jarring was a silent traveller, plodding his way in a thankless attempt to narrow the gap separating the parties to the conflict. Unfortunately, however, the gulf remained as wide as the distances covered by the tireless, roving ambassador.

Before long it became evident to all the participants that this exercise of questions and answers by messenger service was most unlikely to produce meaningful replies. The parties, separated by an impenetrable wall of distrust, were hesitant to convey their true thoughts through a party-line to which the whole of the United Nations listened in. The formulation of the questions and the scrutiny of the answers were particularly attractive to those who believed that sophistry was the highest form of diplomatic agility. On the Israeli side, Minister Without Portfolio but not without influence, Menachem Begin, was in his element. He would argue fervently about the monumental difference between the words 'withdrawal' and 'redeployment'. The term 'implementation of the resolution' was anathema to him, and he regarded any reference to the fact that Israel had accepted the resolution as a frivolous deviation. Not even the slightest punctuation mark escaped his vigilant eye. Although he seemed convinced that his contributions to the textual debates were of historical significance, his influence was more that of a point-setter than of a pace-maker.

After a few more rounds of this futile quiz programme, Jarring understood that the time was ripe for a change of direction. From now on he centred his efforts on reaching an agreement on the initiation of negotiations between the parties. At the beginning of March 1968 he presented them with a proposal which he hoped would merge the views and reservations of both sides into a combination likely to unlock the door to the negotiating chamber. The wording in itself is noteworthy for the convoluted style of United Nations communications designed to accommodate conflicting objectives under the same roof. Its substance was significant because it responded essentially to Israel's request for direct negotiations. In a meeting in Jerusalem on 10 March Dr Jarring informed us that he had presented to the Egyptian Foreign Minister a few days before the following text for an invitation to a peace conference:

The governments of Israel and Egypt (respectively Jordan) have both indicated to me that they accept Security Council Resolution 242 for achieving a peaceful and accepted settlement of the Middle East question and intend to devise arrangements, under my auspices, for the implementation of the provisions of the resolution.

In view of the urgency of the situation and with a view to expediting efforts to reach a settlement, I have invited the two governments to meet with me, for conferences within the framework of the Security Council resolution, in Nicosia. I have pleasure in informing you that the two governments have responded favourably to this invitation.

But Jarring was denied the pleasure of Foreign Minister Mahmoud Riad's favourable response. He was surprised by the Egyptian rejection because he had felt certain that the text corresponded to the views expressed in his prior consultations in Cairo. He tried to rationalize the sudden change by attributing it to student riots in Cairo, which had caused some discomfort to the regime. Most probably, however, this was one of Nasser's habitual evasions from implementing previous commitments.

Be that as it may, at our meeting with the Special Representative on 10 March Eban expressed his personal view that the text of the letter would be acceptable to Israel if it led to negotiations between the parties. Subsequently Ambassador Jarring was officially informed of Israel's acceptance. Jordan tried to modify the wording of the invitation by shifting the emphasis from the convocation of a conference, as proposed, between the governments in Nicosia to arrangements for meetings between their representatives with Ambassador Jarring in New York. Although it was clear that Egypt had backed out, the indefatigable UN Representative continued to commute between Cairo, Amman and Jerusalem. Having run out of diplomatic fuel, he asked Washington to provide some other propellent. The traditional reflex of the State Department was not to apply its persuasive talents to make the refusing Arab side reconsider its position, but to prod Israel to make another concession.

President Johnson intervenes

One quiet Sabbath afternoon in April, Ambassador Barbour arrived in Jerusalem with the request for an urgent meeting with the Prime Minister. Such unscheduled visits by the American envoy, who preferred sedentary to itinerant diplomacy, normally presaged an emergency or a brewing crisis.

We assembled at Eshkol's home. Barbour handed the Prime Minister a letter from President Johnson. The President urged the government to reiterate publicly Israel's acceptance of Resolution 242 and its willingness to implement its provisions by mutual agreement. King Hussein was ready to negotiate, but his situation was precarious. Israel should understand his predicament and be forthcoming. The Jarring mission was probably the only barrier to the renewal of war. The letter concluded with an ominous warning that Israel should not forget that its relations with the United States should have preference over any variations of Dr Jarring's formulations.

Eshkol replied that Hussein's situation had been precarious from the beginning of his reign and would remain so until its end – hopefully a happy one. Israel had always been understanding and had pleaded with Hussein at the outbreak of the hostilities with Egypt not to participate in the war. He had dismissed Israel's appeal and that was the only reason for his present distress. He compared the King's plea now with that notorious defendant who had murdered his father and mother and begged mercy because he was a poor orphan. As a parting shot Eshkol said that he had thought that when Barbour had asked for an urgent appointment he was coming as a messenger of good tidings, bringing Johnson's consent to sell us the Phantom fighter planes which the Prime Minister had requested so urgently in his meeting with the President a few months earlier.

After the ambassador had left, Eshkol asked Eban and myself to stay behind. He was uneasy and began to question us. When had the government declared its acceptance of Resolution 242? Eban patiently reminded him that he had reported fully to the cabinet all his conversations and communications with Ambassador Jarring. As late as 19 February he had handed him, with the Prime Minister's consent, a written statement on Israel's position on the resolution reaffirming 'that the best way to achieve the objective of the resolution is through direct negotiations. However, as a further indication of

Israel's co-operation, we are willing that this be done in a meeting convened by the Special Representative.' The Foreign Minister's communication to Dr Jarring then stated: 'On 12 February 1968, I informed you of Israel's acceptance of the Security Council's call, in its Resolution 242, for the promotion of agreement on the establishment of peace and on our willingness to negotiate on all matters included in the resolution.'

Convinced by Eban's cogent statements, Eshkol directed him to draft a positive reply to President Johnson's requests. At the same time I drafted the text for a statement to be made by our permanent representative at the United Nations. Mindful of the Prime Minister's occasional amnesia, which was of course not a mental affliction but a widely practised convenience of politicians in distress, I asked him to countersign my telegram of instructions. He duly obliged upon the advice and in the presence of his political adviser, Dr Jacob Herzog. Accordingly, on 1 May 1968, Ambassador Tekoah stated in the Security Council: 'In declarations made publicly and to Dr Jarring, my government has indicated its acceptance of the Security Council Resolution 242 for the promotion of agreement on the establishment of a just and durable peace. I am also authorized to reaffirm that we are willing to seek agreement with each Arab state on all the matters included in that resolution.'

Ministerial rumblings

When the press reported the statement Mr Begin, supported by Minister of Defence Dayan, tersely asked the Prime Minister who had authorized its issue. They claimed that the government had never decided to accept the resolution. Eshkol, anxious to avoid a crisis, replied that he would clarify the matter with the Foreign Minister after his return from an official visit to Scandinavian capitals. The two protesting ministers insisted that Eban should cut short his official functions and return immediately. He refused to heed the summons, explaining that the whole thing was a minor storm in a muddy tea-cup. Although the two ministers were sniping at him, their real target was the Prime Minister himself. Eban predicted that the sham attack would blow over by the time of his scheduled return. Eshkol gave way grudgingly. I assured the Prime Minister that, upon his return, Eban would produce the relevant documentary proof to satisfy his inquisitive cabinet colleagues. I suggested that if he played it cool the agitation would soon fizzle out. Eshkol was not convinced. He admitted that Begin might content himself with oratorical flourishes, but Dayan would not yield so easily. Like many others, Eshkol was reluctant to cross Dayan's path, fearful of being run over at a dimly-lit, political street-crossing.

As Eban had anticipated, the cabinet accepted his well-documented version of events, but this did not change the fact that three years later Dayan asserted in a discussion with the American Secretary of State that Israel had never accepted Resolution 242.

In a private talk a few years later with Golda Meir, by then Prime Minister, I encountered the fable of the non-acceptance of the resolution when it had long been overshadowed by far-reaching Israeli concessions. Her relationship with her Foreign Minister, Abba Eban, had never been a particularly happy one. Golda complained that Eban had expressed some independent views not to her liking, and indicated that it did not do me any good to encourage Eban. I responded that in giving advice to the Foreign Minister I was guided by professional judgement which was based on the interpretation, as accurate as possible, of the best available information. It was given to Eban in the same spirit of intellectual independence as I used to offer it to her when she was Foreign Minister. We both tried to implement the government's objectives by means of a foreign policy best suited to Israel's needs and capabilities and we were conscious of the existing international realities. This could only strengthen the process of rational decision-making by the government, which was not infrequently swayed by facile arguments forcefully presented by some of its more persuasive, but not necessarily more thoughtful, members. This was not exactly what Golda wanted to hear. To stress her point she reverted to the legend of poor Eshkol being led down the garden path. At the time she had not been a member of the government but she claimed that she had always been well-informed of all that went on. We had sent instructions to our UN representative to announce Israel's acceptance of Resolution 242 without Eshkol's consent. When I referred to Eshkol's countersignature Golda seemed convinced, but would not admit it explicitly. She only lamented: 'Poor old Eshkol.'

The Jarring stalemate

But back to Jarring and his mission. Early in the summer of 1968 he came to the realization that his proposal to convene the peace conference had foundered. Neither the diluted formula of King Hussein nor the Israeli statement of acceptance were capable of refloating it as long as Egypt was opposed to the very idea of the conference. The timid reluctance of Jarring to press on with his initiative had a decisive influence on the course of events. We prodded him to cut through the diplomatic entanglement by simply forwarding to the Arab capitals and Israel his invitation for the conference, as Dr Bunche had done when he convened the armistice conferences in Rhodes in 1949 – all the Arab delegations had turned up on the day and at the place the UN mediator had invited them to, despite their prior energetic refusal to attend. And, we claimed, they would do it again if Dr Jarring summoned the parties to the peace conference. His reluctance to act decisively was probably the main reason for the failure of his mission, inaugurating a decade of diplomatic deadlock instead of initiating a process of negotiation.

The stalemate was shattered when, in September 1968, Egyptian artillery suddenly and provocatively opened fire across the canal on Israeli positions.

Our losses were heavy because our soldiers, lulled by the continuous quietness of the front-lines, were caught in the open. I had visited the place of the incident, Kantara East, a week before. I returned to Jerusalem with an uneasy feeling that our troops were carelessly exposed to the risks of a sudden attack. I conveyed my worry to the Chief of Staff, but he assured me that sudden opening of fire was a most unlikely eventuality. Preparations for it would be detected in good time for the men to take shelter. Military men do not like civilian advice in matters of their competence. A few days later I visited some of the wounded in their hospital wards. They did not complain and several of them continued to ask questions about Israel's foreign policy, as they had done so eagerly when I had seen them last.

22

War of Attrition

The shelling of Kantara was the opening gambit of a new Egyptian military venture ambitiously named by Nasser the War of Attrition. Israel countered the attacks by constructing fortifications all along its line on the canal, later to be known as the Bar-Lev line. After a winter lull the Egyptian army began, on 8 March 1969, its spring offensive which it called 'active preventive defence'. It laid down a massive artillery barrage on the Israeli positions along the entire length of the canal. In a speech on 30 March, Nasser gave a vivid description of what he called 'the new very important phase of the Middle East crisis'. He said: 'There was a time when we used to ask our soldiers at the front to account for their actions if they fired first at the enemy on sight, for we were not prepared for complications. Now the picture has changed. We ask every soldier at the front to account for his action if he sees the enemy and does not fire at him.' This was the way Nasser interpreted Egypt's solemn undertaking of June 1967 to observe a complete and unconditional cease-fire.

In his May Day address he elaborated on this theme: 'We are in a state of war, and war means that we shall kill our enemies. . . . At the beginning of last month, our armed forces said they were ready. Their objective is to destroy the Bar-Lev line. We have so far been able to destroy sixty per cent of the line. After the destruction of the remaining forty per cent we are prepared to proceed to Sinai to meet the enemy face to face.' Nasser did not live to see that day and before it came, Egypt suffered very heavy losses from Israel's counteractions. Outnumbered in men and fire-power, the only effective recourse open to Israel was the use of its superior air power. Initially the air-strikes were directed against Egyptian artillery batteries which were constantly shelling Zahal's positions, and there were a few airborne penetration raids to demonstrate the army's long and muscular arm. But neither the air nor the commando operations were persuasive enough for Egypt to call off its armed attacks and to return to the observance of the cease-fire. Our military pressed for more spectacular action to bring home to the government of Egypt and to the population in the rear the risks of the continued bombardment of our front-line troops which was causing a mounting toll of casualties.

The government's scrutiny of the international aspects of a proposed course of military action was mostly confined to listening to an authorized version of the current situation in the area presented by the director of military intelligence. The trend of the presentation was to provide political underpinning for the military plans supported by the Minister of Defence. Other considerations, which determined the government's attitude to a proposed plan of action, were the number of estimated Israeli losses, the desire to avoid Arab civilian casualties and the evaluation of the American reaction.

In most instances, however, the outcome of the debate depended on the measure of firmness of the views expressed by the Prime Minister. The unwritten rules, already agreed upon under Ben Gurion after a number of political setbacks caused by the lack of consultation between the Ministries of Defence and Foreign Affairs, envisaged that military counteractions had to be approved by the Premier and the Ministers of Defence and Foreign Affairs. Eshkol, inexperienced in foreign affairs, open-minded and by nature a man of compromise and accommodation, paid greater attention to the views of his Foreign Minister. He valued Eban's professional competence and generally shared his moderate approach. But sensing that he did not have sufficient party support, Eshkol carefully tried to defer a frontal clash with Dayan.

In March 1968 a wave of murderous terrorist raids, carried out from bases in Jordan, had caused a number of civilian losses and aroused strong feelings in Israel. The new Chief of Staff, General Bar-Lev, proposed a major operation against a Fatah base located inside the perimeter of the refugee camp, Karameh, on the east bank of the Jordan near the Dead Sea. Washington, anticipating strong military and political repercussions, exerted considerable pressure on the Prime Minister to desist from action, more so since King Hussein had asked the United States to inform Israel of his determination to put an end to the attacks. Eban and some of his cabinet colleagues strongly urged Eshkol to reconsider his prior consent to the planned action. They argued that its scope was exaggerated, its target was unsuitable, it unnecessarily endangered lives of uninvolved refugees and its political risks were disproportionately high. While the deliberations were in progress Ambassador Barbour kept on transmitting messages from Washington, which culminated in a warning from President Johnson strongly urging that no action of this kind be taken: 'It would have most destructive consequences for our common hopes for peace and for the future of our own, as well as your, position.' Eshkol was wavering. Suddenly the news arrived that Dayan had been hurt in one of his private and lonely archaeological digs and been rushed to hospital in a serious condition. The outcome of the discussion was still in the balance. Some of us thought that the incapacity of the Minister of Defence would provide the Prime Minister with a good, face-saving reason to postpone the operation. But Eshkol's mind worked differently. Defiantly he replied: 'Do you want the Arabs to believe that there is no action when Dayan is ill?'

A few hours later the forces went into action. They met with unexpected and stiff resistance from the Arab Legion and suffered heavy losses. Together with the terrorists entrenched in the refugee camp, many civilians were hit. More than a hundred prisoners were taken. After a few weeks of detention, the majority of them were returned to Jordan after their non-affiliation with terrorist organizations had been established, but it was later reported that most of them joined these organizations after their repatriation. The United States, true to its usual practice, did not take any open steps to show its displeasure; it just delayed the supply of some urgent Israeli requirements.

The operation gave an enormous uplift to Yassir Arafat's Fatah organization and irrevocably implanted the Palestine problem onto the international agenda, no longer as a humanitarian issue of homeless refugees, but as a claim to Palestinian statehood. One thing appears certain: the Karameh operation was more of a boost than a blow to the terrorist organizations. It did little to stop the recurrent incursions but much to swell Arafat's ranks. The Israeli Ambassador in Washington, Yitzhak Rabin, reported to the Prime Minister that the Karameh action had produced a worldwide reverberation for the cause of the Palestine liberation movement.

Escalation

Golda Meir, as Prime Minister, had her own personal way of handling defence matters. Dayan recognized from the outset of her premiership – which he had not supported in the party caucus as she had objected to his appointment to the defence post two years earlier – that for his proper functioning as Defence Minister he had to gain her goodwill and confidence. Whatever he thought or said about her in unguarded moments, he showed her all the outward signs of deference. He would not surprise her in cabinet with controversial plans and oppose her with contentious opinions. Before seeking cabinet approval he would try in private consultation to gain her prior support for his proposals. When she was firm in her opposition, he would drop the matter and not appeal to cabinet. When she had doubts, she would consult with a few of her intimate friends, weighing the arguments but rarely checking the facts which formed the basis for the proposed plan of action. When she agreed with her Minister of Defence – the case in most instances – she would give him firm backing and a free hand and the cabinet decision became a foregone conclusion. In this set-up the Foreign Minister's influence was naturally severely curtailed. Eban sometimes rebelled but generally felt that he had to accept this situation unless he should decide to resign, a step he used to contemplate with more frequency than consequence. His position was doubly difficult. Not only was there a lack of affinity between him and Golda, but her prime-ministerial authority combined with her experience as Foreign Minister predestined her to run the foreign affairs of the country with a firm hand and a great attention to detail. The Foreign Minister was not in a position to curb or even balance the strong influence held by his defence colleague.

The more Nasser stepped up his war of attrition, the more he exposed Egypt to Israeli counter-strikes of mounting severity and scope. The supersonic boom of its fighter-bombers over Cairo reminded its inhabitants, visibly and audibly, that their town was within range of the Israeli air-force. The intensification of the fighting in the canal zone prompted Israel's military planners to seek authorization to extend the air-raids in strength, frequency and depth. The war virtually reached Cairo, Alexandria and Aswan and severely hit the canal towns of Port Said, Ismailia and Port Suez. The government rarely engaged in a wider discussion of the overall strategy. Questioning occurred only when something unforeseen or unpredicted had happened: an exorbitant number of casualties suffered by our forces or some major international complication incurred.

In one of its bombings of Port Said the air-force hit targets apparently in close vicinity to some Soviet naval vessels at anchor. The Soviet government sent a stern note of protest to Jerusalem through Finland, which represented its interests in Israel. It claimed that bomb fragments had hit two Soviet warships in the harbour of Port Said, but did not explain what the naval craft of a formally neutral power were doing there right in the centre of an active war zone. It concluded with a warning of possible Soviet action. The communication stirred up considerable excitement among the members of the government. Some of them were fascinated by the mere fact that the Soviet Union had deigned to address Israel; others indulged in lengthy disputations on the meaning of the veiled threat; but none of them questioned the wisdom of or authorization to bomb targets so close to foreign warships. The ministers contented themselves with the laconic reply of the Chief of Staff that it was for the Soviets to worry, and not for Israel, if they exposed their naval craft to risk.

Anyway, it was not the task of the Foreign Ministry to devise a military reply to a possible Russian threat, but to draft an answer to the Soviet note. We compared it with a Soviet warning presented to the United States on the occasion of a recent similar incident, where American bombers had inadvertently hit Russian ships in Haiphong harbour. We found that the Soviet threat to the United States was even more strongly worded than that delivered to Israel. Comparing notes with Washington, in the true sense of the word, we jointly reached the conclusion that the Soviet missive was not meant to be the prelude to military action, but merely a warning against repetition. With this in mind we drafted a restrained reply, refraining from legal or other annoying arguments, stating simply that Israel had neither knowledge nor intention of hitting Soviet vessels. It was neither apologetic in its tone, nor strident in its content. It closed the incident until the next one occurred a year later, when Israeli fighter-planes shot down four Mig 23s flown by Soviet pilots over Egyptian territory. But on that occasion Moscow chose to take no notice of the embarrassing encounter. It apparently considered disregard of the occurrence the better part of political valour.

Deep-penetration bombing

The lack of effective Egyptian air defence gave Israel's air force virtual freedom of action over all the Egyptian territory within its flying range. Washington, so it appeared at least to Jerusalem, watched the extension of the hostilities with equanimity. Ambassador Rabin's dispatches encouraged the government to believe that the United States was in favour of Israel's hard-hitting air strikes. As former Chief of Staff, it was only natural for Rabin to follow military activities with an acute professional interest from his ambassadorial post, remote from the centre of military decisions but close to the seat of decisive political power in Washington. In his frequent and always very detailed telegrams he offered military advice and commented on actions, not always complimentary. Those in government who advocated carrying the war deeper into Egypt were content with Rabin's urging for more vigorous action, but those who felt bound to counsel restraint, such as the Foreign Minister and his staff, whose inherent duty it was to underline the international consequences of military overaction, were dismayed by the Ambassador's communications. To their sceptical, but cautious, probing whether the opinions he attributed to high officials in Washington represented the authentic position of the United States government, he would reply with an even measure of anger and disdain. At a rather early stage of his mission he had come to the conclusion that his Minister and his associates were unable to understand the intricacies of foreign affairs, which he had mastered with rocket speed.

The upshot of his messages was that Washington wanted Israel to hit Nasser so hard that he would either regain his senses or succumb to his losses. Rabin drew his impressions mainly from private meetings with Assistant Secretary of State, Joseph Sisco, a highly qualified professional, skilful and friendly interlocutor. Rabin used to expound his views to him, and Sisco would carefully absorb his analyses, commenting here and there, but normally avoiding serious argument. Rabin interpreted this, in a number of cases, as tacit agreement with the views he had proffered. In one of their conversations Rabin ventured to suggest that the Israeli army might have to march on Cairo. In his report he described Sisco's reaction – 'he did not fall from his chair' – concluding from the Secretary's sedentary stability that the United States was in sympathy with such far-reaching Israeli action. This assumption was received in Jerusalem with considerable scepticism.

Meanwhile, Egyptian attacks in the canal zone continued with undiminished vigour while Israeli bombing reached the suburbs of Cairo. The

American Ambassador conveyed to the Foreign Ministry Washington's reactions, ranging from the expression of displeasure to outright censure. When bombs had fallen near a school in a suburb of Cairo where 200 American children were studying, the State Department called in one of the embassy's top-ranking officials to launch a strong protest. They were as stupefied at his riposte as was the Foreign Minister in Jerusalem at his report. Our man in Washington recommended that, if the Americans felt that the school was in danger of being hit, they had better remove it from its present location. This advice made the rounds as one of the great Israeli diplomatic sayings.

The first Israeli delegation to the United Nations, May 1948. *Left to right:* Gideon Rafael, Arthur Lourie, Abba Eban and Moshe Sharett.

Golda Meir and Gideon Rafael, the first envoys of the State of Israel, *en route* from Haifa to New York, 18 May 1948.

Trygve Lie, UN Secretary-General, and Warren Austin, US Permanent Representative, 1949.

With Abba Eban and USSR UN representatives, Jacob Malik (*left*) and Seamyon Tsarapkin (*right*), 1950.

Above left With Charles Malik, Foreign Minister of the Lebanon, 1953.

Above right Ben Gurion and Moshe Sharett with British Foreign Secretary Selwyn Lloyd (*left*), March 1956, prior to the Suez campaign.

Ben Gurion visits the United Nations Headquarters, 1955.

Digging for victory, 1956.

With Queen Elisabeth of Belgium and Isaac Stern, 16 May 1959.

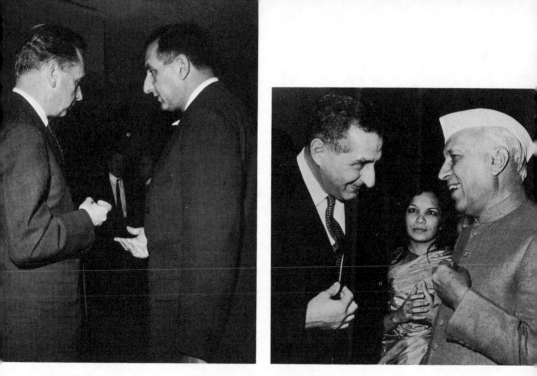

Above left With UN Secretary-General Dag Hammarskjöld.
Above right With Pandit Nehru, 1961.

Below left The author presents his credentials to UN Secretary-General U Thant, May 1967. *Below right* At this meeting with UN Undersecretary-General Ralphe Bunche, Gideon Rafael informed him of Egyptian troop movements threatening Israel, 15 May 1967.

UNION O
SOCIALIST

In conversation with
Nikolai Fedorenko,
24 May 1967.

Ambassador and Mrs
Gideon Rafael at a
reception with UN
Secretary-General and
Mrs Kurt Waldheim,
1967.

The author standing on a captured Soviet tank on the Golan Heights during his service in the Yom Kippur War, 1974.

With Romanian Deputy Foreign Minister Gheorge Macovescu on his arrival at Ben Gurion airport, 1971.

'Number one on the Palestinian terrorists' hit list' – arriving under heavy guard at Heathrow airport, London, January 1971.

Below left Gideon Rafael *en route* to Buckingham Palace to present his credentials as Ambassador to the Court of St James's, February 1971.

Below right With Prime Minister Harold Wilson, 1976.

23

The Rogers Plan – First Steps

While the United States kept a close watch on the military developments, it engaged in a political dialogue with the Soviet Union on a possible joint course of action. Already early in 1969, when the Foreign Minster sent me to Washington to brief the new foreign affairs team appointed by the newly installed Nixon administration and to elicit their views, Undersecretary of State Elliot Richardson had indicated that the White House felt that it had to keep in touch with Moscow on the Arab-Israeli conflict. He doubted whether they could come to an understanding in an area where the views and interests of the two countries differed so widely. But the new administration was of the opinion that because of the unacceptable risks of a superpower confrontation resulting from miscalculation, misunderstanding or sheer irresponsibility by their respective regional friends, the two governments had to keep in close touch, to avoid rash action in case of an emergency. Of course, we did not contest the necessity for the two principal nuclear powers to maintain their lines of communications intact, but we doubted whether the Soviet Union was willing to play a positive role in the resolution of the Arab-Israeli conflict. There were two keys, we argued, which could unlock the deadlock in the Middle East. One was global, held by the United States. The other was regional, held by Israel. Nothing could happen internally in the area against Israel's will, because of its military preponderance. All that the United States was asked to do was to hold on firmly to its key and resist the Soviet Union in its attempt to turn it, while keeping Israel's arm strong enough to deter any regional aggression.

While exchanges on a joint political initiative proceeded between Washington and Moscow, four other developments took place simultaneously. Firstly, the fighting became increasingly severe and menacing. Secondly, the United States supplied important new weapons-systems to Israel, recognizing that it acted in self-defence against the massive breach of the cease-fire by Egypt. Thirdly, the Soviet Union, which had replenished the Egyptian arsenals depleted by the losses of the Six Day War, now took upon itself to equip and organize Egypt's air defence which was virtually devoid of any means to stop the continuous pounding of the deep-penetration raids. And fourthly, Washington pursued its efforts to prepare the ground for a new political initiative.

Contrary to the opinion held by our embassy that the US government welcomed a policy of bombing Nasser into submission, Washington in fact became increasingly concerned with the strategic and political implications of the air-strikes. Instead of reducing the Soviet commitment to Egypt and making Nasser more pliable to American designs, the Soviet Union became increasingly involved in the War of Attrition. Yielding to Nasser's pleas, the Soviet government established an air-defence system, covering the principal urban centres and extending the deployment into the area between the Suez Canal and the Nile delta. It introduced with remarkable speed its most advanced SAM anti-aircraft missiles, dispatched thousands of military technicians, training staff and operational planners – an expeditionary corps amounting at its peak in 1972 to approximately 20,000 men. It stationed on Egyptian air-bases Russian-manned combat and reconnaissance planes, not only to help defend Egyptian airspace, but also to monitor the movements of the United States fleet in the Mediterranean.

The growing Soviet military presence changed not only the bilateral military balance between Israel and Egypt, it also prompted the United States to urge Israel to act with greater circumspection, and expedited American diplomatic preparations for the presentation of an American solution to the conflict. But in a way the prominent Soviet military presence in Egypt was a mixed blessing. By initiating his war of attrition Nasser had intended to force Israel's hand, but in reality he drove Egypt into Russia's arms. In trying to compel Israel to return the lost territories without peace, he mortgaged his freedom of independent action to a foreign power. The constant flow of Soviet armaments, covering the full range from rifle to rocket, was accompanied by a massed influx of Russian military personnel. It created more than the habitual friction between the odd allies. Where Rommel's Afrika Korps had failed, the Soviet expeditionary force succeeded. It reached Cairo and the Suez Canal. The Soviet Union, as a superpower, kept its eyes steadily on Washington, adjusting the scope of its intervention to the degree of American response. It was careful not to get directly engaged in the fighting. It confined its active participation to advising, training and supplying the Egyptian army, as well as operating the SAM missile installation.

The Israeli air force recognized the deadly potential of the Soviet missile system after its first encounter with it. While trying to knock out the newly installed missiles and the sites under construction, the air force incurred losses. They were not large in numbers, but they were painful because they affected its most advanced equipment and its best-trained pilots. Israel's urgent requests to Washington to expedite the delivery of the promised Phantom fighters to replace those lost in action and to supply electronic equipment and anti-missile weapons were met only with partial responses. Yet they added momentum and motivation to the administration to accelerate the preparation of its diplomatic initiative.

After the first Soviet SAM missiles had been installed for the protection of

Cairo and Alexandria, Israeli intelligence and foreign affairs experts reached the conclusion that for reasons of military effectiveness alone, the Soviets would press for the forward deployment of the SAM missiles into the area of the canal, where the main ground-fighting took place. They warned that such an extended missile defence system would create considerable difficulties if the air force needed to prevent an Egyptian attempt to cross the canal in strength. The events of the opening days of the Yom Kippur War fully bore out the accuracy of this assessment. At the time of our deliberations at the end of 1969 we agreed to recommend to the government to centre its military and political efforts on the establishment of a missile-free zone approximately twenty-five miles deep west of the canal.

Golda goes to Washington

The American political move came earlier than expected. At the end of October 1969, Secretary of State William Rogers surprised Israel with the presentation to the Soviet Union of a detailed plan for a peace settlement between Israel and Egypt. It envisaged the restoration of all of Sinai to Egypt, as part of a binding peace agreement which included the lifting of the maritime blockade and the establishment of demilitarized zones. The government of Israel resented the American initiative for three reasons: its surprise, its contents and its evidence of US–USSR collaboration on matters which vitally affected Israel's future.

Only a few weeks had passed since Golda Meir had returned from her first visit to Washington as Prime Minister. She had approached her mission with apprehension. It was her first test on the highest level of governmental responsibility and her first encounter with President Nixon. For weeks before her departure she discussed with us a large variety of problems which she expected to be raised at her meetings. She decided to give first priority to arms procurement and related aspects of Israel's security, and relegate the political issues to the bottom of the agenda. She suspected, correctly, that any discussion of a peace settlement would add to the administration's insistence that Israel should specify its territorial claims. Knowing that her government was fundamentally divided on this and other peace terms she had decided, perhaps instinctively, from the very start of her premiership, to avoid any national or international debate on the specifics of peace. She entrenched herself, and with her the government, in a position marked with the motto 'the time has not yet come to draw maps'. Direct negotiations without preconditions was the password for leaving the trenches.

In Golda's talks with Nixon, both leaders skirted, though for different reasons, the sensitive political subject. They focused on what Golda used to call with housewifely joviality 'her shopping list'. She deduced from her talk with the President, who evoked hopes of a satisfactory response to Israel's defence requirements, that the political issues were not of primary presidential concern. These were left to Secretary Rogers. His adamant prodding annoyed her a little, but did not worry her much. She dismissed the Secretary's exertions as normal State Department practice, doomed to founder on the rocks of the White House. She was strengthened in her belief by Ambassador Rabin's general aversion to institutions entrusted with the conduct of foreign affairs, and Dr Kissinger's advice to pay attention only to what the President said. But the presidential security adviser failed to enlighten her that presidents in meetings with foreign heads of government prefer sometimes to leave certain controversial matters untouched, relying on their Foreign Secretaries to fulfil the less pleasant duties. Henry Kissinger later, in his capacity as Secretary of State, distinguished himself in the art of performing such assignments with roles divided between himself and the President.

Be that as it may, Golda was unimpressed by the entreaties of Secretary Rogers to proceed with the American peace plan. Upon her return to Israel the Prime Minister declared herself pleased with her talks with the President. 'We have a friend in the White House,' she exclaimed. She indicated that her shopping bag was heavier now than when she had left, but she did not reflect any apprehension at possible American political moves. Because of Israel's predominant and understandable preoccupation with its defence capacity, it was only natural that parliament, press and public judged the success of prime-ministerial missions to Washington by their achievements in the field of military procurement. Ben Gurion had returned from his meeting with President Kennedy with a promise on the supply of ground-to-air Hawk missiles. Eshkol had brought home from his visit with L.B.J. an undertaking to sell Phantom fighters to Israel. Golda received from Nixon a pledge for more aircraft and electronic warfare equipment deliveries.

Rogers moves in

Regardless of the strong objections voiced by the Israeli government to the step taken by the State Department in inviting the support of the Soviet government for its peace plan, Washington proceeded with its initiative. After Moscow had delayed its reply on the proposals, Secretary of State Rogers published them on 9 December 1969 without prior notification to Israel. The government, aroused, called Ambassador Rabin home for consultations. He urged a vigorous public rejection of the Rogers plan, which he castigated as an attempt on the very existence of Israel. He advanced a somewhat astonishing explanation for the American initiative. He now claimed that the reason for Washington's unforeseen initiative was the refusal of the government to heed his advice to inflict a heavy blow on Syria. He argued that in the absence of such military action, the United States felt constrained to act politically. The cabinet, with all its antagonism to the Rogers plan and procedure, was more inclined to accept the interpretation of the Foreign Minister that the diplomatic stalemate of the Jarring mission had produced the American move. Furthermore, explained Eban, Washington was afraid that the present fighting would degenerate into a major conflagration, unless curbed by political action. He pointed out that the Rogers plan, although hurtful and unacceptable to Israel, constituted the basic concept and specific prescription of the United States for the solution of the conflict. It was not a compact of improvised ideas cherished by the Secretary of State or his Middle East experts, but a considered policy developed by the United States government.

In its meeting of 22 December the cabinet decided to reject the Rogers plan stating 'that it prejudices the chances of establishing peace; disregards the essential need to determine secure and agreed borders through the signing of peace treaties by direct negotiations; affects Israel's sovereign rights and security in its proposals for the solution of the refugee question and the status of Jerusalem. If these proposals were carried out, Israel's security and peace would be in grave danger. Israel will not be sacrificed by any power policy, and will reject any attempt to impose a forced solution upon it.'

It was evident that the government did not realize that the Rogers initiative was a warning sign, pointing to Washington's resolve to terminate the escalation of the fighting and the widening of the Russian involvement. It chose to believe that it was one of those sporadic and misguided outbursts of pent-up State Departmental energy destined to evaporate under the heat of Arab-Israeli contrariness. Having rejected the plan, the government returned to the immediate concerns of the War of Attrition.

Whither Russia?

Watching the accruing military and political strength of the Soviet Union in Egypt, we felt strongly at the Foreign Ministry that the Minister should acquaint the cabinet with the inherent dangers. We prepared a detailed memorandum, outlining Soviet policy in Egypt, the scope of its military commitment, eventualities of its direct intervention and the location of the trip-wire which could trigger forcible Soviet intervention. We estimated that the Soviet Union would intervene if Zahal crossed the canal in strength with the aim and capacity of destroying the bulk of the Egyptian army. As long as the hostilities remained within their present bounds, the Soviet Union would confine itself to reinforcing Egypt's air defence and fire power and to inflicting such losses on Israel as would make it amenable to accepting a cease-fire when Egypt or the two superpowers felt that the War of Attrition had served its purpose.

After Eban had added his own comments, he presented its contents to his colleagues at the end of December. His lucid submission lasted more than an hour. They followed him with varying degrees of attention. Those who generally shared his concerns were impressed by the cogency of his exposition. Others, surprised by the Foreign Minister's deviation from his usual practice of surveying the diplomatic scene, chose to ignore his exposé, considering it an intrusion into a closed area habitually preserved for military intelligence. Moreover the Prime Minister was not an admirer of penetrating analyses. She preferred action. At the end of lengthy presentations, she would ask the speaker: 'So, what do you propose to do?' Only someone endowed with exemplary courage would dare to answer: 'Nothing at this stage besides giving the matter more thought.'

Eban was disappointed. He had expected that his presentation would evoke a discussion on the wider aspects of Israel's policies and strategy, but Golda proposed to take up the next item on the agenda.

At the beginning of the 1970s Israel faced two major diplomatic problems, which coincided with two serious military concerns. Politically it struggled against the Rogers plan and at the same time tried to avert its convergence with the completely one-sided Soviet Middle East policy. Militarily, the continued Egyptian attacks goaded Israel to take increasingly stronger and extended counteractions, resulting again in a fast-growing Soviet involvement in the hostilities.

The Soviet government's primary concern at this stage was how to respond to Nasser's urgent appeal for equipment to protect Egypt against Israel's hard-hitting air-strikes. The Egyptian leader left secretly for Moscow on 22 January 1970. In four days of tough talks with the Soviet leaders, he revealed that Egypt's defences were completely inadequate, and that the Soviet equipment supplied so far was no match for the sophisticated American material employed by the Israelis. He asked not only for the latest Soviet anti-aircraft missile systems, but also for long-range bombers for retaliatory raids on Israeli urban centres. Moscow refused the latter request, but promised to dispatch sufficient modern weapons for the defence of civilian and economic targets within thirty days.

Apprehensive that such a step might evoke strong negative reactions in Washington and prompt it to respond positively to Israel's pending request for additional Phantom fighters and Skyhawk bombers, Premier Kosygin sent a personal note to President Nixon on 31 January. In the Soviet view, Israel was responsible for the increasing tensions in the Middle East. 'We would like to tell you in all frankness,' wrote the Soviet Prime Minister, 'that if Israel continues to bomb the territory of Egypt and other Arab states, the Soviet Union will be forced to see to it that the Arab states have the means at their disposal with the help of which due rebuff to the arrogant aggressor could be made.'

The President, in his reply of 4 February, dismissed the Soviet allegation of Israel's sole responsibility for the fighting and called for the restoration of the cease-fire and an agreement on the reduction of arms deliveries to the area. He expressed his regret at the Soviet lack of response to the American peace proposals and concluded: 'A more constructive Soviet reply is required if progress towards settlement is to be made. We do not believe peace can come if either side seeks unilateral advantage.'

24

Suspension of Arms Deliveries to Israel

A day before the Kosygin letter was made public President Nixon startled Israel with an announcement that he would delay for thirty days his reply to Israel's arms requests – the famous shopping list which Golda had presented to him during her visit a few months earlier. The President's statement came at a critical time. Israel's air force had escalated and extended its action to the interior of Egypt, to force Nasser to de-escalate his attacks in the canal zone. It hoped to impress the Egyptian people with the inability of its regime to cope with the war situation. The flow of Soviet arms into Egypt was growing steadily. France's decision to sell 100 Mirage fighters to Libya – some of which it had previously contracted to Israel and later refused to deliver – aggravated the arms race. The United States feared that the vehemence of the hostilities and the increasing Soviet involvement were introducing a global strategic dimension into the conflict – a danger which the administration, in view of its mounting difficulties in Vietnam, wished to avoid by all means.

Washington assumed that the thirty days' delay would have a restraining influence on Israel, induce Egypt to accept a cease-fire and the Soviet Union to reduce its arms shipments. But the American tranquillizer had exactly the opposite effect. Egypt continued the fighting, Israel escalated its responses and the Soviet Union sped up its shipments of arms. At the beginning of March alarming information reached Jerusalem that the President was contemplating the suspension of the promised aircraft deliveries for an undetermined period. At the same time the first hard evidence became available that the Russians had started to deploy in Egypt their latest type of SAM 3 missile, operated by Soviet crews. Doubly perturbed by Washington's suspension and Moscow's extension, the mood of the Israeli government swayed between apprehension and defiance. Any reduction of military action was considered to be a sign of weakness in the face of mounting pressure, but at the same time thoughtful members of the cabinet warned that bombing a Nasser shielded by the Soviet Union into submission, in defiance of the American administration, surpassed Israel's potential.

After the presidential announcement of 30 January, Foreign Minister Eban concluded that the principal cause of Israel's difficulties in Washington was the bombing of the interior of Egypt. Though he had previously doubted the soundness of Ambassador Rabin's assessment that Washington favoured the devastating strikes and the wisdom of his repeated urgings for even stronger military action, he was now convinced that the immediate aim of the US government was to bring the fighting to a halt. On 8 February 1970, therefore, he proposed to the government that they accept a cease-fire, even if of limited duration, and that they should couple their acceptance with an appeal to open negotiations on a peace settlement. A number of ministers, among them the powerful Pinchas Sapir, supported the idea. But Golda firmly opposed it. She claimed that Nasser would only agree to negotiations if Israel were to announce its acceptance of Resolution 242. Her argument startled the gathering. Eban and others, referring to Ambassador Tekoah's statement in the Security Council on 1 May 1968, reminded her that Israel had made such an announcement long before; but the Prime Minister would not budge. Confronted with her resistance, Eban and his supporters retreated.

A last-minute attempt to smooth ruffled feelings failed as well. A suggestion was made that Israel should unilaterally halt its air attacks for forty-eight hours. Defence Minister Dayan reassured the meeting that he was fully aware that critical decisions were under consideration in Washington during the month of February. Accordingly he had imposed three restrictions on the air force: it would refrain from bombing objectives in the vicinity of Cairo, avoid civilian targets and any other activities likely to be interpreted as pre-war softening-up blows.

Four days later, on 12 February, bombs fell on the El-Khanka factory near Cairo, causing considerable damage and heavy loss of civilian life. The Minister of Defence immediately expressed his regrets, stating that the mishap was due to a navigational error. Moreover, he informed the Egyptian authorities that one heavy bomb had hit the ground without exploding and advised them how to defuse its secret detonating device. But the fact of the bombing remained and the high death toll not only aroused fury in Egypt, but also pronounced indignation in Washington. Sources close to the administration later asserted that the unfortunate incident had a major influence on Nixon's decision to extend the suspension of aircraft deliveries to Israel beyond the original planned limit of thirty days.

The officials in Washington initially evaded any explicit explanation of this step. They hinted here and there that the suspension was intended to induce the Soviet government to reduce its arms deliveries to Egypt. It appeared, however, most unlikely that the administration believed that by punishing its friends and rewarding its foes, it could make the Soviet government more co-operative. Long-standing experience pointed to the contrary.

To those of us who had watched the unfolding of the American moves in the preceding months, the 'moratorium' meant that the government was on notice from Washington to bring the fighting to an end. Already at the end of 1969 Nasser had intimated his interest in a new United States initiative. He seemed to be looking for some relief from the continued Israeli military pressure. He also sensed that his exclusive engagement to the Soviet Union strengthened the American commitment to Israel. Not long after Nasser had sent out his feelers to Washington, Dr Kissinger recommended to Israel to accept a cease-fire of ninety days' duration and the reactivation of the Jarring mission, a proposal presented by General Bull, the UN military representative in the area. He implied that Egypt would be amenable and offered his good offices to negotiate the agreement, as he had done in the past on smaller, but no less sensitive, issues. Golda resolutely rejected the idea, not because she favoured the continued fighting, reaping its daily crop of casualties on both sides, but because she suspected that Nasser would use the breathing spell to renew his attack with reinforced vigour. She had the habit of expressing her aversions in Yiddish sayings, dismissing the proposal with her favourite 'in this wood one gets strung up'. Such an *obiter dictum* of hers usually prevailed over sophisticated arguments and normally settled the issue.

However, the United States had its own idiom, which was more of a sign language. Certain things which were expected to happen, just did not happen. Rarely would the administration inform Israel that it had taken counter-measures because of a certain action or policy disapproved by it. American diplomacy preferred the silent treatment, and it was often rather late in the day before its meaning dawned on Israel's policy-makers. Suddenly certain delivery schedules would be delayed. Financial aid, previously promised on the highest level, encountered unexpected obstacles and the whole matter had to go through new processing. At particularly critical stages of gaping differences, the administration would announce the inescapable necessity of reappraising the situation, meaning: let the other side stew in its own juice until it has reconsidered its position. The administration's method of persuasion was not to cancel its promise, but to withhold its fulfilment. It operated a mechanism of parallelism, adjusting the speed of its advance towards the other party to the progress that was made in conforming with Washington's requests. In applying the subtle squeeze, it produced in the first instance more misgivings than apprehensions.

It usually took some time for the decision-makers in Israel to realize the linkage and draw the necessary conclusions. In general, the Israeli government was more impressed by blunt talk and unenigmatic action sparing it the burden of guessing, than by refined diplomatic ambiguities covering up preconceived action. The standard vocabulary of diplomatic intercourse, such as 'My government views with grave concern', rarely had a shattering effect. Especially in its Hebrew connotation of 'being worried', it provoked sometimes mildly sarcastic reactions from Prime Ministers and politicians, who would advise the American Ambassador to calm his government and stop worrying. The bemused diplomat would only occasionally be prepared to explain to his interlocutor that Washington thought that, under the circumstances, it would be advisable for Jerusalem to worry. Although Israel's politics appear sometimes rather convoluted and opaque, plain talking befits better its style of life.

A private talk with Golda

In the course of the month of March, the State Department slowly lifted the veil of obfuscation. It intimated to our embassy its intention of making a public announcement about the holding in abeyance of Israel's arms requests for an undetermined period. But it also dropped mild hints that the administration would nevertheless try to accommodate us secretly on a number of vital items. When it became clear that, regardless of Israel's representations in the highest quarters, the administration was determined to proceed with its decision, influential advisers of the Prime Minister urged Golda to counter the impending announcement of the suspension with an angry rebuttal. This advice was, as in most cases, accompanied by the suggestion that public protest should be mobilized.

I felt that such a step would be as harmful as it was useless in the given situation. The steam let off in Jerusalem would not move the wheels in Washington. Golda was, in general, more open to advice offered in private than that expressed in debates in a larger forum. This was a trait she had in common with other political leaders who do not like their authority challenged or their loss of direction exposed in front of others. I called Golda at her home. She usually answered the phone herself and responded readily to my request to see her. Regardless of the urgency of a situation she would never fail to treat her visitors to a cup of strong and tasty American coffee, brewed by herself in her own special way which was her best-guarded secret. She was gravely disturbed at our failure to change the administration's decision to continue the suspension of aircraft deliveries. She admitted that we had exhausted our powers of persuasion with the White House. Influential friends of the President had also been unable to change his decision. She was inclined to accept the rather sweeping opinion of Ambassador Rabin that Nixon had lost interest in the Jewish electorate, after having gained surprising strength in the southern states and feeling assured that there was no serious Democratic contender in the offing to defeat him in the next elections. Moreover, according to Rabin, the President was irritated at the number of Jews who played a prominent role in the struggle for civil liberties in America and were against America's involvement in the Vietnam war.

I doubted whether this was a correct reading of the reasons for the President's decision. In my view the administration wanted to persuade Israel to de-escalate its air-strikes, Egypt to agree to a cease-fire and the Soviet Union to desist from further involvement in the hostilities. It wielded its stick against Israel and dangled its carrots before Cairo and Moscow. Nonetheless, I advised Golda to avoid an open clash with the President. We had nothing to gain from it. I reminded her of a saying of her good-humoured predecessor, Levi Eshkol: 'This is a kind of fight I like, where I know the other fellow can't win.' In this case the other fellow was Israel and not the American President. I suggested that we should highlight in our reply to the expected American statement the part which reiterated the readiness of the United States to meet Israel's defence requirements at a suitable time and to ensure the military balance. The Soviet Union would anyway not co-operate with the United States to limit arms supplies to the Middle East and Washington's insistence on an early cessation of the fighting was unalterable. A cease-fire agreement would greatly increase the propects of lifting the ban. It would not only be factually wrong, but also psychologically ill-advised, to create the impression that the United States had divested itself of its commitments towards Israel. This would harden Nasser's position and encourage the Russians to believe that they could act with impunity. Meanwhile, until the publication of the announcement, we should continue trying to improve it and, more important, obtain an unpublished pledge of the continued shipment of specific items.

Golda agreed with this reasoning and the suggested line of response, but she thought that our people would expect the government at least to express its disappointment at the American decision. This was incontestably right. She asked me in preparing our draft reply to stress, besides a short expression of regret and restrained criticism, the positive American commitments towards Israel. Of course she had not lost sight of the fact that, after she had pointed to her bulging shopping bag upon her return from her meeting with the President, it would be politically unwise and diplomatically harmful to divulge that its size had dwindled.

Rogers lifts the veil

Secretary of State Rogers made the long awaited statement on Israel's arms requests on 23 March. Referring to the application made in the previous year to purchase twenty-five additional Phantoms and 100 more Skyhawks, he announced that in the judgement of the United States: 'Israel's air capacity is sufficient to meet its needs for the time being. Consequently, the President has decided to hold in abeyance for now a decision with respect to Israel's request for additional aircraft. The United States will be in a position to provide additional as well as replacement aircraft promptly if the situation requires it.' The statement then mentioned that the Soviet Union had recently introduced SAM 3 missiles and additional Soviet personnel, but it said nothing about the steps the United States contemplated taking. On the other hand, the United

States government responded positively 'to certain of Israel's short-term financial requests while studying further its longer-range needs'.

The statement assured Israel of the United States' continuing concern for its security. The President would not hesitate 'to reconsider the matter of Israel's arms requests, if steps are taken which might upset the current balance or if in our judgement political developments warrant it.' In its summation the statement revealed the direction of Washington's renewed diplomatic efforts. It would urge the parties to restore the cease-fire, reappraise their positions on peace, support Jarring's efforts to launch a process of negotiations and engage the major arms suppliers to the Middle East in early arms limitation talks. To leave no doubt about the seriousness of the United States' intentions, the announcement urged all those concerned to respond to these serious initiatives 'with the sense of urgency which the present situation demands of all responsible governments'.

This was the final accord of a carefully orchestrated piece of policy. Only a non-musical ear could miss the strength of its tone and the power of its theme.

When Ambassador Barbour personally handed the text of the statement to the Prime Minister, he was equipped with two additional briefs which were meant to soften the blow. The first one was an exegesis, whittling down negative parts of the announcement and sprucing up its more promising points. The language of the statement, explained the ambassador, was designed to warn the Soviets and the Egyptians that the President would make his eventual decision on Israel's arms requests in the light of their political and military behaviour. He did not say that this criterion was meant to apply to Israel likewise. He relied on the Prime Minister drawing her own conclusions. To allay Israel's apprehensions of a basic change in America's attitude, the ambassador assured the Prime Minister that the relations between the United States and Israel were to remain as steadfast and firm as they had been during all the years of Israel's nationhood.

But the ambassador had something more to communicate to the government. As an experienced diplomat he knew that good timing was as essential a requisite of his craft as it was for other performing arts. The sweetener he kept for the end. The President informed the Prime Minister with the greatest discretion that, in view of current attrition and losses of Israeli combat aircraft, competent US authorities would discuss with the Israeli government at an early date the replacement of lost Phantoms and Skyhawks and make additional deliveries as part of the existing contracts. Furthermore he undertook to keep open the pipeline of other military equipment, as in the past. In addition the message specified that the promised economic assistance would amount to $200 million, equivalent to the total sum Israel had requested in grants and credits.

Golda immediately grasped the importance of this part of the presidential message and dealt with it first. She appreciated the promised military and financial aid and noted the positive aspects of the President's pledge. However, in Israel's view the introduction of highly advanced Soviet weapons and first-class military personnel had already changed the military balance. Unless the United States took immediate steps to equalize the situation, Israel considered its security endangered. The public announcement of the intention to hold Israel's arms requests in abeyance was not only disappointing as such, but it was harmful to the very objectives it professed to serve. Instead of trying to convince Moscow and Cairo of the futility of changing the situation created by the Six Day War by military means, the Washington statement was likely to strengthen their hope that they might achieve their aim by continued military pressure. The ambassador preferred to avoid further argument. He assumed that the government would realize that the purpose of the American measure was to convince Israel to reduce its military pressure on Egypt and to agree to renew the cease-fire. To line up the two other parties it would use different methods: it would serenade Nasser and, when necessary, hector Moscow.

Israel's subsequent reply, published by Foreign Minister Eban, reflected the line of restraint, disappointment and appreciation we had previously recommended to the Prime Minister. It recognized that current American supplies continued, it noted that the President's decision on the supply of aircraft was defined as an interim decision and emphasized the danger evolving from increased Soviet involvement. The Foreign Minister expressed his appreciation for the favourable response to Israel's financial requests and his expectation that the United States government 'would soon take steps to prevent the increase of the dangerous imbalance and supply Israel with the aircraft so vital for her security'.

25

Cease-Fire and Diplomatic Deadlock

From now on the four sides participating in this risky tug-of-war began to heave harder and faster. They knew that they were approaching the end of the game. The Soviet Union accelerated its dispatch of arms and men; Egypt stepped up the scope and strength of its attacks; Israel hammered away full blast against the forward deployment of the SAM missile sites; and the United States shifted its diplomatic efforts into top gear.

Assistant Secretary of State Joe Sisco visited Cairo in the middle of April. Nasser took the bait which the Americans offered of pulling him out of the troubled waters with political gain. Sisco left Cairo confident that Nasser was willing to co-operate with the United States to bring the fighting to an end. He had realized that the use of Egyptian force and Russian aid were not sufficient to compel Israel to withdraw from Sinai. For that he needed powerful American support; but before extending that, Washington wanted to be sure that Nasser, who had disappointed it invariably in the past, would not let it down again. Sisco asked for a public statement inviting the United States to take a new political initiative. In his May Day speech Nasser complied with the request. As usual he coupled his vague promise with an outspoken threat. 'We will not close the door finally to the USA,' said el-Rais. But the resumption of aircraft deliveries to Israel, he thundered, 'will affect the relations of the USA and the Arab nation for hundreds of years. There will be either rupture forever, or there will be another serious and defined beginning.'

The State Department was satisfied. It accepted Nasser's bluster as a prelude to peaceful dialogue. It now turned its attention again to Israel. The stick of the suspension of the arms shipments was not sufficient in itself to obtain Israel's compliance. The carrot of the prospect of their resumption was needed to persuade the Israeli government to adjust its policies to the wishes of Washington. On 21 May, President Nixon received Foreign Minister Eban. He assured him that the suspended supplies would be discreetly resumed. He warned against any publicity; it would jeopardize his delicate diplomatic moves. But America also required some assistance from Israel. Nixon asked for a public statement indicating Israel's readiness to compromise on a peace settlement. Prime Minister Golda Meir responded immediately. On 26 May, in a speech in the Knesset, she stated that Israel continued to adhere to

Resolution 242 and agreed to enter into negotiations on a settlement by a procedure similar to the one followed in 1949 in the Rhodes armistice talks.

Two days earlier Eban had returned from Washington. Flushed with the good news he brought from his meetings with the President he hurried to take the tidings straight to the Prime Minister. He asked me to join him. After Golda had listened to his report, she asked him one single question. Why had the President failed to comply with our repeated urgings to issue a stern public warning against the mounting Soviet involvement in the hostilities? She had no comment or word of appreciation for the good news Eban had brought with him on the resumption of the aircraft deliveries. She probably doubted whether Nixon would keep more faithfully a promise given to Eban than the one she had received from him a few months earlier. The rambling conversation was interrupted by a telephone call from Defence Minister Dayan asking for authorization to bomb installations in the vicinity of Port Said. Golda asked whether there was any danger of Soviet ships being hit. Dayan reassured her and received his permission with a deep prime-ministerial sigh. It was not the first time that I had witnessed the casualness with which important military and political decisions were taken at top level. I was worried by the lack of reflection on the possible effect of decisions of such importance.

There was a curious tailpiece to the story. When Eban reported to his colleagues the success of his mission, telling them that the argument which had impressed the President most was that an adequately armed Israel was capable of defending itself alone without the aid of American forces, Dayan surprisingly took exception. He claimed, contrary to his previous declarations, that a situation could arise where Israel might need American soldiers. He did not elaborate, but his startling remark reflected his apprehension that Israel might get caught in a clash with Soviet forces. This anxiety was perhaps the key to the understanding of some of his attitudes. At the height of the fighting in 1967 he opposed the advance of Israeli forces to the Suez Canal; he feared that their deployment along the waterway could only create international complications for Israel and strengthen the Soviet position in the area. Likewise he was reluctant until the very last moment to agree to an assault on the Syrian positions on the Golan Heights; he was wary of the possibility of a sharp Soviet reaction. In the final hours of the Yom Kippur War, when powerful Soviet pressure supported by the United States denied Israel the decisive victory, Dayan warned the government that they should not ignore the possibility of open Soviet military intervention. Perhaps he sensed intuitively what Dr Kissinger later revealed in his memoirs about a talk with Ambassador Anatoly Dobrynin on the possibilities of Soviet intervention against Israel. On 8 May 1972 Kissinger advised the Soviet Ambassador of the blockade measures President Nixon had decided to take against North

Vietnamese harbours. When he asked Dobrynin how the Soviet Union would react if its 15,000 soldiers in Egypt were in imminent danger of being captured by Israelis, the Soviet Ambassador became uncharacteristically vehement and revealed more than he could have intended: 'First of all, we never put forces where they can't defend themselves. Second, if the Israelis threaten us, we will wipe them out within two days. I can assure you our plans are made for this eventuality.'

By the middle of April 1970 Israel had detected for the first time the participation of Soviet pilots in operational missions. On 4 May Dayan confirmed publicly that Israel had irrefutable evidence that the Soviets had taken upon themselves the responsibility for the air defence of the Nile delta, stating that 'the Russians are not only defending Cairo, but are relieving Egyptian forces of the job of defence so that they may be free to attack Israeli forces all along the canal. I would prefer to wait and see what we can and ought to do.' With its rear covered by Soviet defences the Egyptian army became increasingly emboldened along the Suez front line. Its artillery pounded the Bar-Lev fortifications incessantly, its air force attacked Israeli positions in Sinai in strength and its commandos raided targets across the canal. They culminated at the end of May in a successful assault on a supply convoy moving north along the east bank of the canal. Israel's losses were high – nineteen casualties in all, including eleven killed.

Public opinion was anguished and the military were concerned for the safety of our troops and our exposed positions. In a consultation convened by the Prime Minister, the Chief of Staff voiced the idea that these positions should be moved to safer and more accessible ground some ten miles away from the canal. The Minister of Defence cautiously supported the suggestion, but Golda rejected the very thought of moving any of Zahal's positions from their present location, even if tactical considerations favoured such a step. She argued forcefully that any withdrawal from the present lines would prejudice Israel's prospects of peace. It would encourage the Arab states to insist on their demand for an unconditional and complete withdrawal to the pre-1967 lines. The first retreat, even if only to a distance of ten miles, would be the beginning of a roll-back, ending who knew where. She would have nothing to do with such dangerous ideas. Instead of introducing the element of flexibility to our defence dispositions, the government decided – in the light of the Prime Minister's opposition to mobility – to reinforce the static defences of the Bar-Lev line. Golda believed that a number of strong points on the east bank of the canal was Israel's most effective defence line against any military or political onslaught.

But events did not stand still. At the beginning of June the deployment of Russian missiles had advanced close to the limit set by the air force as endangering the defence of the Bar-Lev line. Massive air-strikes, though inflicting devastating damage on Egypt, failed to halt the missile progress.

Simultaneously, the Soviets moved on the diplomatic front. On 2 June, Ambassador Dobrynin informed Secretary Rogers that the Soviet Union had obtained from Nasser certain concessions, facilitating the conclusion of a cease-fire agreement. But Washington was not keen on Soviet participation in its cease-fire initiative, which had reached its final preparatory stage.

The final thrust

On 19 June, Ambassador Barbour asked for an urgent meeting with the Prime Minister. She received him that same afternoon at her private home in a Tel Aviv garden suburb. Eban, who had just returned from London, and I joined her. While Golda served her celebrated coffee and cake, we engaged in relaxed conversation about the astounding news of the election victory of the British Conservatives which had been as much of a surprise to Golda as it had to Prime Minister Harold Wilson. Little did I suspect at the time that four years later I would take up the post of Ambassador to the Court of St James's only a few weeks before Wilson was returned to office.

When the pleasant preliminaries were over, the Ambassador came to the purpose of his visit. He rarely plunged straight into a subject, usually he approached it gingerly. A heavily-set man, he moved slowly, but his intellectual agility was as impressive as his easy-going and confidence-winning manner was endearing. He unfolded the new American cease-fire initiative with deliberate care, peeling it off like an onion and holding it far enough away from the Prime Minister's face to avoid unnecessary tears. In essence it was a two-point plan: a cease-fire of at least ninety days' duration and the resumption of the stalled Jarring talks.

The extension of the cease-fire was to be linked to the progress of the negotiations, and again the touchy question of additional aircraft delivery was vaguely related to the outcome of the talks. The message, as usual, did not fail to assure Israel of the steadfast support of the United States in its quest for security and well-being. The Prime Minister did not leave any room for uncertainty about her negative reaction to the new Rogers initiative. She was irritated by the limited and qualified nature of the cease-fire and the nebulosity of the American pledge of continued military aid. She claimed that Egypt would use the ninety days of the cease-fire to recover from Israel's heavy blows, absorb more Soviet arms and personnel, and renew the next round of fighting from better positions. At the same time Israel's defence potential would be weakened by the continued American denial of vital armaments and its negotiating position would be prejudiced.

The Prime Minister was less outspoken in her criticism of the political part of the suggested text. The United States proposed that Ambassador Jarring should report to the UN Secretary-General informing the Security Council that Egypt, Jordan and Israel had agreed:

1. To hold discussions under the auspices of the Special Representative, according to such procedures and at such places he may recommend, noting that the parties have accepted and indicated their willingness to carry out Resolution 242 in all its parts;
2. To reach agreement on the establishment of a just and lasting peace based on the provisions of the resolution;
3. To facilitate the promotion of such an agreement, the parties will strictly observe for at least ninety days the cease-fire resolutions of the Security Council.

The Prime Minister, supported by the Foreign Minister, made it clear that she did not expect the government to accept the plan, but Ambassador Barbour strongly urged that Israel should not be the first to reject the initiative. It should concede this dubious privilege to Nasser who, in his view, would not accept the proposal. I found this argument rather unconvincing and differed from his assessment. Secretary Rogers would not have approached Israel without having previously ascertained Egypt's views. The wording of the proposed announcement to be made by Jarring sounded too much like Egyptian Foreign Ministry language. Golda supported my assumption that Egypt would accept the deal and stated that the government would not base its decision on a bet. The embattled ambassador realized that, in the final analysis, Israel's response would depend less on the duration of the cease-fire and the text of the Jarring statement than on the resumption of the shipment of the aircraft and other defence equipment. An unguarded remark of his that perhaps the consolidation of the cease-fire would make the deliveries unnecessary had the Prime Minister up in arms. If that was the purpose of the whole exercise, she exclaimed, how could he expect Israel to co-operate? In less than twenty-four hours the ambassador had this matter cleared up with Washington. On the Saturday night preceding the weekly Sunday cabinet meeting, he asked me to tell the Prime Minister that he had received a positive clarification on the arms issue which should lay her apprehensions at rest.

The message did not sway the cabinet. It decided unanimously to reject the plan. A strongly worded reply was sent to Ambassador Rabin for submission to the State Department, but he refused to transmit it because in his view it was ill-advised and harmful to Israel's best interests. He advised the government to concede to Egypt the right of first refusal, being convinced also that Egypt would reject the plan.

The not-very-rigid rules of our budding foreign service allowed its representatives a large measure of freedom to express their views on matters within their competence and often also beyond it. It left them considerable tactical liberty in the execution of policy directives. Ambassadors were used to making major policy speeches without prior clearance from home. It would have been difficult otherwise. Unless the speech was intended beforehand for wide media circulation, very few took the time and adopted the recommendable habit of preparing a written text. Ambassador Rabin added a new dimension to this liberal practice. He also commented, for home consumption to the Israeli media, on the wisdom of the policies of his own government and the alleged errors of its Foreign Minister. His barbs evoked regular irritation, occasional reprimands and eventually resigned despair. But his refusal to convey a government decision on a crucial issue transcended the level of tolerance which the Prime Minister was ready to accept. She summoned him to Jerusalem for consultations. It was a useful step, not for its disciplinary effect but for the opportunity it afforded Rabin to persuade the government to reconsider its first rather impetuous decision and to tone down its reply.

Secretary Rogers' public announcement on 25 June of the new American initiative, without disclosing its contents, had naturally stirred up widespread public interest in Israel and much unfounded political guesswork. After considerable internal pressure on the Prime Minister to reveal the details of the American proposal and disclose Israel's reply, she accepted the view that a public debate at this stage could only cause harm to Israel and unnecessarily burden its relations with the United States. She contented herself with a short and general statement in the Knesset on 29 June. Refusing to discuss the substance of the initiative, she firmly took Nasser to task for propagating the idea of a conditional and limited cease-fire. He required such a transitional period, she declared, 'to prepare for the renewal of the war in a more intense form'.

From this point on the administration in Washington engaged in a cautious but steady course of diplomatic attrition. It tried to reassure Israel by the shipment of sophisticated electronic countermeasure equipment and please it by calling Syria and Egypt 'its aggressive neighbours'. It urged Soviet restraint, with Dr Kissinger going as far as to say to the press 'we are trying to expel the Soviet military presence from Egypt, its combat personnel, before they become too firmly entrenched'. It worked on Egypt to obtain its support by sponsoring its formulations for the resumption of the Jarring talks.

Meanwhile the War of Attrition continued with undiminished fury. Egypt increasingly felt the weight of the air-strikes and Israel encountered mounting difficulties from the greatly improved air defences. In the course of the month of July it lost five Phantom fighters. The government debate on the Rogers initiative reached, at times, apocalyptic heights. Cabinet minister Begin predicted that the implementation of the plan would expose Israel to unthinkable perils. It would lead, he exclaimed, to a new Auschwitz or Masada. He was particularly apprehensive about the political consequences of renewing the Jarring talks on the basis of the proposed formula. The wording of 'carrying out Resolution 242 in all its parts' and 'withdrawal from territories' were anathema to him. A few weeks later the adoption of these words by the government impelled Mr Begin and his colleagues to leave the Government of National Unity. Eight years and one war later Prime Minister Begin signed the Camp David agreement which contained these very same formulations and others which went even farther than the Rogers text of 1970.

Meanwhile, part of a Soviet fighter squadron had been transferred from the interior of Egypt to an airfield close to the canal zone. On 30 July, a flight of Israeli fighter planes encountered a number of Soviet aircraft, piloted by Russians, some thirty kilometres west of the canal. They shot down four of the Soviet planes and the others dispersed. It was the parting shot of the War of Attrition. The government received the news with a mixture of awe and admiration and decided to suppress any publicity of the incident. However, a few months later, on 25 October, Prime Minister Meir told a startled audience of Jewish students in New York who had criticized her policy: 'We know there are Russians in Egypt because we shot down four of their pilots.'

On 31 July, the day after the dramatic combat, the government informed Washington of its acceptance of the Rogers plan. From the end of June Nasser had spent several weeks in the Soviet Union for medical treatment and political consultations. On 11 July, Moscow published a plan for the settlement of the conflict on lines similar to the original Rogers plan of December 1969. While in Moscow, Nasser received the agreement of the Soviet leadership that he should respond affirmatively to the new American initiative. On 22 July, shortly after Nasser's return to Cairo, Foreign Minister Mahmoud Riad officially notified Secretary Rogers of Egypt's acceptance. His letter, containing more reservations than affirmations and obviously co-ordinated with the State Department, was accepted by it as a satisfactory reply.

The administration was not too keen on active Soviet partnership in its initiative, but thought it advisable to insure itself against Russian obstruction. The observance of the cease-fire required at least a measure of Soviet restraint. Assistant Secretary of State Sisco consequently informed Ambassador Dobrynin of the details of the agreement. After consultation with his government Dobrynin informed the State Department that Moscow had no objections. He read his statement from an unaddressed and unsigned sheet, a 'talking paper' in American foreign service jargon. Astute Joe Sisco asked him to leave it with him as a cherished memento and kept it on file as an insurance against future Soviet disavowal.

Presidential persuasion

The Egyptian acceptance placed the Israeli government in a dilemma as it was deeply split in its attitude. Even those ministers who tended to accept the plan had grievous doubts about its usefulness. Immediately following Egypt's acceptance, President Nixon dispatched a reassuring letter to Prime Minister Meir. It was meant to strengthen her hand, allay the fears of the opponents and persuade the doubters. The President pledged the continued supply of arms and substantial economic aid, assured Israel of his rejection of the Arab interpretation of Resolution 242, and said that he would not ask Israel to move from the present lines 'until a binding contractual peace agreement satisfactory to Israel had been achieved'. Furthermore, the President promised not to support a solution of the Arab refugee problem which would fundamentally alter the Jewish character of the state and endanger its security.

The message had its intended effect. It contained sufficient inducements for the majority of the cabinet to recognize that it was safer for Israel to comply with the President's request than to defy it. The argument in the government was sharp. Those who looked for consolation asserted that the Rogers June initiative eliminated the Rogers plan of the previous December. As Dean Acheson once said, what seemed to be policy in the winter was a hallucination in the spring. Yet the United States plan in winter for an overall settlement, made public by Secretary Rogers in December 1969, was far from being a mirage. It was shelved in preference of the cease-fire proposal which, of course, had a claim to priority. At every deadlock or turning point the old plan reappeared, and it finally made the grade when parts of it were incorporated into the Israeli-Egyptian framework agreement concluded at Camp David in September 1978.

At this stage the Prime Minister concluded that Israel had exhausted its leverage and recommended to the government to accept the cease-fire proposals coupled with renewed Jarring talks. It succeeded in obtaining an important addition which improved the cease-fire arrangement: Egypt and Israel agreed 'to refrain from changing the *status quo* within zones extending fifty kilometres to the west and east of the cease-fire line'. Both sides undertook not to introduce or construct any new installations in these zones. The purpose of this addendum from Israel's point of view was to halt the forward deployment of the Russian SAM missiles, which had caused so many difficulties and unexpected losses to the Israeli air force. The missile standstill was to become a cardinal point in the implementation of the Rogers plan.

Begin leaves the government

By a vote of seventeen in favour and opposed by the six Gahal members – forerunners of the Likud Party, some of them reluctantly following Begin's lead – the government accepted the American proposal six weeks after it had been submitted to it. The decision brought the War of Attrition and the Government of National Unity to an end. But before the government finally broke up, the Prime Minister made a last-minute attempt to improve the political terms relating to the resumption of the Jarring talks. She appointed a special drafting-group, chaired by herself, to iron out certain terminological idiosyncrasies. Golda was aware that the margin for change was minimal because the wording reflected basic American positions, formulated to make them acceptable to Cairo and tolerable to Moscow. But when the ministerial working-group tried to amend some of the formulations, it met with unforeseen opposition from Dayan. He rejected the text altogether and insisted on a new home-made version. It became obvious that the principal purpose of Dayan's intervention was a last-minute attempt to avoid Begin's departure from the government.

In any event, the prime-ministerial committee drafting Israel's reply was not in a philosophical mood. The ministers were aware that no formula could be devised that would both satisfy Begin and be acceptable to Cairo, Washington and Moscow. Moreover further delay was costly in lives which could be spared by a cessation of the fighting, so close at hand. Still, Dayan managed to delay the reply for two more days. Only after he had convinced himself that Begin's decision was irrevocable did he support an insignificantly amended text.

It has become an Israeli national pastime, cherished by many and loathed by others, to figure out the true intentions behind the surprise moves of Moshe Dayan. Some appear to be so involved that seasoned Dayanologists believe that he himself is not always clear at the onset of an opaque move of the end he strives for. Rocking the boat is his favourite tactic, not to overturn it, but to sway it sufficiently for the helmsman to lose his grip or for some of its unwanted passengers to fall overboard. His reactions sometimes appear to represent more an urge to contradict for the sake of opposition than a reflection of a considered opinion. When he attempted to stall the acceptance of the American cease-fire plan, the leadership of the Labour Party tried to accommodate him, fearing his defection from the party ranks. They suspected that together with a few of his friends in the Knesset, Dayan might vote with Begin's Gahal Party to unseat the government. They were determined to avert such an eventuality. In this respect Israeli politicians are no different from their fellow practitioners elsewhere: retention of power is their *ultima ratio*.

Golda was in an unenviable position. Torn between the desire to keep her government intact and Israel's relations with the United States unharmed, she turned in her distress to Ambassador Barbour. Late in the evening of 5 August she made him privy to her dilemma. She asked him to explain to his government the domestic difficulties which had compelled her to dispatch a reply which was slightly different from the text proposed by Washington. After all, an internal upheaval was not likely to serve either Israel's or America's best interests. Barbour assured her of his personal sympathy and support and expressed the belief that as long as Israel's reply responded to the original Rogers initiative of 19 June, he did not expect any trouble.

Missed missile standstill

Meanwhile the Minister of Defence was supposed to work out the detailed arrangements of the cease-fire with the representatives of the US embassy. It was of particular importance to demarcate clearly the fifty-kilometre-wide special zones. In view of the agreed prohibition to advance and introduce new missile installations, it was vital for the observance of the standstill that Israel should have a clear picture of the missile deployment on the Egyptian side at the hour the cease-fire agreement took effect. But as General Yariv, then chief of military intelligence, later revealed, Dayan dismissed his reminders that the existing dispositions should be mapped and attached to the agreement to prove any possible violation of the missile standstill. The Minister of Defence, apparently too deeply immersed in his other preoccupations, discarded the advice with the curt and ominous remark that, in any case, he expected the Egyptians to move their missiles into the prohibited zone. And so they did. The night the cease-fire came into force, the Egyptian army with the help of Soviet crews advanced numerous new missile installations into the vicinity of the canal.

On 7 August, the day the cease-fire became operative, the State Department authorized the Secretary-General of the United Nations to publish the original text of the Rogers initiative for the resumption of the Jarring talks, disregarding the wording of the Israeli reply which the Prime Minister had made public in her statement to the Knesset on 4 August. Golda made a last-minute attempt to prevent the discrepancy. In a rather emotional telephone conversation with Sisco she accused the State Department of bad faith and asked him to defer the publication of the statement. The Assistant Secretary of State protested innocence and explained that, anyway, it was too late for changes. Secretary-General U Thant had already authorized the publication of the original Rogers text.

As on previous occasions when similar 'misunderstandings' had occurred, the State Department assumed that Israel would calm down after a while and accept the accomplished fact. But the Egyptian violation of the missile stand-still still aggravated Israel's differences with the United States. For three weeks Washington declined to confirm the hard evidence which Israeli intelligence submitted to it, proving the forward movement of the SAM missiles. On 6 September the government submitted to Dayan's strong urgings to delay Israel's participation in the Jarring talks until the missile crisis had found a satisfactory solution. By that time the State Department had recognized that Egypt had violated the agreement, but had no remedy to offer.

A year later George Macovescu, Deputy and later Foreign Minister of Romania, told us during a visit to Jerusalem that he had discussed the missile crisis with Nasser on 5 September 1970, a month after the conclusion of the cease-fire agreement and three weeks before Nasser's death. Upon instructions from President Ceausescu, he had asked the Egyptian leader whether Israel's claim was true that Egypt had moved missiles forward after the agreement had come into force. Nasser flatly denied the allegation. Macovescu commented: 'I looked at Nasser, and he knew that I knew that he had not told the truth.' The Romanian Minister was not a man to be easily fobbed off. His President was very concerned, he insisted, and wanted to know all the facts. Did Nasser really want him to tell Ceausescu that no movement of missiles had taken place? Nasser, lowering his head and his voice, replied: 'That night we only moved one battalion of missiles.'

The three-months' cease-fire holds three years

Autumn passed in futile efforts to break the deadlock on the diplomatic front and to remedy the violation of the missile standstill on the ground. But by September the crisis which broke out in Jordan overshadowed all other events. In November, Dayan had reached the conclusion that the time was ripe to terminate the boycott of the Jarring talks, although earlier in the month he had sternly opposed Eban's appeal to change the government's decision. In a speech in Haifa, the Minister of Defence's recommendation that Israel should resume the Jarring talks surprised not only his audience. His splashing metaphor that Israel 'should jump into the icy water' chilled the Prime Minister's fascination with her Minister of Defence and turned it into angry consternation. Not unnaturally Golda had held the view that when the necessity arose to switch policy, she would have the privilege to announce it after having consulted her cabinet. But Dayan's initiative forced the government's hand and after a few more weeks of hesitation it decided to return to the Jarring talks. It was not so much Dayan's concern for progress of the stalled Jarring mission that had prompted his surprise move. He was pursuing a new idea for which he tried to obtain American support. He hoped to consolidate the cease-fire by a new agreement providing for the re-opening of the Suez Canal, to be linked to the withdrawal of Israeli forces from the east bank of the waterway. At the beginning of February 1971, President Sadat, who had succeeded Nasser in September, responded favourably to a plan for a peace settlement launched by Ambassador Jarring. Although the plan in itself did not lead the parties to peace negotiations, it provided sufficient reason for Sadat to agree to the extension of the cease-fire. Indeed, it survived its three-month deadline by more than three years, until it was obliterated by Egypt's surprise attack on the day of Yom Kippur.

The violation of the missile standstill undertaking of 1970 gave Egypt a substantial tactical advantage when it decided in 1973 to break the cease-fire agreement. Its anti-aircraft missiles, moved into the prohibited canal area, reduced effectively the freedom of action of the Israeli air force over the battle zone. This handicap not only lessened the losses of the Egyptian forces crossing the canal but enabled them to accomplish the daring operation, an act of far greater political consequence than of military significance. Israel's lack of alertness in 1973, and the role and responsibility of its political and military leaders in the calamitous state of affairs, became the central theme of a fierce national debate from which the nation slowly emerged in a more sober and chastened mood. The 'mechdal', as the initial failings of the Yom Kippur War were euphemistically termed, was the aggregate of a wide variety of shortcomings, one of which was the failure to map and certify the Egyptian missile deployment prior to the cease-fire.

26

US–USSR: Common Denominators and Conflicting Objectives

The Mediterranean and the Red Sea washing Israel's western and southern shores are its natural outlet to the oceans of the world. But for more than thirty years Israel had been politically a land-locked country, cut off from all peaceful communication with its immediate neighbours.

Situated at the fringe of the vast desert lands extending eastwards to the Euphrates river and south-westwards to the Nile delta, the unimpaired flow of fresh water had been the country's life-blood from time immemorial. It was as scarce as all Israel's other natural resources. Perhaps this paucity of natural wealth produced the richness of its history. It certainly made a vigorous physical effort indispensable for survival and spurred the human mind to refine its ingenuity.

The availability of sweet-water sources and the access to salt water oceans have been two principal concerns of Israel's political action and military defence. Any threat directed against these two vital points has always evoked alarm in Israel; any tampering with them by hostile neighbours has eventually led to war. Their denial strikes at the roots of Israel's existence as a country capable of providing a livelihood for its people and of sustaining its links with the outside world, where its main human and material reserves are stored.

While the first war, waged by the Arab states in 1948 against Israel, had been an all-out attempt and subsequent failure to wipe the Jewish state off the map of the world, the reasons for the outbreak of the three major wars of 1956, 1967 and 1973 were the interference with maritime freedom and the threat to the free flow of the Jordan waters, the principal source of Israel's irrigation needs. In 1956, Israel joined battle against Egypt when it added the blockade of the Straits of Tiran to its continued closure of the Suez Canal to Israeli shipping, at a time when the flow of Soviet arms to Egypt and stepped-up terrorist activities had created a situation of grave peril to Israel's security.

The war of 1967 was preceded by a Syrian attempt, endorsed by a summit conference of the Arab League, to divert the headwaters of the Jordan river. It broke out when Egypt reimposed the blockade of the Straits of Tiran, which had been kept open since 1957 by a United Nations force stationed at Sharm el-Sheikh.

The Yom Kippur War was initiated by Sadat after Egypt and Israel had failed to agree on an American-negotiated arrangement to re-open the Suez Canal, subject to the withdrawal of the Israeli forces to a certain distance from their positions along the east bank of the waterway.

The threat to the water supply and the denial of access to the sea, although recurrent and pre-eminent themes in the Arab-Israeli conflict, were surely not an exclusive cause of the protracted struggle. Their activation, however, raised the temperature of over-heated tensions to boiling-point.

In his book *Foreign Policy System of Israel*, Professor Michael Brecher quotes my views on the principal flashpoints which I summarized for him in August 1966:

There are four Arab acts which would constitute a *casus belli* for Israel; two are on water, two on land. One is the attempt to divert the waters of the Jordan, the other the closing of the Straits of Tiran, the third is control of the West Bank by a state or united command more powerful than Jordan, and the fourth is the concentration of Egyptian military power in the Sinai desert.

Cease-fire agreements

There are other common features peculiar to the pattern of the conflict. All the military encounters culminated in tangible military decisions, and ended in political deadlock. The superpowers, watching carefully the evolution of the fighting, intervened decisively through the Security Council or directly when the situation seemed to be spreading into a wider conflagration. All the four major Arab-Israeli wars, as well as the War of Attrition, were terminated by a cease-fire agreed between the United States and the Soviet Union and imposed upon the warring parties by their joint action inside or outside the United Nations. The state of relations prevailing at the time between the two powers, and their commitments to the parties involved in the fighting, determined the intensity of their diplomatic action but not its ultimate outcome.

In the War of Independence of 1948, the United States and the Soviet Union supported Israel against Arab aggression. They had no difficulties in expediting cease-fire decisions, although at certain stages the Soviet Union showed greater reluctance than the United States to break the momentum of a successful Israeli counter-offensive.

In the Sinai and Suez campaign of 1956, America and Russia again co-operated effectively to bring the fighting to a halt. But this time they took the Arab side and forced Israel, Britain and France to halt operations and to evacuate the occupied territories. Acting jointly with the Soviet Union, the United States frustrated the intentions of its close allies to put an end to Nasser's harmful policies. Thus American misjudgement carried in it the seeds of further wars, accelerating Soviet penetration of the Middle East and North Africa and weakening established Western influence in the area.

The errors of 1956 came home to roost in the Six Day War of 1967. Supported by the Soviet Union, Nasser embarked on a course of action which inexorably led to war. The United States, aware of its miscalculations in 1956 and convinced, as enlightened opinion was throughout the world, of the justice of Israel's action in self-defence, resisted rash and drastic decisions urged on it by the Soviet Union. This time the Soviet Union had to accommodate itself to the timing and the terms of an American cease-fire resolution, which neither hampered the Israeli forces reaching the Suez Canal, nor called for their withdrawal from the territories evacuated by the defeated Arab armies. The resolution confined itself to a call for the cessation of the armed hostilities. Only on the sixth day of the fighting, when the Israeli forces in pursuit of the Syrian army advanced in the direction of Damascus, did the United States add its weight to the continuous Soviet pressure, expressed in thinly veiled threats of intervention, and insist on an immediate termination of all military activity.

The Yom Kippur War of 1973 produced the sharpest polarization and the nearest confrontation that had ever happened between the Soviet Union and the United States in the Arab-Israeli conflict. In addition to the total political support which the Soviet government gave to the Arab side – a policy which it had religiously followed since 1956 – it operated, from the beginning of the combined Arab attack, a steady sea and airlift of massive arms supplies to Egypt and Syria. The United States responded after a short delay with sizeable emergency shipments to Israel. In view of the initial Arab military successes the Soviet Union delayed any initiative by the Security Council to adopt a cease-fire injunction. The United States also assumed a reserved attitude in expectation of an Israeli counter-attack. When the fortunes of war changed at the end of the second week of fighting and sizeable Israeli forces had succeeded in crossing the canal, the Soviet Union invited Dr Kissinger to go with utmost urgency to Moscow to discuss the immediate cessation of the hostilities. Less than forty-eight hours later the Security Council fulfilled its duty. It supported a joint United States-Soviet resolution calling for an immediate cease-fire concurrent with the opening of peace negotiations.

Throughout the thirty years of conflict the estimated timing of intervention by the Security Council in the fighting had engaged the closest attention of the military planners of both sides. Strategists and field commanders planned and conducted their campaigns virtually with an eye on the ticking of the United Nations clock. They accelerated the advance or slowed down the retreat of their forces in synchronization with the movement of the clock's hands. The ringing of the Security Council bell was never absent from their mind because they knew that military means would not finally decide the outcome of the conflict. While Israel had always been conscious that a lost war meant the end of its political and probably physical existence, the Arab states never thought that a defeat would deprive them of the chance to recover in the political arena what they had lost on the battlefield. They remained convinced throughout of their capacity to turn military failure into political success.

The attitude of the great powers strengthened Arab belief in their political invincibility. While the Soviet Union and the United States had jointly applied their influence at every critical stage to bring major Israeli-Arab fighting to a halt, they continuously failed to agree on the termination of the state of war and its substitution by a permanent peace. They were unable to agree on a common denominator because they pursued conflicting objectives. Even when it sympathized with Israel in its fight for survival in the early period of its independence, the Soviet Union refrained in the ensuing years from lending any noticeable support to its struggle for peace. Despite innumerable tactical changes of its Middle-Eastern policy, Soviet strategy was unalterably aimed at a state of permanent instability in the area. The consistently one-sided political and military assistance which the Soviet Union granted to the Arab states strengthened their defiance of Israel's peace initiatives. The Russian policy of no-lasting-peace and no-lengthy-war helped fan the smouldering flames into sporadic conflagrations, never to be extinguished completely but only to be dowsed by the diplomatic fire brigades of the two superpowers until a new spark would reignite the embers.

Avoidance of confrontation

However, the danger of confrontation between the Soviet Union and the United States in the Middle East was not only inherent in the Arab-Israeli conflict. There were numerous situations where the interests of Moscow and Washington in the area clashed openly, beginning with Soviet reluctance to withdraw their occupation forces from northern Iran in 1946, and extending to Soviet military intervention in Afghanistan in 1980. Only two years after their joint action against Israel, France and Britain in 1956, the two superpowers were again at loggerheads when the United States landed forces in the Lebanon to assist its government to protect the independence of the country threatened by Soviet-Egyptian subversion. The Soviet government reacted with threats of counteraction, moving troops into its southern regions bordering Turkey. In practice it confined itself to an outpouring of invective against the 'American aggressors'. A specially convened General Assembly of the UN, after a routine exercise of tumult and shouting, relegated the issue to the no less agitated intimacy of the Arab League.

The American show of force reduced the acute inflammation in Lebanon, but did not remedy the malady of foreign subversion against Western-orientated regimes in the area. It erupted with regularity and reached a new high-point of crisis in the rebellion instigated by Yassir Arafat against the Hashemite monarchy in Jordan. The happenings of September 1970 became a hideous landmark in the turn of events in the region. When Palestinian armoured forces, trained by the Syrian army and equipped with Soviet tanks and ammunition, crossed into Jordan and advanced on Amman, its capital, the United States felt constrained to intervene again. Its action was threefold: it flexed its muscles by moving units of the Sixth Fleet closer to the eastern shores of the Mediterranean; it supported Jordanian requests for Israel's assistance; and it cautioned the Soviet Union to exercise restraint and to exert its influence on the government in Damascus to withdraw instantly the Syrian-controlled forces from Jordan. The multiple American prescription worked wonders. It saved Jordan, defeated Arafat, deepened the rift in the Arab ranks, persuaded Syria to desist from military adventures and warned the Soviet Union of the inherent dangers of supporting them.

In the contest which the great powers have been waging in the Middle East for the last three decades, they have evolved a set of rules for East and West to abide by in times of crisis. The Soviet Union advances as long as the going is good. When it encounters determined American resistance, it either tries to consolidate its newly gained positions or limits its direct involvement. Soviet daring has increased over the years but so have the risks incurred. On occasions when Soviet policy had overreached itself and created a direct threat to vital Western interests in the area, the United States managed to rally and curb the Soviet challenge. Just as all the full-scale wars between the Arab states and Israel have been halted by cease-fire orders agreed upon by the United States and the Soviet Union, so were all major confrontations between the two superpowers, even when they culminated, as in October 1973, in an American nuclear alert, resolved by the mutual withdrawal from the brink, but not by an agreed political accommodation of their interests and aspirations in the area.

27

Upheaval in Jordan

A different set of rules governed intra-regional relations. Since the Arab states lacked a common policy, apart from their rejection of Israel, they reacted to crisis situations in their own individual ways. The localization of fighting in one sector and its eventual suspension reduced endemic regional tensions only in a few cases. Cease-fire agreements in one sector frequently sparked off flare-ups on other fronts, not necessarily between Israel and one of its other neighbours, but also between the Arab states themselves. Each Arab-Israeli war left behind its crop of political casualties. Every Arab-Israeli accord with one part of the Arab world released shockwaves of fierce discontent in another.

In the wake of the disastrous outcome of the military intervention launched by six Arab states against the fledgling State of Israel in 1948 and the armistice agreements concluded with it a year later, the Syrian government was overthrown by a military coup; the Egyptian monarchy was replaced by Nasser's revolution; Riad el Solh, the Premier of Lebanon, was assassinated; and King Abdullah of Jordan was shot dead at prayer in the El Aqsa mosque. In the ensuing years, chain reactions of similar severity repeated themselves after the other wars and agreements, some not related to Israel at all. In Baghdad, the regime of Nuri Said was wiped out together with the dynasty; in Damascus, one military *putsch* succeeded another with seasonal regularity; and in Beirut, parliamentary government was torn asunder by civil strife and the national cohesion of the country was threatened by Arab intrusion. The misfortunes of the Arab-Israeli conflict were not the root cause of the regional turbulence. They were no more than a contributory element which acted like yeast in the general process of fermentation.

There was one lonely ruler, however, who, with amazing persistence, managed to emerge unscathed from the perennial ordeal. King Hussein of Jordan became the modern political Noah of the great Middle East flood. On his ark he paired the dove with the hawk and sent them out to scout for firm ground and a safe anchorage. He is the great survivor on the fast-spinning oriental turntable. He was standing next to his grandfather when he was murdered in the mosque; he emerged from the war in 1948 with most of the territory allocated by the UN to the Palestinian Arabs conquered and annexed by the Hashemite Kingdom of Jordan; he survived the loss of his Palestinian conquest when he was rash enough to join Nasser's war against Israel in 1967. He was never choosy in the choice of his allies when the existence of his regime was at stake. They formed a broad spectrum of swiftly changing colours. At the hour of his gravest peril the nimble King did not hesitate to invoke the aid of Israel when Yassir Arafat and his cohorts rose to overthrow him.

Black September

Barely a month had passed since 7 August 1970, the date the Egyptian-Israeli cease-fire agreement had become effective, when Arafat and his forces decided to open up a new front. His PLO dreaded nothing more than the idea of tranquillity descending upon the area. To rekindle the flames, they hatched a weird combined air and land operation aimed at hitting Jordan, harming Western countries and provoking Israel.

The fifth of September was D-day for the terrorist spectacular. September, in general, is an eventful month. After a leisurely summer recess, not only the peace-makers but also the men of violence are intent on resuming their activities. The latter prepare their actions with an eye on the propaganda stage which the annual session of the UN General Assembly so generously offers. For them the United Nations is not a deterrent to the use of force, but rather a vehicle for the propagation of violence.

At the Foreign Ministry we had no definite information about any operational plans. Our intelligence services shared our assumption that something was brewing, but were not in a position to identify the nature and timing of the anticipated operation. At noon-time on 5 September the members of the government and a great number of personalities from all walks of life in Israel were assembled in Jerusalem to attend the funeral of Zalman Aranne, Minister of Education and a highly respected labour leader, who had belonged to the select group of old-timers influential in the affairs of the nation for more than four decades. Whether it was a feeling of premonition which made me abandon the funeral procession and return to my office, is hard to say so many years after the event. Be that as it may, I had just settled down behind my desk with a pile of telegrams in front of me, when the head of my private office rushed in with the news that an El Al plane on its way from Amsterdam to New York had been hijacked. Chanan Bar-On had no peer in the Foreign Ministry in the speed of gathering information, reliability in checking it out and practicality in handling it.

In quick succession the news followed of three more hijackings. This then was Arafat's autumn offensive. The El Al crew, after having succeeded in subduing the two attackers, landed the plane safely at London airport. We asked our embassy to transmit to the captain the government's instructions to take off immediately for Ben Gurion airport, but the British authorities refused permission. They insisted that the body of the hijacker and his wounded woman companion be taken off the plane, and the incident, as they preferred to call the attack, fully investigated. They had worked out that it must have happened within the jurisdiction of British airspace. Had they realized that only a few days later PLO terrorists holding nearly 300 air passengers hostage in Jordan would compel the British government to release Leila Khaled without due process of law, they might well have preferred not to have interfered with our instructions.

The hijackers forced two of the other captured airliners to land at an abandoned desert airstrip near Zerka in Jordan. The third one, a Pan American jumbo, came down in Cairo, to be blown up by the terrorists immediately after its passengers and crew had been evacuated. The fourth plane, the El Al craft, had successfully resisted being diverted to Arab territory. The list was impressive: about 200 passengers held hostage in the Jordanian desert, two planes seized and one demolished. But this was just the curtain-raiser for a dizzying round of events.

Two days after the multiple hijacking, PLO men seized a British Airways plane in Beirut, and forced it to join the other two at Zerka, augmenting the number of hostages by roughly 100. The purpose of the exercise was to raise the stakes and to exert special pressure on the British government to dispense with legal proceedings against Leila Khaled, the woman hijacker removed from El Al captivity to British custody. She was an experienced operator, having gained notoriety in previous exploits of air piracy. Her capture was a matter of high priority for the police in a number of countries and by the same token her release a matter of utmost urgency for the leaders of her organization.

The PLO, having completed the first stage of their operation with three planes and more than 300 hostages in their bag, now announced their conditions. Israel was to set free some 200 security detainees, and Britain, Switzerland and Germany were to release from prison all Arab terrorists, convicted or awaiting trial. Unless the governments complied within seventy-two hours, all the passengers and crew locked up in the planes would be blown up together with the aircraft. The heat was on – in the true sense of the word. The hapless people, incarcerated in the unventilated planes, virtually broiled in the desert sun while the officials of the governments involved seethed under the responsibility weighing upon them.

The governments whose planes and nationals were involved tried to impress on Israel that its decision would decide the fate of the hostages. Either it should yield to the demands of the terrorists or launch a daring rescue mission. Entebbe was then still far away; the cabinet was divided. Golda Meir felt that, although no Israelis were among the captives, an outright refusal to release Arab detainees would place a grave responsibility on the government. After consulting my colleagues at the Ministry who were well versed in Arab affairs, I advised the Prime Minister that all concerned should refrain from any move in any direction for the duration of the seventy-two hour ultimatum. If we were all to sit it out calmly, eyeball to eyeball, so to speak, the hijackers would be the first to blink.

As I used that by now proverbial saying, I remembered when I had heard it for the first time. At the height of the Cuban missile crisis I had met Joe Sisco in the delegates' lounge adjoining the Security Council. I had asked him how things were going, and he told me that he had just attended a meeting in Washington, where Dean Rusk had assessed the situation: 'We are eyeball to eyeball with the Soviets, and they are blinking.' 'But we have a problem with the governor,' added Sisco somewhat mysteriously. He steered me into a quiet corner and explained that Adlai Stevenson, the United States permanent representative, insisted on fighting the confrontation between the two titans on the battleground of the United Nations. After the anticipated Soviet veto, Stevenson wanted to continue the discussion in the General Assembly under the provisions of the ill-famed 'Uniting for Peace Resolution'. 'Do I have to explain to a representative of Israel, what it would mean to leave the management of this momentous crisis to the whims of 120 governments? Most of them would try to assume the role of the mediator and all of them would aspire to a compromise, injurious to the national security of the United States and the safety of the free world.' Recalling Israel's plight in 1956, when the United States and the Soviet Union put the screws on it using that same resolution, I realized the irony of the present situation. But in view of its gravity, I refrained from making any commemorative comment. I confined myself to endorsing Sisco's view and to commiserating with him in his professional predicament. But he was too much a man of action to leave it at that. 'I think you could do a lot of good if you talked to the governor. He may listen to your experience.' I waited until Stevenson got up from his seat during an interpretation interlude. 'Governor, what do you expect to be the outcome of this Security Council debate?' I asked him innocently. 'A Soviet veto', he snapped back. 'And then?' I continued probing. 'Then we go to the General Assembly under "Uniting for Peace",' he answered unhesitatingly. 'Wouldn't that be a rather more dividing than uniting step?' I plodded cautiously on my set course. 'What do you mean?' asked Stevenson, slightly puzzled. I explained that to have 120 mediators at his neck, all shoving in different directions, did not appear to me the most enjoyable prospect. He scratched his head and stared vacantly into the bustling Council chamber. 'What would you suggest I do?' he asked, giving me the cue. 'I would try to prolong the debate in the Council until Washington and Moscow have found a solution to the crisis. I would filibuster, exposing the machinations of the Soviet Union and the falsehoods of its representatives. In any case I believe it is worth trying to avoid the vote as long as possible. If the two sides reach agreement, it may need some UN wrapping, but if, God forbid, they decide to step forward over the brink, no force in the world will be capable of holding them back.' The next speaker on the list was the representative of the United States.

Stevenson pressed his Soviet colleague heavily to state clearly whether there were Soviet missiles deployed in Cuba or not. Ambassador Zorin took evasive action. He resented the interrogation. This was not a courtroom, he exclaimed. But Stevenson continued doggedly: 'I shall sit here and wait for your answer until hell freezes over.'

Before the seventy-two hours were up, the hijackers at Zerka began to quiver. They asked for food and water to be delivered on board and threatened to blow up the planes at the slightest movement of the Jordanian forces which surrounded them. From information reaching us, we gathered that King Hussein wanted to liberate the hostages by military assault. His forces were closing the ring around the planes, a move which had been noticed by the terrorists. We suggested to the American embassy that they advise the Jordanian government to refrain from any precipitate action and maintain the siege of the planes from a safe distance.

While our attention at the Foreign Ministry was focused on the events in Jordan, news reached us unexpectedly that there was some trouble on the Lebanese border. Our UN representative asked for information and instructions. On the latter we were able to oblige. Debates at the United Nations were conducted by a rule best described by Beaumarchais' remark: 'One does not have to know the facts to argue about them.' The request for information, however, created more of a problem. Our urgent inquiries at the Ministry of Defence elicited some excuses about misunderstandings which had caused the news black-out, and some assurances that our forces were on the point of winding up the operation and thus details were immaterial.

However, international attention remained centred on the situation at Zerka. After the expiration of the deadline, the hijackers indicated their readiness to reduce their demands as well as the stakes. Eventually they disembarked the passengers, sending the women and children to a hotel in Amman and the rest, as hostages, to a secret location. After the last crew member had descended the ramp, the terrorists detonated the explosives placed in the planes. Three huge columns of smoke blackened the same desert which, half a century earlier, had been the scene of the 'Seven Pillars of Wisdom' of T. E. Lawrence fame.

Diplomatic interlude

The countries affected by the abduction of the airliners had set up, in Berne, a co-ordinating team composed of the ambassadors of the United States, Britain, Germany and Israel, chaired by a high Swiss official. Because of the time difference between America and Europe they met at night, an unheard-of extravagance in early-to-bed Switzerland, clearly demonstrating the gravity of the crisis. After each meeting, our ambassador would regularly phone me to report. Long after midnight some of the other ambassadors, accredited to

Israel, would also call after they had received their nightly instructions from their capitals. The gist of their communications was to urge Israel to release a number of detained terrorists in addition to those their governments had agreed to free. The British government was particularly keen to get Leila Khaled off their hands and to exchange her for the hostages taken in the British plane. She was a double embarrassment to them, having been caught red-handed in mid-air in the El Al plane and removed from it against the express will of the Israeli government.

The night the British Ambassador called me, the negotiations with the hijackers had reached a critical stage. John Barnes, normally an example of diplomatic courtesy and calm, snapped without introduction: 'I am instructed by my Prime Minister to demand the immediate release by your government of a number of Arab detainees in order to complete the arrangements agreed between all the other parties concerned.' The style of the message evoked the memory of bygone days. 'Listen, John,' I replied slowly, 'I want to remind you that the British High Commissioner departed from these shores on the 14 May 1948.' The ambassador recovered his good humour quickly. 'All right then, Gideon, if you prefer: The Ambassador of Her Britannic Majesty expresses his compliments to the Government of Israel and has the honour to solicit its co-operation in the humanitarian effort to free the hostages, etc., etc.' I countered by reminding him of our request for the extradition of Leila Khaled in accordance with the existing treaty between our two countries and assured him that I would advise our Prime Minister of his amended message first thing in the morning.

Five years later, when I served as ambassador in London, I dined with Ted Heath, by then ex-Prime Minister. We reminisced about the black days of September 1970, when we were on opposite ends of the line. 'Was Leila Khaled really so important?' he asked gingerly. 'Important enough for the terrorists to make her release a prime condition for the freeing of the hostages and for HMG to make light of the hallowed British institution of due process of law. After her release she went back to her bloody *métier*. But perhaps more dangerous than the terrorist coercion', I added in a philosophical vein, 'was their subversion of the system of justice which guarantees our democratic liberties.' Ted Heath was too pragmatic a man to spoil his dinner with metaphysical contemplations on events of the past. He said that in those days he had had to make painful decisions. One of them was to deprive himself of the pleasure of attending a concert by Isaac Stern which he was to have hosted at Chequers, the Prime Minister's country home. Torn between his love for music and his prime-ministerial responsibility, he stayed that evening at his crisis command-post at Number Ten.

At our crisis centre in Jerusalem, working round the clock, we processed a steady flow of incoming information. It reached us from the scene of the hijacking, from the counsels held in Amman, the cabinet deliberations in the capitals concerned and, with Swiss punctuality, from the co-ordinating group in Berne. We analysed the reports in minute detail to discover the weak spots in the behaviour of the terrorists, the positions of the diplomats and the moves of the military. At what point would the governments yield or the terrorists break? Recalling the methods employed by the Palestinian hijackers in previous instances – their pattern of behaviour under stress, their ways of negotiation, their reaction to counteraction, their mental stamina during the period of the ultimatum – our emergency group urged all concerned to refrain from precipitate action, to avoid provocative moves and to ignore the ultimatum. In other words, to keep cool and gain time – to act like the traveller in the old Jewish story who is held up at a lonely spot by an armed robber, with the proverbial command: 'Your money or your life.' Baffled and frightened to death, the good man faces his attacker, speechless and motionless. 'Come on, you heard me', hollers the hold-up man, shoving his gun into his victim's ribs. 'Wait a minute', puffs the hapless traveller, regaining his wits. 'Do you really think, mister, that one can decide on such an important proposition on the spur of the moment?'

Hussein takes action

Ten days had passed since the beginning of the crisis. The fate of the majority of the passengers and crews was still in jeopardy. Their exact place of detention was not known. Three foreign airliners had been demolished on Jordanian territory and Yassir Arafat had openly defied the Jordanian government, calling for its overthrow. Civil war was imminent. The fighting between the terrorist groups and the Jordanian army broke out on 16 September. The PLO forces were well entrenched in refugee camps in and around Amman.

King Hussein moved against the camps in an attempt to suppress the terrorist rebels and to free the hostages. President Nixon had from the outset taken a firm stand against surrender to blackmail. He supported Israel's refusal to release security prisoners as ransom for the recovery of the hostages. To demonstrate the determination of the United States, the President dispatched two aircraft-carriers to the eastern shores of the Mediterranean, placed the 82nd Airborne Division on the alert and ordered a number of military transport planes to be flown to Turkey. These movements were meant to be more a show of force than a decision to apply it.

On 17 September Acting Prime Minister Allon, Dayan and myself discussed the situation. Golda was in Washington and Eban at the United Nations in New York. We considered the possibility of Syrian and Iraqi military intervention on the side of Arafat. This could result in the carving-up of Jordan between Syria and Iraq. On previous occasions, when the continuity of the Hashemite dynasty seemed threatened from inside and the territorial integrity of the kingdom from outside, Dayan had advocated that the IDF should take far-reaching action against Jordan to protect Israel's security. Yet in our consultation on the present crisis he favoured a cautious approach. He doubted whether an opportunity would arise to justify Israeli intervention; in any event he recommended that no action be taken without American consent. Allon, being more inclined towards activism, was slightly disappointed. I reminded the two ministers that Hussein had unexpectedly weathered many a storm in the past. Anyway, Golda and Eban were in the United States and would keep in close contact with the White House and the State Department.

Indeed, the next day, Golda met first with Rogers and then with Nixon. The relations between Washington and Jerusalem had cooled off considerably. Israel's refusal to attend the Jarring talks and the US administration's reluctance to confirm the obvious Egyptian violation of the missile standstill agreement had contributed to the mutual ill-feeling. The Secretary of State urged Israel to resume its participation in the Jarring talks and to be flexible on the outstanding issues. The Prime Minister complained about the delayed American confirmation of the violation of the missile standstill. Their new deployment, she argued clairvoyantly, would make the fighting more costly for Israel should a new war with Egypt break out. On the substance of the settlement she reiterated her view that 'nobody in Israel would agree to leave Sharm el-Sheikh and depend on UN forces'. Israel must have some land connection with it from Eilat. What she dreaded most, she said, was what had happened in 1956 – withdrawal under pressure.

But the most vexing difference remained the continued American restraint in supplying the promised armaments. At the Prime Minister's meeting with the President on 18 September, the two leaders did not discuss military options in Jordan. It appears that at this stage the President wanted neither to encourage an Israeli intervention, nor preclude it, if need arose. However, the President assured the Prime Minister that from now on the delivery of the contracted Phantom fighters would be accelerated and $500 million in military credits be made available to Israel. This undertaking lifted relations from their doldrums just at the time when the gathering storm in Jordan demanded intimate understanding between the two governments.

Syria invades Jordan

The day after this auspicious meeting, sizeable Syrian tank formations crossed the Jordanian border. Nixon ordered a high state of alert for the 82nd Airborne Division and some units in West Germany. Moreover, he strengthened the Sixth Fleet by sending a third aircraft-carrier, *John F. Kennedy*, and the helicopter carrier, *Guam*, with 1,500 marines on board into the Mediterranean. The same morning Assistant Secretary Sisco gave a stiff warning to the Soviet chargé d'affaires. He intimated that unless the Soviet

Union bridled its Syrian warhorse, an intervention by both the United States and Israel was not excluded. Vorontsov protested, as good diplomatic form required, Moscow's complete innocence of the Syrian attack, although it was carried out with Soviet tanks and ammunition, military advisers and strategic planners. In the course of the day about 300 tanks had invaded the northern part of Jordan. They rolled forward painted with the insignia of the 'Palestinian Liberation Army'.

King Hussein, battling in the capital against the PLO forces, became increasingly alarmed at the Syrian advance. By the end of the day he had lost the district town of Irbid to the Syrian tank columns, which threatened to move forward the next day on the open road to Amman. Hussein reckoned that without outside help he would be unable to halt the Syrian advance, protect his throne and prevent the occupation of his country. The fact that the attitude of the commanders of the 20,000 Iraqi troops stationed in Jordan was uncertain, made the King's position even more precarious. On the evening of 19 September he ordered his close friend and adviser, Zaid Rifai, to appeal to the American ambassador in Amman for urgent military intervention by air and land 'from any quarter'.

Kissinger decided to inform Golda Meir of Hussein's call for help. He contacted Ambassador Rabin, who was in New York with the Prime Minister, and asked him to fly back to Washington the same night. He put the problem before the Ambassador bluntly. The United States, unable to intervene directly, would not be displeased if Israel were to take appropriate action. The administration would be ready to make good any material losses incurred and take steps to fend off Soviet interference. Rabin asked some searching questions to clarify the American commitment. Would the US umbrella extend also to the Suez front, in case the Soviets supported Nasser in a diversionary move? Would the undertaking to compensate Israel for losses entail a generous response to Israel's supply needs in general? Would the United States provide political backing to Israel in the Security Council's resolutions? Kissinger claimed that the urgency of the situation excluded the possibility of a detailed and leisurely negotiation. He referred Rabin to Sisco for further talks.

It turned out that the Americans wanted Israel to confine its intervention to an air-strike. Rabin, however, relying on a briefing he had received from the General Staff in Tel Aviv, stressed that air action unaccompanied by the operation of ground forces would be ineffective. He advised Jerusalem that in his opinion the government should turn down the American request. The employment of our forces could be costly and the reaction of the Soviet Union risky. But Syrian pressure on Jordan mounted and so did Hussein's despair. The air-strike was indispensable, he urged, and if Israel thought the use of land forces was unavoidable, they should attack Syria but not operate on Jordanian territory.

The cabinet shared Rabin's reluctance, but nonetheless authorized him to be available to the US government for further discussions. While Kissinger reiterated the King's urgent appeals, Rabin repeated Israel's request for binding back-up assurances. The President's security adviser became impatient with the 'procrastination from Jerusalem'; he complained that there was too little discipline and too much talk on the Israeli side. All matters concerning an Israeli intervention and its implications must be handled only through the President to ensure its success. 'Only we can run the thing,' insisted Kissinger, 'and we will do it just as we did it in the Cambodia operation. If we decide to go, the President will be tough.' He did not make it easier for Rabin when he added that Washington had indications that the Soviets were on a collision course. Facts count, he exclaimed, and if Israel beats the Syrians that will count – not formal undertakings from the United States.

Allon, Dayan and I met again in the early morning of 21 September. The previous day, units of the reinforced Sixth Fleet had moved still closer to the Syrian and Lebanese coasts. A United States naval plane had landed with marked ostentation at Lod airport. Press and radio were prompted to leak the story that the mission had come to discuss operational plans with officers of the General Staff. At the same time, with no less conspicuousness, Israel moved two armoured brigades from their position in the West Bank up the Israeli side of the Jordan valley to battle stations in plain view of the Syrians at Irbid. The State Department again warned the Soviet Union to exert a restraining influence on the leadership in Damascus and insist on the immediate withdrawal of the Syrian forces. At the meeting convened by Allon, Dayan maintained his reservations about military action as long as Jordan was not actually in danger of being split up between Syria and Iraq. It was decided to recommend the cabinet not to go beyond the movement of the armoured brigades which was proceeding for all to see and defer further action until the imminent return of the Prime Minister.

Hussein, heartened by the impressive display of combined American and Israeli military and political resoluteness, ordered his small air force to attack the Syrian tank columns and sent armoured units north to halt the Syrian advance towards Amman. Both operations made their mark. Syrian tanks began to turn back across the border. The next day the situation improved further. Hussein was gaining the upper hand in Amman against the PLO uprising and the Syrian withdrawal was now in full swing. King Hussein now signalled Washington that Israel should refrain from an action on Jordanian territory, yet he would not be averse to the IDF administering a memorable blow to the Syrian forces returning to the Golan. Neither Washington nor Jerusalem were keen on such a venture, spectacular in its design but superfluous in its military and political usefulness. The Israeli government was convinced that it had made its contribution, and a rather decisive one, to the safeguarding of the Hashemite Kingdom of Jordan.

The United States government shared this view. On 24 September Kissinger told Rabin that the President wanted him to convey to the Prime Minister that he would not forget Israel's behaviour that week and that he thought that the United States was very lucky that Israel was there. Sisco added that the steps Israel had taken had contributed measurably to the Syrian withdrawal. The government appreciate Israel's prompt and positive response to its approach.'

The events of September were not only a landmark in King Hussein's turbulent struggle for survival, but also a turning-point in Israel's relations with the Nixon administration. Washington had realized that it could rely on Israel at a critical juncture, on the muscle of its military arm and the mature judgement of its political leadership. His hands free and his flanks covered, Hussein now mercilessly smashed the rebellious terrorist organizations. His forces unhesitantly shelled refugee camps where the insurgents had their strongholds. The number of casualties soared into the thousands. There were estimates of more than 15,000 people killed in the fighting, many of them uninvolved civilians and refugees. Arafat managed to escape with the remnants of his followers to the Lebanon, where he set up his headquarters and transformed that unhappy land into a hotbed of internal and external turmoil.

Nixon regarded his handling of the emergency as a personal triumph. Without firing a shot, the United States had forced the collapse of the Syrian attack, backed by the Soviet Union. He had demonstrated to the countries in the Middle East leaning towards the United States that they were in safer hands than those courting the Soviet Union. He had found in Israel a valuable and responsible ally. In a jubilant mood, the President paid a flying visit to the flagship of the Sixth Fleet cruising in the central Mediterranean.

The successful suppression of the PLO uprising also brought the weird hijacking affair to a fortunate end. None of the hostages was harmed and all were freed, but not before Britain, Germany and Switzerland had yielded to the terrorists. One bleak day in September an RAF plane took off from London with a single passenger, Leila Khaled, deported without trial. It landed in Munich and Zurich to pick up other PLO terrorists released from prison where they were serving long-term sentences for murderous attacks against embarking El Al passengers, a group of people to which I had the dubious distinction to belong myself when our plane was attacked on the runway of Kloten airport the previous year. The RAF plane delivered its high-priced cargo to Qaddafi's safe haven in Tripoli. The flight will hardly enter into the proud annals of the valiant Royal Air Force as one of its finest missions.

That same day, 27 September, Arab kings and presidents gathered in Cairo. Nasser had invited them for a meeting of reconciliation. Droves of armed bodyguards dominated the scene which was charged with high tension. Nasser moved between the contending camps with untiring zest. He goaded, he threatened and he pleaded until Hussein shook hands with Arafat. It was a meaningless gesture, for the fury of their hatred continued unabated in the years ahead. The following day, after Nasser had seen off the last departing ruler, he returned to his home a stricken man. His heart failed him when he saw his great Pan-Arab dream dissipate in blood and bluster. The turbulent Nasser era had come to an end.

28

The Ascension of Sadat
and the Decline of Jarring

The new Egyptian President, Anwar al-Sadat, had grown more in the shade of Nasser than under his sun. Although he had been a founding member of the Free Officers Revolutionary Group, his influence on the policies of the new regime appeared to be modest. His more prominent qualities were a pronounced religiosity and a sturdy political durability. He was useful to Nasser, so it was said, more for his unfailing loyalty and smooth adaptability than for the prowess of his intellect and the weight of his advice. He was known to keep his thoughts much to himself and thus his opinions were not well known.

His political background was rather checkered. Imprisoned by the British authorities in Egypt for participation in pro-German intelligence operations during the Second World War, he never denied, even in later years, his early sympathy for Hitler. In a television interview with Lord Chalfont in July 1975 he admitted frankly: 'I was fascinated with Hitler and the way he had done his best to improve his country and build up the Third Reich.'

Sadat's home was the delta of the Nile and his roots its fecund soil. He reflected his attachment to the simple virtues of village life more in an idealistic way than in his personal life-style. Whether his presidential duties drew him away from the hovels to the palaces for which he came to show a distinct proclivity, or whether it was his inclination for pageantry, remains to be judged by researchers into the character of politicians. Anyway, Sadat was no exception in this respect.

Sadat's pre-presidential record on Israel was not exceptional. As an officer in King Farouk's army, he was scarred by the humiliation of its defeat by Israel in 1948. Nasser's military *débâcle* in 1967 cracked this wound wide open. His speeches against Israel were tainted with Koranic aspersions against the Jews, and his unguarded comments were sometimes tinged with anti-semitic slurs. But if a general trend could be detected in his speeches, a difficult undertaking in an emotional environment, they indicated a greater concern for the well-being of Egypt than the prosperity of Pan-Arabism.

Like any successor to an authoritarian leader, trying to acquire the power and authority of his demised or deposed predecessor without shaking the existing regime, Sadat embarked subtly on a course of de-Nasserization. While outwardly continuing to venerate the lost leader, though with an ardour that swiftly cooled off, the new President removed, one by one, Nasser's trusted aides from their positions of influence. He proceeded with a remarkable mixture of caution and resolution, always dividing his antagonists while building up strongholds of military and political support. His political cunning was remarkable and his firmness impressive when he felt strong enough to dispose of the hard core of Nasser's former associates and commit them to trial and prison in one well-aimed stroke.

It had become a ground rule of Israel's diplomacy to greet leadership changes in neighbouring, but politically still so distant, Egypt with expressions of goodwill. Thus did Ben Gurion when Naguib came to power at the head of the Free Officers Revolutionary Group. When the news of Nasser's sudden death reached us, I directed our information services to refrain from vilification as much as from glorification. On the latter we had a little problem. The then President of Israel, Zalman Shazar, debarred from attending the funeral, wanted to pay homage to Nasser in a radio broadcast. It was not that he had loved the man, he simply loved eulogies. It was not easy for Golda to dissuade her old friend and comrade. Soon after Sadat's accession to the presidency I drafted a message on the following lines to be sent to the new President by Prime Minister Golda Meir: The period which had come to an end was marked by great expectations and grave disappointments. Israel had initially welcomed the Egyptian revolution for its constructive and progressive aims. Unfortunately however, Egypt, instead of devoting its efforts to the promotion of its own progress, had used up vital resources in an attempt to deny Israel's right of existence.

It appeared that Nasser himself in the last period of his life had reached the conclusion that the Arab-Israeli conflict could not be solved by military means. Israel had been willing to meet Nasser half-way in a common search for a political solution. The government of President Anwar al-Sadat might wish to open a new chapter for Egypt and the Middle East. The experience of the past had shown that the road of armed conflict had not only been extremely costly to Arabs and Israelis alike, but also futile since it had always ended in a complete impasse.

Furthermore, it had become evident that the conflict could not be settled by foreign intervention, but only by the parties themselves. Therefore, the government of Israel proposed that the two countries explore, sincerely and conscientiously, ways and means of solving by pacific means the problems outstanding between them, in order to establish a just and lasting peace.

As a first step towards this end it suggested removing the obstacle to political talks created by the non-implementation of the missile standstill agreement. Israel was prepared to discuss this problem and any other matter with representatives of the government of Egypt. The consolidation of the cease-fire was not only a compelling necessity as such, but also the only secure foundation for the erection of the structure of peace.

The people of Israel wished nothing more than to advance together with the Arab peoples towards a future of independence, prosperity and security for all people of the Middle East which only peace can ensure.

Eban who had approved the idea, as well as the outline of the message, passed it on to Golda. We never heard of it again nor did Sadat ever see it.

Resumption of the Jarring talks

Although the co-operation between the United States and Israel in the Jordanian crisis had improved the climate and in a way the nature of the links between the two governments, easing in particular the flow of promised arms deliveries, some of the central diplomatic differences remained unresolved. The State Department did not relent in its efforts to crank up the stalled diplomatic machine and get the Jarring talks back on the road. In his meetings with representatives of Israel, Secretary of State Rogers pressed hard. If the idea of discussing peace was out of question, he argued, then the parties would again proceed on a course to war. He warned of the consequences: 'The Russians are in Egypt for the foreseeable future. Even if Nasser wants to, he cannot get rid of them,' he declared in mid-September 1970, ignoring the dangers of prophecy. Nasser departed from this world two weeks, and the Russians from Egypt two years, later.

In the following months Washington increased its exertions to break the deadlock. After Dayan had, in his speech in Haifa, invited the reluctant government to jump into 'the icy water' of the Jarring talks, it was a foregone conclusion that with some presidential push the cabinet would take the dive. Nixon offered a helping hand. In December, he reiterated in a firm but friendly letter to Golda the American commitments to and expectations from Israel. He reiterated his assurances that the continued strength of Israel was in the United States' national interest; that the solution of the Arab refugee problem should in no way change the Jewish character of Israel; that arms would be supplied on an on-going relationship; and that the territorial situation created by the Six Day War should remain intact until the Arab states agreed to sign a peace treaty. On the other side of the ledger the mediator, Ambassador Jarring, featured prominently. The talks must be resumed, urged the President. They were the only available way to proceed towards a peaceful solution.

On 28 December 1970 the government decided to lift its ban, responding to Washington's urging and irrespective of Cairo's refusal to withdraw the illegally deployed missiles. I suggested inviting Jarring to come to Jerusalem for the re-opening of the talks. Golda agreed, partly because she wanted personally to be in command of the negotiations, and partly because she believed that Jarring would refuse the invitation. But the mediator accepted with alacrity and arrived in Jerusalem on 8 January 1971. At the Foreign Ministry we prepared three position papers, entitled 'Essentials of Peace', to be submitted by Ambassador Jarring to the governments of Egypt, Jordan and Lebanon. They were identical in their general principles and differed only where they related to specific issues pertaining to the respective country.

Our proposals contained all the elements of the future peace settlement between Israel and Egypt which, alas, was to elude the parties for another eight years. Though not committing itself to specific territorial dispositions without negotiations, Israel explicitly endorsed the withdrawal as well as all the other provisions of Resolution 242. It linked the demarcation of the final boundaries to the nature and substance of Israel's future relationships with its Arab neighbours. Territory versus peace and security remained its negotiating stance, from the time of the resumed Jarring talks until the signing of the peace treaty with Egypt. The mediator refrained in the Jerusalem meeting from expressing any opinion of his own on the merits of our proposals; he simply promised to submit them to the governments concerned. The Prime Minister emphatically and repeatedly urged him to place the new proposals before a conference attended by the two sides and chaired by him. He neither discouraged the idea nor promised to act upon it. We were somewhat puzzled by this evasiveness. He was apparently then already committed to a quite different procedure with which he surprised Israel exactly one month after his visit to Jerusalem.

All in all, the talks had been satisfactory and were likely to help improve Israel's international standing, which had somewhat suffered from its refusal to participate in the Jarring round. The day after his departure, Golda was expected to make her customary report on the talks to the cabinet. But she also had a surprise in store. Without any introduction she announced that she had decided on a new procedure for the conduct of the contacts with Dr Jarring. She read out a well-formulated paper. It stipulated that from then on the Prime Minister would direct and supervise all activities connected with the Jarring mission. The Foreign Minister would be consulted. Those who had been authorized to deal with the UN representative would report directly to her. The only person allowed to make statements in connection with the Jarring mission would be the cabinet secretary in his capacity as spokesman of the government. In conclusion she admonished the ministers and their officials to abide strictly by these rules which she called her 'new constitution of 10 January'. Stunned silence followed the prime-ministerial proclamation; but there were neither questions nor comments, only a flow of little notes fluttering between the ministers across the table. Eban, the minister directly concerned, did not stir. He sat as if thunderstruck. He patiently answered the little chits of paper tossed to him over the table by his inquisitive colleagues but he did not budge.

He wrote a note also to me, telling me that Golda's announcement had hit him without forewarning. He would not react in cabinet but would also not take it lying down.

What motivated Golda to take that step at all, and at this stage in particular, has never been made clear. A sudden pique, a suspicion nursed by her advisers that the Foreign Ministry was not firm enough in its dealing with Jarring, a fit of personal antagonism, a premonition that Israel was soon to be on a collision course with the Jarring mission – who knows? Probably it was a bit of everything. In any case, whatever the motives behind her 'new constitution', it neither improved Israel's foreign environment nor the climate of interministerial relations, nor did it affect Jarring's course of action.

An unexpected initiative

On 8 February the UN Special Representative made his surprise move. The fact that in the wide-open United Nations a secret could be kept was in itself an astonishing act. But Ambassador Jarring's plunge into a new initiative, without prior notification of the parties, was an astounding feat for a diplomat who was as cautious as he was. He presented to the UN representatives of Israel and Egypt identical memoranda outlining his own proposals for the solution of the outstanding questions between Israel and Egypt. They reflected Israel's position on contractual peace relations, Egypt's territorial claims and the United States views as embodied in the Rogers plan. The unexpected move as such irritated the Israeli government, and its substance upset it even more. In its first reaction it challenged the authority of Dr Jarring in venturing into the field of mediation when his mandate limited him to the role of provider of good offices to the contending parties. This argument did not carry us very far. It created more personal and international support for Ambassador Jarring than disapproval of his proposals. It was obvious that he had not acted on the spur of the moment.

Sadat had prodded the United States to activate the mediation effort. The ninety-days' cease-fire, once extended, was to expire on 7 February 1971. Counting on the apprehensions of a State Department anxious to prevent a renewed flare-up, Sadat proclaimed that the year of 1971 was the year of decision. He remained somewhat vague on the nature of the decision and on how he intended to implement it, but he implied that a lack of diplomatic motion would result in a rush of military movement. Washington, considering the Jarring mission to be the best available diplomatic channel and concerned at the approaching date of the expiration of the cease-fire, had asked the Ambassador to change his role from that of a mailman delivering messages from one party to the other to that of an active promoter of proposals. In the heat of the argument which his initiative provoked on the Israeli side, Jarring admitted to us that he had been in close touch with the State Department on the preparation of his memorandum, not only on its timing but also on its substance.

Ambassador Jarring submitted his proposals one day after the ninety-days' cease-fire deadline and three days after Sadat had announced his willingness to extend it for another month. He assumed that the deadlock had resulted from the unwillingness of the parties to commit themselves to specific provisions of the peace settlement, before having exchanged reciprocal undertakings on the issues which counted most to them. He therefore asked each side to make to him 'the parallel and simultaneous commitments which seem to be inevitable prerequisites of an eventual peace settlement between them, which was subject to the eventual satisfactory determination of all other aspects of a peace settlement, including in particular a just settlement of the refugee problem.' The equivocacy of this formula would have done honour to his great compatriot, the late Dag Hammarskjöld, a craftsman of unparalleled skill in the art of obfuscation.

On the specifics, however, he was unequivocal. Israel should withdraw its forces from all the occupied Egyptian territory to the former international boundary on the understanding that demilitarized zones would be established; freedom of navigation in the Straits of Tiran would be guaranteed by the stationing of United Nations forces at Sharm el-Sheikh, and free passage through the Suez Canal would be ensured.

Egypt for her part should give a commitment to enter into a peace agreement with Israel and explicitly undertake, on a basis of reciprocity, to terminate all claims of belligerency; to respect each other's sovereignty, territorial integrity and political independence; to acknowledge each other's right to live in peace within secure and recognized boundaries; and to do all in its power to ensure that acts of hostility were not committed from its territory against the citizens or property of the other party.

In essence Jarring blended the Egyptian demand for the total evacuation of its territory with Israel's claim for a contractual peace. For this purpose he used most of the principles contained in Israel's memorandum, 'Essentials of Peace', but skipped over those provisions which, in his view, were not to Egypt's liking, such as the termination of all manifestations of economic warfare and the non-participation in hostile alliances.

The US government, which had prior indications of Sadat's responsiveness to the Jarring initiative, advised him to express explicitly his readiness to conclude peace with Israel under the terms outlined in the memorandum. He hastened to do so. On 14 February the government of Egypt confirmed in its reply its acceptance of the proposed undertakings and declared that 'Egypt will be ready to enter into a peace agreement with Israel containing all the aforementioned obligations as provided for in Security Council Resolution 242'. It was a far-reaching development. For the first time, the government of an Arab state had publicly announced its readiness to sign a peace agreement with Israel in an official document. Although the full implications of this new departure remained obscured for many more years of diplomatic probing, nurtured by deep-seated distrust and continued hostility, it was undeniable that a new seed was sprouting from the scorched earth of Egyptian-Israeli relations.

The Israeli reply

The Israeli government, though considerably impressed by Egypt's intention to conclude peace, was flustered by its territorial conditions. Yet there was little reason for surprise. Its territorial claims were not new. As a matter of fact, immediately following the Six Day War, the Israeli government had itself proposed to evacuate all of Sinai and establish the former international boundary as the new recognized border, subject to such minor alterations as were required by security. Under internal pressure – exerted principally by a combination of three ministers, Begin, Dayan and Galili – and due to Egypt's refusal to negotiate peace, the cabinet had altered its original decision in October 1968. Still, the record was indelible and so was Egypt's persistent demand for total withdrawal.

In formulating its reply to Jarring, the government found itself hard-pressed. There was the obvious attraction of Sadat's willingness to conclude a peace agreement, there were the objectionable territorial conditions and there was strong American urging to give a positive reply. In a memorandum to Eban I recommended that the government should proceed from the assumption that on the principal issue, the conclusion of peace, Egypt had been responsive. In our reply we should refrain from exegetic quibbling and present the framework of a draft peace treaty, which we had prepared for the occasion that had arrived at long last. I suggested that we should draft our reply to Jarring's proposals on the following lines:

a. Israel welcomes Egypt's readiness to conclude a peace agreement.
b. It proposes to discuss with Egypt all points contained in her reply to Ambassador Jarring, as well as all topics mentioned in Israel's memorandum 'Essentials of Peace' and any additional questions mutually agreed upon.
c. In these negotiations, to be held on the level of Foreign Ministers and under the auspices of Dr Jarring, both sides will present their detailed positions on the territorial, demographic, military and other outstanding issues.

The first result of the convoluted cabinet discussions was delay and their final outcome was a decision to reiterate the principles presented to Jarring at the Jerusalem talks. The crucial withdrawal paragraph, however, was the catch. Originally, the government was inclined to accept Eban's non-committal formulation: 'Withdrawal of Israeli armed forces from the cease-fire line with Egypt to secure, recognized and agreed boundaries to be established in the peace agreement.' But Israel Galili led a move to add a decisive qualification. Supported by Ambassador Rabin and Defence Minister Dayan, Galili succeeded in persuading his colleagues not to leave any doubt about the boundary issue. Rabin had maintained since the promulgation of the Rogers plan that it corresponded with President Johnson's principles and that the United States would stick to it all along the way as its basic policy for the settlement of the conflict. Even at the peak of the intimate understanding between Washington and Jerusalem in the wake of the events in Jordan, Rabin warned at the end of September 1970 that the American position had not changed. 'The lines that existed before the Six Day War', he stated, 'will in the American view form, with minor adjustments for security requirements, the basis for the establishment of the final boundaries.' Was it this assessment which motivated the Ambassador to encourage the hard-liners in the cabinet to take an adamant stand on the border issue? Did he believe that by drawing the line at this stage, the United States would abandon its position? Perhaps, but it seems more likely that Rabin at the time shared the scepticism of some of the politicians, Golda Meir foremost among them, that the risks of the peace settlement outweighed its blessings.

Be that as it may, the government decided to add to Eban's withdrawal clause a short but highly significant sentence: 'Israel will not withdraw to the pre-5 June 1967 lines.'

There was one noteworthy point in the three documents – the Jarring memorandum and the two replies. They relegated the Palestinian refugee problem to a subsidiary position on the peace agenda. The term Palestine was not mentioned in any of the documents, just as it had been omitted from the text of Resolution 242. The later transformation of the refugee problem into the claim for the recognition of the 'legitimate rights of the Palestinian people' became one of the major stumbling-blocks for the future peaceful settlement of the conflict.

The Jarring initiative, instead of priming progress, had deepened the deadlock. Its failure sealed the fate of the UN Special Representative's mission. It was never wound up officially, it just wilted away, overshadowed by more dramatic events.

29

Suez Approaches

Coinciding, but obviously unco-ordinated with Ambassador Jarring's surprise move, President Sadat launched his own initiative. Concerned about the diplomatic stalemate which had been caused by the wide gap between the positions of Egypt and Israel and the temporary nature of the cease-fire, Sadat looked for a new opening. He seized upon an idea which Dayan had been quietly and privately exploring.

On 15 January 1971 Sisco informed Ambassador Rabin of a secret communication he had received from Donald Bergus, the State Department's representative in Cairo. He had been approached by a close friend of Sadat trying to find out whether Israel would be interested in a proposal based on Dayan's reported readiness to consider a partial withdrawal from the Suez Canal. The Egyptian contact suggested that Israel should withdraw its forces to the Mitla pass, a distance of forty kilometres from the canal. Egypt would not be able to effect a complete pull-back to an equal distance. But it was prepared, in return, to thin out its ground forces within a forty-kilometre-wide zone west of the canal. It would, however, leave its air defences in that area intact. It would also agree to exchange prisoners-of-war captured in the post-1967 fighting, and negotiate through Jarring a cease-fire agreement of longer duration, including a prohibited zone of aircraft approach of ten kilometres on both sides of the canal which would be opened to free passage for all ships. Rabin conveyed the message to Jerusalem and advised the government to inform Sadat of its readiness to examine the plan following an Egyptian reply to Israel's peace principles transmitted to Cairo through Jarring earlier that month.

The Prime Minister was far from happy with the Egyptian proposal. She saw in it the beginning of the withdrawal of Israel to the old international boundary without the equivalent of a peace treaty. She had noted that Sisco had communicated it without a favourable American comment and assumed that the United States, for global strategic reasons and especially because of the war in Vietnam, was not interested in the opening of the Suez Canal at this time. She therefore decided that before replying Rabin should discreetly ascertain, at the highest level, the US position. Dayan strengthened Golda's scepticism. He inferred, so he claimed, from his private sounding out of

Secretary Rogers in December, that the United States government was not keen to support any move which was likely to facilitate the unblocking of the canal. Dayan's discouraging comments were somewhat incongruous in view of his own personal initiative in this matter; but perhaps he felt it politic not to reveal too much initial interest, assuming that if Sadat was keen on his proposal he would pursue it anyway. For three weeks both Israel and the United States hedged. Washington was hesitant to offer its advice. Kissinger intimated that if the President were to inform Israel that the opening of the canal did not serve an American interest, he would take upon himself a serious responsibility. In case of the resumption of hostilities, Israel could justifiably present heavy claims and charges to the United States.

Rabin, on his part, urged the government to come forth with a positive, though qualified, reply. On 1 February he cabled his recommendations accompanied by some general reflections. He believed that if, as the result of the political deadlock, fighting should recur and the Soviet Union should intervene militarily in a way that threatened Israel's very existence, Nixon would meet the head of the Soviet government and propose a joint imposed settlement in the Middle East. The opening of the canal would defer for a long time the danger of renewed war and was likely, in the long run, to promote peace.

Dayan was correct in his assumption that Sadat would follow up his first soundings with additional steps. Indeed, on 4 February, the Egyptian President made a public statement linking the re-opening of the Suez Canal to a partial withdrawal of Israeli forces from its east bank as the first stage of the implementation of Resolution 242.

The announcement, not exactly couched in the most appealing terms, provoked an angry, negative reply from Golda in a television interview with an American CBS reporter. But Sadat remained undeterred. On the eve of a statement the Prime Minister was scheduled to make in the Knesset on 9 February, Sadat sent a message to the State Department which conveyed it to Jerusalem. He explained that the principal motive for his proposal was to defuse the prevailing danger. His proposal was neither a tactical nor an academic exercise. He wanted a serious discussion with Israel conducted through the good offices of the United States and not through Jarring. In passing the message on to Rabin, Sisco lifted for the first time the veil that had covered the American attitude to the proposal itself. He recommended that the Prime Minister should react to Sadat's initiative positively and constructively in her Knesset speech. With considerable encouragement from her Foreign Minister she complied and cautiously intimated the government's willingness to discuss the Egyptian initiative under certain stringent conditions. She had adopted this line half-heartedly, more as a tactical accommodation than a desirable objective.

Sadat had revealed for the first time a political style which was to become the trademark of his future behaviour: meticulous secret preparation and public surprise to force the issue either by military or by political means, or a combination of both. In a sequence of successes he refined his method, crowning it with his sudden but extremely well-prepared visit to Jerusalem. The initial American reaction to Sadat's Suez initiative also disclosed a pattern which was to repeat itself eight years later when he consented to open bilateral peace negotiations with Israel. In both instances the first reaction of the State Department had been tepid, but it soon warmed up. In a meeting with Eban in March 1971, Rogers stated that he strongly favoured the conclusion of a Suez agreement. It would, in his view, facilitate the extension of the cease-fire and open up a prolonged period of diplomacy. Referring to a view Eban had expressed to a group of US Senators that Israel could not co-operate with Sadat's proposal if the United States government believed that the opening of the canal would prejudice American strategic interests, the Secretary of State emphasized 'that the United States favours the opening of the Suez Canal. There might be a slight disadvantage, but in the overall picture it would not be a net disadvantage.' Already, in mid-February, in reply to Rabin's discreet inquiry, Kissinger had replied that the President had no objection to Israel examining Sadat's proposal.

Still the Israeli government sustained its reservations on the Sadat proposition. The Jarring plan, however, which was either contradictory or complementary to the Egyptian proposal depending on one's viewpoint, induced the government to seek a way out, bypassing the Jarring mission which, in the opinion of Israel, had outlived its usefulness. Accordingly, Eban sent Rabin more substantive directives concerning the Egyptian approach. The State Department was requested to relay to Sadat the government's willingness to discuss the Egyptian proposal in a constructive spirit as outlined by the Prime Minister in her speech in the Knesset. The re-opening of the Suez Canal was welcome and should provide for the freedom of passage of Israeli ships and cargoes. It should be accompanied by the resumption of civilian life in the canal area. The reconstruction of the devastated towns would be an indication of Egypt's future peaceful intentions. This was an idea cherished by Dayan, who held the view that the shelling of towns in times of war would hasten its termination and the rebuilding of the ruins prevent its resumption. To ensure the normal functioning of the canal and encourage the restoration of civilian life, Israel would agree to a mutual reduction of military forces and installations. Since Sadat's proposal was not sufficiently detailed, Israel welcomed the suggestion made by the United States to lend its good offices for the clarification of the issues.

Sadat's sounding through Bergus and Israel's reply through Sisco paved the way for an intensive American involvement. At the beginning of March Sadat was ready with 'preliminary ideas', which apparently had matured in the incubator of the State Department. Israel should withdraw its forces to a distance of forty kilometres from the canal; the evacuated area would be demilitarized; Egyptian civilians and personnel required for the clearing, operation and safety of the canal would be allowed into a ten-kilometre-wide strip along its east bank. Six months after the agreement became effective, the canal would be opened to shipping, including that of Israel. The agreement would constitute a first step towards the full implementation of Resolution 242; both sides would be free to review the cease-fire after one year in the light of the progress made in the implementation of the resolution.

The US reaction

As in numerous other instances, American 'first thoughts' on Arab-Israeli problems did not differ much from the end product, presented to the parties at the last stage of a patient negotiating process. Nor were these 'preliminary ideas' far removed from the final Arab fall-back positions. The Sisco suggestions contained many of the bones of contention unpalatable to Israel for many years, until it felt constrained to swallow most of them in the after-shock of the Yom Kippur War. The idea of withdrawal without peace was anathema to the Prime Minister. Even if it was limited to a relatively small area, it would dislodge Israel from its strategic stronghold – the Bar-Lev line – which, so went the argument at the time, prevented the Egyptian army from crossing the canal. But, worse than that, any movement from the existing cease-fire lines would also undermine Israel's political position, anchored in President Nixon's pledge of 4 December 1970, that no Israeli soldier should be withdrawn before the conclusion of formal peace. Even if the government were to consider a limited redeployment, the distance of forty kilometres was unthinkable. It would deprive the army of the control of another vital strategic position: the Sinai passes of Mitla and Gidi. The Egyptian demand for a forty-kilometre retreat from the canal was not an innovation in the context of Sadat's initiative in 1971. It had appeared for the first time in a confidential Soviet peace plan submitted to the United States in 1968. It had stipulated that Israeli forces should, as a first stage, withdraw to an intermediate line thirty–forty kilometres from the Suez Canal, whereupon Egypt 'will bring its troops into the canal zone and start to clear the canal for the resumption of navigation'.

The second sticking-point in Sisco's opening gambit was the linkage of the Suez agreement to the implementation of all the provisions of Resolution 242, an Arab code-term for the demand for complete evacuation of all the territories occupied in the Six Day War. The Prime Minister, backed by a cabinet majority, refused to tie the partial agreement in any shape or form to the implementation of Resolution 242.

The third controversial issue was the stationing of Egyptian personnel, in other words a small military or police force, on the east bank of the canal. Golda's opposition on this point was adamant. Even when, in the course of the later negotiations, the Americans whittled its size down to 700 policemen equipped with sidearms only, the government maintained its strict objection.

In the agreements concluded between Israel and Egypt subsequent to the Yom Kippur War, the three contentious issues were resolved to the full satisfaction of Egypt and above and beyond its expectations of 1971. Under the agreement of 1975, Israel withdrew its forces to about forty kilometres from the canal, accepted linkage with Resolution 242 and resigned itself to the permanent presence of sizeable Egyptian military forces east of the canal. It was the premium paid to prime the peace process with Egypt, consummated by the signature of the peace treaty providing for the complete withdrawal of Israeli forces from all the occupied territory of Egypt.

Sadat campaigns for the Suez agreement

Soon after Sadat's accession to power, Washington registered some signs of his inclination to revamp Nasser's policy and establish a new relationship with the United States. These impulses released responsive reactions in the State Department and one of the first was to support Sadat's initiative on the re-opening of the canal. The more the clarification of the proposal progressed, the more the State Department participated in its promotion. It elaborated its own proposal and prodded the Israeli government, still divided on the merits of the move, to go ahead.

Sadat did not remain idle. He gave interviews to American magazines, travelled secretly to Moscow and, upon his return at the beginning of March 1971, wrote confidentially to President Nixon. In his interview, published in *Newsweek* on 15 February 1971, the Egyptian President asked for a first-stage withdrawal of the Israeli forces to a line stretching from Ras Muhammad on the Red Sea to El Arish on the Mediterranean as part of a Suez agreement. Although at the time it was meant to be Egypt's opening gambit, this line became a permanent feature on Egypt's list of claims. Early in 1980 the Israeli forces completed their withdrawal behind the Ras Muhammad-El Arish line in implementation of the first stage of the peace treaty. What Sadat discussed in Moscow has not been officially disclosed. But there is sufficient indication for the assumption that his principal aim was the amplification and acceleration of Soviet arms shipments. Presumably he also tried to cover his back in Moscow while testing new approaches to Washington and preparing the ousting from government of influential friends of the Soviet Union whom he had inherited from Nasser.

In his letter to Nixon, Sadat explained why he could not formally extend the cease-fire, but at the same time did not threaten to resume the fighting on the expiration date of 5 March which he had proclaimed a month earlier. But the main purpose of his communication was to solicit the active support of the President for his Suez plan, which Nixon extended by the end of the month. With the green light of the White House signalling an all-clear to the State

Department, it now sped up its moves. It proceeded on three tracks: it urged Israel to produce its peace map, specifying its territorial claims; it goaded the government to present its own proposals on a Suez agreement, and it put the brakes on the shipment of contracted armaments. To release some steam from the mounting pressures, Golda decided to open the territorial valve slightly.

Golda's peace map

In an interview she gave on 13 March to Louis Heren, then foreign correspondent and later deputy editor of the London *Times*, Golda divulged her territorial concepts. The gist of it was that Israel must retain Sharm el-Sheikh and a connecting land road; border changes around Eilat were indispensable; Sinai must be demilitarized; Gaza should not revert to Egyptian rule; the Golan Heights should remain under Israeli control; the 1949 armistice lines on the West Bank must undergo changes; and Jerusalem would remain united under Israeli jurisdiction. Although the picture was still rather blurred, it revealed enough to provoke critical comment in Israel and a moderately favourable reaction abroad.

A few years later in London, the day Golda announced her resignation as Prime Minister, I happened to lunch with Heren. He was eager to know whether her resignation was definite, a legitimate question in view of her former reversals. When I told him that in my view it was what was known in American newspaper jargon as the 'final final edition', he told me that the reason for his inquiry was a story which he wanted to reveal in a piece he was going to write for the occasion. On the day she had given him that famous interview in 1971 he had found her in a highly fraught state of mind. At one point of the conversation tears came into her eyes and she muttered: 'Why can't they let us live in peace like any other people? Haven't we suffered enough?' She immediately regained her composure and apologized for her emotional outbreak. She had just come back from a military funeral of a young soldier. He was a third-generation sabra from one of the old pioneer families, the nobility of the country. His grandfather, Chaim Sturman, a founder member of Kibbutz Ein Harod, had been slain in the Arab riots of the 1930s. His father fell in the War of Independence and the son, serving in the army, had been killed now. 'I just could not hold back when the sight of the grandmother standing at the grave flashed through my mind,' said Golda, wiping away her tears.

Heren, moved by the emotional eruption of the old lady so admired in public for her self-control, put his arm on her shoulder and said that he would not mind if she wished to delete from the record the configuration of Israel's peace map which she had volunteered with such frankness but which might cause her domestic trouble. He realized that she had spoken while under considerable emotional strain and he would not like to embarrass her. Golda warmly dismissed this admirable display of journalistic chivalry and assured him that she would uphold every word she had said, provided of course, she added with a whimsical smile, that it was accurately reported. When the interview was published she came under heavy crossfire from the opposition party in the Knesset. She stood by every word of her interview and did not dodge a single query. In his article on Golda's resignation, Louis Heren paid generous tribute to the steadfastness of the former Prime Minister.

But Golda's peace map neither appealed to Sadat nor comforted the State Department. Sadat replied with his own claims that there should be total withdrawal from Sinai, which was only to be partially demilitarized, and Sharm el-Sheikh should be supervised by UN forces. And Washington, realizing that the gap between the basic positions of the two sides was still too wide, decided to concentrate its efforts on the attainment of a Suez interim agreement. Responding to Rogers' and Sisco's urging of Israel to submit its own proposals, the government reluctantly complied, but not before it had sought Kissinger's advice. On the one hand he did not concur with the State Department's position; on the other he did not believe that some of Israel's major points had a chance of being accepted. But, normally having a third hand in reserve, he expressed the view that Jerusalem would commit a serious error by stalling. Without any progress on the diplomatic front, he maintained, the possibility of a renewed outbreak of hostilities by the end of 1971 could not be excluded. He foresaw that in such an eventuality the Soviet Union would not stand idly by; it would intervene to save Egypt from another defeat. In such an emergency there was only one man who could make the decision to come to Israel's aid, but President Nixon and the American public had to be convinced that Israel had not neglected any opportunity to avert the military confrontation by sufficient political flexibility. Kissinger's advice was that Israel should stand firm on its position and when it felt that it had to yield on certain points, it should never make the concessions to Foggy Bottom (which was bottomless in its capacity to ask for more), but only to the President, who was the supreme arbiter of US foreign policy. He would appreciate concessions made personally to him and was politically too experienced to exact too heavy demands.

Israel's Suez memorandum and the Rogers-Allon dialogue
On 19 April, the Israeli embassy submitted to the State Department a detailed memorandum outlining the views of the government on the principal points of a Suez agreement: the clearing and opening of the canal by Egypt for the use by ships and cargoes of all nations within six months after the conclusion of the agreement; the unlimited duration of the cease-fire; the withdrawal of Israeli forces from the east bank of the canal to a distance to be specified; provisions for the crossing of Egyptian civilians required for the operating of the canal, but prohibition of introduction of military or irregular forces into

the area evacuated by Israel; reduction of Egyptian forces west of the canal; and the exchange of all prisoners-of-war.

To allay Egypt's apprehension that Israel would refrain from further withdrawal of its forces, the memorandum stated explicitly that when agreement on a final boundary was reached in the framework of a peace treaty, the Israeli forces would withdraw to the final boundary established in a peace treaty. But it contained also a passage designed to allay Israel's fears. It asked for assurances from the United States government that the pledges in the President's letters to the Prime Minister in 1970 remained in force; and that the withdrawal should not be construed as a stage for further evacuation in the absence of a peace agreement and in no case as a commitment of withdrawal to the international boundary. In view of possible dangerous Soviet moves in and across the canal, 'ways and means should be found to deter such moves'. Israel felt bound to ask for these American assurances since 'to give up the strategic advantages of a water obstacle and a line of fortifications before final peace would be a grave matter'. Tragically, this assessment did not stand the test of the calamitous day of Yom Kippur.

A day after the presentation of the memorandum Yigal Allon, the Deputy Prime Minister in charge of education, met Secretary Rogers in Washington. Allon was interested to know how the whole Suez proposal had originated: where, when and who had brought the matter up. His opening shot was straight on target. He told the Secretary of State that Dayan had reported that the re-opening of the Suez Canal did not, in the view of the United States, serve its interests. The government was surprised when Washington changed its mind. Rogers was perplexed, for Dayan had explained that he did not speak for his government when he brought the matter up. Therefore, Rogers had seen no need to give much thought to the whole thing. An agreement between Israel and Egypt would contribute a measure of stability and provide time to work out a full settlement.

Having cleared up the matter to his satisfaction, Allon now embarked on a detailed exegesis of the Israeli memorandum. He wanted it to be absolutely clear that such an agreement could not be considered as part of a total withdrawal from Sinai. Israel would never agree to this. The Secretary replied that the administration did not like Israel rejecting everything. It should have some regard for the interests of the United States too. Allon tried to reassure the Secretary that Israel did not seek a confrontation with the United States, but Rogers remained undeterred. The confrontation already existed, he stated. If Israel insisted on major territorial changes, the United States would vote against Israel in the Security Council. Sisco added his punch. In 1967 Israel had informed the United States that it did not want any Egyptian territory and would return most of the West Bank to King Hussein. It was not the American position that had changed. If Israel asked for changes of sovereignty, there would be no peace. And then he added gravely: 'Weigh what will be the results of a new war: it will last only a few weeks before the United States will be called in to defend you against the Soviets.'

Rogers led up to the climax. With undisguised anger he jabbed: 'None of us understands why your answer to the Jarring proposals was given in such arrogant and adamant terms. We want to support you but we have also other interests.' Allon valiantly tried to calm Sisco's anxieties on a possible Russian intervention. 'What can they do to Israel? They'll have to bring in half a million men and we are no worse fighters than the North Vietnamese.' Rogers was unimpressed. He shook his head and sighed: 'What baffles me is why a nation that is so smart with words, comes to stand so alone in the world.'

A few days after this unusual bout, the State Department replied to Israel's memorandum in its customary smooth and measured style: the United States government subscribed to a peace settlement based on Resolution 242; it supported any step advancing this objective and diminishing the risks of renewed hostilities. In this context it would favour the interim agreement. It believed that the Israeli proposal provided a basis for a negotiated agreement and would convey it to Egypt. It contained, in the view of the US government, some constructive elements and some points that Egypt would not be able to accept. But more important for Israel was the announcement, preceding Washington's reply, that twelve more F-4s would be released to Israel. Phantom fighter planes had already in the past been shown to possess as much persuasive diplomatic potential as they had striking power.

Rogers' visit to Cairo and Jerusalem, and the Bergus paper

Egypt's answer to the Israeli proposal was not long in coming. Sadat informed Donald Bergus that he insisted on the crossing of Egyptian forces; that Egypt must control the strategic Sinai passes; that certain demilitarized zones would be acceptable; and that in the first stage Israel could remain in Sharm el-Sheikh, but a full settlement must be reached within six months. Without Israel agreeing to yield the passes, there was no point in the United States pursuing its efforts. His terms, unacceptable to Israel, appeared to be the end of the Suez initiative to those who were not too familiar with Sadat's intricate ways of operating, Sisco's boundless enthusiasm and Dayan's astonishing inventiveness. Rogers and Sisco decided that they could move the parties by talking directly to their leaders. They arrived in Cairo on 4 May and a few days later went to Jerusalem. It was the first visit to the Middle East in eighteen years by an American Secretary of State.

Shortly before Rogers' arrival, Sadat removed Ali Sabry, a former influential aide of Nasser and trusted friend of the Soviet Union. He assumed that this step, inevitable for his political survival, would enhance his standing with the United States government. Sadat, skipping skilfully over the details of the Suez proposal, tried to reach a large measure of conceptual understanding with the Secretary of State. Rogers was impressed by his moderation and flexibility. He was as keen, if not even more so, as Sadat to come to an understanding with him. He saw it as an essential part in his endeavours to improve the relations between the United States and the Arab world, an objective which he said President Nixon had instructed him to pursue vigorously. On the other hand, the White House, i.e. Henry Kissinger, had been sceptical about the need and utility of the present visit which it considered premature and ill-prepared. But the success of the Secretary's mission did not depend exclusively on the charm of Sadat and the courtesy of the American envoys. It required, to no less a degree, the readiness of the Israeli government to compromise on the specific issues which it regarded as essential for the safeguarding of its vital needs.

For this purpose, Sisco met privately with Dayan, who indicated his willingness to support under certain conditions a re-deployment of the Israeli forces at the entrance to the Sinai passes, at a distance of thirty–forty kilometres from the canal. Golda was demonstrably irked when Simha Dinitz, the head of her private office, reported Dayan's retreat from the official government line. She sternly admonished her cabinet to stick to its guns and Dayan returned to the fold from his sortie without firing a single verbal shot in his defence. It appeared that some of his colleagues were more pleased with his cave-in then worried by the possible collapse of the negotiations. When Rogers left Israel, the key questions remained unanswered: the distance of withdrawal, the linkage to the final 'peace agreement, the passage of Israeli shipping through the canal and its crossing by Egyptian forces. Sisco returned to Cairo to work out some solutions. Back in Washington he reported to Rabin with pointed optimism that Sadat had shown sufficient flexibility to justify the continuation of the effort.

But when, a few days later, Foreign Minister Mahmoud Riad handed Bergus a document specifying Egypt's official position on the major points at issue, the American representative realized that under those conditions an agreement was unattainable. Bergus decided, as he later claimed on his own initiative and without prior authorization from Washington, to re-draft Riad's paper and submit it to one of the Minister's aides. But before he received any reaction, Sadat sprang one of his surprises for which he became feared and famous. He announced that Soviet President Podgorny would arrive in Cairo on 25 May. Or was it perhaps that this time Sadat had become a victim of surprise? In any case, he later remonstrated that the Soviet leader descended upon him self-invited and with only a few days' prior notice. He had no advance knowledge that Podgorny would present him with a ready-made treaty of friendship and co-operation, gift-wrapped in promises of a swelling flow of arms and continued vigorous political support. Sadat claimed that he tried to wriggle out of the bear-hug – perhaps; but on the third day of the visit he signed on the dotted line. The Soviets have little use for lengthy procedures à la Camp David when they feel they have the upper hand. They use their camps for other purposes. The treaty was intended to last for fifteen years. It came to a sudden end after fifteen months.

The Bergus text was even more short-lived. Still, it created sufficient commotion, not easily forgotten. Sadat, who considered it as an authorized communication, adopted it with minor changes. He informed the United States government that his signature of the Soviet treaty had not altered his desire to conclude the Suez Canal agreement. Rogers and Sisco were inclined to accept Sadat's assurance, but Nixon was not keen to give him further credit. He directed the Secretary of State to refrain, for the time being, from any further action.

The Bergus initiative had meanwhile become known not only to his superiors in Washington, but also to our Foreign Ministry in Jerusalem. One fine morning in June I found copies of the Sadat-Bergus exchange in my in-tray. They had reached my desk not exactly by the courtesy of the authors. The authenticity of the papers was vouched for and admitted some time later by the State Department. The surreptitiousness of the American move in Cairo not only aroused our dismay, but the contents of the Bergus proposals justifiably outraged the Prime Minister.

The Bergus paper, on which Egypt had modelled its propositions, not only stalled the whole proceedings, but understandably produced an angry crisis of confidence between Jerusalem and Washington. It was impossible for us to believe that the American representative in Cairo, even if not explicitly authorized, could be so completely ignorant of State Department policy as to draft a collection of inexplicable absurdities. The White House, involved in much more dramatic events, decided to relegate the interim agreement to the 'backburner'. The President had much higher priorities at the moment: since February, Kissinger had been negotiating with North Vietnamese delegates in great secrecy in Paris and had been preparing his covert mission to China.

The re-opening of the canal or a renewal of hostilities

Sisco, endowed with admirable zest, believed that diplomacy in the Middle East was best practised by the rules of tight-rope walking – standstill came before the fall. He advocated continued movement, even if its destination remained sometimes obscure. He convinced the Secretary of State and the

President that he should have another go at the Suez negotiations. He came to Israel at the end of July determined to mollify the ruffled government and to modify its position. He was, however, handicapped by two seemingly converse directives: not to exert undue pressure and not to make any commitments on the delivery of the F-4s which had been held up. He concentrated his thrust on three points: Israel should agree to the crossing of a token Egyptian force, say 700 policemen; it should remove its own forces as close as possible to the Sinai passes; and it should accept some vague wording establishing by reference to Resolution 242 some connection between the interim agreement and the final settlement. In five long meetings, presided over by the Prime Minister and attended by three of her cabinet colleagues, Sisco was at his persuasive best. But he was not good enough, without presidential backing, to overcome Golda's resistance. From the outset she had detected the chink in his armour and hammered away at it all through the talks. She asked for an explanation for the delay in the delivery of the Phantoms. Sisco, now walking the tight-rope himself, tried to evade the issue. He did not stumble, but neither did he advance. He realized that the release of the aircraft was the key to possible progress. His recommendation to Washington to yield fell on deaf ears.

But Golda had yet another arrow in her quiver. What about the Rogers plan, she wanted to know. Will America forget about it or at least undertake not to activate it? This was another catch from which Sisco tried to free himself, but Golda did not loosen her grip. He was constrained to say 'the United States will not and cannot drop the plan in the foreseeable future'.

At the final meeting he made a last attempt to breach Golda's ramparts. The Prime Minister had told the ministers in attendance to leave the conduct of the talks to her. They were expected to behave like well brought-up children in the presence of adult company: to be seen, but not heard. Throughout the meetings they had shown exemplary discipline and forbearance, only letting off steam in the protected recesses of their offices. Turning directly to Dayan, Sisco said pointedly: 'It is our judgement that there is a likelihood of the resumption of the hostilities if no practical progress is made on the interim agreement. What is your opinion as Minister of Defence?' Dayan replied calmly: 'This might happen; either by the end of this year, or some time next year the Egyptians might open fire, if no progress is made.' Eban, trying to bolster Dayan's statement, said: 'We all share Dayan's estimate of Sadat's action, if no agreement is achieved.' Sisco was satisfied and pushed on: 'If it happens', he declared, 'the Russians will feel themselves more responsible for the results of the battle. We have to do everything possible to prevent the resumption of the war.'

Whether Golda was impressed by this fateful forecast we could not discern. Summing up the talks, she explained that Israel had agreed in principle to conclude a special agreement. She doubted whether the government would now endorse the position she had stated in her speech in the Knesset on 9

February. She was ready to consider a withdrawal from the canal but nothing so dramatic as the kind of distance which had been mentioned. She would under no circumstances agree to the crossing of Egyptian forces in any form, shape or size. A direct or indirect link of the agreement to Resolution 242 was unacceptable. To ease the tone of finality she said: 'We do not think the canal proposal is dead.' As far as Sisco's exertions were concerned the proposal had come to a dead end. He went back to Washington without even stopping over in Cairo. From Israel he had obtained too little to fulfil Sadat's expectations and the concessions he could expect from him were too insignificant to affect Israel's position.

During the meeting of the United Nations in September, Secretary Rogers tried to rekindle the cold embers. In his address to the Assembly he described the existing differences as bridgeable and presented a blueprint for the building of the bridge. In his private and separate talks with the Foreign Ministers of Israel and Egypt, he suggested a new form of procedure: proximity talks, a refined sort of negotiation by proxy. When it came to pouring old wine into new vessels, American ingenuity was peerless. It designed not only the vessels but also relabelled the wine. Eban, keen to avoid the impression of complete diplomatic stalemate, perfected the proposal. From the rostrum of the General Assembly he called upon his Egyptian colleague to meet him under the roof of the United Nations and to discuss the terms of an interim agreement. His move helped alleviate allegations of Israeli intractability, placed Egypt in a tight corner and aroused the ire of Ambassador Rabin.

A new arms accord with the US

Rabin protested in a cable to the Prime Minister that Eban's proposal had harmed his efforts to break the ban on the delivery of the F-4s and other vital equipment and had taken the wind out of the sails of his public campaign. He complained that Eban's reaction to Rogers' new proposals had been weak and indecisive and his whole appearance at the United Nations useless.

This was not the first or the last time that Rabin criticized the Foreign Minister and his colleagues. It normally ended with a verbal shoot-out between the two, with Golda sometimes acting as the soft-spoken sheriff. But this bang contained an innovation: it censured Eban, widely admired as the 'voice of Israel', for the quality of his performance at the United Nations. Since his masterly speeches had always evoked universal admiration from friend and foe alike, Rabin had touched on Eban's most sensitive nerve. His wrath was biblical and the 'percussion of his sound' Shakespearean. Rabin's opinion on the speeches of Israeli representatives at the UN, Eban thundered, was immaterial because all opinions prompted by extremism and exaggeration became an obsession which blurred rational advice. It was an unusual practice for an ambassador to reprimand the members of his own government. The Ambassador in Washington was not in charge of the government. Nobody forced him to represent a government whose decisions were, in his retroactive view, one continuous chain of errors.

A few days after this exchange the Ambassador signed at the State Department a memorandum of understanding on arms supplies which had been the subject of extended negotiations. Its most important point was the American agreement to allow the sale to Israel of jet aircraft engines for its new fighter plane Kfir, an improved version of the French Mirage. Apparently, Eban's reasonable stance at the United Nations had not impaired the accord; it might even have facilitated it.

In December, the Prime Minister revisited Washington. She pleaded the case which Dayan had presented to the White House a year earlier – that of a long-term agreement on arms supplies. At every stage of a renewed Israeli request difficulties had arisen which were unpleasant for both governments. The vital requirements of Israel's security should not be used as diplomatic levers. They deserved the United States unreserved consideration, based on objective needs. Her argument was effective with the President who was, as any incumbent of the office, alert to the exigencies of domestic politics. Needless misunderstandings with Israel were harmful to both of them. On 31 December 1971, the administration announced its agreement in principle to resume the shipment of the F-4s, and a month later it signed a new memorandum of understanding on the sale of forty-two additional Phantoms and eighty-two Skyhawks.

Sadat was disappointed in many ways. His Suez initiative had run aground. His friendly approaches to Washington had failed to produce practical results. His treaty with the Soviet Union had not expedited the promised deliveries of arms and had impeded the improvement of his relations with the United States. And, last but not least, he had failed to dislodge Israel from its entrenched positions along the canal or any other part of Egyptian territory lost in the Six Day War.

The war between India and Pakistan, which broke out in December, provided Sadat with a plausible excuse for postponing his threatened action against Israel. It also afforded a welcome reason to the Soviet Union for retarding its shipments of arms to Egypt. Sadat explained it himself in an interview he gave in August 1972 shortly after his eviction of the Soviet advisers. He had gone to Moscow in October 1971 to insist on the delivery of Mig 23s, solemnly promised by President Podgorny. 'For this reason, I had decided to sign the treaty with the Soviet Union. I felt this would finally convince the Russians that I was not America's man and that they could trust me. But four months went by and nothing happened. The Russians knew that I had made 1971 the year of decision for the liberation of our occupied land, but it was becoming increasingly clear that they did not want to help us solve the problem with the equipment we needed.' In Moscow, Sadat received a renewed promise that the armaments would reach Egypt by the end of the year. 'November passed and nothing – except a Soviet airlift to India via Egypt, where some Soviet equipment was picked up for the Indians for their war against Pakistan, a country backed by America. This showed', concluded Sadat, 'that when the Russians want to throw their weight behind a country at war, they are not necessarily deterred by the fact that the United States stands behind that country's opponent.'

1971, which Sadat had proclaimed as the 'year of decision', faded out as a year of continuing indecision.

30

The Great Surprise

The Soviet presence in Egypt constituted one of the major concerns of the United States in the Middle East at the beginning of the 1970s. Naturally it also engaged Israel's strategic and political considerations. The Soviet military involvement in men and material was not only of preponderant assistance to the modernization and fighting strength of the Egyptian army, but it also directly affected the United States' military posture in the area. From bases in Egypt, Soviet-manned Tupolev planes took off on their surveillance flights of the Sixth Fleet. The Soviet navy, which had considerably increased its strength and activities in the Mediterranean since the Six Day War, enjoyed the unimpeded use of Egyptian port facilities.

Sadat realized that he had to put some distance between himself and the Russians if he wanted to achieve some *rapprochement* with the United States. In the talks on the Suez agreement, he had dangled before his American interlocutors the prospect that Soviet military advisers would leave Egypt after Israel had completed the first stage of withdrawal. When the negotiations had come to a virtual standstill, Kissinger felt the time had come for the White House to play a more decisive role in the direction of the triangular American-Israeli-Egyptian affair.

Kissinger was critical of the negotiating tactics employed by the State Department. In his opinion the withholding of arms from Israel was likely to stiffen its attitude. The more insecure Israel felt, the less it was inclined to compromise. The impressive Soviet involvement justified Israel's reluctance to embark on a process of withdrawal, not knowing where it would end. It had a right to be assured that the evacuated territories would not serve as a launching-area for a new assault against it. Kissinger recommended reversing the order of business. The first stage should be what he called the expulsion of the Russians by Sadat. Only then should Israel withdraw its forces to the lines agreed upon in an eventual Suez accord.

Kissinger saw to it that Sadat was not left uncertain about the change of wind in Washington and from where it was blowing. Sadat soon adjusted his sails and established contacts with the White House through a secret channel. Moreover, 1972 was a presidential election year with its traditional limitations on initiatives or controversial foreign policy issues. There was no sense in creating difficulties for Israel when the result of its concessions might not only weaken it, but also evoke displeasure among its numerous supporters. But beyond these domestic considerations, Nixon had become convinced that an Israeli withdrawal, preceding the departure of the Soviet advisers from Egypt, would neither strengthen Middle-Eastern stability nor further United States interests in the area.

1972 was also the year of a summit meeting, scheduled to take place in Moscow in May. In anticipation of that conference, the President wanted the Soviet leaders, as well as the American public, to be apprised of his policy and concerns in the Middle East. In his foreign policy review, submitted to Congress on 9 February, he stated that 'The Soviet Union's effort to use the Arab-Israeli conflict to perpetuate and expand its own military position in Egypt has been a matter of concern to the United States. The Soviet Union has taken advantage of Egypt's increasing dependence on Soviet military supply to gain the use of naval and air facilities in Egypt.' The President expressed the hope that the avoidance of a major conflict in the Middle East was a Soviet interest which would best be served by 'restraint in its arms supply, refraining from the use of the conflict to enhance its own military position and encouraging the negotiation of peace'. He then warned that: 'Injecting the global strategic rivalry into the region is incompatible with Middle East peace and with détente in US-Soviet relations.'

After he had made his point regarding Moscow, Nixon departed for Peking. His visit to China at the end of February 1972 transformed the existing polarized US-USSR relationship into a triangular power constellation. The United States expected that this fundamental change in the balance of power would have a restraining effect on Soviet policies in various parts of the world, hopefully including the Middle East. Indeed, the Middle East section of the joint statement issued on 29 May at the end of the Moscow summit conference was rather innocuous. It reaffirmed the adherence of the two powers to Resolution 242 and their support for the Jarring mission. It emphasized that a settlement of the Arab-Israeli conflict would promote the normalization of the Middle East situation and assist a process of military relaxation in the area.

On the sidelines of the conference, Kissinger and Gromyko agreed on a set of guidelines for the negotiation of an Arab-Israeli peace settlement. Although the aim was the attainment of a comprehensive agreement, it could be achieved in stages: it should provide for the withdrawal of Israeli forces from occupied Arab territories and the establishment of de-militarized zones and the stationing of UN forces at Sharm el-Sheikh; freedom of navigation in the Straits of Tirán and the Suez Canal should be guaranteed; changes of boundaries should be subject to agreement between the parties; the settlement should terminate belligerency and establish a state of peace recognizing the right of independence and sovereignty of all states in the Middle East, including Israel. Two points remained open: the problem of the Palestinian refugees and the need to bring the parties together in direct negotiations at the final stages of the peace process.

Both sides kept strict confidentiality on the existence of the agreement. Whether it was Kissinger's intention to secure the co-operation of the Soviet Union in the implementation of the set of principles is an open question, given his later practice of excluding the Soviet Union from active participation in the peace process. In any event, the policy Moscow continued to pursue in the Arab-Israeli conflict scarcely indicated that it felt itself bound by these guidelines. It persisted in its strong anti-Israeli bias and exclusive support of the Arab side. Whatever Kissinger's initial intentions may have been, in practice he tried to limit Soviet participation to a minimum, indispensable to avoid harmful interference with his own schemes. On his step-by-step journey he preferred to travel alone. Until the tensions in the Middle East worsened in 1973 he proceeded slowly and waited patiently for Sadat to make a complete u-turn. The Soviets for their part were, during this period, principally concerned with protecting their faltering position in Egypt and bolstering their waning influence in other parts of the region. This was, for them, an objective of much greater immediacy than playing an active role as Middle East peace-maker, an activity which had never ranked very high on the list of their political priorities.

How much they were concerned in 1971 about the uncertainty of their continued military presence in Egypt under Sadat can be deduced from an unusual Soviet initiative. At the end of December Anatoly Dobrynin, the Soviet Ambassador in Washington, intimated to his Israeli colleague that the Soviet Union was prepared to withdraw its military advisers from Egypt. It would content itself with leaving only 600 experts behind, attached to the Soviet embassy. This would be an identical arrangement and equivalent to the number of military personnel which the United States maintained in Iran. The comparison was no less startling than the proposal itself. The admitted concept of trading off the Russian presence in Egypt with that of the United States in Iran fitted our assessment of Soviet primary aims in Egypt and other Arab countries. Kissinger, informed of the Dobrynin sounding, interpreted it as a feint and an indication of Soviet uneasiness about its position in Egypt. He advised the Israeli government to ignore the Soviet approach.

He revealed later in his memoirs that when he met Gromyko at the Soviet Embassy in Washington on 30 September 1971, the Soviet Foreign Minister had broached the subject: 'In the event of a comprehensive settlement the Soviets would be prepared to withdraw their forces from the Middle East . . . And even then the Soviets made their withdrawal from Egypt conditional on the withdrawal of American advisers from Iran.'

Sadat ousts Soviet advisers

It appears that Sadat was unaware of the secret Kissinger-Gromyko understanding, arrived at during the Moscow summit meeting, but the joint statement by the leaders of the United States and the Soviet Union alarmed him. He thought it was likely to frustrate the prospects of achieving his central aim: the restoration of the territories lost in 1967. He concluded that in view of the trend towards détente, the superpowers were disinterested in any precipitate action in the Middle East and that Soviet-American antagonism was no longer a powerful lever to be used to Egypt's advantage. He felt that the Soviet Union had let him down, first by foisting the treaty on him, then by granting priority to India for the delivery of armaments, and finally by making common cause with the United States in freezing the Arab-Israeli conflict. He now realized that, without gaining the sympathy of the United States, his cause was condemned to hopeless stagnation. Sadat supposed that, without the elimination of the substantial Soviet presence in his country, the United States would hardly budge from its reserved attitude. But, at this stage, he was not convinced of the utility of an exclusive liaison with Washington. He doubted whether he could achieve his main objective without employing military means and he knew he could not count on the United States in this respect – it was firmly opposed to the renewal of the hostilities. For the use of the military option he needed the Soviet Union. The Egyptian army was nearly exclusively Soviet-equipped and trained. For the resumption of the war, Egypt depended on a continued flow of Soviet military supplies, but not on the massive presence of Russian troops on its soil. On the contrary, this could present a handicap for the initiation of the hostilities. It could cause an American intervention on the side of Israel and conjured up the threat of a US-USSR confrontation, played out on Egyptian territory.

Sadat chose the middle way. He would demand the repatriation of the bulk of the Soviet military adviser force, but not cancel his permission for the Soviet use of Egyptian air and naval facilities. This was strategically far more important for the deployment of Soviet power in the Mediterranean basin than the stationing of their troops in a foreign country, where they had became more of a political liability than a strategic asset. But to impress the United States and its allies with the impact of his decision, Sadat staged it as a sudden outburst of fury. He always had a flair for dramatic display, and would not miss an effect where he could produce one. He applied this talent with equal skill in war and peace.

He launched his thunderbolt against the Russians on 18 July 1972, out of a clear sky, as the world was given to believe. But ten days before his public announcement, he had informed the Soviet Ambassador of his demand for the evacuation of the Russian military advisers. From Moscow's restrained diplomatic reaction he gathered that the Soviet government would absorb the blow without retribution provided that its continued access to the air and naval facilities remained intact. Sadat gave this assurance. International comment was rampant on Sadat's daring expulsion of the Soviets. The opinion which prevailed in Israel among the policy-makers, political commentators and military strategists, was that the action would cause irreparable harm to Egypt's military strength, virtually incapacitating its army to fight, let alone to launch another war in the foreseeable future. It had invoked the wrath of its main supplier of arms and the Soviet government would not hesitate to chasten Sadat. For the years ahead, so went the argument, Israel had nothing to fear from its erstwhile most powerful neighbour.

I did not share these confident interpretations nor the serene outlook of their authors. I was in Europe on some Foreign Ministry business when Sadat made his sensational announcement. After a day or two of reflection I sent my assessment to Foreign Minister Eban I argued that the reason for Sadat's step was to find a way out of the impasse in which Egypt was presently stuck. He wanted to prove to his critics on the domestic front that it was the Soviet Union that prevented Egypt from taking military action, while Moscow was not in a position to impose on Israel a political settlement. He intended to increase the pressure on the Soviet Union to supply the required military equipment and economic aid, and to induce the United States to work for a political solution favourable to Egypt, assuming that only Washington was able to alter Israel's positions.

The Soviet Union would be cautious in its reaction to the eviction of its advisers and not precipitate the end of its relations with Egypt. It would change its attitude towards Israel only when it considered its position completely compromised.

Egypt was now preparing the ground for decisions it intended to take next year. Meanwhile it would intensify its activity among the West European states, to enlist their pressure on the United States. It would concentrate on France by fostering its hopes that it would replace the Soviet Union as principal arms-supplier.

Israel should be alert to the possibility that in due time Egypt might renew the hostilities with limited extension. It would act under the assumption that the United States would restrain Israel from using its full strength in a lengthy campaign to defeat Egypt decisively. Sadat possibly supposed that after a short and violent conflagration, where he had proved his readiness to fight, the United States would put its full weight behind a political solution. These views I communicated to Jerusalem on 20 July 1972.

Upon my return I had a series of discussions with the Minister on the implications of Sadat's new policy. Eban, supported by the senior staff, among them the experts on Arab affairs, tended to accept the sanguine view that Sadat's blow to the Russians would boomerang. It would hit Egypt and its diminished strength would fortify Israel's position. But Eban did not share the opinion that the new situation vindicated the advocates of a policy of diplomatic standstill. He warned that a diplomatic vacuum was likely to create political turbulence in the area.

I shared his opinion of the dangers of immobility, but adhered to my view that the main purpose of Sadat's anti-Russian exercise was to bring the Americans in on his side for a more or less imposed – more on Israel and less on Egypt – political settlement. But at the same time Sadat was preparing substantive military action in case the United States did not act with the resolve and speed he desired. For such an eventuality he had decided to clear the Egyptian deck of cumbersome Russian passengers. With the presence of nearly 20,000 Soviet military personnel he could not navigate at will. The war he had in mind was to be a short but sharp clash with Israel designed to trigger off American political intervention. The involvement of Soviet troops would either frustrate his plan or turn Egypt into a theatre of superpower confrontation. Sadat feared both eventualities. The eviction of the Russians was the prelude to his major combined politico-military offensive.

The Foreign Minister and my colleagues listened patiently to my argument, but remained unconvinced. They were not alone in their reservations. Their judgement of the effects and motives of Sadat's initiative was shared by the Prime Minister, the defence establishment and the intelligence community. The latter used to brief the senior staff of our ministry from time to time. The briefing would display impressive charts, real works of art from the school of military realism. They represented a constantly mounting Arab arms superiority alongside disproportionately inferior Israeli arsenals. The acceptable disproportion, so we were told, was one to three in favour of the Arab states. Where this equation was disturbed by Arab progress and Israeli shortfall, there was the flashpoint of a possible new military conflagration. The graphs presented in 1973 were to prove that until the year 1975 such a possibility was excluded. More so, the expected slowdown in Soviet deliveries to Egypt would delay this date. Unfortunately, there were no charts to predict the working of the minds of the decision-makers which, by and large, were governed by less lucid rules.

In our councils I remained a minority – in fact a minority of one. Attempting to share my concerns with a wider public, I published a few articles in the Israeli and foreign press. It was an unusual procedure for a civil servant on active duty, but the articles did not cause any undue commotion, probably because they were written more in a scholarly than a polemic vein. They made reasonably good reading in the 'I-told-you-so' file of later years.

The leadership of Israel might well have been stirred from its complacency had Sadat helped them at the time to understand his moves and motives as he disclosed them after the Yom Kippur War in an interview with *Newsweek*, published on 25 March 1974: 'No strategist in America or Israel guessed correctly why I asked Soviet military advisers to leave in July 1972. Everyone thought that I had abandoned war as a way of breaking the deadlock. They all said that without Soviet advisers I could not go to war. Well, with the Russian military out of the country, I was making sure that no one could claim that what we did in the future was inspired by the Soviets. If Arab victory there was to be, it had to be clearly Arab.'

Egypt's new diplomatic strategy

On one point at least there was tacit understanding in 1972 between the leaders of Egypt, Israel and the United States. They recognized that the presidential elections precluded any serious American moves in the Middle East. The Israeli government believed that the period of respite could be extended beyond the American elections until after the Knesset elections in October 1973.

Sadat, however, used the waiting period of 1972 for a thorough preparation of his action planned for 1973. Tense as his relations with the Soviet Union were, he did not relax his pressure to obtain the pledged armaments, indispensable for the Egyptian army to fight a new war. Even if there had been delays in delivery and the Soviet Union had withheld some of the offensive weapons Egypt had asked for, enough arms were supplied to equip the Egyptian and Syrian armies to launch such a war.

Politically Sadat embarked on a wide-ranging and well-synchronized campaign to separate Israel from its friends in Africa and Europe. He knew from previous experience that an Israel connected with the world community by a far-flung network of mutual ties was a difficult target to attack. World opinion was on the side of Israel, as the Six Day War had shown, and active support in times of crisis from those states that counted in this regard – the United States and the European community – added considerably to its defensive strength. The international isolation of Israel was a prerequisite for a successful assault on it. In the countries of the Third World, Egyptian propaganda portrayed Israel as the tool of Western imperialism and in the West it depicted it as the sole obstacle to better relations with the Arab world. For special use in Africa, Israel was tainted with racism. Sadat did not expect the Western countries to turn against Israel; he was satisfied if, in an emergency, they would deny Israel their practical assistance and public support. Egypt, acting with remarkable professionalism and planning, and working in conjunction with other Arab states, attained an astonishing degree of success in its political objectives. When the Yom Kippur War broke out, nearly all the African countries which had not already done so severed their relations with Israel. The heads of state of the non-aligned nations, at their conference in Algiers, unanimously supported Sadat's plea to ostracize Israel. As he later conceded, their aid and comfort gave him added encouragement to go to war.

Yet Sadat focused his principal attention on the United States. After the re-election of Nixon he mustered all his available capacity of lure and stratagem, Third World backing and European fear, the Arab oil and the Soviet threat, into one combined thrust for a breakthrough in Washington. After Rogers and Sisco had proved to be ineffective, he concluded that Henry Kissinger was the man to win over. At the end of February 1973 Sadat sent his security adviser, Hafiz Ismail, to Washington to meet Kissinger. He first met the President. They discussed a two-tier strategy of negotiations on an Egyptian-Israeli settlement: public talks at the State Department and the second-tier secret meetings with Dr Kissinger, modelled somewhat on the Vietnam negotiations. In two days of talks Kissinger, assisted by Harold Saunders, discussed with the Egyptian special envoy ideas of substance and procedures of an eventual peace settlement. His formula was composed of two basic elements: Israel recognizing Egypt's full sovereignty over Sinai and Egypt acknowledging Israel's security concerns. The settlement would be implemented in stages over a lengthy period of time. Hafiz Ismail showed interest in the general idea, but refrained from taking a position on the specific security arrangements which Kissinger considered Israel would require. The two men agreed to meet again some time later in the year. Kissinger was in no hurry. He probably thought the project needed a longer period of gestation.

From the President's and his own talks with Golda Meir, who visited Washington shortly after the departure of Hafiz Ismail, Kissinger concluded that her priority was not a renewed US mediation effort, but rather a substantial supply of American arms. Moreover, 1973 was an election year in Israel. The Prime Minister had to cope with enough domestic controversies without adding international complications. Standstill appeared to her the simplest way of avoiding difficulties. But simplicity was not always the essence of political wisdom. One of its distinguishing marks is foresight.

In the following months Sadat became increasingly convinced that nothing but a violent eruption or at least the threat of it was likely to prompt a shift in Washington's policy. He intensified the frequency and visibility of his warning signals. In an interview he gave to Arnaud de Borchgrave which *Newsweek* published on 9 April 1973, he declared: 'The time has come for a shock. Diplomacy will continue before, during and after the battle. All West Europeans are telling us that everybody has fallen asleep over the Middle East crisis. But they will soon wake up to the fact that America has left us no other way out. The resumption of the hostilities is the only way out. Everything in this country is now being mobilized in earnest for the resumption of the battle which is inevitable.'

Indeed the signs of Sadat's preparations became more and more evident. At the beginning of May, Egypt and Syria carried out noticeable troop movements in the vicinity of the cease-fire lines, causing Israel to mobilize some reserves. Counting on the effect of the short but nonetheless sharp crisis,

Sadat sent Hafiz Ismail to Paris for another meeting with Kissinger at the end of the month. But he was not authorized to discuss details of a possible Egyptian-Israeli settlement. He only repeated Egypt's public stance that the complete evacuation of all the territories and the solution of the Palestinian problem were Egypt's immutable conditions for peace with Israel. His brief was to explore the prospects of US support for Egypt and the denial of a continuous sale of American arms to Israel, rather than to clarify the specific conditions of peace.

Sadat, disappointed with the results of Hafiz's special mission, not only dispensed with any further serious attempts to woo the United States until he had administered his great shock, but also with the services of his security adviser whom he appointed as ambassador to the Soviet Union. The Egyptian leader now took his next step on the steadily moving escalator. Unable to force America's hand by private diplomacy, he decided to force the issue by submitting it to the Security Council. He apparently hoped that a public debate would compel the United States to adopt a more dynamic role or, in case it refused, to move the Arab states and their allies, ranging from Cuba to Cambodia, to blame the United States for Israel's 'intransigence' and provide Egypt and Syria with an alibi for their planned military action.

The debates in the Council dragged on for several weeks in the charged UN atmosphere and the hot and humid summer climate of New York. The representatives of Egypt did not show any inclination to settle on a compromise resolution. The Israeli embassy in Washington was instructed to press hard for an unequivocal American stand even if it necessitated the casting of the veto, a prospect far from cherished by the State Department. Finally the US delegation did cast its veto. It hit where Sadat wanted it to: the United States and Israel.

Our permanent representative to the United Nations, Ambassador Joseph Tekoah, saw it differently. He had played a prominent part in overcoming the reluctance of the United States to use its veto. In this respect the defeat of a strong anti-Israeli resolution was a creditable personal success. In an exultant telegram he called the outcome of the debate 'the greatest Egyptian defeat since 1967'. It taught them that all escape hatches from negotiations with Israel were now locked, Israel's position was firmly anchored in US support and the present territorial and political situation would last until Egypt, or for that matter any other Arab country, would deign to negotiate with Israel. The continued stalemate would erode Arab resistance to a directly negotiated peace settlement. I annotated his dispatch at this point: 'or lead to war'.

Complacent Israel
More and more indications reinforced my earlier conviction in these summer months of 1973 that the diplomatic deadlock, which was taken for granted, if not even welcomed, by our decision-makers, could become a sudden death-

trap. Many of our political and military analysts had long since adopted the attitude of reading statements by Arab leaders as if they were a form of mirror-writing. They meant the converse of what they were saying. Protestations of peace meant preparation of mischief and threats of war were the expression of impotence. I had always thought that there was nothing wrong in taking a person's word, and even a politician's pronouncement, at its face value, unless obvious facts repudiated them. Sadat's declarations since the beginning of 1971 revealed a remarkable consistency. He was prepared to enter into a peace agreement with Israel, he said in his reply to Dr Jarring's proposal in February 1971; he would contemplate the conclusion of an interim agreement on the Suez Canal as a first step. He persisted in his conditions with amazing perseverance, whether it was the withdrawal to the Sinai passes in the first stage or the total evacuation. He knew that the Soviet Union would provide him with an amount of equipment sufficient to start a new war, but that only the United States had the capacity to supply the political leverage to remove Israel from its present positions.

As late as 21 September 1973 General Eli Zeira, director of military intelligence, assured a closed conference of Israeli ambassadors meeting in Jerusalem that there was no real energy crisis, just an atmosphere of it. In 1974 the United States might prod Israel to create an appearance of negotiations but not pressure it to make concessions against its will. Sadat was satisfied with the present situation, it was the lesser evil for Egypt. The cease-fire would continue because of the existing power equation between the opposing forces. Egypt was aware that the ratio of military strength was to its disadvantage. By 1975 Egypt might reach the conclusion that Israel's deterrent balance was at a point where Egypt could wage war. Until then no combination of Arab states would dare to initiate hostilities.

Some of us ventured to differ from this outlook. Regardless of the developments discernible from the beginning of 1973, intelligence assessments had become increasingly and infectiously self-assured. They invariably predicted the undisturbed continuation of the cease-fire. Who influenced whom is hard to tell. The question of whether it was the military who set the minds of the politicians at rest or the national mood of complacency which dulled the alertness of the military mind will remain a subject of historical and psychological speculation. At any event it was a process of cross-fertilization breeding disaster.

On 5 October Henry Kissinger, by then Secretary of State, discussed with his Israeli and Egyptian colleagues respectively the possibility of launching the new negotiation model in November, shortly after the Knesset elections. Little did he or Eban suspect (and perhaps not even Zayad, the Egyptian Foreign Minister) that Sadat would launch quite a different kind of proximity talks the day after these meetings. He ordered his guns to speak.

The preparations for the elections had dominated Israel's political scene from the beginning of the year until the outbreak of the Yom Kippur War. In the ruling Labour Party everything turned around the question of whether Golda would agree to serve another term as Prime Minister. She kept her cards close to her chest and the aspiring competitors for succession dangling like marionettes. The only one who was kicking his heels was Moshe Dayan. He had always been a solo performer, partly admired, partly feared for his political stunts. To ensure his place in the party power structure he would try to assume a position which allowed him to tip the scales. Commanding a group of loyalists, small but decisive in the parliamentary balance, he would try to set off the rival party factions or candidates. If necessary he would cast suggestive glances at the Opposition, to frighten the wits out of the Labour leadership. He would oppose a moderate platform and inject a radical stance, which would appeal to one side and distress the other. At the party convention in April he proclaimed that he would prefer war to a return to the previous borders. In the debates in August he raised the banner of extended settlement in the West Bank; the right for private individuals to acquire land in the administered territories and the development of the Rafiah salient, west of the old Egyptian-Israeli boundary in Sinai.

His most controversial demand was for the construction of a new port city, Yamit, on Egyptian territory. The town should become Israel's principal deep-water port in the newly settled areas of Sinai and eventually accommodate a population of 250,000 inhabitants. Dayan's plan, presented with the pointed emphasis of 'take it or lose me', aroused the strong but rather ineffective opposition of the moderate but numerically predominant centre of the party. Sapir and Eban attempted vainly to commit the party to a realistic policy which would neither ruin the prospects of a peaceful settlement, nor overtax Israel's political and economic capacity. Golda, traditionally bound to the centre group, but emotionally attracted by Dayan's activism and politically concerned at his possible defection, supported the hardliners with some reservations. Galili, her astute mentor, wrapped up the glaring differences in a neat package which carried Dayan's indelible imprint. The Jerusalem correspondent of the *New York Times* wrote that 'the new platform represented a victory for the hardliners led by Moshe Dayan. It is likely to have a profound impact on any future peace map that Israel negotiates with the Arab countries. Supporters of the platform maintain that it is based on the realistic premise that there will be no peace between Israel and the Arab countries for at least the next four years.'

No war, no peace in the foreseeable future – this was the relaxed view of most of the people in Israel in these days of wilting summer heat and pre-election fever. Over their heads the sky looked clear, under their feet the ground felt firm. The Arab states were incapable of taking up arms against the far superior Israeli forces; the borders were quiet; the United States was in no hurry to press for a political settlement; the Jarring initiative had petered out and Security Council intervention had been prevented by the American veto. The Europeans appeared to be apathetic; the Soviet Union had not yet recovered from Sadat's blow; the number of immigrants from the USSR was swelling; and a steady flow of US arms and credits were being supplied to Israel. Economic difficulties admittedly existed, but they did not affect the euphoric feeling of general well-being; the political infighting was lively and offered an outlet and distraction for the more combative part of the electorate. The warnings from a handful of people that the awakening from this pleasant midsummer night's dream could be rough and sudden, met with polite disbelief from the more gentle souls, and stringent rebuff from the less tolerant ones.

Pinhas Sapir, Minister of Finance at the time and fly-wheel of the Labour Party machine, was among those who were tormented by forebodings. Shortly after the new platform had been adopted, we had lunch *en famille* at our home in Jerusalem. He had asked that no other guests be invited. He was in a sombre mood and was smarting under the defeat of his moderate line. He had been let down by Golda, he grunted, and led down the garden path by Galili, who had made common cause with Dayan. But as long as he was Minister of Finance, they would not get a penny for their absurd Yamit scheme. The whole country was a fools' paradise. The people were completely unaware of the real situation and we were sliding down inexorably into an abyss. 'We are facing an economic catastrophe,' he exclaimed. '*Shuah kalkalith*' (an economic holocaust), he hollered, as if in pain. 'They have dreams of new settlements while I have nightmares about how to raise funds for our basic needs, for bread and arms, for housing the newcomers and repaying our foreign debts.'

I did not argue with him about the gravity of his forecast. If he did not know the facts, who else did? But I felt that he judged the situation only from his particular vantage point, and the view from there appeared terrifying. Before we slid down into the abyss, I said, the volcano on which we were sitting might erupt. We were facing a military blow-up in the near future and, if we were unprepared for it, it would be a greater calamity than the economic disaster he foresaw. Sapir asked me for the facts on which I based such an assertion. I gave him my assessment of Sadat's motivations and moves since the eviction of the Soviet military experts from Egypt and the accumulating evidence of hostile military preparations. He wanted to know what Golda thought about this. I answered that he should know better than I. He was a member of her cabinet and a personal friend. Sapir retorted: 'You see her more often than I do.' I told him that Eban and I had tried on several occasions over the last few months to alert her to the dangers inherent in a protracted diplomatic deadlock. She did not share our apprehensions. She preferred the assessment of the defence establishment, which dismissed the existence of a military threat for the next two or three years. Why should Kissinger remain so passive, if he believed that a diplomatic vacuum was militarily dangerous? Apparently he saw nothing wrong in a stalemate and certainly did not expect the collapse of the cease-fire, adjudged Golda. Our explanations for Kissinger's unusual immobility had not swayed her. And even if Kissinger was preoccupied with other matters, we persisted, or saw the situation differently from Israel, why should this prevent the government from pursuing policies which were in the country's best interest? Golda determined that Israel's best interest was to sit tight. Any move was fraught with danger.

I told Sapir about a memorandum I had written in March 1973 in which I had outlined the reasons why Israel had reached the optimum of its political strength and suggested that it should try to settle the conflict now by compromise, before the Arabs generated sufficient power from international currents likely to favour their cause. The Arab world was divided: King Hussein was firmly in the saddle and ready to make peace; the PLO had caused harm but lacked political strength; the Soviet Union was handicapped in the Middle East by its difficulties with Egypt and its Chinese concerns in the Far East; China's role in the Middle East was still insignificant; the energy crisis in the United States had not yet assumed serious proportions and future priorities of America's foreign commitments might change after the conclusion of the Vietnamese peace agreement. Israel had reached the peak of its international potential. This and the compactness of its military strength were the prerequisites for the best compromise settlement it might ever be able to attain. My principal purpose in writing this memorandum was to warn against the closure of the openings created by Sadat's Suez initiative and King Hussein's readiness to negotiate. Of course, they wanted agreements on terms most favourable to themselves, but so did Israel. The important matter was that the permafrost of hopeless hostility had begun to thaw. Nobody knew whether or when it would melt altogether, but I believed it was worth stimulating the process.

Sapir left no more cheerful than he had arrived. We had hardly touched on the subject which had been the original reason for his visit: his forthcoming meeting with the British Chancellor of the Exchequer in London, where I was soon to take up my new ambassadorial duties.

The dangers of deadlock

In preparation for the new moves in the Middle East which Kissinger was planning for the end of 1973, he explored again with Gromyko at the summit meeting at San Clemente in June whether the Soviet Union could possibly play a positive role in the settlement of the Arab-Israeli conflict. His conclusions were not encouraging. Brezhnev had stressed at the conference the mounting dangers of a new crisis. He warned Nixon that, in the absence of the prospect of a political solution, Egypt and Syria were preparing to renew the hostilities. The Soviet Union was not in a position to dissuade them. American pressure on Israel to withdraw, claimed the Soviets, was the only way to stave off a new war, while in reality their accelerated arms deliveries made the war imminent. But this was not a point to be sharpened, when the two leaders were keen to create a climate of détente.

The professionals in the State Department were not indifferent to the signs of an approaching crisis. At the end of January 1973, Ephraim Evron, assistant director-general in charge of North American affairs at the Foreign Ministry, discussed the then prevalent official Israeli views with Joe Sisco in Washington. He dutifully argued that after the expulsion of the Russians, Egypt no longer constituted a military threat. The more Sadat was made aware of Egypt's impotence, the earlier he would agree to a reasonable settlement with Israel. The worst the United States could do, asserted Evron, would be to interfere in this ripening process by untimely diplomatic activity. The password to peace was to sit tight.

Sisco differed as strongly with the prognosis as he opposed the prescription. In his view this was an overly complacent philosophy. Since their ejection from Egypt the Russians had been busy consolidating their positions in Syria. The present *status quo* was untenable and he hoped that Israel had not opted for it. And then he asked more rhetorically than operatively, but with a remarkable degree of foresight: 'Are not negotiations in February 1973 a better proposition than they might be in February 1974?'

The oil weapon

The Arab states, however, were in no mood to acquiesce in the existing situation. Sadat, in his relentless endeavour to gather every grain of support for the forthcoming battle, devoted immense efforts to beating the oil wealth of Saudi Arabia into a mighty weapon. The Saudi dynasty had always been reluctant to expose itself by threatening openly to use its oil as an instrument of Arab political warfare. Yet in July, King Feisal intimated in a statement that he would no longer hesitate to use the oil weapon against the supporters of Israel. His threat flashed a warning-light in Washington. Heads of major American oil companies operating in the Persian Gulf area had repeatedly alerted the administration to the danger of the interruption of oil supplies to the United States and some of its allies from Saudi and other Arab sources in case of a new outbreak of hostilities.

On 30 July 1973 Sisco invited Israel's new ambassador, Simha Dinitz, for a meeting. He wanted to acquaint him with America's present predicament in the Middle East. After the veto the United States 'stood naked before its Arab friends and especially before Saudi Arabia'. The administration had clear indications that Saudi Arabia, under Sadat's pressure, would politicize the oil. It was not precluded that King Feisal would freeze oil production, with tremendous consequences for Western Europe and the United States. This was a serious US concern which could lead to a major reassessment of its policy.

Sisco wanted Israel to do something that would help the United States to convince Feisal that there would be progress in the Middle East conflict. He needed such evidence because of Sadat's unrelenting pressure. Sisco admitted candidly that he was not authorized to make any specific proposal, but he was sure that Israel would know what steps it could take to help the United States.

Dinitz was baffled by the intensity of Sisco's appeal and the vagueness of his request. He sensed the urgency but could not make out what he was aiming at specifically. Dinitz contented himself with the routine replies that he did not know what more Israel could do than it had already done. It was ready to open negotiations with any Arab state which so desired. But he would, of course, report to Jerusalem. There the matter was dismissed as one of Sisco's not unusual reconnaissance missions, meant to probe the solidity of Israel's position.

Obviously the Israeli policy-makers believed that the oil threat was either an empty Arab boast or a political plot, hatched by the State Department and the oil companies. They failed to recognize the real and imminent danger of an effectively prepared Arab plan of action, well orchestrated by Sadat. After Sadat had visited Saudi Arabia and other Arab oil states during the summer, it was officially stated that his tour was aimed at 'co-ordinating Arab policies for the use of oil in the struggle against Israel'. Sadat had also received pledges to the amount of several hundred million dollars for his war chest. However, as Sadat later disclosed in a speech made at the end of August 1974, he did not receive a single dollar of the promised Arab aid until he had started the war in October: 'In the first week of the fighting our Arab brethren sent us the promised $500 million. Without it, we would not have been able to provide a piece of bread. This grave economic situation was one of my considerations in making war.'

Israeli leaders were not alone in underestimating the potential of the oil weapon. The newly nominated Secretary of State, Dr Henry Kissinger, replying to a question in the course of the Senate Foreign Relations Committee's hearing on his appointment in September 1973, said: 'We have excellent relationships with our principal Middle Eastern suppliers of oil, Saudi Arabia and Iran, and we do not foresee any circumstances in which they would cut off our supply.' The new Secretary was right with regard to Iran, but the circumstances, unforeseeable in September, became strikingly visible in October when Saudi Arabia led the Arab oil boycott against the United States.

Yom Kippur

On 6 October, the day of Yom Kippur, Sadat hurled his armies against Israel. They crossed the Suez Canal with relative ease and remarkable speed. The 'impassable' water barrier and the 'impregnable' Bar-Lev line succumbed to the massive Egyptian assault and the incredible Israeli surprise. Sadat, a daring strategist and a skilful schemer, had laid his plans and synchronized his timing with painstaking precision. He had measured not only the tides in the canal but also the international currents favouring its crossing. He had manifested undeniable talent in the military and political preparation of the war. He had managed to isolate Israel in the non-aligned world, to malign it in the United Nations, to alienate it from its European friends. He had quarrelled with the Soviet Union, but obtained from it arms to fight a friend of the United States. He had improved his relations with America by professing peace, while preparing war. He had promised the United States a beneficial relationship with the Arab world, while organizing the use of the oil weapon against it. He succeeded in disguising his masterly military preparations and on the day he had chosen for the great assault he sprang his surprise on Israel and the world at large. 'Surprises are the most delightful things in life,' wrote Moshe Dayan three years later in his autobiography. Are they, indeed? Surely nobody in Israel will ever relish the memory of the one on Yom Kippur.

31

The Watershed

Was the Yom Kippur attack really a surprise? It was and it was not. In pure military terms it was: in its scope, thrust, co-ordination with Syria and its timing. On 5 October 1973, on the eve of the outbreak of the hostilities, the Prime Minister of Israel sent a message to the US Secretary of State Kissinger drawing his attention to the enlarged troop movements along the Suez Canal and the Syrian lines on the Golan Heights. Golda Meir asked Dr Kissinger to convey to the governments of Egypt and Syria that Israel had no hostile intentions and could not see any justification for their troop concentrations. In a last-minute attempt to avert the war the Prime Minister sent another message to Washington the next morning, when Israeli intelligence had received confirmed information that Egypt and Syria would attack Israel simultaneously that same day at six p.m. Again she requested Washington to apprise the two countries of Israel's peaceful intentions and assured the US government that it would not strike pre-emptively at the hostile concentrations.

Two hours after the receipt of the message in Washington, Egypt and Syria began the bombardment of the Israeli positions, moved their massive armoured formations and began the crossing of the canal. It was two p.m. Israeli time, four hours before the anticipated time of the attack. It was another surprise and a very costly one. During the twenty-five years of Arab-Israeli hostilities alerts had, of course, occurred on numerous occasions. Likewise, the dispatch of emergency signals to the other side had not been an innovation. On 15 May 1967, when Egypt began transferring considerable forces into Sinai while Syria and the Soviet Union alleged that the Israeli army was poised to attack in the north, I was instructed to ask the Secretary-General of the United Nations to transmit to Cairo a message assuring the Egyptian government that Israel had no hostile intentions, either north, east or south of its borders. Nasser's response came the following day in the form of an ultimatum to the Secretary-General to withdraw the United Nations forces stationed in Sinai and Gaza since 1957. Sadat reacted similarly to Israel's message in October 1973. The guns sounded his reply, probably a few hours earlier than planned, when he and his Syrian partner realized that Israel had finally grasped what they were up to. In our experience last-minute messages, whether couched in friendly terms or as stern warnings, had been of little value. At best they placed on record Israel's intentions, and at worst they actuated its opponents to advance zero hour.

But it appeared that Washington was no less surprised than Jerusalem. Despite its far-flung intelligence machinery – ranging from surveillance satellites to earthly agents, all of them registering unusual military movements in Egypt and Syria – the combined wisdom of the US intelligence community dismissed the possibility of large-scale military operations. When the Washington Special Action Group (WSAG), chaired by Dr Kissinger, met in the White House situation room an hour after the beginning of the hostilities on 6 October, it summed up its evaluation: 'We can find no hard evidence of a major co-ordinated Egyptian-Syrian offensive across the canal and in the Golan Heights area. It is possible that the Egyptians or the Syrians, particularly the latter, may have been preparing a raid or other small-scale action.'

The CIA bulletin of 6 October 1973, obviously prepared before the beginning of the war, stated:

Israel, Egypt and Syria are becoming increasingly concerned about the military activities of the other, although neither side appears bent on initiating hostilities. For Egypt a military initiative makes little sense at this critical juncture. It would almost certainly destroy Sadat's painstaking efforts to invigorate the economy and run counter to his current efforts to build a united Arab political front, particularly among the less militant oil-rich states. For the Syrian president, a military adventure now would be suicidal.

Why did neither the Americans nor the Israelis see the approaching tempest? In fact they noticed and recorded some visible signs, yet they failed to forecast its direction and force. The mere collection of bits of information and their collation into a pattern does not necessarily ensure the accuracy of the picture. What counts is the interpretation of its meaning and not the reading of its details. The trap of intelligence is to search for evidence to support your own views and exclude evidence which contradicts them. To understand human behaviour it is not enough to observe the symptoms of man's actions. To penetrate the hidden recesses of the mind, where the motivations are stored and the decisions are made, remains, despite the discoveries of modern psychology, an uncertain journey. It becomes even more enigmatic when political or military strategy is involved using dissimulation as one of its weapons. To substitute the knowledge of the working of one's own mind with that of one's opponent is a risky venture when the fate of nations is at stake.

Israeli assessments

The United States government could ask, with some justification, why it should have taken a stricter view of the facts than Israel which knew them at least as well. It was a question which has not ceased to harrow the minds of the Israeli people to this day. But what did the Israeli government actually know in those days preceding the war? It was aware of the troop concentrations along the Egyptian and Syrian cease-fire lines; of the stepped-up Soviet arms shipments; of Sadat's publicly stated willingness to renew the hostilities; of large-scale amphibious exercises to cross water obstacles; of the reinforcement of front-line positions. Yet it dismissed all this staggering activity as extended autumn manoeuvres. It noted with some concern the swift deployment of ground-to-air missiles and the positioning of substantial armoured formations on the Syrian front.

As a matter of fact Zahal took certain precautionary measures, not in anticipation of imminent war, but in expectation of a Syrian retaliatory raid. On 13 September, one day after the decisive summit meeting in Cairo, Israeli fighter-planes shot down twelve Syrian Mig 21s in one afternoon without a single loss to themselves. The air force supposed that the action would serve as an adequate reminder to any Arab state bent on mischief of Israel's uncontested air superiority. But instead of sobering the enemy, it dulled Israel's perspicacity.

Actually, in the course of 1973 two other unusual air incidents had occurred. In March a Libyan airliner had strayed over the Sinai and had disregarded air-force orders to land for identification. Instead it made itself suspicious by turning back and was downed after having ignored warning shots. The death toll of more than 100 passengers shocked and saddened the Israeli public as much as it infuriated the Arab world. The tragedy was caused by the extraordinary tension created by previous acts of terrorism, such as the killings at the Munich Olympics, and new threats of spectacular suicide missions from the air against Israeli urban centres. The terrible experience of the past and the danger of future actions of even greater virulence constrained the security forces to maintain a state of tight vigilance.

Somewhat different, perhaps not in motivation but in implementation, was the grounding of a Lebanese passenger plane. According to Israeli intelligence information it was supposed to carry George Habash, the chief of the extreme wing of the Palestine terrorist movement, the PFLP. Whoever endorsed the idea of capturing him on Israeli ground by forcibly diverting a civilian aircraft, assumed that his detention in Israel would be a tremendous blow to the terror organizations and an invaluable boon to Israel's security. Public opinion doubted and criticized the wisdom of the enterprise. The Foreign Minister, on a visit to Latin America, voiced in a terse personal cable to the Prime Minister his stringent objection to the operation. He described it as being as mindless as it was useless to the very objectives it planned to serve. It had harmed Israel's position as the stalwart of the freedom and safety of international air traffic and as a protagonist of joint action against hijacking. As it happens the whole affair was a double fiasco. Habash was not among the passengers on the plane and Israel was condemned by the International Civil Aviation Organization for forcible diversion of a commercial aircraft. The paltry outcome of the venture sobered even the most ardent of the activists. Only Dayan kept a stiff upper lip when he declared to the press on 23 August that 'similar raids would be carried out when the government deemed them necessary'. It was the last support for an ill-conceived idea. Ever since, successive Israeli governments have not deemed such raids necessary.

Yet the three air incidents were indicative of the priority of concerns which prevailed in Israel in the months before the renewal of hostilities. After the outrages committed by the terrorists and the painful losses sustained by Israeli citizens, the Prime Minister understandably diverted a considerable section of counter-intelligence to the prevention of further attacks and the neutralization of their perpetrators. The government held the view that acts of terrorism were the most acute danger from which it had to protect the population. The overall military situation, it believed, was well in hand. It was confident of the decisive superiority of the Israeli army. The administered territories would serve in any emergency as a shock absorber, a protective belt for the mainland of Israel. The argument that the longer lines of communications delayed the deployment of forces and added to their vulnerability was discounted by the military. The conviction reigned that no Arab state would start a war as long as it lacked control of the sky. The Arab air forces were still remote from reaching such an advantage. If proof was needed, claimed the experts, the twelve Syrian Migs shot down on 13 September were convincing evidence. Ingrained military concepts had the right of way, even when they were on a clear collision course with visible facts all pointing to the imminence of war. The sanctity of the doctrine prevailed over the observance of the time-honoured maxim of military prudence: when in doubt assume the worst and prepare for it. But as Joseph Conrad said in his eerie *Heart of Darkness*, we were 'cut off from the comprehension of our surroundings'.

Although the situation reports and their assessment had become the near-exclusive prerogative of the defence establishment and their views carried decisive weight in most cases, if not with all the members of the government then predominantly with the Prime Minister, it would be incorrect to acquit other branches, including the Foreign Ministry, from all responsibility for the misjudgement of the unfolding events. The very fact that the Foreign Ministry did not ring the alarm signal loud and clear after the tripartite summit meeting in Cairo on 12 September was in itself a grave failing. Since the bloody clashes in Jordan in 1970, relations between King Hussein and the rulers in Damascus had remained strained and tainted by reciprocal recrimination. Hussein's ties with Sadat were no better. The King had little confidence in the Rais, and the lack of esteem was mutual. The September meeting held in Cairo against the background of intensified military preparations was like a replica of the gathering which had taken place on the eve of the Six Day War between the heads of the same countries at the same place. There King Hussein had joined Nasser's war coalition, closing the ring around Israel. That act, more than anything else, had convinced Israeli policy-planners that war was inevitable.

The trilateral meeting in Cairo was the culmination of a process soon to reveal itself in its full ominous significance. It was preceded by a series of Egyptian diplomatic moves not unnoticed by the Foreign Ministry, but essentially misinterpreted by it. None of its analysts would have accepted at the time the explanation which Sadat himself offered later in his autobiography with such chilling frankness: 'Three weeks before D-day', he wrote, 'the support of more than 100 countries was guaranteed. It took me many months, from January to September, to prepare the world for the war.'

The prevalent Israeli opinion was that Egypt's diplomatic activity was a substitute for war, not a prelude to it. The eviction of the Soviet advisers had deprived Sadat of his military option, so reasoned the experts. His courting of the United States was thought to be an attempt to gain politically what he had lost militarily. The mobilization of the Third World was interpreted as an attempt to reduce Israel's international standing, but not to generate moral and political support for the coming war. The defeat of Egypt's appeal to the Security Council by the American veto, however, was not an incentive to enter into negotiations with Israel, but a pretext to open hostilities against it. The let-up of France and her other partners in the European Economic Community from pushing pro-Arab solutions to the conflict was not so much the result of Israeli persuasion, but rather a change of direction of Arab diplomacy, which had selected Europe as one of the target areas of the oil weapon. It was more important to intimidate European governments into withholding aid from Israel in case of war than to prod them into producing peace plans.

The looming threat of an oil boycott was dismissed by the Israeli experts as empty bluster and the signs of an approaching energy crisis as symptoms of monetary manipulations rather than of mineral shortages. As late as 30 September 1973 the Foreign Ministry distributed to its missions information guidelines stating: 'The strategic balance between Israel and the Arab states is disadvantageous to the latter. And should they start war, they will be defeated. No Arab leader has an interest to make war, in order to lose it. Because of Israel's strength and deterrent power, Israel has succeeded in thwarting the danger of war.' It concluded, therefore, that Arab war threats were empty.

The Foreign Ministry, as well as the Ministry of Defence, had seen the trees but got lost in the woods. Notwithstanding some occasional, solitary voices of warning sounding within their walls, both failed to put the pieces together into their right and proper setting. The thunder of the October guns caught the officers of the defence establishment and the foreign service off-guard as it did most of the Israeli people.

And what about the Russians? Were they surprised? It is hard to believe.

Brezhnev had already forewarned Nixon at the San Clemente summit in June 1973. Many signs indicate that the Soviet Union was well aware not only of the preparations for the war, but also of its impending outbreak. On 4 October, two days before the beginning of hostilities, a fleet of Soviet transport planes evacuated Russian civilians from Damascus and Cairo. On the day the Arab armies opened fire a number of Soviet freighters, carrying heavy armaments for Egypt and Syria, left Russian Black Sea ports. Five days later in his message of 9 October to Boumedienne, Brezhnev urged Algeria to join 'in the just struggle against imperialist Israeli aggression'. And last but not least, Sadat disclosed after the war that President Assad himself had informed the Soviet government of the date of the planned offensive. Why then did Moscow remain silent? Under the terms of the 1972 summit agreement the Soviet Union and the United States were bound to consult on developments likely to endanger international peace. Although the Soviet government must have been aware at least at the beginning of October that war was in the offing, it shunned any private or public discussion of the situation. Unlike 1967 when Soviet propaganda poured out an endless stream of specious allegations of Israeli aggressive intentions, in 1973 it watched the Arab war preparations with a complete information black-out. It knew that Egypt and Syria were set on attaining their objectives by a war of surprise prepared under a blanket of silence.

Haykal's prediction

As early as March 1969 Hassanain Haykal, the talented and versatile Egyptian journalist and at the time the editor of *Al-Ahram* and intimate of Gamal Abdul Nasser, had charted Egypt's future strategy in two substantive articles: 'In the coming battle', he wrote, 'neither we nor the enemy will be taken by surprise. The battle I am speaking about is one in which Arab forces might destroy two or three Israeli divisions and force the Israeli army to retreat from positions it occupies to other positions, even if only a few kilometres back. Such a battle and its consequences would cause the United States to change its policy towards the Arab-Israeli conflict in particular, and the Middle East in general. It would shake the Israeli belief in the ability of its army to protect it. Israeli society once shaken would set in motion a series of reactions with unpredictable consequences.' This battle began on 6 October, the day of Yom Kippur and the tenth day of Ramadan, the month of fasting. Egypt and Syria waged it, as Haykal had predicted. But it did surprise Israel, contrary to Haykal's assumption, and thus it shook Israeli society and changed the course of events in the Middle East as he had foreseen.

Military historians, strategic analysts, political pamphleteers, generals and ordinary soldiers, journalists and jurists have described and dissected in minute detail the military developments of the war. Nothing escaped their scrutiny and judgement. The Yom Kippur shock released a tidal wave of literature as sweeping as befitted the cataclysmic effect of the event. But long before the writings saw the light of day it had dawned on the people throughout the country that something unbelievable, something enormous, had happened: Israel had lost the opening battle. How many times had we all postulated that a lost battle is Israel's last battle? Like all slogans it covers only a stunted part of the truth. But now with the reports of the initial set-backs seeping through to the home front it disillusioned more than it disheartened, it agitated the people more than it stupefied them.

View from the battle front

At the front we were too involved in our hourly chores to discuss the long-term effects of the events unfolding before our eyes. Ten days after the beginning of the war I left the Golan Heights for a day's leave in Jerusalem. The fighting up in the north was still heavy and on the southern front our forces were regrouped to launch a decisive offensive to carry them across the canal. I drove through the Jordan valley. It was all quiet. King Hussein, who had precipitately rushed into the Six Day War, was now biding his time, waiting for the clouded fortunes of war to clear. He was ready to stand up, but not to be counted. Jordanian troops were in sight all along the eastern slopes of the mountains of Gilead and Moab, facing our sparse positions along the river. Any attack on the central front would have caused serious difficulties for our forces, hard-pressed as they were on the Golan Heights and the Suez Canal area.

The tranquillity I sensed in the Jordan valley on my journey south to Jerusalem was somewhat eerie, though life seemed to proceed normally. Farmers were working in the fields, sheep were grazing among the scarce shrubs and spreading thistles. Now and then sprinklers swivelled, refreshing the green fields which the new settlers had wrested from the parched land. But the most unusual sight was the two open bridges over the Jordan, teeming with civilian Arab traffic. There was war to the north, there was war to the south and in between flowed a stream of peaceful citizens back and forth between two countries which were officially in a state of war that might erupt at any time into open hostilities. I was reminded of the chassidic story of the rabbi whose community had asked him to explain why he had committed the unpardonable sin of travelling on the sabbath. His defence was as bizarre as his offence had been. Where he was travelling, he said, there was no sabbath. There was sabbath to the left of the road and there was sabbath to the right of the road and his wagon had travelled in between, just in the middle.

Jerusalem looked oddly different. Nothing had changed in its outward appearance. Its beauty was as radiant as ever. The iridescence of its autumn sky with its confluence of bluish-green mediterranean and brown-and-purple desert shades was as exciting as always. But its human face had changed. The men had gone. The pace of the town had slowed down. People walked. Most of the buses had been requisitioned. Arabs continued to mingle with Jews, but a cloud hovered over them. It had wrapped the town in a mantle of anxious uncertainty. Jerusalem had become a very quiet city.

Even the customary bustle of the Knesset had subsided. It had yielded to a poignant sense of common responsibility and a mood of fraternal comity. I spoke to a few Knesset members and some journalists covering the home front. The parliamentarians and some ministers were eager to know what the soldiers were saying. Did they rail at the defectiveness of our military preparations for which they had been the first to pay a terrible toll? I was bewildered by these sharp-edged queries. They revealed a state of anxiety among the politicians which I had not expected. They certainly knew more about the shortcomings and worried more about their effect than we did. Perhaps the troops were too close to the scene of action and too occupied with the task of winning and staying alive.

I told my interlocutors that our soldiers were swearing like soldiers did everywhere, no less and no more. The misreading of the enemy's visible war preparations and the inadequacy of measures taken to counter them puzzled them more than it incensed them. Why were the supply dumps located so far in the rear? Why did tanks have to travel on their tracks long distances from their emergency depots and consequently require repairs when they arrived at the front, instead of being carried on transporters? Why were we short of 105mm armour-piercing ammunition, so urgently needed to knock out the Soviet tanks the Syrians were moving against our front-line troops? The explanation that the British government had embargoed the shipments when the war broke out did not convince them. Why didn't we lay in sufficient stocks in advance?

It was the lack of foresight which caused the grumbling but not the conduct of the war. The fighting morale was undiminished. In a way everybody tried to make good for what had gone amiss by added effort. One day I had travelled with one of our convoys for twenty-four hours in search of artillery ammunition. Our orders directed us to a depot nor far from Haifa. We had a lengthy and variegated shopping list. The ordnance men hurried to fill the order, but quite a few items were out of stock. They sent us to another depot, miles away. It was the same story there: only part of the merchandise, as it was called in army jargon, was available. We contacted our headquarters. They ordered us back with what we had already got. But the commander of the convoy would not give up; the drivers insisted on continuing the search. Some of them knew the location of other ammunition dumps. Late at night we had finally found nearly everything we had been looking for. The last place had been a kind of self-service store. With the help of a sleepy reservist, who in civilian life was a respectable accountant, we picked up what we believed was needed and useful and loaded it ourselves. Sympathizing with our plight and desirous to contribute to the success of our expedition the good man suggested that, in the absence of what we were searching for, we might prefer some other ammunition, of a different calibre, but no less effective, he assured us.

I was reminded of a meeting in 1947. It was the decisive year before Israel's independence. The responsible leaders – foremost among them Ben Gurion – expected that the Arab states would wage war against the Jewish state. They tried to gather every ounce of strength for the coming ordeal. Haganah, the Jewish defence organization, was not yet a regular army and besides it was poorly equipped. The acquisition of armaments and their landing in the country, still under British administration, was a very costly enterprise. At that meeting the chief of procurement presented the list of shipments on order and their costs. He asked for the allocation of the necessary funds. Eliezer Kaplan, the treasurer of the state-on-the-way and later its first Minister of Finance, was appalled. The sums required exceeded anything within his reach. 'I won't argue with you', he said, 'about the number and size of the artillery pieces, but can't you buy some smaller and less expensive shells?'

In the small hours of the morning our convoy, brimming with its deadly load, climbed the hills of Galilee. At certain points women and children from near-by villages had set up roadside-stands laden with fruit, doughnuts and piping-hot coffee. It was their contribution to the war effort. We were touched and revitalized. When we arrived at our destination on the Golan Heights, the commanding officer proposed to relieve the entire crew. But the exhausted men refused. They quipped that they would not entrust their precious cargo to bloody newcomers who didn't know how hard it had been to scrape it together. They carried it to the front line where the shooting was pretty rough and supervised its safe unloading. They had ample reason for resentment, I assured the inquiring politicians, but little desire for sterile argument.

What struck me most in my talks with friends in Jerusalem during that short leave was that they were speaking more about the failings of the opening phase of the war than about actions needed now to bring it to a successful end. I was stunned by the remark, which I had heard several times, that there would be a political earthquake in Israel after the return of the soldiers. Their stories of heavy losses incurred by negligence, military mismanagement and political misjudgement would arouse the public. An outcry would go up to oust the people responsible for the muddle, if not the whole government altogether.

A short visit to the Foreign Ministry did not lift my spirits. Its staff was enveloped in a thick fog of frustration. The action had moved to Tel Aviv, where the government was in temporary residence and permanent session. Abba Eban, the Foreign Minister, was still in New York. All important communications and confidential information by-passed Jerusalem and flowed directly into the Prime Minister's office and the Defence Ministry in

Tel Aviv. Two or three senior officials operated out of Tel Aviv as some sort of liaison with our missions abroad and kept in perfunctory touch with the Ministry in Jerusalem. Several others, attracted by the action, had ventured down on their own to Tel Aviv to make themselves useful, but spent their time walking the corridors, unable to penetrate the inner sanctum. Most of the other officials were sitting behind their empty desks in Jerusalem or flocking together in small groups to swap scraps of information or analyse the latest rumours. The Ministry in war-time was a melancholy sight.

On the road to Damascus

The war had shattered the stillness of the Day of Atonement and had roused a placid nation to face the spectre of supreme danger. But worst of all, the war cut short the lives of thousands of young people. I had been on the point of leaving for London to take up my new post as Ambassador to the Court of St James's, but now I felt the right thing to do was to volunteer for the army. I knew well enough that my service was not likely to add anything to the war effort. My military experience was of Second World War vintage and my age qualified me more for the rank of senior citizen than that of warrior, but I thought it was a fitting expression of identification with the young people who bore the brunt of the fighting. The statesmen, the politicians, the diplomats and, last but not least, the military bore by commission or omission their share of responsibility when the young had to shed their blood. I had always pondered on the terrible injustice of the sons having to suffer for the faults of their fathers. They were the victims of our errors. I loathed the idea that some people were considered indispensable and were empowered to decide who was expendable. How many who were classified as indispensable, or claimed to be, were really irreplaceable? In my experience very, very few. In many cases there was more self-seeking than self-sacrifice in the claim.

During the Six Day War I had battled in the sometimes stormy, but always safe, precincts of the United Nations, where even the most venomous verbal attacks were never lethal. I had been commended then for coolness under fire and awarded the distinction of the Stephen Wise Award by the American Jewish Congress. In my acceptance speech I had tried to express, however inadequately, what had inspired us and given us the strength to repel the verbal assaults in the Council: 'We tried to be in the Council of the nations the voice of our sons and daughters fighting for the very existence of us all. They were always before my eyes. I saw them in their tanks and soaring in their planes; I saw them storming the hills of Golan and crossing the wilderness of Sinai. They were with us and we were with them when they fought in the streets of Jerusalem, reuniting our people with the birthplace of its nationhood.'

Six years later I wanted to be with them not only in spirit and words, but also in action. I called the Prime Minister's military aide, a veteran officer of singular composure and practical sense, and asked him to get me enrolled in the army; but it seemed that he had at the time other more urgent preoccupations. He promised to call me back. He did, and delicately tried to make me understand that my enlistment would not materially change the fighting strength of our armed forces, while my presence in London might perhaps help lift the British arms embargo. I was touched by his faith in my professional ability, but disappointed by his answer. I was determined to make my way to London via the Golan Heights or Sinai. I called Lieutenant-Colonel Seevik Peleg, a good friend who had never let me down. We had first met in 1968 during the War of Attrition. He served then as chief education officer at Southern Command and had escorted me round the canal area, where I spoke from time to time with the troops on our international situation. I remember that one of the recurrent questions soldiers used to ask me was, how long are we going to stay here? It was normally not homesickness or ordinary boredom that motivated the question. They were annoyed by the bleak desert and felt an irresistible urge to make it blossom. But was it worth sowing a patch with vegetables here and planting some grass there, if we were soon to withdraw from the area?

Now Seevik was serving in the north. In no time at all I got my orders to report to a transport unit in his area. If I could bring a lorry it would be greatly appreciated, otherwise my small car would do. I called the new Director-General of the Ministry, who was in Tel Aviv, to inform him about my change of address. He took the announcement with his customary equanimity and reminded me only to be back in time for London. I reassured him by quoting the memorable words of the brave soldier Schweik, fixing an appointment with a friend in Prague: 'Let's meet at six o'clock after the war.'

We were a small unit which controlled the traffic on the access roads to the front on the Golan Heights and escorted convoys hauling ammunition. We fulfilled the combined functions of a traffic cop and a sheepdog, guiding the erring and gathering in the straying vehicles. Our group was a mixed bag: a timber merchant and a trade union official; a manufacturer of liquor, who kept our spirits high, and a stern kibbutznik, who acted likewise for our morale; a lieutenant born in Morocco, who was highly admired for his proficiency in French, and a young rookie from Argentina, who was still wrestling with the Hebrew tongue. In short we were a cross-section from all walks of life and age-groups. The no-nonsense spirit which reigned and the nonchalant but conscientious manner with which everyone went about their business, were a refreshing experience. What a relaxing change from my professional environment where so many talked so much and said so little. Naturally we had our problems. We operated mostly under rather general orders. Their execution was normally left to the ingenuity and enterprising spirit of the officers and men.

I faintly remembered the terrain in which we were operating. During the Second World War, I was stationed for some time in Damascus. We frequently made the run with our heavy trucks from Haifa via Damascus to Deir-ez-Zor on the River Euphrates. Now, thirty-two years later, I again travelled the same road in the direction of Damascus. The Israeli army in its counter-attack had thrown the Syrian forces back from a position which, in the opening days of the fighting, had come dangerously close to the pre-1967 border. They were now regrouping some twenty-five miles west of Damascus. From our forward positions we could see the outskirts of the Syrian capital. But to reach it, we would have to fight a very tough battle or wait many more years until peace opened it to a friendly visit.

The roadside was strewn with burned-out tanks and abandoned pieces of artillery. The barren plain was dotted with empty bunkers. The unfinished meals and the personal belongings left behind testified to a post-haste retreat. I picked up an abandoned letter and asked one of our Arab-speaking men to translate it for me. It was like any other letter sent anywhere by a worried wife to her man at the front. It told him about the children and the hardships at home and all the friends who cared for him. She implored him to be careful, she longed to see him back soon. No exhortations to smite the evil enemy, no outpouring of patriotic balderdash.

Scorched bodies were lying here and there along the road – Syrian soldiers, un-buried yet, who had jumped from their burning tanks. They looked like grotesque dummies, twisted human flotsam washed ashore by the cruel sea of war.

Our command car had stopped at one of these burned-out tanks. There were eight of us on patrol. Our little Argentinian, like any good Israeli going to war, was equipped with three indispensable utensils: an Uzi machine-pistol, a transistor and a camera. He was all excited. He had to take a picture of some dead bodies lying next to their tank. Our patrol-leader, a man with the mien of a pirate and the reticence of a trappist monk, tapped him on the shoulder. No pictures, he snapped. But the young photographer was undeterred. 'What a sight,' he exclaimed. 'I must keep a souvenir of it.' The patrol-leader, a captain, looked at him as if he was sizing him up and said slowly: 'Listen my boy, these men had a mother and a father, like you have, perhaps they had a wife and children. They're not an object for tourist snapshots. And now let's get going.' We climbed into our car silently and proceeded on the road to Damascus.

In the evenings, my friend Seevik would take me to advance headquarters where we heard the news of the day and the plans for the morrow. Seevik was a remarkable man. As a matter of fact there were two of them. His twin brother Chazi looked like him, spoke like him, moved like him and thought like him – and both were serving with the same rank and in the same command area. Rarely have two men caused so many good-natured practical jokes and so much amusing confusion. They never had a problem with duty or leave. They were interchangeable. Seevik, a man in his middle thirties, was a professional soldier and a born educator. He exuded natural authority, professional competence and human understanding.

One evening he took me to the Sieff hospital in Safad. It was the forward medical station for the casualties from the Golan Heights. Seevik wanted to show me what he called a marvel of medicine, and meet a surgeon who performed miracles. In the dim corridor stretchers were wheeled in and out of the operating rooms like a conveyor belt: young faces, waxen, with feverish eyes and lost looks, their limbs mangled – the toll of war. After some time a doctor came out. His face half-hidden behind his surgeon's mask, his head covered by his pale green cap, he slouched down on a sofa. Seevik nudged me to approach him. The man looked so completely worn out that I hestitated to disturb him. Suddenly he pulled himself up and rushed towards me. He had recognized me despite my novel military attire. Professor Howard Rosen, an old friend from New York, was indeed a miracle man. He was an outstanding orthopaedic surgeon, renowned for his skill, innovative methods and his infectious cheerfulness. The day the war broke out, he packed his instruments and took off with his wife on the first available flight to Israel. Since then he had operated in Safed. He was pained by the great number of casualties and appalled by the severity of the injuries. Some cases had arrived virtually in severed parts which he and his colleagues had managed to piece together. He was full of praise for the high standards of the front-line medical posts, which had saved many lives by their proficient first aid and fast removal by helicopter to the base hospital. But above all Dr Rosen admired the fortitude of his patients. Some of them had apologized for causing him so much trouble, others had reassured him when his face had apparently betrayed some doubt that they would be all right. With such people Israel cannot fail, he said. I thought to myself, with men like him caring for them it surely will prevail.

Zahal had steadily harnessed its strength and gathered its wits. It had crossed the Suez Canal and nearly surrounded the Egyptian Third Army entrenched on its east bank. All the territory lost to Syria in the initial fighting had been recovered and our forces had made deep dents in the Syrian lines. Only the position on Mount Hermon, lost on the day of the outbreak of the war, had still not been recaptured. Its 8,500-foot peak was a coveted vantage-point. It dominated the Syrian plain, Israel's northern and Lebanon's southern valleys. Its reconquest necessitated not only daring uphill fighting in open view and close range of the well-fortified Syrian positions on the summit, but also round-the-clock pounding from the air. The Russian missiles, and new AA guns, had caused far higher losses to our air force than anticipated. It was not in a position to support big battles simultaneously on the two fronts; it had to rotate its participation in the fighting in the south and in the north in accordance with the pressures and priorities of each front. The operation to re-take Mount Hermon had therefore been deferred until the army had gained the upper hand on the Egyptian front.

Northern command had to wait until 20 October before everything was ready for the attack. The night the operation got under way I spent at headquarters.

It was a new experience to watch a battle conducted by electronic remote-control. There was a lot of activity in the large operations room. Everything seemed to work smoothly. Orders were transmitted calmly and messages recorded impassively. The progress of the forces was marked on the maps without comment. Commotion was noticeable only when casualty reports came in. When morning came the reports indicated fierce fighting, slow progress and heavy casualties. I returned to my station. We had been ordered to bring up relief forces. Before night fell our commandos had reached the peak in very costly hand-to-hand fighting. We carried back a company of battle-worn soldiers, together with the prisoners they had taken. The men were either too tired to display any emotion of just uninterested in their Syrian co-passengers. When we disembarked the prisoners, some soldiers offered them cigarettes while others helped them board the waiting trucks. A few received a hefty shove to speed up the transfer. Nearby I heard a stocky commando growl: 'Don't touch that man. I took him prisoner. He was a good fighter.'

The next morning, bent as always over our transistors to listen to the early news, we were startled by the first item. Secretary of State Henry Kissinger had reached an agreement in Moscow with the Soviet government on the text of a cease-fire resolution which the Security Council would most probably pass within the next twenty-four hours. On his way back to Washington Kissinger would stop over in Israel for a few hours. I had some difficulty in convincing my comrades that I was as startled by the news as they were. They thought that I had a secret line to the Foreign Ministry which had kept me well-informed. Not only had I been without any news from the office but, much more important, the government had been without any news about Kissinger's movements until shortly before his departure for Moscow and it only learned about his dealings there when they were completed. On 21 October, the day before the cease-fire agreement was announced, Deputy Prime Minister Allon visited the Egyptian front and assured the commanding generals that they had ample time still to roll back the Egyptians before a cease-fire resolution would be adopted.

We were amazed by the sudden turn from war to peace; but would it be peace, or just another interval between wars? Of course we all wanted the fighting to be over. Although our unit had not suffered any casualties, besides one or two road accidents, we had seen enough human wreckage and widespread devastation to be weaned for ever from any romantic sentiments about war, if they had ever existed. Anyway, the men I had met had not harboured notions of that sort. War was bloody business. They went about it with a matter-of-fact sense of duty, trying to get it over as quickly and as thoroughly as possible. But without having the slightest knowledge of the circumstances that had brought about the Moscow agreement, our instinctive feeling was that it had stopped Israel short of decisive victory.

The idea of communicating with the Foreign Ministry now began to intrigue me. After all, momentous things were happening. Eban had just returned from his lonely watch in New York. I reached him in Tel Aviv on a poor military line from advance headquarters. He could not make out where I was speaking from and I was not supposed to reveal my location. He wanted to know why I was not in Tel Aviv where everybody who was somebody had arrived. I told him that I was otherwise engaged. It did not make sense to him, but he tried to explain the situation to me. I understood only half of it, the other half fell prey to interruptions by field security. Here and there I tried in vain to argue. 'Where do we go from here?' I cried so loudly into the defective telephone that he could almost have heard it in Tel Aviv without recourse to the instrument. Eban's answer came back fast: 'I'll tell you where you go, you come to Tel Aviv right away. We'll have a lot to discuss and plan in the days to come.' A Foreign Minister can recall an ambassador at his pleasure or displeasure, but not demobilize a soldier. Seevik, as always, was helpful again. Two days later I reported for duty in Tel Aviv.

32

Airlift, Cease-Fire and Oil

The political battle in the international arena had proceeded in step with the military developments in the field. It centred on five themes: arms supplies, the timing of the cease-fire, the politics of the powers, the oil weapon and inter-Arab relations. The moves on the cease-fire in the Security Council were closely linked to the sway of the battle on the ground. Egypt, encouraged by the impressive success of its opening attack, was not interested in a cease-fire before its troops had at least reached the strategic Sinai passes. Israel was disinclined for exactly the opposite reasons. It first wanted to recover from its initial set-back and then throw the Egyptian forces back over the canal. Syria, apparently attentive to Soviet advice, contemplated a cease-fire in the first days of the war after its armoured corps had substantively penetrated the Israeli lines. The United States stood by watching the military situation without making a serious move in any direction. Kissinger accepted the Israeli assertion that Zahal, fully mobilized, would soon recover the lost ground. Its successful counter-offensive on the Golan Heights seemed to bear out these expectations.

Before the first week was over it became clear that this was not to be a short war. Israel's losses in men and material were far higher than it had ever experienced in the past. Repeated attempts to dislodge the Egyptian forces had failed. Israel was short of certain categories of ammunition and equipment for conducting a prolonged war. The disproportionately heavy loss and attrition of aircraft called for swift replacements. The United States was the only available source for the replenishment of the arsenals. Israel, which during the first days had not pressed hard for major shipments, now began to urge Washington to supply immediately substantial quantities of armaments. At the same time it confirmed its readiness for a cease-fire based on the pre-October lines.

The United States government allowed Israeli aircraft to carry supplies but was reluctant to permit an airlift by American transport. In the face of this dilemma it intensified its efforts to bring the fighting to a halt. Contrary to Israel's wishes, Kissinger now tried to obtain the agreement of Egypt and the Soviet Union on a cease-fire-in-place. The actual position of the forces at the time of the cessation of the hostilities would constitute the new cease-fire line.

The proposal was advantageous for Egypt in Sinai and for Israel in the Golan, but both sides rejected it. Israel sought the restoration of the post-1967 lines while Egypt aspired to the recovery of the territory it had lost in 1967. Not that Sadat hoped to achieve this by an all-out military campaign. He rather relied on the success of diplomatic action following the fighting.

The Israeli government now pressed its request for a massive American emergency airlift with urgency mounting from hour to hour. Controversial interpretations of the US response have ever since excited publicists, scholars and diplomats into passing judgement on the responsibility for the delay. Was it Schlesinger's, the Secretary of Defense, or Kissinger's? Had the bureaucracy of the Pentagon or the animosity of the State Department put on the brakes? Or had the Israeli embassy neglected to pull out all the stops early enough, being lulled by dilatory promises? Was it Kissinger's intention to take advantage of the military predicament of both sides to extract maximum political mileage, before extricating them from their dilemma by an American compromise settlement? There were as many versions as there were personalities and authorities prepared to volunteer answers. Those who believed that demons were the moving forces of history would choose their particular villain. Others who saw Machiavelli as their mentor, generally taking his irony at face value, would interpret every diplomatic action as the opposite of what it was really meant to be. Yet the commentators on historic events have two decisive advantages over the practitioners. They enjoy the comfort of opinion, while the practising statesman has the burden of decision. Historians roam in the open plain of hindsight, while mountains of uncertainty obscure the view of the decision-maker.

Whether satisfactory answers can ever be given to these intriguing questions is in itself questionable. Anyway, until all the records are available no one will be able to disentangle the web of contradicting versions and pass a reasonably objective judgement on the decisions and their makers in those crucial days. And even with complete freedom of access to the records it will still be difficult to judge, because policies are rarely the product of a single-track process. They are not made up by rational conclusions alone – calculable, measurable and recordable – but are determined by a series of accidentals and imponderables. Passing moods and deep-seated prejudices, mental fixations and volatile tempers form the components of political decisions by public bodies as much as they influence the actions of individuals. What was done will always be more clearly discernible than who did what to whom. In the matter of the airlift to Israel the established facts are: that Jerusalem realized only two or three days after the outbreak of the war the urgency of the supply situation; that Washington hesitated to get directly involved in the re-supply operation; that Kissinger urged Israel to agree to a cease-fire based on the actual lines of fighting and hoped to turn the initial Egyptian success and the eventual military stalemate into diplomatic leverage to break the political deadlock; that the Soviet Union fuelled the fires with a massive injection of arms supplies and that President Nixon ordered on 13 October an all-out effort to rush deliveries to Israel. As a matter of fact, when Dr Kissinger recommended the President to dispatch initially only three giant Galaxy transport planes with armaments, Nixon is reported to have reacted: 'If we send three we may as well send fifty. I do not believe in half-hearted response.' In less than six weeks the American airlift flew to Israel more than 22,000 tons of equipment on 570 flights.

It was a strange situation. Internally Nixon was in deep trouble, but externally he was in control of events. While the hostilities in the Middle East attracted the attention of the world community, the growing difficulties of the Nixon administration at home perplexed the American public. Allegations of fraudulent activities compelled Vice-President Agnew to resign on 10 October. A few days later, Nixon's personal involvement in the Watergate affair became transparent, and the day Kissinger reached a cease-fire agreement in Moscow became better known in American chronicles as the Saturday-night massacre than the dawn of peace in the Middle East. Of course, when the Watergate affair had gained full momentum, culminating in Nixon's resignation, it harmed America's international position and restricted its freedom of action in foreign affairs, but when the first act of the drama was played out in October 1973 it did not have any noticeable repercussions in our area. Regardless of what was happening on the disturbed domestic scene, the President ordered the airlift; Kissinger concluded the cease-fire agreement with the Soviet Union on amenable terms for the United States; a few days later Nixon confirmed the alert of the armed forces; and when it came to the crunch, to make Israel lift the siege of the encircled Egyptian forces, the presidential backing which the Secretary of State invoked was as effective as ever.

A curious episode showed how much some Israeli leaders believed in Nixon's strength and durability until the end. Early in July 1974 Yitzhak Rabin, newly installed Prime Minister, visited London. At a reception we held for him at the embassy he agreed to answer questions from the assembled guests. One questioner wanted to know how much longer, in the opinion of the Prime Minister, Nixon could last in view of the possibility of his impending impeachment. Without batting an eyelid, Rabin replied that he was ready to bet everyone present ten pounds that the President would serve out his full term of office. Six weeks later Nixon resigned.

The American airlift had two immediate effects. It bolstered Israel's dwindling reserves and its counter-offensive capacity, and it prompted the Arab oil-exporting states to reduce their production and impose a selective embargo, aimed mainly at the United States and Israel's European friends. This produced a scramble among the European countries for Arab favours and dissent between them and the United States. None of America's Western European allies was prepared to grant facilities for refuelling its transport planes, except Portugal after considerable pressure. The British government, traditionally sensitive to Arab exactions, refused permission to the United States to use its own air bases in England or alternatively the British ones on the island of Cyprus, much needed for American reconnaissance flights over the battle area. American resentment over the lack of support from its closest ally at the height of a severe international crisis continued to mar the relations of the two countries for a considerable period of time.

Cease-fire negotiations in Moscow

Three days after the beginning of the airlift, substantial Israeli forces crossed the Suez Canal. Zahal, now fully mobilized and regrouped, in control of the situation on the Syrian front and reassured of the re-supply of vital material, had gone over to an all-out counter-offensive. It aimed at knocking out the principal enemy forces with one blow. The Egyptian high command had failed to recognize the scope and significance of the counter-strike. But not so the Soviet government. On 17 October, Prime Minister Kosygin flew hurriedly to Cairo to advise Sadat of the precariousness of his military situation. The Russians, grandmasters of chess as they were, had a much clearer view of the position on the board than Sadat and his generals. They knew that Egypt was trapped and would not escape total defeat, unless saved by a quick move.

Kosygin urged Sadat to agree to a cease-fire imposed by the Security Council with both sides remaining in their present positions. But Sadat stuck to a proposal he had enunciated in a speech a day before Kosygin's arrival. He would agree to a cease-fire provided that it was followed by Israel's withdrawal, within a given period, to the pre-1967 lines. After its completion the state of belligerency would be terminated, and within a specified period the UN would convene a peace conference attended by the parties to the conflict, including the Palestinians and all members of the Security Council. The Soviet Premier worked hard to convince the Egyptian President that under the circumstances his plan did not exactly fit the existing realities. It seemed that, when he left Cairo on 19 October, he had succeeded in enlightening Sadat on the hopelessness of his military prospects and had obtained his consent to an immediate cease-fire-in-place linked to the implementation of Resolution 242. In a press conference in Kuwait held on 14 May 1975 President Sadat revealed Egypt's plight in the final days of the Yom Kippur War:

Premier Kosygin came to Egypt where he stayed four days in order to persuade me to accept a cease-fire. I rejected all these requests. But on the 19th of October and after ten days of confrontation with the USA [sic], I was not prepared – as I pointed out in my message to President Assad on the 19th – to bear the historic responsibility of destroying my people and armed forces once again. I agreed to the cease-fire.

Now we must on no account boycott any [negotiating] forum as we did in the past when we said No, No, No, until first half of Palestine was lost, then the rest of it, and then Sinai, and the Golan, as a result of our No, No, No.

Upon Kosygin's return to Moscow, Brezhnev proposed to Nixon that urgent consultations be held. Either Gromyko should go to Washington or Kissinger come to Moscow. The Secretary of State preferred a meeting in the Russian capital. Before his departure he sought the views of the Israeli government on a cease-fire-in-place linked to Resolution 242, obviously after the Soviet government had sounded out Washington on such a possibility. Prime Minister Meir instructed Ambassador Dinitz to reject the idea and asked instead to tie up the cease-fire with an agreement on direct negotiations. While Israel would accept a cease-fire on the lines of the present fighting, it was still eager to end the war with a convincing Egyptian defeat. With the present momentum of the fighting it looked as if this objective was within Zahal's grasp.

Kissinger's explanation that he had decided to go to Moscow in order to provide more time for the Israeli forces was in reality meant more to allay the fears of the Israeli government of a let-down in Moscow than to spur its army to achieve total victory. Kissinger assumed that diplomatic initiatives would be feasible and promising only if the war ended in a draw. But this does not explain why he preferred Moscow to Washington as the venue for the cease-fire negotiations. What prompted the Secretary of State to rush to the Soviet Union was not his desire to prolong the fighting, but his eagerness to bring it to an immediate end, because, in his judgement, the military situation was ripe for a political break. And besides, Kissinger was not the man to miss the opportunity of a dramatic lift-off, which promised a sensational splash-down.

The text of the cease-fire resolution was hammered out in less than twenty-four hours. It was built on four pillars, each representing a preferred position of one of the parties. The immediate cessation of all armed hostilities was the common ground. The call for the implementation of Resolution 242 was to satisfy Egypt; the insistence on negotiations for the establishment of peace was meant to be a concession to Israel; and the provision that such a conference was to be held 'under appropriate auspices' was designed to ensure the role of the two superpowers in the peace-making process. Israel was informed of the results of the Moscow talks only after their conclusion and presented with the cease-fire text as an accomplished and unalterable fact. Nonetheless Golda Meir made a last effort to defer the final decision for a few days. Zahal was at the crest of its forward thrust. The rout of the Egyptian forces and perhaps also those of Syria was in reach. The White House adamantly declined Golda's plea for delay and further negotiation. The only thing the President conceded was a short stop-over in Israel by the Secretary of State on his way home to Washington. The purpose of his visit was to smooth some ruffled feathers and reassure the government of America's unwavering support for Israel. Before he had left for Moscow, Kissinger pointed out to his Israeli hosts that the White House had submitted to Congress a request of $2.2 billion aid for Israel and he assured them that arms would continue to arrive. In any case, when Kissinger arrived in Tel Aviv on 22 October at noon, the cease-fire Resolution 338 had already been adopted by the Security Council twelve hours earlier with the consent of the government of Israel.

Yet fighting continued for another three days like a dying forest fire, going out in one spot and flaring up in another, until the two superpowers brought it finally under complete control.

The Soviet threat

24 October was one of the most critical days of the war which had formally ended two days earlier. Fierce fighting was still raging along the Suez front. Each side accused the other of violating the cease-fire. Israeli forces were closing the net around the Third Army, cut off from the main body of the Egyptian forces. A parachutist battalion was fighting in the streets of the town of Suez. President Sadat had appealed to President Nixon and to the Security Council to stop the advancing Israeli forces. The Council had passed another resolution calling for an immediate halt of the fighting and withdrawal to the cease-fire lines of 22 October. Washington urged Israel to comply, but Jerusalem claimed that the lines had not been demarcated. The Soviet Union alleged that the United States was conniving with Israel. While its threats against Israel mounted in vehemence, Moscow dispatched a military group to Cairo to form part of a hastily established United Nations observer contingent.

When night fell on 24 October the Israeli forces had virtually severed all the supply lines of the Third Army, but had still not occupied the town of Suez. There was no immediate end to the fighting in sight. Tel Aviv was like a beehive, but with more hum than honey. Zahal was racing against the clock and the ministers were rushing back and forth to cabinet meetings with retinues of officials at their coat-tails. In between, Eban gave me hurried briefings. The acceptance of the Moscow award was inevitable. Israel was internationally isolated and politically outmanoeuvred. Resolution 338, conceived by Kissinger and Gromyko and delivered by the Security Council on 22 October, was a success for Israel's diplomacy, claimed the Foreign Minister. It made the implementation of Resolution 242 contingent on the conduct of direct negotiations. This had been Israel's long-standing objective, now for the first time endorsed by the highest international forum. It was a turning-point, dramatically improving the prospects of peace. The continued fighting worried the Foreign Minister. He thought that in no time the United States and the Soviet Union would jointly clamp down on us. It had happened before. When Kissinger had stopped over in Tel Aviv on his way back from Moscow, he had tried to assuage the dissatisfaction of the military who complained that a cease-fire at this stage would again leave the outcome of the war in abeyance. The Secretary of State held the view, without expressing it explicitly, that breaking the military momentum would eventually break the political deadlock. However, he felt that he should make some concession to the army's concerns. Casually he said to the Chief of Staff that he realized there was always some tidying-up to be done before a cease-fire became fully effective. Obviously he had underestimated Zahal's sense of tidiness.

When Israel woke up on the morning of 25 October the Middle East crisis had assumed threatening proportions. Overnight Brezhnev had sent a stern – Kissinger described it as a brutal – message to Nixon. He asked the United States to intervene together with the Soviet Union to stop the fighting immediately. If not, and that was the alarming part, 'the Soviet Union would be faced with the necessity urgently to consider the question of taking appropriate steps unilaterally. Israel cannot be allowed to get away with the violations.'

United States intelligence reported that seven Soviet airborne divisions had been put on instant alert. At least two landing-craft were spotted steaming towards Alexandria, together with a number of ships from the Soviet fleet in the Mediterranean. Suspicious radiation had been detected coming from a Soviet freighter passing the Bosporus. Were the Soviets sending nuclear weapons to Egypt? Or was this a ploy of psychological warfare? It has never been authentically established what the freighter carried to Alexandria. Was it conceivable that the Soviet government would apply atomic bluff in a situation where a measured manifestation of conventional strength would have been sufficient for its purpose? Hard to believe. Was there any evidence that the seven airborne divisions or even a fraction of them ever intended to take off?

Neither Kissinger nor Schlesinger were sure about it, but they were determined to meet Brezhnev's challenge. Upon their advice the President raised the state of alert of the US armed forces. It was not a spectacular act, but it was emphatic enough to demonstrate the will of the United States to counter any ill-considered Soviet unilateral intervention. No doubt Moscow got the message.

While the Israeli government was discussing the danger of the country's growing political encirclement and the risks of a clash with Soviet forces, the United States considered emergency plans for the dispatch of American forces to the Middle East and stepped up its diplomatic moves to terminate the fighting without further delay and complications. The first step the Secretary of State took was to declare at a press conference the strong opposition of the United States to unilateral Soviet action. Having made his point he continued on a more conciliatory note. The Soviet threat did not impair the process of détente. The prospects of peace in the Middle East were better than ever. He showed understanding for the reasons which had prompted the Arabs to resort to military action: 'The conditions which produced this war were clearly intolerable to the Arab nations.' This was indeed a far-reaching departure from previous American policy which had held Egypt responsible for the situation which had caused the war in 1967. 'In the process of negotiations', continued Kissinger, 'it will be necessary for all sides to make substantial concessions. The Arab concern for the sovereignty of the territories will have to be related to the Israeli concern for secure boundaries.'

A day later the President himself elaborated on the same theme at a press conference held in the White House. 'The outlook for peace is the best that it has been in twenty years,' said Nixon. 'The United States and the Soviet Union have different objectives in the Middle East, but agreed that it was not in their interest to have a confrontation which might lead to nuclear confrontation. It is necessary for us to use our influence more than in the past, to get the negotiating track moving not simply to a temporary truce but permanent peace. One of the major factors, which gives enormous urgency to our efforts to settle this particular crisis, is the potential of an oil cut-off.'

The stage for the Secretary's next move on this critical day, 25 October, was the Security Council. Less than twenty-four hours after the crisis had climaxed, it adopted its third cease-fire resolution ordering in the strictest terms the immediate cessation of all fighting. Both Israel and Egypt announced their compliance. The Yom Kippur War had come to an end. But before the political process could begin, a number of military matters arising from the war had to be settled. The fate of the Third Army was vital to Egypt, for it was by now completely cut off. Kissinger assumed that its surrender to Israel would strike a severe blow to Sadat's regime, while its rescue through American pressure on Israel would give powerful leverage to the United States in Egypt. The Israeli government initially rejected the American demands to allow supply convoys to pass through its lines. It regarded the besieged army as a pawn which Sadat would eventually redeem by the withdrawal of all the Egyptian forces from the territory they had occupied in Sinai. But Kissinger would not relent. Any further refusal, he warned, would jeopardize Israel's relations with the United States – words strong enough to make the government yield and rescue the Egyptian forces in distress. As Dayan later explained to an embittered Knesset, Israel could not conduct war at the risk of a rift with the United States.

The oil weapon

But the oil embargo continued. Contrary to the expectations of the Secretary of State that Saudi Arabia would not interrupt the flow of oil to the United States, but true to the warnings Assistant Secretary Sisco had conveyed to Ambassador Dinitz two months before Sadat's attack, King Feisal did lead the embargo syndicate. Its methods of operation were more sophisticated and better orchestrated than at any previous oil boycott. It reduced the output and quadrupled the prices. It selected its targets not only in terms of their political affinity with Israel, but taking into account their economic vulnerability as well. Holland was not only one of Israel's closest friends in Europe, but Rotterdam was one of the main continental oil-ports and distribution centres. Its shut-down was meant to have a triple effect: dissociation of the Netherlands from its support for Israel, dislocation of the Western European oil supply and discord between the members of the European Economic Community. To sow dissension among the partners of the Western alliance had been a long-standing objective of Soviet foreign policy. The stronger the differences between Russia and China, the more the Soviet Union increased its efforts to weaken the strength and cohesion of its Western neighbours. The oil and monetary squeeze exerted by the Arab states against the West perfectly suited these aims.

The less secure the Soviet Union considered its positions in the Arab countries after the expulsion of their military advisers from Egypt, the more it intensified its exhortations to the oil-producing states 'to turn the oil weapon against the foreign exploiters'. The imperialists having lost the keys to Arab oil 'would be forced more and more to yield and to retreat'. This *leit-motiv* of Soviet propaganda became the signature tune of Moscow's Arab broadcasts, increasingly amplified since the October war.

After the Arab proclamation of the oil embargo during the Yom Kippur War, the Soviets' main concern was that the Arab governments should lift it at the end of the hostilities. They should not content themselves with the embargo; they should nationalize their oil industries and 'withdraw all the Arab accounts from banks in the United States and other protectors of Tel Aviv; they should raise the price of their scarce product now in such high demand'. That advice needed very little Soviet persuasion to be followed. The idea of taking advantage of the growing energy distress had occurred to the oil-producing countries long before the Yom Kippur War. In fact Colonel Qaddafi can claim rights to its authorship. In 1970 the accidental rupture of the Tapline, carrying oil from the Gulf to the Mediterranean via Syria and the Israeli-occupied Golan Heights, and Syria's refusal to allow the necessary repairs, had caused a temporary oil-supply problem for Europe. Qaddafi seized the opportunity to increase the price of Libyan oil. It was the first turn of the spiral, which in the years to come reached dizzying heights and caused the steady decline of the world economy, sparing neither East nor West, countries poor nor rich.

In the course of the twentieth century oil has become not only the principal moving force of machinery and source of human comfort, but also a mainspring of regional and international conflicts. The greater the concentration of oil resources in a given geographical area, the more inflammable that area becomes in political and military terms. The combustibility has been heightened in the Middle East by the additives of its contested strategic situation, its fierce intra-regional rivalries, and the enduring Arab-Israeli conflict. Without subscribing to the Soviet simplification of the mythical powers of foreign oil interests, it cannot be denied that oil has played a significant role in the origin, extension and termination of armed hostilities in the Middle East.

In 1973 the oil factor figured prominently in Sadat's preparations and the conduct of the war. The use of the oil weapon, with all its ramifications and implications, became one of the most powerful after-effects of the Yom Kippur War, perhaps even more far-reaching than the initiators of its use had reckoned or wished. The selective oil embargo and production cut-down proclaimed by the Arab oil-producing states on 19 October 1973 became a turning-point in world affairs, as the war itself had changed the fortunes of the Middle East.

The first peaceful encounters

At the end of the fighting the positions of the Egyptian and Israeli forces were scattered. In many places they faced each other within shouting-distance, sometimes causing a sporadic outbreak of shooting, but in many others leading to neighbourly visits. The ordinary soldiers from both sides started the process. Their first steps were hesitant – they were guided more by curiosity than by fraternity. But human contact fast melted the ice of enmity. Both sides discovered that they shared common sentiments: the senselessness of the bloodshed and devastation, the longing for peace, the urge to return to their families, and the yearning for a better life. They looked at each other in wonderment and spoke to each other with respect. Were these the first buds sprouting from the scorched earth? Did the fighting men in their first peaceful encounter after they and their fathers had been engaged for more than a quarter of a century in intermittent battle, sense that they were the pathfinders for approaching peace? Probably not, but perhaps they felt in their tired bones the coming change of climate.

Reviewing the Arab-Israeli conflict in 1972, I concluded that the most significant recent development had been Sadat's repeated declarations of his readiness to make peace with Israel. Although his statements were pronounced in terms which were mostly unacceptable to Israel at the time, the very fact that the leader of the most important Arab country had spoken publicly of his desire for peace with Israel appeared to me to be a spark of hope worth fanning.

In the absence of other means of direct communication with Egypt I published an article in an Israeli paper in February 1972, reproduced in the *New York Times*, entitled 'Letter to a neighbour'. I spoke in it of the political, human and psychological wilderness which separated the people of Egypt and Israel, the oldest and most creative peoples in the region, who had met in triumph and tribulation since their first encounter more than three millennia ago. I spoke about the futility of the present hostility and commended Sadat's vision of peace. We had to face the choice between living in constant peril on the edge of a precipice or building a bridge over the abyss. I advocated, as a first step, secret preparatory talks between the representatives of both governments, saying 'that once such contacts have been established the political and psychological landscape between our two countries will change. When we see the first sprouts of understanding piercing the scorched earth and each of us coming out from his trenches, we shall see our world in a new perspective. Let us act intelligently so that the next encounter between Egypt and Israel shall take place not on the battlefield but at the negotiating table. I am certain that, when we rise from that table, our two ancient and proven people will go forth towards a new life.'

But before coming to that conference table Sadat had chosen again to try the fortunes of the battlefield. He claimed that the direct road to negotiations had been barred by Israel's refusal to accept his terms. More likely, he calculated that the sharp shock of a short war was needed to set the peace process in motion. He took an enormous risk from which Egypt narrowly escaped. In reality both sides came out of the war thoroughly sobered. Israel was shocked by the way it opened and Egypt by the way it ended. but whilst the highly articulate and open society of Israel made no secret of its sentiments of pain and frustration, the strictly regimented Egyptian mass media directed the Egyptian people to rejoice in the initial victory of the canal crossing and to pass in silence over the presence of considerable Israeli forces on its west bank at the end of the fighting. Egypt had regained its self-esteem while Israel was deeply shaken in its self-confidence. It had lost not only the aura of invincibility of its army but also the trust in the competence of its leaders.

But above all the people of Israel were anguished and deeply wounded by the loss of so many of its sons. The death-list recorded nearly 3,000 lost lives. They were all a part of our lives. They had carried the brunt of the assault and paid the irredeemable price of our lack of preparation. They had turned back the tide, and the nation's grief was as gripping as its gratitude was compelling. Its mood was grim. It questioned itself and challenged its leaders.

33

Disengagement

The Israeli government and people had lulled themselves into a sense of immunity from peril secured by an unchallengeable military deterrence. They mistook the post-1967 war boom for solid economic growth and the wave of the worldwide feeling of relief at its deliverance from the threat of extinction for a permanent tide of support and unmitigated admiration. The government saw sporadic disturbances of the calm as passing gusts, and not as a change of wind. It believed that with some zigzagging here and there, it could continue to sail the international waters quietly, until its Arab neighbours agreed to make peace, acquiescing in or compromising with the situation created after the Six Day War. The energy crisis was annoying but not alarming. As Prime Minister Rabin put it, it might bring upon Israel seven politically lean years, but it would dissipate and Israel would re-emerge with renewed vigour.

The Israelis, so well known for their individual assertiveness, their boundless energy of expression and their zeal for controversy, lived – strange as it may seem – in an essentially conformist society. They were more inclined to endorse what their leaders said and did than to contest their wisdom by collective action. This they reserved for the great moments of the external struggle, when the existence of the country was at stake. Up to the very day of the outbreak of the Yom Kippur War their leaders had regaled them with assurances that Israel was safe from attack. Only ten weeks before the beginning of the fighting, the Minster of Defence had unequivocally declared, in an interview published in *Time* magazine of 23 July, that he did not expect any major war between the Arab states and Israel in the coming years. And General Ariel Sharon had boasted, as late as September, that Zahal could reach the Atlantic and the Persian gulf in two weeks without encountering any major obstacles. A month later his forces were halted not at the gates of Casablanca, but in the outskirts of the town of Suez by the combined Soviet-American political intervention. However, the popular attitude of the ordinary citizen was: if the ministers and the generals did not know, who would? The shock of the Yom Kippur War shattered this myth.

It was not a downfall but rather a climb down from the clouds to solid ground. It was neither precipitate nor violent, each step being accompanied by manifestations of popular discontent. The democratic life-style of the people, the uncertainty of the cease-fire, the great number of soldiers still mobilized, the expectations raised by the forthcoming peace conference and the election campaign all served as an outlet for the pent-up frustrations and exerted a restraining effect. Protest movements sprang up which were completely separate from the established political framework; but the demonstrations, held mostly in front of the Prime Minister's office, were generally well-disciplined and dignified. Letters appeared in the press from officers blaming the Minister of Defence for the lack of military preparedness and demanding his resignation. An open letter to Dayan published in *Yedioth Aharonoth*, a mass circulation paper, said: 'You have prided yourself that you attained your high office by the will of the people. But the people are loath to see you continue. Strange are the ways of destiny. The entrance of Egyptian divisions into Sinai in 1967 brought about your appointment then and their return in 1973 calls for your resignation now.' These statements made little impression on Dayan. Indeed, he even seemed to derive satisfaction from the idea that his return to office in 1967 was the result of the positioning of massive Egyptian forces near Israel's border. In his memoirs he cheerfully referred to the fact that it needed 80,000 Egyptian soldiers deployed in Sinai to bring him back into the government in 1967. But he declined to draw the parallel with their successful re-entry in 1973, and their continued stay there after the war had ended. However, the fate of Yacob Shimshon Shapira, Minister of Justice in Golda Meir's cabinet, was quite different. Shortly after the end of the fighting, he had publicly asked for the resignation of his colleague, the Minister of Defence. The Prime Minister dissociated herself sternly from her old friend and veteran party comrade, forcing him to resign instead of Dayan. Large areas of the public and the press commented critically on the injustice done to the Minister of Justice.

Still, the Knesset elections held on 31 December returned the Labour Party under Golda Meir's leadership to power, though with a reduced number of seats. It was remarkable how orderly and uneventful the election day was, given the agitated state of mind of the nation. After the elections the display of popular dissent became more and more widespread. The turmoil rendered the formation of a new government more difficult than ever before.

Responding to the clamour of the protesters, whose demands were shared by large sectors of the population and the press, the outgoing government empowered Chief Justice Agranat, President of the Supreme Court, to set up a commission of inquiry into the state of Zahal's military preparations on the eve of the war and the course of the fighting in its opening days. The government had carefully drafted the terms of reference, enabling the commission to avoid in its findings, if it so desired, judgements on the political and parliamentary responsibility and competence of its ministers. The commission was directed to investigate the conduct of the generals and not the performance of the politicians, with the result that it recommended the resignation of the Chief of Staff, General David Elazar, and reserved its judgement on the responsibility of the Minister of Defence. Moshe Dayan interpreted the report as a complete personal vindication. However, neither the press nor the public shared this view. It ran against its ingrained belief that in a parliamentary democracy the minister carried full responsibility for the commissions and omissions of the department he headed. To dismiss the head of the army who after the initial set-back had shown remarkable resilience in recovering lost ground, and ignore the responsibility of the Minister – a professional military man at that, known for the active part he took in operational planning and decisions – evoked a pained outcry of favouritism and miscarriage of justice. The Commission's preliminary but momentous report, instead of setting the anxieties at rest, raised them to new heights.

Three years after these turbulent months I had a private talk with Golda. We used to meet occasionally in the years of her retirement. It was election day 1977. Golda was in a sombre mood. The Labour Party was a house divided; its floors were creaking and through its open windows blasted draughts of dissent. Whatever the numerical outcome of the elections, Golda predicted that Labour would pay a heavy price for its iniquities. It might even lack sufficient strength to form the government – a heretical thought she had never entertained before. We contemplated the possibility that a few members of the labour faction in the Knesset might cross the floor, enabling Begin to form a government, but she dismissed the never-absent speculation that Dayan might be among the defectors. He was capable of performing many surprising twists, she said, but he would not leave the party. Though their ways had parted, in the wake of the Agranat report, she would not believe that he would uproot himself from the labour movement. Before the report was published he had indeed offered her his resignation. He had come to her office straight from a military funeral, all shaken. Bereaved parents had shouted at him that he was the murderer of their sons. Golda refused to accept his resignation. But the day the inquiry commission had asked for the dismissal of Dado, as the Chief of Staff was popularly known, she expected Dayan to share the responsibility and resign with him. It would have been the only right thing to do. He disappointed her beyond recovery.

The reactions to the Agranat report made not only Dayan's political future uncertain, but also the longevity of the new post-war government formed by Golda Meir in March 1974. Eban, who had played a prominent role in the election campaign, featuring as his central theme the promising prospects of peace, had devoted his attention to the Geneva conference and the ensuing negotiations. He felt no need to participate in the customary Derby for cabinet positions. He was sure that Golda, even if her personal preferences were different, would reappoint him as Foreign Minister. But he was innocent of the machinations that cabinet aspirants and makers were apt to engage in. He narrowly escaped political demise, as the Prime Minister later admitted. The renomination of Dayan gave her so much trouble that she felt incapable of undergoing the additional agitation which Eban's exclusion from the cabinet was likely to cause.

But just as the collective survival of the new government was uncertain, so was Eban's ministerial future. At the time of his reinstallation I was already in London. The view from abroad afforded sometimes a better picture of the Israeli political scene than actual immersion in it. On Eban's next visit to London I carefully broached the subject. I asked him casually whether he had ever contemplated taking a sabbatical from politics. The political instability at home caused by the Yom Kippur shock would continue to bedevil the government. Eban's reputation had remained unblemished by the events; people knew he had advocated a different course, but had not prevailed. But they wanted to see a change of leadership. Now that he had been reaffirmed in his office, wasn't this a good moment to step down – not in protest and opposition, not slamming the door, just to prove that not all politicians cling inexorably to their seats? It would set a refreshing example. Eban did not hide his consternation. 'I'm used to better advice from you,' he retorted. Didn't I know that whoever gave up his cabinet post hardly ever returned to it? Better times would come and open the way for him to assume an even more important task in the direction of the affairs of the country.

A month later Golda Meir stepped down. She was worn out by the incessant manifestations of discontent, the rigours of her responsibilities, the dissent in her party and the strains of age and disease. Her successor did not include Eban in his new government.

To Geneva and beyond

The adoption of Resolution 338 calling for immediate peace negotiations opened completely new vistas and challenges to Israel's foreign policy. A peace conference where the delegations of Israel and Arab states sat together under the watchful direction of the representatives of the United States and the Soviet Union, with terms of reference agreed in advance, was certainly an epoch-making innovation. It required meticulous preparation and high professional standards. The Israeli delegation was facing not only skilful and obdurate Arab negotiators, but highly experienced and agile masters of diplomacy in the persons of Kissinger and Gromyko. They were backed up by a team of experts versed in the art of negotiations between hostile parties and familiar with every detail of the dispute. They were as apt in formulating the fine points as in skipping over the more intractable large issues. They enjoyed the benefit of access to both sides and had a sound appraisal, at least as evidenced by Kissinger, of the available options.

Abba Eban saw in the opening session of the conference, held in Geneva on 21 December 1973, a unique historic opportunity to present Israel's case to an attentive world audience in a sweeping speech ranging from Abraham, the founding father of the nation and its faith, to Ben Gurion, the progenitor of its rebirth; from the prophetic visions of the Bible to Israel's actual peace proposals.

Following his idea that the Geneva meeting would offer a forum of exceptional reverberation for Israel's views, Eban added to the delegation a sizeable number of journalists, academics and public relations experts. Assuming that the negotiations would be conducted in Geneva over a considerable period of time, Eban instructed the administration of the Foreign Ministry to rent a small office building and to install there an adequate number of officials, headed by a permanent representative. But Kissinger had quite different ideas about the way to peace. He preferred to proceed step by step, securing limited areas of bilateral agreement to be extended in scope and substance in negotiations which would probably drag on for several years. The Geneva conference would serve as a repository of their legitimacy and be convened for the signing of accords, but not for the process of their attainment. It would serve as a kind of glorified registry office where the couples could consecrate their marriage contracts after a prolonged courtship.

Although step-by-step diplomacy was from now on the chosen instrument, the United States was far from contenting itself with a leisurely pace. Unlike the period preceding the war, Kissinger now began to drive hard for fast progress. He drove himself the hardest, jetting unrelentingly between the capitals of the opposing camps. His performance never lacked suspense and his staging was always superb. The American administration, stirred by the enormous risks of superpower confrontation, economic dislocation and political differences in the Western world accentuated by the war, was now resolved not to let diplomatic action stagnate again.

The Secretary of State realized that he would have to cover much ground on both sides before the Arab states were ready to end the conflict and Israel to make the necessary concessions. In the first instance, the United States had to strengthen its influence in the relevant Arab countries, keep the Soviet Union at bay and reassure Israel of unwavering American support for its security. Kissinger was careful not to annoy the Israeli government unnecessarily by insisting on a comprehensive settlement which would inevitably require Israel to make extensive concessions for which it was not yet ready. He therefore presented to its government his step-by-step procedure as a means of staving off such an agonizing choice, while he wooed the Arab governments to accept it as the safest way of achieving their ultimate goal. It would be inaccurate to describe his method as diplomatic duplicity, because both his arguments were meant to serve the same purpose – to set in motion the peace process which would eventually lead to the resolution of the conflict. The peace train starting from Geneva would pass through many stations on its long journey until it reached its ultimate destination.

After two days of sparring and speeches the Geneva conference adjourned with not a single handshake being exchanged between the delegates of the two hostile camps. An empty table had represented Syria, which had made its attendance conditional on the prior evacuation of its territory occupied by Israel in the 1973 fighting. It had also refused to hand over the lists of Israeli prisoners-of-war who, by all accounts, were suffering severe maltreatment. For the first time since the Soviet Union had severed its relations with Israel in 1967, the Foreign Ministers of the two countries held a private meeting in which they discussed their policies in the area and the prospects of their bilateral relations. Gromyko gave Eban a vague promise that the Soviet Union might restore diplomatic ties after Israel had made an important step forward at the Geneva conference. He carefully avoided specifying its nature. Silence settled over the Geneva conference, not to be disturbed by another plenary meeting in the years to come. The permanent representatives, left behind as the guardians of the spirit of Geneva, faded away when the spirit and the diplomatic action moved to the capitals of the contenders.

Step by step

The first item on Kissinger's long agenda was the separation of the forces on the Egyptian front, entwined at the end of the fighting like chessmen at an advanced stage of the match. The two sides had two immediate concerns. Egypt sought the relief of its Third Army and Israel was anxious to have its prisoners-of-war repatriated. Golda Meir's visit to Washington at the end of October and Kissinger's visit to Cairo a week later afforded the Secretary of State the opportunity for a practical and highly successful application of his diplomatic method. Israel yielded on the transit of supplies to the Third Army; Egypt promised to lift maritime restrictions at Bab el-Mandeb and agreed to the exchange of the prisoners-of-war. And both governments agreed to negotiate an accord on the separation of forces – a euphemism for the withdrawal of Israeli forces from the territory they were holding on both sides of the Suez Canal.

But Kissinger did not content himself with the solitary practice of his step-by-step procedure. He insisted that the two sides should step towards each other and negotiate face to face. Two weeks after the end of the fighting, delegations from Israel and Egypt met in a tent in the desert at kilometre 101 on the road from Cairo to Suez.

Kissinger extended his first journey to Cairo to include visits to Jordan and Saudi Arabia. In his talks with the Secretary of State King Hussein stressed his continued opposition to PLO rule over the West Bank, although at the time Arafat had already attained widespread support from other Arab countries. 'I will reclaim', said Hussein, 'the occupied territories as part of the Hashemite Kingdom of Jordan and demand Israel's complete withdrawal to the pre-1967 borders.' At one stage of the confidential exchange of views which had been held sporadically over a length of time, Israel had proposed the reinstatement of the administrative control of Jordan over the West Bank while retaining its responsibility for the defence and security of the territory and leaving the question of sovereignty in suspense. On other occasions Israel had indicated on the highest level its readiness to restore the Moslem holy places in Jerusalem to Jordanian sovereignty and to evacuate the densely Arab-populated areas of the West Bank. But at no point had the government renounced its resolve to regard the Jordan river as its first line of defence.

King Hussein was not disinclined to regain the West Bank in stages. After the Yom Kippur War he proposed that Israel withdraw its forces from the Jordan river along a twelve-kilometre-wide strip. This would be the Jordanian equivalent of a separation of forces agreement. To all intents and purposes this proposal was the antithesis of Israel's security doctrine. Israel rejected it as non-negotiable. Another idea, attributed to Allon, to return the town of Jericho and the adjacent area, linking it to the Trans-Jordanian territory of the Hashemite kingdom, as a first instalment, found favour with neither the Jordanian nor the Israeli governments. Hussein, who had been cautious enough not to intervene directly in the Yom Kippur War, lamented repeatedly that he was the only one to be punished for his prudence, whereas his warring Arab neighbours had been rewarded by the withdrawal of Israel from parts of the territory that the Arabs had lost in the fighting of 1973.

But neither Jordan nor the Palestinians preoccupied the thoughts of Washington at that time. Progress with Egypt and Syria and renewed co-operation with Saudi Arabia took a much higher place on its list of priorities. The more the prospects of arrangements with Egypt and, in a more limited sense, with Syria improved, the more Israel's interest in an accommodation with Jordan receded. Not only did King Hussein's uncompromising stand on the restoration of the pre-1967 border, perhaps with some minor adjustments, impair the possibility of an overall agreement with him, but Israel's leaders doubted to various degrees his personal reliability and political durability. In a way they underestimated his ability to extricate himself from tight corners and to change his political liaisons. He was the Houdini of oriental politics, an escape artist unsurpassed by his contemporaries. Small in stature, he impressed by the wholesomeness of his personality, the resonance of his voice, the reasonableness of his argument, the naturalness of his manner and the dignity of his posture. He would break out easily into hearty laughter but without any intimation of frivolity. Western in his upbringing and bedouin in his character, he exuded a special charm. He impressed his Jewish interlocutors by the genuineness of his respect and goodwill towards Judaism and the Jewish people. Like his grandfather, whom he revered, he abhorred religious fanaticism and political extremism. But this was exactly his problem. He ruled in an environment of constant excitation. He had an innate skill in navigating these torrents and keeping his leaky ship afloat. Where he was destined was anyone's guess. Was it peace with Israel? Was it the sheer desire for survival? Probably both, but he knew that only when calm settled over the waters was his survival assured and peace possible. Meanwhile he kept his options open. Nobody should despair of him, neither Carter, Sadat, Arafat nor Begin.

Oil and the PLO

The more the chances of an agreement with Hussein faded, the higher the influence of the PLO among the Palestinians in the West Bank and the international standing of the organization rose. Although it did occasionally inflict painful casualties on the civilian population in Israel, its operations never constituted a military menace to the country nor did they disrupt its normal way of life. Arab leaders, however, felt themselves increasingly threatened by the gunmen of the terrorist organization and the political agitation unleashed by it against unco-operative Arab governments. They easily acceded to the proposition of insuring themselves against the PLO by paying it political ransom and protection money. The Soviet Union soon recognized the inherent destabilizing potential of the PLO. It generously provided it with assault arms and sabotage equipment, training facilities for its cadres and political guidance for its leaders. Although Moscow was aware that the PLO was in no position to influence the military situation and make any significant contribution to the war capacity of the Arab states, it could always serve Soviet policy as a handy tool to keep Arab-Israeli, and if necessary inter-Arab, relations in a state of constant unrest.

The oil crisis and in particular its financial implications hit the weaker economies of the developing countries with greater force than those of the industrialized world, which possessed a large capacity of shock-absorption. Most of the non-aligned oil-importing countries believed that they would be rewarded with guaranteed supplies and preferential prices if they were to back Arab hostility against Israel. They supposed that the *nouveaux riches* of the non-aligned fraternity would willingly share some of their windfall wealth with their less fortunate brethren. Their leaders were given to understand that a quick political and ideological adjustment to Arab policies would help expedite the transaction. Liberation was the hallmark of the era and the essence of the struggle of the developing countries against colonialism. Thus the battle cry of 'Palestine liberation' evoked in them familiar associations, even if in reality it meant the subjugation of Israel and the denial of its right to liberty. But oil has the singular quality of not only moving the wheels of transport and industry but also removing the scruples of morality. It was the PLO who cashed in on this dupery and not the hard-pressed treasuries of the gullible governments. It took them some time to realize that political sell-outs are not necessarily rewarded by bargain sales of oil and generous foreign aid.

But the attitude of some of the industrialized Western countries was basically no different. Perhaps they were a bit more reluctant to succumb to Arab temptations. But essentially they stood more on ceremony than on principle. They reasoned that if the Arab governments cowered from fear of Arafat's strong arm, the Europeans could at least humour them by a display of goodwill towards the PLO. Slowly but markedly they helped confer international standing on an organization that instigated and collaborated with like-minded practitioners of international terror, and helped them in their operations on European soil. Yet the PLO had as much influence on the production, pricing and distribution of oil as the Red Brigades had on the manufacture of motor-cars. The PLO dealt in blood and not in oil. Its international elevation retarded the inevitable progress towards peace in the Middle East and advanced Soviet aspirations in that area.

When Dr Kissinger paid his first visit to Saudi Arabia shortly after his meeting with Sadat in November 1973 the oil crisis was uppermost in his mind. He was fully aware that the continuation of the embargo would seriously hurt Western prosperity and political cohesion. Only very few people perceived at the time the disastrous consequences which reduced production and inflated prices would have on the world economy and stability as a whole. Saudi Arabia was a land barred to Jewish visitors. Old King Feisal was not only a faithful adherent of the austere cult of Wahabism, an Islamic sect, but also a firm believer in the existence of a communist-zionist world conspiracy. He used to present his distinguished visitors with a farewell gift of an ornately leather-bound copy of the *Protocols of the Elders of Zion* fabricated in Czarist Russia.

Henry Kissinger was the first Jewish Foreign Secretary to be received by the formidable monarch. In true bedouin tradition and not oblivious of the fact that he spoke to the representative of a pretty powerful country, Feisal preferred to greet his visitor with the good graces of Arab hospitality. To ease the first awkward moments of the encounter, so the story goes, the old king opened the audience with the words: 'Mr Secretary, let's talk man to man like human beings.' Whereupon Kissinger, the quick-witted, is said to have replied with a straight face: 'Your Majesty, some of my very best friends are human beings.' The Secretary of State returned from Riyadh with a vague promise that Saudi Arabia would try to be helpful provided that the United States induced Israel to start its withdrawal. Kissinger assumed that King Feisal's assurance of alleviating the oil crisis was related only to the current Egyptian-Israeli negotiations and the meeting of the Geneva conference.

However, the day after the first session of the peace conference had adjourned, OPEC, upon the initiative of the Shah of Iran and with the concurrence of the King of Saudi Arabia, doubled the price of oil – a rise that initiated the decline of the Western economy and spurred the fall of the Persian ruler.

The Kissinger shuttle takes off

It prompted Kissinger to expedite the conclusion of the agreement on the separation of the entangled Egyptian and Israeli forces. He returned to the Middle East in January 1974 and inaugurated his shuttle service between Cairo and Jerusalem. Israel linked its readiness to undertake limited withdrawal to the termination of the state of belligerency. Egypt insisted on the retreat of the Israeli forces to positions east of the Sinai passes and an undertaking on a timetable for the full implementation of Resolution 242. In his travels and travails Kissinger became an expert not only on the physical but also the human topography of the area. He learned to discern the weak and strong traits of the leading figures in both camps as intimately as he became familiar with every rise and depression on the ground.

His negotiating technique was finely honed. He would present the more unattractive features of a proposal in their most flattering light and offer foregone concessions as hard-won victories. His art was the nuance of emphasis, but not the wile of double-dealing. He was too experienced to try to sell one thing to one side and the opposite to the other. A horse was a horse. If it limped on one leg, it still had three other healthy ones. Where his power of persuasion failed, his tireless tenacity worked wonders of attrition. He soon realized that crude pressures were more likely to stiffen the resistance of his negotiating partners than to break it. He skilfully employed the system of the American bonus. Advantages which the opposing sides were unwilling to grant one another, he would provide in the form of an American compensation. Undertakings to which the parties felt unable to commit themselves directly, one towards the other, the United States would accept in escrow.

The Secretary of State employed this system successfully in bringing about the conclusion of the first Israeli-Egyptian disengagement of forces agreement. It became the model for the others which followed. Egypt would commit itself to the United States on the measure of demobilization of its forces, the strength of its troops in Sinai, the rebuilding and repopulation of the towns in the canal zone, the transit of Israeli cargoes through the reopened canal and the continuation of the cease-fire. Israel signed with the United States a ten-point memorandum of understanding in which it undertook to continue negotiations on further withdrawals also on the Syrian front, and proceed with the implementation of Resolution 242, while the United States undertook to respond to Israel's defence requirements on a continuing and long-term basis. The United States also stated formally that it regarded the Strait of Bab el-Mandeb as an international waterway with all that that implied for the freedom of passage. Furthermore it pledged its assistance in monitoring the new agreement by an increased number of reconnaissance flights over the area of disengagement.

The new agreement initiated the process of Israeli withdrawal before the termination of the state of war, let alone the conclusion of peace. It was a bitter pill for Israel's public to swallow. Its government – and the United States government also – had in the years before the Yom Kippur War staunchly declared that withdrawal should take place only within the context of contractual peace. 'Withdrawal should never occur', stated Secretary Rogers on 29 January 1970, 'before there is a contractual agreement entered into by the parties and signed by them in each other's presence, providing full assurances to Israel that the Arabs would admit that Israel had a right to exist in peace.'

But the Yom Kippur War had changed many things. Some of us remembered Sisco's forebodings, when he had asked Evron whether Israel was so sure that in a year's time it could expect to reach a better agreement with Egypt than was possible at the beginning of 1973. No, was the answer, it was not sure that it could reach any peace agreement, but it was confident that the recurrence of war was excluded in the foreseeable future. The new deployment of forces and weapons which both sides were permitted to keep in the zones of forces limitation separated them beyond the shooting-range of the ground-arms. Since the implementation of this agreement in February 1974 not a single shot has ever again been exchanged between Egypt and Israel. It was the first peaceful engagement after nearly a quarter of a century of hostilities, setting in motion a process of military and political disengagement that led to the first encounter between the leaders of Egypt and Israel in Jerusalem four years later, culminating in the first treaty of peace concluded between the Jewish state and an Arab country.

Negotiations with Syria

However Syria, Egypt's ally, was not eager to become its partner in peace. Unlike Egypt, its political and emotional commitment to fierce Arab nationalism was an inherent trait of its national character. President Assad was quite different from Sadat. He was a cold, calculating, humourless man, suspicious not only of foreigners but also of the loyalty of his own people. Although he held the dubious record of the longest tenure of a military dictator in Syria's *putsch*-ridden establishment, he had to be on the constant look-out for plotters. He hardly fitted into the Sadat-Kissinger mutual admiration society, of which Begin was later to become a prominent member. Assad was impervious to the Secretary's charms and this seemed to be based on reciprocity.

Israel was deeply disturbed by reliable information in its possession that its prisoners-of-war had suffered severe maltreatment at the hands of their Syrian captors. Assad was determined to squeeze every drop of political advantage from Israel's compassionate desire to obtain their repatriation. He refused to submit the lists of the prisoners to the International Red Cross nor would he permit its representatives to visit them. Syria was prepared to exchange the prisoners, so the President informed the Secretary of State, if Israel would withdraw not only from the territory it had occupied in the 1973 fighting, but also from that taken in the Six Day War. Only on that basis could he envisage an agreement on the separation of forces – an utterly unrealistic proposition, as Kissinger admitted and Assad realized. More shuttle between Damascus and Jerusalem resulted in February in the first movement on both sides. Syria would content itself with the evacuation of half of the occupied area on the Golan Heights and hand over to the United States the list of the POWs if Israel would give an affirmative declaration of intent on withdrawal. Kissinger returned to Washington, letting the two governments sweat it out. He would be pleased to receive their envoys whenever they were ready to submit more promising proposals.

But instead of talking to Israel via Washington, Syria tried to make its point by renewing the shooting. Intermittently, but heavily, Syrian guns shelled Israeli positions on the Golan Heights. Zahal riposted with restraint in order to avoid an extension of the fighting. What Syria wanted to prove was not clear. It had only recently experienced a failure to drive Israel from the Golan Heights. Its recourse to military action seemed to be motivated by a number of reasons: to serve as a smokescreen for the home front, covering up the ongoing diplomatic contacts; to spite Sadat for the signing of an agreement with Israel; to keep up pressure on the United States government to adopt a more favourable position; and to counteract Washington's efforts to end the oil embargo.

In fact the Saudi government had already informed the administration that it would have difficulties in persuading its friends to lift the embargo before Israel started to withdraw from Syrian territory. Kissinger, realizing that the waiting game was too risky, turned to a number of Arab countries to exert their influence on Damascus and intimated to Israel that the United States would have to re-examine its policy if it failed to show more flexibility. Sadat promised his support and advised the Secretary of State that Syria would eventually agree to a compromise provided that its control over the town of Kuneitra was restored. Saudi Arabia convinced its Arab associates to suspend the oil ban for a period of three months in anticipation of a satisfactory solution of Syria's claims. Israel also showed signs of compromise.

There remained Damascus and Moscow. At the end of March Kissinger departed for a visit to the Soviet capital. This time the going was rough. Brezhnev accused the Secretary of State of trying to eliminate the Soviet Union from the peace process and acting against its legitimate interests in the Middle East. He insisted on the resumption of the Geneva conference under the joint auspices of the two governments. He referred to Iraq's good relations with the Soviet Union and Assad's forthcoming visit to Moscow, in order to impress on the Secretary of State that without Soviet co-operation his efforts in Damascus were bound to flounder. But despite these differences both sides preferred to remain in touch and to continue their search for a common approach.

In the course of April, Gromyko and Kissinger met again. The Soviet Foreign Minister proposed a four-point understanding: a joint Soviet-American policy on the Syrian-Israeli disengagement agreement; Israel's partial withdrawal as an integral part of its eventual total evacuation of Syrian territory; Syria's participation in the reactivated Geneva conference; and co-ordination by the United States and the Soviet Union of their overall policy in the Middle East. This was a tall order and went far beyond Kissinger's limited objective which was to neutralize harmful Soviet influence in Damascus. Gromyko urged that the two ministers should come out with a joint statement in which the Soviet Union would explicitly say that the independence and sovereignty of Israel should be assured like that of all other states in the area. As he put it, the Soviet Union had no intention of pulling the rug out from under the existence of Israel. Besides the withdrawal there were other issues such as Jerusalem, Gaza and the Palestinian question, but it would be easier to deal with these matters later within the framework of the Geneva conference and in parallel bilateral Soviet-American talks. But Kissinger avoided committing himself. He only agreed to remain in touch with his Soviet colleague for an exchange of information about the situation and the progress of his efforts. After his unilateral diplomacy had proved itself so successful with Egypt, he felt little inclination to facilitate active Soviet involvement in the negotiations with Syria. After all, the intentions of the Soviet Union were obvious. It sought the co-operation of the United States to oust Israel from the occupied territories and the collaboration of the Arab states to oust the United States from the Middle East.

By the end of April Kissinger believed the situation was ripe for a final assault. He decided to return to the Middle East, determined to clinch the agreement in a few days of shuttle between Damascus and Jerusalem. Dayan had visited Washington at the end of March with a new map which indicated some possible openings for success. But he had also brought disquieting news. Israeli intelligence had detected the presence in Syria of Cuban crews manning tanks, of North Korean pilots flying Syrian Migs and of Polish and East German military instructors. Washington responded that it lacked independent confirmation from its own sources. In any case to speak of the presence of an international brigade (as Dayan had called it) was in its view an exaggeration.

Kissinger realized that the negotiations would be very difficult. The Israeli government was shaky. Golda Meir had resigned and presided over a caretaker government until the new Prime Minister designate was able to form his government. Manifestations of protest against the outgoing government did not abate and now extended to Kissinger personally, whom extremists accused of leading Israel towards untold new perils. Nixon's prestige was sinking in the spreading morass of Watergate. However, to ease Kissinger's mission in Israel, the President equipped him with a sizeable incentive in the form of a waiver of $1 billion on the repayment of the $2.2 billion aid loan. Regardless of his domestic preoccupations the President did not hesitate also to wave the stick, by letting it be discreetly known that he was reviewing the aggregate of aid that Israel received from governmental and private American sources.

The concerted Arab influences which Kissinger had managed to line up made the desired impression on Damascus. At the decisive moment of the negotiations, which had entered their fourth week, Sadat's assistance became invaluable. He dispatched his Chief of Staff, General Gamassi, to Damascus with a face-saving compromise proposal which after some minor alterations and two more shuttles became the key to the new agreement. Kuneitra and three hills west of it, overlooking the town, had been the main stumbling-blocks since the negotiations had moved from idle posturing to the stage of busy bargaining. Understandings on zones of forces limitations and UN supervisory functions had been eked out laboriously, but the future of the town of Kuneitra assumed for Syria the proportions of a key to its national survival, and for Israel the gauge of its international strength. To move mountains went beyond even Kissinger's formidable talents. Yet in arranging climb-downs he was unsurpassed. Goading Israel to come down from its position on the hills, he induced Syria to resign itself to some Israeli presence on its slopes.

The two sides edged forward inch by inch. But at every turn there loomed the danger of another derailment. The massacre of Israeli schoolchildren at Ma'alot by terrorist infiltrators came as a terrible shock to the country and endangered the continuation of Kissinger's efforts. With much tact towards Israel and marked firmness towards Syria Kissinger navigated his way through the turbulence. Golda Meir insisted on the inclusion in the agreement of a Syrian undertaking to prevent the mounting of terrorist operations from its territory. Assad refused to commit himself in writing but was ready to give the Secretary an oral assurance of his compliance. President Nixon endorsed the Syrian pledge in a letter to the Israeli Prime Minister confirming that terrorist raids were a violation of the cease-fire, entitling Israel to exercise its right of self-defence. After two more acts of ostentatiously packing his suitcases and preparing departure statements, after promising US aid to Syria and threatening to withhold support from Israel even in times of war, Kissinger had finally lined up both sides. On 29 May, thirty days after the indefatigable Secretary of State had set out on his eventful journey, after innumerable false starts and bumpy landings, he could announce with justified pride that Syria and Israel had agreed on the terms of an agreement on the disengagement of forces. Two days later the representatives of the two countries signed the accord in Geneva. The Syrians kept their pose until the very last. They refrained from exchanging a single word, let alone a handshake with their Israeli co-signatories. It was a shot-gun marriage, but it lasted. Dr Kissinger, the accomplished matchmaker, had established a new endurance record not only for itinerant diplomacy, but also for the co-existence of unwilling partners.

Six years after the signature of the agreement, defined in its preamble as a first step towards peace, Syria and Israel have remained as remote from the conclusion of final peace as they were when they signed the accord. With the exception of Kuneitra, Israel has retained all its positions on the Golan Heights. Its forces are well entrenched and its settlers have extended the cultivation of the barren plateau. How long Syria can persist in its hostility to Israel, and in its refusal to enter into peace negotiations, does not solely depend on the durability of its regime, but also on the changes the Arab world is undergoing, the steadfastness and prudence of Israel and the evolution of the policies of the superpowers in the Middle East.

In early summer 1974 the prospects for regional stability and the extension of American influence in the area looked brighter than at any time before. Nixon, exposed in Washington to the cold fury of his adversaries, felt the urge to warm himself in the sun of Kissinger's success in the Orient. The President departed at short notice for a visit to five Middle East countries. His progress through Araby and Israel was impressive. In Egypt the government staged his visit like a superproduction of *Aida*, with millions of jubilant descendants of the pharaohs cheering all along his route. In Israel Nixon's reception was warm and cordial, but not tumultuous. Mass turnouts of chanting multitudes were not customary and the system of rent-a-crowd by government order unknown in the country. Still the popular and governmental expression of gratitude was ubiquitous and abundant for the help the President had extended to Israel when it needed it most.

34

London – The Last Post

The elections to the Knesset on 31 December were the closing event of the momentous year 1973. Most of the men were still in uniform. My wife and I voted dutifully and a week later we departed for London with a heavy heart. Not that the post of Ambassador to the Court of St. James's was unattractive – far from it – but we had never enjoyed bidding a long farewell to Jerusalem. This time the parting was more difficult than ever. The country was in a sad state. The death of so many of our young people pained all of us like a personal loss. The main effort of human and political post-war recovery had to be made in the country itself.

But Israel had also suffered an alarming set-back in the international arena. To recover the lost ground or at least to halt the erosion became one of the primary objectives of Israel's foreign policy. Anglo-Israeli relations, which had been in a state of constant decline since the beginning of the 1970s, had taken another downturn with the Yom Kippur War. Israel considered Britain's position to be pivotal between the friendly United States and the frosty European countries. And Britain still wielded some influence in the Middle East due to its long-standing involvement in the area and its far-flung network of trade relations. It was a vantage-point which should not be neglected.

After the tiring travel preparations, the restful El Al flight to London was a welcome relaxation until a well-meaning passenger drew my attention to a story in the *International Herald Tribune*. In bold letters it reported that a sizeable contingent of a special security force had been ordered to London airport to protect the new Israeli Ambassador on his arrival. His safety was imperilled because he figured as number one target on the list of the Palestinian terrorists. I tried to allay the fears of my co-traveller who seemed to be torn between feelings of awe for my unexpected distinction and compassion for our well-being.

As soon as the plane landed we were greeted by a group of hefty security men who bundled us off in a limousine waiting at the bottom of the stairs. A phalanx of photographers surged forward. It was obvious that their congregation was not inspired by their pictorial interest in the arrival of the new ambassador, but rather by their expectation of recording his sensational dispatch to a better world. As far as we could see from the car there were indeed soldiers posted on the roofs of the airport buildings and armoured cars patrolling the tarmac. The gathering of dignitaries and heads of all Jewish organizations, which welcomed us in the reception lounge, was more reassuring and heart-warming. But the press and television were still not satisfied. The BBC interviewer in particular was curious to know how it felt to be number one on a hit list. I assured him that I could probably live more comfortably without this distinction and thanked him for his amiable message of welcome to Britain, reserving my more outspoken comments for the condemnation of the evil of international terrorism.

On the way to our new residence we paid a brief visit to Teddy Sieff, the venerable and brave community leader who was recovering in hospital from a terrorist attempt on his life, presumably committed by Carlos, the notorious PLO hit-man, who later achieved the height of his fame when he led the assault on the OPEC oil ministers assembled in Vienna.

London looked bleak in these days of January 1974. Its lights burned dimly and the wheels of its industry turned slowly. A coal miners' strike and the fear of an oil shortage were taxing Britain's energy reserves to a degree that had forced the government to decree a three-day working week. The people appeared more listless than discontented. The public accommodated itself to the inconveniences more in a sullen fashion than in the defiant mood of 'Britain can take it'. Although the oil embargo affected the country only marginally in real terms, psychologically it hit it with full force. It was not the lack of incoming oil supplies but the missing information on the movement and discharge of oil-shipments that caused the near-panic situation. The oil companies had kept the government so completely in the dark about their transactions that it was constrained to gather intelligence by its own means in order to check on the destination of tankers sailing through the Persian Gulf. As it turned out sufficient quantities of oil reached the British ports. In reality the crisis was the result of a sudden formidable increase in the price of oil and the attempt to lower the cost of energy by increased coal production. The miners' strike compounded the difficulties.

I made the customary round of visits to cabinet ministers and opposition leaders. A sharp scent of an approaching election filled the air. Sir Alec Douglas Home, the Foreign Secretary, received me with old world courtesy and quick British wit. When the photographers came in for the customary picture-taking he asked me tongue-in-cheek, alluding to the poor state of relations between the two countries, whether I would take the risk of being photographed with him. The picture might spoil my political career. I assured him that I had never entertained political ambitions. I was certain that our public would enjoy seeing the Secretary in his familiar attire shaking hands amiably with the Israeli Ambassador, after it had viewed with various degrees of admiration the picture of Sir Alec, robed in Bedouin garb, stroking a camel in front of the pyramids.

This little exchange of pleasantries led us straight to our subject. Sir Alec was eager to explain that the arms embargo that his government had imposed at the outbreak of the war was not meant to harm Israel. They had thought that it would affect Egypt much more. I told the Secretary, from personal experience, how badly we had missed the impounded spare parts for the British Centurion tanks and the 105mm armour-piercing ammunition for their guns and how relieved we felt when the first airlifted shipment reached us on the Golan Heights – unfortunately not from a British arsenal, but from a remote US depot in Alabama. Sir Alex replied that the military experts had assured the government that the Israeli army was amply supplied and would not suffer any shortages of British material. I explained that the ammunition spent in the Yom Kippur War in one hour of fighting equalled the amount used in the Six Day War in one day. Sir Alec assured me that after the signing of a separation of forces agreement between Israel and Egypt, HMG would lift their arms embargo and business would return to normal all along the line. On 21 January the government cancelled the embargo. Asked by the press to comment I described it as the right step away from a wrong direction, suspecting that it was prompted more by an eagerness to sell arms to the Arab states than to replenish Israel's arsenals.

My first encounter with Prime Minister Edward Heath was a chance meeting at a press luncheon. To the ritual question about whether we had settled in, I replied that all that I had done so far was to fasten my seat-belt in expectation of a bumpy ride, as I had been advised to do by my knowledgeable superiors in Jerusalem. Heath surprised me with a hearty outburst of his peculiar body laughter and said that, after the conclusion of the agreement with Egypt, Israel's situation in Britain and the European community would become much easier. By the time the accord had come into effect in February, Ted Heath had ceased to be Prime Minister. During my years in London we used to meet from time to time to discuss the Middle East situation. Before we left he arranged a little farewell party and reminded me of our first meeting. 'I told you that you would soon be able to unfasten your seat-belt. You had a smooth ride, because you steered remarkably well' – a compliment not to be sneezed at, coming from an old sailor.

Harold Wilson received me in his room in the House of Commons. He immediately told me of his fight against the embargo. Before the government had made its decision public, he had personally intervened with the Prime Minister, but to no avail. The Foreign Office was insisting on the measure, hoping to score points with the Arab governments. His own shadow cabinet was divided and most of its members were lukewarm in their support of Israel. He decided to force the issue. He told them that as leader of the party he had yielded on quite a few matters for the sake of party unity, but the support of

Israel in its struggle for life or death was for him a matter on which he could not compromise. In the vote in the House against the embargo he was backed by the vast majority of his party.

Naturally the uncertain situation in Britain preoccupied the leader of the opposition most when we met on that shivery mid-January day. There would be an election in the near future, he predicted. The situation was worsening from day to day and the government had lost its grip. He was not trying to precipitate things.

By the end of February the country had gone to the polls. Harold Wilson moved back into No. 10 from where he had been surprisingly evicted in June 1970. Although the new Prime Minister was known in Israel for his ties of friendship with its labour movement and for the valuable support he had extended to Israel in the past, the feeling of scepticism on the Middle East policies of the Labour Party in office was deep-seated. Bitter disappointment at its previous performances – especially that of the Attlee-Bevin administration – had left its scar. Israeli public opinion welcomed Labour's return to power with marked reserve. The popular answer to the perennial question of which was the best party for Israel in Britain had always been: the party in opposition.

A few days after the elections I sent Jerusalem a first assessment of the main problems which would engage the attention of the new government. Not commanding an absolute majority in the House, its first concern was parliamentary survival. Domestically its priorities were: the termination of the miners' strike; the return to the full working week; and the halt of the inflationary spiral. Abroad it would concentrate its efforts on obtaining a loan of £2–3 billion sterling to cover the trade deficit; overhaul the Anglo-American relationship; and try to attain some favourable changes in its contractual obligations towards the European Economic Community without jeopardizing Britain's continued membership. It would press hard for the reduction of EEC prices for agricultural products and for regional financial aid. In the Community it would follow a more independent political course than the previous government.

In Middle Eastern affairs the government would act with caution and restraint, striving to reassure the oil-producing Arab states and Egypt that Wilson's pro-Israeli reputation would in no way harm Arab interests. But the Arab governments would not be satisfied with general declarations of friendship. It was a fair assumption that they would use oil and their sterling deposits as a means of pressure to induce the government to refrain from active and open support of Israel. It was not excluded that the terrorist organizations would play their part in the intimidation effort.

I recommended that our government should be reserved in its welcome of the changes and allow the embassy to work quietly and methodically towards the improvement of Anglo-Israeli relations.

My Arab colleagues in London seemed to share my view that the new government might offer a reasonable chance for the improvement of Anglo-Israeli relations. What we considered a hopeful opportunity, they regarded as a dreadful prospect. They concluded that Wilson had to receive an early warning by press and private influences of the enormous harm to British economic interests which a more friendly policy towards Israel would entail. An editorial published by *The Times* on 21 March 1974 was the first warning-shot: 'It is not surprising that Mr Wilson's return to power should have caused apprehension in the Arab world, and also in the Foreign Office, where some officials were heard to wonder how soon Britain would be put on the Arab blacklist and subjected to the oil embargo.' The writer accused Mr Wilson of having offended the Arabs 'by his tactlessness in praising Arab-Jewish co-operation at a non-political Christmas Eve banquet in occupied Bethlehem'. To speak of peace on earth in Bethlehem on Christmas Eve was indeed an unpardonable indecency in the eyes of writers who preferred the dictates of oiliness to the commands of holiness.

But the only effect *The Times* leader and similar press exhortations had on the Prime Minister was to strengthen his resolve to watch the Foreign Office more closely. He claimed that he had learned his lesson from the leniency he had shown during his first tenure of office towards 'the Arab Legion', as he liked to call the Foreign Office officials dealing with Middle Eastern affairs. When forming his new government Wilson had made it clear that matters of substance concerning Arab-Israeli affairs should not be decided without his prior consent. The Foreign Office was advised that the ambassadors of three countries were allowed direct and unimpaired access to the Prime Minister. Israel was among the three.

The Anglo-Israeli agenda

Before my departure from Jerusalem I met Abba Eban and a few senior officials of the Ministry to discuss the guidelines and central objectives of my mission. It was a copious bill of fare, consisting of main courses only. When we drafted the embassy's work programme, we did not anticipate an early change of government in Britain.

In the political arena we were to induce HMG to refrain from special initiatives in the Arab-Israeli peace process and from interference with the delicate American diplomatic efforts. We should support moves aimed at closer understanding and the co-ordination of Anglo-American policies. The British alignment with France in the Community on Arab-Israeli issues had not only been detrimental to Israel, but had also affected the intimacy of relations between London and Washington. It was obvious that Britain could expect more effective sustenance from the United States than from France.

Britain's susceptibility to Arab oil and financial pressure had become an increasingly influential element in determining its attitude towards Israel. Admittedly we could not countermand these influences, but we should endeavour in London and Washington to limit their potentially harmful effect on British policies in connection with the Arab-Israeli dispute. This was more easily decided than implemented, but the unexpected change of government facilitated our task.

Of course close co-operation with the Jewish community figured high on our agenda. The closer the community felt attached to Israel and worked for it, the more it expected the ambassador to participate in its activities. British Jewry had made outstanding contributions to the struggle for Jewish statehood and held a proud record of generous material support for Israel. Their devotion to and concern for the well-being of Israel was ardent. It was as stimulating as it was demanding. The organizational diversity of the Jewish community, counting less than half a million members, was prolific. Not always seeing eye to eye on religious, political or organizational matters, all the organizations were united in their unqualified support of Israel.

In the economic field we were concerned with three major issues: the gap in Anglo-Israeli trade, British complacency on the Arab boycott, and EEC policies concerning Israel. Britain was Israel's third largest trading-partner. It exported to Israel three times as much as it imported from it. Our economic ministries strongly urged us to make sustained efforts to bring about a change in this disturbing and costly imbalance.

The effect of the Arab boycott was not striking, but its very existence was vexing. Our ceaseless representations to the government to adopt protective measures against this illegal practice of trade discrimination were met invariably by the assertion of HMG's opposition in principle to the boycott, and a profession of helpless inability to abolish it in practice.

Our concerns relating to the European Economic Community met with greater understanding. Israel's trade with the nine member states of the community amounted in 1974 to around $1\frac{1}{2}$ billion, of which only $500 million was made up by Israeli exports. For several years our government had been negotiating a treaty relationship with the Community, designed to improve the conditions of access to European markets. France, although recognizing the justice of Israel's case in principle, hampered the progress of the negotiations in practice. It feared that the Arab states would look askance at an agreement between the Common Market and Israel. The British government was less affected by such considerations. Its economic interests and trade relations with Israel favoured a preferential accord which would lower the tariffs on Israeli agricultural products, a measure concurring with overall British policy of reducing the costs of imported farm products. Still, the Conservative government, trying to keep in line with the policy that France was pursuing, carefully avoided differences with her ally on issues concerning Israel. The new Labour government was more forthcoming in this respect and, in the course of time, we obtained its active and effective support.

The area of military affairs was by its very nature a sensitive one. When the

British government imposed the arms embargo, Vickers shipyards were building three small submarines of a special design for the Israeli navy. Their construction was not affected by the embargo. In the past, Britain had sold Centurion tanks to Israel which, after conversion in our army workshops, became a valuable part of our armoured corps. One of the main efforts of our military procurement mission in London was to secure the supply of a given number of discarded Centurion tanks. In its search the mission encountered more obstacles than tanks. The removal of the obstructions required constant ambassadorial prodding, not infrequently at the highest level. After the lifting of the embargo the acquisition of spare parts and ammunition for Zahal's British equipment went ahead without any special difficulties.

In general Israel's interest in the procurement of British war material diminished markedly after the Yom Kippur War for two reasons: the arms embargo had revealed Britain as an unreliable supplier and the United States had become the main source for Israel's purchases of armaments. Their quality and availability were unmatched and the financial facilities for acquiring them unobtainable elsewhere. But Israel could not afford to remain indifferent to Britain's arms sales to the Middle East. Apart from its traditional Arab customers, Egypt, and to a lesser degree Syria, became actively engaged in preparing the ground diplomatically and commercially for major arms purchases in Britain. This was a matter the embassy followed closely and a subject of frequent discussion with the British government.

Meetings with the new Foreign Secretary and the new Prime Minister

At my first meeting with James Callaghan, the new Foreign Secretary, I had planned to give a general review of Anglo-Israeli relations, outlining perspectives for a more favourable evolution and laying the groundwork for more positive discussions of specifics in the future. But a day or two before the appointment the Foreign Office unexpectedly issued a statement which virtually re-endorsed a policy declaration of 6 November 1973, adopted under considerable Arab pressure by the Foreign Ministers of the European Community at the height of the oil crisis. That statement, which had caused strong Israeli misgivings and to a lesser degree also American displeasure, endorsed a number of principal Arab claims.

The British Labour Party in opposition had criticized the statement and we had reason to hope that in office it would refrain from endorsing it. The unexpected Foreign Office reaffirmation reminded Israel abruptly of the disappointments it had suffered from previous Labour governments. The Foreign Ministry sent me firm instructions to express the dismay of the Israeli government at this most unfortunate first official pronouncement on Arab-Israeli affairs by the new British government. Instead of opening the new season on a harmonious note I now had to start it with a resounding drum-roll.

After an introductory remark on the change of programme, I said my piece.

Callaghan looked at me with a completely blank expression. It was obvious that he had not the slightest idea of what I was talking about. One of his assistants rushed to his aid, explaining to him the history of the EEC statement and the innocence of the Foreign Office – it had only confirmed what the previous government had accepted. The Foreign Secretary was visibly and audibly annoyed. It was up to him, he grunted, and not the officials, to decide which policies the new government was going to endorse, change or reject. The new statement was a regrettable mistake and we should not draw from it any wrong conclusions on his policy. He had learnt a lesson and would apply what he had learnt. When I tried to press the issue, asking for some public amend to correct the wrong impression the statement had created, he replied with a ring of finality in his voice: 'I told you it was an error which will not recur in the future.' His blunt words sounded more like an instruction to his officials than an answer to my suggestion.

We had lost some time by the prologue, which however had a salutary effect on our future dealings with the Foreign Office. To catch up I condensed my review of the issues and left the answers for a later meeting. After the formal end of the conversation I stayed alone with Callaghan. Eban had asked me to convey to him the gist of an exchange of views on Europe that he had had with Kissinger. He had recommended his American colleagues to be responsive to Callaghan's intentions of strengthening Anglo-American ties and mentioned his pro-Atlantic orientation. It would be advisable for the United States not to blame indiscriminately all of Western Europe, but to co-operate more closely with the more positive governments of the alliance. The new British government merited Washington's friendly support, especially in its endeavour to overcome the country's formidable economic difficulties. Callaghan, pleased with Eban's message, said it encouraged him in his resolve to give top priority to the strengthening of Anglo-American relations and his personal ties with Dr Kissinger. He reiterated that he was 'terribly sorry to have upset us' on the statement; we should rely on him as a sincere friend. He would keep in touch with me personally to avoid such 'road accidents' in the future. There were wider issues than the Arab-Israeli conflict on which the two governments could fruitfully work together.

A month after the meeting with Callaghan, Ted Short, the Lord President of the Council and Leader of the House, invited my wife and myself for a family dinner with Harold Wilson. The Shorts occupied a little official flat on the top floor of Admiralty House. In the absence of Mrs Short, who was a teacher in Newcastle, the Lord President acted as his own cook and housekeeper; but for this event she had come to London to help her husband host the dinner.

Wilson arrived a few minutes late. He explained that when he arrived at Admiralty House, he was mistakenly directed by a guard to the ground floor reception rooms where people from the Department of Defence were giving a party, apparently for an Arab arms-purchasing mission. He had just escaped before being recognized. I had not expected that he would touch on this sensitive subject which figured high on my agenda so early in the evening. I told him what we knew about British-Egyptian negotiations on the sale of arms which included purchases of missiles. Our government was seriously concerned at the possibility that Britain would help rearm an Arab country which was still in a state of war with Israel. Wilson said that he understood our apprehensions, but was it not better for Israel if the Arab states were to purchase their arms from Western rather than from Eastern Europe? We had heard this argument repeatedly from France, I said, but the facts were that the arms the Arab states received now from the West were in addition to the shipments that continued to reach them from the East. To top it all France persisted in its arms embargo against Israel. The Prime Minister, showing signs of discomfort, responded eagerly to the dinner-bell.

At the table he switched subjects. He felt he owed us an explanation of the unfortunate incident of the Foreign Office statement. David Ennals, Minister of State, had dined with a few Arab ambassadors who had made some threatening noises and asked for a reaffirmation by the new government of Britain's position in the Arab-Israeli conflict. The tough diplomats had put the fear of Allah into Ennals' tender heart. The next morning he had convened the Foreign Office Arabists and they had come up with the idea of the statement. Neither he, the Prime Minister, nor his Foreign Secretary had been consulted. He had taken the necessary precautions to avoid any recurrence of such unpleasant surprises.

Wilson was interested in the state of Syrian-Israeli negotiations on the separation of forces agreement. Kissinger had informed him that they had reached crisis point and asked him to press Golda Meir to yield on Kuneitra, the key to the agreement, and a small adjacent area. Of course he would like to be helpful, but not on the basis of such desultory appeals. Kissinger was orbiting the globe and on his infrequent and hurried touchdowns in London, he had not shown any inclination to discuss his overall strategy with HMG. The Prime Minister was not prepared to play the role of Kissinger's PPS (Principal Private Secretary).

President Nixon had also brought up the matter the other day, when they had met in Paris at what Wilson called 'the working funeral' of President Pompidou. Nixon had left him with the dismal impression of a man who had not much rope left. His memory was clear and his talk was coherent, but his mind was absent. He would not last through the summer. Nixon suggested that he be invited to London on his return from a summit meeting in Moscow. Wilson thought that the President would never make it to Moscow and thus would spare him the embarrassment of playing host to him in London. He underestimated Nixon's tenacity. At the end of June he reached Moscow, but skipped London on his way home and resigned at the beginning of August.

I raised the problem of Soviet Jewry. Wilson explained that he was willing to support American efforts to open the gates of emigration, but he preferred to do it by quiet persuasion. On his last visit to Moscow in 1971, as leader of the opposition, he had discussed the matter with Kosygin. He presented him with a list of Jewish activists, imprisoned only because they had insisted on leaving for Israel. A leading figure among them was Ruth Alexandrovitch. As the result of Wilson's entreaties she was released and permitted to leave. But only later he learnt that she had been the beneficiary of a curious misunderstanding. Shortly after Wilson's return to London, the government expelled a batch of 102 Soviet intelligence agents. When Wilson was in Moscow he had not been aware of his government's intentions, but the Soviet government had already been advised of the coming expulsion. Kosygin assumed that Wilson knew what he did not know, and regardless of the awkward situation had not cancelled his visit. The Soviet government interpreted this as a deliberate demonstration of goodwill and decided to reciprocate with a gesture on its part. It released Ruth Alexandrovitch. At that meeting in 1971 Kosygin had also urged Wilson to meet Yassir Arafat. He had politely declined the dubious offer and contented himself with seeing Arafat's representative in London, Said Hamami.

Now, after his return to the premiership, the Soviet government had asked him to pay an early visit to Moscow. He believed that after the differences which had cropped up between the Soviet leaders and Kissinger on his last visit to Moscow, they were interested in enlisting Wilson's good offices as mediator in the Arab-Israeli conflict. They thought that his close relations with the leadership of Israel would be useful. Wilson hardly concealed his eagerness to follow the call and play the assigned role. He thought this would be a welcome occasion to discuss the situation of the Soviet Jews and obtain some alleviations. But Ted Short dampened the Prime Minister's enthusiasm for travel, reminding him of his party's narrow parliamentary margin of survival. Every single vote counted. On his way to the Kremlin the Prime Minister might get lost in Westminster, warned Short.

After dinner, I broached the subject I had intended to make the central theme of our conversation. Mutual friends had advised me that I should use the occasion to make an impassioned appeal to Wilson to lend Israel his unreserved support. I could forgive them their ignorance of my aversion to high-flown oratory but they should have known Harold Wilson better. I opened my allocution with the description of the effects of the Yom Kippur War on Israel, abandoned by its friends in the hour of its greatest peril; the icy spell of solitude repeating itself so soon after the torments of the Nazi period; the shock of the initial disarray and the high losses. Living in a hostile environment and an indifferent world, we were anxiously looking for friends. We hoped that his long-standing friendship would manifest itself now that he was again at the helm, at a time vital to the destiny of Israel and peace in the Middle East.

At one point Wilson interrupted me, saying with feeling that he had first-hand knowledge of the cruel losses Israel had suffered. During the war his son Giles had been at Kibbutz Yagur, which had lost seven of its members in the fighting. He had described in his letters the grief of the kibbutz and the grim mood of the country. The people had lost their self-confidence.

Wilson heard me out with polite attention, but after a short while his look became forlorn. Queen Victoria's famous saying about Gladstone crossed my mind: 'He speaks to me as if I were a public meeting.' When I had ended he simply said to our host: 'We should soon have a cabinet discussion on our whole policy in the Middle East.'

Harold Wilson had a compelling interest in Israeli politics. Undoubtedly it was a fascinating subject for any curious observer and even more so for such a master practitioner as Harold Wilson, whose acquaintance with many Israeli leaders augmented his friendly interest. The evening we dined together, Golda Meir had resigned and Rabin had been entrusted with the formation of the new government. Wilson praised Golda's virtues and regretted that his close friend Yigal Allon had failed to realize his life's aspiration. His hopes of succeeding Eshkol had been crushed by Golda's unexpected return to the political stage, and his rivalry with Dayan had foiled his chances of succeeding Golda. While Wilson obviously commiserated with Allon's misfortune, he relished the political drama. Undoubtedly he was really fond of Allon and would have cherished his accession to the top post. But with a resigned shrug he passed judgement: 'Well, Yigal is not made of prime-ministerial timber, he is not ready to go for the jugular.' This startling insight into the making of Prime Ministers concluded the evening.

Allon and Rabin visit London

Three weeks later Allon visited London. He still held the position then of Minister of Education in the outgoing caretaker cabinet. He told me that he was hesitant to join Rabin's new government but that, whatever his final decision might be, he would not accept the post of Foreign Minister and relieve Abba Eban of office. Allon had come at the invitation of Harold Wilson to address the Richard Crossman memorial meeting, to be held by the Labour Party on 15 May 1974. But in the early hours of 15 May Jerusalem informed us of the terrorist attack on the schoolhouse at Ma'alot, a small town in western Galilee. Allon decided to return home immediately. He gave me the notes he had prepared and asked me to address the memorial meeting in his place. Explaining Allon's absence I informed the audience that: 'In the early hours of this morning a group of about a hundred Israeli schoolchildren fell into the hands of a terrorist gang. They belong to an organization which has a blood-stained record of infamy. They have proclaimed in the past their responsibility for the murder of Israeli schoolchildren and for the massacre at Lod airport. Do I have to tell you what anguish the attempt on the lives of children evokes in a people which has lost in this generation one million of its children who perished in the gas chambers and the furnaces?' Before the day was over twenty-seven schoolchildren had been murdered.

At the end of June the new Prime Minister, Yitzhak Rabin, came to London to attend a leadership meeting of the Socialist International. Harold Wilson had invited his colleagues to Chequers, mainly for the purpose of rallying support for the Socialist Party in Portugal. Of course, Wilson was aware that hosting a gathering attended by a number of prestigious heads of government would have political side-effects on his personal and international standing. Wilson received Rabin at Downing Street immediately upon his arrival. The meeting attended by Callaghan, the personal secretaries of both Prime Ministers, and myself passed off to the satisfaction of both sides. Rabin made a detailed *tour d'horizon* of the Middle East situation, the future of the peace negotiations, Israel's relations with the United States and its concerns in Europe. He took the European Community to task for its weak-kneed policy during the Yom Kippur War and its surrender to Arab pressures ever since. The only contribution the Europeans could make to the peace process, said Rabin briskly, was to stay out of it. Their intervention added weight to Arab obstructionism but nothing else.

Both Wilson and Callaghan had apparently agreed in advance to avoid arguments with the new Prime Minister. They contented themselves with informative questions. Only once did Callaghan inject a more lively comment, maintaining that without an understanding between Israel and the Palestinians no real peace could be secured. But when Rabin energetically dismissed this view as conflicting with the true nature of the struggle, the Foreign Secretary did not press his point. All in all it was a relaxed session and Rabin had good reason to be satisfied with his first Prime Minister-to-Prime Minister talk.

At the Chequers meeting Rabin was cordially welcomed as the new member of the club and thoroughly sized up by its old-timers. The socialist leaders were used to Golda Meir. Not always in full accord with her, they felt personally at ease with her. She had commanded their respect as a single-minded leader and their admiration for her home-spun attachment to the outmoded tenets of the old socialist faith. Rabin represented the new generation of Israel, hardened in its struggle for survival rather than formed by ideological debates on socialist doctrine. She appealed to the emotions and he to the logic of his listeners. Rabin gave a short presentation of Israel's views on the topical issues, ending with a positive outlook on peace which was to be achieved not by leaps and bounds but by gradual steps. His sober approach left a favourable impression.

As always the Jewish community excelled in its attentions to a Prime Minister of Israel. The heads of organizations virtually besieged the embassy with their demands to honour Rabin, while others jammed our switchboard with their requests for invitations. Neither time, nor the Prime Minister's wishes allowed for more than one festivity. The audience which had come to hear Rabin compared him, as was only natural, with Golda. Rabin's matter-of-fact style was very different from her emotional flamboyance which the community had adored. Carried along by the waves of the audience's enthusiasm for Israel, the Prime Minister reached the safe haven of warm acclaim.

At the end of July, Yigal Allon came back to London, this time as Foreign Minister. Wilson invited him to go to Chequers on a Sunday morning. The two friends talked for an hour alone, then they asked me to join them. Allon presented me to the Prime Minister as if this were our first meeting. He enumerated with embarrassing effusion the qualities of his ambassador. The compliment I liked best was that I was 'a man of high principles motivated by moral values'. Wilson should feel absolutely free to discuss with me any matter of state or to offer me his personal views and advice on Israeli affairs. He could send through the ambassador, who enjoyed his personal trust, any communication to him he wished.

After this elating prologue we got down to brass tacks. The conversation ranged from the deficiency in arrangements for Israeli security personnel to Ceausescu's eagerness to play an important mediatory role in the settlement of the Arab-Israeli conflict; from Wilson's suggestion of an official visit to Israel by his deputy, the Lord President of the Council, to the rumours of the opening of an official PLO representation in London. Wilson noted the items he had promised to deal with and in due course I received the answers, some of them satisfactory, some of them dilatory.

Arms sales

In the following months our discussions with HMG centred on three subjects: British arms sales to Arab states, Israeli arms purchases, and the growing international strength of Arafat's PLO. The interest of the British government focused essentially on one problem: its parliamentary frailty which made the holding of new elections unavoidable.

Contacts between Egyptian arms-procurement missions and the British authorities had intensified markedly since the end of the Yom Kippur War. Egypt showed an increasing interest in the acquisition of sophisticated British equipment and HMG a growing eagerness to meet their demands. But they were mindful of the Labour Party's aversion to the supply of arms to states at war with Israel. To overcome the opposition of Israel and its friends, Wilson assured Jerusalem that these sales to Egypt and some Gulf states would remain limited in quantity and be defensive in nature. If the Israeli government were to acquiesce in these transactions, Britain in return would respond favourably to Israeli requirements. Wilson and Callaghan, who dealt personally with this delicate matter, had gained the impression that the responsible Israeli ministers had accepted their proposal.

At various occasions when we made representations against British arms sales to Arab countries, the Foreign Secretary would refer to Jerusalem's vow of silence, as if we had never clarified that it was based on a misunderstanding.

Wilson also was not much impressed with our interpretation. In an interview with the editor of the *Jewish Chronicle* in October 1974, he told him, fortunately not for the record, 'you know that after consultation with Israel we are supplying some arms to Egypt. We asked Israel's view first. This is an attempt to lure Egypt away from dependence upon the USSR. The Americans feel the same.' However, the reports on British-Arab arms deals under consideration by far exceeded the sales eventually transacted. The obstacle was the lack of funds. The gap between Saudi Arabian promises to finance Egypt's purchases and its actual performance was as wide as the amounts in question were high. Besides, Egypt was eager to publicize its intentions to buy British in order to obtain more advantageous conditions in France and to induce Washington to sell arms to it. When Sadat eventually surmounted this hurdle in 1978, the quantities and quality of armaments Egypt contracted in the United States surpassed anything it had been able to purchase in Europe after the Yom Kippur War.

The PLO to the fore

The extension of Arab propaganda in Britain became a matter of increasing preoccupation for the embassy. Among the many new trends the Yom Kippur War had set in motion, the interest in the Palestinian problem was one of the most prominent features. Combined with the oil weapon it became a powerful, and for Israel worrisome, tool in the arsenal of Arab political warfare. A well-orchestrated and skilfully conducted propaganda campaign, supported by an ably organized and financed lobby, succeeded in generating growing sympathy for the Palestinian cause. Its impact was felt in the first place in France, where it fell on the fertile ground cultivated by the government. In Britain the Labour government was far more reserved and balanced in its attitude. It did not yield to the unrelenting pressures of the PLO and its supporters to accord official status to Said Hamami, its unofficial representative in London. He was a capable man. Posing as a moderate, he succeeded in widening the circle of the traditional supporters of Arab causes. His relations with the press were notable and his influence on Foreign Office orientalists was indisputable. He moved in the twilight of Arafat's approval of his unpublicized achievements and the disavowal of his public statements. A few years later he fell victim to the dichotomy of his diplomacy. He was assassinated by a gunman from a rival Palestinian organization which regarded his dialectic subtlety as treason to the cause.

The embassy was constantly on the alert to mend the political fences through which the able PLO representative had slipped. The PLO was a staple item on the agenda of our meetings with the officials of the Foreign Office. In particular our first secretary, Oded Eiran, made valiant efforts in this and related fields. Thanks to his knowledgeable presentation and amiable disposition he made many friends among his professional colleagues and gained a fair hearing of our views. Still the answers we received were not always reassuring. At certain critical junctures we felt bound to bring the matter to the attention of the Prime Minister. Wilson's and Callaghan's positions were firm: HMG would not recognize the PLO, nor grant official status to its representatives, until it radically changed its policy towards Israel and abandoned its support of terrorist activities. Their public statements frustrated not only the attempts of the PLO in Britain, but rendered its efforts to attain recognition in the other EEC countries more difficult.

In October 1974 the Arab summit conference in Rabat decided to recognize the Palestine Liberation Organization as the sole legitimate representative of the Palestinian people. It was an impressive victory for Yassir Arafat, regardless of the fact that a number of participants in the meeting had capitulated to his pressures and the veiled threats of his henchmen. King Hussein was among those who surrendered. He divested himself of any official responsibility for the fate of the West Bank. Sulking in his tent, he declared that from now on it was Arafat's responsibility to liberate the occupied territories. Nonetheless he did not discontinue his contacts with his Israeli neighbours, hoping that in the long run the strength of Arafat and his organization would be decimated. Meanwhile, however, Arafat continued to climb up the ladder of fame – others would say notoriety – and international recognition. A month after his success at Rabat the United Nations permitted him to address the General Assembly. Britain voted with the minority opposing the invitation which not only violated the statute of the United Nations, but outraged public opinion in the few remaining free democratic member states of the organization.

In an article on a tripartite Jordanian-Palestinian-Israeli solution which I wrote for the *Guardian* in February 1975, I commented on Arafat's appearance before the United Nations: 'The spectacle of a terrorist chief toting his gun from the rostrum of the highest peace forum, threatening to bomb out of existence a sovereign state if it refused to liquidate itself, was an experience no less chilling and sickening than the outrage committed by the gunmen of the self-same Arafat against the schoolchildren of Ma'alot. They, like their master, wielded in one hand the blackmailer's stick and in the other "the liberator's gun".'

Following Arafat's UN appearance the organization granted observer status to the PLO. The United States and a number of other states, among them Britain, voted against the resolution. This was the prelude to the adoption of a more far-reaching resolution conceding to 'the Palestine people the inalienable right of self-determination and calling on Israel to terminate the illegal occupation of the territories held since the Six Day War.' The United

States voted against this, but all the members of the EEC, including Britain, abstained on the resolution.

Golda comes to London

In October Wilson gained his second election victory that year, and the Labour Party was returned with a small working majority. Shortly after the disappointing British vote at the United Nations, Golda Meir came to London. It was her first private visit after a lifetime in office. Wilson welcomed her, in the true sense of the word, with open arms. When they met at a dinner of the Labour Friends of Israel, they fell into each other's arms. The morning after, the picture of the affectionate encounter adorned the front page of *The Times*. Photo interpreters were divided on the question of who tilted towards whom. But a few Arab ambassadors had no hesitation in branding Wilson's embrace of Israel's grand old lady as an unpardonable sin.

The following day Wilson hosted a luncheon in Golda's honour at Downing Street attended by thirty-eight guests, among them four cabinet ministers. The Prime Minister had obviously been impressed by the hard-hitting speech Golda had delivered the previous evening in his presence. She had denounced the UN appeasement policy which Britain had not opposed. Wilson dispensed with the customary after-dinner toasts and instead engaged his guests in a kind of panel discussion around the luncheon table. It turned into a tense but friendly dialogue between him and Golda. He wanted her to understand that his government would remain loyal to its friendship with Israel. Its policy would continue to be based exclusively on Resolutions 242 and 338 as interpreted by him in the past to Israel's satisfaction. Britain's vote at the UN was meant to bring France, the pro-Arab outsider, into the fold. His government would not recognize the PLO. These were difficult times for all of Israel's friends, but in five years Britain would be independent of Arab oil. He had taken care that its oil stocks were at record high to weather any new Middle East crisis and to avoid a repetition of the Yom Kippur panic, which had prompted the former government to take steps inimical to Israel and harmful to Britain's relations with the United States.

In her reply, Golda exhorted her Labour friends around the table to take the lead in the European Community by supporting Israel instead of endorsing the pro-Arab policy of France. It was Labour's proclaimed responsibility to refrain from policies harmful to Israel. This was the test now. A firm stand by the British government would bring Germany to its side. Wilson interjected a reservation. In matters of the Middle East, Bonn paid far greater attention to the French position than to that of Britain. Golda, undeterred, continued alternatively to pound and appeal. She had expected more from Wilson, a proven friend in the past, but she had not given up hope that after more reflection he would proceed in the right direction.

It was obvious that Golda had touched a sensitive nerve. Wilson did not keel over under Golda's punches, but they left their mark. He promised to reconsider Britain's stance in the EEC and its voting at the United Nations. He also thought that he could exert some influence in Moscow to moderate its anti-Israeli bias. The subject of Soviet policy had figured only marginally at the table talk. Perhaps the reason for Wilson's remark was an occurrence that had happened three months earlier.

The Panov reception

In the summer of 1974 the Soviet government, yielding to a sustained public campaign conducted in the West and with particular zest in Britain, permitted Valery and Galina Panov, celebrated members of the Kirov ballet in Leningrad, to leave for Israel. The day they had made known their desire to emigrate, they were dismissed from the company. Despite harassment and hardships suffered over a period of years, the Panovs had not wavered in their resolve. Valery's valiant struggle to go to Israel and the ardent encouragement he received from his non-Jewish wife, Galina, stirred the compassion of many leading artists and public figures in Britain. Wilson himself had intervened with the Soviet government on their behalf. The retention of the Panovs became an embarrassing *cause célèbre* to the Soviet government.

At the beginning of August the couple came to London to express their gratitude to the many friends who had fought for their release. We arranged a garden party at our residence so that they could meet them all. Harold Wilson had promised to attend; but after the appointed hour of his arrival had passed, the gathering of actors, dancers, ministers, parliamentarians and all the other good helpers in the cause showed signs of impatience. The drinks and snacks had been dispensed, there remained only the speeches. I delivered the prologue, thanking all to whom tribute was due for the role they had played in the Panov passion play, from the Prime Minister to Galina, the petite lady with the great heart. Lord Olivier followed. He spoke with emotion and great warmth. He admonished the couple not to fall for the blandishments of Western affluence. An artist must have roots. Israel was their new soil. Valery Panov answered, overflowing with emotion and gratitude to the legion of 'Free the Panovs' militants.

There was still no sign of the Prime Minister. Finally, his private secretary called. The PM had been detained by an overlong cabinet meeting and had asked him to present his greetings to the Panovs and regrets to me. He would like to see me that afternoon at Downing Street. Without preliminaries Wilson went straight to the point. He wanted me to know the real reason for his absence from the Panov party. The cabinet meeting *had* lasted longer than normal, but this had not been the decisive impediment. The day before, Callaghan had summoned the Soviet Ambassador to the Foreign Office in connection with the veto that the Soviet Union had cast in the Security Council on a resolution designed to calm the situation in Cyprus. Using the occasion, the Ambassador delivered a message from Brezhnev to Wilson in which he warned him that the Soviet Union would regard the Prime Minister's presence at the Panov reception as an unfriendly act. His attendance would be doubly resented after he had boycotted the London performances of the Bolshoi ballet.

Wilson was stunned by the sharpness of the message, but summoned the Ambassador the next morning, the day of the reception, to find out for himself the real reasons for this unusual warning. Ambassador Lunkov arrived with a long list of complaints, headed by the PM's intention to honour the Panovs with his presence at the Israeli embassy reception. This was adding insult to injury. Not only had the Royal Family and the government spurned the Bolshoi visit, but the authorities had refrained from interfering with the demonstrations against it. He was instructed to repeat his government's insistent request that the Prime Minister and other members of his cabinet should refrain from attending the Panov party. It still did not make sense to Wilson why a London welcome for two ballet dancers, who after all had been allowed to leave Russia, was an exciting enough event to prompt the Soviet government to go to such lengths. However, he reached the conclusion that a social occasion was not of such overriding importance that it was worth risking an estrangement with the Soviet leadership. His relationship with them was valuable not only to Britain, but also to Israel; it afforded him the opportunity to intervene on behalf of Soviet Jews. But, of course, he could not submit to Soviet bullying. The attendance at the reception of three of his cabinet colleagues was proof of that. He was grateful for the warm tribute I had paid to him in my speech and would greatly appreciate my understanding of his predicament. What was my explanation for the Soviet intervention, he wanted to know.

I was inclined to quote the French proverb, *'les absents ont toujours tort'*, but felt it was inappropriate to add to his visible embarrassment. Instead I thanked him for his frankness and ventured the view that Moscow might have turned the Panov affair into a major grievance to silence criticism of some mischief it had committed. Be that as it may, ballet had always been a favourite Soviet addiction. Years ago, I remembered, when the Soviet Union had been accused of aggressive intentions in a fierce UN debate, Andrei Vyshinsky blurted out: 'We do not need the Red Army to conquer the world, we will sweep it with a white cloud of dancing ballerinas.' The two Panovs had deserted from the white army.

London, Washington, Moscow – and Jerusalem

His government secured in parliament after the favourable outcome of the October elections, Wilson arranged his visits to Washington and Moscow to take place in February 1975. Gerald Ford had succeeded Nixon for the remaining two years of the administration. There was little more than a year left for the new President to take an active interest in foreign affairs before the domestic issues of the election year would engage his principal attention.

Wilson was well aware that Britain had little freedom of manoeuvre between Washington and Moscow. Still, he would try to make the best use of the narrow space that remained. Israel's position in the United States in those years was influential. The policy it pursued in the Middle East conflict was not without consequences for the fortunes of the Western world, and Wilson's concern for the well-being and security of Israel was a factor which motivated him to maintain a continual dialogue with representatives of Israel. He would meet us before and after his meetings with foreign leaders and seek out our views on Israel's concerns and its assessment of the Middle East situation. Above all he wanted to be well briefed before he heard the other side. Whenever possible he would ask Allon to come to London for such consultations. The pattern was for them to spend the first hour or two in a secluded session which Wilson called 'Allon alone', and then ask me to join them. Occasionally the Foreign Secretary would be present.

In the middle of January 1975 Wilson invited us to Chequers. He told us how he had surprised Giscard d'Estaing at the last EEC summit in Paris by his sharp dissent from the biased position which France tried to impose on the Community as a whole. Britain favoured the harmonization of the views of its members on international questions, but not the unification of their decisions based on a denominator contrary to its fundamental policy principles. The last vote in the United Nations on a resolution which was harmful to Israel and to the peace efforts was a case in point. In future Britain would cast its vote in accordance with the merits of the case and not with the preferences of France. The Prime Ministers of Holland and Denmark mildly supported him, but Helmut Schmidt was surprisingly critical of Israel. The Germans still adhered to their Hegelian *weltanschauung*, explained Wilson. The Chancellor conducted his policy like a streetcar, always straight on the rails from its departure at the depot to its arrival at the terminal. It had the right of way and whoever carelessly crossed the rails risked being run over. Wilson knew that Golda had had a rather rough talk with Schmidt at their recent meeting in London. He had accused her of intransigence and she had resented his callousness. 'I wouldn't have liked to be passenger', gibed Wilson, 'when those two streetcars collided.'

Then the conversation turned to the principal subjects: the Middle East, the United States and the Soviet Union. Wilson probed into the prospects of an additional partial agreement between Israel and Egypt. At a recent stopover in London Kissinger had predicted a new blow-up in the Middle East in 1975, unless the parties made visible progress in their negotiations. What was Allon's estimate, the Prime Minister wanted to know. We were seated in front of the open fire in the long gallery, a restful place for reflections on war and peace. Allon analysed the Egyptian and Israeli positions. The main difficulty was that Israel linked the next step of withdrawal to the termination of belligerence, and Egypt to an Israeli undertaking on the eventual complete evacuation of Sinai. Still there was sufficient room for mutual accommodation, but the next round of the negotiations would be protracted and required all of Kissinger's skills.

Wilson asked whether there was still a danger of a new war. Allon explained that he could not dismiss it. He probed how Britain would act in case of war. Would Wilson's government assist Israel or would they repeat the grievous error of the former government by denying facilities to the United States in England for the purpose of rushing military aid to Israel?

The Prime Minister did not answer directly. It was obvious he could not. This was a matter of such gravity that he had to discuss it first with his colleagues and then with the President of the United States. When he returned from his visit to Washington, he gave me his reply. It was not disappointing.

Wilson asked whether we had any specific requests for him to take up in Moscow. Allon mentioned three: expression of British concern for the situation of Soviet Jewry; assistance in the restoration of diplomatic relations; and the obtaining of Soviet consent for Jewish immigrants to fly directly to Israel. On the first point Wilson replied that, true to his previous practice, he could not commit himself to making public statements. If the circumstances permitted he would express his concern in private to the Soviet leaders. He thought he could act more effectively on behalf of individual cases, and requested to be furnished with a list of names of people for whom he should intercede.

Allon also had Africa on his list of requests. The Foreign Minister was anxious to rebuild Israel's relationship with a number of African countries, which had severed their ties with it. As a first step he would like to meet two of their eminent leaders: Kaunda, the President of Zambia, and General Gowon, the head of the government of Nigeria. The idea intrigued Wilson. He was ready to help. Perhaps the best way would be for Allon to make a tour of the Caribbean and to arrive in Jamaica when the Commonwealth conference met there in the spring. There, Wilson thought, he could perhaps arrange the meetings. The Foreign Office, however, did not favour such imaginative improvisations.

Yet Wilson was more enterprising. At the beginning of June he invited my wife and me to a private party at Downing Street, to watch the annual parade of Beating the Retreat at the Horse Guards' grounds. The guest of honour was General Gowon. Wilson introduced me to him. I had met him before in Israel when he visited the country as a member of the African Presidents' mediation mission. He politely inquired about his Israeli friends and regretted the unfortunate complications in the relations of our two countries. I told him insofar as the government of Israel was concerned, it would gladly help disentangle them. Would it not be useful, I asked, to restore the dialogue between the two governments which had proved itself so fruitful in the past? In fact nothing would please our Foreign Minister more than to have the honour of meeting the President and discussing with him matters of mutual concern. At this point General Gowon motioned the Nigerian High Commissioner to join us. He informed him of my suggestion and advised him to keep in touch with me, so that he could transmit the President's reply. The Prime Minister, who had watched our animated conversation from the side-lines, asked whether he could butt in. He only wanted to make sure that his guests had enjoyed a friendly chat. If it would not be seen as an interference into the affairs of two sovereign states, said Wilson with a knowing twinkle, he would wish to second the proposal of the Ambassador of Israel. Then he led us to watch the military display. It was General Gowon's last parade. While still in London, enjoying the honours bestowed on him, he was overthrown. He remained in England, his High Commissioner departed and the prospect of the ministerial meeting vanished.

Shortly after the Prime Minister's return from Washington we met in Leeds, where we were both to speak at a dinner organized by the Labour Friends of Israel. Before the beginning of the function he gave me a briefing on his talks in Washington. Ford had spoken warmly of Israel and his long-standing support of it in Congress. But the President and Kissinger emphasized that they would not let 1975 pass without a major effort to achieve an additional Arab-Israeli agreement. Stagnation in the Middle East was dangerous. The United States would vigorously proceed with its step-by-step policy. It opposed the early reconvening of the Geneva conference, which did nothing but serve Soviet interests. Sadat favoured the American approach. Wilson assured the President that he subscribed to this policy and both governments agreed to co-ordinate their policy in the Middle East. Kissinger had not failed to refer to the rift between the two countries during the Yom Kippur War caused by the former British Prime Minister's refusal to co-operate with Washington in a situation of emergency. Wilson indicated that there would be no recurrence of such deep misunderstanding in a future crisis.

Wilson was soon to leave for Moscow. I gave him the names of people for whom we asked him to intervene there. Wilson confirmed his willingness, but added something to the effect that the Jackson amendment of linking American credits for the Soviet Union to a Russian undertaking to permit substantial emigration to Israel and elsewhere, had materially complicated matters. He mumbled, if I understood him correctly, that he wanted to explore in Moscow a way out of this dilemma. I had already noticed the habit the Prime Minister had of lapsing into his Yorkshire drawl and addressing his pipe rather than his interlocutor when he was not particularly keen on making himself comprehensible. In cases where I thought elucidation was essential I would ask him to repeat his words. He would oblige if it was a mere matter of acoustics, and ignore the request if he thought the smoke-screen was more convenient. His comment on the Jackson amendment went up in smoke.

The result of his visit to Moscow gave an indication of what his casual remark could have meant. The Soviet Union concluded with Britain a wide-ranging trade agreement under which HMG opened to the Soviet Union a credit line of about £1 billion sterling for the financing of its purchases in Britain. Such credits were unavailable to the Soviet Union in the United States because of the Jackson amendment. Trade and human rights were, in the opinion of the British government, two separate categories. Linking one to the other was detrimental to both, or so they believed.

After his return from Moscow Wilson invited me to inform our government of the outcome of his talks on the subjects of interest to Israel. Callaghan also participated in the meeting, as well as Zvi Kedar, the minister at the embassy. The Middle East had not been the central theme of the Moscow conference. The Soviets were carefully avoiding harsh differences with their guests. They insisted on the immediate reconvening of the Geneva conference, but in the official communiqué compromised on the British wording of 'very soon'.

Such hair-splitting, irrelevant as it appears to the outsider – and indeed it is irrelevant – is the daily bread of diplomatic negotiators. They can spend days, if not weeks, on such haggling exercises although well aware that an 'immediate reconvening' is no more realistic than a meeting convened 'very soon'.

I asked how they had dealt with the problems of Soviet Jews and Soviet-Israeli relations. Not directly and not officially, replied Wilson. He had mentioned privately a certain name to Kosygin, who assured him that he would try his best for the person. Hadn't he proved in the past, said the Soviet Premier, that he could be relied on in these things more than any of his colleagues? Nonetheless, on the occasion of a meeting with Gromyko, one of the British officials casually submitted our full list. Gromyko put it into a file, commenting with a wry smile that he hadn't seen or heard anything. Hardly hiding my disappointment I asked how and when they expected to hear from him. Wilson replied that he had learned from experience that it was hard to predict the Soviet reaction in these matters. Sometimes after a long period of silence, a positive reply would arrive unexpectedly. I continued my probing. Had the question of emigration been touched upon in their discussion on the human rights part of the Helsinki draft declaration? Wilson replied that he had intended to discuss the whole Israeli and Jewish question with Brezhnev alone but, when they met, the Soviet leader steered away from the subject. Moreover, Kosygin had clearly expressed the Soviet resentment at Senator Jackson's mixture of trade with politics. The British delegation gained the impression that this was one of the reasons the Soviet Union was interested in strengthening its commercial ties with Britain. The results of Wilson's talks in Moscow were undoubtedly tangible for Britain, but meagre for Israel. I thanked the Prime Minister for his goodwill and frankness. This ended the first Wilson round on the London-Washington-Moscow circuit.

At the end of the meeting Callaghan asked us to advise our government to put its faith in Kissinger. He was Israel's best hope, at least for the next eighteen months until the presidential elections. A few days later Henry Kissinger passed through London on his way to Cardiff where he received, together with Callaghan, the freedom of the city. From there the Secretary of State proceeded to the Middle East where he encountered unexpected trouble.

The Kissinger shuttle grounded

The day Dr Kissinger enjoyed the hospitality of the Welsh capital, a PLO commando raided a beach-side hotel in Tel Aviv, killed a number of its occupants and seized the others as hostages. Jerusalem instructed me to ask Kissinger to publish a strongly worded condemnation not only of the act as such, but of its PLO perpetrators. In the absence of the Secretary from London, I met with Sisco. He promised to contact him, but hoped that the terrorist action would not bring about a change in Israel's readiness to pursue the negotiations on a new agreement with Egypt. Arafat's very purpose in mounting such terrorist operations was to sabotage the negotiations.

Later that evening Sisco reported that he had reached the Secretary somewhere between Cardiff and London. He would consider making an appropriate statement to the press the next morning before his departure. But while Kissinger was considering, Israeli security forces were acting. That same evening they overpowered the terrorists and freed the hostages.

At the end of March 1975 the Secretary of State landed again at London airport. He was on his way from Jerusalem to Washington at the end of a desperate shuttle between Egypt and Israel. Callaghan met him at Heathrow. If the steam which the frustrated Secretary of State let off could have propelled his plane, it could have circled the globe without a single drop of jet-fuel. It was all Israel's fault that his mission had failed, he exclaimed. Its leadership was narrow-minded and divided. Instead of seeing the new horizons he was opening up, they looked backwards to make sure their political rear was covered. He would have never gone to the Middle East at this crucial juncture were it not for the explicit undertaking he had received from Allon in Washington that Israel was ready to compromise. But in Jerusalem he had met the intransigence of Rabin and Peres. Sadat had been ready for a deal, but Rabin would not yield the five-odd miles in the area of the Sinai passes necessary to conclude the transaction. The United States would, for the time being, refrain from any further initiative; it would let the two sides stew in their own juice. After Kissinger had vented his anger and his plane had been refuelled, he took off for Washington's clouded skies. Not only had his Middle East mission run aground, but his South-East Asian peace plan had capsized. He failed to recognize the causal connection between the two events.

Callaghan, perturbed by Kissinger's fulminations, reported immediately to the Prime Minister. Wilson called me in to hear our side of the story. Before I obtained the information from Jerusalem, the Foreign Office had already received a detailed report from Washington. After Wilson had studied both versions he expressed his perplexity at their striking divergence on a number of essential points. He felt that Israel's credibility and good faith were in jeopardy. It could imperil its vital interests in the United States and alienate its friends in Britain. He thought it was imperative for Allon to come to London to clarify the situation and he should bring all the relevant documents with him. He and Callaghan would compare notes with us. From Allon's reply I gathered that he was not too happy at the summons. After some more urging from Wilson the meeting was set for 14 April.

For reasons of informality Wilson invited us to his private home in Lord North Street. Callaghan and Allon arrived with bulky files looking like court-room lawyers, but in the course of the proceedings neither of them even consulted his collection of documents. Wilson opened by pointing out the existing crisis of confidence. Allon delivered a vivid account of every phase of the recent Kissinger round. There had been considerable give on Israel's part in the advanced stages of the negotiations and, while the Secretary was still waiting in Jerusalem for Sadat's reply on Israel's latest compromise proposals, Cairo abruptly broke off the negotiations. Instead of returning to Egypt for another try, Kissinger left for Washington in a black mood of despondency and foreboding. Pressure would be exerted on Israel, he predicted, to force it back to the 1967 borders, a dilemma he had tried to forestall. It was a tragedy to see a government doom its people to a future fraught with unthinkable danger.

Wilson, seemingly impressed by Allon's spirited defence, ventured the opinion that Kissinger's dejection had perhaps been caused by the accumulation of recent American set-backs in Indo-China, Turkey and Portugal. Israel should spare no effort to encourage Kissinger to resume his mediation. The present mood in Washington was ugly towards Israel. What the President had called a reappraisal of US policy meant in reality a suspension of economic and military aid to Israel, until it readjusted its own policy to the needs of the United States in the Middle East.

But Callaghan was more reserved about accepting Allon's explanations. He had been given three versions, he said, of the failure of the recent negotiations: an Israeli, an Egyptian and an American. On some points they coincided but on others they diverged widely. He was dealing with realities and not with research. It was clear that the American version appealed to him as the most acceptable. Israel was in a tight corner not only in America, but also in Europe. Allon reiterated Israel's willingness to reach an agreement with Egypt. He was ready to leave a memo with Callaghan in which he would unequivocally reaffirm this. The Foreign Secretary seized the offer with alacrity. He would use it to uplift Kissinger's morose mood, to answer the criticism of his European partners, and to reassure Sadat of Israel's positive intent.

Wilson seemed satisfied. It was clear that he had been interested more in what was going to happen than in a disputation on what had occurred. The same afternoon we dispatched to Callaghan an innocuous *aide-mémoire*. It reaffirmed the government's willingness to reach either an interim or a comprehensive agreement; it hoped that Egypt would be more forthcoming; and it invited the United States to continue its mediation effort after a period of calm counsel and mutual reflection. The same evening Callaghan transmitted a copy of our paper to his German colleague, Genscher, who was scheduled to leave for Cairo the next morning.

The breakdown of Kissinger's spring shuttle was not the result of one traceable defect. The failure was more a matter of adverse atmospherics than of bad strategy. In Israel the feeling had gained ground that Kissinger was pushing a feebly resisting government too far. Rabin apparently felt that a resounding 'No' could not only strengthen his domestic posture, which indeed it did, but also his government's negotiating stance, which it did not. Yet what influenced Israel and Egypt most in their decision to stall was the American *débâcle* in South-East Asia. Less than two years had passed since the Americans had guaranteed peace in Indo-China, when it caved in under the blows of the North Vietnamese and the Khmer Rouge armies, burying under its debris the freedom of the Republic of Vietnam and the Kingdom of Cambodia.

The disaster struck while the Secretary of State was assiduously travelling between Cairo and Jerusalem, trying to convince the two governments of the credibility and durability of American commitments. The agreement stood and fell with their faith in the reliability of bilateral American undertakings. Why should Washington, which had not lifted a finger in defence of a solemn international peace treaty, be relied upon in the observance of its obligations under a local interim agreement? Psychologically the question seemed justified, although internationally the realities were different. Kissinger could have avoided the crisis in the Israeli-Egyptian negotiations had he himself suggested suspending them for further consultation, honestly admitting that his presence in Washington was indispensable in view of the events in Indo-China. But the worse things became in the Far East, the harder he tried to succeed in the Middle East.

In the course of May, Wilson met Ford and Kissinger twice, first in Washington and later in Brussels. His American friends made a special effort to impress him with their determination to impose an overall peace settlement in the Middle East. The President indicated that under the present circumstances the United States could not underwrite the inviolability of Israel's frontiers. Kissinger assumed correctly that Wilson would convey the warning to his Israeli friends. And indeed he did, adding his personal emphasis. He foresaw the danger of a frontal clash between the United States and Israel, which would leave Israel not only totally isolated in the world but perhaps even prostrate. Wilson thought that he should warn Rabin personally. He met him at London airport as Rabin was on his way to Washington in mid-June. When Rabin stopped over again on his way back to Jerusalem a few days later, he assured Callaghan that nothing that Wilson had feared had occurred.

There were a number of reasons for Washington's changed attitude. Ford had met Sadat in Salzburg at the beginning of the month. The Egyptian President had confirmed his continued interest in an interim agreement, though he had not budged essentially from the terms which had frustrated Kissinger's mission in March. Yet Israel had begun to yield gradually on the two essential points on which Sadat had remained adamant: the nearly complete withdrawal from the Sinai passes and his refusal to terminate formally the state of belligerency. Moreover the reopening of the Suez Canal on 5 June, before the conclusion of a new agreement, was seen in Washington and London as an indication of Sadat's positive intentions. In Israel's favour there was the growing congressional dissatisfaction with the administration's pressure tactics. A letter sent by seventy-six senators to the President urged him 'to be responsive to Israel's military and economic needs'.

The agreement was signed on 1 September, the day that Nazi Germany had started the Second World War thirty-six years before. It was an ominous date for an auspicious event. In an article I wrote for the *Daily Telegraph* called 'September the first, the day the war ended' I dwelt on the coincidence of the events: 'The new Israeli-Egyptian agreement was initialled on a date of sombre memories. Seeds of hope are implanted in it which may usher in a new era in the fortunes of the Middle East, portending the end of the old rancours and the beginning of new understandings.'

Earlier in the summer at one of Lord Weidenfeld's parties, famous for their relaxed conviviality, stimulating company and informed conversation, I met Helmut Sonnenfeldt, Dr Kissinger's assistant for European affairs. Inevitably, we spoke about Henry's grounded peace shuttle. What would I suggest to get it airborne again? asked Sonnenfeldt. The needless clamour still ringing in my ears after Kissinger had aborted his mission in March, I suggested a formula for more unostentatious diplomacy: 'Motion but no commotion; prodding but no pressure; progress but no precipitation.'

The equanimity with which the Soviet government had watched the progress of the negotiations in 1975 was surprising. The Helsinki summit had replaced the Middle East on the list of Soviet priorities. Both Moscow and Washington timed their moves, without openly synchronizing them, to a time-table fitting their own principal priorities: the Helsinki summit declaration early in August and the Egyptian-Israel interim agreement one month later.

The repercussions of the Israeli-Egyptian accord

At the Helsinki conference the Soviet Union attained its principal goal: the recognition and legitimization of its new post-war borders in Europe. They were the result of the pre-war Stalin-Hitler accords which partitioned Poland and conceded the Baltic states to Russia, and of the territorial conquests made by the Soviet armies when they defeated Nazi Germany. In the Middle East, however, the Soviet Union posed as the champion of the ambiguous principle of the non-acquisition of territories by war. In Europe détente served it as an instrument to consolidate its territorial gains; and in the Middle East tension was its means of supporting Arab territorial claims.

Together with Syria, the PLO and other extremists in the Arab camp, the Soviet Union assailed the Israeli-Egyptian agreement. It selected Libya as its central base in North Africa, Syria as its strong arm in the Middle East and the PLO as its chief agent of violence and subversion. The Lebanon became the theatre of a new war by proxy.

The three-pronged Arab strategy was simple and therefore powerful: it aspired to Israel's isolation, defamation and eventual elimination. Israel was first to be separated from its friends in the world, an operation which Sadat had initiated with considerable success. The campaign of defamation reached its climax in the United Nations resolution of 10 November 1975 which branded Zionism as a form of racism. The resolution was strongly contested by Israel's friends in the West, among them Britain which vigorously opposed it. Patrick Moynihan, the American Ambassador to the United Nations, proclaimed: 'The United States does not acknowledge, it will not abide by, it will never acquiesce in this infamous act.' The adoption of the resolution came as a terrible shock to Jews everywhere. It electrified them and they closed ranks in self-defence.

British Jewry excelled in its vigorous and dignified reaction to the challenge. It formed an all-embracing solidarity movement. Twice during my term in office, the heads of all the Jewish organizations and leading Jewish personalities from all walks of life participated in an emergency meeting at the embassy. The first time they met in protest against Yassir Arafat's appearance at the United Nations. Now they came together to seek counsel as to how to stem the new offensive against Judaism. The gathering distinguished itself not only by the eminence of its participants but also by their resolve to stand together in joint action.

Two weeks later the Albert Hall overflowed with an excited crowd which was addressed by Golda Meir. Visibly enjoying the tumultuous applause which greeted her, she dryly opened her speech: 'Had the architects of this huge hall been able to foresee the enormity of infamy the United Nations were capable of committing, they would have built a hall twice as large to hold the multitudes of protesters!' The defamation campaign backfired on its instigators. It scandalized enlightened public opinion, induced democratic governments to express their repugnance and evoked sympathy for Israel.

Although under the September agreement Egypt had undertaken to moderate its anti-Israeli propaganda, it did not dissociate itself from the UN drum-beating in November. Sadat was cautious about moving away from his old comrades-in-arms towards his new Western friends. Shortly after the conclusion of the agreement, he made his first presidential visit to Washington. His aim was to enlist goodwill, the prerequisite for political support and economic and military aid. He did not fare badly in his first attempt to gain public attention, congressional understanding and presidential support. He succeeded in breaching the unwritten ban maintained by all American administrations on arms deliveries to Egypt. President Ford informed Congress of his intention to permit the sale of six Hercules transport planes to Egypt. In less than four years Sadat accomplished a complete breakthrough. At the military parade held in Cairo in 1979 to celebrate the October war, American F-4 phantom fighters piloted by Egyptians soared in the skies of Egypt for the first time.

On his way home from Washington, Sadat paid an official visit to London. Press stories of planned multi-billion dollar Egyptian arms purchases preceded his arrival. Jerusalem got excited. The Foreign Minister sent a strongly worded reminder to his British colleague of previous promises to refrain from substantive arms sales to Egypt. Sadat succeeded in gaining more sympathy in London than in Washington. His progress from Buckingham Palace to Fleet Street via Downing Street was warmly acclaimed. His public appearances were well staged. His pensive silences between puffs on his pipe and his studied hesitancy of speech conveyed to his British television audience the comfortable image of a statesman of moderation.

Wilson was obviously impressed with Sadat's personality. When he briefed me on the talks, he praised Sadat's desire for peace and his great intelligence. Sadat claimed that the principal aim of his policy was to free Egypt from Soviet tutelage. For this he was in need of Western technology and the diversification of his sources of arms supplies. The naval equipment he had bought from the Soviet Union ten years before was already antiquated. The Soviets had, however, recently transferred modern naval craft to Libya. Mig 23s which they had withdrawn from Egypt were now stationed there.

On Israeli-Arab issues Sadat had spoken with restraint. Though making a point for another Israeli-Syrian interim agreement, he sounded more as if he were making the plea on Kissinger's than on Assad's behalf. On the PLO his discussion was likewise low-key. A Jordan-type solution would afford the best settlement of the Palestinian question. He was highly critical of the outside intervention in the affairs of Lebanon. Egypt and Saudi Arabia were trying to counteract these influences.

Wilson asked me to inform the Israeli Prime Minister that the British government had not entered into any new commitments or signed any new contracts for the supply of armaments to Egypt. He would not deny that strong commercial and political pressures were exerted from inside and outside the government, but any British decision in this field was co-ordinated in all its details with Washington. Kissinger had strongly advised HMG to assist Egypt in its endeavour to free itself from its dependence on Soviet arms. Britain would be guided in its decision by three considerations: promoting the joint Anglo-American objective of assisting Sadat in the diversification of his sources of supply; maintaining the balance of armaments in the Middle East while mindful of Israel's security and the prospects of peace; and strengthening the group of moderate Arab states which included Egypt, Saudi Arabia and Kuwait.

I asked him to issue a statement on Britain's policy on arms supplies in order to dispel the rumours of imminent massive sales to Egypt. He agreed to reply to a question on the subject in the House of Commons. Meanwhile, he authorized me to state that the Prime Minister had assured the Israeli government that Britain had not entered into any new commitments and contracts on arms sales. I published the statement the same evening. It was received with some relief and cautious satisfaction in Jerusalem.

Courting Europe

Allon recognized the damage caused to Israel by the erosion of its European relations. He devoted considerable personal efforts to stemming the tide. Unlike Prime Minister Rabin, who since the Yom Kippur War had written off Europe as a significant factor in world affairs, Allon realized that Israel's position in Europe had a direct bearing on its economic and political fortunes. Repeatedly Washington had pointed to the lack of European support for Israel as a handicap to the United States in granting its own.

The strengthening of Israel's relations with the European community as a whole, and the normalization of relations with European countries which as yet had refrained from establishing diplomatic ties with it, became a major objective of Israel's foreign policy in the post-Yom Kippur War period. In the course of 1975 it could register noteworthy successes in both areas. In May Allon signed in Brussels Israel's first global agreement with the EEC, as part of a comprehensive Mediterranean accord. It was the first agreement the Community had signed in this context with a non-member Mediterranean country. Arab objection, which had held up the conclusion of the agreement for more than three years, soon gave way to their willingness to sign similar accords.

In the field of bilateral relations our targets were: Spain, which had never recognized Israel nor established any form of relationship with it; Portugal, which maintained consular relations but hesitated to elevate them to the embassy level; and Ireland, which had recognized Israel *de jure*, but had shied at establishing diplomatic relations. The efforts with Spain, before and after Franco's demise, were fruitless. The new democratic regime in Portugal agreed to the opening of embassies on the basis of reciprocity. But it went only half of the way. It welcomed the Israeli Ambassador in Lisbon, but refrained from sending its own envoy.

The setting up of the Irish connection was more successful. After Allon had done some straight talking with his Irish colleague when they met at the United Nations in autumn 1974, I visited Dublin for the follow-up. In December the Irish Ambassador in London exchanged letters with me, formalizing the agreement to establish diplomatic relations at embassy level and 'to exchange ambassadors initially on a non-residential basis'. In March I presented my credentials to President O'Dalleigh. Undeterred by my Flemish fiasco at a similar occasion in Brussels two decades earlier, I opened the act with two sentences in Gaelic followed by a short speech in Hebrew. Having paid tribute to the two revived ancient tongues, I asked the President for permission to translate the Hebrew part into English. He declined politely, drawing from his pocket the text of his reply – in Hebrew. The solemnity of the occasion was shattered by the roar of our laughter. But for the sake of historical accuracy, it must be recorded that the President's Hebrew was by far more perfect than the Ambassador's Gaelic – though we both admitted that only after we had exchanged our written texts did we get an idea of what we had meant to say. The ceremony in Dublin and the parallel performance with a different cast in Jerusalem a few weeks later closed the ring of Israel's diplomatic relations with all the nine members of the European Economic Community.

The budding ties with Ireland grew in a climate of warmth and ambivalence, affinity and oddity. Both people had attained their independence in a struggle against British rule. This created common links and memories. Both countries had been partitioned: the Republic of Ireland refused to recognize the partition, Israel had accepted it, but the Arabs had rejected it. Which one was Northern Ireland and which was the Republic? – the question became even more confusing after the 1967 war, which extended Israel's control over the whole territory of former western Palestine. Israel was a secular Jewish state and Ireland a Catholic republic with strong clerical marking. Both had reinstated their native language, but in Ireland English remained the vernacular while in Israel Hebrew had become the common language. Both were interested in co-operation with developing countries, but while Ireland progressed in this area, Israel's relations declined. Trade between the countries was moderate, mainly Israeli citrus fruits for Irish meat, vitamin C for protein, a healthy barter but only of minor economic consequence. At the United Nations Ireland voted more often for the French pro-Arab ticket than with the more friendly group of EEC states to which Britain and the Netherlands belonged. But altogether there was more consent than dissent in our bilateral relations. In the spreading wilderness of Israel's diplomatic landscape, Ireland in any case was a welcome oasis. Even if its waters were not always calm, it was a pleasant place to visit.

Wilson's resignation

Wilson had planned an official visit to Israel early in 1976. Actually the date had been fixed for the end of January, but when Rabin received an invitation from President Ford coinciding with this date, he asked Wilson to postpone his journey. Wilson regretted this, but said he understood the presidential precedence. I tried to arrange another date but he was evasive. He had intended to make two trips to the Middle East at the beginning of 1976, one to Israel and Iran and the other to Egypt and Saudi Arabia. The rescheduling would make it necessary to change his programme, he observed opaquely.

I wondered at the reasons for his vagueness. Had he taken umbrage at the postponement? I did not gain that impression. On a number of occasions he had told us of his ambition to be the first British Prime Minister in office to pay an official visit to Israel. Our country had not been deprived of the pleasure of welcoming British Prime Ministers, but they had all come either before their appointment or after their resignation. Wilson liked to establish historical records – the youngest cabinet minister, the longest-serving Prime Minister of the century, the first British head of government to visit Israel. I consulted a close mutual friend, a wise and well-informed man. His reply was oracular. It was unfortunate, he said, that our Prime Minister had to defer the visit. The new date he had proposed, in September 1976, was shrouded in the mists of the future. If he were in my place, said my perspicacious friend, he would do everything possible to fix the date before the ides of March. Was there any Brutus hiding in the wings, I asked jokingly. My friend dismissed such a preposterous assumption. 'Mind you, Harold Wilson is not Julius Caesar.'

My recommendation to Jerusalem to reconsider the date of the visit remained unheeded. Having promised the oracle not to breathe a word of its prediction, my arguments for reconsideration were rather thin and unconvincing. On 8 March, I called on the Prime Minister at Downing Street. We were alone. Would he lift the veil? Of course it would be most inappropriate to ask him any direct question. He wanted to discuss the anticipated American moves after Rabin's recent visit to Washington. Did the administration give Israel explicit undertakings that it would not sell arms to Egypt, besides the six Hercules transports? I confirmed this in accordance with information we had received from Jerusalem. Would the United States persist in its exclusion of the PLO from the peace process? Again I confirmed that it would not change its position as long as the PLO refused to accept Resolution 242 with all that that implied for the recognition of Israel's rights to sovereignty and secure boundaries. Washington supported a Palestinian solution within the context of an Israeli-Jordanian peace treaty.

This was not the assessment, said Wilson, that Callaghan received from his associates in the Foreign Office. But the Foreign Secretary had recently rejected certain recommendations which he considered detrimental to Israel; a

Palestinian breeze was wafting from the monumental building across from No. 10. But Wilson wanted to assure me that Jim Callaghan viewed Israel's basic concerns with friendly understanding and tended to be helpful. He hastened to add that Denis Healey was also sympathetic to Israel. This sudden praise puzzled me. Not that I thought it was undeserved, but I wondered why Wilson wished to make the point at this particular moment. Were these the men standing in the wings, of course not wielding a dagger, but perhaps waiting for the Prime Minister's exit?

Wilson murmured something about the rumblings in the party. The dissent of the left-wing back-benchers irked him. There was a mood of unrest, he said. He would have to calm it, but he loathed the idea of turning against those with whom he had been politically associated in his earlier years. Interrupting his ruminations he said distinctly: 'I don't want to preside over a divided party.' Was this the cue? I felt that it was. I said, 'I hope you will not spring a surprise on your many good friends.' Wilson was startled for a short moment and then casually continued our conversation by turning to the Arab boycott and British arms sales. I should inform Jerusalem that nothing had changed since our last conversation on the subject. He brought up a few other matters which had been on the agenda of our recent talks. It strengthened my impression that he was clearing his desk.

When I returned to the embassy I cabled Allon 'eyes only' that from my talk with Wilson I gained the impression that he would soon announce his resignation, probably in the course of the coming week. This was the first time I had mentioned to Jerusalem the possibility of the Prime Minister's resignation. Bound by the pledge to my knowledgeable friend I chose to wait for a sign from the protagonist himself. The following weekend, Allon made one of his touch-downs in London on his transatlantic run. Between planes we drove out to Chequers. Wilson was in high spirits. His family had assembled to celebrate his sixtieth birthday. On our way back to the airport we mused upon Wilson's next move. He had not given the slightest indication of his intentions.

Three days later, on the morning of 16 March, a messenger from Downing Street brought a rather bulky envelope to the embassy. It contained two ties and a letter from the Prime Minister:

Dear Gideon,

In the rush of departure, I forgot my intention to present you both with a special tie. Roy Mason, our Defence Minister, designs ties for a hobby. Two or three months ago I asked him to design one with the Chequers crest which I proposed to give to all surviving ex-Prime Ministers who had used Chequers. In the event, I got about fifty ties.

So far the only recipients have been members of what *The Times* called 'the most distinguished club in Britain', members of the family, and one or two recent visitors.

I should be grateful if you would receive one, and send the other to Yigal Allon, together with a copy of this letter, so that he will know the background.

Yours Harold

I duly dispatched to Allon the tie, the background and a forecast on successors and their future policies.

Callaghan seemed to have the best chance of obtaining the party nomination. His Middle-Eastern policy would not deviate essentially from that of his predecessor. He would conduct it in close co-ordination with Kissinger, whom he held in high esteem. The press was rife with speculation about Wilson's resignation. He was the first Prime Minister in living British memory to step down in mid-term, undefeated either by Parliament, public hostility or ill-health. His own explanation did not go beyond his official statement. In the absence of personal revelation, public guessing flourished. There is always a tendency, stimulated by the media, to brighten the political darkness with flashes of illuminating insights. To attribute ordinary human motivations to public figures is not sufficiently exciting. The fact that a political leader can get tired, lose bounce or simply get fed up, lacks the drama expected from his performance while holding or leaving office.

The olympian calm of No. 10, pleasant as it was, seemed to me sometimes unreal. One evening Wilson asked me at short notice to see him as soon as I could get away from a dinner party I was attending. It was at the height of some serious trouble the British were having with Idi Amin. He had condemned Denis Hill, a British national, to death, but was ready to stay the execution on condition that the Prime Minister visited him in Uganda equipped with a petition for mercy from the Queen. Public opinion was agitated and the government was considering how to save Hill's life without bowing to the mad tyrant. Time was running out and decisions had to be taken. The Prime Minister kept me for nearly two hours. He did not refer to the emergency with a single word, nor did anyone intrude with a late item of crisis information. Two days later the Foreign Secretary went to Kampala and returned with Mr Hill. This showed that quiet efficiency was not a bad recipe for success. When Israel sent its commandos to Uganda a few months later, it proved that its own formula was no less salutary.

War in the Lebanon

Until the rescue mission at Entebbe sent Israel's popularity soaring it was steadily losing ground in the international arena. At the United Nations anti-Israeli resolutions were piling up; the press found fault with its lack of diplomatic dynamism; friendly governments criticized its alleged intransigence and its pungent anti-terrorist operations. Fervent advocates of the Arab cause cast aspersions on Israel's attitude towards the civil war in the Lebanon. An editorial in *The Times*, produced by its Arab expert Mr Edward Mortimer, out-classed in its malice even the outpourings of the professional Arab propaganda mills. In analysing the underlying reasons for the tragic events in the Lebanon the editorial concluded: 'And the Israelis are almost dying of laughter.'

Writing letters to *The Times*, a cherished British custom, was not my favourite pastime. I preferred to publish our views in the form of articles which a number of British and Irish national papers were kind enough to feature occasionally. Fully aware that it was easier to write leaders than to lead writers, I was under no illusion that a letter would have the slightest influence on the editorialist known for the courage of his prejudices. Still his insinuation could not be left without reply. Referring first to some of the basic misconceptions and erroneous perspectives of the author, I wrote:

Sir, the Israelis are not 'almost dying of laughter' in watching the Lebanese tragedy. When our people were dying in their millions to the hollow laughter of our tormentors, the outside world was deaf at the sound of horror. No, Sir, Israelis are not dying of laughter. They have been dying, men, women and children, at the hands of the same murderers causing the present untold suffering to the tormented Lebanese people. But what apparently is dying, too, is common decency, as so grievously revealed in the insidious affront of your editorial – and that is certainly no cause for laughter.

It was indeed a curious situation. Less than six months had passed since Israel had concluded the agreement with Egypt under which it withdrew its forces from a strategically important part of Sinai and returned the oilfields at Abu Rodeis, but the mass media sounded the hue and cry of Israel's uncompromising rigidity. The chanceries in the capitals of Europe, fearful of a diplomatic void and the aggravation of the civil war in the Lebanon, urged new initiatives. But the presidental elections had considerably reduced the momentum of Dr Kissinger's step-by-step progress.

The Soviet Union, a steadfast ally of Arafat, stepped up its arms deliveries to the PLO, reinforced its links with Iraq, armed Libya and gained a strategic foothold in the Red Sea area. Israel felt threatened by the intrusion of considerable Syrian forces into the Lebanon and their deployment in the vicinity of its northern border.

Late one evening in April 1976 I got a call to meet urgently that same night an eminent Arab personality at the house of a mutual friend. My nocturnal interlocutor was deeply concerned about the mounting tension in the area. It was in our mutual interest, he argued persuasively and with amiable sagacity, to keep the situation under control and contain the present fighting in the Lebanon. A few hours after this appeal my wife and I were on our way to Israel for a previously planned visit. Upon our arrival in Jerusalem I reported to the Prime Minister. Rabin appreciated the message. A few days later I returned to London with his reassuring answer, which I promptly dispatched to its destination where it was anxiously awaited. In conformity with my instructions I also informed privately Prime Minister Callaghan of Israel's response. He praised the wisdom of our government's position.

After Syria had delivered some punitive blows against the PLO formations in the Lebanon, it soon ceased fighting them. Riyadh had impressed

Damascus with its threat to suspend all financial aid to it. Shielded by the oil power of Saudi Arabia the PLO soon recovered and continued the war in the Lebanon and its terrorist attacks against Israel.

On stalemates and initiatives

Israel's envoys abroad were engaged in a running battle with the political detractors of the Jewish state. The Arab propaganda machine, lubricated with petrodollars and equipped with the well-orchestrated techniques of communist agitprop, working directly or through a network spreading from new-left to ultra-right organizations, was a formidable opponent.

It was in the nature of the electronic mass media that they were more interested in the spectacular staging of a discussion than the prosaic presentation of a case. Our repeated challenges to our Arab opponents to meet us in free and open debate had always been more attractive to television networks than to Arab governments. They maintained a strict ban on face-to-face discussions between their representatives and envoys of Israel.

The first to break the ban, anywhere, was the Egyptian Ambassador to the Court of St James's. General Sa'ad el Shazly, chief of staff of the Egyptian army at the beginning of the Yom Kippur War, relieved of his post by President Sadat in the course of the fighting and later tucked away in diplomatic exile in London, accepted with nonchalance a BBC invitation to appear with me on the same programme. He dismissed the warnings of his Arab colleagues and disdained Cairo's disapproval.

This *première*, which took place on 12 February 1975, attracted considerable attention. Opening my introductory remarks with an Arab proverb 'A greeting starts a conversation, and a conversation leads to understanding', I turned towards my Egyptian colleague with a friendly smile and the customary greeting in Arabic. General Shazly stared straight ahead, ignoring the presence of the moderator and his discussion partner. He presented the habitual arguments and I the usual replies. It was a dialogue cut into two monologues with the able moderator trying valiantly to establish a connecting link.

The only human emotion the General displayed was when Arafat, appearing on a filmed insert, claimed that the Palestinians were better educated than the Egyptians. Shazly shook his head in disbelief and raised his arms in a gesture of resignation at such offensive ignorance.

At the end of the performance, which was more an exercise in shadow boxing than a verbal duel, Ambassador Shazly withdrew without a word of greeting, let alone a handshake.

The press reviews were not too charitable with the General-turned-diplomat. One notice in particular apparently irked him: 'General Shazly', it said, 'had shown greater ability in crossing the Suez Canal than coming over the TV channel. He should have observed the elementary courtesy of responding to the friendly greeting of the Israeli Ambassador.' Shazly relieved his anger in a lengthy letter to *The Times*, ending with an appeal to the readers: 'After having had a chance to explain my behaviour I should like to hear your opinion. Now the verdict is yours. Please send me your opinion whether with [sic] or against, and if against please give reasons. Long live justice and the democratic way of dialogue between democratic people.' The verdict the editor passed in his wisdom was to stay any further proceedings.

The Egyptian Foreign Ministry felt that Lisbon was a more adequate place than London for the display of Ambassador Shazly's diplomatic talents. His TV debut became his swan song, but not his last word. Three years later he fiercely attacked President Sadat's peace initiative and was dismissed from his post. He joined the ranks of Colonel Qaddafi with the proclaimed aim of overthrowing the Egyptian government. Time will tell whether the general will fare better as a rebel than as a diplomat.

Whenever I found a suitable occasion I would use it to expound Israel's basic policies. But what the media wanted was a bill of particulars. An invitation by the Diplomatic and Commonwealth Writers' Association to address their monthly luncheon on 13 May 1976 provided me with a suitable forum to summarize Israel's position in the form of an eight-point peace plan: the termination of the state of war and actions emanating from it; the explicit recognition of the sovereignty, territorial integrity and political independence of the contracting parties; withdrawal of forces to secure and recognized boundaries; special arrangements to ensure mutual security; freedom of navigation in international waterways; mutual obligations to settle the refugee problems; balanced reduction of armaments, aimed at the cessation of the uncontrolled arms race in the Middle East; the establishment of a peace fund, to which Israel and the Arab states would contribute a sizeable percentage of the funds they had been allocating for armaments. The fund would finance projects for the settlement of refugees, the accelerated improvement of the standard of living, and scientific and technological co-operation for the advance of the whole area.

News agencies reporting the speech presented it as a new Israeli peace plan. Saul Bellow commented on it in his book *To Jerusalem and Back*: 'These latest proposals by the Israeli Ambassador in London will probably be ignored by the Arabs, but they indicate that Israel has not become immobile, inflexible, paralysed by the stubbornness of political rivals, or lacking in leadership.' It encouraged me to believe that our initiative had at least fulfilled one purpose: it had helped mitigate the widespread criticism of Israeli intransigence.

A presidential visit

In June, Professor Ephraim Katzir and his wife came to London. It was the first visit to Britain by an incumbent President of Israel. Although it was not a state visit, Her Majesty's Government went out of their way to receive the

President with special courtesy and great warmth. President Katzir had come to London to honour Sir Ernest Chain on the occasion of his seventieth birthday. The famous scientist, a Nobel prize-winner for his contribution to the discovery of penicillin, was closely associated with the Weizmann Institute of Science, home base of Professor Katzir, himself a biochemist of international repute.

It was a week of pleasant festivities code-named by us at the embassy 'Operation TIOBE' – 'The Importance of Being Earnest'. The atmosphere of a *première* enveloped the visit. For the first time a British sovereign held a luncheon in honour of the head of the Jewish state. The atmosphere at Windsor Castle was relaxed. The Queen was, as always, well briefed. At the table she engaged the President to her right in lively conversation on the state of scientific research in Israel and the ambassador to her left on the state of affairs in the Middle East. Prince Philip across the table added his succinct comments, which are precluded by royal privilege from being recorded for posterity.

Prime Minister Callaghan's luncheon at Downing Street was another pleasant affair. After a few sentences he discarded the text of his prepared speech, remarking with a broad smile that it was not his favoured vintage. Then he continued without notes. Known to most of his guests as a down-to-earth politician, he surprised them by the almost emotional expression of his personal commitment to Israel. Its security and well-being, he said, were a tenet of his political faith, shared by his government and party. Scientists like the President might in the long run make a greater contribution to the peaceful development of the Middle East than the statesmen looking for momentary solutions.

Noting that Professor Sir Ernest Chain was the reason for President Katzir's visit, the Prime Minister stressed that the British people should always appreciate and never forget the formidable contribution Jewish immigrants had made to the scientific, economic and intellectual progress of Britain. Men and women who had grown up in Whitechapel were today outstanding parliamentarians and members of the government or presided over prestigious universities. They could well be the precursors of immigrants from Asia, today populating London's East End. Nothing was more debilitating to a free society than racial prejudice. The audience, ranging from the Foreign Secretary to the captain of a leading soccer team and from the Chief Rabbi to the government's chief scientist, applauded the Prime Minister warmly.

The Jewish community was elated by the President's presence in their midst and immensely proud at the honours conferred on him by the Queen, government and academic community. It fêted the presidential couple at banquets and in synagogues. The President radiated warmth and good humour even when he had to make long marches on the sabbath from his hotel in Mayfair to the synagogue in St. John's Wood, escorted by a phalanx of security men. The President reciprocated the hospitality at a dinner held at the embassy residence. We invited primarily the leaders of the community in order to pay tribute to them for the splendid reception they had afforded to the Katzirs. We dispensed with the tiresome after-dinner speeches in favour of a more pleasurable entertainment.

Pinchas Zukerman, the brilliant young Israeli violinist, and his radiant wife, an accomplished flautist, were to play for our guests. My wife and I had heard Pinki, as he was known to his friends, for the first time when he was a boy of ten. We had arranged for him to be auditioned by Elisabeth, the Queen Mother of Belgium on the occasion of her visit to Israel. She was the patron of the Queen Elisabeth musical competition, a music lover *par excellence* and an enthusiastic violin-player. She was enchanted by Pinki's performance and predicted that with his talent he could become one of the outstanding violinists of our times. Playing for the President and his guests that evening, Pinchas Zukerman proved that he had lived up to the Queen's expectations.

The joy of Entebbe

Three weeks after this enjoyable musical *soirée* the Zukermans visited us again – this time on the spur of a very special moment. They just couldn't be alone on such a night, exclaimed Pinki, they had to celebrate the rescue at Entebbe with us. On 4 July 1976 the United States celebrated the 200th anniversary of its independence and Israel the deliverance of its hostages from the clutches of Idi Amin. It had been a week of almost unbearable tension until the newsflash arrived at the embassy at 4 a.m. that day informing us that the freed hostages were on their way home.

The day Idi Amin's first ultimatum was due to expire, the High Commissioner of Mauritius asked to see me at the embassy most urgently. I hoped he might be the bearer of good news; the President of his country had been designated to take over the chairmanship of the Organization of African States (the OAS) from Idi Amin at the beginning of the coming week. But as soon as the High Commissioner stepped into my office I perceived from his embarrassed mien that he was a messenger of bad tidings. He announced that his government had decided to suspend its diplomatic relations with Israel. This step was inevitable, he said, in view of the forthcoming meeting of the OAS in his country under the chairmanship of his President. He hoped that the Israeli government would understand the predicament of the Republic of Mauritius. I assured him it would not, got up, accompanied him to the door and said that the message was a disgrace. Its delivery on the very day the mad president of the OAS threatened to execute nearly 200 of our people was a painful provocation.

Then, brimming with wrath and anxiety, I went to a luncheon with the editorial board of the *New Statesman*. The editor, Tony Howard, was friendly and understanding, but some of his smug colleagues, closer to modernistic

Trotskyism than to old-fashioned Marxism, were more concerned with the motivation of terrorism than the fate of its victims. Paul Johnson, former editor and author, his face as red as his hair and boiling over with anger, launched a salvo of expletives at his callous colleagues which forced them to take cover behind specious assertions of misunderstanding.

On Sunday, when the good news broke, the telephones did not stop ringing with messages of jubilation and relief. We had never experienced anything of this sort. The Jewish community was overjoyed. They felt like both the hostages and their liberators. Cabinet ministers and citizens from all walks of life called. A bishop told us that he was ringing the church bells and the Chief Rabbi invited us for a thanksgiving service. A general was in a hurry to know all the operational details and an ex-commando wanted to enlist in the Israeli parachutist corps. Bartenders offered free rounds and amateur poets composed ballads. An inquisitive BBC interviewer asked me by what right Israeli forces had operated in a foreign country. By Amin's summons, I replied. Hadn't he said, a day before, that Israel should do something about the situation? How could we refuse such an invitation?

People everywhere cheered the David who had dared Goliath; the little man had stood up to the bully. The frustrated dream of multitudes of decent people had come true. Shortly after the successful rescue mission I attended, as I did every year, the miners' gala at Durham – the traditional festival of the coal-miners of Britain. After the festive dinner, Jim Callaghan took me aside and said in a conspiratorial whisper: 'When I heard the news on that Sunday morning, I understood what you had meant at that dinner in your house on the eve of my departure for Uganda, when I asked you what your government would do in such a situation, and you answered cryptically: "It would put the fear of the God of Israel into the heart of that brute." ' Idi Amin never recovered from the raid at Entebbe. It was the beginning of his end.

Winding up

In January 1977 we began the preparations for our return to Jerusalem in the spring. Every foreign service knows the problem of the rotation of its top echelons. In April 1976 Allon had appointed a new Director-General of the Foreign Ministry. Shlomo Avneri, a professor of political science, was a newcomer. It was his first opportunity to practise political science on the living object. His appointment created some discontent among the professional foreign service officers. In particular, the incumbent Deputy Director-General, Ephraim Evron, resented that he had been passed over. The practice in such cases was to compensate the disappointed diplomat with an appoint-ment to an attractive foreign post. London was a much-coveted embassy, but Evron preferred Washington. His candidature, however, failed to meet with Prime Minister Rabin's approval. Evron reluctantly accepted London. He was in no hurry to leave. With equal reluctance the new Director-General agreed to defer Evron's departure until April 1977. He never reached London, but eventually arrived in Washington, benefiting from the change of government.

In February Callaghan received me at No. 10. Reviewing the relations between our two countries, the Prime Minister noted with satisfaction their remarkable recovery from their low point in 1973. Harold Wilson, his predecessor, he himself and the ambassador had contributed their share to this achievement. The Labour government had pursued a stable course of friendship and concern for Israel, despite the pressures exerted on it.

The Prime Minister asked what we knew about the Middle East policy of the new administration in Washington. The assumption of UN Secretary-General Kurt Waldheim that Europe could ease the burden of the Arab-Israeli conflict was preposterous. Genscher's recent flair of activism was due more to his personal political ambitions than to Germany's desire to play a role in the peace process. As in the past Britain would not engage in any initiatives and would instead try to curb the zeal of its European partners. For this reason he had opposed the issuing of a new EEC statement on the Middle East. Only American muscle could move the Arab-Israeli conflict towards a solution. Washington was not likely to take any steps before the elections to the Knesset in May. There was no reason for nervousness. No state in the area, besides Israel, was in a position to make war.

I assured him of Israel's peaceful intentions. We needed peace to direct our strained resources to the development of the country and the integration of the new immigrants. Sadat had recently stated that Egypt needed peace, because the heavy military expenditure foiled its economic and social progress. If this reflected correctly what he thought, there was a spark of hope for peaceful accommodation between the two countries.

The change of direction in Britain's foreign policy in the course of 1974 had helped to improve its stranded relations with Israel. Britain had mended its fences with the United States; reinforced its position in the European Economic Community; the first flow of North Sea oil had reached its shores, heralding the end of its dependence on Arab oil; and its government felt less inhibited in pursuing a policy of active friendship with Israel. In the Middle East it discontinued the policy of either Israel or the Arab states, which had previously led it into a dead-end street of neither-nor, reducing Britain's influence on both sides.

At a press luncheon in March 1977 I summed up the state of Anglo-Israeli affairs:

The relations between our two countries are solid and comprehensive. They are conducted in a spirit of mutual confidence, on all levels of our contacts. Intimate exchanges of views between the leaders of our two countries have become an established and fruitful practice. The great wealth of Middle East experience, accumulated by Britain during its long presence in the area, enabled it to interpret events in their true meaning. British decision-makers were not impressed by political programmes which proposed the solution of the Arab-Israeli conflict by means of the dissolution of Israel. Britain's policy shied away from ill-conceived and ill-timed initiatives, taken for the sole purpose of scoring points of popularity with one side while upsetting carefully planned peace moves.

When I saw Foreign Secretary David Owen two weeks later he told me that he had read my statement. It was a fair assessment and reflected accurately the state of relations between our two countries. Sir Michael Palliser, the Permanent Undersecretary, added that Britain was now glad to follow the United States on the list of Israel's best friends in the world.

On matters of substance the expansion of Anglo-Israeli trade was especially fortunate during the period 1974–7. British exports to Israel increased from £128 million to £250 million sterling, while Israel's exports to Britain rose from £70 million to £128 million sterling. However the dilatory manner by which the British government dealt with the Arab boycott remained a source of dismay, mitigated occasionally by some verbal muscle-flexing, but never producing incisive measures.

The sale of arms to Arab countries remained a subject of vigilant Anglo-Israeli dialogue. The talk about projected purchases went far beyond their actual realization. Since the abolition of the arms embargo early in 1974, Israel did not encounter insurmountable difficulties in the procurement of the limited amounts of equipment it was interested in.

Cultural exchanges were lively, but their extension was hampered by lack of funds. Still the Israel Philharmonic Orchestra and soloists were always welcome and warmly applauded guests in England. So were the excellent representatives of the British performing arts on their visits to Israel. Centres of Judaic and Hebrew studies existed at a number of British universities, and the Bible remained the most abiding spiritual and cultural link between the two peoples.

In the previous decade the structure and composition of Jewish leadership had undergone changes. The majority of the Jewish population had climbed, by hard work and austere tenacity, from the bottom of the social ladder to a comfortable middle-class level. Quite a few of them occupied positions in the liberal professions and some of them were active and influential in the political and academic life of the country. They would normally be available to assist Israel, but preferred individual and discreet action to collective and public manifestations.

A thin layer formed the top of the pyramid. These people were prominent in business, banking, industry and public service. Two families were leading in their contribution to the British economy and the well-being of Israel. The Rothschild involvement in the settling of the Land of Israel and in the social and educational improvement of the state had been unique in its scope and fruitfulness and continuous for a whole century. The Sieff family had been a pillar of strength of the Zionist endeavour in Britain since the arrival of Chaim

Weizmann in Manchester in 1904, and constructively supported the ideals he fought for. They were the trend-setters of fund-raising and the leaders in the expansion of Anglo-Israeli trade. The distinction and prominence of the 'family', as it was known, made it the natural and unchallenged leader of the community in all undertakings on behalf of Israel.

Since the middle of the 1960s new leaders gradually took over. They belonged to the younger generation imbued with new communal concepts, influenced by innovative American methods, keenly interested in Israel's domestic politics, but above all as fervent in their devotion and zealous in their work for Israel as their parents and mentors had been. They aimed at wider participation in the fund-raising campaigns and mass manifestations of solidarity with Israel.

Every aspect of Israeli life – its domestic problems and foreign difficulties – was a matter of personal concern to British Jews. They expressed their solidarity not only in mass manifestations, but in a constant drive to mobilize aid. In its fund-raising campaigns for Israeli causes Anglo-Jewry occupied a leading place among the communities of the world. And at times of crisis several thousand young people went to Israel to support the war effort on the home front. We spent much effort in transforming this volunteering spirit into a movement of personal commitment, to increase the relatively small number of people set on settling permanently in the country to which they were bound in soul but not yet in body.

Action on behalf of Soviet Jewry had become a common cause enjoying the whole-hearted support of the entire community and, beyond this, of the general public, the press, parliamentarians, artists, writers, trade unionists and clergy. The spectre of Jewish discrimination and persecution evoked deep anxieties and eagerness to help among the British people. The situation of the Jews in the Soviet Union was a matter of our constant concern and rarely left unmentioned in our conversations with the Prime Minister and the Foreign Secretary, their associates and a wide range of public figures.

At the beginning of 1977, Jimmy Carter had been inaugurated as the new President of the United States. In Israel, Prime Minister Yitzhak Rabin prepared for new Knesset elections. The traditional Labour-National Religious Party coalition had collapsed. The violation of the sabbath by a thirty-minute delay in the arrival from the United States of the first batch of F-15 fighter planes, due to transatlantic headwinds, had aroused a parliamentary storm in the Knesset. The three ministers belonging to the National Religious Party declined to support the government in a vote of confidence. Rabin fired the triumvirate, who had abided by the commands of their convictions but broken the rule of collective cabinet responsibility. As usual, in the wondrous ways of Israeli politics, the government had fallen, not because of differences on a major issue of domestic or foreign policy, but because of a completely unforeseen hazard which aroused religious emotions.

It was not the first time that an Israeli government had slipped on such a banana peel. Veteran politicians had learned how to keep their balance when they stepped inadvertently on the treacherous object. The Knesset set the date of the elections for 17 May. The Labour Party confirmed Rabin with a narrow majority over Peres as its candidate for the premiership.

Opinions were divided on whether it was wise for the outgoing Prime Minister to visit the new President in Washington before the Knesset elections, but in the end the two governments agreed on a short visit in March. On their way home Mr and Mrs Rabin stopped for an hour or two at London airport to meet the leaders of the Jewish community in a nearby hotel. Callaghan, who had wished to meet him, had himself gone to Washington, accompanied by his Foreign Secretary, David Owen. Rabin gave a short report to the assembled Jewish dignitaries, factual in those parts he chose to disclose and careful in his assessment of the future. He assured his audience that the new President would pursue the traditional friendly American policy towards Israel and that no new diplomatic moves should be expected before the summer, because of the need for the new administration to familiarize itself with the Middle East issues and the forthcoming elections in Israel. We had only a few minutes for a private talk on our drive from and to the airport. I found Rabin in a rather glum mood, but attributed it to travel fatigue. Little did I suspect that he had run into serious trouble in Washington.

Three weeks later, when I paid a farewell call on Foreign Secretary David Owen, I got to understand better – though still only partially – what had troubled Rabin. Immediately following his visit to Washington, Callaghan and Owen had met President Carter. After his return, I had spoken with the Prime Minister, who gave me his impression of the new President. He was struck by his steely eyes which were unmatched by his toothy grin. He advised me to hear more from David Owen about Jimmy Carter's prospective policy in the Middle East.

Indeed, said the Foreign Secretary, they had a long session with the President on the Middle East. Israel was in for a bumpy ride in the coming year. The words reminded me of my first encounter with Ted Heath. Although, continued Dr Owen, Carter had not yet fully worked out his course, it was clear that he would give the Middle East a high priority. The problem of the Palestinians worried him and he was determined to pay more attention to its solution than his predecessors. Rabin had shown little readiness to accommodate on this point. Israel would be ill-advised to assume a hard-line stance. In case of differences, the President would try to mobilize public opinion in support of his position and to the detriment of Israel. Carter's commitment to the existence and security of Israel was firm, but he expected the Israeli government to be forthcoming and open-minded. Britain, the Foreign Secretary assured me, would not meddle in the peace-making process. It would be in touch, as always, with the parties concerned and closely co-ordinate its policy with Washington.

Then he asked what I had meant by my enigmatic remark in my recent conversation with the PM that I would not be surprised if the next peace move came from Cairo in the course of 1977 rather than from Geneva. I said it was no more than a hunch. In any case, nothing eventful would happen until after our elections. My assessment was that conditions were maturing for a breakthrough on the Israeli-Egyptian front rather than for progress all along the line. The year 1977 might be decisive.

Farewell to Britain

We used to spend the Jewish holidays alternately with the Ashkanazi and Sephardic communities. And for good measure we spent our first Yom Kippur in London, the second year in Dublin and the last with the lonely community in embattled Belfast. But Pessach we celebrated at home in Israel. We had hoped to return in time to keep to our custom, but the winding-up in London took longer than we had envisaged. Mrs James de Rothschild asked us to spend the days of passover with her at her country home. We would be alone with her and Miss Brassey, her friend and companion. Dollie, as our hostess was known to her friends, asked me to hold the traditional seder service, reading from beginning to end the hagadah – the story of Israel's exodus from Egypt. We sang with fervour the timeless prayer, 'Next year in Jerusalem', a vow which all present duly fulfilled in the coming year. It took another year for the other prayer to be answered – 'Oh Lord lead the children of Israel safely out from Egypt'.

Dorothy de Rothschild's dedication to Jewish causes is legendary. Invariably shunning the spotlight, she is always there where she is needed. The work of rebuilding the Land of Israel, begun by her father-in-law, Baron Edmond de Rothschild, and continued faithfully by his son James, was carried forward with unbounded commitment and energy by his widow. The settlements founded by Baron Edmond not only helped regenerate the dispersed Jewish people in its redeemed homeland, but also shaped the configuration of the future State of Israel. The work of land reclamation and colonization advanced by James de Rothschild and his support of Dr Weizmann in his political endeavours furthered significantly the attainment of Jewish statehood.

The Knesset building, educational television, Everyman's University, the beautification of Jerusalem and the restoration of some of its most venerable synagogues, community centres, institutions of higher academic and religious studies and hospitals – all bear the imprint of Dorothy de Rothschild's unsparing dedication to the well-being of the people and to the growth and consolidation of Israel's social, political and cultural structure.

There could be no place more relaxing and enjoyable to bid farewell to England than Dollie's country home, overlooking the green meadows, neatly tilled fields and rolling hills of Buckinghamshire. It was an island of tranquillity and a delight of hospitality.

My wife and I were leaving Britain with a store of rewarding memories. We had seen the country at work and at play, and sometimes in an intermediate stage between the two: the spring rites of the football Cup Final resembling a mixture between a revivalist meeting and an agitated street demonstration; the Oxford-Cambridge regatta, a fine display of superior academic muscle; the television news presented in a masterly fashion with that occasionally raised eyebrow which says more than any sophisticated commentary; an afternoon with Henry Moore at work in his village studio; the enlightened dinner conversations at Lord Goodman's, an inexhaustible source of human wisdom and sagacious advice. We had gone down into the pit of a coal-mine and come up with a vivid experience of the hard lot of the miners. We flew out from Aberdeen to the North Sea oil-rigs and admired the lonely and tenacious efforts of the men searching for energy supplies to make Britain self-sufficient. We met our communities throughout the land and were inspired by their devotion to Israel. We were impressed by the regularity of the annual party conferences and amazed by the degree of election fever which, by Israeli standards, rarely rose above a mild rash. We cherished the exquisite performances of drama and music. We carried with us the treasured memory of innumerable friendly encounters with open-minded and tolerant citizens in a land that had remained one of the last citadels of civility.

All packed and ready for an early departure on Good Friday, 8 April, I waited for the midnight news before retiring. A momentous event was taking place that evening which kept every Israeli, wherever he was, at the highest state of alert – Israel's leading basketball team was playing against Yugoslavia in the final match of the European championship. Eagerly, we waited for the result. And the BBC newscast did indeed open with an item on Israel. It was stunning: Prime Minister Rabin had resigned from the leadership of the Labour Party. He would take leave of absence until the elections and would not run for the premiership.

His decision came like a bolt, but not out of a clear blue sky. A watchful Washington correspondent from an Israeli newspaper had discovered at the time of the Prime Minister's recent visit to the United States that Mrs Rabin was keeping an account in an American bank without authorization from the Israeli controller of foreign exchange. This was a serious offence against the then existing currency regulations. In the ensuing investigation, Leah Rabin had given contradictory explanations and her husband had publicly sustained her statements. The Attorney-General decided to prosecute Leah Rabin and she was sentenced to a heavy fine. Yitzhak Rabin, strongly criticized by press, public and party for his conduct in the affair, had become an electoral liability. He resigned and Shimon Peres replaced him as the new leader of the party.

We were perturbed and pained by the news. Not even the announcement of

Israel's victory in the European championship was able to comfort us. The circumstances of Rabin's fall deeply disturbed the country. We left London with a sense of foreboding for the future of Israel's political life. We were glad to be back in Jerusalem at this time of crisis and change.

35

Inside the Foreign Ministry

In our conversation in 1961 Pandit Nehru had asked me how Israel, with a population two hundred times smaller than that of India, managed to find so many suitable heads of mission to man such a variety of posts. India's Department of External Affairs was still wrangling with the problem. I admitted that it was not easy for Israel either, but assured him that the moment his government announced its readiness to receive a resident Israeli ambassador in Delhi, a choice of good candidates would be available. The Prime Minister, nonchalantly ignoring the passing shot, persisted in his inquiry about our system of recruiting and training foreign service personnel.

He was astonished to learn that quite a few of Israel's ambassadors had graduated from kibbutzim rather than from professional schools for diplomats. The man from behind the plough who was familiar with the intricacies of modern rural economy, who understood how to get along with his Arab neighbours and to negotiate with hard-headed bankers and thick-skinned bureaucrats, who had innate intelligence and human culture, was at least as good ambassadorial timber as the professional diplomat reared in the precincts of academic exclusivity. Some of our best people had a background of both. They were deeply immersed in the life of the country, had toiled and fought for it, grown up and gained experience in its struggle for independence, were educated in the ways of other nations and imbued with the knowledge and sense of the history of their own people. Most of them had swiftly acquired their professional polish, others had remained rough diamonds, attractive and valuable in their own way.

As Director-General of the Foreign Ministry, I was frequently subjected to the 'friendly advice' of dispensers of political patronage soliciting a comfortable embassy post for one of their protégés. The candidates represented a wide, but not always colourful, selection of the country's political spectrum, ranging from unsuccessful candidates for the Knesset to meritorious ex-generals, from redundant party functionaries to faded underground fighters. It was not easy to hold the line against the political encroachment of the foreign service, but we always tried to make the best of an unavoidable compromise.

Despite the perennial handicaps of a mini budget incommensurate with the

Ministry's task, lack of adequate modern office facilities and working conditions incomparably inferior to any other foreign service, the Ministry functioned on a high level of efficiency. The standards of responsibility, devotion and proficiency of its staff evoked the admiration of other foreign services more senior and richer in resources and experience.

When I relinquished my post of Director-General at the end of 1971, Israel maintained nearly ninety diplomatic and consular missions abroad. Evaluating the work of the Ministry in this field, Abba Eban wrote on 23 November 1971:

Since 1967, the fostering of foreign relations, in most difficult circumstances, has meant for our Ministry an arduous task of which it had never previously borne the like. Yet the fact today is that far from being isolated and ostracized, as was the aim of our adversaries, Israel, after these years of tension, and notwithstanding numerous handicaps, maintains throughout the world a far-flung network of fruitful and substantive relationships. They have been extended and reinforced by the establishment of relations with additional countries.

You played a major part in the endeavours that brought those results about, and in managing the Ministry's work efficiently, in introducing organizational innovations, in promoting new and qualified personnel and, above all, in wise and lucid political thought that has proved a significant asset in shaping the policies of Israel.

Policy making

What Eban so generously called 'lucid political thought' had only limited influence on the shaping of Israel's foreign policy. This was formed more by the flow of events than by premeditation. Its conduct was more in the nature of accident prevention than of traffic planning. From his vantage point the Director-General, with the extensive information at his disposal, was reasonably well equipped to foresee possible collisions and sound the warning signal. It was not always appreciated, especially by those who were eventually booked for reckless driving.

We learned that, in reality, foreign policy was not made by lucid thinkers and contemplative planners, but by choices of priorities; reaction to events; aspirations and opportunities; decisions and avoidance of decisions; adherence to moral values and consideration of domestic issues. The management of foreign policy required alert and skilled navigators. They had to know the direction, chart the currents and measure the winds to reach their destination.

Israel, constantly poised on the precipice of war, was constrained to concede primary priority to its defence requirements. The access to sources of arms supplies and the effort to secure their unimpeded flow formed one of the principal objectives of its security and foreign policy. It determined more than any other factor its international conduct and the nature of its open or covert domestic wrangles. The Foreign Ministry operated on the assumption that a successful arms procurement policy depended largely on the quality of the overall relationship existing between Israel and the supplier state. In countries like the United States, Britain and to a lesser degree France, where public sentiment and parliamentary opinion exerted a considerable influence on the decisions of the government, it was essential to cultivate wide public sympathy for Israel's needs and aspirations and understanding between the governments of their mutual concerns.

This required a methodical preparation of the ground and sometimes the renunciation of actions which encumbered the relations. The defence establishment, hard pressed by its urgent needs and frequently oblivious of the international effect of military actions, was often impatient with the Foreign Ministry's *modus operandi*. It regarded it as cumbersome and looked for its own shortcuts, occasionally creating not only inter-ministerial friction, but inter-governmental confusion to the detriment of the cause both branches were bound to serve.

During my term of office as Director-General I endeavoured to establish, on the professional level, close working relations with the military. Chanan Bar-On, the trusted, well-liked and alert head of the Director-General's Office, was of particular help in raising the standards of confidence and co-operation between the two ministries. We had to rely on patient persuasion, rather than on the weight of the Foreign Ministry's authority. The big battalions were with defence. They would normally carry the day when differences of opinion were submitted to the Prime Minister's decision.

The Prime Minister's role in foreign affairs

It was self-evident that the head of government would put his stamp on the foreign and defence policy of the country. Until the outbreak of the war in 1967, with a short interval in 1955, the Prime Ministers of Israel had always held the post of Minister of Defence. Their direct involvement in the conduct of foreign affairs depended on a number of factors: their personal interest; the forcefulness of the Foreign Minister; the professional competence and reputation of the Ministry's top echelon; international circumstances; and unforeseen crises – which in our case were the rule.

Ben Gurion would generally deal only with issues which he thought to be of major consequence. The views of his Foreign Minister, Moshe Sharett, although often differing from those of the Prime Minister, carried weight with him, if only for the fact that Sharett occupied an influential position in the cabinet and in his party and did not shy from mustering voting majorities against Ben Gurion's plans of action. Although this went against the grain, Ben Gurion accepted this situation, until he reached the conclusion that the influence of his Foreign Minister was likely to frustrate his major policy and military objective at the time: the elimination of the offensive potential of the Soviet-equipped Egyptian army. At that point he forced the resignation of his Foreign Minister.

Ben Gurion refrained from intervening in the day-by-day work of the Ministry and its initiatives in areas peripheral to his central aims. During the period of his premiership Israel's foreign policy focused, willy-nilly, on the happenings at the United Nations. Ben Gurion was hardly impressed with the proceedings at the United Nations. He treated them with the same detached disdain, whether they reinforced Israel's struggle for international recognition as they did in the years preceding and immediately following its independence, or whether they aggravated its international situation. Only in exceptional circumstances would he desist from some action in deference to the difficulties it would create for Israel at the United Nations. It usually required a major effort of persuasion by his Foreign Minister, supported by like-minded cabinet colleagues and compounded by strongly worded exhortations from Washington.

Ben Gurion was far from being insensitive to the positions of the major powers in a given situation: they exerted a weighty influence on his decisions. Not only had the experience of the 1956 Sinai campaign reinforced his reluctance to support action evoking the combined opposition of the United States and the Soviet Union, but he also disapproved of any major pre-emptive military venture, justified as it may be, without at least the tacit understanding of the United States. The man who did so much to stimulate Israeli self-reliance and harden it to resist pressures was remarkably prudent in delineating the perimeters of Israel's power. Within these limitations he would operate with audacity, sometimes greater than his cabinet colleagues would have liked and friendly powers were willing to put up with. More than any other temperamental and visionary statesman he had the ability and strength to come down from dazzling heights of exaltation and perform a soft landing on the solid ground of international reality.

Ben Gurion's successor, Levi Eshkol, was an earthbound man, a farmer by heart and profession, economist by experience and realist by nature. He was not given to dramatic take-offs into the unknown spheres of foreign policy. He relied more than any Prime Minister, either before or after him, on the professional skills, international reputation and experience of his Foreign Minister and the ability of his professional staff. His premiership was Eban's halcyon days. The Prime Minister respected the advice of his Foreign Minister, supported him substantively in cabinet against criticism, gave him considerable scope of independent action and refrained from interfering with the work of his Ministry.

In his endeavour to introduce a greater measure of checks and balances into the decision-making process, Eshkol was prepared to consider unorthodox ideas and discuss regularly current defence and foreign policy issues. He acted less as an ultimate decision-maker than as a patient conciliator, bridging the different viewpoints or choosing between them by the application of his innate astuteness and common sense.

He was elated by the victory in 1967, but not intoxicated by it. He saw in the territories which had come under Israel's control, currency to be converted into peace. Only ten days after the end of the fighting Eshkol steered through his cabinet – of which Menachem Begin was a prominent member – peace proposals, with certain safeguards, which envisaged the withdrawal of Israel from Sinai and the Golan Heights. They were ignored by the Arab States and later tightened up by the Israeli government. In November 1968 he confided to a correspondent of *Newsweek* his willingness to make far-reaching concessions also on the West Bank. The report evoked a storm of indignation from the right wing of his cabinet and insipid defence from his own party colleagues.

A few months later Eshkol died, a disheartened man. He knew that continued diplomatic immobility could lead to a renewed outbreak of hostilities of more devastating force and momentous consequences than any previous war. But he lacked the strength to rally his government around a realistic compromise plan supported by the United States and attractive to the neighbouring Arab countries. If level-headedness, human insight, perception of realities and liberality were the attributes of a peacemaker, Eshkol was richly endowed with them. At any event under his premiership the foreign policy of the country was conducted with as much rationality and proficiency as the limitations of a heterogeneous government allowed.

Golda Meir had been recalled from retirement to succeed Eshkol. Her ascent to the premiership at the age of seventy did not come as a complete surprise to the initiated of her party. A few months before Eshkol's death a few intimate and influential party friends had made it clear to her that she was their choice to succeed the ailing Prime Minister. She arrived at the summit imbued with awe at the magnitude of the responsibility, pride at her summons and the resolve to write her own page in the history of the Jewish people.

As Foreign Minister under Ben Gurion she was exempt from formulating foreign policy. The Prime Minister laid down the ground rules and initiated the great decisions. Her task was to present and defend the policy in the international arena. Relying on Ben Gurion's sense of history, intuition and political judgement, she advocated his policies with emotional simplicity and hefty practicality. Sustained by an unwavering faith in the incontestable justice of the cause, she had little use and patience for the refined counter-argument. There were only two sides to the case: the right one and the wrong one. There were only two political species: the friends of Israel and the foes of Israel. Her approach to problems was functional. The evolution of events and their future implications were not a matter of primary interest to her. She wanted to know what should be done, rather than what could happen. To her mind analysis was an intriguing intellectual exercise, but of little practical value.

As Prime Minister, Golda Meir retained an abiding interest in the working of the Foreign Ministry – the more so because matters of defence were firmly in the hands of a strong-willed minister. Dayan was not the man to take interference with his authority lightly. Their relationship was ambivalent. Golda was impressed with his pluck, prowess and originality, but dreaded the opaqueness of his thoughts, often camouflaged by seeming outspokenness, and the unpredictability of his moves, often taken on the spur of the moment.

Golda Meir was well acquainted with the senior staff of the Foreign Ministry, their way of thinking and operating. She respected their proficiency and appreciated their workmanship. But, as she repeatedly stated in and out of office, she never felt really at home in the Foreign Ministry. Diplomacy, in the true sense of its meaning, was neither her style nor her method. The well-prepared brief, the refined speech, the subtle negotiation, the detached weighing of all the elements involved, the precisely formulated summary were foreign to her. What Edmund Burke described as the heart of the art of diplomacy, 'to grant graciously what you no longer have the power to withhold', sounded to her more like effete defeatism than an enlightened maxim. To hold on doggedly to concepts, even if they had long been overtaken by events, was Golda's perception of leadership. It endowed her with a singular strength of resistance – a quality much needed by an embattled people – but it impaired her resilience to adapt her policies to changing circumstances.

Golda Meir devoted particular attention to two main areas: Israel's ties with the Jewish communities and its relations with the United States. In many ways they were interrelated. The intimacy of the relationship between the diaspora and Israel constituted for Golda the spiritual foundation of Jewish existence, while she symbolized for multitudes of Jews the living reality of Israel.

The interdependence between Israel and the United States was somewhat more complex. There was the enormous difference of dimension in every field: of needs and aspirations, and of foreign policy priorities. What seemed to Israel an immediate and overwhelming danger, appeared to the United States to be a passing turbulence. What Israel regarded as inescapable necessity in asserting itself militarily, America dismissed as rash and ill-conceived reaction. But beyond the occasional differences of views, all administrations remained loyal to the United States' commitment to Israel's existential needs. Golda Meir was fully aware of the centrality of Israel's relations with the United States. With all her firmness in defending Israel's positions, she would know how to yield when differences approached the danger-point

As Prime Minister, Golda Meir chose to direct personally nearly every aspect of Israel's American policy, often down to minute details. Not that she acted singlehandedly. She conferred extensively with close cabinet and party friends and consulted the Foreign Minister, without necessarily following his advice nor always entrusting him with the implementation of her decisions. She maintained her direct lines of communications with the embassy in

Washington, instructing the ambassador and receiving personally and sometimes exclusively his reports and evaluations. This practice not only reduced the influence of the Foreign Minister on the policy-making process, but deprived the Washington embassy of normal professional guidance, necessary for its proper functioning in the many fields of its responsibility.

Golda Meir's successor, Lieutenant-General Yitzhak Rabin, was a complete innovation in the political life of the country. He was the first Prime Minister who had been born in Israel, and the first to come up from the ranks of the army and not the cadres of the party. He was the first to be elected in a party contest instead of being selected as customary by leadership consensus. His nomination was a deliberate departure from worn-out political practices. High hopes accompanied his appointment that he would save the ailing Labour Party from decline.

The composition of Rabin's cabinet mirrored more the chart of the party power-grid than the Prime Minister's personal choices, a not unusual situation in a country where not only governments but also parties were composed of coalitions. But on two appointments his personal preferences prevailed. He excluded Dayan from his government and replaced Abba Eban with Yigal Allon as Foreign Minister.

The new Prime Minister had undergone a period of intense apprenticeship in foreign affairs when he served as Ambassador to the United States. It was only natural that in his vision of world affairs he was influenced by American perspectives and dimensions. He was firmly convinced that Israel's fortunes were tightly linked to the goodwill and strength of the United States. His ambassadorial relations with the Foreign Ministry had left much to be desired.

As Prime Minister his attitude changed in this respect. Yigal Allon, the new Foreign Minister, had been his former commander in the War of Independence and had played an important role in his nomination to the premiership. Like every Prime Minister, Rabin took a primary interest in the conduct of the country's foreign policy, but considerably reduced direct interference in its management. Ambassador Dinitz in Washington communicated from that time on directly with the Foreign Ministry.

Rabin's pre-eminence in foreign affairs was somewhat curbed by the influence Shimon Peres, the Minister of Defence, exerted on policy decisions. Rabin's nearly exclusive concentration on Israeli-United States issues, and first and foremost on Dr Kissinger's mediation efforts, gave Allon free rein to direct the Foreign Ministry's work in Europe, Latin America and the United Nations, and to try to recuperate lost ground in the developing countries.

Unlike Allon, who by disposition tended to activism also in foreign affairs, Rabin was more hesitant and less enterprising. He devoted a great deal of thought to analysing world affairs, but less to synthesizing processes of action. He was a great believer in gaining time, hoping that changing circumstances would do more for Israel than its own initiatives.

His political calendar consisted of two seasons: the pre-election and the post-election years. In the four-year cycle of American politics two years were essentially inactive ones in which Israel was more or less immune from troublesome American initiatives: the year of the electoral campaign and the year needed by the new administration to get organized. In Rabin's rhythm theory it was the art of statecraft to get unharmed over the two fertile and potentially dangerous years, until the approaching elections slowed down or halted undesirable initiatives. But international affairs do not proceed with the regularity of army route marches. As Disraeli once said: 'What we anticipated seldom occurs; what we least expected generally happens.'

At the beginning of 1977, the Israeli government anticipated that the new Carter administration would refrain from new initiatives in the Middle East during its normal warm-up period. Yet when Prime Minister Rabin met the new President in March, he found him all set to get things going: the Geneva conference; the recognition of Palestinian rights; the withdrawal from territories and the conclusion of a final and comprehensive peace between Israel and its neighbours. But the Labour Party also anticipated, when it advanced the Knesset elections by six months, that the voters would return it to office. The least expected thing happened – the ailing but durable opposition leader, Menachem Begin, defeated Rabin's successor, the energetic and unspent Shimon Peres.

Was it coincidence or a phenomenon of politics that in the year 1977 three leading parties – Congress in India, Socialist in Sweden and Labour in Israel – which had held power continuously for thirty years or more, lost it? Had democratic societies established a retirement age for ruling parties?

A new government

When we returned from London in April 1977, our fifth homecoming from prolonged service abroad, I had just one more year to complete my thirty years of service and the government just one more month to reach the end of its term of office.

The pulse of the country was beating so fast that it afforded little respite for decompression and readjustment. As always during election time, the Foreign Ministry was orphaned and its activities limited to routine. Whatever the outcome of the elections would be, a change of Foreign Minister was anticipated. In the reshuffle of the Labour Party leadership following Rabin's resignation, Allon was marked down to take the Ministry of Defence in Shimon Peres' administration, and Eban was supposed to return to the Foreign Ministry.

In the previous decade Israeli politics had become highly personalized. In these pre-election days, speculation on the prospects of ministerial candidates was running higher than on the outcome of the vote. One could not attend a social event without being asked the opinion of the Foreign Ministry staff on

Eban's anticipated reinstallation. Normally I would avoid the subject, but a few days before the elections I succumbed to a pointed question from Gideon Hausner, a cabinet minister and good friend. I ventured the view that Eban would not return to his former post because the next Foreign Minister would be Moshe Dayan. Hausner asked me on what fact did I base such a bizarre forecast. Simply because, I replied, Moshe Dayan wanted to be Foreign Minister, a good enough reason for a man like him to use or create the opportunity to get his way. And if he could not get it from Peres he might not hesitate to cross the floor and obtain the appointment from Begin.

Dayan was determined to make a come-back because he was loath to close his life story marked by the events of the Yom Kippur War. He wanted to vindicate himself and finish his career on a positive note. Begin afforded him the opportunity. In June, Dayan took charge of the Foreign Ministry. I was abroad at the time on a mission to the United States. Begin's electoral victory was as stupefying to his admirers as it was to his adversaries. The former were carried away by high expectations, the latter by deep anxieties, and both were stunned by Dayan's appointment. Upon my return in July I presented myself to the new Foreign Minister. I had known him for nearly forty years as a neighbouring farmer, as Haganah commander, as Chief of Staff, freshman politician and seasoned cabinet minister, at the height of his influence under Ben Gurion and in the years of his political wilderness. But I had never served under him.

Under the first impact of the election results a few of us old-timers had wrangled with the idea of resignation. We could not imagine being able to adjust to the unaccustomed style and way of thinking of the new government. But after some reflection we felt that such a resignation would be interpreted as a demonstrative political act contrary to the tradition of our non-political civil service. It could be taken as disregard for the democratic process by which the government had been legitimately elected.

I reported to Dayan my impressions of my visit to the United States. The new American President would strive vigorously to revive the Geneva conference on the basis of Resolution 242 and insist on the discussion of all outstanding issues with the participation of all parties to the conflict, including the Palestinians. He would try to co-operate with the Soviet Union in the solution of the problems. The Jewish community was swayed between uncertainty about Begin's future policy and uneasiness about Carter's basic attitude towards Israel; but its support of Israel was unswerving.

I informed the new Minister of a number of confidential contacts I had maintained in London with representatives of countries which had no relations with Israel. Then I evolved some ideas on how to avoid the reconvening of the unproductive Geneva conference by launching a new, direct and secret initiative towards Egypt. Dayan listened impassively. Other proposals on how to re-activate the Ministry's staff, which had been suffering in recent months from under-employment and intellectual malnutrition, also failed to elicit any noticeable response. Dayan was not in the mood for dialogue. It was clear that he was going to play his cards close to his chest also in his new post, and perhaps even more so since the stakes were high and the track new to him.

Five Foreign Ministers in search of peace

Since its inception the Foreign Ministry had been headed by a succession of four men and one woman. I had been associated with them over a period of thirty years. They were as different as any five human beings could possibly be: in background, upbringing, temper, human qualities and intellectual capability. The ideological roots of all of them had been in the Israeli labour movement, but its various currents determined the political outlook of each of them. All of them corresponded partly to Talleyrand's description of the perfect Minister for Foreign Affairs, but none of them was flawless:

He must have the faculty of appearing open, while remaining impenetrable; of masking reserve with the manner of careless abandon; his conversation should be simple, varied, unexpected, always natural and sometimes naive; in a word, he should never cease for an instant during the twenty-four hours to be a Minister for Foreign Affairs. Yet all these qualities, rare as they are, might not suffice, if good faith did not give them the guarantee which they almost always require. Diplomacy is not a science of deceit and duplicity. If good faith is necessary anywhere it is above all in political transactions, for it makes them firm and lasting. Good faith never authorizes deceit but it admits of reserve; and reserve has this peculiarity that it increases confidence.

Moshe Sharett was the ardent believer in good faith and perfection; Yigal Allon the practitioner of natural conversation and careless abandon; Golda Meir appeared open, while holding back; Abba Eban was Foreign Minister for twenty-four hours a day; and Moshe Dayan was impenetrable. Their qualities taken together would have excelled even Talleyrand's most fastidious demands of perfection.

Different as their personalities were, all Israeli Foreign Ministers had to cope with the same challenges and chores. The emphasis and priorities changed from time to time, but the basic objectives remained the same: to secure Israel's place in an inhospitable environment and change its adversity; to repel hostile attacks and fortify the defence of the state; to offset its regional isolation by a worldwide network of fruitful relations of mutuality; and to realize its supreme national aim: the physical, cultural and social anchorage of the dispersed Jewish people in its revived ancient homeland.

Israel accorded high priority to specific Jewish concerns. The representatives of Israel took a vigorous stand with individual governments and in international forums on the promotion of Jewish immigration and the struggle against obstacles put up against it; on the oppression of Jews and racial discrimination; and on the reawakening of neo-Nazism and the suppression of human rights and religious freedoms wherever they occurred.

There were also dilemmas of choice between purely Israeli interests and the wider Jewish responsibility of the state. During Nasser's War of Attrition an unusual point in case arose. Zahal had captured a number of Egyptian pilots. The military authorities in Cairo were especially interested in the repatriation of two or three of them who had high-ranking family connections. United Nations sources intimated to us that the Egyptian government might permit the departure of 500 Jews in exchange for the pilots. Supporters of the exchange argued that it was the duty of Zahal not only to fight for Israel, but also to save the lives of Jews endangered by hostile governments. As if foreseeing 'Operation Entebbe' the protagonists claimed that if a group of Jews were exposed to mortal danger, the government should not hesitate to order the air force to rescue them. But the Prime Minister rejected the proposal. Only when the fighting ended in 1970 were the Egyptian pilots exchanged for Israeli prisoners-of-war.

It would be wrong to conclude from the unusual decision taken in this case that an 'Israel first' attitude dominated the policy of the Jewish state. Of course, there were instances of parochialism, understandable when judged in the light of the extraordinary stresses to which the state was exposed. But Jewish responsibilities and concepts fundamentally motivated the Israeli decision-makers. Despite the cynicism and expediency governing the affairs of the world, they strove to uphold moral values in the conduct of Israel's policy and remain cognizant of its spiritual heritage which it shared with a large part of enlightened humanity.

But the realities the Jewish state had to face during the first thirty years of its existence bore little resemblance to the precepts of the UN Charter and the visions of the prophets. The hostility of Israel's neighbours, the indifference of the world and the memory of Jewish suffering formed Israel's national character and its policy no less than the tenets of its faith. Israel's national compactness, its sense of direction, its physical prowess, its rallying in times of emergency, its innate anxieties and its creative zeal were in no small measure the result of the immense vitality of its people and the reaction to past persecution and present pressures. Arab hostility, designed to stifle the growth of the nation, in fact spurred its energies, strengthened its resilience, steeled its resolve and forged its solidity and national coherence.

The cycle of war and cease-fire determined the rhythm of Israel's policy. It revolved around pre-war and post-war periods. The wars ended in impressive military victories, but not in decisive political changes. Israel's military power was not commensurate with its political strength. Its military swiftness was not matched by its diplomatic mobility. International diplomatic intervention succeeded in most cases in bringing the fighting to an end but failed to terminate once and for all the continued state of war. The efforts of the international community to persuade the belligerent parties to enter into meaningful peace negotiations were half-hearted and ineffective. Peace opportunities offered by the outcome of the fighting withered away, because the Arab governments believed that a lost war was only an unfortunate and temporary setback, to be redressed by the next round of fighting. In their view cease-fire and even formal armistice agreements were no more than breaks in a prolonged fight to the end.

36

Peace

Israeli diplomacy following the fighting focused on consolidating the cease-fire; seeking economic aid to alleviate the economic burdens of the war; obtaining arms to replenish the depleted arsenals; and sending the peace doves out to reconnoitre the flooded land for some firm ground. And, after thirty years, the first bird returned from Egypt carrying an olive branch. Future historians will debate what made the floods recede, as theologians and natural scientists still argue about what caused the waters of the Red Sea to part.

When Begin triumphed in the Knesset elections in May 1977, he appealed to the leaders of the neighbouring Arab countries to meet him in their capitals, in Jerusalem or at any other convenient place, to discuss the conclusion of a final peace. But so had all his predecessors, without ever evoking a positive echo from the other side of the valley. The idea was not new – it was the quintessence of Israel's foreign policy. Yet in order to burgeon, it had to fall on fertile soil at an opportune moment. The frustrations and ravages of a generation-long conflict had prepared the ground in Egypt and the ascendency of a new government in Israel had created the opportunity. Whether Begin initially meant more than customary rhetoric, or Sadat was animated by the lofty ideal of everlasting peace, is immaterial. The confluence of anxieties and constraints, incentives and hopes, initiative and response created favourable conditions for peace.

The forces which changed the course of the current were a combination of negative and positive impulses. Israel's neighbours were deeply apprehensive about the ultimate intentions of the new government and feared its militant background and activist ideology. Sadat was resolved to recover the territories lost in 1967 and understood that he could achieve this only by political means. He realized that in the face of the growing threat of the expansion of Soviet power in the Middle East, it was essential to eliminate potential flash-points. He endeavoured to gain massive American support to alleviate Egypt's economic and social plight, and recognized that a comprehensive peace conference would neither benefit Egypt's national needs nor advance the peace process, but rather serve Soviet interests.

The factors which prompted Begin to embark on the road to peace were no less complex. There was the deep yearning of the people of Israel for peace; the government's concern that the United States might collaborate with the Soviet Union on a solution establishing Arab sovereignty over the West Bank; Begin's assumption, originally conceived by Dayan, that the restoration of Sinai to Egypt would ensure Israel's continued control over Judea and Samaria and their eventual inclusion in the sovereign territory of Israel; his hope that peace with Egypt would induce the other Arab states to follow suit or at least reduce their capacity to wage war; and last but not least his burning desire to crown the story of his life, rent with struggle and strife, with the accomplishment of peace.

Jerusalem, the turning-point

When Begin met Sadat in Jerusalem both knew where they wanted to go, but not how to get there. When they set foot on peace-land, they looked at the new landscape with bewilderment. After the preparatory meeting in Morocco between Foreign Minister Dayan and Deputy Prime Minister Hassan el Tohami, they had a general idea of what they could expect from each other, but were uncertain about each other's motivations and ultimate objectives. They had little clarity about the scope of the agreement they intended to reach. Would Egypt content itself with Israel's withdrawal from Sinai or seriously insist on Israel relinquishing its control of the West Bank? Did Sadat pay only lip service to the 'legitimate rights of the Palestinian people', or would the conclusion of a peace treaty be contingent on the prospect of their realization? The elucidation of these questions caused the major snarls in the negotiations and prolonged them far beyond the time anticipated.

President Sadat's visit to Jerusalem in November 1977 surprised Washington no less than all the other capitals, including Jerusalem. Although at the end of September, Dayan had privately informed President Carter of his secret meeting with the Egyptian Deputy Prime Minister held two weeks earlier, neither of them anticipated the bold step which Sadat would take two months later. It took the administration a few days to recover from its initial consternation, for it rated the risks of Sadat's audacity higher than his chances of success. But accomplished facts in war as in peace create their own momentum. They are met either with resistance or with resignation. It was inconceivable that the United States government could oppose an Arab peace initiative launched with such boldness and ostentation, even if it deviated completely from any sort of scenario ever designed by Washington. But it was also improbable that the United States would remain a passive observer of the momentous developments. Even if it had preferred to remain uninvolved, Egypt and Israel would not let it stay aloof. Sadat counted on Washington's active support, and both sides needed it to surmount the many obstacles barring the progress of the negotiations.

The American role in the talks changed gradually from that of reluctant participant to active mediator and eventually to supreme arbiter. It is an open question whether a settlement could ever have been achieved without energetic American intervention. In the first flush of excitement of the encounter in Jerusalem Begin, more than Sadat, believed that he had found a shortcut to peace, avoiding a detour via Washington. This might have been possible had both sides conceded to each other at the beginning what they were ready to yield at the end, but it soon became evident that American leverage was indispensable. The attainment of peace, its growth and viability required the sustained support of the United States. It is not accidental that the direct meetings in Jerusalem, Ismailia and Cairo failed to produce agreement, while the negotiations at Camp David and in Washington were crowned with success.

In the tedious process of peace-making, the Foreign Minister was the leading man of the Israeli cast. Moshe Dayan acted alternately with dash and deliberation, advancing and stalling, vacillating between surprising compromises and inexplicable intransigence. Although Dayan and Ezer Weizman, the two chief negotiators, enjoyed considerable prestige, Begin kept them at short rein. Unlike the Egyptian delegation which stuck to its brief, Israel's team distinguished itself by its versatility and originality. Its script was loosely written and Jerusalem's reaction to its moves was not always predictable. Dayan conducted the talks with his customary aloofness. His strategic objective, the conclusion of peace, was manifest but his tactics were inscrutable. In his moves he was usually ahead of his Prime Minister and government and often ran into opposition when he tried to cut corners. If the odds were too strongly against him, he either retreated or induced the American intermediaries to take the initiative.

The Foreign Ministry as such played only a marginal role in the negotiations, although for thirty years it had prepared itself and worked for the day when Arab and Israeli representatives would negotiate peace. Since the end of the Six Day War the Ministry's planning, political and legal staff had been actively engaged in elaborating proposals for the settlement of all aspects of the conflict. The plans ranged from the territorial issues to mutual security arrangements; from joint development projects to the settlement of the refugee problem; from freedom of navigation to the establishment of land and air communications. These drafts were of minimal use at the negotiations, not because they failed to provide the sought-after answers, but because they were left to slumber untouched in their filing cabinets.

Still, one of our blueprints saw the light of day. It was the draft peace treaty which we had prepared in 1971. It dealt with all outstanding questions apart from the delineation of the final boundaries and the details of the security dispositions. On various occasions – the last time when the Geneva peace conference first convened at the end of 1973 – we had recommended the presentation of the document as Israel's starting-position. Eventually Dayan took up the idea and submitted the draft to the State Department in advance of his first contacts with Sadat's emissary. Although the final text of the Israeli-Egyptian treaty was quite different from our first draft, it fulfilled a useful purpose as a basis and guide-line for the negotiations. The only section of the Foreign Ministry, apart from its technical services and the Minister's personal staff, which was actively and continuously involved in the peace process was the legal department. It was headed by Dr Meir Rosenne, an able and tenacious jurist who distinguished himself by the wealth of his knowledge of precedents, his skill in sealing loop-holes and detecting flaws in the fine print.

In the course of the negotiations I had two private talks with Dayan, one shortly after Sadat's visit to Jerusalem, and the other a few months later. In our first conversation I asked him whether he believed that Sadat was prepared to sign a separate peace agreement without an agreed solution of the Palestine issue and in defiance of the other Arab states. Dayan admitted that the problem of the Palestinians could become a sticking-point, but he did not think that Sadat would make it an insurmountable stumbling-block. How much the rejection of the other Arab states would figure in his considerations depended mainly on the attitude of Saudi Arabia. Dayan assumed that Washington's influence on Riyadh was sufficiently strong to dissuade it from causing trouble to Sadat. He returned the question to me.

My view was that Egypt would not disavow 'the legitimate rights of the Palestinian people'. It would insist on their recognition in one form or another by Israel, but not necessarily make the conclusion of peace contingent on a detailed plan for their immediate realization. A declaration of intent by Israel, admitting the validity of Resolution 242 also in regard to the West Bank and Gaza and the right of its inhabitants to participate in the determination of the future status of these territories, might be the indispensable minimum at this stage. The opposition of the other Arab states would not deter Sadat, but be used by him as a bargaining-counter in his negotiations with Israel. The fear of radical Arab elements would influence the position of the Saudi dynasty more than its friendship with the United States.

The Soviet pincer
When we met again at the end of March 1978, on the eve of my retirement, the negotiations with Egypt had come to a standstill. The positions of the two sides were diametrically opposed on the Palestine issue. That spring the Israeli government had rejected as heresy texts which in the autumn it accepted at Camp David as binding policy. Dayan asked me whether I believed in the sincerity of Sadat's intentions. I answered that I would advise respect for him for his audacious initiative and his proclaimed peaceful intentions and suspicion of him until he gave convincing proof of his readiness to achieve peace by mutual accommodation.

I asked what was going to happen next. 'How would I know,' growled Dayan, rocking in his ministerial swivel-chair. 'I wouldn't even know how much longer I'll occupy this seat.' By some artful swivelling he held on to it for another eighteen months. When he eventually resigned in November 1979 the discussions between Israel and Egypt on the establishment of full autonomy for the inhabitants of the West Bank and the Gaza area, as envisaged in the Camp David agreement, had reached a complete impasse. Realizing that his original hypothesis – the acceptance of Israel's rule over Judea, Samaria and Gaza for the return of Sinai to Egypt – did not work, he withdrew from the scene.

In our talk Dayan was obviously disinclined to discuss the state of the stalled peace negotiations. He said some amiable words in connection with my retirement, intimating that he himself longed for that blissful state of freedom from bondage. I suggested that we use the quiet hour he had set aside for our last meeting to discuss some wider aspects of the strategic developments in our part of the world. The government, I began, immersed as it was in the immediate issues of the Arab-Israeli conflict, seemed to pay little attention to the changes in power relations occurring in the Middle East. They could become more decisive for Israel's future than many of the issues which preoccupied the government at present. Naturally, governments were more concerned with actualities than with eventualities, but in our area both were on the point of converging into a new reality more perilous than the Arab-Israeli conflict *per se*.

The northern tier, a John Foster Dulles creation erected in 1955 to protect the Western sphere of influence in the Middle East against Soviet encroachment and to shore up NATO's south-eastern defence line, had caved in. The Russians had vaulted over it, first by establishing themselves in Nasser's Egypt, the back door to the Middle East, the gate to Africa and the maritime link between Europe and Asia. For two decades Egypt's Russian connection had determined the direction of the Arab-Israeli conflict until Sadat, realizing the danger, denied the Soviet Union the use of the territory of Egypt as a spring-board for its further expansion. The tools which Soviet strategy selected for the implementation of its grand design were exchangeable, and so was the location from which they launched their forward thrust. But its direction was pre-targeted. One of the Soviet's main objectives in the Middle East was already defined in the Molotov-Ribbentrop agreement as 'the extension of Soviet influence in the direction of the Persian Gulf'. In actual terms this meant the creation of a Soviet capability to interfere with the free movement of oil shipments from the principal production sites in the Middle East to the centres of consumption in Europe, Japan and the United States. There were two neuralgic points along this route: the Horn of Africa and the Strait of Hormuz, with South Yemen serving as a bridge-pier. Along that line the Soviet Union was erecting its southern tier.

Dayan was familiar with the situation in the Red Sea, where the Soviets had intervened in the fighting between Somalia and Ethiopia by arms deliveries, advisers and Cuban military proxies. But the Strait of Hormuz was *terra incognita* to the Foreign Minister. He asked me to point out its location on the large map which covered part of one wall of his office. Dayan looked at the spot with curiosity and asked what was so special about it. I explained that through this narrow waterway nearly all the oil produced in the Persian Gulf area had to pass to reach its destination. Every fifteen minutes a fully loaded oil-tanker went through the Strait of Hormuz. Whoever dominated it controlled the flow of Gulf oil. It was the jugular vein of the Western world and future trouble in the region would focus on this artery. In a year or two all eyes would be on the Strait of Hormuz while the Straits of Tiran would revert to being a forgotten backwater.

Dayan queried how all this would affect Israel. I listed a number of implications: Russian advance in the area would upset the global strategic balance; the United States and its allies would increase their efforts to strengthen their ties with the Arab and Moslem world and press Israel to make more concessions to achieve a speedy conclusion of an agreement with Egypt; upheaval in Iran would affect the oil supplies to the Western world and foremost those of Israel.

Yet the Soviet Union progressed not only in the southern part of the region, but also in its northern approaches. Iraq, once the hub of the Baghdad pact, was now tied to the Soviet Union which had become its principal arms-supplier. Soviet political and military influence in Syria was growing. The presence of Syrian armed forces in the Lebanon and possible changes in northern Iran would extend the Soviet zone of influence from the Caspian Sea to the Mediterranean coast just north of the Israeli-Lebanese boundary. The emerging southern and northern tiers formed two arms of a powerful pincer designed to secure Russian predominance over the Middle East and the Persian Gulf area. The prospects of this strategy depended on a variety of factors: the internal stability of Iran; the development of Soviet-Arab relations; the strength of the American commitment to Israel's security; the future relations between Egypt and Israel; the solidity of Israel's internal and external position; and above all the assessment by the Politburo of the determination of the United States to resist the execution of the Soviet grand design.

Dayan thanked me for the survey. The only contribution he could make to improve the situation was to persevere in the peace negotiations with Egypt. Whether they would succeed only Sadat and Begin knew.

Peace: a lifelong journey

On this note of uncertainty I took my leave of the Ministry. Thirty years had passed since the day I had first entered that ramshackle little house on the beach of Tel Aviv, which we had proudly named 'Ministry of Foreign Affairs of the State of Israel'. War was imminent then. Departing now from the pleasant, though still temporary premises of the Ministry in Jerusalem, clouds were still hovering over Israel but peace was in the offing.

It had been a long, strenuous, exciting, exhilarating and, at times, amusing journey. A little episode of bygone days came to my mind. In August 1953 the *New York Times* reported that I had been appointed to a new post in Jerusalem 'to prepare specific plans for settlement of some of Israel's disputes with the Arabs, against the day when agreement seems near. Israeli sources said that the Foreign Ministry wanted to be ready for the time when an Israeli-Arab peace became a reality.' The day the story appeared my friend and neighbour at the United Nations, Charles Malik, Ambassador of the Lebanon and later its Foreign Minister, came up to me in the delegates' lounge, his face beaming. 'My heartiest congratulations on your new appointment,' he exclaimed, pumping my hand to the consternation of his Arab colleagues. 'You are a lucky man to have landed so early in your career a nice and quiet lifetime job.'

Indeed, the quest for peace has been a lifetime job. Although most of the time the glare of war has obscured the vision of peace, we have never lost sight of it. When I reached the end of my journey, peace was clearly in view. It took another year of arduous negotiations before the treaty was solemnly signed and sealed on the south lawn of the White House.

It was delivered a month later when the representatives of Egypt and Israel exchanged the instruments of ratification at a United States surveillance station in the heart of the Sinai desert. It was the most unusual ceremony I have ever attended. The parking-lot of the American compound had been transformed into a parade-ground. A reviewing dais where the plenipotentiaries were to solemnize the act was facing the grandstand from where the invited notables from Egypt, Israel and the United States were to witness the event.

At the appointed hour Egyptian and Israeli military bands drew up, followed by the guards of honour. They lined up in front of the guests, a mixed gathering of parliamentarians, army officers and government officials. For the first time Egyptian and Israeli soldiers stood shoulder to shoulder. It was an unprecedented sight, a living testimony to the absurdity of war. For a whole generation they had faced each other in battle. Now they stood together to salute peace.

The diplomats exchanged the documents of peace. The bands intoned the national anthems. The flags went up and the silent desert resounded with cheers. Night fell over the wilderness of Sinai. When morning dawned the fires of war had burned out. Egypt and Israel had arrived at destination peace.

Index

Abdullah, King, of
  Jordan, 30, 74, 238
Acheson, Dean, 228
Adenauer, Konrad, 108
Africa: Israel and, 78–85,
  123 (Uganda, 111, 363,
  367–9); China and, 95
Agnew, Spiro, 306
Agranat, Simon, Chief
  Justice, 316
Albert Hall, Golda Meir
  addresses meeting at, 356
Alexandretta district, 121
Alexandrovitch, Ruth, 339
Algeria, 79–80, 106
Allon, Yigal, 385; posts in
  Eshkols's cabinet, 160,
  169; Acting Prime
  Minister, 245; and Jordan
  crisis (1970), 245, 247;
  discusses Suez-Sinai with
  Rogers, 265–6; not Prime
  Minister, 340; visits to
  London (1974–6), 340,
  342, 349–50, 354, 362–3;
  Foreign Minister in
  Rabin's cabinet, 342, 382;
  and relations with Europe,
  359–60; mentioned, 302,
  321, 369, 383, 386
Amin, Idi, 362, 368–9
Amir, Shimon, 158
Anderson, Robert, 45, 49,
  49–52
Aqaba, Gulf of, 30, 39, 64,
  65, 76, 138, 151
Arab League, 8, 73, 79
Arab states: hostility to
  Israel, 30, 74; Soviet
  support for, 115 (see also

under Soviet Union);
  optimism of, 236, 387;
  lack of cohesion among,
  238; see also Egypt;
  Jordan; Syria and other
  Arab states
Arafat, Yassir, 203, 237, 239,
  244, 248, 249, 339, 344;
  see also Fatah; Palestine
  Liberation Organization
Aranne, Zalman, 92, 239
Argov, Colonel Nehemia,
  42–3
Armenia, Rafael's visit to,
  131–3
Arms, armaments: for
  Egypt, see under Britain;
  Soviet Union; United
  States; for Israel, 377–8
  (see also under Britain;
  France; United States); for
  Libya, 214, 358; for Syria,
  246; Middle East arms
  race, 174, 188
Asia, Israel's relations with,
  86–90, 123
Assad, Hafez, President, of
  Syria, 325–6, 328
Aswan Dam, 54
atom bomb, 22–3
'Atoms for Peace', 23–4
Attlee, Clement, 56
Attrition, War of, 201–32, 234
Austin, Senator Warren, 13
Avigur, Shaul, 3
Avneri, Shlomo, 368
Avon, Lord, see Eden, Sir
  Anthony

Bab el-Mandeb, 320, 324

Baghdad pact, 35, 40
Bandung conference (1955),
  45, 93
Bar-Lev, General Haim, 202
Bar-Lev line, 201, 223,
  261, 287
Bar-On, Chanan, 239, 378
Barbour, Walworth, 182,
  197, 202, 219, 224, 225,
  230
Barnes, John, 243
Battle, Lucius, 182, 184
Baudouin, King, 84
Beeley, Harold, 16
Begin, Menachem: and
  Israel's rapprochement with
  Germany, 107, 110; and
  peace moves after Six Day
  War, 170; and Jarring
  proposals, 195–6, 256; and
  Resolution 242, 198;
  opposes Rogers plan,
  226–7; and Camp David
  agreement, 227; resigns
  from Meir government,
  229; becomes Prime
  Minister, 383, 384; and
  peace negotiations,
  388–90; mentioned, 79,
  380
Belgium, 83–4, 100–103
Bellow, Saul, 365
Ben-Elieser, Aryeh, 176
Ben Gurion, David, 378–9,
  380; and arms for Israel,
  4, 51, 52, 125; and cease-
  fire proposals (1948), 15;
  and policy of retaliation,
  30, 31, 32, 33(2); in
  retirement, 35; his views

on Egypt not known
(1954), 35; recalled as
Minister of Defence, 41;
and Jackson mission, 42;
and Gaza raid (summer
1955), 42–3; Prime
Minister again, 47; and
Kinnereth action, 47, 48;
warns about arms for
Egypt, 48; and Anderson
mission, 49, 50, 51–2;
prepares for war, 53;
dismisses Sharett, 55–8,
378; and Suez, 58, 59–60,
62, 64; resigns, 76–7, 109;
on China, 98–9; on
relations with Western
Europe, 100–101; and visit
of Queen Elisabeth, 101,
103; and Israel's
rapprochement with
Germany, 107–8, 109;
letter to President
Kennedy, 125–6
Ben-Zvi, Isaac, 102
Bergmann, Professor Ernst,
24
Bergus, Donald, 258, 266,
267–8
Bernadotte, Count Folke, 13,
17–18
Bernadotte, Countess, 18
Bevin, Ernest, 21
Birnbach, Dr Kurt, 110
Borchgrave, Arnaud de, 280
Brandt, Willy, 111–12
Brezhnev, Leonid, 294, 308,
310, 326–7
Britain: end of Palestine
mandate, 3, 5; recognizes
Israel, 7; withdraws from
Egypt, 35–6; and arms for
Egypt, 48, 336, 359; and
Suez, 54–5, 58–63; and
Jordan, 71, 73, 74;
improving relations with
Israel, 123; withdrawal
from Middle East, 129–30;
and re-opening of Suez
Canal, 184; and
Resolution 242, 187–90;
and Leila Khaled, 239–40,

243, 248–9; and Yom
Kippur War, 307, 332;
relations with Israel,
330–75 *passim* (arms, 342);
Jewish community in, 331,
335, 342, 357, 367, 371;
arms sales to Arab states,
332, 336, 338, 342–4, 370;
trade agreement with
Soviet Union, 351–2
Brown, George, 184
Bulganin, N. A., 120
Bull, General Odd, 163, 165,
216
Bunche, Dr Ralph, 17, 136,
137–8, 139, 140, 147, 148,
193
Burke, Edmund, quoted, 381
Burma, Israel and, 86–7

CIA, *see* Central Intelligence
Agency
Cairo trial, 37–8, 40–2,
44, 194
Callaghan, James, 336–7,
341, 344, 347–8, 352,
352–3, 353–5, 361–2, 363,
366–7, 368–9, 369, 373
Cambodia, Israel and, 86–7
Camp David agreement, 227,
228
Caradon, Lord, 185, 187–9
Carlos (terrorist), 331
Carter, President Jimmy,
372, 373, 383
Ceausescu, President
Nicolae, 96
Central Intelligence Agency
(CIA), 290
Chain, Sir Ernest, 366–7
Chamoun, Camille, 71
China: UN representation, 26,
92, 93–4; and Korean
War, 27–8; and Israel,
91–5, 96, 97–8; and United
States, 94, 96, 97, 98–9;
and Africa, 95
Chou En-lai, 45, 91, 92, 93
Common Market (EEC),
Israel and, 103–5, 109–10,
123, 335, 359
Conciliation Commission,

see Palestine Conciliation
Commission
Congo, Belgian (later Zaire),
83–4
Conrad, Joseph, quoted, 292
Cuban missile crisis, 241–2
Cyprus, Israel and, 89
Czechoslovakia, arms for
Egypt from, 45–7

Dayan, Moshe, 229; and
policy of retaliation, 31;
and Kybia strike, 32, 33,
34; and Lavon, 36, 41; and
Gaza raids (1955), 40,
42–3; and Suez, 58; and
China's UN representation,
94; and Israel's
rapprochement with
Germany, 107; and Six
Day War, 153, 162–3, 165;
insists on being Minister
of Defence, 160; and peace
moves after Six Day War,
169, 170, 198–9; relations
with Eshkol, 202; injured
on archaeological dig, 202;
relations with Golda Meir,
203–4, 381; and War of
Attrition, 215, 222, 223,
229, 232, 386; fears Soviet
military intervention,
222–3; and Jarring
proposals, 231, 256, 257;
and Jordan crisis, 245,
247; and proposal to re-
open Suez Canal, 258,
258–9, 260, 265, 267, 269;
his activist policy, 283,
292; fond of surprises,
288; public criticism of,
316, 317; visits
Washington (1974), 327;
Foreign Minister in
Begin's cabinet, 384–5,
385, 389, 390, 390–1,
391–3; mentioned, 311
Developing countries,
Israel and, 78–9, 81–3, 85,
86–7
Dinitz, Simha, 267, 286–7,
308, 382

Diplomatic and Commonwealth Writers' Association, 365–6

Disraeli, Benjamin, quoted, 383

Dixon, Sir Pierson, 60

Dobrynin, Anatoly, 178–9, 223, 224, 227–8, 275

'Doctors' plot', 34

Douglas-Home, Sir Alec, 331–2

Dulles, John Foster, 25, 28, 35, 47, 54, 54–5, 59, 64(2), 65, 73

Eastern Europe, Israel and, 113, 124; see also under Soviet Union

Eban, Abba, 379, 385; Israel's spokesman at UN, 8, 12; and armistice plan (1949), 17; and Israel's admission to UN, 19; and atomic energy, 24–5; and Korean War, 27; and policy of retaliation, 34; has to defend Kinnereth action, 48; and Suez, 60, 62–3, 64(2), 65–6; and Middle East crisis (1957), 71–3; and relations with China, 92(2), 94; visits Germany (1970), 110; on Soviet-Israeli relations, 120–1; convenes ambassadorial meeting in Warsaw, 124; and Rafael's appointment as ambassador to UN, 129; and Six Day War, 136–7, 137, 140, 141, 143–6, 158–60, 161, 166; and peace moves after Six Day War, 168–85 passim, 195–9 passim; relations with Golda Meir, 199, 204, 253–4, 317–18; and War of Attrition, 202, 211, 212, 214–15, 220, 221–2, 224–5; and projected message to Sadat, 252; and resumption of Jarring

talks, 253–4, 256–7; and proposal to re-open Suez Canal, 260, 269, 270–1; and Sadat's expulsion of Russians, 277–8; opposes Dayan's activist policy, 283; and Yom Kippur War, 297, 303, 309; replaced by Dayan as Foreign Minister, 318, 383–4; and Geneva peace conference, 319; and Rafael's London mission, 334, 337; on Israeli Foreign Ministry, 377; mentioned, 139, 245

Eden, Sir Anthony (later Lord Avon), 59–60, 60–1

Egypt: Tel Aviv bombed by (1948), 7; accepts armistice (1949), 17; British withdrawal from, 35–6; Cairo trial etc., 36–9; territorial link with Jordan, 50; southward ambitions of, 73–4; arms for, 108 (missile programme; see also under Britain; Soviet Union; United States); economic plight of, after Six Day War, 184; see also Independence, War of ; Nasser; Sadat; Six Day War; Suez; Yom Kippur War

Eilat (port), 63, 64, 151, 245, 263

Eilat, sinking of, 185

Eilat, Eliyahu, 12

Einstein, Albert, 23

Eisenhower, President Dwight D., 24, 44–5, 48–9, 51, 58–9, 62, 65

El-Khanka factory, 215

El-Khuni, Ambassador, 161

Elazar, General David, 162–3, 317

Elisabeth, Queen Mother, of Belgium, 101–3, 367

Elizabeth II, Queen, 366

Ennals, David, 338

Entebbe, Israeli rescue mission at, 111, 367–9

Eshkol, Levi, 202, 379–80; and China, 93; and EEC, 105; and Six Day War, 143–5, 160–1; and peace moves after Six Day War, 169, 170, 171, 197–8, 198–9; relations with Dayan, 202; and Karameh raid, 202–3; mentioned, 218

Ethiopia, Israel and, 78–9, 124

European Economic Community, see Common Market

Evron, Ephraim, 286, 368

Eyskens, Gaston, 83

Eytan, Walter, 41

Faluja, 15–16

Fatah organization, 130–1, 202–3

Faure, Edgar, 46

Fawzy, Mahmud, 42, 44

Fedorenko, Nicolai, 122, 133, 135, 136, 143, 146, 156, 159, 161–2, 186

Feisal, King, of Iraq, 71

Feisal, King, of Saudi Arabia, 286–7, 312, 323–4

Fischer, Maurice, 12

Ford, President Gerald, 348–9, 351, 355, 356, 358

France: relations with Israel, 46–7, 79–81, 100, 106, 123, 335 (armaments, 46, 53, 58, 79, 81, 214; Suez, 54–5, 58–63 passim); relations with Arab states, 80, 112 (arms for Libya, 214)

Galili, Israel, 169–70, 256, 257, 283

Gamassi, General, 328

Gaulle, Charles de, 79, 80, 123, 143

Gaza, 15, 40, 42–3, 44, 64–7, 138, 183, 263

Geneva: foreign ministers'

meeting at (1955), 46–7;
peace conference at, after
Yom Kippur War, 318–20,
329, 384
Genscher, Hans-Dietrich,
354, 369
Germany, West, 98–9,
106–10, 111–12, 349
Gibli, Colonel Benjamin,
36–7, 41
Golan Heights, 47, 161, 162,
222, 263, 289, 326, 329
Goldberg, Arthur: and Six
Day War, 140, 141, 145,
146–7, 148(2), 149, 153,
154(2), 156, 157, 158,
158–9, 164–5; and peace
moves after Six Day War,
177–87 passim
Goodman, Lord, 374
Gowon, General, 350–1
Gromyko, Andrei, 13,
116–17, 121, 171, 180, 274,
275, 309, 318, 327, 352
Guinea, 95

Habash, George, 291–2
Hacohen, David, 91–2, 92–3
Haganah, the, 3, 5, 18, 297
Haiphong harbour, Soviet
ships accidentally bombed
in, 204
Hallstein, Professor Walter,
104
Hamami, Said, 339, 343
Hamilton, Sir Dennis, 76
Hamilton, Tom, 26
Hammarskjöld, Dag, 60,
63–4, 64, 73, 84, 138, 254
Harel, Isser, 108–9
Harman, Abe, 143, 177
Hausner, Gideon, 384
Haykal, Hassanin, 294
Healey, Denis, 361
Heath, Edward, 243, 332
Helsinki summit meeting,
355–6
Heren, Louis, 263–4
Hermon, Mount, 301
Herzog, Jacob, 42, 43, 57,
73, 144–5, 198
Hijacking, 111, 239–44, 248

Hill, Denis, 363
Hormuz, Strait of, 392–3
Horn of Africa, 392
Howard, Anthony, 368
Hungarian uprising (1956), 61
Hussein, King, of Jordan,
321–2; British support for,
71, 73; and West Bank,
73, 320–1, 345; staying
power of, 178, 184, 238–9,
320–1; and Resolution
242, 186; and PLO
hijacking, 242; and PLO
uprising (1970), 244–9;
relations with Sadat,
292–3; and Yom Kippur
War, 295; see also Jordan
Hussein, Ahmed,
Ambassador, 42, 54
Huysmans, Camille, 105–6

Independence, War of, 8–9,
11–12, 13–17, 30, 234
India, 87–90, 187, 376
Iran, 78, 79, 124, 324, 393
Iraq, 71–2, 73, 75–6, 393
Ireland, 75, 359, 360
Ismail, Hafiz, 280, 280–1
Israel: establishment of state
of, 3, 5, 5–7, 7–8, 11, 12;
and Arab belligerency, see
Arab states; admitted to
UN, 19–20; foreign policy
of, 21, 22, 25, 385–7;
ambassadors of, freedom
allowed to, 225–6;
importance of Jordan and
maritime freedom, 233;
Prime Ministers of,
378–83; Foreign Ministers
of, 385

Jackson, Elmore, 42, 43–5,
45
Jacobson, Per, 193
Japan, Israel and, 86
Jarring, Gunnar, Jarring
mission/proposals, 193–8,
199–200, 216, 224–5, 231,
245, 252–7, 258, 260
Jerusalem: control of, 17, 50,
161, 167–8, 171, 176,

177–8. 263; an African
view of, 83; White Russian
church in, 120; freedom of
worship in, 171, 174, 176,
177–8
Jessup, Philip, 17
Jews, Jewish community, see
under Britain; Soviet
Union
Johnson, President Lyndon
B., 124, 126, 141, 145,
148–9, 156–7, 174, 183,
185, 189, 197–8, 202
Johnson, Paul, 368
Jordan (state): accepts
armistice (1949), 17;
Britain and, 71, 73, 74;
Israel and, after Suez, 75;
and Six Day War, 157,
163; and Jarring mission,
196–7; PLO offensive
against (1970), 237, 244–8;
see also Abdullah, King;
Hussein, King
Jordan, river, 32–3, 233; see
also West Bank
Juliana, Queen, of the
Netherlands, 103

Kantara East, 200, 201
Kaplan, Eliezer, 297
Karameh, 202–3
Kassem, Colonel Abdul
Karim, 73
Katz, Katriel, Ambassador,
131
Katzir, Professor Ephraim,
(President), 366–7
Kedar, Zvi, 351
Kennedy, President John F.,
108, 124–6
Khaled, Leila, 239–40, 243,
248
Khan Yunis, 43–4
Khrushchev, Nikita, 60–1
Kinnereth action, 47–8
Kissinger, Dr Henry: on
Czech arms deal, 46; visits
Peking (1971), 94, 96, 97,
99, 268; and Meir's talks
with Nixon (1969), 210;
and Middle East, 216, 223,

226, 273–5, 280, 280–1, 282, 285; and Jordan crisis (1970), 246–7, 248; and proposal to re-open Suez Canal, 259, 260, 264; foresees no difficulties over Middle East oil, 287; and Yom Kippur War, 289, 290, 302–11 passim; and peace negotiations after Yom Kippur War, 318–21, 324–9, 338, 350, 352–3, 353–6; and Saudi Arabia, 323–4
Kollek, Teddy, 9, 10
Korea, South, Israel and, 86–7
Korean War, 24, 25–9, 91
Kosygin, Aleksei Nicolayevich, 156–7, 171, 173, 175, 185, 189, 212–13, 307, 339, 351
Kuneitra, 164, 326, 328, 338
Kuznetsov, Vasili, 186
Kybia strike, 33–4

Laos, Israel and, 86–7
Lavon, Pinchas, 32–3, 36, 37, 41, 92
Lebanon: Israel and, 17, 74, 242; US intervention in, 71, 72, 119, 236
Lewin, Daniel, 92–3
Libya, 21–2, 214, 312, 357
Lie, Trygve, 19, 27–9
Lloyd, Selwyn, 58
Lodge, Henry Cabot, 64, 65
Lourie, Arthur, 57
Lumumba, Patrice, 84
Lunkov, Nikolai, Ambassador, 347

Ma'alot, terrorist attack on, 328, 340–1
Macmillan, Harold, 47
Macovescu,George, 96, 97, 231
Malik, Charles, 74, 394
Malik, Jacob, 26
Marcus, Colonel David (Mickey), 9
Marshall, George, 3, 4

Mason, Roy, 361
Meir, Golda, 380–2, 385; fund-raising mission to US (1948), 9, 10; ambassador to Moscow, 12, 117; urges return of Ben Gurion, 41; on threats of resignation, 57; becomes Foreign Minister, 57–8; relations with Ben Gurion, 57–8, 380; and Suez, 63–7; and relations with developing countries, 82; and China's UN representation, 94; and Israel's rapprochement with Germany, 108–9; becomes Minister of Labour, 117; and Ben Gurion's letter to Kennedy, 125; and Galili, 170; fund-raising mission to US (1967), 187; relations with Eban, 199, 204, 253–4, 317–18; relations with Dayan, 203–4, 381; visits Nixon (1969), 209–10; and War of Attrition, 209–31 passim, 386; and PLO hijacking, 240; meets Nixon and Rogers (1970), 245–6; and projected message to Sadat, 251–2; and resumption of Jarring talks, 252–4, 257; and proposal to re-open Suez Canal, 258–9, 259, 261–2, 263–4, 267, 269–70; and Louis Heren, 263–4; visits Washington (1971), 271; another visit (1973), 280, 320; another term as Prime Minister?, 283; and 'hard-line' policy, 283; does not expect war, 284–5; and Yom Kippur War, 289, 307(2); and resignation of Shapira, 316; post-war government of, 316, 317–18; resigns, heading caretaker government, 328(2); succeeded by Rabin, 340;

private visit to London, 345–6; addresses Albert Hall meeting, 356
Menon, Krishna, 87
Menon, Mrs Lakshmi, 87
Micunovic, Veljko, 61
Molotov, V. M., 47, 113
Moore, Henry, 374
Morocco, Israel and, 81
Mortimer, Edward, 362
Moynihan, Patrick, 356
Mulki, Fawzi, 75
Murville, Couve de, 149–50

Naguib, General, 36, 251
Nasser, Gamal Abdul, 30, 49; in War of Independence, 15–16; and British withdrawal from Egypt, 35; and Cairo trial, correspondence with Sharett, 38–9, 40; his deviousness, 39; opposes Baghdad pact, 40; and Jackson mission, 42, 43–5; and Czech arms deal, 45; his surprise moves, 45; attends Bandung conference, 45, 93; and Anderson mission, 49–52; proclaims Egypt's power, 53–4; and Aswan Dam, 54; and Suez Canal, see Suez Canal; relations with Israel after Suez, 71, 76–7; and Six Day War, 133, 138–9, 139–40, 141–2, 148, 161; and peace moves after Six Day War, 186, 196; War of Attrition, 201–32. 234; visits Moscow (1970), 212; succeeded by Sadat, 231; attempts Arafat-Hussein reconciliation, 249; his death, 251; mentioned, 119; see also Egypt
navigation, see shipping
Navon, Yitzhak, 48
Negev, 15(2), 17, 32, 35, 50
Nehru, Pandit, 87, 87–90, 376

Nervo, Padilla, 25, 28
Nesterenko, Aleksei, 163
Netherlands, Israel and, 103
New Statesman, 367
Nixon, President Richard
  M.: and Romania, 97; and
  arms for Israel, 126, 209,
  210, 214, 215, 245–6;
  meets Meir (1969), 209–10;
  and War of Attrition,
  209–10, 212–13, 214, 215,
  217–18, 221–2, 228; and
  PLO hijacking, 244–5; and
  Jordan crisis, 245–6, 246,
  248; urges resumption of
  Jarring talks, 252; and
  Sadat (1973), 268, 279–80;
  does not favour Israeli
  withdrawal, 274; and Yom
  Kippur War, 306, 309; on
  US-Soviet common interest
  in Middle East, 311; and
  Kissinger's Israel mission,
  328; visits Middle East,
  329; resigns, 338
'non-alignment', 82–3, 124
'non-identification', 22, 25
nuclear weapons, *see* atom
  bomb

Odessa, Jews of, 114
oil, 286–7, 293, 306, 311–13,
  322–4, 326, 334–5, 393
Olivier, Lord, 346
Olympic Games (Munich,
  1972), 111
Owen, David, 370, 372

PFLP, *see* Habash, George
PLO, *see* Palestine Liberation
  Organization
Pachachi, Adnan, 131
Palestine Conciliation
  Commission, 18, 75
Palestine Liberation
  Organization (PLO),
  239–49, 322–3, 331, 342,
  344–5, 353; *see also*
  Arafat, Yassir
Palliser, Sir Michael, 370
Pandit, Mrs, 87
Panov, Valery and Galina,

347–8
Pauls, Rolf, 110
Peace Observation
  Committee, 27
Pearson, Lester, 16, 17, 25,
  153
Pedersen, Dick, 181
Peleg, Chazi, 300
Peleg, Colonel Seevik, 299,
  300–301, 303
Peres, Shimon: and Lavon,
  41; Director-General of
  Ministry of Defence, 58;
  and Suez, 58; and Isser
  Harel, 109; succeeds Rabin
  as party leader, 375;
  Rabin's Minister of
  Defence, 382; defeated by
  Begin in Knesset elections,
  383
Philippines, Israel and, 86–7
Pinay, Antoine, 47
Pinneau, Christian, 58
Podgorny, N. V., 267–8
Poland, Israel and, 124
Port Said, Soviet ships hit by
  bomb fragments at, 204–5
Port Suez, shelled by Israel,
  185
Portugal, Israel and, 123,
  358–9

Qaddafi, Colonel, 312

Rabin, Yitzhak: Israeli
  general, 144–5, 162;
  ambassador in
  Washington, 203, 205,
  210, 210–11, 217, 225–6,
  246–7, 257, 258, 259, 270;
  Prime Minister, 306, 315,
  340, 341–2, 353, 355,
  355–6, 359, 372–3, 375,
  382–3
Rabin, Mrs Leah, 375
Rafael, Gideon: Sharett's
  assistant at Foreign
  Ministry, 3–7; to UN to
  assist Eban, 8–10, 12–13;
  and cease-fire proposals
  (1948–9), 13, 15, 16–17;
  received by Countess

Bernadotte, 18; and
  'Atoms for Peace', 23,
  23–4; and Malik's Security
  Council appointment, 26;
  and UN Peace Observation
  Committee, 27; and
  Korean peace plan, 27–9;
  and policy of retaliation,
  Kybia strike, 30–2; and
  Cairo trial, 37–8; and
  Gaza raid (summer 1955),
  42–3; and foreign
  ministers' Geneva meeting,
  46; and Anderson mission,
  49; and Sharett's
  resignation, 56, 57, 57–8;
  and Lord Avon, 59; and
  Suez, 60, 62–3, 66;
  ambassador to Belgium
  and Luxembourg, 71, 100,
  105–6; and Middle East
  crisis (1957), 71–3; some
  personal relationships at
  UN, 74–5; permanent
  representative to UN, 77,
  103–4, 129, 134–5; on
  French attitude (1966), 80;
  and Belgian Congo, 83–4;
  and India, 87–90; and
  China's UN representation,
  94; visits West Africa
  (1960), 95; and Romania,
  96–7; permanent observer
  to EEC, 103–5, 106; on
  terrorists at Munich
  Olympics, 111; visits
  Odessa, 114; visits
  Moscow (1967), 122, 129,
  131–5; and Ben Gurion's
  letter to Kennedy, 125;
  and Syrian crisis (1966),
  130; and Six Day War,
  136–66 *passim*; and peace
  moves after Six Day War,
  167–71, 177, 182, 186, 187,
  197, 198, 199, 200; visits
  Washington (1969), 207;
  and War of Attrition,
  217–18, 224–5; and PLO
  hijacking, 240–4, 249; and
  Jordan crisis (1970), 245,
  247; and death of Nasser,

251; and resumption of
Jarring talks, 252, 256;
meets Louis Heren, 263;
on Sadat's expulsion of
Russians, 277–9; and 1973
negotiations, 281, 281–2;
fears war, 284–5;
ambassador to London,
285, 318, 330–75; and
Yom Kippur War, 289,
295–303; given Stephen
Wise Award, 298; on
relations with Egypt,
313–14; suggests Eban's
resignation, 318; Director-
General of Foreign
Ministry, 376–7; returns to
Jerusalem (1977), 383–4;
visits US (1977), 384; and
peace moves, 391, 391–2;
retires, 392, 393–4;
mentioned, 41, 317
Rafael, Mrs Nurit, with
Countess Bernadotte, 18;
with Lord Avon, 59; with
Queen Elisabeth of
Belgium, 101; arrival in
London, 330; with Harold
Wilson, 337; departure
from Britain, 374
Rafiah salient, 283
Rau, Sir Benegal, 25, 28
refugees, Palestinian, 18–19,
50, 170, 174, 176–7, 190,
203, 228, 257
'Regatta' (US naval plan),
150, 153
Resolution 242, 190, 193–200
passim, 215, 225, 227, 228,
259–62, 266, 269–70,
307–8, 324
Resolution 338, 190, 309(2),
318
retaliation, policy of, 30–5
Riad, Mahmoud, 140, 186,
194, 196, 227, 267
Richardson, Elliot, 97, 207
Rifai, Zand, 246
Rikhye, General, 137
Rogers, William, the Rogers
plan, 209, 210, 210–11,
218–19, 224–5, 226, 227,

228, 230, 245, 252, 260,
265–6, 266–8, 270, 325
Romania, 96–7, 113
Roosevelt, President
Franklin D., 23
Rosen, Professor Howard,
301
Rosenne, Dr Meir, 391
Rosenne, Shabtai, 150
Rostow, Eugene, 144, 145,
182, 183, 184
Rothschild family, 370,
373–4
Rouleau, Eric, 138
Rusk, Dean, 130, 144, 177,
177–8, 179, 241
Russia, see Soviet Union

Sabry, Ali, 267
Sachs, Alexander, 23
Sadat, President Anwar,
250–1; his mastery of
surprise, 45, 259–60; heads
Egyptian delegation to
Soviet Union, 133;
succeeds Nasser, 231; and
Jarring talks, 231, 254,
255–6, 282; and Yom
Kippur War, 234, 282,
287–8, 289, 293, 307, 309,
313–14; his proposal to re-
open Suez Canal, 258–72;
and expulsion of Russians
from Egypt, 273–4, 276–9;
approach to US, 279–81;
and oil boycott of US, 286,
287; relations with
Hussein, 292–3; and peace
moves after Yom Kippur
War, 328, 356, 358,
369–70, 388–90; see also
Egypt
Said, Nuri, 71
Sapir, Pinhas, 57, 105, 215,
283, 284–5
Sasson, Moshe, 165
Saudi Arabia, 130, 286–7,
312, 323–4, 391
Saunders, Harold, 280
Scheel, Walter, 98–9, 110
Schmidt, Helmut, 349
Schuetz, Klaus, 110

Security Council (see also
United Nations): and War
of Independence, 13, 16,
16–17; paralysed by Soviet
veto, 25; and Korean War,
25–6; condemns Kybia
strike, 34; condemns
Kinnereth action, 48; and
Suez, 60; debate on Syria
(1966), 80; and Fatah
organization, 130–1; and
Six Day War, 143, 145–6,
146–7, 148–51, 155–6, 158,
161–6, 168, 235; session of
1967, 185, 186–90;
intervention of, watched
for by Middle East
combatants, 235–6; Middle
East debate (1973), 281;
and Yom Kippur War,
302, 304, 309(2), 311; see
also Resolution 242;
Resolution 338
Semyonov, Vladimir, 122(2),
133
Sèvres, pre-Suez meeting at,
58, 59–60
Seydoux, Roger, 149–50
Sforza, Count, 21
Shapira, Eiga, 5
Shapira, Yacob Shimshon,
316
Sharef, Seev, 7
Sharett, Moshe, 3, 55, 385;
meets Marshall in
Washington (1948), 3–5;
requests recognition of
Israel, 5–7; Foreign
Ministry appointments by,
8, 9–10, 12; and War of
Independence, 13, 15, 17;
and Israel's admission to
UN, 19–20; and Libyan
trusteeship, 22; and
Korean War, 28–9; and
policy of retaliation, 32;
acting Prime Minister, 32;
and Jordan project, Kybia
strike, 32–4; Prime
Minister, 36; and Cairo
trial, 37–8, 40–1; end of
his premiership, 40–1, 47;

and Jackson mission, 42, 44; and Gaza raid (summer 1955), 42–3; and foreign ministers' Geneva meeting, 46–7; criticizes Kinnereth action, 48; and Anderson mission, 49, 50; dismissed by Ben Gurion, 55–8, 378; and Nehru, 87; and Korean War, 91; and relations with China, 92, 93

Sharm el-Sheikh, 64, 138, 139, 141, 151, 234, 245, 255, 263, 274

Sharon, General Ariel, 33, 315

Shazar, Zalman, 251

Shazly, General Sa'ad el, 364–5

Shchiborin, Ambassador, 134

Shiloah, Reuben, 5, 92

shipping, navigation, international waterways, 188, 233; see also Aqaba, Gulf of; Bab el-Mandeb; Eilat; Sharm el-Sheikh; Suez Canal; Tiran, Straits of

Shishakli, Adib, 36, 74

Short, Edward, 337, 339

Sieff family, 331, 370

Sinai, 58–67, 71, 234, 263

Sisco, Joseph, 180–1, 206, 221, 227–8, 230, 241, 246, 248, 258, 259, 266, 266–8, 268–9, 286, 286–7, 352

Six Day War, 113, 136–66, 235; peace moves after the war, 167–90

Solh, Riad el, 238

Solod, Ambassador, 95

Sonnenfeldt, Helmut, 355

South America, Israel and, 123

Soviet Union: recognizes Israel, 7, 116–17; opposes Arab attack on Israel (1948), 14; absent from Security Council, 25–6, 26–7; diplomatic relations

with Israel severed then restored (1953), 34; and arms for Egypt, 45–7, 48, 53, 207–9, 212–13, 214, 221, 223–4, 227, 228, 230–1, 235, 262, 271–2, 273–4, 275, 276–9, 285–6, 306; and Sinai-Suez campaign, 60–2, 113; and Ethiopia, 79; and Syria, 80–1, 120–2, 129–31, 246, 393; deteriorating relations with Israel, 106, 113–22, 124; Jews in, 114–16, 120–1, 133–5, 338–9, 350, 352, 372; Middle East policy of, 117–22, 129, 236, 237, 392–3; and Six Day War, 143, 146, 154, 156–8, 159, 161, 162, 163; and peace moves after the war, 171–90 passim; and War of Attrition, 204–5, 207–9, 211, 212–13, 214, 221, 223–4, 227–8, 230–1; relations with US in Middle East, 234–7; and Yom Kippur War, 294, 302, 307–8, 309–10; and oil boycott, 311; and peace negotiations after Yom Kippur War, 318–20, 322, 326–7, 356; and Panovs, 347–8; trade agreement with Britain, 351–2; and Helsinki summit, 356–7

Spaak, Henri, 63, 72

Spain, Israel and, 123, 358

Springer, Axel, 108

Stephen Wise Award, 298

Stevenson, Adlai, 163–4, 241–2

Strachey, John, 56

Sturman, Chaim, 263

Suez Canal: Israeli shipping, 30, 38, 39, 44; British military presence in, welcomed by Israel, 35; nationalized by Nasser (1956), 54; Israel, France and Britain mount expedition to, 58–67, 71,

234; re-opening of, mooted, 184, 194–5, 234; blockaded by Egypt (1967), 194; Israeli forces deployed along (1967), 194, 222, 234; negotiations concerning (1971), 258–72; Kissinger-Gromyko proposals (1972), 274; re-opened (1975) 320, 355

Syria: accepts armistice (1949), 17; and Jordan headwaters, 32, 233; relations with Israel, 47–8, 74, 80–1, 120–2, 129–31; and Soviet Union, 80–1, 120–2, 129–31, 246, 393; dispute with Turkey over Alexandretta district, 121; and Six Day War, 136, 161, 162, 163, 165–6; invades Jordan, 237, 246–8; and Yom Kippur War, 289; and peace negotiations after the war, 320, 325–9

Tabor, Hans, 154, 155, 162, 164, 165–6

Talleyrand, quoted, 385

Tekoah, Joseph, 154, 198, 281

Tel Aviv: bombed by Egypt (1948), 7; PLO raid in (1975), 352

Television, 364–5

terrorism, 18, 111, 291; see also Fatah; Palestine Liberation Organization

Thailand, Israel and, 86–7

Thant, U, 136–42 passim, 145, 147–8, 151, 193, 230

Times, The, 334, 362–3

Tiran, Straits of, 64, 65, 138, 141, 147, 150, 154, 174, 233–4, 255, 274

Tito, President, 61

Tohami, Hassan el, 389

Tome, Ambassador, 163, 164

Toukan, Ahmed, 75

Toure, Seku, 95

Truman, President Harry S.,

7, 23
Tunisia, Israel and, 81
Turkey, 78, 121, 124

USSR, *see* Soviet Union
Uganda, *see* Amin; Entebbe
United Nations Emergency
    Force (UNEF), 76, 137–8,
    139–40
United Nations
    Organization: fails to curb
    Arab belligerency (1948),
    8, 11; and armistice
    (1949), 17, 18–19; Israel
    admitted to, 19–20; and
    Korean War, 24, 25–9;
    China's representation, 26,
    92, 93–4; and Suez, 60–7
    passim; and Hungarian
    uprising, 61; and Middle
    East crisis (1957), 73;
    Ireland admitted to, 75;
    Israel's declining position
    at, 124; Special Assembly
    after Six Day War, 171,
    173–82; and Lebanon
    crisis (1958), 236;
    addressed by Arafat, 345;
    Zionism deemed racist by,
    357; *see also* Security
    Council
United States: and arms for
    Israel, 3–4, 46, 51, 53, 125,
    126, 207, 208, 209, 210,
    214–20, 221–2, 224, 225,
    235, 245–6, 252, 269,
    270–1, 273, 304–5, 336;
    recognizes Israel, 7;
    opposes Arab attack on
    Israel (1948), 14; approach

to Nasser, 35; tries to
    arrange Israeli-Arab talks,
    42; and arms for Egypt,
    45, 46, 344, 358; and Suez,
    58–9, 60, 61–2, 62–7; and
    Lebanon, 71, 72, 119, 236;
    and China, 94, 96, 97,
    98–9; and Romania, 96–7;
    relations with Israel, 124-
    6, 130, 381–3; and Six Day
    War, 140, 141, 143–5,
    146–7, 150, 153, 156–8,
    159, 164–5; and peace
    moves after the war, 169,
    174, 177–90, 197–8; wider
    concerns of, 183–4; and
    War of Attrition, 202–31
    passim; relations with
    Soviet Union in Middle
    East, 234–7; and Jordan
    crisis, 245–8; and
    resumption of Jarring
    talks, 252, 254, 255; and
    proposal to re-open Suez
    Canal, 258–63, 264–72;
    and Middle East in early
    1970s, 273–5, 279–81, 282,
    285–6; and Yom Kippur
    War, 290, 302, 304–7, 308,
    309–11; and peace
    negotiations after the war,
    318–21, 324–9, 338, 351,
    352–3, 353–6, 384, 389–90

Vietnam, 130, 214, 223, 268,
    354
Vyshinsky, Andrei, 347

Waldheim, Kurt, 369
Washington Special Action

Group, 290
Watergate, 306, 328
waterways, *see* shipping
Weidenfeld, Lord, 355
Weizman, Ezer, 390
Weizmann, Chaim, 23–4, 79,
    370, 371
West Bank, 73, 161, 170,
    177–8, 183, 263, 321, 322,
    345
Western Europe, Israel and,
    123; *see also individual
    countries*
Wigny, Pierre, 101
Wilson, Giles, 340
Wilson, Harold, 123, 143,
    332–63 *passim*
World Health Organization,
    Delhi conference of, 87, 90

Yadin, Yigael, 9, 15, 170
Yamit, 283, 284
Yariv, General, 230
Yom Kippur War, 222, 232,
    234, 235, 287–314;
    Moroccan support for
    Syria in, 81; peace
    negotiations after the war,
    190, 262, 318–29, 349–50,
    351–6, 373, 384, 388–90,
    393–4; non-aligned states
    oppose Israel, 279
Yugoslavia, 61, 113, 175–6

Zaim, Colonel Husmi, 74
Zaire, *see* Congo, Belgian
Zeira, General Eli, 282
Zionism, deemed racist by
    UN, 357
Zukerman, Pinchas, 367